PAUL LAURENCE DUNBAR

PAUL LAURENCE
DUNBAR

The Life and Times of a Caged Bird

GENE ANDREW JARRETT

PRINCETON UNIVERSITY PRESS

PRINCETON AND OXFORD

Published by Princeton University Press
41 William Street, Princeton, New Jersey 08540
99 Banbury Road, Oxford OX2 6JX

press.princeton.edu

Library of Congress Cataloging-in-Publication Data

Names: Jarrett, Gene Andrew, 1975– author.
Title: Paul Laurence Dunbar: the life and times of a caged bird /
    Gene Andrew Jarrett.
Description: Princeton: Princeton University Press, 2022 |
    Includes bibliographical references and index.
Identifiers: LCCN 2021033992 (print) | LCCN 2021033993 (ebook) |
    ISBN 9780691150529 (hardback; acid-free paper) | ISBN 9780691235158 (ebook)
Subjects: LCSH: Dunbar, Paul Laurence, 1872–1906. | Poets, American—
    19th century—Biography. | African American poets—Biography. |
    LCGFT: Biographies.
Classification: LCC PS1557.J37 2022 (print) | LCC PS1557 (ebook) |
    DDC 811/.4 [B]—dc23
LC record available at https://lccn.loc.gov/2021033992
LC ebook record available at https://lccn.loc.gov/2021033993

British Library Cataloging-in-Publication Data is available

Editorial: Anne Savarese and James Collier
Production Editorial: Ellen Foos
Text Design: Karl Spurzem
Jacket Design: Lauren Michelle Smith
Production: Erin Suydam
Publicity: Jodi Price and Carmen Jimenez
Copyeditor: Daniel Simon

Jacket image: Paul Laurence Dunbar at age 19. Paul Laurence Dunbar Collection / Ohio History Connection

This book has been composed in Arno Pro with Helvetica LT Std

Printed on acid-free paper. ∞

Printed in the United States of America

10 9 8 7 6 5 4 3 2 1

For the Boynton-Jarrett Family

and

in memory of

Toni Morrison

(1931–2019)

FIG. 0.0. Paul Laurence Dunbar, circa 1890. (Paul Laurence Dunbar Small Picture Collection, Ohio History Connection)

I know what the caged bird feels, alas!
    When the sun is bright on the upland slopes;
When the wind stirs soft through the springing grass,
And the river flows like a stream of glass;
    When the first bird sings and the first bud opes,
And the faint perfume from its chalice steals—
I know what the caged bird feels!

I know why the caged bird beats his wing
    Till its blood is red on the cruel bars;
For he must fly back to his perch and cling
When he fain would be on the bough a-swing;
    And a pain still throbs in the old, old scars
And they pulse again with a keener sting—
I know why he beats his wing!

I know why the caged bird sings, ah me,
    When his wing is bruised and his bosom sore,—
When he beats his bars and he would be free;
It is not a carol of joy or glee,
    But a prayer that he sends from his heart's deep core,
But a plea, that upward to Heaven he flings—
I know why the caged bird sings!

—PAUL LAURENCE DUNBAR, "SYMPATHY,"
LYRICS OF THE HEARTHSIDE (1899)[1]

CONTENTS

List of Illustrations   xi

INTRODUCTION   1

PART ONE: BROKEN HOME, BEGINNINGS TO 1893

CHAPTER 1. Broken Country   15

CHAPTER 2. Broken Home   47

CHAPTER 3. Public Schooling   77

CHAPTER 4. The Tattler   91

CHAPTER 5. A Superior Gift   110

CHAPTER 6. Career Choices   131

CHAPTER 7. The White City   152

PART TWO: A TRUE SINGER, 1893 TO 1898

CHAPTER 8. Chafing at Life   173

CHAPTER 9. The Bond of a Fellow-Craft   188

CHAPTER 10. Heroine of His Stories   206

CHAPTER 11. A True Singer   217

CHAPTER 12. England as Seen by a Black Man   239

CHAPTER 13. East Coast Strivings   263

CHAPTER 14. The Way Is Dark   278

CHAPTER 15. The Wizard of Tuskegee   294

PART THREE: THE DOWNWARD WAY, 1898 TO 1906

CHAPTER 16. The Wedding of Plebeians   307

CHAPTER 17. Our New Madness   327

CHAPTER 18. Still a Sick Man   351

CHAPTER 19. A Sac of Bitter Sarcasm   372

CHAPTER 20. Old Habits Die Hard   390

CHAPTER 21. The Downward Way   408

CHAPTER 22. Waiting in Loafing-Holt   421

Epilogue   449
Acknowledgments   461
Notes   467
Index   523

ILLUSTRATIONS

Fig. 0.0. Paul Laurence Dunbar, circa 1890.   vi

Fig. 1.1. Matilda Dunbar, circa 1890.   21

Fig. 1.2. Fugitive slave paths through Kentucky and beyond.   24

Fig. 1.3. Routes of fugitive escape on the Underground Railroad, 1860.   25

Fig. 2.1. Conservatory and garden of Dayton's Central Branch, circa 1876.   70

Fig. 2.2. Belva Ann Lockwood.   73

Fig. 3.1. Central High School, Dayton, Ohio, 1857–1893.   80

Fig. 3.2. Paul and his Central High School classmates, with Orville Wright in back row, center, circa 1890.   85

Fig. 3.3. Orville and Wilbur Wright, circa 1897–1899.   90

Fig. 4.1. Paul and classmates in Philomathean Society, Central High School, 1890.   95

Fig. 4.2. First issue of the *Dayton Tattler* (December 13, 1890).   98

Fig. 4.3. Dayton Central High School commencement program, June 16, 1891.   108

Fig. 5.1. James Whitcomb Riley, circa 1898.   114

Fig. 5.2. Paul Laurence Dunbar, circa 1892.   117

Fig. 7.1. Exposition grounds, World's Columbian Exposition in Chicago, 1893.   154

Fig. 7.2. Frederick Douglass, 1893.   159

Fig. 7.3. Will Marion Cook, n.d.   162

Fig. 9.1. Alice Ruth Moore, circa 1895.   189

Fig. 9.2. Dr. Henry A. Tobey, n.d.   197

Fig. 11.1. Front page of *Harper's Weekly*, June 27, 1896.   221

Fig. 11.2. William Dean Howells, circa 1900.   223

Fig. 11.3. Frontispiece of *Majors and Minors* (1895).   226

Fig. 11.4. Paul with Brand Whitlock, mayor of Toledo, Ohio, outside the home of Major James Pond, Paul's literary agent, 1896.   232

Fig. 12.1. Samuel Coleridge-Taylor, circa 1905.   246

Fig. 12.2. Frontispiece of *Lyrics of Lowly Life* (1898).   252

Fig. 12.3. Paul with friends in England, 1897.   254

Fig. 13.1. Paul at Berean Baptist Church, Washington, D.C.,
  November 14, 1897.   271

Fig. 15.1. Booker T. Washington, circa 1895.   297

Fig. 16.1. Advertisement of *Clorindy* in *Harper's Weekly* (1898).   314

Fig. 16.2. Charles Waddell Chesnutt, n.d.   318

Fig. 17.1. Thomas Jefferson Building of the Library of Congress,
  Washington, D.C., circa 1897.   331

Fig. 17.2. Sample decorated page and photograph from "The Deserted
  Plantation," in *Poems of Cabin and Field* (1899).   349

Fig. 18.1. Theodore Roosevelt, circa 1906.   354

Fig. 18.2. James Weldon Johnson, circa 1900.   358

Fig. 18.3. Paul with his mother, Matilda, circa 1896.   359

Fig. 18.4. Paul and Alice Dunbar en route to Colorado, 1899.   360

Fig. 18.5. Paul Laurence Dunbar on horseback, circa 1900.   362

Fig. 20.1. Paul and friends with his mother, Matilda (back row), n.d.   393

Fig. 20.2. Paul with a friend outside of Dayton home, circa 1905.   394

Fig. 22.1. Bert Williams and George Walker, *In Dahomey*, with words
  by Paul Laurence Dunbar and music by Will Marion Cook (1902).   423

Fig. 22.2. Home of Paul Laurence Dunbar, 219 North Summit Street,
  Dayton, Ohio, circa 1900.   427

Fig. 22.3. Advertisement for Paul's recital with Joseph Douglass,
  Atlantic City, New Jersey, 1901.   434

Fig. 22.4. Paul giving a recital at the National Cash Register Company,
  Dayton, Ohio, January 6, 1903.   435

PAUL LAURENCE DUNBAR

Introduction

In the October 1914 issue of the *A.M.E. Review*, an author named Alice M. Dunbar (1875–1935) published "The Poet and His Song," reflecting on the "life and character" of her former husband, the legendary African American poet Paul Laurence Dunbar (1872–1906).[1] When they first corresponded in April 1895, she went by the full name of Alice Ruth Moore; she was nineteen years old, he twenty-two. Their epistolary courtship lasted nearly two years, until they became engaged in early February 1897. In March 1898 they married; and in January 1902 they separated abruptly, without having children together. Despite his pleas for forgiveness, which she unfailingly ignored, they never reunited.[2] In print and in person, turbulence described the six years and nine months of their relationship: infatuation and love, admiration and encouragement, but also suspicion and frustration, exasperation and fury, as well as intimidation and violence.

Even though Alice published "The Poet and His Song" almost nine years after Paul's death, she retained the surname "Dunbar."[3] In fact, the essay marked her first-ever published study of why Paul perceived the world the way he did. "So if one wishes to get a correct idea of any poet whatever," she explains at the outset, "he must delve beneath the mere sordid facts of life and its happenings; of so many volumes published in such and such a time; of the influence upon him of this or that author or school of poetry; of the friends who took up his time, or gave him inspiration, and, above all, one must see what the love of Nature has done for the poet." Alice's essay seeks to render more human, if more profound and complex, a person she once loved but later came to resent during his lifetime—and after his death in 1906, a person she had eventually come to appreciate. The title "poet laureate of his race," which Paul assumed during the height of his professional career, underestimated the sophistication of his poetry.[4]

In lyrical prose, Alice describes the poems Paul wrote that best mirrored his unique literary sensibility.[5] One of these poems was "Sympathy," published in his fourth book of poetry, *Lyrics of the Hearthside* (1899). The bird's cage, according to Alice, actually referred to the "iron grating of the book stacks in the Library of Congress," where the "torrid sun poured its rays down into the courtyard of the library and heated the iron grilling of the book stacks until they were like prison bars in more senses than one." Paul worked at the Library of Congress from September 1897 through October 1898; during this period, a series of illnesses cut short his employment there. (The "dry dust of the dry books . . . rasped sharply in his hot throat," she remembered.) What had initially been the proverbial job to die for turned into a job that was killing his body and spirit. Being "a poet shut up in an iron cage with medical works" was "ironic incongruity," Alice wrote. Among the stacks Paul was not a patron but a prisoner; now he "understood how the bird felt when it beat its wings against its cage."[6]

Alice could very well have been overstating the misery surrounding the nature of Paul's job in the Library of Congress. Others who witnessed him there tell a different story, suggesting that the Library of Congress, for all its faults as an oppressive work environment, could never truly suppress Paul's brilliant sense of not only literary time and place but also how distinctive forms of art, such as music and poetry, could converge, stimulate his imagination, and move audiences.[7]

Although its autobiographical basis in Paul's stint at the Library of Congress may be debatable, the poem "Sympathy" nonetheless testifies in profound, existential ways to the miraculous and transcendent bond between the poet and the world. The poem highlights the "direct ratio" of the poet to sympathy—to the knowledge, as the poem's speaker puts it, of three refrains: "what the caged bird feels," "why the caged bird beats his wing," and "why the caged bird sings." Paul struggled with the belief that he lived and wrote like a bird trapped in a cage, however gilded it might have been by the acclaim of admirers. The poem would reverberate in the century after its publication, its lyrical poignancy and thematic cogency extended in Maya Angelou's *I Know Why the Caged Bird Sings* (1969).[8] In its depiction of how a young black girl could grow and achieve a personal sense of dignity in the face of rampant racism and sexism, Angelou's autobiography reveals the perennial relevance of Dunbar's original song: a caged bird beating its wings is the story of the individual imprisoned by societal preconceptions and struggling to escape.

Describing the life and times of Paul Laurence Dunbar requires that we tell this story. Prodigious and prolific, he was a serious professional writer for a total of eighteen years, from 1888 until his death. During this time he released fourteen books of poetry, four collections of short stories, and four novels, a body of work that showcased his mastery of literary genres—the Western lyric, the Romantic poetry of England, the "Fireside" or "Schoolroom" poetry of the United States, the realism and naturalism of American fiction, the racial uplift of African American literature, and the dialect of informal English. Newspapers and magazines across the country syndicated many of the individual texts in his eighteen books of poems and short stories. Across various mainstream and obscure periodicals, he also published essays on the progress, productivity, and challenges of African Americans from the era of slavery to newfound franchise and freedom in the decades after the Civil War. (For Paul himself, the achievements of his life and literature, whether accurately or not, served as his benchmarks of racial progress.) To wide acclaim, he recited his poems or delivered speeches in private homes, churches, schools, and auditoriums across America's East Coast and Midwest as well as in England's cities. And he drafted experimental works, including librettos and drama, that exhibited his prodigious artistic versatility. The quality, breadth, and diversity of his literature inspired countless people around the world.

A biography of Paul Laurence Dunbar, however, cannot be merely a story of the intellectual ideas that informed the way he wrote literature. Nor can it be only an exploration of the mental, emotional, and moral compass by which he oriented himself in the world. It must also recount the wider historical forces that inevitably shaped his personality—the forces that guided the various personal and professional choices that lay before him and that, he believed, would determine the course of his life, career, and legacy. One must tell the full story of an African American who privately wrestled with the constraints of America in the Gilded Age, but who also sought to express or mitigate this strife through the written and spoken word.[9]

Reared during and after Reconstruction, Paul belonged to a generation of African Americans—of so-called New Negroes—whose parents had been enslaved and who were adjusting to the capitalist modernity of America. It was a time when "the man of letters" had to become "a man of business," as William Dean Howells—the so-called Dean of American Letters, a renowned critic and writer who had become one of Paul's most influential patrons—acknowledged in 1893: "unless he sells his art he cannot live, that society will leave him to starve if he does not hit its fancy in a picture, or a poem, or a statue; and all this is bitterly true."[10] But it also was a time when such an edict leaned on an expectation that African Americans who sought to make a living through literary writing had to tailor it to racial stereotypes. Professional opportunities for such writers were limited to certain types of writing, including the depiction of undereducated dialect or African Americans in the racist mold of blackface minstrelsy. Auto-biographical undertones about how Paul himself faced this conundrum can be found in his poem "The Poet," included in his 1903 collection *Lyrics of Love and Laughter*:

> He sang of life, serenely sweet,
>   With, now and then, a deeper note.
>   From some high peak, nigh yet remote,
> He voiced the world's absorbing beat.
>
> He sang of love when earth was young,
>   And Love, itself, was in his lays.
>   But ah, the world, it turned to praise
> A jingle in a broken tongue.[11]

Paul resented how much the world underappreciated his literary skills and creativity. The facts corroborate his belief. Critics, editors, publishers, patrons, and fellow writers rarely acknowledged publicly, or even privately, Paul's ability to experiment with the various traditions of Western poetry in formal English—from the lyric to the ballad, the rondeau to the sonnet—beyond the stereotypical language of African American dialect he likewise happened to know and write so well. To Alice especially, he complained about how these circumstances so unfairly limited him, about how they forced him to bear a burden of racial authenticity more onerous than what any other African American writer of his era had to shoulder.

Nonetheless, and perhaps ironically, Paul overcame these personal reservations and social conditions to write and recite dialect in ways unprecedented in their artistic excellence and commercial success.

————

To make proper sense of Paul Laurence Dunbar, one has to begin his story well before his birth on June 27, 1872. One must understand the antebellum lives of his parents, Joshua Dunbar and Matilda Murphy, as Kentucky slaves; their separate experiences during the Civil War; their acculturation to the postwar city of Dayton, Ohio, where Paul was born; and their combustible marriage, violent exchanges, and eventual divorce. As Paul matured, he came to embody contradictions while rebelling against the world's stifling expectations. He tried to be a faithful boyfriend or husband to women, but his wandering eyes betrayed his pleas of fidelity. Alcoholism afflicted his father and eventually overtook him, too, to the horror or fascination of sober onlookers. Paul enjoyed reading, writing, and reciting literature in formal English, but the commercial vogue for the persona and dialect of the so-called Old Negro, or of the undereducated, docile slave, pressured him at times to change course to improve the sales of his published literature. Racial politics divided the African American intelligentsia into partisan camps either supportive or critical of the industrial ethos of the most famous African American educator at the turn of the twentieth century, Booker T. Washington. As Paul's perspective on racial progress evolved, he would come to support both camps at different times. Under such duress, the conflicted dimensions of Paul's personality became more manifest. He was a temperamental judge of others' failings, yet he himself was insecure. Toward the patrons of the white literati he was obsequious, yet with the patriarchs of the black intelligentsia he ingratiated himself. And to multiple women he wrote private letters that alternately expressed extremes of excessive love and merciless condemnation.

The remarkable life and times of Paul Laurence Dunbar break down into three main parts. Against the backdrop of the Civil War, Reconstruction, and the rise of Jim Crow segregation, the first section, "Broken Home," describes the early lives and eventual challenges of Joshua and Matilda, Paul's parents; the circumstances and consequences of Paul's birth and his fatal inheritance of Joshua's virtues and vices; his rearing in Dayton, Ohio, where he entered an entrepreneurial newspaper partnership with his high school classmate Orville Wright, who would later be known, along with his brother Wilbur, as a coinventor of the first airplane that could achieve controlled, sustained, and powered flight; and the years leading to 1893, when he published his first book, *Oak and Ivy*, and befriended the legendary African American abolitionist and statesman Frederick Douglass at the World's Columbian Exposition in Chicago. Spanning five eventful years, the second section, "A True Singer," bookends the era when Paul entered his literary prime and tried to grasp what being a professional African American writer meant. Literature authored by African Americans most excited mainstream audiences when it portrayed the stereotypical dialect of slaves, which became the mythical object of white nostalgia once the Emancipation Proclamation liberated 3 million slaves in 1863 and portended the metaphorical disappearance of their racist caricatures and vernacular. This section traces the origin and growth of his infatuation with Alice, leading to their tumultuous courtship and engagement; and it highlights the extent of Paul's personal and professional reach to the era's rising political stars.

The final section, "The Downward Way," begins in 1898 with his marriage to Alice, the joy of which was tempered over time by episodes of his grave illnesses, his confusing negotiations with editors and publishers, his financial obligations to support his mother, and his erratic behavior worsened by an irrepressible and obscene addiction to liquor.

A prominent part of this book involves analyzing Paul's volatile relationship with Alice, whose own comprehensive biography is long overdue and which accrues more information from the research I have conducted. I plumb his professional networks, which included patrons and politicians on both sides of the so-called color line. White men whom he came to know and admire included the writers James Newton Matthews, James Whitcomb Riley, and William Dean Howells; the medical doctor Henry Archibald Tobey; and Theodore Roosevelt, a government official he revered and reached out to—a gesture that this governor of New York and, later, president of the United States reciprocated. Others in Paul's orbit were legendary African American intellectuals of his time, including Frederick Douglass and Booker T. Washington above all, and to a lesser degree the musician Will Marion Cook, the writer James Weldon Johnson, the activist Alexander Crummell, the author Victoria Earle Matthews, and, in England, composer Samuel Coleridge-Taylor. Paul's countless interactions with editors and publishers, from the renowned Major James Pond and his daughter, Edith, to Frank Dodd of the publisher Dodd, Mead, reveal how he navigated the perks and pitfalls that accompanied his sudden rise to literary celebrity.

In portraying Paul's life, I attend especially to how broad historical forces shaped his personal, public, and professional identities. Newspapers, magazines, and recitals, in the United States and during his six-month tour of England in 1897, dictated his tactics and strategies to broaden his literary appeal for commercial gain. Political factors in the postwar stability of American society—including the period of Reconstruction (circa 1865–1877), the nomination of William McKinley for president (in 1896), and the gubernatorial and then presidential rise of Theodore Roosevelt (from 1899 to 1901)—played a hand in his access to elite constituencies of readers and sources of political power. The customs of racial taxonomy defined and authenticated his "blackness," to be sure, while segregationist policies for public interaction between blacks and whites limited his social mobility and his professional opportunities. And he gravitated to the great minds of literature in the extensive library that he built over time and collected in Loafing-Holt, the second-floor study in his final Dayton home, where he died on February 9, 1906.

Paul Laurence Dunbar was the first African American born after slavery—that is, the first modern African American writer—to achieve commercial prosperity and international stature exclusively by his literary works. But he was not just a writer of literature. Although only an occasional librettist and lyricist for musicals, he nevertheless helped achieve two unprecedented milestones in the history of American culture: he wrote the libretto for the first musical with a full African American cast to appear on Broadway, a one-act show called *Clorindy, the Origin of the Cakewalk,* which premiered in 1898; and he wrote the lyrics for *In Dahomey,* which debuted in 1902 as the first full-length Broadway musical to be both written and performed by African Americans.

Despite these accomplishments, the blessing and curse of Paul's celebrity status compelled him to behave in extreme or unpredictable ways, ranging from his poised and gentlemanly decorum during his trip to England to the shameful misbehavior in—to repeat Alice's lament—"the mere sordid facts of life and its happenings." Like a poem, the essential meaning of Paul's life and literature defies easy paraphrase.

———

Since the late 1960s, academic and public interest in Paul Laurence Dunbar has steadily risen, coinciding with the centennial of his death in 2006 and the sesquicentennial of his birth in 2022.[12] The election of Barack Obama as the first African American president of the United States likewise inspired scholars of American history to examine precedent circumstances under which African Americans aspired for high political office and intellectual leadership. Many scholars have gravitated toward Reconstruction, the era lasting roughly from 1865 to 1877, when Dunbar happened to be born and reared and when his early mind matured. During this time, the federal government sought not only to restore to the Union the eleven southern states that allied with the Confederacy during the Civil War (1861–1865) but also to consummate the constitutional franchise of African Americans in the wake of their emancipation from slavery.[13] My biography hinges on the very cultural, political, and ideological implications of Reconstruction for Paul's phenomenal emergence in the late nineteenth century as a leading writer, intellectual, and spokesperson for his race.

During Reconstruction, so-called Radical Republicans employed a vocabulary of higher law that anchored the arguments for African American franchise to the idealistic republican principles of the nation's founding almost a century prior, during the Revolutionary War. Although not unanimous in strategy or conviction, the Radical Republicans objected to the immorality of slavery and its denial of the natural rights of African Americans to "life, liberty, and the pursuit of happiness." Even though federal emancipation in 1863 undermined slavery, ingrained prejudice after the Civil War perpetuated the constitutional disfranchisement of African Americans. The Radical Republicans turned to an obscure provision in the Constitution that assured each state a Republican government. In another sense, the provision granted the federal government and its supporters license to intervene in state practices and enforce the entitlements of citizenship. According to historian Eric Foner, "A government that denied any of its citizens equality before the law and did not rest fully on the consent of the governed could not be considered republican."[14]

A host of constitutional amendments established the newfound franchise of African Americans after the Civil War: the Thirteenth Amendment in 1865, which formally ended slavery; the Fourteenth Amendment in 1868, which accorded citizenship to African Americans and certified the rights of citizens to due process and equality before the law; and the Fifteenth Amendment in 1870, which declared the rights of citizens to vote regardless of their "race, color, or previous condition of servitude." The Civil Rights Acts of 1866, 1871, and 1875 aimed to add further legal protections and assurances of equal treatment for African Americans. For a time, the core equivalence between Revolutionary-era republicanism and Reconstruction-era radicalism governed the progress of African Americans in the postbellum era. Under these postwar circumstances, African American men who served in the Union Army returned to their home states to reunite with family members (if they could be found) and look for work.

However, the notion that the federal government could control the conduct of individual states, particularly those in the South, fueled controversy. As the postwar tool of Radical Republicans to enfranchise African Americans and protect their rights as citizens, Reconstruction could not progress unencumbered. Constitutional cornerstones began to crack and buckle beneath the pressure imposed by the more resentful and retrogressive elements of American society, jurisprudence, and politics. For example, in December 1874 the Forty-third Congress assembled in the wake of Democratic domination of that year's elections, weakening the grip of Republicans on both the White House and Congress. (Ten years would elapse before the Republicans again commanded both branches.)

For each electoral advantage that Democrats gained, African Americans despaired that the nation took one step closer to the reinstitution of slavery. Slowly but surely, Democrats were reassuming the governmental helm of southern states. In April 1877 the southern Democrats conceded that Rutherford B. Hayes, the Republican candidate for president the previous year, could be declared winner over their own candidate, Samuel Tilden, under two conditions: first, southern and northern capitalists had to work together to ensure the industrial and economic revitalization of Confederate territories, and second, Hayes had to remove federal troops from southern state capitals, where they had been sent to supervise contentious gubernatorial and legislative elections. The so-called Compromise of 1877 began to nullify the Republican principles of Reconstruction that ultimately secured the political franchise of African Americans. As one Kansas Republican stated in February of that year, "I think the policy of the new administration will be to conciliate the white men of the South. Carpetbaggers to the rear, and niggers take care of yourselves."[15]

Juridical rollbacks accompanied the electoral compromise. Most notably, in the 1873 Slaughter-House cases and the 1876 cases *United States v. Cruikshank* and *United States v. Reese*, the Supreme Court weakened federal ability to uphold the liberties and due process of citizens, their right to assembly, and their right to vote, especially when these entitlements, in this court's view, conflicted with the individual jurisdiction and will of the states. Ironically, the very laws that once shielded the lives and franchise of African Americans in the South now exposed them to terrorist violence. Random white mobs and formalized, paramilitary organizations like the Ku Klux Klan plundered the homes of African Americans and castrated, raped, and lynched African American men with impunity. Additional laws designed to save citizens from being victims of fraud and corruption seemed inapplicable to African Americans.[16]

Political disfranchisement amplified the legal vulnerability of African Americans in postbellum times. During this period, as historian Nell Irving Painter rightly notes, "blacks never held political office in proportion to their numbers," and "any black representation at all was a novelty."[17] The electoral relegation of African Americans to the lower congressional chamber—the House of Representatives, as opposed to the upper one, the Senate—starkly attested to this disproportion. For African Americans and their supporters, minimal representation was better than no representation at all.

Most whites believed, in contrast, that they would suffer if the political status quo improved or even remained the same for African Americans. As the

Reconstruction period of emancipation and enfranchisement faded in national memory, racist efforts to undo these political attainments grew emboldened and systematic. Eventually, these efforts became victorious in their own right. Discouraging African Americans from running for the House of Representatives and relegating them to less prestigious and powerful posts, such as state legislatures and city councils, were tactics espoused by vocal Democratic constituencies and neglected by the deafening silence of Republican acquiescence.

By the Compromise of 1877, anti-Reconstruction sentiment in the media had reached a crescendo. Punditry in periodicals and books ranged from the Democratic criticism of government to the broader allegation, condoned by many white conservatives and liberals, southerners and northerners alike, that African Americans were fundamentally incapable of representing themselves in the realm of intellect, much less politics. The hallmark egalitarianism of Reconstruction gave way to the purportedly more realistic and practical, but essentially white-supremacist, doctrine of Redemption. Spearheaded by secessionist Democrats and Union Whigs, Redemption sought to ensure Reconstruction's utter failure.

Historians have shown that racial progress in the nineteenth century culminated with the Reconstruction-era electoral victories of the first African American congressmen and judges. Politicians and, less directly, cultural leaders emerged from African American communities to guide ideological discussions on how electoral politics could combat racial prejudice, injustice, and inequality, and how laws could work on behalf of African American progress toward complete civil rights.[18] Recent scholarship has enabled the discovery of new archives and literary forms emergent during and in the wake of Reconstruction, such as in association with the African American writers Charles W. Chesnutt, Frances Ellen Watkins Harper, Pauline Hopkins, and Paul Laurence Dunbar himself. The "unfinished revolution" suggested by Eric Foner in his classic 1989 book *Reconstruction* encourages a historiography that extends the story about the analogous opportunities and challenges of African Americans from the postbellum nineteenth century into the twentieth and twenty-first centuries.[19]

A comprehensive biography of Paul's life and times enables us to grasp the personal and creative choices he made while maturing into a professional literary writer on the heels of Reconstruction, when he became an emblem of modern African American letters but also a key protagonist in the epic story of race relations in America. Only recently have literary experts begun to pursue this wider lens of analysis, revising the long-held premise that his "dialect poetry" waged merely a "masked critique of the white racism, invisible to white readers but legible to black audiences."[20] The meaning and consequences of his life and literature turned out to be more complex than that.

———

Writing a biography of a famous American writer—especially in the case of Paul Laurence Dunbar, born of African descent less than a decade from slavery's end—invites a host of challenges. Some difficulties include the process of selecting the most relevant details for biographical inclusion; overcoming the practical limits suffered by the African American archive during the era and aftermath of slavery; cutting through the myths of his celebrity to the facts of his life; and capturing the essence of his writings, despite how numerous, dispersed, and sensationalized their publications. Perhaps the greatest challenge was documenting only the portion of the literature, life, and legacy of his wife, Alice, that revolved about his experiences, even though recent scholarly interest, including my own, in her historical significance and literary accomplishments continues to grow, and even though she deserves her own independent biography, one comprehensive enough to tell her life story in all its complexity, wonder, and inspiration. I describe these largely academic issues in the epilogue to this biography, whose conceptual and methodological puzzles rivaled the various puzzles embodied by Dunbar himself.

By the end of this book, new features in Paul's portrait should emerge even for experts in his life and literature. First, he was more concerned and frustrated with the plight and practices of African American communities than the standard record suggests. Evidence of this sentiment appeared in the editorials he wrote for the *Dayton Tattler*, the newspaper he edited and circulated for the African American Dayton community in December 1890; in the frequency with which he wrote poems in formal English, not in the dialect suggestive of African American vernacular; in his resistance to using African American protagonists in his early novels; in his and Alice's private rebukes of fellow African Americans; and in his oscillations between agreement and disagreement with Washington's doctrine of racial uplift. Second, he was more mentally and emotionally unstable than the standard record suggests. Private letters of correspondence between Paul and Rebekah Baldwin tell us that she, a lesser-known girlfriend on the margins of previous biographies, is crucial when attempting to fathom the unpredictable personality and behavior that he would demonstrate later in his more notorious relationship with Alice. His letters to Alice reveal that he expressed suicidal thoughts in regret of having committed violence against her. And throughout his life, he expressed deep disappointment with the course and outcome of his career.

Just as the "caged bird," as Paul deploys the term in "Sympathy," represents a biographical metaphor of the societal constraints on his life and literature, "For the Man Who Fails," a poem also appearing in *Lyrics of the Hearthside*, reveals his inner turmoil. In this poem, the speaker addresses "the noble heart and mind / Of the gallant man who fails," not only the man "who wins the game" and earns "Fame." An intervention of sorts, the closing of the poem imagines a tale of redemption before it is too late, before history casts a fatal glance upon the life and legacy of "the gallant man":

We sit at life's board with our nerves highstrung,
    And we play for the sake of Fame,
And our odes are sung and our banners hung
    For the man who wins the game.
But I have a song of another kind
    Than breathes in these fame-wrought gales,—
An ode to the noble heart and mind
    Of the gallant man who fails!

The man who is strong to fight his fight,
    And whose will no front can daunt,
If the truth be truth and the right be right,
    Is the man that the ages want.
Tho' he fail and die in grim defeat,
    Yet he has not fled the strife,
And the house of Earth will seem more sweet
    For the perfume of his life.[21]

PART ONE

Broken Home, Beginnings to 1893

CHAPTER 1

Broken Country

And their deeds shall find a record,
  In the registry of Fame;
For their blood has cleansed completely
  Every blot of Slavery's shame.
So all honor and all glory
  To those noble Sons of Ham—
The gallant colored soldiers,
  Who fought for Uncle Sam!

—PAUL LAURENCE DUNBAR, "THE COLORED SOLDIERS,"
MAJORS AND MINORS (1895)[1]

Paul Laurence Dunbar was quite bright for a four-year-old. At this age he was learning to read and write, a process his mother, Matilda, began before his formal schooling even started. As a child, he used a slate tablet on which he learned the typography, enunciation, and meaning of letters and words. Close to the end of his life, he recalled that his mother watered the seeds of his early literacy: "My mother, who had no education except what she picked up herself, and who is generally conceded to be a very unusual woman, taught me to read when I was four years old." Matilda could have been deemed "unusual" for a host of reasons—her indefatigable will, at the end of the Civil War, to flee her birthplace in Kentucky for a small town in Ohio, all while being a single mother expecting her second child from her first husband; her temperamental flashes; her hard-nosed protection of her family; her vulnerable acceptance of a troubled and troubling man, in Joshua Dunbar, who became her second husband and Paul's father. Equally unusual was her

15

educational resolve, which she shared with Joshua despite the strain in their marriage and the domestic malaise resulting from it. "Both my father and herself were fond of books," Paul recalled, "and used to read to us as we sat around the fire at night."[2]

The semicircle of Paul and his older half-brothers, Robert and William Murphy, created the audience. Matilda's handwritten letters to Paul and her relatives prove that she commanded literacy, which legend says she accumulated over time letter by letter, word by word, ranging from her access to other schoolchildren to her forays into night school. According to Paul, both of his parents valued education; he asserted that his father even played the role of an instructor.[3] Despite their domestic hard times, Matilda and Joshua still managed to bring themselves and their sons together, to huddle and cherish stories and language, as a family trying to grasp what had been penned about their race or their times, about their town or their country, while continuing to understand one another.[4]

The stories Paul heard from his mother about the South, about how she survived and left Kentucky, prescribed his vision of the world as long as he lived with her. "Here, in the evening, around the fireside," an earlier biographer wrote, "was an environment of study, of song, cheer and the lore and romance which had been the background of their forebears." Another wrote that, from his father, Paul obtained a deeper sense of the ways of the South. The voices of Joshua, Matilda, and those "friends" who were "former house slaves and field hands from Southern plantations," and to whom Matilda introduced Paul, inflected the vernacular wisdom "in the old plantation language," regaling him with "stories entailing humor and pathos." Looking back, Paul attributed the tenor, the music, the ethos of his poetry about the lives of his parents, about their circle of friends, to his memory of these voices. "I have heard so many fireside tales of that simple, jolly, tuneful life. Down in the country districts of Kentucky I have seen it all." But the journey of his parents, Joshua and Matilda, was far more complicated than merely a "simple, jolly, tuneful life."[5]

Indeed, the story of Paul's life, of how his characteristic mind and heart evolved from childhood to adulthood and expressed themselves in his personal conduct or literary writings, must begin with the largely untold and difficult story of how his parents survived slavery in Kentucky and, as freed people, built their lives in Ohio, first independently, then together, then apart. Part of this story—particularly, that early period about his father, once an artisanal slave in search of freedom—Paul himself recounted for the sake of his family's legacy and embellished on behalf of his literary craft.

———

Joshua was born in Garrard County, Kentucky, sometime between February and June of 1816.[6] Established in 1796 as the state's twenty-fifth county, in commemoration of James Garrard, its second governor, Garrard thrived as one of the most tillable counties in the state.[7] Joshua's early life there was comparable to those of Africans and their descendants enslaved in the antebellum South. Typically, the slaves acquired their first names in the English language, as opposed to the native language of an African nation-state, from the merchants that sold them or the masters that afterward owned them. If they did not devise their own names, as Frederick Douglass and William Wells Brown eventually did, slaves "often retained surnames identified with early owners," states historian Hebert H. Gutman, "and they and their descendants carried them from the eighteenth century into the nineteenth century, from one owner to another, and from the Upper South to the Lower South."[8]

As a slave, Joshua was counted as property by the state or federal census—if he was even counted at all. Slavery turned millions of Africans and their New World descendants from human beings into a mere "type," according to scholar Ian Baucom: "a type of person, or, terribly, not even that, a type of nonperson, a type of property, a type of commodity, a type of money."[9] If Joshua worked as a field hand, he did not do so for long. He was trained as a plasterer, a member of the rarefied class of skilled laborers that distinguished about one out of every four slaves in the antebellum South. They were not the workers whose toil amid fields of crops and cattle, or whose drudgery within and around their masters' homes, was simply manual in nature and menial in stature. Nor were they of the semiskilled or domestic group of coachmen, gardeners, house servants, and teamsters. Instead, they were the most dignified barrel-makers, blacksmiths, carpenters, coopers, harness-makers, masons, millers, painters, plasterers, shoemakers, tanners, wagon-makers, wheelwrights—the artisans and mechanics who, early in life, likely first served their owners as apprentices. Masters only reluctantly sold away their apprenticed or artisan slaves. Hiring local white craftsmen tended to be more expensive. Renting the slaves out to owners or businesses enabled masters to skim off the earnings while retaining their property.[10]

By the time Joshua was born, plastering was a special skill in America. The last decade of the eighteenth century had already witnessed the hiring of slaves to help build the District of Columbia's capitol. (For a little more than the next half-century, the slaves were denied the rights and privileges of the government whose buildings they helped construct.) Artists and scientists alike, plasterers were attentive to the aesthetics and geometries of artisanship. Peter Nicholson, in his 1831 "mechanics companion" to learning several professional kinds of "art," insisted that plastering was useful "in the finishing of buildings, and furnishes the interior with elegant decorations, and conduces both to the health and comfort of the inhabitants."

Plastering could be arduous labor. Plasterers mixed and mastered the ingredients of their material. A compound of lime, hair, and sand were boiled down, turning plaster into paste. Slender strips of wood, known as reeds or laths, were latticed across ceilings to support surfaces soon to be plastered. Trowels and hawks carved plaster into globs of paste, to be layered and smoothed over and along walls and ceilings. Maneuvered hand, quirk, or derby floats helped lay down the second coat of plaster. Screeds guided the creation of running moldings. The plaster dried and hardened under watchful eyes. The stucco, the ultimate and finest layer, consummated the artistry. Plastering skill made Joshua invaluable to a slaveowner.[11]

Plastering deepened Joshua's view of slavery. Though his ability to read and write was functional at best, his life likely resembled those of other slaves skilled and lucky enough to leave written records of their lives.[12] Joshua was not unlike a young William Wells Brown, of Fayette County, who became the most famous Kentucky-born former slave of the era.[13] He was like an adolescent Henry Bibb, of Shelby County, the next most widely read slave from the state.[14] And he resembled Lewis Garrard Clarke, of Kentucky's Madison County, early in life.[15] Skilled slaves were more likely than any other kind not only to desire and imagine freedom but to strategize ways to achieve it. Such behavior was illegal, but its autonomy and ambition were common traits of slave artisans, as was the intelligence to see the link between labor and wages, to imagine ways of taking advantage of this link, and to develop exit strategies in case their slaveowners could not or would not meet their demands as workers.[16] Simply because slave artisans were privileged did not mean that they were satisfied with their lot. Being hired out to other plantations or cities strained their bonds to their families, left them vulnerable to exploitation by new employers, and subjected them to worse conditions of labor.[17]

Closer to the end of the nineteenth century, when he was in his late twenties and in his literary prime, Paul published a short story, entitled "The Ingrate," set in antebellum Kentucky and recounting the life of Josh Leckler, a slave hired out as an underpaid plasterer and sharing an abbreviated first name. Both of these details coincided with the qualities of Paul's own father.[18] Josh, according to the story, learns from his master, James Leckler, how to read, write, and cipher, skills that he redeploys to help himself strategically discern whether his contractors are ripping him off. With this learning Josh repays his master not with obedience but with deceit, with being an "ingrate": he forges a traveling pass in James's hand, flees Kentucky, finds his way through Ohio, reaches Canada as a freeman, and returns to America to enlist as a "colored soldier" in the Union army.

In a fanciful way, "The Ingrate" enables one to envision Joshua's whereabouts as a slave, fugitive, and freeperson. Although mostly fiction, the story leans on the actual facts that Paul had gathered over time as a student of African American history and as a child of former slaves. Artisanship, for example, granted both Josh Leckler and Joshua Dunbar exceptional privilege in their slave communities, resembling the stature of Dave the Potter, a legendary slave who worked in South Carolina in the two decades before the Civil War and whose mastery of reading and writing (such as by designing ceramic pottery, etching verses on them, signing them, and financially speculating on his artwork) boosted his social authority.[19]

Artisanship also granted slaves practical chances to be free. William Wells Brown, upon being hired out at one point in his life, knew that the "opportunity of getting to a land of liberty was gone, at least for the time being." Later, around 1840, he knew the moment had come:

During the last night that I served in slavery," he reflected, "I did not close my eyes a single moment. When not thinking of the future, my mind dwelt on the past. The love of a dear mother, a dear sister, and three dear brothers, yet living, caused me to shed many tears. If I could only have been assured of their being dead, I should have felt satisfied; but I imagined I saw my dear mother in the cotton-field, followed by a merciless task-master, and no one to speak a consoling word to her! I beheld my dear sister in the hands of a slave-driver, and compelled to submit to his cruelty! None but one placed in such a situation can for a moment imagine the intense agony to which these reflections subjected me.[20]

Artisan slaves were most likely to occupy the class of managers, rebels, and leaders within their communities. They were also likely to demonstrate ingenuity and persistence in running away, reaching free land, and avoiding capture. The coincidence resulted, in part, from the ability of runaways to act as hired-out or self-hired slaves in search of a job, or their ability, while at work, to exploit the time and distance away from their masters that they regularly enjoyed and then slip away. Artisans took advantage of this skill set and class status within the slave community to escape.[21] Skilled in this respect, Joshua, probably in the early to mid-1840s, or in his mid- to late twenties, fled northward when bondage became too much to bear.[22]

———

On October 5, 1845, Willis and Elizabeth Porter Burton, a married couple enslaved on Squire David Glass's farm in Fayette County, Kentucky, gave birth to Matilda Jane Burton around the same time that Joshua, nearly thirty years old, was fleeing northward.[23] She was said to have possessed Cherokee Native American ancestry, potentially inherited from her grandmother, Rebecca Porter. By the time Matilda turned five, she was one of fifteen slaves who lived on the farm and one of the eleven children under the age of twenty. In the course of her life, Matilda came to know, to the extent that she could, seven siblings: three brothers, called Alec, Robert, and Willis; and four sisters, named Ann, Ellen, Rebecca, and Priscilla.[24]

Matilda's contact with her father, Willis, was superficial. Owned by a different master, Willis dropped by to see his children only periodically, such as Saturday afternoons in the summer. Even so, few things pleased Matilda more than seeing him these afternoons. Jubilant, she and her siblings would sing and dance: "Here comes Pappy, here comes Pappy!" Still, Matilda could not connect with him. Even Willis's final reunion with her and her mother, Elizabeth, in Dayton did not leave a lasting impression. Fleeting was his time in her home and in the lives of those Matilda was closest to, such as Elizabeth and her grandmother Rebecca.[25]

Matilda and her fellow slaves did not "love" the farm's owner, "Master David." He was an "old man," "so irritable and hard to get along with," she later remembered. But they loved his son, Thompson, who "managed" the plantation. (Sarah, the mother, also lived there.)[26] Around the age of six, about four years younger than slaves typically began regular work as field hands, Matilda was assigned to minor tasks inside the house.[27] Then Thompson fell ill while

FIG. 1.1. Matilda Dunbar, circa 1890. (Courtesy of the Paul Laurence Dunbar Collection, Ohio History Connection)

drinking water in the field and was confined to bed. By his bedside Matilda tended to him. She used an asparagus branch to shoo flies away. His health continued to decline until he died before her eyes. Afterward, she witnessed the grief of Mrs. Glass, who became "hysterical," and of Mr. Glass, "his old father, who had been so cross with him." Tragedy in the Glass family had been steady, with earlier deaths of their other children: Marshall, at about twelve months in 1827; Sarah Agnes, at age three in 1834; Joseph, at fifteen, in 1835; James, at thirty-one, in 1848; and now Thompson, at twenty-eight, on August 14, 1852.[28] Shortly after Thompson died, Mr. and Mrs. Glass—respectively seventy-two and sixty-five in 1852—sold their farm, which they could not manage on their own. The sale of the property tore apart the Burton family, and Matilda was forcefully separated from her mother.[29] Matilda moved with Mr. and Mrs. Glass to the farm of Glass relatives Jack and Margaret Venable, in Lexington, the seat of Fayette County and one of Kentucky's major cities.[30]

Matilda's labor in the homes of the Glasses and the Venables attested to the hardship enslaved girls and women faced in antebellum Kentucky. The home was the locus of the slave girl's obligation to the master's family, which in turn imposed a set of duties that stressed both her lower status and the vulnerability of her own enslaved family. "A compact, volatile, and somewhat isolated society," writes historian Jacqueline Jones, "the slaveholder's estate represented, in microcosm, a larger drama in which physical force combined with the coercion embedded in the region's political economy to sustain the power of whites over blacks and men over women."[31] Matilda worked to preserve the quality of life of her master's family or of his extended family. She had to tend to the sick, as she previously had done for Thompson; care for any small child; serve the master and mistress individually, along with any relatives residing on the estate; cook the meals, often with dangerously sharp knives, sometimes over open hearths; clean the house and all its recesses; launder clothes in tubs and pots or in the creek outdoors; iron the garments while not getting burned, and hoist loads of them throughout the residence. Domestic work rivaled the strain of fieldwork.[32]

Matilda also faced, as many female slaves did, the seasonal move from housework to harvesting. (Children her age often were told to act as scarecrows or lug water to field hands.) From July or August to December of every year, for about fourteen hours per day, she faced the prospect of accompanying the male slaves in handling the plow, the hoe, or the sack of 150 pounds of cotton. And she likely knew that even pregnant women were not absolved of this task. Every one of them was still counted as at least half a hand. They had to do the backbreaking outdoor labor like everyone else.[33]

In 1853, after having lived at the Venable home in Lexington for no more than a year, Matilda moved to Louisville, about eighty miles west, to the home of Robert K. White, whom she would later call a "son-in-law" of deceased Thompson Glass. From here she was hired out to a number of other homes in Louisville, the first belonging to William and Elizabeth Timewell. When Colonel White first took Matilda to Elizabeth Timewell, the elderly lady—who, like her husband, had been born in England and was then about seventy years old—surveyed the child. "How old is this girl?" Mrs. Timewell asked. "She is seven," Mr. White replied. This was the first time Matilda realized her own age. It marked the year to which she would later refer in calculating her birthdate, her movements as an adolescent from one master or employer to the next, and her age at any subsequent moment in history. For the next three years, Matilda worked mainly for Mrs. Timewell and continued to see her even when she moved on to the service of different masters. On occasion she took up residence in Mrs. Timewell's home.[34]

From about 1854 to 1859, Mr. White hired "Tillie," as Matilda was also called, to perform a range of odd jobs for other families: she nursed a two-year-old, shoveled snow, got an employer's relative ready for a wedding. Her jobs varied in location: some were in Louisville, which was in Jefferson County; others were in Shelby County, the eastern neighbor. "I had a number of places," Matilda once reflected, regarding this time. "Some of the people I worked for were not good to me; but the people who owned me were kind and indulgent and would not compel me to stay at a place if I didn't like it." If at any time an employer were cruel, Matilda would soon inform Mr. White, who would return with her the next workday and correct the misconduct. "She is nothing but a child," he would admonish.[35]

———

Joshua chose the most historic, if most perilous, kind of flight. By leaving permanently, he defied not only his master but also the laws that defined him as property subject to the discretion of a slaveowner. Early Kentucky slave statutes and the "extradition clause" of the United States Constitution established, certainly by 1850, the classification and prosecution of slaves as runaways whenever they abandoned plantations for free territories. Urgency fueled his escape. Aside from lashings, both public and private, he likely feared being sold to a state farther south, where flight to free soil would have entailed much longer travel across slave territories.

No other free state was more enticing to Joshua and other Kentucky runaways than Ohio, where antislavery and abolitionist policies dated back to the time of its admission as the seventeenth state in the Union in 1803. African descendants constituted merely 1 percent of the state's total population,

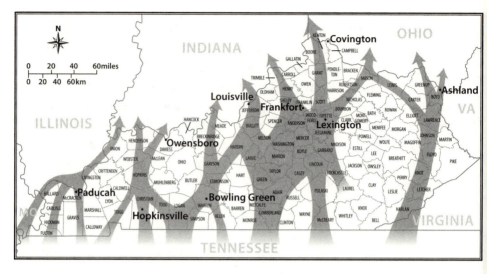

FIG. 1.2. Fugitive slave paths through Kentucky and beyond.

congregated mostly in northeastern Wayne County, after they had fled the South and landed among Native Americans.[36] The jurisdiction of Ohio Territory had been adhering to Article VI of the Northwest Ordinance of 1787, which outlawed slavery in the broader region demarcated by the western and eastern boundaries of the Mississippi River and Pennsylvania and, on the other side, by the northern and southern boundaries of Canada's rim (above the Great Lakes) and the Ohio River. Fifteen years later—or the year before Ohio entered the union—the Constitutional Convention upheld the law establishing a legislative linchpin of antislavery and abolition rhetoric for decades to come: slavery was prohibited in the Northwest Territory.[37]

The cultural and political ideals of Ohio complemented the edict. Former white residents of the South, seeking to be rid of slavery, crossed the border of the Ohio River to settle in the state. New England residents who were far less exposed to slavery than the expatriated southerners also formed a substantial part of Ohio's diverse migrant community and imbued the state's community with another facet of largely antislavery sentiment. Only a brief period passed after the 1802 constitutional enforcement of Article VI when slaveholders began to transport their chattel to Ohio and, almost repentantly, relinquish ownership of the human property. Freed, the slaves held dear the official certificate indicating that they would "not become a charge of this county" in Ohio as long as they henceforth remained in it.[38]

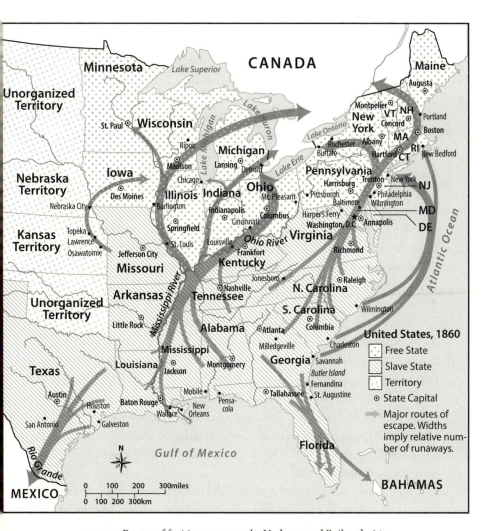

FIG. 1.3. Routes of fugitive escape on the Underground Railroad, 1860.

Kentucky slaves gravitated to the Ohio antislavery sentiment, societies, statutes, and advocacy for civil rights. In 1841 a "personal liberty" guarantee for slaves came from the case *State v. Farr*, in which an abolitionist was charged with abduction and larceny for telling slaves that they were manumitted once they stepped foot in Ohio. Ultimately, the state's supreme court ruled in favor of Ohio's status as free territory and overturned precedent legal opinion to the contrary.[39] Since then, free African American communities proliferated throughout the state and identified with the fellow free states of the North.

Ohio was accessible only after crossing the Ohio River, also called the river of democracy.[40]

Crossing the Ohio River and navigating the adjacent main streets, however, were exceedingly difficult for runaways like Joshua. Most could not swim, and they did not have time to learn how to do so during their journey. Forging the common border between Kentucky, on one side, and Ohio and Indiana on the other, the treacherous river ranged between one and two miles wide. Tributaries cut into and out of the river's steep banks, which often rose four hundred feet above water level and in which efflorescent forest trees had taken root. Slaves had to plot how to descend and ascend those banks nimbly and quickly.[41]

Joshua and fellow runaways could not ignore the weather's impact on the Ohio River. The Ohio Basin's weather was more temperate than the warmer region west of the Mississippi River and the cooler region east of the Appalachian Mountains. Still, the weather fluctuated enough for slaves to consider flight as a seasonal opportunity, just as merchants and tourists regarded their commercial expeditions on the Ohio River. Extreme cases of sweltering summers and frigid winters made flight nearly impossible. Excess precipitation in the spring months of March through May and the autumn months of September through November threatened to flood the main channel and the tributaries with levels of water so high that the weaker and shorter embankments could not restrain the flow. The river became so choppy that flatboat and steamboat captains refrained from navigating upstream or downstream. In such conditions the water was so dangerous that tree debris, like planters and sawyers, lay scattered across it.

Under these circumstances runaways had to sneak onto barges, ferries, and steamships as hirable laborers. Some slave-catchers counteracted this stealth with their own knowledge about the riskiest ravines, the social exclusivity of vessels, and the sometimes equally mindful officials who ran or worked aboard them or along the waterways full-time.[42] Weather dictated the probability of successful flight. Relative to summer and winter, the autumn months provided runaways the best weather conditions to travel long distances by foot. Ironically, the moderate temperatures also facilitated the ability of slave-catchers to pursue them. As they accounted for this probability, runaways necessarily resorted to the uncomfortable winter months of December through February. The harsher conditions of cold and snow meant that winter could discomfort, disorient, and discourage slaves and slave-catchers alike. The frozen Ohio River inspired slaves to skate across its frozen surface from the Kentucky shoreline, even at the risk of crashing through a fragile section of ice and drowning or dying of hypothermia. Summer was the next most desirable season. From June through August, shrubs were bushiest, tree branches yawned widest with mature leaves; the backwoods sprawled to obscure footpaths. Finally, the spring months of March through May attracted those slaves who, perhaps regrettably, had stayed behind the previous season, in many cases one season too long.[43]

Upon exiting Kentucky, Joshua and other runaways trained their eyes not only on Cincinnati, the nearest major city in Ohio, nor only on the smaller stopping points in Ohio associated with the so-called Underground Railroad, such as Moscow, Felicity, Williamsburg, Ripley, Springboro, Xenia, and Mechanicsburg, but also on one or more of the twenty-six counties, located in south-central and southwestern Ohio, where free African Americans settled before the Civil War and returned afterward—including Dayton, the largest city in Montgomery County. In all these cities and counties, slaves knew they could rest and recover on their own before heading to other free states north of Kentucky, like Michigan or Pennsylvania. They knew they could find communities of freed slaves and stay in Ohio until they decided what to do and where to go next.[44]

Some runaways turned to another country, like Canada—where Joshua ultimately went. First, he had to cross the Ohio River.[45] Dodging the slave-catchers who policed the Ohio River perilously complicated any fugitive's northward pursuit of free soil. He likely tried to reach one of the major crossing points in Kentucky, cities situated as close as a quarter mile to as far as five miles from the river banks. Joshua likely trudged fifteen miles per night by foot—sometimes farther, depending on preparation, health, desperation, and luck.[46] Trekking runaways were wise to choose the relatively quiet weekends over the weekday traffic. They paid attention to when and where the Ohio River, during a cold season, froze solid enough to traverse. For the decade and a half after 1850, many slaves turned to the Underground Railroad of former slaves and Quakers.

Joshua settled in the Ohio town of Troy, about twenty miles north of Dayton. From the 1820s onward, Troy was a hub of citizens and commerce. The Erie Canal connected the Hudson River to Lake Erie; the Ohio Canal linked the Ohio River to the lake; and the Miami Canal, beginning in Cincinnati, about fifty miles south of Dayton, went through Dayton and by way of Troy. As canal towns, Dayton and Troy abounded with flour, textile, and sawmills and enjoyed modern transportation. Starting in 1837, the din of Miami Canal boats was Troy's industrial soundtrack. About a decade and a half later, in March 1853, the first train—an outcome of the boom in railroad construction—disembarked in Troy. The fifteen months of railroad construction now joined Cincinnati, Dayton, and Troy.[47]

Two years after the first boat traversed the Miami Canal, African American families had begun to settle in the west end of Troy and established the St. James Methodist Episcopal Church. While African Americans congregated in their own geographical sanctuaries, the larger Troy community of Methodists, which comprised abolitionists, grew divided over the moral problem of slavery in the early 1840s. (As the Civil War approached, ministers praised the Union while denouncing the secessionist slaveholding states, and they urged the congregants to help defeat the Confederate Army any way they could.) Troy was hospitable to African Americans precisely because most townspeople were Republican abolitionists. Even before its rise as a canal and railroad town, Troy was essentially a stop on the Underground Railroad.

For Joshua and other slaves fleeing Kentucky, the paths via Dayton to Troy, then to Canada, were logical. By the time the abolitionist cries amplified in the 1840s, slaves were already exploiting the Miami Canal boats in which they could lay low in the secret cargo holds and await disembarkation at Troy, where they might rest, recover, and find work and a nearby place to live—or where they could proceed on their course, as Joshua had, toward Canada.[48]

Joshua's path to freedom recalls those of other Kentucky slaves who cut through Ohio and settled in Canada.[49] Since the early decades of the nineteenth century, Canada was one of the lands of opportunity and equality for which runaways, especially those coming from the Upper South, longed. But the region was difficult to reach. Only the most clever, motivated, and, yes, fortunate slaves stepped onto Canadian soil with the energy and motivation to start their lives anew. "And because they could stop their flight short of the Canadian border and find a degree of freedom," writes historian Robin W. Winks, "to continue to British territory was an act of conscious choice, in part a positive decision rather than a negative impulse arising from fear, as it would become after 1850," when the U.S. Congress passed the Fugitive Slave Act (as part of the compromise between the southern and northern states) mandating that law-enforcement officials or marshals across the country had to apprehend anyone suspected of being a fugitive slave.[50]

As one of the slaves determined to travel and settle in Canada—probably in nearby Ontario, at that time Canada's most populous province and one of its largest in square miles—Joshua faced the practical questions of how to get to this "promised land" and what to do once he got there. Which Ohio cross-ing points of the Underground Railroad were most secure—the cities of To-ledo and Cleveland, or the lesser-known Sandusky, Huron, Lorrain, Sheffield Village, Ashtabula, and Conneaut? By float or ferry, was Lake Erie as troubling to cross as the Ohio River? And which Ontario border town was safest—the outermost Fort Malden? Or the inland towns of Amherstburg, Sandwich, and Windsor (only about five miles from Detroit, Michigan)? Or those towns running along the Thames River, parallel to Lake Erie's shoreline, such as Elgin, Chatham, Dawn, and Longwood? Further questions abounded. How worthwhile was navigating the recesses of Ontario if doing so demanded a lot of money and equipment? If it detracted from an ability to return to America on short notice? If it led to landscapes and villages uncomfortably foreign? Or if it led to places where no other runaways could be found, or where no one looked like him?[51]

In the mid- to late 1840s Joshua found his way to Canada. Free African Amer-icans had already blazed the trail there: large contingents of slaves had already fled antebellum Ohio, rejecting its enforcement of the "Black Laws" or "Black Codes," which denied "mulatto" or "black" persons residence in that state with-out an authentic certificate of manumission if formerly a slave; without an of-ficial attestation of actual freedom if not an ex-slave; or without the registration of family members at a courthouse. (The codes were not repealed until 1849.) Some runaways sought the more hospitable environs in neighboring northern states—Indiana or Michigan to the west and Pennsylvania to the east. Others corresponded with Sir John Colborne, a lieutenant-governor of Upper Canada, asking permission to relocate there. Usually he agreed, alluding to their entitle-ment to "all the privileges of the rest of his Majesty's subjects." In the two de-cades leading up to America's Civil War, acres of land were allocated to the Cincinnati settlers intermittently, their exodus speeding up or slowing down according to whether their treatment in Ohio was worsening or improving.[52]

In the 1840s and 1850s, runaways settled near or within exiled communities located in cities like Colchester, Amherstburg, Windsor, London, Chatham, and Dresden. The neighborhoods tended to be homogeneous and segregated from white Canadians. Informal separation of black and white students in schools slowly crystallized into law. The goodwill white residents initially showed African American settlers gave way to feelings of resentment. The local government felt pressured to stem the tide of immigration. Once again, the settlers from Ohio had to deal with discrimination, even as they took solace in having fled its more profane and deadly manifestations on native soil.[53]

Work opportunities greeted Joshua by the time he arrived in Ontario. While most Kentucky runaways had to work as farmhands upon their arrival in Canada, skilled laborers could expect to find better jobs if they were willing—as the settled African American immigrant communities already were—to abide by the provincial laws of a foreign land. The runaway slaves also could serve in the Canadian military, where settlers or citizens of African descent had been stationed as far back as 1793 at Kent, 1807 at Fort Malden, 1812 at the Niagara border, and 1837 during Upper Canada's own rebellion. To be sure, their actual service was devoid of romance; they took up the mundane tasks of guarding bridges and buildings, patrolling canals, clearing roads—of volunteering in ways that would not be impeded by their overall lack of education or literacy. Throughout the rest of the nineteenth century, they were more likely to be celebrated as military heroes or veterans in Canada than their fellow runaways were after fighting for the Union in the Civil War.[54]

For runaways living and finding work in Canada, the allure of returning to family, friends, and familiar American surroundings was difficult to overcome. Nor could the runaways help but view themselves ambivalently, betwixt and between old and new worlds. The enslaved descendants of Africa had every reason to flee northward, yet British protectionism had far fewer, but still justifiable, reasons to accommodate them. One question was unclear, however: Would Canada welcome the fugitive immigrants to the country and ensure them proper claim to all the rights and privileges of Canadian citizens or long-time residents? Strains inevitably afflicted any bond that formed between the fugitive settlers and the African and indigenous natives of Canada already struggling to assert and enjoy their own civic rights. Certain slaveholding jurisdictions in America began to request diplomatic assistance from the Canadian government to extradite runaways and return them to their rightful owners. Within a decade after the initial panic of the Fugitive Slave Law in 1850, Canada's influx of runaways had subsided to a crawl. By this time, the Civil War was about to begin. Runaways living in Amherstburg and elsewhere in Canada were trying to decide when was the best time to return to their house divided and fight in the Civil War.[55]

———

The Confederate attack on a Union base at Fort Sumter, South Carolina, on April 12, 1861, forever altered the lives of Joshua and Matilda, just as it had the lives of all African Americans seeking to survive the era of slavery. Also called the War of the Rebellion, the Civil War extended the long-standing American conflict between the North and the South. Having African or African American men, women, and children in bondage was crucial to the South's quality of life, its economic prosperity, and its hierarchy of the races, whereby the Anglo-Saxon immigrants and descendants of Europe could allege and affirm their own superiority. The South perceived that the federal government, under the presidency of Abraham Lincoln, was guilty of "the oppression of the Southern slaveholding states." Unless actively counteracted, the oppression would upend the southern order. The southern states' rebellious plan to secede from the Union triggered the war that would last four years.

For a slave like Matilda and a runaway like Joshua, the Civil War pivoted on the practical and moral question of slavery. Slavery would have been upheld in perpetuity if the Confederate Army had won; overturning it would require not only victory by the North's Union Army but also the federal government's ability to reconstruct the South, preparing it for life afterward. New World Africans were already accustomed to getting involved in America's military conflicts, such as the Revolutionary War and the War of 1812. The Civil War's political meaning hit closer to home.

———

When Matilda, at the age of fifteen or sixteen, married another slave, Wilson Murphy, "at Marse Jack Venable's" Lexington estate, their time together lasted barely a year, since he would leave to enlist in the Union Army as soon as African Americans were permitted to, in 1862.[56] Indeed, only with its back against the wall, staring at defeat, did the Union Army allow the enlistment of African Americans—whether slaves or fugitives, freed or born free—given that carrying out the new policy exacerbated entrenched racist attitudes and practices. Short-term policies were already in place, in the war's early months, by which the federal administration and Union Army officials demonstrated an eerie compliance with southern slaveholding ideology. During the arrival of the Union Army in Confederate territory, for example, if slave uprisings happened to explode in their midst, Union soldiers would consider helping to quell them. The Union Army's initial aversion to helping slaves accorded with its early reluctance to recruit them. Tightened during the antebellum era, wartime policies denying the military enlistment of African Americans were reaffirmed by Secretary of War Simon Cameron.

Over time, such icy treatment of African Americans continued to thaw. The increasing military and social tensions between southerners and northerners seeped into the Union ranks enough to discourage compliance with slaveholders. A host of military actions and federal decrees paved the way toward allowing African Americans to enlist, albeit only in racially segregated regiments. The First Confiscation Act, passed in August 1861, denied a slaveholder ownership of those slaves permitted to assist the Confederate Army. Almost a year later, in July 1862, the Second Confiscation Act more explicitly manumitted slaves during the course of the Union Army's military seizure of property (which may have included these very slaves) belonging to supporters of the Confederacy. The Militia Act of 1862 was, to date, the most forthright expression of the Union Army's willingness to permit "persons of African descent" to enter "the service of the United States, for the purpose of constructing intrenchments, or performing camp service"—that is to say, "any military or naval service for which they may be found competent." Finally, President Lincoln signed the Emancipation Proclamation on January 1, 1863, formally freeing all the slaves in southern states and decreeing that these slaves would be "received into the armed services of the United States to garrison forts."[57]

Wilson Murphy thereby became one of the 93,000 African American men enslaved in the Confederate states who went on to enlist in the Union Army.[58] The mothers, wives, and daughters of these men, not to mention the slaveholding families for whom they continued to work, all buckled beneath wartime's duress. Masters and mistresses grew anxious over the fate of the privilege and entitlement of their livelihoods. Women slaves grew even more fretful over the fate of their own families. Short-term responsibilities to those who could not care for themselves—small children or the elderly—preoccupied women slaves as much as, if not more than, the long-term prospects of freedom that Washington, D.C., anticipated if the Union Army conquered the rebellion.[59]

———

Former slaves, like Joshua, sought to join the Union Army for their own sake or, like Matilda, were left behind to tend to families and wonder what fate had in store for them when the war came to an end. Slaveholders witnessed the deterioration of their way of life—the demise of an Old South whose very reliance on slavery for custom and commerce the Confederate Army fought desperately to preserve; the death of over a quarter of a million soldiers stood as one measure of that decline. The Civil War also galvanized northerners. Their collective goal was military victory over the South, not the abolition of slavery, but the federal emancipation of slaves in southern territories implied a deep-seated connection and circularity between the two: the Emancipation Proclamation of 1863 authorized the full-scale enlistment of African Americans in the service of the Union Army.[60]

With the proclamation in effect, Joshua could depart Canada without fear of recrimination. Newfound humanity and citizenship were possible. He was one of about 200,000 African Americans (out of a total of 100,000 free blacks plus 800,000 slaves available) constituting the 163 units of the Union Army. He set his sights on Readville, Massachusetts, where he could enlist and muster into service.

Remarkably flat, prone to spring mud, dreadful in the winter, Readville was known as Dedham Low Plain, about ten miles south of Boston along the eastern side of the Boston and Providence Railroad, before it was renamed in honor of James Read circa 1850. Fifteen years later, by the time the cherished cotton mill owner died, Readville became the site of Camp Meigs, a complex of about 125 acres on which stood soldier barracks; a cook house; company headquarters; a hospital; a pesthouse for the ill; a mortuary; a prison; a chapel; a store run by a sutler, or a man who orbited the soldiers and sold them supplies, ranging from merchandise to food; storehouses; and, by the war's end, a stable for horses. John Albion Andrew, Republican governor of Massachusetts, first erected these facilities for "the most important corps to be organized during the whole war," the Fifty-fourth Regiment of Massachusetts Volunteer Infantry.[61]

The Fifty-fourth Massachusetts exerted such a gravitational pull that aspiring African American soldiers in the North found it irresistible. Despite early skepticism, they flocked to it, acting upon the words of antislavery leader Frederick Douglass encouraging them to join. A local periodical like the *Anglo-African* likewise exhorted them to "prove" themselves as "men." Along with their wives or women in their communities, African American soldiers or interested onlookers donated funds to buy an American flag or facilitated recruitment to raise a regiment in the Fifty-fourth Massachusetts. Just as Joshua was being drawn to this infantry, Readville, instead of Canada, was becoming the final stop for the Underground Railroad. The rates of enlistment and publicity for the Fifty-fourth Massachusetts soared—as did, however, the swirling of epithets like "colored children at camp Africa" in the mouths of cynical observers near and far.[62]

On June 2, 1863, Joshua formally enlisted in the Union Army. Unfortunately, the Fifty-fourth Massachusetts had just closed its doors to further recruits about one month earlier, on May 11. At camps like Readville, one hundred men enlisting in one region formed a company and ten companies formed a regiment—several of which made a brigade, several of these a division, a handful of divisions a corps, and multiple corps the whole Union Army. The actions of regiments within one brigade complemented one another. Part of a bigger web of military interconnections, the Fifty-fourth Massachusetts was capped in size and function, even as it was fabled as the first unit of African American soldiers raised in the North. In fact, its very attractiveness caused it to burst at the seams. Officers and privates were transferred from the Fifty-fourth Massachusetts to accompany the surplus of recruits to the old Readville camp of the Second Massachusetts Cavalry, where they set up base, on May 12, for the Fifty-fifth Regiment of Massachusetts Colored Infantry.[63]

Enlisting for a term of three years, Joshua became one of the ninety-nine men to serve in Company F of the Fifty-fifth Massachusetts. Records say he was forty years old upon enlistment, but he was more likely closer to fifty, certainly not a typical private: the regiment's soldiers were in their early twenties, on average. At five feet, ten inches, he stood about two inches taller than the average fellow soldier. The word "dark" was scrawled in the enlistment ledger to describe his eyes and complexion. He was in need of new clothing. He declared that he had become "free" a little more than two years earlier—on or before April 19, 1861—which happened to be one week after the attack on Fort Sumter. He was part of a distinct numerical minority of Fifty-fifth Massachusetts enlistees who were former slaves.[64] Just as he was the peculiar soldier, Joshua was the peculiar ex-slave. Unlike the great majority of soldiers who formerly called themselves farmers, he was one of the few who had mastered an artisanal skill as specialized as plastering, and he listed it as his occupation.[65]

If Joshua did share a trait with his comrades, it was that he claimed Troy as his current residence. He stood in a long line of fellow Fifty-fifth Massachusetts soldiers who claimed Ohio, more than any other state, as either their birthplace or their home. In Company F, four hailed from Troy, twenty-four from Ohio alone.[66]

———

Matilda spent the time while Wilson was in battle working for different masters and mistresses between Fayette, Shelby, and Jefferson Counties, alternately working and returning to Mr. and Mrs. White's Louisville home. Her uncertainty over whether Wilson would return was resolved in the spring of 1863, when she once again came face-to-face with her husband of three years, two of which he had spent serving in the Union Army.[67] Approaching her eighteenth birthday in October of that year, Matilda and her husband had some catching up to do. Months earlier, on New Year's Day, Lincoln's executive military order emancipating slaves residing in the Confederate states had officially gone into effect. (The decree took a little while to roll out across the South.) The event was more than a relief.

"If freedom hadn't come," Matilda once remarked, "I'd been killed."[68]

Matilda heard first through hearsay from fellow slaves that they were free. The slaveholders confirmed it. Filled with elation and ecstasy when she realized the news one early morning, she "jumped up and down from the loft with a whoop and a holler, singing hallelujahs as bold as a mockingbird."[69] However, the persistence of Matilda's joy was put to the test by Wilson's arrival. Both got off to a rocky start. Though husband and wife, they hardly knew each other. Prior to Wilson's departure a couple of years earlier, Matilda recalled a formative strain in their trust that was still having an impact. "Before I was emancipated, he gave me a watch," Matilda remembered. "Working with it all the time, I broke the hands, and he took it and said he would have it fixed; but I never got it back; he said somebody stole it. When he come back from the army he had another watch, a great, big, heavy man's watch. I saw a guard string around his neck and I jerked it out right quick, and there was a watch." Then they had a tempestuous exchange attesting to the marriage's fragility:

"That's my watch," Matilda insisted.
"How's that?" Wilson questioned.
"You took mine, so this one's mine now."

"He took the guard off and handed it to me," Matilda later said. "When he didn't get work and I didn't have support, I told him that I was going to sell the watch and take the money and go to my mother's, which I did."[70]

Matilda sold the watch for fourteen dollars. The cash helped hold her over while she tried to make ends meet in a Confederate state whose economy was reeling from the war. The money also represented her independence from Wilson, whose detachment from the marriage and whose employment woes denied him the status of breadwinner. Matilda fretted that since Wilson "didn't do his duty" financially, the instability of their family resulted as much from the tension between husband and wife as from the unsettling rebellion and its economic consequences.[71]

Life would not get any easier for Matilda. After emancipation, she had rejected the money her mother, Elizabeth, had sent down to her while she was staying in Mrs. White's Louisville home. She was supposed to spend that money to make her way toward reuniting with her mother and grandmother Rebecca in Dayton. But Matilda preferred to stay at Mrs. Timewell's. She wanted Wilson to return from the army, regardless of the problems they had prior to his departure.

That choice proved fateful. Within one year of Wilson's return, in Shelbyville, Matilda, aged nineteen, gave birth to their first child, William Travis Murphy, on February 12, 1864. (The date also happened to be Lincoln's birthday.) Far more than their free white contemporaries, women slaves like Matilda tended to suffer high rates of miscarriage, infant mortality, and fatal illness. Masters expected their slaves to procreate to enhance their financial capital or fill the ranks of laborers, even as they imposed backbreaking work on their women slaves who were already weary in the months leading up to and in the wake of childbirth. Matilda and her son William were fortunate to have survived these conditions.[72]

Mrs. Timewell dedicated valuable time to William's care, even though she was still recovering from the death of her own husband, also named William, an England-born cabinetmaker who had died of dropsy. (The ailment, which had led to his sharp two-month decline in health and his death in June 1860, would afflict Matilda's own child a decade and a half later.) Mrs. Timewell dutifully nursed "Buddy," the nickname for Matilda's baby boy. "I would go in," Matilda recalled decades later, "and she would be settin' in the rockin' chair— maybe he would be asleep in her lap or maybe she would be asleep and he'd be standin' by, holdin' onto her." Ever grateful, Matilda was never reluctant to heap praise onto one of her most generous mistresses. "God bless her! God bless her!"[73]

———

Three weeks following Joshua's enlistment, the Fifty-fifth Massachusetts was mustered into service. Joshua's uniform comprised an overcoat, dress coat, pants, a pair of jackets, a cap with visor, and shoes, along with a haversack containing his bayonet, blanket, and cooking and eating supplies.[74] He was prepared for the long journey ahead of him.

On July 21, 1863, Company F—along with Companies A, B, C, D, E, G, H, I, and K in the Fifty-fifth Massachusetts—left Boston on the steamer *Cahawba*, set for Morehead City, North Carolina. Nearly a week later they landed in Morehead City. By rail they proceeded to New Berne and then set up camp on a riverbank near Fort Spinola. Another four days passed. They marched out of North Carolina and toward Charleston, South Carolina, where they hopped aboard the steamer *Maple Leaf*. On August 3, *Maple Leaf* landed on Stono Inlet, off Folly Island. The men made their way along the beach toward the island's north end, bivouacking in the sand.[75]

The two-week trip from Boston to Folly Island by foot, rail, and boat covered about one thousand miles. From their arrival on August 3, about four hundred soldiers had to do continuous fatigue duty each day on Morris Island—a nearby territory in South Carolina—for the rest of the month.[76] Their tasks, as Major Charles Barnard Fox of the Fifty-fifth Massachusetts wrote, included "cutting timber, making gabions [i.e., wirework containers for constructing retaining walls], building wharves, loading and unloading stores, artillery, and ammunition, hauling heavy guns to the front, and working in the trenches on Morris Island. The greater part of the work was under fire." Only in September, after the soldiers in the regiment had spent enough time together to improve their military discipline, did the tasks begin to lighten up.[77] When Joshua and the rest of the Fifty-fifth Massachusetts arrived on Folly Island, they were "introduced to Messrs. Shovel and Spade," in the words of James Henry Gooding, a Fifty-fourth Massachusetts corporal. Weakening, the men indeed were struggling to adjust to the warmer southern climate. The men had to travel almost everywhere by foot, their leg pain the inevitable price of fatigue duty.[78]

Fatigue duty was endemic to the African American regiments of the Union Army. It was noncombat work and the least appealing: in principle it recalled the drudgery of slavery, and in practice it kept African American soldiers away from the battlefield. "The spade and the shovel is their only implement of warfare," wrote one Civil War chronicler in regard to the Fifty-fourth Massachusetts. In his view, these troops were "in a state of demoralization."[79] Fatigue duty as heavy as the kind Joshua faced on Morris Island tended to exhaust, debilitate, and even kill African American soldiers, whose morbidity and mortality rates were higher than those of any other defined group in the Union Army.

On August 24, 1863, Joshua was declared unfit for duty on account of "injuries received, by lifting, while on fatigue duty."[80] He was marked present on the muster rolls of September and October, but on October 23 he received his certificate of disability of discharge, filled out by a surgeon at the Folly Island medical headquarters. During the sixty days prior, the surgeon wrote, Joshua had been unable to work as a consequence of the "varicose veins of the left leg, which he has been liable for eighteen years, and which have prevented his doing duty during the past six weeks."[81]

Fatigue duty ended Joshua's career as a Civil War soldier. It had inflamed the varicose veins that had likely developed in the mid-1840s, during his long flight, largely on foot, toward freedom. And it relegated him to a rare group: the 10 percent or so of Fifty-fifth Massachusetts soldiers whose disability on account either of sickness or of wounds received, in action or by accident, led to their discharge. As far back as the preparation in Readville, the African American regiments of Massachusetts were at higher risk for sickness and death than white soldiers, North and South, even before they went into battle.[82]

Joshua had "served honestly and faithfully," according to the certificate of discharge. Aside from serving his country, he received no benefits from his stint in the Fifty-fifth Massachusetts. He was a private who lacked either the time or the ability to ascend in rank. Upon discharge he had not yet received any compensation, such as the bounty of fifty dollars he was due for his service, after his enrollment in Readville. Withheld or erratically disbursed "bounties" for African American soldiers—that is, the sums the state promised to pay them upon their enlistment—were the subject of protests in the Fifty-fourth and Fifty-fifth Massachusetts Infantries; and when they were paid, it was consistently, and unfairly, less than what their fellow white Union soldiers earned.[83] Service records show that upon discharge Joshua was still "entitled to pay and subsistence for traveling to place of enrollment," to the tune of thirty-nine dollars for clothing.[84] But he still owed two dollars to D. W. Johnson, a sutler—or "Company," as Johnson called himself. In August 1863 Johnson had propitiously pitched his tent at the Fifty-fifth Massachusetts campsite and sold provisions to the soldiers. The soldiers were running out of supplies, and Johnson sold other valuable items ranging from literature and food to tobacco and alcohol. Excessive drinking was common among Union soldiers, including the Fifty-fifth Massachusetts.[85] Alcoholism would plague Joshua in the years after his service, well into his marriage and parenthood, and near the time of his death.

Once again, Joshua was in Massachusetts. In the opening weeks of 1864, despite his disability diagnosis, he sought to rejoin his fellow African American soldiers in the fight against the Confederate Army—against slavery. He knew that Massachusetts was the hub of recruitment for colored soldiers. On

Long Island—the one located in Boston Harbor—resided a number of draftees into the Fifty-fourth and the Fifty-fifth Massachusetts Infantries. In January 1864 recruits were being sent down to the Fifty-fifth Massachusetts in South Carolina, just before the infantry moved on the following month to decamp in Florida.[86] Some recruits not yet sent southward, backlogged in the Long Island "Camp for Drafted Men," were eager to serve a new regiment being raised in the state: the Fifth Regiment of Massachusetts Cavalry Volunteers, whose headquarters were located nearby at 21 School Street.[87] On January 9 Joshua traveled to Ward 6, in Boston's North End, and enlisted in the Fifth Massachusetts Cavalry.[88] He was then sent about ten miles south, back to the more familiar grounds of Readville. Merely seven months after he had gone there to enroll in the Fifty-fifth Massachusetts, he was back, awaiting further instructions on the nature of the Fifth Massachusetts Cavalry's involvement in the War of the Rebellion.

On November 28, 1863, the Fifth Massachusetts Cavalry welcomed its first volunteer to Company A. Cavalry companies—each ranging between sixty and seventy-eight troops—filled up at a steady pace. The First Battalion, including Companies A, B, C, and D, reached its limit by February's first week. The Second Battalion, comprising Companies E through H, was ready after about forty days, by mid-March. The Third Battalion, Companies I through M, after a little over fifty-four days, by early May. Within six months the Fifth Massachusetts Cavalry, which ended up having about 1,200 men, was fully staffed.[89]

Joshua was welcomed to a three-year term in Company F. His age was now listed as forty-two, although two years had not yet passed since his first enlistment. He was now an inch and three-quarters shorter than before. His eyes were "dark," his complexion "cold"—more likely an abbreviation for "colored" (the handwriting left out the apostrophe) than a description of his temperament. Yet his birthplace (again misspelled as "Garrett," rather than "Garrard"), hair ("black"), occupation ("plasterer"), and rank ("Private") went unchanged. Also relatively unchanged was Readville, whose muddy flatlands provided little resistance against the freezing winds that whipped across the state in the first weeks of 1864, which only worsened the winter discomfort in which he and his comrades writhed.[90]

———

Matilda's husband turned out to be nowhere near as involved as Mrs. Timewell was in raising newborn William. In fact, Wilson decided in either late 1864 or early 1865 to reenlist in the Union Army. He promised to reunite with Matilda if she held true to her plan of leaving Kentucky for Dayton, Ohio, where her mother and grandmother lived. In the meantime, the pull of the Civil War was irresistible. "Willis said it was his war and he had to get in it," Matilda remembered. "He said if he was to live through the fighting and all, he'd go to Dayton, and I must go there and find my mammy and wait for him. Well, I couldn't go right away, because Buddy was just a baby."[91] Wilson likely left in late 1865, as the war was ending. The Union Army no longer needed his services, or the services of other former African American slaves, as it had at the war's outset, when it was incurring innumerable casualties.

As her husband's image and import faded, Matilda had two goals: keeping her toddling son and unborn child safe and healthy, and getting to Dayton as soon as possible.

———

Between February 1864 and October 1865, the months in which Joshua was mustered into and out of service, his own journey through the Civil War was less eventful than those of the Fifth Massachusetts Cavalry and the broader Union Army. Like most African American Union regiments, the Fifth Massachusetts Cavalry worked far from the front lines. In March and April, the Fifth Massachusetts remained at Camp Meigs in preparation. The regiment's officers were scrambling to find horses. (The federal Cavalry Bureau, only a year old, was struggling to meet the high demand for them.) The soldiers were also learning to use their new firearms, such as carbines and revolvers, the typical artillery of Union cavalries.[92]

Joshua was detailed at the washhouse. At best, he accompanied the troops on trips. On May 5, 1864, he went with the Second Battalion on its two-day journey on the Boston and Providence Railroad toward the District of Columbia. Once there, for two months Company F was stationed aboard steamer *Dictator* in James River, Virginia. Soon it would advance through the state, onward to Petersburg and, in mid-June, its very first conflict at Baylor's Farm. When the cavalry was in position to strike, the Confederate Army had retreated and no attack was needed. "In the beginning the men were exposed to a severe cross-fire," wrote Charles P. Bowditch, who must have crossed Joshua's path multiple times as the first and second lieutenant and captain of the Fifty-fifth Massachusetts Infantry and again as captain of the Fifth Massachusetts Cavalry. Simultaneous with the crossfire, Bowditch went on, "sharpshooters in the woods around made it extremely nasty. Only one of my men was wounded and not that seriously."[93] If Joshua's battalion lacked military engagement, the men likely witnessed the typical distractions of desertions and training accidents, and the usual horrors of injury, illness, and mortality that befell combat and noncombat soldiers alike. A shortage of horses meant that Joshua and his comrades marched interminably, it seemed. His varicose veins likely continued to encumber, if not debilitate, him.

From July 1864 to February 1865, Joshua and his fellow soldiers were stationed at Maryland's Point Lookout. The period ended with their guarding Confederate prisoners of war. In March and April the company sailed on the *Red Jacket* steamer to Deep Bottom, Virginia, from which it embarked on a number of sites to encamp. Along Charles City Road the men marched into the outskirts of the city of Richmond, from there into Petersburg, then to Sutherland's Station on the South Side Railroad, next to Varina Landing on the James River, then to a camp just one mile outside Petersburg. After one more month of marching to and encamping at Light House Point and City Point in Virginia, Company F boarded the *McClellan* steamer, sailed a little over two weeks, and ultimately landed in Brazos Santiago, Texas, a small island at the opening of the Rio Grande River. Here they were folded into the Cavalry Brigade of the Twenty-fifth Army Corps.

Morale began to decline in proportion to the incessant fatigue duty and repeated bouts of dysentery, typhus, and scurvy. Many of the white officers in the Fifth Massachusetts Cavalry promptly resigned as the regiment withered beneath the scalding Texas sun. On September 28, 1865, the War Department rescued the men by ordering the brigade to be mustered out as soon as possible. On October 31 the men sailed back home to Massachusetts, landing on Gallops Island in Boston Harbor. Within a month they were to be paid and discharged.[94]

Joshua happened to make personal strides in this second, and final, military stint. Secretary of War Edwin Stanton had been slow to promote African American officers up the ranks. In response to Governor Andrew's inquiry into the matter, Secretary Stanton responded that such stature should not be accorded "except, possibly, for a few cases of plainly competent persons, recommended by the field officers, who shall be gentlemen and soldiers of the highest merit and influence." Joshua, according to historian A. W. Drury, was "an intelligent man of quiet and dignified bearing."[95] Unlike the other men who served the Fifth Massachusetts Cavalry from start to finish, Joshua was promoted to corporal on October 30, 1864, and again to sergeant on May 1,

1865.[96] His military distinction and discipline buoyed the lofty diction he would use to talk to his future wife, children, and acquaintances.

Joshua ascended the ranks at a time when the distinction between enlisted men and officers was not only one of military rank, dress, obligations, and compensation; it was also one correlated with racial difference, social segregation, and unequal pay. The commissioned, usually white, officers did not interact much with the African American soldiers. The discrimination and distrust that had long alienated the races from each other in the outside world bled into the relationship between the officers and the soldiers in the Massachusetts colored regiments. But some of the older enlistees, such as those in their forties and fifties, displayed the maturity and wisdom to adjust to these conditions and receive promotion. Joshua turned out to be one of those "gentlemen," said Stanton.[97]

In October 1865 Joshua's Company F of the Fifty-fifth Massachusetts was mustered out in Texas, his regiment's final place of deployment. Afterward, the regiment returned to northeastern headquarters—Gallops Island in Boston Harbor. Joshua was due almost seven dollars for clothing, eleven dollars for arms and equipment, and three hundred dollars in bounty payment.[98]

———

After mustering out of the Union Army in 1865, Joshua returned to Troy, Ohio. Aside from his place of birth and early rearing in Kentucky, Joshua knew Ohio best. (Incidentally, his enlistment records listed Troy as his permanent residence, although it remains unclear why.) The state was perfect for him. African Americans were flocking there: in the 1860s, its African American population grew by 72 percent. By 1870, Ohio was second only to Pennsylvania among the northern states in the size of its African American population, and second only to New Jersey in terms of having the largest percentage of African Americans in its total population.[99]

Joshua might have been aware that the increasing settlement of African Americans in Ohio led to vocal and conniving efforts by some lawmakers and politicians to stem their influx into the state, or to deny their sense of freedom within it. Controversies distinguished the political culture of Ohio. African Americans found encouragement in advocating for better labor opportunities, constitutional franchise, the racial desegregation of public spaces, and higher education.[100] Yet they encountered statutes—the so-called Black Laws—that discouraged them from settling in the state. They also realized the ambivalence many Democratic and Republican politicians expressed toward enforcing the legal protections African Americans needed to survive there.[101]

Joshua returned to Troy. As a civilian once again, he hoped that he could resume the life he left behind.

———

Sometime between February and April 1866, Matilda made the move from Louisville, Kentucky, to the eastern side of Dayton, Ohio, in a section once called the Haymarket area. Dayton was meaningful to African Americans precisely for its geographic accessibility. From the time the first African Americans settled in Dayton in 1798, controversy and transience coexisted. Some residents fled to Haiti by the end of the 1820s. Conflict arose by the early 1840s across the color line in the southwestern part of the newly incorporated city, when white mobs burned down the homes of African Americans. In the years before the Civil War, Dayton was a site of permanent disembarkation for slaves who had just crossed the Ohio River. The city also was a detour for slaves on their way to Canada. In any case, Dayton was a place where abolitionists met, antislavery societies formed, and manumitted or fugitive slaves fled, just as they did in adjacent Ohio cities like Piqua and Xenia, in the cities slightly farther away, like Sidney and Troy, as well as in the larger cities of Cincinnati and Columbus.[102]

Matilda's mother, Elizabeth, owned property in Dayton on 47 Howard Street, as did her grandmother Rebecca on 311 Howard Street. Matilda was already three to five months pregnant with her second child. Her husband, Wilson, had taken up a second stint with the Union Army and had yet to return. Another renter in the Louisville house where Matilda and her son lived happened to work for a steamboat that regularly took passengers from Kentucky, across the Ohio River, to Ohio. The man was generous with his time and help. Not only did he tend to Matilda's baggage as she tried to corral her son William, he guided her to the steamboat on which they traveled overnight, across the river, to Cincinnati, and he helped her secure a train ride from there to Dayton.[103]

When Matilda and her son joined her mother and grandmother to live in Dayton, they defied the odds. Slavery notoriously tore families apart, and their inability to reunite became a fact of life in the postbellum years. Freedwomen faced other postwar afflictions: illiteracy and poverty; declining biological fertility, even as they presided over households with six or seven children on average; cultural obstacles blocking their children who needed to attend school; and the burdens borne both inside and outside the home to maintain even a meager living.[104]

Matilda's sense of domestic obligation to take care of her children, of strengthening the bonds of family, was rooted well before the Civil War, albeit under very different conditions. African American women, particularly in the South, were charged to take care of whites—the children, the elderly, the sick—even more during the Civil War than before it. Masters and physicians in wartime were drawn away from their plantations to the battleground. The Union Army, on the other hand, encouraged African American women to convene their own families and abandon the relationships with whites that had been imposed on them—relationships that were asymmetrical in power and, hence, fragile.

The preference by African Americans to work either in the home or in the field, either on their home plantation in the South or somewhere in the North, was bound up with political questions of agency and freedom. Matilda's own desire to travel from Kentucky to Ohio, to reunite with those who had left her behind and awaited her eventual arrival in Dayton, resembled the aspirations of countless other African American women of her time: to do what was in the best interest of her life and her family, now that bondage as they knew it had ceased.[105] Matilda's reunion with her mother and grandmother was also imperative. She and fellow freedwomen who were single mothers regarded rural life financially untenable. Like most African American migrants from the South, they sought employment in cities.

Life remained stressful for Matilda as she, along with other freedwomen in her situation, moved from slavery—from beneath the thumbs of masters, mistresses, and overseers—to a freedom that put them under the contractual oversight of landlords, which not infrequently replicated slavery's duress.[106] But her decision to work in the domestic sphere was deliberate. Now manumitted or emancipated from bondage, many African American women embraced the idea that field labor was a job more than worth leaving behind.

In the years spent at her mother's house, Matilda knew domestic work best.[107] Work of this kind was not without its problems. Freedwomen trying to make ends meet while working for white men or women often had to tend to their every need, vulnerable to their whims, almost as if slavery were reborn in postwar form. Freedwomen regularly complained to the Freedmen's Bureau that their employers refused to pay them what they earned.[108] Despite these problems, many African American women had to accept low-wage work—as domestic servants, laundresses, nurses, cooks—if only because they wanted the autonomy to deposit earnings in bank accounts held by the Freedman's Savings and Trust Bank, when it was stable before the Panic of 1873, and to develop greater self-reliance. Servants and laundresses accounted for 70 percent of African American women working in cities during the couple of decades after the war. Likely to work long and hard their whole adult lives, African American women, by 1870, were three times more likely than white women of leisure or means to report having an occupation, even as, on average, the income of an African American family was about half that of a white family. Living under these conditions, married or not, mother or not, was not by any means easy for African American women.[109]

Life took another turn for Matilda on August 1, 1866. Two months from her twenty-first birthday, she gave birth to a second son, Robert Small Murphy, in her home on Howard Street. The father was nowhere in sight. But at least her mother and grandmother were there. Child mortality was especially high among African Americans, but Matilda, resilient and blessed, was able to nurture this newborn to full health.[110]

———

As Joshua wended his way back to Troy, he was aiming to resettle into a civilian world that likely had little room for him. A veteran soldier, he represented a class of individual that, in the decade after the war, found difficulty assimilating into broader society. Some were disabled, others disoriented, but all veterans needed help securing medical services, transportation, and places to live and work over the course of their "demobilization," as historian James Marten puts it. In some civilian quarters, the idea of returning soldiers provoked anxieties both during and after the war. In the wartime era, one Iowa newspaper described how civilians "look[ed] forward with dread to the restoration of peace and the disbanding of the army." A northerner noted that "the moralization of the soldier is the demoralization of the man." Public apprehension continued into the postwar era. The United States Sanitary Commission was compelled to establish a Bureau of Information and Employment to mitigate the potential "pauperism and crime, necessarily more or less a consequence of war," of which the veteran would be culpable, according to prejudicial eyes.[111]

Beyond public life, the veterans needed to reacquaint themselves with private life, with casual or intimate conversation with regular folk at home and work. And they had to assume habits antithetical in most ways to the restless chaos of military life they might have grown accustomed to, even if they did not enjoy being immersed in the chaos itself.[112] Stories of public opinion and private circumstance were prone to exaggeration during the early postwar years. The problems veterans faced, however, were very real. "Although many men returned to their homes and picked up careers and occupations where they left off," writes Marten, "others found themselves facing at least temporary dislocation," to the degree that "soldiers believed that their prospects for prospering seemed grim." Potentially compounding this dismay was disability. Maimed veterans tried to persuade society to overlook their physical afflictions. Joshua belonged to a population of physically disabled veterans who had to overcome the newfound stigma that observers foisted upon them: "a stereotype of noble sacrifice and deserving pity."[113] Tensions erupted between ex-soldiers and civilians, based on their contrasting outlooks on the meaning of the Civil War, and their assertion of political franchise in the wake of it.[114] By the time Joshua returned to Troy, the religious fervor of the Methodist population that had so inspired abolitionism before the war had in the postwar years invigorated a local temperance movement. Groups that included the Miami County Temperance Society, the Troy Total Abstemious Temperance Society, and the Troy Sons of Temperance sought to deter alcoholism by invading saloons and keeping a watchful eye on returning veterans.[115]

The Fifty-fifth Massachusetts Colored Infantry exposed Joshua to the culture of heavy drinking that afflicted the Union Army. Five years after his arrival in Troy, his own heavy drinking would lead to unpredictable and abusive behavior that would threaten his marriage.

CHAPTER 2

Broken Home

I don't think he was right in his mind. He had some of the worst spells—came home ravin'. When he had one of his tantrums, he threatened to kill me. I got afraid of him—and I had a nasty temper. I still think he wasn't right in his head. Poor man! He had been through the war and so much; and around the can[n]on! And he drank! Sometimes he wouldn't go to bed at night. He would walk the floor. Maybe I would wake up and he would be standing over me, saying, "I'll get you yet!"

—MATILDA DUNBAR (1933)[1]

On Thursday, June 27, 1872, Matilda gave birth to her and Joshua's first child, a boy. Over the weekend, Joshua hovered over Matilda's bed as she held the newborn; he spoke to her in a lofty tone, admiring the baby's resemblance to himself, as Matilda later recalled, while she teased him about it:

"Madame, that's my baby; he has my hands. Yes, that's my baby—
    the little rascal!"
"Well, what are you going to call *your* baby?"
"Oh, Madame, I know nothing about naming babies."
"I have named a couple; you name this one," Matilda remarked, in
    reference to her previous naming of her first two sons, William
    and Robert.
"Madame, have you named your baby?" he inquired, after having
    deliberatively left the room and returned.
"No, I haven't."
"Well, I have a name."
"What is it?"

"Paul."

"What? Paul? That old name?" she fussed.

"Madame, that is a fine name! That's a great name! Why don't you know that Paul was a great man?"

"I will never call this little baby Paul! That old name for this little baby!"

"Why, Madame, that's a fine name! You will like that name!"

"Well."[2]

Matilda relented. Her sister Rebecca (who had the same name as their grandmother), who came to visit in these early days, suggested Laurence as a middle name. Matilda relented there, too. So be it: Paul Laurence Dunbar was the boy's full name. The baby joined Matilda's other two sons, William and Robert, at 311 Howard Street, a home once owned by Matilda's grandmother Rebecca and which Matilda now shared with Joshua. The house stood near the prominent Church of the United Brethren in Christ on Wayne Street, which ran parallel to Howard and also intersected McLain.[3]

Little is known about exactly where and when Joshua and Matilda met. Most likely, they met in Dayton just before or in 1871, by which point her previous husband was no longer a part of her life. What is certain is that they became intimate by autumn of that year, around the time they conceived their first child and prepared to marry. What is equally certain is that the home awaiting this boy was a broken one: he would have to compete with his two older half-brothers for his mother's affection. Later he also would have to witness the illness that befell his newborn sister, and he would endure the violence that accompanied his father's intermittent presence in the family's life. In his early adolescent years, the volatility of his family left a deep impression on him, precisely when his independence and his attraction to literature and the life of the mind began to grow.

———

The bad luck of family strife that would trail Paul from childhood to adulthood began before he was born—in late 1870 or early 1871, when Joshua and Matilda decided to get married. At this time, Matilda technically was still married to Wilson Murphy. Her first two sons, William (then eight years old) and Robert (five), lived with her when she and Joshua began their courtship. Because Wilson had never returned from the war, Matilda did not know how to pursue a divorce or annulment; nor was she certain that he would not one day return and expect her to welcome him home. Despite this, two days before Christmas, in 1871, Matilda and Joshua were technically married by Dennis Dwyer, probate judge for Montgomery County, and Jacob Stephans, the deputy clerk. Both "being duly sworn," Matilda "deposeth and saith" that she "is more than eighteen years of age and has no lawful husband living," and Joshua "is more than twenty-one years of age and has no lawful wife living." For the public record, Matilda decided to assume Wilson had died.[4]

On the following day, the weather was cloudy and hazy, the wind light and calm. Thicker clouds were advancing from the South Atlantic coast, portending rain. Pastor Milton Wright married Joshua and Matilda in a religious ceremony at the United Brethren Church, where Reverend William McKee signed their marriage certificate. ("But it was Bishop Wright who married us," Matilda recalled, in a 1933 interview.) On that day, Joshua and Matilda invited to their home another reverend, named "Mr. Nichols," from the church. (Joshua wanted Reverend Nichols to preside over the wedding ceremony, but he did not get his wish.) As the group sat at the table, Matilda remembered, "they told the funniest stories." So humorous were they that, in her words, "I could hardly restrain myself from laughing out loud." The laughter had to be bridled, though. Otherwise, "I knew my husband wouldn't like it." After Reverend Nichols left, Joshua, in what would become his customary high-minded diction, congratulated Matilda for her restraint. "Madame," he smiled, "I owe you a thousand thanks; you laughed just enough."[5]

Joshua was the typical patriarch. "He liked a lady in a lady's place," she recalled later in life.[6] Laws, demographics, and economics conspired after the war to reinforce Joshua's authority over Matilda. The Freedmen's Bureau declared men the head of the African American household: only men could sign contracts binding the labor of their families, and it condoned the unequal pay that segregated the work of husbands and brothers from that of their wives and sisters. Only men could be delegates to political conventions. During Reconstruction, men could, in theory, participate in the political system as voters and office-seekers and in the courts as jurists. And men could thrive in a world where churches, newspapers, and public debate explicitly urged women not to seek equivalent franchise but only to bear and rear sons and daughters.[7] By 1870, about 80 percent of the African American households in the Cotton Belt—a geographical triangle in the South that stretched from Maryland down to Florida, then westward to Texas—had a male head of household and a wife, a ratio equal to the white households in this region. Most of the husbands were significantly older than their wives.[8]

As much as Christmastime in 1871 marked the apex of Joshua and Matilda's marriage, the foundation of their relationship also began to crack at this time. Beneath the innocence of Matilda's restraint and Joshua's relief, of her laughter and his compliments, their bond evolved misshapen, unmoored from the affection that first brought them together. There were the natural rumblings of conflicting personalities. But there was also the omen of domestic earthquakes: the destructive kind that erupted when one spouse yelled at the other, when both were coping with what it meant for a veteran to return to civilian life after the trauma of war.

Close to the end of her life, Matilda recollected that in the course of their marriage, she "got afraid of him":

> I don't think he was right in his mind. He had some of the worst spells— came home ravin'. When he had one of his tantrums, he threatened to kill me. I got afraid of him—and I had a nasty temper. I still think he wasn't right in his head. Poor man! He had been through the war and so much; and around the can[n]on! And he drank! Sometimes he wouldn't go to bed at night. He would walk the floor. Maybe I would wake up and he would be standing over me, saying, "I'll get you yet!"[9]

The domestic feud between Matilda and Joshua prompted her, though increasingly slowed by her pregnancy, to gather her three sons—Robert, William, and Paul—and leave home to live with her mother, Elizabeth, at 47 Howard Street.

———

On October 29, 1873, Matilda gave birth to Elizabeth Florence Dunbar in her mother's house, the same residence where she had delivered her second son, Robert, when she first arrived in Dayton.[10] But short-lived was any bliss that Matilda enjoyed from Elizabeth's life on earth. In the brief time that she was alive, Elizabeth suffered swelling in her legs and belly, which was treatable but not yet curable by medical science. Lying supine caused fluid to fill her abdomen and impair her respiration so much that she became asthmatic. She had to be held upright to breathe freely, eventually confined to a chair or an adult's lap for rest or sleep. Her muscles stiffened, then withered. Doctors knew that only ridding her body of this accumulating fluid would provide relief. Remedies of the time included paracentesis, the puncturing of the belly to allow the fluid in the abdomen to dribble out; diaphoretics to induce perspiration; jalap, elaterium, or dwarf elder shrubs for their laxative properties; and emetics for their ability to induce vomiting. Doctors might even have suggested a costly trip to a warmer location—supposedly conducive to sweating.

Elizabeth's steady decline in health resulted mainly from the insufficiency of medicine at the time to treat her illness, then called dropsy.[11] She had been born to a family less than one decade removed from slavery: travel to a warm climate for her health was not possible. Moreover, the mortality rate for African American toddlers was disproportionately high compared to other ethnic groups at the time.[12] Alas, she died only five months past her second birthday, on May 30, 1876. She was buried in Potter's Field at Dayton's Woodland Cemetery.[13]

What Elizabeth could have become was now a dream deferred to the afterlife. Matilda was wounded. "We called her mistress and sister as a baby," she remembered. "She was always brighter than Paul," even though he was a little more than a year older. "If only my little girl had lived."[14]

Joshua had nothing to say or do while Elizabeth's health declined, because he did not see it: he had abandoned the family the year she was born and did not return until half a decade later. In the interim, he wrestled with his own demon: alcoholism. In the postwar years, ex-soldiers bore extra scrutiny in the public eye whenever the media bemoaned the cultural rampage of alcoholism. Legend had it that, just as inebriation was a hallmark of camp lore and persisted afterward, the soldiers' moral turpitude threatened to infect society like a cancer. Alcoholism pervaded soldiers' homes, large residences where many veterans retired to and sought health care. Retirees not infrequently checked into and out of these homes, in lockstep with the arrival of pension checks, only to cycle back and seek readmission—their wallets emptied of money, their liquor bottles dried up. Later, with the arrival of the next paycheck, some would expect a discharge to pursue this "riotous living," as one Midwestern newspaper reported in 1869, starting the miserable alcoholic cycle of independence and dependence once again.[15]

Drinking was the salve for physical and mental pain. It helped assuage the worries of some veterans about their permanent injuries. It helped mitigate the depression that grew from the inability of some veterans to live alone or with others. And it helped some of them withstand the memories or the imaginings that became as terrifyingly real as the actual world in which they lived.[16]

Matilda witnessed Joshua's postwar syndrome in all its guises: the insane ramblings, the paroxysms of vehemence, the will to violence, the insomniac episodes, the vengeful hallucinations, including Joshua's embrace of drinking, either to withstand some of these symptoms or with the faintest predilection that he would be vulnerable to the more dangerous ones and that there would be little he could do to stop his own misbehavior.

———

Paul would never turn out to be as close to his half-brothers as he was to his mother, but all three boys shared the same mother and home, the same father for a time, the same devotion to learning at home and school alike. Not only did the parents read to the boys, the latter later read to the former. "I worked hard to educate my boys," Matilda remembered. "My boys read and explained things to me."

The exchange of lessons and learning, of love and discipline, strengthened Matilda's bond with her sons. "No, I never had any trouble bringing up my boys," she remembered. "They obeyed me; they knew what they would get if they didn't. They loved school. In the morning I gave them their breakfast and I said, 'Boys, you have to do the house work before you go to school.'" In fact, by the time Robert and William, five and eight years Paul's senior, were old enough to move out of the house, Paul would continue to read to Matilda and relate what he had learned at school.[17]

Yet Paul sensed that home was not always the best place for him to develop his intellect. "To this I owe a great deal," Paul admitted late in life, in reference to the experience of "family readings" by the fireside, "but, generally speaking, the influences surrounding me during the 'formative period' were not conducive to growth, and any development in myself came from fighting against them." Just as he was learning to read the written word, anticipating the day when he would write it at least equally well, he was also learning to interpret his private and public worlds, ones in which his parents warred with each other in the home and his race struggled in a political war outside it.[18] "Through the family readings I was introduced to 'Robinson Crusoe,'" he later recalled.[19]

———

The fact that Paul encountered *The Life and Strange Surprizing Adventures of Robinson Crusoe of York, Mariner* was not unusual. Ever since William Taylor published Daniel Defoe's novel in London in April 1719, it was an instant success. Written in autobiographical form with the real life of sailor Alexander Selkirk in mind, it tells the story of a young man who, against his parents' wishes, abandons home to go sailing, only to end up a castaway for close to three decades on an island nearby Trinidad, where he survives encounters with cannibals and pirates before his rescue. By the end of its first year of release, *Robinson Crusoe* was an extraordinary bestseller, and it appeared in six editions, in pirated form, in serial format, and as a precursor to the "farther adventures" and the author's "serious reflections" on the tale. More than any other book in Europe and North America, it had augured alike the English traditions of the novel and children's literature, even as its compelling narrative of action and violence encapsulated a more harrowing story, seen in Robinson Crusoe's appreciation of slavery and, more broadly, in the novel's prognostication of economic colonialism in the modern world.[20]

The gravitas of *Robinson Crusoe* held an allure for the serious reader, but other virtues and traits inhered in the novel's appeal to an impressionable youth like Paul. Over time illustrated editions emerged, with vivid drawings as well as textured binding and pages, that afforded an instructional feel and layout for parents or teachers and their children. Myriad other forms, ranging from chapbooks to songs and shows, not to mention the hundred different abridgments of the novel on the market by 1830, encouraged generations of people, across a range of literacies, to enjoy Defoe's story. Chapbooks, inexpensive pamphlet-like volumes, circulated inexpensively and literally on the street, among the lower classes, and among adults still struggling to read and children just starting to acquire the skill. The version of *Robinson Crusoe* that Paul, in his words, "never read for myself" but engages secondhand was likely a chapbook, a digestible edition that his parents, both "fond of books," could sink their teeth into. *Robinson Crusoe*'s condensation into chapbook form meant that underdeveloped literacy did not automatically hinder former slaves and their ambitious children from grasping and relaying something so child-friendly.[21]

Paul's memory resulted not just from the accessibility of *Robinson Crusoe* to the Dunbars as a family of fledgling readers. Nor did it only have to do with the persistent traction of Defoe in American culture, which compelled Thomas Macaulay to wonder in an 1858 essay, "I can not understand the mania of some people about De Foe," whom all acknowledged was "a man of the first order of genius, and a paragon of virtue," but also whose literary greatness the incessant popularity of *Robinson Crusoe* had overinflated, in his view. Rather, Paul's memory stems from the resonance of Robinson Crusoe in his own adolescence, much as the character did for other boys his age, and as it did for Macaulay, something the British historian had in common with an African American boy in Dayton, Ohio: in "That awful solitude of a quarter of a century—the strange union of comfort, plenty, and security with the misery of loneliness—was my delight before I was five years old, and has been the delight of hundreds of thousands of boys."[22]

For Paul, alongside William and Robert, now between the ages of six and the midteens, *Robinson Crusoe* was a tale of independence, shown when Robinson wishes to go to sea, when he leaves against the wishes of his parents, and when he survives in solitude on a remote island. Like Paul, Robinson had two elder brothers as well as a mother and father at home. (Robinson's father died before he went out to sea.) "Being the third Son of the Family, and not bred to any Trade," Robinson muses, in an original edition:

> my Head began to be fill'd very early with rambling Thoughts: My Father, who was very ancient, had given me a competent Share of Learning, as far as House-Education, and a Country Free-School generally goes, and design'd me for the Law; but I would be satisfied with nothing but going to Sea, and my Inclination to this led me so strongly against the Will, nay the Commands of my Father, and against all the Entreaties and Perswasions of my Mother and other Friends, that there seem'd to be something fatal in that Propension of Nature tending directly to the Life of Misery which was to befal me.

Boys who saw themselves in Robinson Crusoe embarked upon errands into the wilderness. Scavenging the woods, hunting and capturing animals, dwelling alone in makeshift sheds—such activities were irresistible. The story instilled in them a youthful resentment toward their dependence on the home. They were boys who sought to escape the shadow of domesticity for the enlightenment of adventure. If adventure was impermissible, they were boys who could "enjoy much more Solitude in the Middle of the greatest Collection of Mankind in the World." In "serious reflection" Defoe wrote these words, even amid the hustle and bustle of early eighteenth-century London.[23]

Robinson Crusoe intrigued Paul as much as it interested any American boy. The novel charted the path from the dependence of boyhood to the independence of manhood. It was also a cautionary tale about being a castaway: about the figurative and literal price a boy may have to pay in his solitary quest for maturation, a cost spanning the consequences of defying the will of family and heritage and of imagining a place for oneself in a rapidly changing world.

Paul was willing to take the risk. His boyhood education cut both ways: it elevated the life of his mind, but he also sensed that his surroundings delimited, if not denied, his potential. In the postbellum era, there was a difference,

on one hand, between his course of life and, on the other hand, the clash between a boy's ideas of becoming a self-made man and of living in a home so
oppressively matriarchal that he could not yet become a true man.

———

Some African American women in Matilda's situation tried to weather the
storm and stabilize their home. Some were outright fighters. Matilda admitted
that she "had a nasty temper" around Joshua, one that might have surfaced
much earlier. Legend has it that when she was enslaved and peeling onions in
the plantation kitchen one day, a mistress entered the room asking invasive
questions. Matilda "talked back." After the mistress struck her, Matilda threw
the onion at her head. Running away, she knew that she could not return, having "broken the law" and realizing that "going back would mean the whipping
post." Though this legend, told by a previous biographer, does not perfectly
comport with Matilda's own recollections, it does support the prevailing impression that, all her life, from Kentucky to Ohio, Matilda took risks, aware of
the consequences but perseverant nonetheless.[24]

Some women also fought back by turning to others for help. Stacks of complaints at the Freedmen's Bureau described intolerable conditions at home:
husbands who abused their wives, cheated on them, mismanaged their wages,
or were deadbeat fathers. Women were willing to disclose such details, even
at the expense of privacy, to improve their lot. Matilda formally complained
to shed light on her suffering as a "battered woman."[25]

Neither did Joshua endear himself to Matilda by his absence from 1873 to
1877. He never came by to see his daughter, Elizabeth, live or die; to bond with
his son, Paul; or to help raise his stepsons, William and Robert. This was the
last straw for Matilda.

———

Almost one month after Elizabeth died, Matilda filed a petition for divorce
from Joshua and for custody of Paul, the one remaining child they had together. Filed in the clerk's office of Montgomery County in Ohio on July 1,
1876, the petition pitted the couple against each other as "plaintiff" and "de-
fendant," exposing their marriage to the scrutiny of the Court of Common
Pleas. But Matilda, also called the "petitioner," wanted to expose the marital
havoc Joshua had wrought during the previous three years.

In court, Matilda asserted that, since her marriage to Joshua around Christmastime in 1871, she had "conducted herself" as a "faithful, obedient wife." His behavior was quite the opposite. In subsequent years, not only had he failed to be "right in his mind," to recite her remembrance elsewhere, since 1873, he had been "wrongfully and willfully absent" from their home, even though together they had a terminally ill daughter and three small boys to take care of. Despite their problems when they were together, his absence was especially unbearable to Matilda at the time of her greatest need.

Represented by local attorney John M. Bond, Matilda asked the Montgomery County's sheriff's office to issue the divorce petition to Joshua, calling him to court and demanding that he answer to the charges. She also sought sole custody of Paul. And there was one last request in her petition, less pressing than the divorce and child custody, but crucial to her future: she wanted to restore her maiden name, Burton. She no longer wanted in the legal record any association with "Murphy" or "Dunbar," the surnames she acquired in her marriages to Wilson in Kentucky and Joshua in Ohio. They chained her to pasts from which she sought official severance.

The Montgomery court eventually restored Matilda's maiden name. (Incidentally, she continued to use the surname Dunbar, more in association with her son Paul, to whom she would remain close in the decades following her divorce from Joshua.) Six months after the initial petition, on January 9, 1877, Matilda's divorce and child custody were officially granted.[26] In total, the marriage had lasted just under six years; and Matilda, now thirty-one, planned to move on with her life in Dayton. She and her sons lived at 311 Howard Street.

Months after the divorce, Joshua reappeared, claiming to be a changed man. Despite the trouble he had caused Matilda in the past, they began seeing each other again. In their separate lives, during slavery, Matilda and Joshua had contended with the precarious state of marriage in the slave community, when African American men and women had to submit to social unions that could only approximate marriages, from living together in the same household on the same plantation to living in different households on plantations far apart. After slavery, African Americans held ambivalent views toward marriage and its worth. Many were as dedicated as Matilda and Joshua initially were to the formal ceremony and legal execution of marriage. Others were not, opting instead for informal unions that sometimes proved as resilient as official marriages, if not more so. In this postbellum world where the union and disunion of African Americans did not always involve legal marriage, their reunion as domestic partners, therefore, was not unusual.[27]

By the time of their divorce, Matilda thought she would never see Joshua again. "But, after I got my divorce," she said, "and was all settled, he fixed himself up, had his hair all parted and got to be my beau again."[28]

———

Paul began his formal education in 1878, about one year after Reconstruction ended. While the public education of African American students after constitutional emancipation threatened the status quo of white supremacy, their parents embraced it as a long-awaited leap from enslavement to liberation, in body and mind alike. In Dayton, African Americans believed that formal education was the key to both civic and intellectual franchise after slavery. Racially desegregating public schools could help achieve that goal, but the "racial mixing" of students in the Dayton schools did not happen until 1887.

For schooling at home, Paul read with his family. Along with Defoe's *Robinson Crusoe*, he "did run through 'Uncle Tom's Cabin.'"[29] Subtitled "Or, Life Among the Lowly," *Uncle Tom's Cabin* was written by famed author Harriet Beecher Stowe, based on the life of ex-slave Josiah Henson. She first serialized the novel in 1851 and 1852 in the antislavery newspaper *The National Era*, then in 1852 published it in book form with the Boston publisher John P. Jewett. Also like Defoe's novel, in which youthful adventures so straddle life and death that they stretch historical reality to the edge of fairy tale, Stowe's novel refreshes the tradition of such children's tales as the sixteenth century's "Babes in the Wood" and the early nineteenth century's "Hansel and Gretel," even as Stowe uses the child protagonists—the enslaved children Harry and Topsy—to steer readers toward abolitionism and Christian evangelism. In the couple of decades after the initial release of *Uncle Tom's Cabin*, that formula, and the firestorm it provoked among the media and readers, made it the best-selling book next to the Bible.[30]

By different routes, *Robinson Crusoe* and *Uncle Tom's Cabin* reached the adolescent imagination of Paul and his half-brothers, William and Robert. While the countless editions of Defoe's novel took more than a century to evolve into a children's book, the original serialized edition of Stowe's novel concluded with an explicit appeal to the "dear little children who have followed her story." For children, *Uncle Tom's Cabin* circulated in condensed form, reappeared in "pictures and stories" editions with illustrations and verses, and exhibited a style of storytelling at once so vivid and moving that adult readers marveled at the novel's ability to captivate them just as a fable or legend would.[31]

If Stowe's interweaving of legend and myth, fable and fairy tale impressed the childlike sensibilities of all readers, it was a riveting literary means to a sensational political end. "The poet, the painter, and the artist," she writes in a preface to the novel, "now seek out and embellish the common and gentler humanities of life, and, under the allurements of fiction, breathe a humanizing and subduing influence, favorable to the development of the great principles of Christian brotherhood." Stowe presents Christian mercy as the potential cure for slavery: "The object of these sketches is to awaken sympathy and feeling for the African race, as they exist among us; to show their wrongs and sorrows, under a system so necessarily cruel and unjust as to defeat and do away the good effects of all that can be attempted for them, by their best friends, under it."[32]

Child readers, black and white, perhaps not only empathized but also identified with Harry and Topsy. In one storyline, Harry is the adolescent son of a maid, Eliza, enslaved on a Kentucky plantation whose owner, Arthur Shelby, sells him to pay back massive debts. Upon learning the news, Eliza escapes with Harry to the North, eventually to Canada, to be free, averting capture from his new owner, Mr. Haley, and a return to slavery. In another storyline, a New Orleans slaveowner named Augustine St. Clare purchases Topsy, a young girl abused by her previous master, for his cousin Ophelia, who needs to engender, in his view, greater compassion for slaves. By educating the new girl, both Ophelia's and Topsy's lives are changed for the better: Ophelia acquires newfound understanding of blacks; Topsy learns to trust whites.

As compelling as these two interwoven stories may be in the novel, evangelical and political symbolism emanates crucially from the portrait of Uncle Tom, a middle-aged enslaved man. To cover his debts, Shelby also decides to sell Tom, who is not able to escape as Harry does; instead, he is separated from his wife and children. On his way down the Mississippi River to his new owner, Mr. Haley, Tom befriends a little white girl named Eva whom he rescues from falling into the river. Mr. St. Clare, Eva's father, decides to buy Tom from Mr. Haley. Within a couple of years, after the unfortunate deaths of Eva and Mr. St. Clare, Mrs. St. Clare sells Tom to Simon Legree, under whose harsh, unrepentant oversight Tom is abused and beaten to death. Just as a divine aura envelops Eva and her father upon their deaths, Tom's unwillingness to reveal the whereabouts of Legree's enslaved concubines (who flee) results in his unwavering faith in God and his extraordinary forgiveness of his murderers, even as his overseer seeks directly, and unsuccessfully, to destroy Tom's faith. Christian devotion and expatriation to Liberia conclude *Uncle Tom's Cabin*: a pair of religious and racial solutions to slavery and the immoral callousness of men and women.

"How was I impressed by it?" Paul asked, reflecting on his reading of *Uncle Tom's Cabin*. "Well, it disappointed me."[33] But not for the reasons accounting for the polarizing debates waged during Reconstruction's decline. Antislavery activists cherished Stowe's evangelical encouragement of benevolent white families or descendants to end slavery or disabuse themselves of racial prejudice; proponents of slavery justified the peculiar institution in law and custom, and vehemently opposed the novel's religious miscasting of it as sinful. If anything, they clung to the iconically submissive images of Uncle Tom, consistent with the placating plantation lore and language of African American slaves in the Old South as made famous by Georgia-born Joel Chandler Harris, author of the Uncle Remus tales and a contemporary of Stowe.

In the years after his first encounter with *Uncle Tom's Cabin*, and leveraging his own grasp of the Civil War and his parents who survived it, Paul developed substantive and sophisticated opinions on slavery and freedom, the war and its aftermath. Those opinions would prescribe his literary vision, mindful of the degree of accuracy and the style of Stowe's depiction of the Negro, regarding what made *Uncle Tom's Cabin* a classic or what made it fall short. "The scenes of this story," as Stowe writes in the book's first sentences, "as its title indicates, lie among a race hitherto ignored by the association of polite and refined society; an exotic race, whose ancestors, born beneath a tropic sun, brought with them, and perpetuated to their descendants, a character so essentially unlike the hard and dominant Anglo-Saxon race as for many years to have won from it only misunderstanding and contempt."[34] The angle and purpose by which Stowe held her novelistic brush aloft—to be, as she calls herself, "[t]he poet, the painter, and the artist" of the race—troubled Paul. "I have become a devotee to realism—and there is such exaggeration in it," he once said. "The author looked at things through the lens of her own intense emotion, and they were magnified."[35]

In time, Paul identified less with the spiritual rigor of Stowe's title character than with the moral independence of Robinson Crusoe's. But the hand of conciliation that Uncle Tom, in the novel, extends to whites, and the acts of prejudice that the slave bears from them, had more in common with the story of the Dayton-born poet's life and times than a renowned castaway's return to an imperial mainland.[36]

———

By 1877, Joshua had moved a little over a mile across Dayton, from 311 Howard Street to 116 Sycamore Street. He came by whenever Matilda needed him—or, equally likely, whenever he needed her. Reuniting with Joshua was convenient, Matilda recalled. "He lived in the same neighborhood and when I was so sick he came and spent an afternoon with me."[37] Living as a single mother with three boys and mourning the recent death of her daughter, Matilda initially embraced her ex-husband's return to her life.

Even after their divorce, Matilda and Joshua shared parental roles and bickered like a normal couple. Ever assertive and vocal in her previous marriages, Matilda did not mince words even when her postdivorce bond with Joshua remained fragile. "He used to take Paul to the circus," she recalled one time, when Joshua's anger rose. "Once he came to take him to the circus and Paul was crying. Then his pa said he wouldn't take him. I said, 'You take him to the circus,' and he took him." Sometimes Matilda's own fury escalated. She remembered one of these occasions: "Then one morning I was getting Paul ready for school and he was crying. His father came in." This time, Joshua played peacemaker:

"What's the matter with the boy, Madame?" Joshua asked, in his typically formal way.

"He's a dirty little rascal. If you think he's an angel, he's a dirty little rascal!"

"Give him to me, Madame, and I'll make him a good boy. Let me take him."

"Oh, never mind; I'll 'tend to him."[38]

Joshua's wily presence turned out to be a welcome counterpoint to the mundane work Matilda had to do to make ends meet. Life as a domestic laborer was hardly different at the end of Reconstruction versus the beginning. Just as the vast majority of African American women in the United States working for wages were domestic servants in homes, hotels, and boardinghouses, Matilda continued to shuttle between her mother's home on Howard Street, where her family stayed, and the homes of her employers, scattered across Dayton. Domestic labor, according to historian Jacqueline Jones, replicated "the mistress-slave relationship in the midst of late-nineteenth-century industrializing America," insofar as "the traditional form of 'women's work'—dirty, tedious, low-paying— service lacked the rewards of self-satisfaction and pride that supposedly accompanied such tasks when performed for one's own family."[39] Matilda had to be content with the typical wage for domestic servants of the time, a mere four to eight dollars per month.

Despite Joshua's intermittent presence, Matilda was the sole head of her household. Even if in Reconstruction's wake her family technically was not among the 30 percent of urban African American families abandoned by husbands or fathers at some point, she still had to believe that the divorce fractured her family. But she could not let her tenuous stability distract her from the tasks of domestic labor at hand: she had to balance keeping her family together in the 1870s—just as she tried to do so in the 1860s, when her first husband left behind her and their son (and eventually another on the way) to fight in the Civil War—to ensure that her employers did not think she was failing as a "conscientious" domestic servant, the prevailing myth that African American women had to counteract at the time. Thankfully, her relatives sometimes came to the rescue. "Relatives looked after the offspring of working mothers during the day," writes Jones. "The kin networks that gave shape to black rural life remained intact and in some cases even intensified in the urban environment."[40] Matilda still could rely on her mother, Elizabeth (until her death on May 6, 1877), and her sister Rebecca, who lived nearby, in Dayton. Matilda tried to keep up her home and her employers' while rearing three boys and negotiating a renewed relationship with Joshua. By the time her divorce was made official, her son Robert was ten years old, William close to seven, and Paul four. Though too young to begin attending school in Dayton—the minimum age was six— Paul could still observe his older half-brothers finding their way.

———

Relative to other Ohio towns, Dayton was slow to establish public schools. Not until 1838, when Dayton Township comprised not only what became the city of Dayton but also the townships of Mad River and Van Buren, did a suitable law of levying and collecting taxes—or "school-house tax"—exist specifically for funding the schools. Once the taxation fell into place, the Dayton school system expanded and attracted great demand. The town's swelling population—from about 6,000 in 1840 to 30,500 in 1870—required a graduated curriculum to cater to students of all ages and education. District school extended from first grade through the seventh; intermediate school included only the eighth grade; high school went from the ninth grade through the twelfth; and an extra, subsequent grade in normal school trained the future teachers (mainly, women) of the lower grades.

Dayton's public schools, too, felt the effects of Reconstruction and Redemption that had been sweeping across postbellum America. Jim Crow bridged both periods. An avoidable tale of extremes, the "etiquette of race relations"[41] ranged from the guile of law to the guns of outlaws, from the symbolic origins of fantasy to the practical outcome of reality, all the while ensuring the conquest of whites over blacks in America.[42] Across the nineteenth century, how Dayton schools treated African American students and their families followed the typically delayed and fraught path of the nation's wider racial progress. Not until circa 1848 did a policy exist for the education of African American youth—for the establishment of "colored schools." When the policy did come to pass, it authorized the founding of school districts segregated by race. In line with the taxation-funding model of Dayton public education, African American taxpayers chose the directors who could manage their own districts. In 1853, four years after establishing the colored schools, evidence of the unsustainability of this taxation model vis-à-vis the rising African American population prompted the Board of Education to take over. The board devised the formula that if the number of African American students in any one school district eclipsed thirty, another school district would be formed and subsidized by the board until it reached some state of solvency and stability.

Myths overshadowed the availability of education to all African American students in Dayton. The division of colored schools into districts resorted to the same rationale of Anglo-Saxon superiority that would likewise precipitate both the Civil War and the backlash against Reconstruction, despite the victory of the Union and, secondarily, African Americans seeking emancipation and franchise. Even when the "colored youth," as historian Robert W. Steele wrote at the time, enjoyed "the same facilities of education extended to them as to white," the districting of Dayton schools along the color line persisted well until a decade after Reconstruction's end in 1877.[43]

Controversies swirling about Dayton public education began for Paul at an early age. For him, they started in the fall of 1878, two months past his sixth birthday and when he was entering the first grade at Fifth District School, located at the intersection of East Fifth and Eagle Streets. Paul entered the first grade when Robert, age twelve, entered the seventh grade, which was the senior class at that school. Paul lived at Howard Street for his first two years at the Fifth District School, less than a mile away. When his family moved about three-quarters of a mile southwest, to a new place on the south side of Magnolia Street, he transferred to the Third District School, located at the intersection of South Ludlow Street and Baker Street, where he attended the third grade.

When the family moved again, Paul fell victim to the geographic curse of educational segregation along the color line.[44] This is the period—the years of district school, intermediate school, high school, and even some time afterward—that Paul and his family moved among residences in a Dayton region known as "Little Africa." Hemmed in by the Miami River to the west, the

Miami and Erie Canal to the east, and West Washington Street to the north, Little Africa approximated a triangular landmark (upon the nearby southward intersection of the river and canal) where mostly African Americans lived. Paul's homes on Short Wilkinson, Washington, and Zeigler Streets fell within this region.[45]

When Paul lived at the residences of Sycamore for the fourth grade and Short Wilkinson for grades five through seven, he had to enroll in the Tenth District School—a colored school—located in Dayton's Riverdale section. While the reason for his attendance at a colored school only beginning in the fourth grade, as opposed to the previous three, remains unclear, the effects were palpable: travel between Sycamore and school was more than two and a half miles round-trip, while between Short Wilkinson and school the journey was close to four miles.

The routes to school also were no longer straightforward. From Short Wilkinson, traveling a block northward to Washington Street was the only easy path. But then Paul had to proceed about fifteen blocks northward along Perry Street—crossing the Union Station railroad tracks at the midway point—to Stratford Avenue, which angled northwest across a Miami River bridge to River Street, on which he turned right, toward Great Miami Boulevard, then right on Babbit Street, then left on McDaniel Street. The Tenth District School was nestled here, between Babbit Street and Herman Avenue.

The paths Paul, Robert, William, and fellow students of color traveled in Dayton were on average likely to be longer than those taken by white students. Most Ohio townships during racial segregation tended to have fewer colored schools, which in turn were spread out across the region. On Paul's way to the Tenth District School, for example, he would pass the closer district school at the intersection of Salem and Superior Avenues, which was for white students only. Colored schools, accordingly, handed out a disproportionate number of demerits for tardiness and absenteeism. The racial discrepancies in travel time and penalties, for which racial inequality was tantamount to geographical inequality, justified various Fourteenth Amendment litigations in the 1880s against school districts across Ohio. With mixed verdicts and outcomes, litigation seeking to integrate Dayton public schools pointed as much to the educational inconvenience that African American students faced in trekking to remote schools as to the obvious evidence of impoverished buildings, facilities, classrooms, furniture, supplies, and staff that plagued their schools as well.[46]

By the time Paul finished second grade, he knew he had to learn the ways and means of getting to school on his own. Robert and William soon had to leave school to earn money. Robert elected to leave right after finishing intermediate school, at age thirteen, in 1880; William attended high school for two years before leaving at fifteen. Many African American students abandoned formal education after district school for the same reason. "Some pupils quit school because they didn't like to study," biographer Virginia Cunningham wrote, "but most of them left because they couldn't go to school and work, too, and work meant earning extra money that was sorely needed at home."[47] Paul was an exception.

———

Paul's passion for art increased alongside his education. Family readings of literature continued to fill his mind with visions of worlds familiar and foreign, ordinary and extraordinary. Fictional and historical characters were bedfellows; the personae emerging from the minds of writers stood alongside figures from the Old South, the outlines of whose images alternately becoming ambiguous and distinct, similar and dissimilar, their meanings shifting as often as the cadences of Matilda's and Joshua's voices by the fireside. Legend has it that the other activities Paul shared with his family—such as spelling tricks and the discipline of pronouncing words—helped cultivate his young mind as he discovered new words and their nuances of meaning.

Artistic performance appealed to Paul, too. In fits and starts he took up the violin yet became "no mean performer in his prime," according to one contemporary observer. Evidence of true talent lay in his writing. An inkling started around 1878, when he was in the first grade. "My first attempt at rhyming was made when I was six years old. One day at school I came across something by Wadsworth, and a gentleman living in Dayton [who] happen[ed] to have a similar name. I at once concluded that the verses were written by him."[48]

In the handful of years prior to Paul's death, newspapers reprinted these reflective words multiple times, some of them correcting "Wadsworth" with "Wordsworth." No "gentleman" with the first or last name of Wadsworth, it turned out, was recorded as living in Dayton proper, except for one Bennett Wadsworth, a musician in his early thirties living in the National Home of Disabled Volunteer Soldiers. Nor was there any such man with a first or last name of Wordsworth living in Dayton; there was only one Henry Wordsworth, the head of a household in Cleveland, about fifty years old. Moreover, it was unlikely that Paul was alluding to the American poet, born in Portland, Maine, who was still alive and normally went by his surname: Henry Wadsworth Longfellow.

Most likely, Paul had encountered in school the poetry of William Wordsworth, whose *Lyrical Ballads, with a Few Other Poems* and *Poems in Two Volumes* helped inaugurate the Romantic era of English literature alongside fellow
English poets Samuel Taylor Coleridge, Percy Bysshe Shelley, Lord Byron, and
John Keats. Just as crucial as the impression that Romantic poetry would have
on Paul—impressions that in a couple of decades would reemerge in his own
poetry—was the inspiration that the boy derived from the name. Even if he
naïvely believed, in the first grade, that the poems he relished had been written
by someone who lived in his town, the possibility still prompted him to think
that if the hand of a fellow Daytonian could be so dedicated, so dexterous, in
crafting beautiful verses, so could his own—he just needed to learn how. "This
invested [the poems] with peculiar interest," Paul reflected on the possibility
of a Daytonian penning those verses, "making them seem very wonderful, and
as I crossed the railroad track in going home, I remember trying to put words
together for myself that had a jingling sound."[49]

Reading Romantic poems was enough to drive Paul to write his own verses
in rhyme, with an eye toward achieving the very poetry that stimulated his
creativity in the first place. The family helped cultivate and reward his perseverance as much as it helped in honing his skill as a reader. He knew that the celebration of his artistic or intellectual spirit of expression, of his "effusions," required committing this spirit to "paper," while his mother knew that archiving
it was likewise important. "After that I rhymed continually, my effusions being
committed to paper and carefully preserved by my mother in pasteboard
boxes," he later recalled.[50]

Paul began to mature as a poet. As early as the first grade he was experimenting with rhyme schemes; by the seventh he was learning how to enliven the
written word through recitation. Maturing as a poet was inextricable from maturing as a public speaker. Toward the end of his district school years, on April 13,
1884, Paul participated in a Sunday school Easter celebration run by a local African Methodist Episcopal Church. Located eight short blocks north of his
home, the church happened to be the site of his "first poetical experience," in his
words, "occasioned by an Easter celebration which occurred at the Sunday
School which I attended, when I composed the verses that I had been asked to
recite."[51] A literary graduation of sorts, the poem was titled "An Easter Ode":

To the cold, dark grave they go
Silently and sad and slow,
From the light of happy skies

And the glance of mortal eyes.
In their beds the violets spring,
And the brook flows murmuring;
But at eve the violets die,
And the brook in the sand runs dry.

In the rosy, blushing morn,
See, the smiling babe is born;
For a day it lives, and then
Breathes its short life out again.
And anon gaunt-visaged Death,
With his keen and icy breath,
Bloweth out the vital fire
In the hoary-headed sire.

Heeding not the children's wail,
Fathers droop and mothers fail;
Sinking sadly from each other,
Sister parts from loving brother.
All the land is filled with wailing,—
Sounds of mourning garments trailing,
With their sad portent imbued,
Making melody subdued.

But in all this depth of woe
This consoling truth we know:
There will come a time of rain,
And the brook will flow again;
Where the violet fell, 'twill grow,
When the sun has chased the snow.
See in this the lesson plain,
Mortal man shall rise again.

Well the prophecy was kept;
Christ—"first fruit of them that slept"—
Rose with vic'try-circled brow;
So, believing one, shalt thou.
Ah! but there shall come a day
When, unhampered by this clay,
Souls shall rise to life newborn
On that resurrection morn.[52]

At eleven years old, Paul experienced a poetic epiphany under the watchful eye of the AME Church. The Miami Valley, where Paul was born and reared, had one of the greatest regional concentrations of Methodist and Baptist churches in America, second only to Philadelphia. Paul became a member of the AME Church officially on May 17, 1885, when he received a "Certificate of Church Membership," around the time he was regularly attending Sunday school. Still, Paul's experience of the Easter festivity was not entirely a religious one. Although "An Easter Ode" alludes to the Risen One, Paul realized that his public devotion to the verse he first imbibed from the English Romantics dramatized his own rise as a poet. That religious ambivalence and literary aspiration went hand in hand was only a possibility then; but afterward in his life and literature, their union was a certainty.

Remarkably, Paul could even point to his adolescent years as formative in his growth as a writer, given that the many transitions his household went through between 1878 and 1885 apparently were not a distraction, although understandably they could have been. With his mother and half-brothers, Paul moved from Howard Street in the 1870s to Magnolia, Sycamore, and Short Wilkinson Streets in the early 1880s, all within a stone's throw of downtown Dayton. Paul's schooling likewise moved about. He enrolled in Fifth District School for two academic years (1878–1880); the Third District School for one year (1880–1881); and Tenth District School for the final four years before intermediate school, which started in fall 1885. Paul's father was equally transient during this time.[53]

An accurate portrait of Paul's broken home existed in the 1880 census. Recorded eleven weeks before Paul's eighth birthday, the census for Howard Street identifies Paul (in addition to William and Robert) as Matilda's son. She herself is listed as a Kentucky-born "laundryst," aged twenty-nine. (Her age here was about five years off, since she would turn thirty-five on October 5 of that year; the ages of Paul and William were correctly noted as seven and sixteen, but not Robert's, which was recorded as fourteen, even though August 1 had not yet arrived.) Matilda was the sole head in this household of four that did not include Joshua, although his trace still existed both in her designation of Canada as the spouse's birthplace and in her use of the surname Dunbar, which she would retain for the rest of her life, albeit her court-approved divorce in 1877 restored her maiden surname of Burton.

In contrast, the 1880 census for Joshua's West Fourth Street residence lists him as a "laborer" and as the sole head of household, aged sixty-four, with seven-year-old Paul as his son. The census marks Matilda and Joshua—who lived nearly two miles apart, on opposite sides of the Miami River—as divorced, but each parent still listed Paul as a "Person whose place of abode on the 1st day of June 1880, was in this family." The 1880 census happened to document Matilda's and Joshua's shared parental custody and the mutual commitment they had in the handful of years after their initially acrimonious divorce.[54]

As Joshua hovered around Matilda's home, people in the neighborhood began to wonder whether he and Matilda would remarry. He began to wonder, too, even as he poked fun at the curious onlookers. "One morning he come in so tickled," Matilda recalled of that fateful day: "Matilda, Madame, some people are so funny; some people are the biggest fools. They say that you and I are living together again. They don't know that we would have to get married again." She shut the door and replied: "That don't matter. We have been separated so long, we can spend the remainder of our days apart." Despite their recent time together, the marriage was long over. To consider otherwise was impractical. The schizophrenic rage that would overcome Joshua in his first marriage to Matilda returned with equal fury, exploded with equal venom, precisely when she declared that they could not have a second marriage. His reaction consummated the inevitable. "That embittered him," she realized. "That man turned against me; said some of the awfullest things to me. But something was the matter with him. He wasn't right."[55]

Together for about five years after their divorce, Matilda and Joshua broke up for good, finalizing in practice what had already been done in law. On February 4, 1882, around the age of sixty-five—and months shy of Paul's tenth birthday—Joshua quit his residence in downtown Dayton (near West Fourth Street) and moved three miles across town, to the Central Branch of the National Home for Disabled Volunteer Soldiers. Neither Matilda nor her sons ever saw him again.[56]

———

Congress instituted the National Home for Disabled Volunteer Soldiers just before the end of the Civil War.[57] During the National Home's first phase of development from 1865 to 1870, Congress had a sustained interest in mandating the social welfare benefits of veterans, particularly those who fought for the Union. The National Home took responsibility for Union veterans just "as mothers and wives assumed for their families in the nineteenth-century household economy," offering food, shelter, clothing, and medical care.[58] The civic assimilation and domestic security that Joshua Dunbar and fellow

Union veterans—all adult males—had struggled to achieve right after the Civil War found reinforcement in the National Home. Federal caregiving accompanied the bolstering of pensions and the guaranteeing of government jobs. Newfound social citizenship was granted not only to relatively healthy veterans but also, by 1884, to the elderly and the disabled, the diseased and the depressed.

The Central Branch in Dayton was the best that the National Home had to offer. By the time Joshua lived there, from 1882 to 1885, it was one of four existing branches and a unique, flagship National Home in its own right. Joshua reaped the rewards of the Central Branch well before he even stepped inside the facility. The branch was conveniently located, nearly halfway between Cincinnati and Columbus—the former about fifty-five miles southwest, the latter seventy miles east—and it lay abreast an urban center and farmlands, penetrable by turnpike roads to and from Dayton and Germantown. The Central Branch's topography and altitude oriented it to peer over Dayton and the Miami Valley. Split into two regions by the Main Avenue thoroughfare, the grounds "embrace[d] a tract," gushed the *Cincinnati Commercial* in 1870, subtending "productive land, well watered and timbered."[59] Veterans and local residents felt invited to enjoy the outdoor activities, including a stroll along walkways to behold deer, or a row across the lake. Fountains, mineral springs, and lakes glittered across and adorned the grounds.[60] For the Union veteran, the Central Branch was nothing less than the promise of Edenic life to redress the postwar travesty of social death.

After likely marveling at the flora and fauna, Joshua on his first day encountered an edifice equally spectacular. All in all a village, the Central Branch resembled a practical base or fort designed for military protection, operations, or stagings. At the heart of the botanical campus were the magnificently elegant facilities of Queen Anne, Italianate, or Flemish architecture, each replete with residential amenities. Three-story-high barracks, each floor with anywhere from forty to one hundred beds, took care of the largest population of National Home residents. A Protestant chapel, its pews capable of seating six hundred people, with a remarkably frescoed ceiling and beautifully ornate walls, demarcated an inviting place of worship. An immaculately wood-empaneled and burnished hospital, capable of housing up to three hundred beds, welcomed all kinds of injuries, mental and physical. A farm provided fresh, organic food. A host of shops sold books, brooms, carpentry, cigars, knitwear, shoes, tools. A post office held and relayed letters and packages. Residents communicated through the telegraph office to the outside world, and outside visitors could

FIG. 2.1. Conservatory and garden of Dayton's Central Branch, circa 1876.

enjoy the elegant hotel and restaurant on the branch's grounds. A cemetery unmistakably sprawled across the land with reverential finality.[61]

Despite the Central Branch's splendor, racial segregation governed veteran life within the buildings just as it did social life in the outside world. A color line divided the living quarters, dining hall, and cultural activities. Colored soldiers, as they were called, were underrepresented there, counting for only 2.5 percent of the total Central Branch population, whereas they had constituted upward of 10 percent of the Union Army. They also were not free of the prevailing customs of racial stereotyping and theater: some of them routinely performed in minstrel gear for the home. Still, the National Home was willing to take care of colored soldiers, despite the nation's slide from Reconstruction into Redemption and society's rising expression of antipathy or apathy toward African Americans.[62]

Inebriation in the Fifty-fifth Regiment of Massachusetts Colored Infantry in the 1860s and at the Central Branch of the National Home in the 1880s bookended Joshua's social life with Civil War soldiers. If he unwittingly had to contend with the forces of racism at the Central Branch, he also had to grapple with alcoholism as both a personal disease and a campus culture. Officially, the home sought to rehabilitate and take care of newcomers, who promised to abide by its strict rules of conduct, who received uniform clothes and clinical diagnoses, and who entered an almost military installation, regimented and hierarchical, akin to the kind they left behind during the war. In practice, however, martial discipline succumbed to excessive drinking. By the time veterans enrolled at the home, quite a few were reeling not just from ventures into local saloons but also from a reliance on liquor to survive civilian life. Despite the exaggerations of Daytonians about the rampant sight of drunken "inmates," a former Central Branch manager, quoted in an 1886 U.S. House of Representatives investigation into the National Home, called the saloons of Dayton's West End "the constant enemies of men," corroborated by images of "men lying in fence corners, misbehavior on streetcars, and frequent arrests (five to ten a day in earlier years)," resulting in unequal perception and treatment on account of the allegedly alcoholic predisposition of the veteran.[63]

Notwithstanding the conveniences the National Home provided, despair lingered among the soldiers who sought to reconcile themselves to their newfound condition. Some of them paid for drinking—among other kinds of decadence, it was said—with their pensions. Disposable income—and Joshua had some, about twenty-five dollars per month—enabled veterans to drink and gamble, fulminate and fornicate. By the mid-1880s, the Central Branch officials decided to set up a beer canteen on campus, thinking that, by selling alcohol on site, the veterans would be disinclined to light out for Dayton territory, toward the four-mile road separating the campus and the town that was dotted with brothels and gambling shops. Selling beer and food proved to be a success, but it only reinforced the culture of alcoholism, which became as anathema to the prospects as to the sobriety of veterans. Either way, Joshua could not escape the vices of the past and the present.[64]

―――――

In Joshua's absence, Matilda took solace in the bond that grew between herself and her sons. Between 1880 and 1915, about 30 percent of all African American families living in cities did not have a husband or a father in the household. Although Joshua continued to pretend he was Matilda's spouse for a few years after the divorce, from 1877 to 1882 he did not actually live with the family in any of the three residences she and the boys moved among in those years.

Paul, Robert, and William depended on Matilda for maternal shelter, but she as well depended on her "big boys." She expected them, ages thirteen, nineteen, and twenty-one in 1885, to complete "errands and even more responsible jobs," ranging from chores around the house (like tending to the firewood, cleaning the tubs, managing the chickens, maintaining the henhouse) to paying jobs in downtown Dayton stores.[65] As Robert and William prepared to move on with their own lives and out of the house, Matilda and Paul accordingly grew even closer as mother and son.

On July 10, 1884, about two weeks after Paul's twelfth birthday, when he was looking forward to entering the seventh and last grade of district school, thirty African Americans issued a petition at a meeting of the Dayton Board of Education about the colored Tenth District School. They had had enough. Social and institutional inequality on account of race, they argued, still festered in Dayton's public school system. Even while the extra month of education the white students received over the black students was mostly dissolved after 1875, the unusually long distances most African American students had to walk to school continued to rankle their parents.

Equally frustrating were the limited training and availability of African American teachers in the Dayton public schools. These teachers had to preside over multiple grades; in contrast, white schools commonly had one teacher for each grade. "As one Dayton Negro complained," reports an 1885 article in the *Dayton Democrat*, "he was told by the principal of the colored school that Negro children did not make better progress because the teachers had too many grades to handle; and in turn the white school board said that more teachers could not be hired because the enrollment would not justify it."[66] Cycles of educational delay faced by such children and inadequate teaching staffs so frustrated African American parents that many of them continued to demand better school conditions.

When the African American petitioners came forward, they had specific evidence of the disadvantage incurred by the racial segregation of the Tenth District School. The minutes and newspaper account of the meeting recorded their complaints: the extra financial expense; the low quality of teaching; the school's unenviable distance, in Riverdale, away from African American students, like Paul, who lived on the eastern side of the Miami River; the excessive cases of lateness, relative to local white schools; again, relative to white peers, the poor graduation rate of African American students from the seventh grade to intermediate school.

Fortunately for Paul, by the time he reached the end of the seventh grade, Dayton was already close to disbanding the separate school system, two years before the state mandated it in 1887.[67]

———

In 1885 Belva Ann Lockwood, a Washington, D.C., attorney and solicitor, filed an "agreement for fees," in which Joshua Dunbar permitted her to represent him in his quest to declare and claim an original "invalid" pension. Lockwood was the first woman admitted to the bar of the U.S. Supreme Court and the

FIG. 2.2. Belva Ann Lockwood. (Brady-Handy Collection, Library of Congress Prints and Photographs Division)

first woman to argue a case before it, both in 1879. In the course of her career she advocated for equal opportunities for women in her dealings with the bar, Congress, and newspaper media as well as during her run for president of the United States (which she attempted one year before she worked with Joshua, and again four years later).

Like the other lawyers who practiced on F Street in the northwestern quadrant of the District of Columbia, Lockwood belonged to a legal business that was growing by the month: it concerned debts and deeds, divorces and estates—as well as, in the two decades after the Civil War's end, pensions. Joshua's skin color was not a hurdle to her legal representation. (Just one year after her admission to the Supreme Court bar, she recommended the same privilege be granted to an African American attorney.) Most important was that, by the middle of the 1880s, she was moving out of civil and criminal work in the courtroom and settling into Civil War pension and bounty claims work in the law office, located near the Pension Bureau in Washington.

Lockwood's business consisted primarily of filing pension claims. Within the three decades after the Civil War, her office registered seven thousand pension filings. Traveling the country on a lecture tour, touting her views of women in law and politics while toting luggage stuffed with "Belva A. Lockwood & Co." handbills, she steered herself toward veterans to whom she could advertise her services. In her words, she succeeded in "gathering up and sending home as many claims against the Government as I can find."[68] Her stops included Dayton's Central Branch, where Joshua became one of her clients.

Joshua first received from Lockwood the application for pension and fee agreements on March 20, 1885, instructing him to seek witnesses and a notary for his signature and swearing.[69] On the form, Joshua confirmed his 1864 enlistment in the Fifth Regiment of Massachusetts Cavalry Volunteers. (Apparently, mentioning his 1863 enrollment in the Fifty-fifth Regiment of Massachusetts Colored Infantry was unnecessary.) He also indicated his qualification to apply for "pension under the laws of the United States." (By the way, Joshua did not read the articles of agreement on his own; they were "read over to *him* in the hearing and presence of the two attesting witnesses.") At least three agreements were made. First, Joshua agreed to have Lockwood, for a fee of twenty-five dollars (the maximum allowed by law), bring his application to the attention of the commissioner of pensions. Lockwood promised to "endeavor faithfully to represent the interest of the claimant."[70] Since Joshua already received a Civil War pension of twenty-five dollars per month, this additional claim that his disability "did [. . .] originate in the line of duty" positioned him to earn up to ten dollars more per month.[71]

The status of Joshua's pension was not insignificant. "Upon the death of a veteran, for example," writes military historian Patrick J. Kelly, "his widow and any orphaned children became eligible for a government pension."[72] The eligibility assumed that the veteran died while he was married, just as any request by his wife or children, parents or siblings, for a share of his federal stipends could be met only after matrimonial or parental dependence was proven.

For veterans like Joshua who resided in the National Home for Disabled Volunteer Soldiers, stable cases of marriage and parentage were more the exception than the rule. This institution needed to be a "home" for a glaring reason: in the three decades after the Civil War, more than 60 percent of its residents were divorced, single, or widowed. Either they lacked the resolute family that could have kept them out of the home in the first place, or they enrolled immediately in the wake of the family's collapse. Immigrant veterans, their relatives no longer accessible, turned to the home. Native-born veterans alienated in civilian life needed it. Disabled veterans incapable of taking care of themselves, or of persuading others to help them, ended up there, too.

Pension applications enabled these veterans, of whatever kind, to obtain what they felt was rightfully theirs. To be sure, the number of pension agents initially skyrocketed after the 1879 Arrears of Pension Act, which mandated that the calculation of pensions begin with a soldier's discharge date. Perhaps Lockwood preyed on Joshua just as her fellow Washington pension attorneys had, around the same time, "mounted modern and aggressive marketing campaigns," according to James Marten. All such attorneys left themselves open to the criticism that they had advised "veterans and their families to act on their baser instincts," plumbing the untapped wells of pension money. In any case, Lockwood put Joshua in the position to tap his own well, at the very least for his own personal gain.[73]

———

Across the Ohio Valley on August 16, 1885, Joshua lost his battle against pleuropneumonia, a mix of pleurisy and pneumonia, at age sixty-nine. Yet "the death of the Elder Dunbar made no material difference in the Dunbar family," an early biographer wrote, "for he had not contributed to their support after the separation and subsequent divorce. Thus did the father become a memory in his family."[74]

Robert and William both moved to Chicago, Illinois, around the age of twenty. Matilda and Paul stayed in their home at 121 Short Wilkinson. In the years after Joshua's death, Matilda saw how Paul's embrace of his father persisted into his teenage years:

Paul loved his father, and once when we were at Soldiers' Home attending some affair, Paul went to the cemetery and hunted row after row of graves until he came to his father's grave. He came running to me and said,

"Ma, I have found Pa's grave."

I went with him to it, and as we stood there, tears came to his eyes.

Paul's attachment to his father was undeniable. In his later reflections on his growth as a writer, he remembered the encouraging words his father told his mother about his promise: "My father used to tell her that I was not an ordinary boy, and one of my regrets is that he did not live to realize any of his hopes in regards to me."[75]

Paul would reconcile himself to living the rest of his adult life without Joshua's presence, whose previous intermittence was not unfamiliar. The virtues the father showed throughout his life—in outwitting and fleeing bondage, in fighting on behalf of the Union Army, in resuming civilian life, in becoming a husband and a father—were counterbalanced by the vices of his intemperance and marital indifference. The traits coalescing and clashing in these behaviors—notably, ingenuity and stubbornness, courage and anxiety, conformity and inflexibility, ambition and apathy—would reincarnate in Paul at key moments in his life, on his path toward being a grown man and a prodigious poet.

Joshua died alone, without his son and his former wife and the boys by his side. But at least his burial ceremony was not without the Central Branch's traditional pageantry. Consistent with the military culture that regional branches of the National Home were known for, the Central Branch handled the almost daily reality of death with ritualistic discipline. Like the other veterans who died unclaimed, Joshua was buried at the Central Branch's cemetery. Washed, respectably dressed in a new uniform, and carefully placed in a coffin, his body was the center of attention. Clarion music in the air, uniformed men lined the funeral procession. The chaplain conferred blessings as the coffin descended into the marked pit. The grave was filled with earth, to lie flush with those next to it, awaiting the visits of those in whose hearts and minds the deceased remained indelible.[76]

CHAPTER 3

Public Schooling

If the hills are high before
And the paths are hard to climb,
   Keep a pluggin' away.
And remember that success
Comes to him who bides his time,—
   Keep a pluggin' away.
From the greatest to the least,
None are from the rule released.
Be thou toiler, poet, priest,
   Keep a pluggin' away.

—PAUL LAURENCE DUNBAR, "KEEP A PLUGGIN' AWAY,"
OAK AND IVY (1893)[1]

Two years after Paul was born, the Dayton Board of Education established an intermediate school on the corner of Brown and Hess Streets. By the time Paul became a student there in fall 1885, the school enrolled only eighth-graders. All students had to pass through this intermediate school before going on to high school. The intermediate school welcomed students usually in their early teenage years.[2]

Paul began intermediate school just a few months past his thirteenth birthday. He was already a young man, growing into an adult and investing more and more time in reading and writing poetry. He was scheduled to finish intermediate school in little time: it was designed to last only one year, concluded by a straightforward passing of an exam to graduate.[3] As Paul later reflected, a teacher at the intermediate school named Samuel C. Wilson, "under whose care I was placed when I was thirteen years old did more in the beginning to keep the poetic fire within me burning than anyone else."[4]

———

When Paul enrolled in intermediate school, racial desegregation in Dayton public schools remained two years away. Racial desegregation of public education had both federal and local valences, with winds blowing alternately with and against this mission. For mostly Republican politicians, abolishing the empirical discrepancies in public education experienced by blacks and whites was morally tantamount to blotting out the constitutional disparities in elective franchise resulting from racial discrimination. Shoring up the votes of constituencies sympathetic to African Americans (including African Americans themselves once they were permitted to vote), as well as cutting the costs associated with establishing racially exclusive schools in the service of segregation, factored into calculated support by politicians for antisegregation law and policy. Yet these issues gave only practical leverage to the Radical Republican philosophy of Reconstruction: to implement the Fourteenth Amendment, ensuring the equal protection of African Americans under the law and, necessarily, their right to pursue formal education.[5]

Not all African Americans automatically supported racial desegregation. To W. O. Bowles, principal of Dayton's all-black Tenth District, racially segregated school districts preserved the existence of exclusively colored schools. In turn, this existence assured the employment of the African American staff. Disbanding colored schools for the sake of racial desegregation—including the underperforming ones, such as the one in Bowles's own district—potentially put already downtrodden African American teachers at an even greater disadvantage. The civic prize of racial integration sacrificed, as Bowles said in 1884, "the appearance of thousands of colored teachers in the presence of pupils of the land." Whatever Bowles's political motives, these words echoed the broader and long-running sentiment of African Americans across the North and during the century after slavery. They claimed that maintaining—not ending—racially segregated, all-black schools could work to end "race prejudice," particularly the preconception that African Americans were not themselves educable or qualified enough to educate others.[6]

Under these conditions, with African American teachers instructing exclusively African American students, intermediate school turned out to shape Paul more than the initial circumstances suggested. Wilson was not just a teacher, he was a role model of sorts. The "strong sense of educational mission" encouraged the likes of Wilson to cultivate young men such as Paul, who may not have fully understood their own vulnerability to the fate of history. Wilson's poetic predilection also attracted Paul. "Mr. Wilson was himself a writer of verse," Paul remembered; he was "a refined, traveled, wonderfully well read man, the close contact with whom was of immense value to an impressionable boy." The teacher's cultivation and cosmopolitanism enlightened the fledgling poet; the scribblings atop, across, or alongside the drafts of verse informed him, too. "He criticized my work, encouraged me both to write and recite, and giving direction to the literary impulse. Even after I had left his department I often came back to him," Paul later recalled.[7]

In June 1886 Paul passed out of intermediate school. Legend says that the school principal, by the time of graduation, regarded the fourteen-year-old a "kind gentleman," a "great personality and good literary talent" worthy of his nickname "deacon," thanks to his memorable recitations of poems during the afternoon school assemblies.[8] Aside from arithmetic, Paul had earned grades in intermediate school as consistently high as those he received in district school. More important, Paul held dear to nuggets of advice from Wilson, which complemented what he had learned at that Easter celebration in Sunday school years earlier: writing well requires disciplined, relentless practice, and recitation is crucial to bringing such written verse to public life. As Paul summoned inner strength from the second wind of intermediate school, he would bring this work ethic to bear on his performance in high school.

When Paul matriculated at Dayton's Central High School in fall 1886, he was attending an institution long established by the Dayton Board of Education to teach "the higher branches of an English education, and the German and French languages, besides thoroughly reviewing the studies pursued in the district schools."[9] At the time, it was the only high school in Dayton. Seven to eight years later, the high school was built on Wilkinson Street, between West Fourth and Maple Streets.

Between his matriculation and his graduation in 1891, Paul walked to school from a couple of residences. First, he lived at 121 Short Wilkinson (where he had been living since 1883) until 1887, when he turned age fifteen, the time he was completing his first year in high school. Next, from 1887 to 1891 he stayed on the northern side of West Washington Street. His first residence was 315 West Washington Street, the second house on the block to the west of Perry, a cross street. (In letters he also called this address Washington and Perry Streets.) His second residence was 317 West Washington Street, the first

CENTRAL HIGH SCHOOL.—1857 to 1893.

FIG. 3.1. Central High School, Dayton, Ohio, 1857–1893. (Lutzenberger Picture Collection, Dayton Metro Library)

house west of Perry. In any case, his trek to school was the same: about five blocks, or three-quarters of a mile, northward, across the railroad to East Fourth Street, then one block east.[10]

No other time was more important to Paul's growth as a writer—in terms of his pure talent to write literature, and his practical knowledge to recite and publish it—than his time at Central High School. The school's mission and curriculum imposed even more behavioral rigor than the self-discipline instilled by his own poetic aspirations. A major purpose of the high school was to funnel deserving students into the Dayton Normal School, established in 1869 to train teachers for the city's lower-level public schools. Central High School graduates earned admission to the Normal School without examination; they also formed the bulk of the latter's student body. Students seeking admission to the Normal School outside this route were "required to pass a thorough examination in the ordinary branches of an English education." Curated and updatable, the curriculum of Central High School aimed to shape Dayton's future generation of public school instructors, with the expectation that they would teach students how to excel in the rigorous tradition of "English education."[11] Paul's immersion there exposed him to this tradition.

Paul's course of study was not atypical of what secondary schools across the country were touting. The academic line between secondary schools and higher education (such as normal schools, colleges, and universities) was blurry. Quite a few overlaps of subject matter existed between the two contexts, and the latter was not always more challenging than the former. However, the system of secondary schools—which by the 1880s mainly meant high schools, but until then also included academies, seminaries, and institutes—offered Latin and mathematics as classical standards, Greek for college preparation, and such modern subjects as German- and French-language instruction as well as history, science, and English literature.

Classics fueled nineteenth-century secondary education in the United States, and merely reaching and passing this level of education was a privilege. In 1890 less than 1 percent of the country's entire population—around 203,000 students—attended high school, and only 11 percent of this group finished coursework or graduated in the 1889–1890 academic year. Only the most privileged, the most ambitious, the luckiest, or all of the above made it to and through the American high school.[12] Just two decades removed from slavery, most African American families in Dayton did not expect their children to attend high school. In 1890, of the 6,244 people between the ages of fifteen and nineteen residing in Dayton, only twenty-eight were "colored" people attending school. Paul was the only African American in his graduating class of 1890.[13]

Attending high school lifted Paul's social standing in Dayton, but the classical values of its curriculum enhanced his sensibilities as an artist, and his intellect as a close reader of literature. Classicism in secondary education had long been purported to elevate the sophistication of students, although this reputation did not exist without controversy. Colleges and universities in the antebellum era were home to rising scholars who shifted the focus of classical pedagogy from the grammar of ancient languages, such as Latin and Greek, to the worlds of antiquity, such as the national cultures of Rome and Greece and, within this context, a shift from antiquity to modernity and from republican to democratic societies.

Teachers in the early to the middle part of the nineteenth century did not agree on what a classical education should include. "Shall the student confine himself to the abstract and laborious study of grammar, until every form, inflection and syntactical construction, in all their endless variety and nicer shades, are forced into his memory, as if by the operation of machinery," wondered Robert Patton, a philologist at Princeton University, "or shall he neglect these minutiae of grammar, and plunge into the vast ocean of classical literature, with nothing but the raw materials of his bark, calculating afterwards to form, adjust, and compact it?"[14] This complex question, part of Patton's 1825 lecture on "classical and national education" delivered before the Literary and Philosophical Society of New Jersey, captured the pedagogical crisis of whether grammarians would overcome historians in the battle over the future of American classical curricula. The wrestling match between the cold-blooded analysts of ancient grammar and the romantic arbiters of ancient history implied a bias of favorable perception but also what they believed to be at stake for their students.

Classical education remained central to secondary school curricula in the United States at that time, even as higher education was undergoing changes. High school teachers of the late nineteenth century had been students in the antebellum or mid-century heyday of classical education in colleges and universities.[15] Studies of the languages and literatures of ancient Rome and Greece accordingly gained such a foothold in secondary school education that the number of youths studying Latin and Greek in American high schools consistently rose between 1870 and the end of the century, with the curricular decline of Greek beginning a decade into the following century, and Latin after four decades.[16]

At Dayton Central High School, Paul's coursework from fall 1886 through spring 1891 was firmly rooted in studies of ancient history, even as it also represented a true liberal arts education. During these years of study, he took classes in physiology and algebra, civil government and physics, we well as chemistry and psychology. But in each of his last two years of study, he simultaneously took courses in Latin and Greek and, in his final year, courses in English literature and Virgil. In the most classicist sense of the phrase, Paul imbibed "the higher branches of an English education," as his high school's founding mission stated in 1850.[17]

———

In 1887, two years after his father's death, Paul felt pressure to seek financial support for himself and his mother. He was attending school when many other young men, also aged fifteen, were working full-time. Paul could not drop out of school to do that, at least not yet.[18]

Joshua's Civil War pension held promise—or so Paul thought. On November 4, 1887, Paul wrote a letter to the Record Division of the Bureau of Pensions, within the Department of the Interior in Washington, D.C., inquiring into his father's pension. In the formal request he identified himself as the "son of Joshua Dunbar" and indicated his father's enlistment in the Fifty-fifth Regiment of Massachusetts Colored Infantry and the Fifth Regiment of Massachusetts Cavalry Volunteers. Paul evidently knew little else. He did not know whether his father had any other service in the federal army; he did not know the classificatory number of Joshua's pension claim; he did not know when this claim was filed; nor did he know the agency handling the payments. On the form he left these items blank. Still, the information was enough for William E. McLean, acting commissioner of the United States Pension Office, to reply to Paul's query within three weeks. The news was not what Paul was hoping for, though. "It does not appear from the records of this Office that an application for a pension on account of service of Joshua Dunbar . . . has ever been received." Evidence shows that Joshua filled out and signed his pension application only five months before he died. Quite possibly, Belva Lockwood did not submit it in time for processing.

Paul must have kept to himself the news that the Pension Office declared Joshua's pension application nonexistent. Or, if he went on to tell his family, Matilda in particular, that news must have been forgotten over time. His inquiry in 1887 did not prevent his mother, about two decades later, from inquiring about the pension on her own. Public and personal circumstances added urgency to her request at that time. (Paul was not yet a celebrity in 1887, but he was revered by the time of his death in 1906, shortly after which Matilda's finances began to dwindle and she needed the income.) Although the federal government complied with a thoroughgoing and expedited investigation, the results of her request would not differ much from her son's.[19]

The year 1887 was pivotal for another reason. Paul was being shaped not only by his education inside Central High School but also by the changes to public education in Dayton and in Ohio more broadly. By that time, the city's gradual racial desegregation policies aligned with those of a little more than half of the cities in Ohio. This history may be broken into four periods: the period before circa 1848, prior to the admission of African Americans to public education; the brief period from 1848 until 1853, the period before colored schools fell within the jurisdiction of larger boards of education; the longer, overlapping period between 1848 and 1887, when colored schools were up and running but under racially segregated circumstances; and afterward, when such ostensibly racial districting officially stopped. Prior to 1887, Robert W. Steele, former president of the Dayton Board of Education, stated that, despite the slow pace of ending the racial segregation of public schools by legal means (in 1889), African American parents had the right, in the wake of the 1868 ratification of the Fourteenth Amendment, to enroll their children in hitherto all-white schools. By his count, no parent did.[20]

Local peculiarities distinguished the racial policies of Dayton schools from those of schools in the rest of Ohio or in the rest of the country. Early on, national leaders like Frederick Douglass picked up on the deleterious impact of racially segregated public schools. "We want mixed schools not because our colored schools are inferior to white schools—not because colored instructors are inferior to white instructors," he wrote in 1872 in *The New National Era*, "but because we want to do away with a system that exalts one class and debases another." Public schools must be racially mixed, he also said, "in order that the mad current of prejudice against the Negro may be checked; and also that the baleful influence upon the children of the colored race of being taught by separation from the whites that the whites are superior to them may be destroyed."[21] On the other hand, certain African American leaders in Dayton, like W. O. Bowles, would not necessarily identify educational segregation with the presumptions of racial inferiority. Instead, the impending layoff of the workforce of African American teachers would be the ironic cause for alarm. Even so, the racial segregation of Dayton schools—whether the involuntary or voluntary kind—fizzled by 1887.

After this year, the advanced alignment of de facto and de jure racial integration benefited Dayton. Public opinion here indicated that whites were quite prepared for the racial integration of schools, even as African Americans grappled with the division within their own communities over the issue. The racial mixing of schools was lawful in 1887, but Dayton was still permitting a single racially self-segregated colored school—of the Tenth District—to open that fall. With the appearance of only sixteen students on the first day of class—134 fewer than the previous year on day one—the school shuttered by the end of September. The abolition of racially segregated schools in Dayton, which tended to be one of the more politically progressive cities in Ohio, could have been unanimous two years earlier if not for the ironic conservatism of the African American community that sided with the likes of W. O. Bowles.[22]

FIG. 3.2. Paul and his Central High School classmates, with Orville Wright
in back row center, circa 1890. (Wright State University Libraries /
Ohio History Connection)

As 1887 came to a close, racial segregation no longer affected Dayton public
education. (The existence of only one high school in Dayton when Paul was
enrolled obviated the need to segregate schools at that level.) Yet local school
boards here and elsewhere in northern states exploited one last loophole: racially segregating classrooms within racially mixed schools so as to avoid dis-
playing any open defiance of state law. "The Dayton School Board established
separate classrooms for black children in mixed schools in 1912," legal scholar
Davison M. Douglas wrote, "a practice it had used in the nineteenth century."
Other cities in Ohio—Springfield, to take one example—likewise segregated
African American students within racially mixed schools.[23]

No evidence indicates that Paul, as he turned fifteen and entered the tenth
grade a mere seven months after statewide desegregation, was at all separated
from his classmates at Central High School. (In an official school photograph,
he stands alongside the classmates of his initial cohort, the class of 1890, albeit
he stands rather aloof.) All things considered, his memory of Central High
School turned out to be favorable. He was the only African American in his
class, yet fellow classmates still "were kind to him," he stated later in life. He
also befriended and collaborated with a young white man—the one in the
rear, standing before the central doorway in the class photograph—whose
own zeal for technological innovation would soon reach historic proportions.

The partnership between the two became one of the more fascinating legends of Dayton.[24]

———

Paul did not graduate from Central High School the same kind of student as when he entered it. The school used percentages to assess the performance of students in a "branch of study" as well as their behavior in the classroom. Using numbers "because they are more convenient than words, to express the deportment and proficiency of the pupils," an "excellent" student earned a grade of 95–100; "very good," 90–95; "good," 85–90; "fair," 80–85; "tolerable," 75–80; or "very poor," below 75.

Early on, Paul was "good." Available transcripts show that, in the spring semester of his freshman year—or the ninth grade, in academic year 1886 to 1887— he earned 85 percent in physiology and 77.2 percent in algebra. A year later his grades improved. In spring 1889 he received 84 percent in Latin, 84 percent in civil government, and 85.6 percent in physics. And in the subsequent fall, he earned 85 percent in Latin, 97 percent in English literature, and 81 percent in chemistry. By the time Paul was close to graduation, however, he was near the top of the class. He earned 86 percent in Greek, 92 percent in psychology, 94 percent in Virgil, and 100 percent in literature, which happened to be the only course on record for which he received a perfect grade. In all these classes, his "deportment" was always excellent; he almost always received 100 percent, never falling below 98 percent (which was his score in chemistry).

Perhaps the telltale sign of Paul's intellectual growth was his "habits of application," a category the high school used to evaluate his proper use of the knowledge he was learning. In the semester he took courses in Latin, civil government, and physics, his application habits were "very poor." In the following semester, in which he continued to take Latin as well as English literature and chemistry, those habits were "tolerable," or slightly better. By spring 1890, when he broadened his literary education to include the courses in Virgil, Greek, literature, and another reading course in psychology, his habits of application were now "excellent."

Paul became a model student of scholastic achievement. This stature did not go unnoticed by the principal of Central High School at the time, Charles B. Stivers. He personally signed every one of Paul's report cards but also was his physics teacher and witnessed firsthand how an African American student rose from the bottom to near the top of his predominantly white class, a feat for which the young man would be rewarded when he graduated. Paul's academic excellence would inspire the success of William "Bud" Burns, a special friend and high school classmate (albeit a year younger and one grade behind), who also happened to be African American and with whom he formed a bond that would prove unbreakable until the very end of their lives.[25]

More salient than the comparison of Paul's proficiency, deportment, and habits of application with those of his white classmates was his access to an immeasurably rich legacy of classical education. That he took such courses on the languages of Greek and Latin and the literature of Virgil (especially the *Aeneid*) was not unique. Since the turn of the nineteenth century, these subjects were the cornerstones of the classical curriculum in the United States, as were Cicero's *De Oratore*, Xenophon's *Cyropaedia*, and Homer's *Iliad*. Lessons on Roman and Greek antiquity acquainted American students with the broader Western philosophies of morality, nobility, and cultural self-refinement that supposedly would bode well for them in modern times. The humanities courses Paul took in Latin, Greek, English literature, and Virgil indoctrinated him into what scholar Caroline Winterer has called the "central intellectual project in America before the late nineteenth century."[26]

Classical education distinguished Paul in another way: he emerged in a century when African Americans were identifying a literature that could help them make sense of the racial patterns in their own collective experience in the country. Unsurprisingly, the preponderance of classicists in American secondary and higher education and of individual courses on Homer, Virgil, Cicero, Xenophon, Sallust, Horace, Terence, Quintilian, Longinus, Livy, and Demosthenes reciprocated the intellectual ambition of African American students when the formal education of their communities remained frustratingly stunted overall. Roman and Greek antiquity could not always speak directly to the Jim Crow life that African Americans faced daily, but it did expand the ways that they could apply Christian ideas to their own lives.[27]

Classical literature was not merely a road to academic erudition. It provided nineteenth-century readers a learned take on questions of politics, ethics, religion, and intellection; on the importance of wise or intuitively good judgment; on the meaning of human virtue and resilience. The qualities African Americans could likewise apply included, as historian Eric Ashley Hairston puts it, "heroism and an ethic of heroic response to injustice, civic responsibility, commitment to civil rights, manliness, Christian piety, culture (in terms of the habits and activities of refined society and an appreciation for social, artistic, and humanistic enterprises), and profound and diverse knowledge aimed at discerning the meaning of life and the best and most abundant life for the individual and the race."[28]

African Americans who attended northern high schools and colleges between the Civil War through World War I received the greatest exposure to these classical themes. Political author, editor, and educator W. E. B. Du Bois; philological scholar William Sanders Scarborough; missionary and educator Frances Jackson Coppin; political author Anna Julia Cooper; civil rights activist Mary Church Terrell; literary artist Jessie Fauset—their contemporaneous attainment of the highest levels of formal education and intellectual productivity began with a grounding in classical thought. Likewise prophesied by his excellence in the academic humanities, Paul would enter this hallowed group in due course and discover ways of enfolding the form and spirit of classicism into his creative writing.[29]

————

In June 1869 the family of Milton Wright—the same bishop who would marry Joshua and Matilda two years later—made the first of several interstate moves that would typify its itinerancy for the next decade and a half. The clan moved from Indiana, where Milton was born and raised and became an ordained minister in the United Brethren Church, and where his wife, Susan, attended Hartsville College, a United Brethren school where she and Milton met in 1853. After getting married six years later, they started having children: Reuchlin was born in 1861, Lorin in 1862, and Wilbur in 1867. Two years after Wilbur's birth, the family moved to Dayton—first to Third Street, then to Second Street. In April 1871 they settled in a newly constructed house on 7 Hawthorn Street in working-class West Dayton. ("West" or "West Side" meant west of the Miami River.) Their newborn twins, Ida and Otis, died as infants. A little over one year later, however, as autumn approached in 1871, Orville, their sixth child, was born healthy. After three years, a newborn daughter, Katherine, followed.

For most of his adult life, Milton served the United Brethren Church with almost all his energies. The church, established in Maryland in 1800, was profoundly democratic and individualistic in perspective as well as devoutly egalitarian in pietism, even as it subscribed to a hierarchical governance of an elder, bishops, clerical delegates, minsters, and regional conferences. Specific principles distinguished the church: it opposed secret Masonic societies; it deplored alcoholism; it was decidedly antislavery; and, during the Civil War, it supported the Union.[30]

The church's moral and political stances appealed to Milton. By 1871, he had been a pastor and presiding elder in the White River Conference of the Church of the United Brethren. That year he was elected editor of the *Religious Tele-scope*, the weekly newspaper of the United Brethren Church in Dayton, a central region for religious publications. Although he did not ascend to bishop until 1877, his election to the editorship paved the way. Editorship granted him stature and influence as he espoused the Reconstruction laws and policies supporting the franchise of African Americans. He cultivated a home in which his family appreciated the ethical and political causes of their era.[31]

By the time Milton conducted the wedding of Joshua and Matilda in 1871, the lives of their families were becoming increasingly intertwined. Dayton's "Old-Town Church" of the United Brethren in Christ encouraged a hospitality toward African Americans that Wright showed the newlywed Dunbars. Milton was the ideal man to marry the well-traveled ex-slaves from Kentucky—the groom a two-time Civil War veteran around fifty-five years old, the bride a single mother about half his age, already with two boys of her own from a prior marriage.

Church and editorial business forced Milton to shuttle his family across Ohio, Iowa, and Indiana, and to place his boys in a number of different regional schools. Still, the attachment of the Wrights to West Dayton was unwavering. After years of traveling, during which time they rented their Hawthorn house, the family resettled there in 1884. By the end of this sojourn, Wilbur and Orville were seventeen and thirteen, respectively. Despite the family's size, the "bishop's boys," Wilbur and Orville, the third- and sixth-born of seven children, emerged as the most active Wrights in Dayton lore. (With their eventual innovation of the airplane, they would also become the most celebrated.) From the home, Milton came and went, attending to church and editorial business, while Susan normally stayed behind.[32]

The Wrights were a cerebral family, owing to the intellect of Milton and Susan. In his early twenties, Milton was a reputable schoolteacher in Rush County, Indiana. As biographer Tom Crouch notes, he was not only a "gentleman of good moral character," in the words of a teacher certification board, but also "qualified to teach orthography, English grammar, reading, writing, arithmetic, and geography in the common schools."[33]

Milton became, in 1868, the first professor of theology in the United Brethren Church's history. Susan also attended college in Indiana, studying literature, and developed expertise in mechanical invention and repair. Almost all of their children learned to read before they even entered school, and Milton criticized Dayton school instructors if he sensed they were failing to teach

FIG. 3.3. Orville and Wilbur Wright, circa 1897–1899. (Wright Brothers Collection, Wright State University Libraries)

children up to his own high standards. The children (above all, Wilbur) were disciplined, advanced readers and writers, immersed in Milton's large private library, and attracted to learning, whether by way of private concentration or public schooling.

In the late 1880s, the intellectual tailwind (partly driven by his family) that helped push Orville through Central High School also naturally steered him toward a friendship with Paul, whose own scholastic momentum made him an ideal entrepreneurial partner.

CHAPTER 4

The Tattler

A great mistake that has been made by editors of the race is that they only discuss one question, the race problem. This is no doubt important, but a quarter of a century of discussion of one question has worn it thread-bare; we may venture to assert without fear of refutation, that no new idea has been presented upon this subject for the last ten years, and yet it is hacked at, and tossed about until one is almost prone to say, that more harm than good is being done.

—PAUL LAURENCE DUNBAR, "SALUTATORY,"
THE DAYTON TATTLER (DECEMBER 13, 1890)[1]

Paul and Orville's bond may have been preordained. Orville's father, a United Brethren Church clergyman, had married Paul's parents, two former Kentucky slaves, on Christmas Eve, 1871. Nearly two decades later, both Paul and Orville enrolled in Dayton's Central High School. Initially in the class of 1890, they became entrepreneurial partners in a short-lived newspaper called the *Dayton Tattler*. They genuinely respected each other. In the back room of the Wright & Wright print shop—co-run by Orville and his brother Wilbur, and located on the second floor of a building on the corner of West Third and Williams Streets in West Dayton—Paul reportedly scrawled on a wall:

Orville Wright is out of sight
In the printing business.
No other mind is half as bright
As his'n is.

During Paul's years before the *Tattler*, he was refining his reading and writing of poems with the help of committed teachers in intermediate school and the guidance of classical curricula in high school, although he needed several years to mature into an excellent student in the classroom. These years comprised a period of personal struggle and self-inquiry; he grappled with his father's troubled legacy for him and the rest of his family, and he sought to articulate his memories and imaginings in his early fiction, poetry, and drama. Jim Crow racial segregation was not yet officially dismantled right after Paul graduated from district school; it normally kept students, black and white, like him and Orville apart.

Yet they were "close friends," Orville himself later reflected. "Paul Lawrence [*sic*] Dunbar, the negro poet, and I were close friends in our school days and in the years immediately following. . . . When he was eighteen and I nineteen, we published a five-column weekly paper for people of his race."[2] The improbable publication by two young men, one black, the other white, of a periodical for the African American readers of Dayton was the remarkable backdrop to Paul's transformation into a professional writer—from being the early performer of literature on Easter Sunday in 1884 to an experienced writer and editor by 1891.

Paul's high school years encompassed the story of how two young men discovered common ground across the so-called color line: not merely within high school classrooms, where curricula forced them to learn the same lessons, but outside them, where newspapers instilled a shared sense of fascination. For Paul, the allure was literary. He was drawn to honing further his exceptional skills of editing and creative writing—the ones that in a few years would elevate his poetry to international prominence. For Orville, the attraction was managerial. As much as he wished to help advance the mission of the *Dayton Tattler* to provide "all the news among the colored people," in the words of one motto, he also wanted more business for the fledgling printing press that he and his brother Wilbur co-founded and that helped sharpen the organizational acumen they would bring to aviation in the new century.

Paul's union with Orville closed a chapter of his life as grand for its achievement as for its gateway toward literary self-expression. By the time he graduated from Central High School, Paul was poised to learn from these experiences and experiments, and to make a crucial pivot. "Prepared to cast our moorings free," he wrote, as appointed class poet, in his "farewell song" to his high school commencement audience, "[a]nd breast the waves of future's sea."

When Paul first began the ninth grade in high school in fall 1886, he was scheduled to graduate four years later, by spring 1890. But he delayed his graduation
by a year to pursue an extracurricular interest: newspapers.

Paul was not alone in viewing Ohio as an especially fertile state for newspaper publication. In 1888 a writer in the renowned *Scribner* magazine called the
Midwest "the Centre of the Republic," a hub of newspaper commerce that
served the economic wealth and political influence rising in the "old Northwest
Territory" between the Ohio River and the Rocky Mountains. The commercial
epicenters of Ohio were Cincinnati and Cleveland. Although paling in comparison to these cities, Dayton joined them in being a node of religious publishing and promising to cultivate its own market of newspapers. Journalism in
Dayton began as early as 1808 with competing Republican and Democratic
periodicals. By 1890 the market saw the consolidation of Dayton journalism
with papers like the *Journal, Herald, Morning Times,* and *Evening News,* which
all inherited and modified preexisting local papers.[3]

Still, the newspaper was in vogue. The last decade of the nineteenth century
belonged to the era known as "more of everything." Readers craved information, whether education or entertainment. Periodicals ranging from newspapers to magazines, from monthlies to weeklies to dailies, captured an "interest,"
according to historian Frank Luther Mott. "And every interest had its own
journal or journals—all the ideologies and movements, all the arts, all the
schools of philosophy and education, all the sciences, all the trades and industries, all the professions and callings, all organizations of importance, all hobbies and recreations."[4]

As long-standing Dayton newspapers underwent mergers, rebranding, and
political realignments during the nineteenth century, their African American
readership remained small in number and fragile as a literate community. Paul
continued to write poems but, mindful of these circumstances, anticipated the
need to find places to publish them. The growth of periodicals throughout
the country intrigued him.

The burgeoning opportunities periodicals offered editors and writers appealed to one Mr. Faber, a Dayton resident and publisher of a newspaper he
founded in 1890 called the *Democratic.* Paul had learned through other local
papers of Faber's interest in boosting its circulation, especially among African
American readers. Eventually the two connected, and Paul agreed to help
Faber out.

By early June 1890, Paul wrote to Faber that he had "worked the circulation"
of the *Democratic* up to sixty subscribers, "fifty having been agreed upon and

having placed the paper in a position to increase steadily its circulation." Paul swore he "worked hard" for his "promised wages." So successful was Paul that he boasted: the "little *Democratic* sheet was becoming popular." A bitter sense of betrayal tainted Paul's joy in working for Faber. "I find that you willfully and persistently fail to keep your part of the agreement," Paul complained, "whether your action is either *honest* or *gentlemanly* it is not for one to say." He felt taken advantage of, "to use a very polite word, *induced*," presumably by Faber's failure to compensate him for the work done. For two reasons Paul bemoaned this problem. The first was personal. He had to wait six weeks for pay, but that was too long; in his words, "I couldn't afford to walk and wear out my shoes getting news for nothing." The second reason indicted Faber's hypocrisy. "I knew your mother and the Faber family when you were exceedingly, yes even distressingly poor," Paul reminded him, "and I judge that it is no more than right that you after having struggled up through adversities to a *tolerably fair* place in the world should try to crush and deceive people, who can ill afford to lose, though *not quite so poverty stricken as you were* when I knew you in past years." Paul had to quit. The time forced him to consider another opportunity. "Suffice it to say that your actions added to the fact that I have accepted the editor-in-chiefship of the *High School Times*," the organ of the Philomathean Society of Central High School, a debate club. Eventually, he became the club's president.[5]

Fatefully, Paul's turn toward the *High School Times*—and, separately, *Tomfoolery*, a hand-illustrated periodical where he could publish his work, too—allowed him to affiliate with a more homegrown and predictable paper that offered him not money but experience and positions of leadership, the kind of opportunities that his job as a subscription runner did not provide. He also realized that if he were going to be involved in a newspaper for African American readers, he might as well publish or edit one himself. But he needed help.

Paul's high school classmate came to the rescue. He discovered in Orville an ideal companion in print culture—that is, in the writing and editing of pieces for newspapers, in the enterprise of printing and circulating them, and in the use of them as a vehicle for amplifying an original voice for the good of local readers. Orville had been ensconced in the world of newspapers while growing up. His father, Milton, was editor of the *Religious Telescope*, a periodical of the United Brethren Printing Establishment, from 1871 (the year Orville was born) to 1875. One Wright biographer notes that the enterprise, "based in Dayton, Ohio, was one of the best-equipped religious printing houses in the nation."[6] The Wright family was at the epicenter of the religious printing press, enhanced by Milton's ascension to United Brethren Church spokesman as a result of his editorship.

FIG. 4.1. Paul and classmates in Philomathean Society, Central High School, 1890.
(Dayton Park Aviation Center)

Even at an early age, Orville developed a profound attraction to newspapers. In 1881 Milton Wright had become an editorial activist of sorts, publishing *Reform Leaflets* and founding the *Richmond Star* to promote his opposition to secret societies and to the liberalization of the United Brethren Church. Orville's older brother, Wilbur, built a contraption for folding the pages of the *Star* for mailing, as well as a six-foot, treadle-powered lathe made out of wood. When the Wrights returned to Dayton permanently, newspapers—or, more precisely, the technology of printing—held an allure for the two brothers.[7]

Printing so captivated Orville that by the time he entered the ninth grade at Central High School in 1887, classroom education was secondary in his grand scheme of life. Aside from his reputation as a mischievous boy needing a punitive seat in the front of his intermediate school classes, Orville was neither "outstanding" nor "memorable" as a student, but he was a close reader of the extensive library that his scholarly parents compiled at home. Along with copies of the *Religious Telescope, Reform Leaflets,* and the *Richmond Star,* Milton stacked the shelves with books by the Greek philosopher Lucius Mestrius Plutarchus, English historians Edward Gibbon and John Richard Green, French historian François Pierre Guillaume Guizot, Scottish biographer James Boswell, Scottish novelist Sir Walter Scott, and American writer Nathaniel Hawthorne. The library also included theological, scientific, and encyclopedic texts. If Orville's knowledge of printing was born during his handling of United Brethren Church leaflets and periodicals, it matured with his combing through one particular book: *Cyclopædia: or, an Universal Dictionary of Arts and Sciences*.[8]

Published in two volumes in 1728 by Ephraim Chambers, *Cyclopædia* was a massive book, which Orville plumbed to figure out printing. In the second volume he learned about the "Art of taking Impressions with Ink, from Characters and Figures moveable, or immoveable, upon Paper, Velom, or the like Matter." This section of *Cyclopædia* contained a history of printing, including the distinction between "Common-Press Printing" (for books) and "Rolling-Press Printing" (copper plates for pictures), the origin and invention of printing in the West, and the modern progress of this industry. Orville learned the role of a compositor, the method of printing and making ink, and the components of the printing press. Though the reference work was compiled more than a century and a half before he thumbed its pages as a teenager, Orville, along with Wilbur, discovered in it a theoretical blueprint for them to establish their own printing office.[9]

Over time the Wright brothers came to master the rudiments of the printing business. They learned to divide the business into the three areas of composing, pressroom, and warehouse; to enlist the proper personnel and apprenticeship for the jobs; to allocate workload and hours; and to manage the printing process itself, such as typesetting, composition, correcting in metal type, purchasing and preparing paper and ink, and identifying a warehouse to store the newspapers and ready them for delivery. Over time they would learn the economic risks of printing, such as the engagement of customers, the price of resources and technology, and the scaling of newspaper prices according to supply and demand. Out of the experience of printing short-lived periodicals like *The Midget* and *The Conservator*, or publishing church pamphlets like *Scenes in the Church Commission*, they launched the Dayton imprint "Wright Bros.: Job Printers" out of their home on 7 Hawthorn Street.[10]

By 1889, Orville decided that, more than school, he wanted to be in the printing business. On March 1, 1889, he began publishing the *West Side News*, one year after he had constructed a large press to handle complex or demanding newspaper jobs. Geared for the West Dayton community, the weekly paper ran for a mere thirteen months, but Orville remained committed to newspaper publishing. The paper "was intended to function as the keystone of his small printing enterprise," notes biographer Tom Crouch, "producing enough income to justify his decision to quit school, forego college, and devote all his time to publishing." To Orville, classroom education was a distraction. The motto of his new paper, the *Evening Item*, which appeared less than a month after its predecessor the *West Side News*, was that it would print "all the news of the world that most people care to read, and in such shape that people will have time to read it." It would also cultivate "the clearest and most accurate possible understanding of what is happening in the world from day-to-day."[11] Despite its admirable mission, the *Evening Item* died even faster than the *West Side News*. Lasting only four months, the *Evening Item* closed down in August 1890, unable to hold its own among the Dayton competition, which included more than ten papers. But with the rebirth of the family printing business as "Wright & Wright," Orville's new operation could serve Dayton businesses seeking to publish directories, reports, programs, posters, advertising cards, and letterhead. The printing office moved a little more than a block away, from Hawthorn Street to the corner of Third and Williams Streets.

Within the crucible of the publishing world, Orville and Paul linked up at the outset of academic year 1890–1891. Paul was now a member of the class of 1891, given that he was considerably ill during large swaths of calendar year 1889, likely forcing him to take an academic leave of absence overlapping his original third and fourth years of high school.[12] (Indeed, he started the ninth grade in academic year 1886–1887, so now he would need five years, not four, to graduate.) As they approached the Christmas season of 1890, the white printer and the black editor looked forward to publishing a newspaper for local African American readers.

———

Nearly nineteen years to the day that Pastor Wright presided over the marriage of Joshua and Matilda, the *Dayton Tattler* debuted on December 13, 1890, as the entrepreneurial marriage of their respective sons. The publishing house of Wright & Wright and the editorship of Dayton Tattler Co., which Paul founded to certify the *Dayton Tattler* as a commercial business, joined forces to produce what he thought would be the first of many issues of a weekly newspaper— each unfurling across four broadsheet pages in "bright and newsy" fashion, as he first gleefully said after the initial local reviews of the first issue came in. Paul rightly recognized that circulating the *Tattler* only on Saturdays enabled him to cast it as a weekend paper. By the turn of the century, the weekend was the most lucrative time a newspaper, especially those affiliated with dailies, could hit the stands. Paul was riding that wave.[13]

FIG. 4.2. First issue of the *Dayton Tattler* (December 13, 1890).
(Paul Laurence Dunbar Papers, Ohio Historical Society)

In the first issue, Paul listed himself as editor. In the second issue, the masthead also listed an associate editor, chief and assistant business managers, and local reporters, along with a public appeal: "Good live agents wanted in surrounding towns." The address provided for "all communications" was "Paul Dunbar," at No. 9 West Second Street.[14]

The *Tattler* was the quintessential startup paper. Throughout its pages, readers encountered direct appeals for subscriptions, which in standard fashion offered a discount for longer periods. The newsstand price was 5¢ per issue; a one-year annual subscription, paid in advance, cost $1.50. Rates in the second issue of the *Tattler* offered a three-month subscription for 50¢ and a six-month subscription for 75¢. Plastered across the right side of the first page was an impressive slew of advertising from local businesses—merchant tailors and clothiers, a jeweler, a carpet cleaner, a furnisher, a grocer, restaurants and confectioners, a millinery, a cigar and tobacco house, an artisanal repairman, a pharmacy, a handyman, a shaving parlor. The paper had the feel of a publication mostly by, about, and for the local communities of Ohio.

Indeed, the *Dayton Tattler* appealed to an audience within and beyond Dayton. In the first two issues, published on December 13 and 20, were lengthy columns about marriages, holiday festivities, and the Baptist and Methodist churches in Cincinnati. Stories about the strange and obscure were excerpted from other newspapers around the country. The comical tone of the "Humorous" section and the remarkable tales of oddities in "Items of Interest" blurred the line between objective reporting and tongue-in-cheek entertainment. Readers might have faced difficulty taking seriously the news that "Detroit is not the most cosmopolitan of American cities, but the other day a Hebrew, Arab and an African negro were arraigned in court on the complaint of a Chinaman." Or they might have been unsettled by an ironic view of the ethical quandary afflicting one city's legal system: "In the late trial at Binghamton, N.Y., every juror on the panel who claimed not to have read the case was challenged off, leaving twelve men who had read and discussed it, and court, lawyers, and public are agreed that it was one of the fairest verdicts ever rendered by a jury." These stories, along with brief essays on the likes of "Negro superstitions," showed Paul's interest in delivering important news as well as light entertainment to African American readers.[15]

The *Tattler* was yet another periodical in the great milieu of newspaper publishing, or what the editor of the *Journalist*, a New York weekly, called in 1889 the media's relentless devotion "to the interests of everything under the heavens." The United States had more thirteen thousand weekly newspapers in circulation by 1899, even if, as the editor wrote, "by far the greater number [would] either fail or ruin their proprietors."[16] Demand was great for the news. Doors to editorial desks and publishing houses were open to those creative enough to funnel the news to the masses, especially to urbanites, to whom newspapers were a necessary part of weekly life.

Paul appealed to his urban base of readers by focusing on Dayton news in the regular *Tattler* column "City Items." Here was a record of events, memorial services, children's activities, and incidents of crime. Society news also appeared in its pages, from the trivial to the bizarre: the names of visitors, attractive ladies identified by a man "high in social circles," students maintaining good progress in school, a person suffering from a cold, a baby who suffered a fractured skull after being tossed from a house on fire and whose survival was doubtful. And then there was encouragement for readers to patronize local businesses, echoing the advertisements that they had already encountered on page one.

If the *Dayton Tattler* showcased Paul's entrepreneurial instincts and editorial expertise, it also revealed for the first time his complex stance on race. In an editorial he wrote for the first issue, he stated that the periodical above all catered to and sought to cultivate further an African American readership, which "has for a long time demanded a paper, representative of the energy and enterprise of our citizens." The *Tattler* had two mottos: "Gives all the news among the colored people" and "The *Tattler* should go into every family of our race in this state." But its mission went beyond merely delivering the news; it sought to contribute to the economic, artistic, and political well-being of the race: "to encourage and assist the enterprises of the city, to give our young people a field in which to exercise their literary talents, to champion the cause of right, and to espouse the principles of honest republicanism." Just as remarkably, Paul envisioned the *Tattler* as an informational bulwark against financial corruption in politics, as a means of rescuing "the hearts of our colored voters and snatch them from the brink of that yawning chasm—paid democracy." For the paper to survive and fulfill these goals, readers had to give back in at least one of three ways: pay for a subscription, pay to advertise in its pages, or submit a piece of writing.[17]

Yet Paul's desire to enlighten and uplift "colored" readers superseded his desire to fill the *Tattler* with political opinions about race:

> A great mistake that has been made by editors of the race is that they only discuss one question, the race problem. This is no doubt important, but a quarter of a century of discussion of one question has worn it thread-bare; we may venture to assert without fear of refutation, that no new idea has been presented upon this subject for the last ten years, and yet it is hacked at, and tossed about until one is almost prone to say, that more harm than good is being done. We do not counsel you, debaters, writers, and fellow editors, to throw away your opinions on this all important question; on the contrary we deem it one worthy of constant thought. But the time has come when you should act your opinions out, rather than write them. Your cry is "we must agitate, we must agitate." So you must but bear in mind that the agitation of *deeds* is tenfold more effectual than the agitation of *words*. For your own sake, and for the sake of Heaven and the race, stop saying, and go doing.

At eighteen, Paul had little experience of the world, and his mostly peaceful encounters with whites in Dayton could partly explain his erasure of the "race problem" from the pages of the *Tattler*. But a profoundly racial design motivated his editorial bluster: he wanted to educate his readers to vote with a mind immune to financial corruption, even as he sought to downplay the activism of the written word. He planned to create more space in the *Tattler* for "other things than this one question to talk about." His collection of local and national news, of both serious and silly types, sought to do just that.[18]

Still, Paul's call for readers to "agitate" in public instead of in print affiliated the *Dayton Tattler* with a storied tradition of African American culture.

"Newspapers issued by and for Negroes numbered in the hundreds in the 1890s," according to historian Frank Luther Mott, "but the number of magazines of any considerable circulation and life of more than a year or two is very small." The *Dayton Tattler* predated by a decade the Boston-based *Colored American Magazine*, whose editor, Walter W. Wallace, declared in the first issue (in 1900) that "American citizens of color have long realized that there exists no monthly magazine distinctively devoted to their interests and to the development of Afro-American art and literature."[19]

The *Tattler* highlighted neither the former nor, perhaps, even the latter. The poems and short stories Paul published turned out not necessarily to be "Afro-American" in genre. They did not explicitly communicate such "interests," including the ability of African Americans to cope with and correct the electoral disillusionments and violent repercussions of Reconstruction. The nineteenth-century black press included many publications that promoted such interests: the abolitionism of *Freedom's Journal, National Reformer, Colored American Magazine* (prior to the Boston version), *Mirror of Liberty,* and *Douglass' Monthly* in the antebellum era; the politically diversified corpus of the *Anglo-African Magazine* at the outset of the Civil War; and the racial pride of *Colored American Magazine, Horizon,* and *Voice of the Negro* at the turn of the twentieth century. If it lasted long enough, the *Tattler* could forge a new path: to give "all the news among the colored people" of Dayton, even while subordinating horrific news about race relations to humorous views about social relations. But even its appeal to potential African American writers to "give us a variety and cease feeding your weary readers on an unbroken diet of the race problem" was, in itself, a commentary on the rhetorical narrowness of racial politics in America.

If the "race question" received little attention in the essays on local and national news in the *Dayton Tattler,* it enjoyed even less in the poems, short stories, and drama published in the newspaper. Paul wielded a heavy editorial hand in crafting the mission and structure of the paper. His brief salutary essays apprised readers of the state of the *Tattler,* of the likely changes to its news coverage, of the local reaction to its emergence, of the promise of excellence and entertainment it aspired to fulfill. Yet he controlled its literary nature, too: he wrote the majority of it. The *Tattler* received acclaim from what Paul called "the two leading city papers," the *Journal* and *Evening Herald.* Quoted in the second *Tattler* issue, the *Journal* remarked that the Dayton Tattler Co. was "an organ and representative of the colored population of this city," and its political spirit of "republicanism" and "its proposed good works" should be "encouraged." Likewise, the *Evening Herald* hailed the first number of the *Tattler* as "a bright and newsy issue."[20] Accolades in fellow city papers, however, were not enough to keep the *Tattler* afloat. The final issue appeared on December 27. Looking back, Orville noted: "we published it as long as our financial resources permitted of it, which was not for long!" (three weeks, to be exact). Neither Paul nor Orville could generate enough funds to overcome financial woes. Paul also was not willing to sacrifice his formal education without a worthwhile entrepreneurial opportunity at the level of establishing a newspaper.

Orville did find value in the *Tattler* for his own scientific curiosity. In the *Tattler's* final issue, Paul saw fit to include a small essay, "Air Ship Soon to Fly." Inventor E. J. Pennington had announced to the stockholders at a Chicago meeting of the Mount Carmel Aeronautic Navigation Company that "we will sail into Chicago in the first of our air ships." Paul agreed with his printers, the Wright brothers, that a story about the potential "manufacture of ships for traveling in the air" was news fit to print in a "colored" newspaper. Despite being buried in an issue of a newspaper on the verge of death, this story was one of the earliest seeds of evidence that Orville and Wilbur were conceiving of innovating the airplane.[21]

The three issues of *Tattler* represented neither the first nor the last time and place Paul would publish his creative writing during his years at Central High School for an audience wider than the *High School Times*. At the end of his sophomore year, a couple of weeks before his sixteenth birthday, he published his first individual poems, "Our Martyred Soldiers" and "On the River," in the June 8 and 13 issues of the *Dayton Herald*. Almost two years later, for the final issue of the *West Side News* (April 5, 1890), a local periodical Orville was editing at the time, Paul published a notable poem called "The West Side News." Before Paul worked for the *Tattler*, he was already a prolific author of poems, but also one who sought to circulate his work among a range of intramural and city papers, and to speak to an ever-growing community of readers.

The creative writing Paul published in the *Tattler* was as serious as the work that appeared in other publications, if not more so, because it represented the kind of poetry, fiction, and drama he wanted to read in a newspaper for the "colored people" of Dayton. What we find is a motley literary assortment. Putting aside the poems of cryptic authorship (such as "Now'Days" by A. Opper in *Judge* and "Easily Satisfied" by Everhard Up in *Light*) or those republished from other newspapers (John S. Grey's "The Bogus Baron De Guyn," from the *New York Herald*), a number of poems first appeared in the *Tattler* unsigned and later were attributable to Paul. One of these is "Oh, No," a playful song in which a coveted woman declines flattering overtures of wealth, marriage, and society from men: "I'll bid you all good bye; / And don't you call me back again, / Or I'll be sure to cry." Another is "Christmas Carol," whose speaker extols, reminiscent of Paul's fireside readings with his parents and his two half-brothers during his adolescent years, "Let every heart with joy be singing / Peace sit at every fireside, / For 'tis the merry Christmas tide."[22]

The most distinctive poem Paul likely wrote was "Lager Beer." Credited to the unknown Pffenberger Deutzelheim, a name that contains the anagram of Paul Dunbar, this is the earliest published example of his dialect poetry and gestures to the sizable German community in Dayton. (The German accent is pronounced in the orthographical contrast between the literal title "Lager Beer" and the dialectical refrain that refers to the drink, "mit lager peer.") On a deeper psychological level, the poem's emphasis on how inebriated misbehavior leads to conviction, incarceration, and the dissolution of family bonds recalls the tortured story of alcoholism that beset Joshua Dunbar and that would later afflict Paul, too:

I lafs und sings, und shumps aroundt.
    Und somedimes acd so gueer.
You ask me vot der matter ish?
    I'm filled mit lager peer.

I hugs mine child, und giss mine vife.
    Oh, my! dey was so dear;
Bot dot ish ven, you know, mine friend,
    I'm filled mit lager peer.

Eleetion gomes, I makes mire speech,
    Mine het it vas so glear:
De beoples laf, und say ha, ha,
    He's filled mit lager peer.

De oder night I got me mad,
    De beoples run mit fear,
De bleeceman gome und took me down,
    All filled mit lager peer.

Next day I gomes pefore de judge,
    Says he, "Eh heh, you're here!"
I gifs you yust five-fifty-five
    For trinking lager peer.

I taks mine bocket book qvick oud,
   So poor I don't abbear;
Mine money all vas gone, mine friend,
   Vas gone in lager peer.

Und den dey dakes me off to shail,
   To work mine sendence glear,
Und dere I shwears no more to be
   Filled oup mit lager peer.

Und from dot day I drinks no more,
   Yah, dat is very gueer,
But den I found de tevil lifed
   In dot same lager peer.[23]

Paul also wrote short fiction and drama that appeared in the *Tattler*. An assortment of stories—some sketches, others longer pieces a column or more in length, with curious titles like "His Failure in Arithmetic," "His Little Lark," "A Practical Suggestion," "Kissing as Medicine," "Couldn't Speak from Experience," "A Golden Chance"—appear signed by "*Sel.*," referring either to a selection contributed by a reader (after all, Paul did appeal to readers: "Everyone can give us some aid . . . by contributing") or to yet another smokescreen behind which he could experiment with literary forms (such as dialect, dialogue, plot development, humor) and theme (youthful indiscretion, interpersonal tension, marital woes, novelties). The play on voice and language, oscillating between refined speech and vernacular, was common to these anonymous stories, as well as to "His Bride of the Tomb," by Philip Louis Denterly (which, like Pffenberger Deutzelheim, is an anagram of Paul's full name), and "From Impulse," by Frank Mayne Templeton. Paul used dialect to convey ideas and carry dialogue, even as he argued, in his "The Language We Speak" in the third issue of the *Tattler*, that "all who lay claim to intelligence . . . should at all times endeavor to use the very best language at our command."[24]

Paul's lengthiest piece is "The Gambler's Wife," a work of drama serialized across all three issues but uncompleted (closing with "*To be continued*"), according to the *Tattler's* final issue. He understood, as fellow American writers of his time did, the lucrative potential of serializing long-form fiction. For much of the nineteenth century, writers used the serial publication of long-form literature, including novels, to exploit the commercial demand for exciting literature, since the standard circulation of such literature among libraries—of which readers usually had to be members—was expensive and restricted to the wealthy. Half a century before Paul was entering his literary prime, Charles Dickens had already cracked the code for Victorian writers who sought to release long-form fiction to a wide audience. He had two strategies. "One was part issue, in which fiction was issued in standalone serial parts at regular intervals. Weekly or monthly, often with frontispiece illustrations," notes scholar Laurel Brake; the other was "serialization in miscellanies or serials, similarly weekly or monthly and also relatively cheap." Taking the latter route, Paul could have the best of both worlds: he could publish his fiction in serial format and imagine a future in which his work would thereby become available for an increasingly literate audience that could afford periodicals. Later on, he could also consider combining such serialized parts into a book, for those readers who wished to read the entire consolidated text at one time.[25]

More than any prior poem or fictional sketch, "The Gambler's Wife" confirms Paul's early experiments with form and theme. The play does not represent his finest literary achievement, even if one accounts for space limitations in the four-page *Tattler*. In asides uttered by underdeveloped characters, the play overstates actions that have just passed and those to come; it makes clumsy use of suspense, never quite showing a masterful command of detail and dialogue to lure the reader along; and the individual motifs needlessly fall atop one another, without delineated contours. Still, the play provides evidence that Paul was grappling with the "demon's curses" in his family's past, as the play's narrator puts it at the outset.

"The Gambler's Wife" reveals Paul's early preoccupation with the moral vices that can tear marriages or families asunder, in much the same way the marriage of his parents unraveled. Madge Darrell regards herself as scorned, "accursed," for being married to a husband, Ralph Darrell, whose irremediable gambling entices him often and at great length to visit the club. Believing that "the husband's cruelty teaches the wife's deceit," Madge pursues an adulterous affair with her own "lover," Arthur St. Clair, to whom she is drawn as much for his looks as for his wealth. Ralph becomes suspicious and confronts his wife: "What's to hinder my strangling you here like a rat?" Instead, he demands a portion of the newfound money she expects to receive from Arthur in exchange for her release from the marriage. Madge consents.

Interwoven through this central story are a host of other moral and social challenges. Caesar, the servant of the Darrells, resents a practical joke played on him after he fell into a drunken stupor during his service as a delegate to a prohibition convention. The play illuminates the cultural meaning of racial and ethnic differences between whites and blacks (respectively, between the Darrells and Caesar) and Anglo-Americans and the Irish (between the St. Clairs and their servant Jerry). It also amplifies the class differences in language: the Darrells and St. Clairs speak in formal English, and Caesar and Jerry speak in dialect. Finally, it demarcates the sensibility of living in the country—where Madge feels imprisoned in her marriage to Darrell—and living in the city, to which she plans to escape by marrying Arthur.

By the time the third and final issue of the *Tattler* cuts short "The Gambler's Wife" at the outset of act 2, we can only conclude that this story was, in the main, about the unseemly character, the morally flawed personality, of Madge. The play does not hold women in high esteem, as the lamentation of George St. Clair, Arthur's father and now father-in-law to Madge, articulates: "that wife of his, I've studied her deeply and my knowledge of human character tells me, that though women are at best a bad lot, Madge St. Clair, my son's wife, is the worst of her sex. She's got a bad eye. Any man with common sense could see that she is wicked." Madge is neither heroic nor redeemable, and "The Gambler's Wife" would not be the last time misogyny would take center stage either in Paul's writing or in his actual life.[26]

After the demise of the *Dayton Tattler*, Paul returned to Central High School. He completed his final semester there, in spring 1891, as an exceptional (although not officially an honors) student. Aside from improvement in his grades and deportment, a range of successes and failures had deepened his experience of the world and made him wiser as he entered manhood. By mid-spring, his graduation and nineteenth birthday around the corner, he felt the weight of the future, his mind vacillating between ideas of "Some new weight, soon or late, / On my soul to bind, / Crushing all its courage out, / Heavier than doubt," and, on the other hand, "the world we fear no more, / As here we stand upon the shore, / Prepared to cast our moorings free, / And breast the waves of future's sea."

These lines appear in the last two poems of significance Paul published as a high school student. The first set of lines ("Some new weight . . .") are from "Melancholia," which he placed in the *High School Times*, in a spot long reserved for him if he wished, thanks to his past editorial service. The emotional beauty and centered gravity of "Thinking things unknown and awful / Thoughts on wild, uncanny themes" is a far cry from the technical infelicities and convoluted moral and social humor of his *Tattler* writings. "Melancholia" illustrates "Spectres" with the graceful touch of softened meter, with a delicate balance of middle and end rhymes, assonance and alliteration. The poem opens meditatively:

> Silently without my window
>   Tapping gently at the pane,
>   Falls the rain.
> Through the trees sighs the breeze
>   Like a soul in pain.
> Here alone I sit and weep;
> Thought hath banished sleep.
>
> Wearily I sit and listen
>   To the water's ceaseless dip.
>   To my lip
> Fate turns up the bitter cup,
>   Forcing me to sip.
> 'Tis a bitter, bitter drink.
> Thus I sit and think.[27]

———

On Tuesday, June 16, 1891, the temperature in Dayton reached the high eighties, but the air felt even hotter than that, with high humidity. Under these sweltering conditions, the commencement exercises of Central High School took place at the majestic Grand Opera House, near the corner of North Main Street and East First Street.

If Paul continued to brood in private, he ensured that melancholia did not infiltrate the words he wrote for faculty, staff, and fellow classmates on graduation day, which occurred eleven days before his nineteenth birthday. (Orville was not listed, since he dropped out of high school after the *Tattler* folded.)

Thoroughly musical, commencement was a long ceremony, with school anthems religious and choral, and a song performed by a trio of "young ladies of the graduating class." It featured many speeches: the typical salutatory and valedictory speeches, but also ten essays read by graduating students, plus an extended oration by a student graduating with special honors (bestowed on only ten others as well). The penultimate part was the distribution of diplomas to all forty-three graduating students. As long as the ceremony was, it gave Paul, the sole African American student, the last word. Transcribed in the

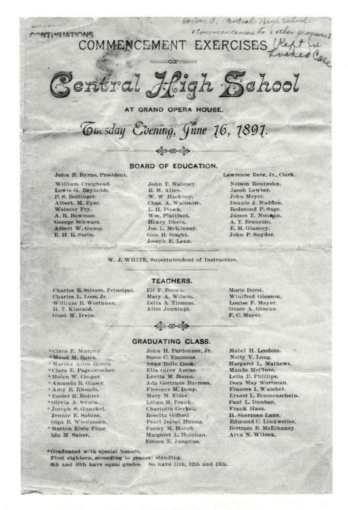

FIG. 4.3. Dayton Central High School commencement program, June 16, 1891. (Paul Laurence Dunbar Collection, Ohio History Connection / Dayton and Montgomery County Public Library)

program was a poem, "Farewell Song," he wrote especially for the occasion. None of the other five songs recited during the event were printed in the keepsake program.

What a fascinating scene! In the heart of a city, in the southern region of a state, whose schools had been only recently desegregated by race; where black and white students could, at last, learn together; where Paul and Orville could collaborate as partners in a business; and where, finally, before the president of the Dayton Board of Education and the principal of Central High School, a young man of once enslaved parents could sing among his white peers, who would accept, if not embrace, his very words. In these words, a young writer wrestled with preconceptions of what the future had in store for him. Whereas "Melancholia" addressed solitary anxiety, in "Farewell Song" he announced, like Robinson Crusoe, personal transcendence from the maternal grip. Whereas the ghastly and ghostly images of the unknown haunted him before, now he stood unafraid, ready to welcome a new world. Spiritual paralysis gave way to a hope whose energies drew upon a restive imagination, a maturation, of what it meant to say "farewell, farewell" to the past. The final stanzas of the song reach a crescendo:

> The wind is fair, the sails are spread,
> Let hearts be firm, "God Speed" is said:
> Before us lies the untried way,
> And we're impatient at the stay.

> At last we move, how thrills the heart,
> So long impatient for the start!
> Now up o'er hill and down through dell,
> The echoes bring our song—farewell.

> The breezes take it up, and bear
> The loud refrain on wings of air;
> And to the skies, the sad notes swell,
> Of this our last farewell, farewell!

CHAPTER 5

A Superior Gift

Certainly your gift, as evidenced by this "Drowsy Day" poem, alone, is a
superior one, and therefore its fortunate possessor should bear it with a
becoming sense of gratitude and meekness, always feeling that, for any
resultant good, God is the glory, the singer but His humble instrument.
Already you have many friends and can have thousands more by being simply
honest, unaffected, and just yourself and the high source of your endowment.

—JAMES WHITCOMB RILEY TO PAUL LAURENCE DUNBAR
(NOVEMBER 27, 1892)[1]

Good luck soon came Paul's way. He remained in touch with one of his former
teachers at Central High School, Mrs. Truesdale. Midway through 1892 she
knew that the Western Association of Writers, whose program committee she
served on, was scheduled to pass through Dayton. She wondered whether Paul,
now twenty, would be interested in attending the convention, whose relevance
was partly due to a coincidence: it was arranged to begin on the same exact day
as his birthday. More than that, he could meet eminent and emerging members
of the association and within his regional circle of influence, where he had been
toiling as a writer for the past couple of years, trying to cultivate a wide following. Mrs. Truesdale remembered Paul as the first African American class poet
who had riveted the audience at his commencement and maintained contact
with his high school alma mater's alumni and newspaper.[2]

Starting Monday, June 27, the Western Association of Writers met in Dayton for five days. Paul received an invitation to deliver a welcome poem on the
opening day. The meaning of the occasion was not lost on him. Not only did
it mark his twentieth birthday, his final turning point from teenager to a young
man; reciting the poem, he knew, also would make him the first African

American ever to earn recognition in the convention's program. Reserved for what an attendee later called the "commodious room" of the 32 East Fourth Street Young Men's Christian Association (YMCA), Paul's recital occurred only one year after he stood during graduation as class poet, likewise an unprecedented accomplishment for someone like him. More than these milestones for his race, the invitation meant that a newfound literary status among the poets of Dayton, if not also the Midwest, was within his grasp. Seizing the opportunity was key.[3]

Prior to the arrival of the Western Association of Writers, in the months following Paul's graduation from Central High School, he and his mother, Matilda, moved from their home at 317 West Washington Street to 818 Linden Avenue, two miles east. As they moved from home to home Paul moved from job to job, to support himself and his mother. Rob had left Dayton for Chicago in 1887 and was living there a married man, with the main concern of supporting his new family rather than continuing to support the one he left behind. Paul took it upon himself to find a line of work for which he was qualified: he had a high school diploma in hand, but, as an African American, he had to contend with prejudicial notions that he was inferior to his white counterparts. By late 1891, Paul could find only a spot in the shipping room of the National Cash Register Company, working as one of thirty African American janitors at the nearly decade-old business that manufactured the newly invented mechanical cash register. When he was not doing the strenuous work the job required, he wrote songs for the company's glee club.

Paul soon quit that job, however. Physically, he could not withstand the strain, given his slight build. "Dunbar stood five feet, nine and one-half inches tall," notes an earlier biographer, "had a thin frame, and high, broad chest. When in good health, which was seldom, he weighed between 125 and 135 pounds." Despite his limitations, the work could never fully distract him from his devotion to songs. For pleasure and as an artist, he loved to hear and write them.[4]

Serendipity opened doors. Occasionally Paul ran errands to the office of Charles W. Dustin, an attorney working in Dayton. Dustin was the agent for banker, stockholder, and manufacturer William P. Callahan. One day Paul, long curious about a career in law, asked whether the law office had any available jobs. No clerical positions were available, so Dustin pointed to the only job he could find for him: elevator boy in the Callahan Bank Building. Located at the intersection of Third and Main Streets, the "Callahan block" was the site of a five-story building, at that time the tallest structure in Dayton. Being an elevator boy was a far cry from being a janitor. The job was less physically taxing, and because an elevator boy's hands were relatively free, Paul expected that he could read on the job. (A little over a decade after Paul's death in 1906, Dustin recalled that he permitted Paul to borrow a law book from his office and take it with him to the elevator, to read while he worked.)[5] Certainly, Paul did not have all the time in the world for leisure; he had to learn to operate the elevator safely and professionally. He had to stay inside the car at all times, in uniform, and he had to report suspicious loiterers in the elevator's vicinity.

Nor did the job itself offer much intellectual stimulus. Passengers were prohibited from speaking to the elevator boy: posted signs inside the car ordered silence. Yet Paul knew that a diligent elevator boy still could instill the sense among passengers that, like the mechanical quality of the ride, the service was excellent. He also knew that being an elevator boy came with a fair share of responsibilities and dangers. The car could malfunction, in which case he would be forced to improvise among the ropes or the machinery within the elevator shaft. But he very much needed the money. So even as he longed for time to read, he had to take the job seriously.[6]

Paul's own words about this job set the tone and topic. In letters he wrote to an acquaintance while working on the elevator, he apologized for his delayed response: "through your knowledge of the difficulties under which I labor, you can easily forgive my negligence."[7] On another occasion, he depicted his invisible shackles more poignantly: "your letter found me still chained to the ropes of my dingy elevator," and "the incongeniality of my work and surroundings cannot but have a depressing effect."[8] Relegation to this part of the working world, where he was earning no more than four dollars per week for a job held by people without his degree of schooling, was unforgiving. The road from elevator boy to professional writer was neither clear nor direct at all.

Aside from the usual times Paul could observe and listen to passengers and ruminate on the subjects of his literary art, the moments of mental and physical respite between and among his tasks were precious. In silence, especially when the elevator was vacant, he could read whatever book, magazine, or letter he had in hand; he could write verses as well. When friends came by, such as Ezra Kuhns, a nearby law student who passed through regularly, Paul enjoyed talking about law or, more to his specialty, classical language, activities that could enlighten him despite his job's monotony.[9]

Midway through 1892 Paul and Matilda moved again, this time to 140 West Zeigler, a few blocks south of their previous homes on West Washington Street. Paul had taken out a mortgage on this one-and-a-half-story house, which cost $950 and belonged to the Mary E. Garst Estate. Paul and his mother would live in the house for the next six years, longer than at any other prior residence. One of the nicer places they had lived in, the residence featured space inside for decorating and land outside for gardening.[10]

As Paul was reckoning with life after high school, he was embarking on the difficult venture of a new professional life. He leveraged his companionship with Orville and Wilbur Wright, who were still running Wright & Wright printers after the demise of their earlier joint project, the *Dayton Tattler*, to help launch his fledgling literary career. Along with the *Tattler*, the brothers assisted Paul's efforts to increase his name recognition by printing advertisements and supplying tickets and handbills on his behalf for local recitals.

Paul was always trying to get his pieces published. He took up invitations extended by editors for his latest poems and stories. He scoured publications after he had sent a piece in but had not yet heard from their editors, for fear that they would go on to release his writings without proper credit or compensation. He sought clarification from editors on whether they wanted "original poetical contributions of a popular or other order."[11] And he diligently archived private correspondence from editors and publishers; these letters traced his attempts as a young man from Dayton to circulate his writings in newspapers and magazines around the country.

Not infrequently Paul defined the language of poetry as either popular or rarefied. That definition pivoted on the question of dialect. As he was struggling to find his identity as a poet, dialect was becoming a popular form of American literature. Two of the most famous poets at the time were Bret Harte of Albany, New York, and James Whitcomb Riley of Greenfield, Indiana. Among the other celebrated writers of prose who mastered or dabbled in dialect were Mark Twain; George Washington Cable, of New Orleans; Stephen Crane, of New Jersey; Abraham Cahan, a Russian-Jewish immigrant; and Thomas Nelson Page, of Virginia. "America was crazy about dialect literature," scholar Gavin Jones notes. Critics expressed fear that dialect signified an increasingly diverse nation of languages and immigrants, and marked the irreversible corruption of English in all its mythical purity. Readers, on the other hand, were insatiable consumers who "could not get enough of black dialect, Appalachian dialect, Pike County dialect, Maine dialect, New Yorkese dialect—every region was mined for its vernacular gold, and every predominant ethnic group was

FIG. 5.1. James Whitcomb Riley, circa 1898. (Library of Congress Prints and Photographs Division)

linguistically lampooned in popular poetry and prose."[12] Periodicals ranging from *The Century* to *Harper's Weekly Magazine* to the *Atlantic Monthly* regularly published special sections devoted to dialect writing. Authors sought publication in the elite magazines to entertain high-class readers who enjoyed the spectacle of ethnic or regional difference, even as such treatment of unfamiliar speech promoted stereotypes of races and regions.[13]

Paul was among the several writers and performers at the time who, to remarkable effect, took advantage of the marked distance between standard and nonstandard English in American popular culture. He also belonged to a race often caricatured in the popular press and to a region not without its own peculiarities. Yet even he was not immune to the prejudices of popular dialect writing and recitals. Paul was not the most qualified to write the literary dialect that readers expected of a person like him: a dark-skinned African American descended from parents who called Kentucky their original home. Readers ignored—or were not aware of—the fact that he was born and reared in Dayton. In fact, he could claim to be the genuine article of the Midwest as persuasively as he could claim African ancestry. And he would assert this claim, well aware that any regional authenticity required he play the part in his dialect writing, in much the same way that Riley caricatured a sort of Hoosier dialect for readers and for audiences who watched him perform.[14]

Still, Paul knew that his likeness and supposed racial authenticity would attract readers and spectators more than his Midwestern ties—although this, too, was a part to be played, an amalgam of race and region that would inform the fantasy of the Negro tongue. To wit, as scholar Nadia Nurhussein puts it, "Dunbar's correlation with his invented Southern black voices was so strong that books and articles sometimes grouped him with southern writers although he never lived in the South."[15] In due course Paul would realize that he needed to exploit this pigeonholing, this reputation for racial authenticity, for financial gain. In the meantime he tried to improve his literary craftsmanship while strengthening his grasp of how the marketplace imbued literature with commercial value.

Up until and including the period Paul was working as an elevator boy, he had begun to build his professional career as a poet with local help, building on his early promise. In addition to his early publications—two poems in the *Dayton Herald*, a poem in Dayton's *West Side News*, edited by his friend Orville, as well as his work in the *Tattler* and in his high school magazine—Paul dipped his toe in musical recitals. On August 12, 1891, he played the role of "dramatic reader" at Diester Hall in Dayton, sharing the stage with "Philodramian" friends from high school who sang and recited humorous poems. ("Philodramian" was Paul's neologism, meaning "fond of drama.") He immersed himself in his own particular interest: the preeminent achievements of literary art about troubled lovers. He recited Edgar Allan Poe's 1849 poem "Annabel Lee," about a maiden's death. He read a scene from the 1838 melodrama *The Lady of Lyons; or, Love and Pride*, by Edward Bulwer-Lytton, about a love triangle defined by deception and redemption. He recited the 1842 Tennyson ballad "Lady Clara Vere de Vere," about a prideful and flirtatious aristocratic lady. And he restaged the argument between Cassius and Brutus in act 4, scene 3, of William Shakespeare's classic 1599 play *Julius Caesar*. Neither this recital nor the minor publications that came before, however, did much to move the needle of fame in his favor.[16]

So aggressive was Paul in advancing his career that he pursued syndication, which other ambitious and strategic authors of the era likewise viewed as a way to enhance literary influence. The term "syndicate" applied to a newspaper publisher that printed material for distribution as well as a company that manufactured the stereo plates, or solid plates of type metal, needed to reprint newspaper pages. For writers it more commonly meant a company that, upon an editor's request, obtained and circulated galley proofs of poems or stories to a series of newspapers for wide, almost simultaneous circulation, anywhere from a couple dozen to upward of a thousand newspapers.[17]

Toward the end of 1891, Paul was more than willing to sell his first short story to the A. N. Kellogg Newspaper Company. Based in Chicago, the company received his manuscript by way of a Cincinnati branch to which he first mailed it on December 13. Although the company was not purchasing original stories ("we are over-stocked") or poems and short articles ("unless by special arrangement"), it was willing to take "The Tenderfoot," a story about a burly college-taught man who rises to prominence in a mining company, for six dollars. Six days before Christmas, it appeared in print.[18]

Syndication was a turning point for Paul. He exacted a price for "The Tenderfoot," just as he would a couple of years later for his sketch "Little Billy," about a remorseful man who accidentally shoots and kills his estranged son and namesake during a hunt for a horse thief. Again purchased by the Kellogg syndicate, "Little Billy" was the second story in his early career for which he was paid. In both cases he started to understand the role newspapers could play in setting the dimensions and demands of a literary marketplace. It also alerted him to the monetary value editors assigned to different genres of literature. Syndicates were especially known for circulating individual stories or

FIG. 5.2. Paul Laurence Dunbar, circa 1892. (Paul Laurence Dunbar Collection, Ohio History Connection)

serializing them if part of a novel. It introduced him to the potential scale of publication, tapping into newspapers that were published daily or weekly, read by both men and women, across levels of society and class, in many regions of the country. And syndication was ideal for elevating to national popularity a diverse stratum of writers, some more obscure than others, but all with coveted real estate on a newspaper's page.[19]

In syndicating his writings, Paul was slowly realizing that to be a renowned American writer meant being not only a professional writer but also a modern one. The rise of the syndicates, typified by the A. N. Kellogg company, attested to the literary industry's modernity. Ansel Nash Kellogg began his printing business in 1861; ever since, his company had grown, printing the insides and eventually the outsides of 53 weekly newspapers by 1865, 300 by 1871, 701 by 1877, close to 1,600 by 1886, and close to 2,000 by 1900. When Kellogg started printing serialized novels by 1870, it became an arbiter of literary fame. Paul's interest in Kellogg implied his intended emphasis on the literary value of his writing at the possible expense of its aesthetic value. But that calculus was required to expand his brand beyond Dayton and the Midwest. After all, could he not always change course down the road, when he could focus exclusively on being a man of letters rather than a man of business?[20]

In the couple of years after Paul's graduation from Central High School, he looked mostly toward the future, with the ambition of becoming a professional writer. But his brief turn to the past, his reconnection to the former students of his alma mater, turned out to be a critical moment in launching his literary career. In summer 1892 students from his graduating class came together for their first alumni reunion. Paul also returned to his high school, in a new building about half a mile northeast of the campus he attended.[21]

In keeping with his legacy as class poet, Paul recited "The Old High School and the New" for the alumni. In the poem, Paul envisioned the old and new buildings as metaphorical chapters in a heartfelt story of a sacred high school, likened to a "mother," that shaped its students. Across the years the story left indelible imprints on the students, a memory that would not be forgotten. The poem's second half especially brought this idea home for the alumni. In rapt attention they listened to Paul, who stood on the auditorium's stage. Over and again he declared that he and his fellow alumni were a community, a fateful "we," with another generation of loyal, intelligent boys and girls to come:

It seems that now some pretty tears the sentiment would garnish
But we're afraid to weep in here for fear we'll spoil the varnish.

So tearless, but with a regret, a deep one and a true one,
We've questioned her identity, of all this change abhorrent,
But on near view she warmer grows. She's not half bad I'll warrant.
She speaks and on her quivering lids the anxious tear drops glisten,
What can we do but pause awhile respectfully and listen?
"Don't let the thought that I have changed with stubborn hearts imbue,
If you'll accept me, children dear, I'll be a mother to you."
We'll do it, won't we, girls and boys, excuse me, men and women,
We'll throw our arms about her neck in spite of all the trimmin',
We'll climb upon her ample lap, turn up our eager faces
And listen to her wisdom in the pause between embraces.
And while we toast the old that's gone, new joys shall make our
    pain sweet
We'll take our love from Wilkinson and move it up to Main Street.
We'll bind this new'made mother's brow with every wreath and token
Of that deep life within our hearts that never can be spoken.
We'll love her as we loved the dear old school or very very near it,
For tho' she's thrown the dress away she's kept the same old spirit;
And of her present boys and girls we'll each prove a believer
That every year she'll turn them out as good and bright as we were.[22]

The audience erupted into applause when Paul finished. Chatter afterward among the attendees fueled his belief that, in the near future, he should publish a book.

In the days following the event, the idea gathered momentum in Paul's mind: a compilation of the more mature poems (relative to the 1884 poem "Easter Ode," for instance) he had been publishing or reciting over the years, plus those he had been jotting down and reciting in between. There *were* enough poems for a book. Encouraged, he banked the idea until the time was ripe.

————

By summer 1892, the Western Association of Writers had been in existence for six years, founded by Indiana writers including James Newton Matthews and Marie Louise Andrews. The goal of the association was to represent a "literary profession for mutual strength, profit, and acquaintance," to focus on "the advancement of literature in America," with an eye toward compiling for release the proceedings and presentations of its annual convention, which rounded up "the writers of the Wabash valley and the adjacent states." In its first years, the association met annually in Indiana, where most of its members lived. For its seventh meeting, the association decided to change the venue to the neighboring state of Ohio. Of great interest to Paul, some of the attendees were likely to be popular writers of the Midwest, led by poet James Whitcomb Riley and poet and novelist James Maurice Thompson of Indiana.[23]

Given that Paul had to recite his poem Monday morning, he knew he had to steal away briefly from his elevator job. He walked a block south, on Main Street, to the YMCA, where he was ushered toward the front of the hot and stuffy hall, crowded with the Dayton elite. As the people fanned themselves, Paul maneuvered his way down an aisle. For many in the audience he was the sole Negro lad many of them had ever seen assume such privileged treatment in a setting for high literature. Paul took his place on the rostrum and faced the audience. The room quieted down. The association's chairman, Dr. John Clark Ridpath, an administrator and English literature professor at Indiana's DePauw University, introduced the slight, obscure young man, who started to read aloud a poem that he would include in his first book a year later:

"Westward the course of empire takes its way,"—
So Berkeley said, and so to-day
The men who know the world still say.
The glowing West, with bounteous hand,
Bestows her gifts throughout the land,
And smiles to see at her command
Art, science, and the industries,—
New fruits of new Hesperides.
So, proud are you who claim the West
As home land; doubly are you blest
To live where liberty and health
Go hand in hand with brains and wealth.
So here's a welcome to you all,
Whate'er the work your hands let fall,—
To you who trace on history's page
The footprints of each passing age;
To you who tune the laureled lyre
To songs of love or deeds of fire;
To you before whose well-wrought tale
The cheek doth flush or brow grow pale;

To you who bow the ready knee
And worship cold philosophy,—
A welcome warm as Western wine,
And free as Western hearts, be thine.
Do what the greatest joy insures,—
The city has no will but yours![24]

For American poets of the late nineteenth century, Bishop George Berkeley
had a prominent place. Born in Ireland in the late seventeenth century and a
philosopher of perception and immaterialism, he published in 1728 *On the
Prospect of Planting Arts and Learning in America*. Berkeley's verses from that
volume appeared in *Poems of Places*, a massive collection Henry Wadsworth
Longfellow edited and published from 1876 to 1879. A wide reader of literature
since high school, Paul probably knew or owned this book. The section "America" in Longfellow's edition gathers the most compelling "introductory"
poems, including Berkeley's, whose ultimate stanza begins with "Westward
the course of empire takes its way." This line led Paul to imagine how the proverbial errand into the wilderness could lead to the cultivation of "Art, science,
and the industries." Focused on the Midwest and titled "On the Prospect of
Planting Arts and Learning in America," Berkeley envisions the irrepressible
creativity of a young nation:

There shall be sung another golden age,
    The rise of empire and of arts,
The good and great inspiring epic rage,
    The wisest heads and noblest hearts.

Not such as Europe breeds in her decay;
    Such as she bred when fresh and young,
When heavenly flame did animate her clay,
    By future poets shall be sung.[25]

What made Paul's own poem so moving was not merely its erudition, its
proof that a young man on the other side of the so-called color line, as most
of the audience saw him, could interpret and redeploy classic literature, history, and mythology for his own purpose. Handling both Berkeley's poetics
of the American West and the botanical metaphor of Hesperides in Greek
mythology showed Paul's intellectual versatility. Yet his reading before the
Western Association of Writers threw down a gauntlet that underscored his
own sense of affiliation with the organization: he was distinguishing the

literature of the Midwest from other kinds of American literature in almost the same way that Berkeley, in his day, was extolling "the rise of empire and of arts" in the face of Old World "decay." Paul's poem closed by pointing to the individual listeners—the historians, the poets, the storytellers, the philosophers—and welcoming them to Dayton.

The acclaim Paul enjoyed after reciting his poem was measurable not only by the applause but also by what happened afterward. The day after his recital, certain people in the audience sought him out: Ridpath along with two men, the Illinois-born poets James Newton Matthews, a medical doctor who wrote poetry and a co-founder of the Western Association of Writers, and William W. Pfrimmer, a Newton County, Indiana, school superintendent who shunned his law degree to write dialect verse.

The three men tracked Paul down at the Callahan building. As Matthews later recalled, "I found him seated in a chair on the lower landing, hastily glancing at the July *Century*, and jotting down notes on a handy pencil-tablet. Not having time to converse with me there, he invited me into the elevator, and during a few excursions from floor to floor I gathered from him the following facts"—namely, about the background of his parents, about his first serious attempts at writing verse at the age of thirteen, about how he was devoting his full pay of four dollars per week (despite working a full eleven hours per day) toward supporting himself and his mother in Dayton. As they continued to talk, Matthews began to delight in Paul's "natural brilliancy," such as his deep affinity for John Greenleaf Whittier, the celebrated poet from Massachusetts, and James Whitcomb Riley, despite being "chained like a galley-slave to the ropes of a dingy elevator at starvation wages."[26]

Matthews transcribed these and other thoughts in a flattering October 2, 1892, essay he published in the *Indianapolis Journal*. He titled the piece "A Negro Poet," subtitled it "A Young Man Whose Literary Talent Shows Itself in Spite of Unfavorable Environment," and described his first interaction with the young poet and introduced him to the world.

Even Matthews's life-changing encounter with Paul was not enough to achieve a self-purging of long-harbored racial stereotypes. He broke the news to *Indianapolis Journal* readers that they should discard the "old idea that no excellence can come out of Africa," that "ignorance has always been associated with darkness, and a white skin has been the index of intelligence." Matthews remarked that, when he first saw Paul at the conference, the poet was "as black as the core of Cheops's pyramid," even though he stood before the audience with "the coolness and dignity of a cultured entertainer." Matthews's admiration for the "poetic taste and ability of a young colored man of Dayton" was enough to cement the bond between him and the newfound poet.[27]

Few people would mean more to Paul's early literary aspirations than Matthews. That summer of 1892 inaugurated private correspondence in which Paul repeatedly thanked him for his introduction to Midwestern literary society. The difference in age was clear—Paul just turned twenty, about half of Matthews's age—but the young man regarded his elder as more than a mere acquaintance. "For friend you have proven to be," Paul wrote. Matthews "came like a ray of light into the darkness of discouragement" during his tenure as an elevator boy.[28]

Paul's time with Matthews marked his first with a patron invested in his future. Patrons like Matthews were known for playing crucial roles in the lives of aspiring authors. They tended to be people of means who helped writers make ends meet—to give them money. In lieu of an onerous job, these writers could now afford the leisure to write beautiful and everlasting literature. Patrons worked in other ways, too: they were willing to stand as interlocutors between authors, on one hand, and editors and publishers on the other. They were like literary agents, brokers, publicists, and, to a different degree, well-connected friends or acquaintances who served as intermediaries of verbal and capital exchange (such as information, money, prestige) within the professional world. Patrons were protagonists in the American literary industry. Paul's friendship with Matthews promised to open doors.[29]

But the connection was more than that. A patron's involvement in a writer's life was a window onto what it meant to be a professional. It was a clue to how a writer's self-conscious sense of artistry, labor, bonds with acquaintances, and pay were tied to a shifting notion of literary value—to how the aesthetics of taste and the economics of the marketplace could unite in deciding the value of a poem or a story. These criteria determined how much a writer like Paul earned for his written work; they explained how much a writer accrued in literary eminence and professional security. Patrons who already had succeeded in securing their own riches or wealth, their own certitude of personal stability in an otherwise unpredictable capitalistic society, knew full well the stakes by which writers aspired to join the world of letters. The "literary networks and partnerships" that formed among the likes of patrons and writers, according to scholar David Dowling, "were based on both common artistic visions and commercial objectives, on both literary and economic interests."[30] No author could proceed autonomously without being part of a broader circle of supporters and expect to succeed in the literary industry.

Paul knew that Matthews had to be more than just an investor, which was what a patron could ultimately be; the elder gentleman had to be a friend in whom secrets, personal and professional, could be confided, with whom the language of intimacy could be shared naturally. In the dozen or so letters they exchanged from 1892 to 1895 (and a few more until as late as 1903), Paul engaged him in this mode. In one of his earliest letters to Matthews, in late July 1892, Paul first only tiptoed, starting with "Dear Sir" yet closing with "Your Friend." By October of the same year, he was beginning his letters with "Dear Friend" and ending with the core phrase "Ever Your Friend," amid a signature embellishment like "With deepest regard," or appeals like "Write to me whenever you can, I am always glad to hear from you" and "Hoping to hear from you soon again."[31]

For Paul and other African American figures of his time, befriending white patrons and philanthropists hinged on a twofold connotation of friendship: community and collaboration. Three years after his first encounter with Matthews, a southern educator would most famously demonstrate this reality. In a legendary speech that Booker T. Washington delivered in September 1895, he stated his "desire to say something that would cement the friendship of the races" to a rapturous audience during the opening of the Cotton States and International Exposition in Atlanta, Georgia. Two years later, in a private exchange, the Midwestern writer and activist Charles W. Chesnutt would send a letter to Walter Hines Page, wishing to obtain the *Atlantic Monthly* editor's "interest" and "friendship." The lives of Washington and Chesnutt became stories of how African American men, in an era of Jim Crow, could earn the trust of white men who themselves or whose ancestors once accepted slavery. Paul led this kind of life at the same time, if not earlier, even if such white benevolence, moral and financial, happened to reify the very terms of racial inferiority he was trying to overcome.[32]

Starting in 1892, Paul's exchanges with Matthews inspired him to endure his job as an elevator boy. Paul's own uncertainty over his excellence as a creative writer brought him closer to the elder gentleman. Early on, failures to get published shook Paul's sense of well-being; they magnified his lack of conviction about his professional future. In one of his first letters to Matthews, in summer 1892, Paul asked, "Can you blame me for doubting my ability when I have never been able to sell a single poem to any paper?" Doubt gave way to despondency a couple of months later; he still found little commercial success while toiling away shackled to his "dingy elevator," overshadowed by "the darkness" of "discouragement." "There have been many things to encourage me," he prefaced the letter, "but the incongeniality of my work and surroundings cannot but have a depressing effect." Thank heavens Matthews, in Paul's view, was the primary "light" of encouragement, the man who continually advised him "to keep plugging away with my pen."[33]

Paul thanked Matthews for having written "an excellent article" for the *Indianapolis Journal*, urging the periodical to publish more of Paul's poetry. Matthews played a double role in Paul's life, in spirit and professionally—the "letter in giving strength to my soul and the article in paving the way for a venture which I am now about to undertake." A few months afterward, Paul began to reap the rewards sown by Matthews's widely circulated words of praise. The young man's confidence rose higher. "I am receiving many letters from different parts of the country now and all through you, my friend." Elated, Paul finally had someone influential in his corner.[34]

Matthews's words were pearls of wisdom and encouragement when Paul faced doubts and criticism about his professional promise. A year and a half after starting the elevator job, he was at a low point, "bemoaning the fact that my own people were growing away from me," he wrote in a letter close to Christmastime in 1893. Referring to fellow Daytonians, Paul complained "that they watched not for my success but for my failure, that they saw in my efforts no worth, only presumption." Writing to Matthews helped Paul put his life in perspective. Matthews's own struggles with "home cares" made Paul's own "burden grow lighter," making him realize that his only main challenge was to be a writer. "I have at present no regular employment but am trying to live by my pen," he conceded, "with nothing beside the scanty returns of my literary and journalistic ventures," and with little beside the mission to "adopt literature as a profession." In Matthews, Paul discovered a true confidant; in his letters the younger man was most open. "I cannot forbear a few words as you have shown such a material interest in my career." Hardly anyone else Paul wrote to in his early twenties received such an honest admission as this.[35]

Amid his disclosures about his own well-being and his aspiration to be a professional writer, Paul used Matthews as a sounding board for circumspection and plotting, for tales of successes and failures, of the viability and sales of his creative writings. Attaching two recently written poems, "Ode for Memorial Day" and "Easter Poem," in a letter to Matthews, Paul disconsolately complained that opportunities just would not come his way. "My hopes are no brighter than when you saw me here, I am getting no better, and, what would be impossible, no worse."[36]

Paul persevered. "I have determined to publish a number of my poems in book form and try to sell them," he wrote to Matthews in fall 1892, "and I would not have wanted a better aid than the write up you gave me," gesturing to the *Indianapolis Journal* article. He was already aware that the benefits must counterbalance the costs in this enterprise. Seeking to sell anywhere from fifty to one hundred of his books in Indianapolis, he issued a bold proclamation: he would not even print one book until he had the "written assurance of sufficient sales to cover all expenses, in the names of subscribers." Although the cost was one dollar to print five copies, his goal was to sell each copy for one dollar. But the cost and effort would be less about reaping a profit than about breaking into the professional world. "It should pave the way toward better things," he hoped.[37]

Those few years following Paul's high school graduation, which coincided with his friendship with Matthews, marked the time when he obsessed most over the commercial viability of his creative writing—over the degree that he could, as the saying went in his hometown, "adopt literature as a profession." Paul wondered whether his race would prompt people to pigeonhole his poetry. Since his days as editor of the now-defunct *Tattler*, his desire that people read his work for its universal meaning, not merely for its testimony to the Negro Problem or for its perceivable caricature of minstrelsy, laced his early professional instincts with anxiety.[38]

Paul was self-conscious about his literary use of dialect. At one point he wished to refrain from writing it to advance his career. In fall 1892, when Thomas Gentry, a friend of Matthews and author of the 1882 illustrated book *Nests and Eggs of Birds of the United States*, reached out to Paul—probably at Matthews's bidding—to ask for a photo (not an uncommon request at the time) to include in a collection of "bird poetry" he was compiling, the request stoked unease in the rising poet over what he saw as the increasing number of solicitations around the country. Paul was worried; he was not sure if, at his level of literary skill, he yet deserved the attention. Even more, he was concerned that his dabbling in dialect was contributing to his own public pigeonholing. To Matthews he floated the idea, "I shall write less dialect." Over time, he would find it nearly impossible to stick to that promise.[39]

Even as Paul wrestled with what writing poetry in dialect meant for him and his career, such as his October 1892 recital at the Dayton YMCA, he paid attention to professional milestones. A few days after Thanksgiving in 1892, one month removed from his meditations to Matthews about being a "black face," he was able to smile on initial success. "Sunday morning, the mail brought me my first money for a poem, two dollars for a little piece to a child's publication in New York." Albeit neither a major poem nor a major periodical, the news brought the sunshine of optimism into what had been a gloomy year in the professional world. "I am beginning to hope and am going to try to improve myself more and more."[40]

Within a year Paul's audience ranged from a Dayton YMCA crowd of six hundred people awaiting the Fisk Jubilee Singers, an African American a cappella ensemble from Fisk University, to a Toledo, Ohio, audience where he boasted that he "read for a very wealthy and aristocratic private club," which received him "enthusiastically." By the end of the year he had developed a full-fledged sense of "hope" about his future prospects. "I am beginning to feel timidly hopeful and at each step I take ahead," he wrote to Matthews; "I thank and bless you for it, for you were the Moses that led out my enslaved powers." So grateful was Paul to Matthews, in other words, that he was not unwilling to deprecate himself and play the obsequious role of protégé to his patron.[41]

During this time, Paul was learning more about the art of public recital: about how to captivate the ears of people as strongly as he was trying to rivet their eyes with the written word. Although he had done quite a few public recitals in his early career, he doubted himself. In a letter to Matthews, Paul communicates these thoughts and feelings about his public reading, on October 18, 1892, with the Fisk Jubilee Singers at the YMCA. He read his poems before a massive audience that reacted "with an unexpected heartiness." Even so, sharing the stage with the singers of so-called Negro spirituals only reinforced his fears. "I hope there is something worthy in my writings and not merely the novelty of a black face associated with the power to rhyme that has attracted attention." Concerned with his professional immaturity as well as the specter of being classified as a dialect poet, Paul's "self-doubts" would remain a recurring theme in his letters as well as his literary writing throughout his life.[42]

The contemporary poet James Whitcomb Riley inspired Paul's own understanding of recitations. "There could scarcely be a better thing than the development of a distinctly western school of poets, such as Riley represents," Paul once explained to Matthews. By the 1890s, Riley had become popular through his written poetry and his public readings. He also had become a cautionary tale for Paul to remember. Dialect partly enabled Riley to depict classes lower than his own to literate readers who were entertained by his caricatured portrayal of illiterate speakers. In his shows he suggested to audiences, "Whatever you are, be that"—in this case, "the gentleman from Indiana"—as one periodical's special issue stated at the time. Yet Riley's popularity on stage left him despairing over how the public viewed his talent. His late-career endeavor to recapture the prestige of print was his turn away from the gimmick of Hoosier performance. Riley's and Dunbar's respective struggles with the craze for regional and racial folklore mirrored each other.[43]

When Paul praised Riley in his July 1892 letter to Matthews, little did he know that, months later, the elder poet would in turn reach out to him. A couple of days after Thanksgiving, a month removed from the publicity Paul received from Matthews's review, Riley wrote to the rising star: "See how your name is traveling, my chirping friend!" The Hoosier poet delighted in uplifting and advising the emerging poet (about whom he would later declare, with dubious accuracy: "I was the first to recognize Paul Laurence Dunbar"). "And it's a good sound name, too," Riley continued, "that seems to imply the brave, fine spirit of a singer who should command wide and serious attention." Riley pointed to a hitherto unpublished poem, "A Drowsy Day," that Paul had personally sent, along with other poems, to Matthews, who transcribed it for inclusion in his *Indianapolis Journal* column:

> Half seen, the bare, gaunt-fingered boughs
>   Before my window sweep and sway,
> And chafe in tortures of unrest.
> My chin sinks down upon my breast;
>   I cannot work on such a day,
> But only sit and dream and drowse.

What may have captured Riley's eye was not "A Drowsy Day" but what Matthews wrote next, right after this final stanza. "Among other unpublished scraps sent me, I find the following neat verses in Western dialect, almost worthy the pen of Riley or Field"—indeed, the verses of "The Ol' Tunes," which began:

> You kin talk about yer anthems,
>   An' yer arias an' sich,
> An' yer modern choir-singin'
>   That you think so awful rich;
> But you orter heerd us youngsters
>   In the times now far away,
> A-singin' o' the ol' tunes
>   In the ol'-fashioned way.

Yet as inclined as Riley should have been to analyze the latter poem in "Western dialect," he praised the former that was written in exquisite English, which he deemed proof that, as a poet, Paul's "gift . . . is a superior one." Riley went on to say that this poem's

> fortunate possessor should bear it with a becoming sense of gratitude and meekness, always feeling, that, for any resultant good, God is the glory, the singer but His humble instrument. Already you have many friends and can have thousands more by being simply honest, unaffected, and just yourself and the high source of your endowment.[44]

The letter from Riley was a note of encouragement. But it was also equivalent to the prophetic hand of an elder, anointing Paul and his poetry as the divine messenger to a newfound generation. Riley turned out to be one of Paul's greatest advocates at an early moment in the poet's career.

———

As Paul continued to explore what it would take for him to publish a book, naturally he turned to those closest to him who had experience in publishing and, incidentally, a connection with his high school alma mater: the Wright brothers, the publishers of his *Dayton Tattler*. By September and October of 1892, Orville and Wilbur were entering a new stage of their lives. They were living alone while their father was working on the road and their siblings were spending extended time together in Kansas City. Wilbur was no longer an editor for the *West Side News* and the *Evening Item*, the two publications on which they had been collaborating. Orville was growing disenchanted with the life of a printer, despite his success in delegating much of the daily work to a faithful co-worker named Ed Sines.

Orville and Wilbur were thinking about other entrepreneurial opportunities. Starting with the "merry wheel" (or bicycle), the world of invention and innovation sparked their imagination.[45] Just before they would change the course of aviation history, Paul asked them for help in locating a printer for his book. Orville's print shop was not equipped to publish such a manuscript: it focused mostly on newsletters and periodicals. Instead, the United Brethren Publishing House came up as an option, an idea Paul readily embraced. Perhaps, he thought, his long friendship with the Wright family would give him sufficient leverage to convince the publishing house to print his book.[46]

Paul dropped by the United Brethren Publishing House, just a couple of blocks from his elevator job. Tales persist on what happened next. There is the story of how Paul, manuscript in hand and brimming with confidence, entered the printing office and faced an uphill battle in negotiating with officers of the publishing house—an editor, a superintendent, a foreman—skeptical about the idea of an African American wanting to publish his own literature. He also had to face the men's pessimism over the commercial viability of poetry. In the end, the quality of the poems—which a printer ascertained on a brief, although still quite close, inspection—convinced the foreman, named William L. Blocher, to publish Paul's manuscript by Christmas of 1892.

A core detail persists in this legend: Blocher expected Paul to pay about one hundred dollars to defray the initial costs of printing the first run of the book, but an exception was made, allowing a sale of the copies first. The poet was highly motivated to drum up interest in his publication, but he would have to do it on his own. The publisher would print the manuscript only; he would neither sell nor control the public relations surrounding it. Paul agreed to re-imburse the publisher in the amount of the first round of royalties he otherwise would have kept for himself. Now that the advance was set, Paul focused on putting the finishing touches on the manuscript and turning it in.[47]

CHAPTER 6

Career Choices

... Oh, circumscribe me not by rules
That serve to lead the minds of fools!
But give me pow'r to work my will,
And at my deeds the world shall thrill.
My words shall rouse the slumb'ring zest
That hardly stirs in manhood's breast;
And as the sun feeds lesser lights,
As planets have their satellites,
So round about me will I bind
The men who prize a master mind!

—PAUL LAURENCE DUNBAR, "A CAREER," *OAK AND IVY* (1893)[1]

By the end of 1892, Paul had put the finishing touches on a manuscript of poems he titled *Oak and Ivy*. The title referred not only to an impressively large tree, bountiful in its production of acorns and resilient in the hardness and durability of its wood, but also to the sprawling evergreen that climbed up or crawled along its adjacent soil. The pastoral iconography of this image—a majestic oak tree, enveloped by leaves and berries of ivy—conveyed the metaphorical fecundity of nature and love in the book. But *Oak and Ivy* also portended a paradox. As much as oak and ivy persisted in botanical embrace, their apparent symbiosis was not necessarily mutual: the resilient tree could be perceived as not welcoming but rather withstanding the parasitical threat posed by the coiling plant, whose toxicity could invade the oak's ecology. To what in Paul's book did oak and ivy so negatively refer?

History does not regard the first book Paul ever published as his most notable. The books he published later—when the literary marketplace was more favorable, when his talent as a writer matured, when his commercial acumen grew savvier—did more to advance his career and solidify his legacy. But *Oak and Ivy* was the soil in which he rooted his intellectual life as a poet and his professional life as an author. Containing fifty-three poems and representing a selection of verses he had recited or written during and after his high school years, this first book of his paid homage to the range of individuals, past and present, whom he revered. It showed his affinity for the places, eras, and ideas that shaped him. Its lyrical modes of experimentation declared his sense of belonging to rigorous poetic traditions of theme and form. But the visible contrast between formal and informal English, between rarefied diction and racialized dialect, generates a palpable hermeneutic tension in the book's literary ecosystem not unlike the organic tension one can envision in nature between oak and ivy. No book captured as much as *Oak and Ivy* Paul's unobstructed perspective of the writer he wanted to become as he entered his literary prime. Specifically, it showcased the metrical rhythms and rhyme schemes that largely informed the prosody he applied to his subsequent poetry, even as it telegraphed the potential challenges he would have to face as he sought the utter freedom of literary expression.

In fall 1892 Paul wanted to compile a manuscript of poems that demonstrated thematic gravity and formal versatility. He hoped the manuscript would document the creative skills he had acquired over the years while reading and writing literature within and outside the classroom. At minimum the book collected and reprinted some poems he had published before. Close to halfway through the book, for example, a reader encounters "Welcome Address," a transcription of the legendary poem that he first recited to the Western Association of Writers and that catapulted him to local fame.

Paul also selected for his new book a handful of poems previously published in periodicals. Some were juvenilia. "On the River" appeared in the *Dayton Herald* in the summer of 1888, less than a month after he had turned sixteen and finished the tenth grade. "Christmas Carol" came out unsigned in the second issue of the *Dayton Tattler*, and its reemergence confirmed Paul's authorship of it. Closer to his current state of literary maturity were "A Drowsy Day" and "The Ol' Tunes," the poems that Matthews released (on his own) in summer 1892 in the *Indianapolis Journal* and that Riley, his interest equally piqued, referred to in his later correspondence with Paul. Also included were "A Summer Pastoral" and "A Columbian Ode," poems that Paul placed, respectively, in the *Chicago News Record* that same summer and the *Chicago Daily News* in fall 1892.

In *Oak and Ivy*, Paul wanted to express his gratitude to the person who most shepherded him through the turbulence of family life: his mother, Matilda. An early page introduces the person to whom he dedicated the corpus: "to her who has ever been my guide, teacher, and inspiration, my mother, this little volume is affectionately inscribed." The dedication was a clue to the predominance of odes in the book, which may be read as a capsule of his poetic talents and promise but also as a willingness on his part to pay respect to those who had made indelible impressions on him.

Inside the book one finds a diverse array of poetic styles. On one occasion Paul decided to strike an elegiac touch, a refined sense of bringing public grief to bear on the crafting of verse, in "On the Death of W. C.," about Walter Clasz, a Central High School classmate who passed away right after his graduation in summer 1890. In the more pastoral celebrations of nature he dedicated numerous poems to the special times and settings of the day ("Evening" and "Sunset"); to the seasons of the year ("A Summer Pastoral," "In Summer Time," "Merry Autumn," and "October"); to the holidays ("An Easter Ode," "A Thanksgiving Poem," "Christmas Carol," "Memorial Day"). The book also includes numerous other ballads that offer individual, discernibly autobiographical, perspectives on love and loss, and on poetry itself.

Above all, Paul wrote odes to the British Romantic poets who filled his assigned reading in district school, all masters of form. Along with "Ode to Ethiopia" and "Columbian Ode," "To the Miami" and "The Old Homestead" celebrate the charming peculiarities of his hometown. African ancestry, New World discovery, and the Midwest likewise inspired him to write verses about how race, history, and region oriented his vision of the world.[2]

Extending the spirit of celebration to Paul's literary times, "Whittier" is named after John Greenleaf Whittier, who died, at age eighty-four, just as Paul was finishing his manuscript in 1892. Paul alludes to the passing early on:

Not o'er thy dust let there be spent
The gush of maudlin sentiment;
Such drift as that is not for thee,
Whose life and deeds and songs agree,
Sublime in their simplicity.

Nor shall the sorrowing tear be shed;
O singer sweet, thou art not dead!
In spite of time's malignant chill,
With living fire thy songs shall thrill,
And men shall say, "He liveth still!"

Whittier belonged to a group, almost a movement, called the "Fireside" or "Schoolroom" Poets, bridging an American literary and social sensibility from the Northeast to the Midwest. The others in this generation included Oliver Wendell Holmes, who was still alive (he died in October 1894); William Cullen Bryant, who died in 1878; Henry Wadsworth Longfellow, who died in 1882; and James Russell Lowell, who died in 1891. Paul's poems also resonated with the song of British Romanticism, its melodies and metaphors embedded early on in his formal education; but this song likewise shaped the Fireside Poets themselves, whose own mastery of poetic form and theme may have helped him digest the previous tradition across the Atlantic even more. As the last stanza attests, Paul's reverence calls attention to Whittier's place among the most storied American poets between the Civil War and the century's end:

Great poets never die, for Earth
Doth count their lives of too great worth
To lose them from her treasured store;
So shalt thou live for evermore—
Though far thy form from mortal ken—
Deep in the hearts and minds of men.[3]

Paul sought to dignify social concerns in elevated literary form, a hallmark of Fireside Poetry and, broadly, American poetry of the late nineteenth century. As scholar Elizabeth Renker states, "workers from across the broad terrain of American labor wrote, sang, recited, printed, and distributed thousands of original poems and songs advocating the cause of workers against capital."[4] At first blush the poems in formal English did not go so far as to convey the angst of "song-poems," a hybrid of "folk songs, hymns, and minstrel tunes" reaching thousands in the American labor press in the three decades after the Civil War. Song-poems indicted the struggles of work and labor strife—at least some of which Paul knew firsthand as an elevator boy and the child of a laundress. More obliquely, he focused on speaking humanely on the plight of the dispossessed. He made this concern the bookends to his manuscript.

On one end, the opening stanza of "Ode to Ethiopia" recognizes the culprit of slavery in the travail of civilization:

O Mother Race! to thee I bring
This pledge of faith unwavering,
  This tribute to thy glory.
I know the pangs which thou didst feel,
When Slavery crushed thee with its heel,
  With thy dear blood all gory.

On the other, "Justice," the penultimate poem, realizes the ineradicable cancer of discrimination born from slavery:

Enthroned upon the mighty truth,
  Within the confines of the laws,
True Justice seeth not the man,
  But only hears his cause.

Unconscious of his creed or race,
  She cannot see, but only weighs;
For Justice with unbandaged eyes
  Would be oppression in disguise.[5]

Paul knew well that slavery ran in his family: at one time his parents were property governed by Kentucky slave statutes. "No persons shall henceforth be slaves within the commonwealth," the 1798 Kentucky statutes declared, "except such as were on the 17th day of October, in the year 1785, and the descendants of the females of them."[6] Later, in 1810, the statutes confirmed that skin "colour, and long possession, is *prima facie* evidence of slavery." The complexions of most Africans and their descendants typically were darker than those of most Europeans and their children who had immigrated to or been born in the state.[7]

Not until fugitive flight, in the case of his father, or emancipation, in the case of his mother, were his parents ever liberated from slavery. Paul also knew that, from the first census in 1790 until 1870, enumerators went every ten years from city to city, county to county, registering members of the population, gathering data for Congress and the Electoral College, but nonetheless counted only the free inhabitants by name. Listed numerically in tables or schedules, the enslaved went unnamed; and the origin and regeneration of enslaved families were always unsettled: relatives, on one hand, traded like commodities or, on the other, living in numerical anonymity. Slavery thrived by these means.[8]

Conscientious indignation at slavery and social injustice was not peculiar to someone like Paul. He knew well the "pang" of Ethiopia: his parents inherited its putative sign on their flesh, he on his own, all confronting the historic specter of "creed or race." But the American poets of his times used literary art to express activism. Lowell and Longfellow eventually came to embrace antislavery; Whittier was even more proactively abolitionist in the prewar era. The Fireside Poets balanced placidity and perseverance, waged a rhetorical power, in measured tone and form, against the era's social inequities.[9]

Perhaps the optimism encouraged by these poets is captured in Paul's "Ode to Ethiopia." The poem pronounces in the final stanza:

> Go on and up! Our souls and eyes
> Shall follow thy continuous rise;
> Our ears shall list thy story
> From bards which from thy root shall spring,
> And proudly tune their lyres to sing
> Of Ethiopia's glory.

A political realist, Paul dedicated a poem, "To Miss Mary Britton," to an African American woman with her own harrowing story, according to the headnote: "When the legislature of Kentucky was discussing the passage of a separate-coach bill, Miss Mary Britton, a teacher in the schools of Lexington, Kentucky, went before them, and in a ringing speech protested against the passage of the bill. Her action was heroic, though it proved to be without avail." Britton debated the law that Kentucky's General Assembly had passed on March 15, 1892. As in the case of Whittier's death, the stipulation of racially segregating passenger trains into "colored" and "white" coaches, and the groundswell of resistance marked by Britton's dissent, drove Paul to write an ode for the woman in her mid-thirties who was an original member of the Kentucky Negro Education Association (founded in 1877) and on a mission to improve teaching in African American schools. Once again in the name of "Justice" personified, Paul penned it as a call to arms:

> Give us to lead our cause
>   More noble souls like hers,
> The memory of whose deed
>   Each feeling bosom stirs;
> Whose fearless voice and strong
>   Rose to defend her race,

Roused Justice from her sleep,
   Drove Prejudice from place.[10]

The Fireside Poets referred not only to those associated with the Northeast—
namely, the core group of Longfellow, Whittier, Holmes, and Lowell of Massachusetts, along with Bryant of New York. They included key poets of the Midwest, such as Eugene Field and James Whitcomb Riley, who may be regarded
a slightly younger generation of this tradition. By the end of 1892, Field had just
turned forty-two and Riley was one year older; together, they were about three
decades the junior of the youngest Fireside Poet (Longfellow).[11]

Paul expressed special affinity for Riley. In private he was honored to correspond with him. His new book afforded him the precious opportunity to
hail his mentor in print, nothing less than in full view of the public, with the
poem "James Whitcomb Riley":

No matter what you call it,
   Whether genius, gift, or art,
He sings the simple songs that come
   The closest to your heart.
Fur trim an' skillful phrases,
   I do not keer a jot;
'Tain't the words alone, but feelin's,
   That tech the tender spot.
An' that's jest why I love him,—
   Why, he's got sech human feelin',
An' in ev'ry song he gives us,
   You kin see it creepin', stealin'.
Through the core the tears go tricklin',
   But the edge is bright an' smiley;
I never saw a poet
   Like that poet Whitcomb Riley.

Whittier and Riley were the two most famous writers of Paul's time to
each earn an ode in his first book. (The subjects of his other odes, "To
Dr. James Newton Matthews" and "To Pfrimmer," were personal acquaintances whose literary careers had not risen to the heights of Whittier's and
Riley's.) Lauding both men captured his reverence for the Fireside generation. But it also suggested that he was a hybrid of the two, a master of both
formal and informal types of English—as cleverly shown in the first stanza

of "James Whitcomb Riley," which alternates regional language and high diction. The subtitle of the poem, "From a Westerner's Point of View," confirms his subjective kinship with the "Hoosier Poet." As Paul asserts in part of the second stanza, the poem displays what the Fireside Poets so prized and promoted:

> If there's a lesson to be taught,
>   He never fears to teach it,
> An' he puts the food so good an' low
>   That the humblest one kin reach it.
> Now in our time, when poets rhyme
>   For money, fun, or fashion,
> 'Tis good to hear one voice so clear
>   That thrills with honest passion.
> So let the others build their songs,
>   An' strive to polish highly,—
> There's none of them kin tech the heart
>   Like our own Whitcomb Riley.[12]

Education was a key feature of Fireside or Schoolroom Poetry, of which Paul arguably became the preeminent extension within his race. The metonyms of fireside and schoolroom in the name of this generation were intentional. Just as Paul, when a young boy, sat by the fireside alongside his half-brothers, William and Robert, as they read *Robinson Crusoe* and *Uncle Tom's Cabin*, children across the country were enjoying American literature by the hearth. The line blurred comfortably between the home and the classroom. Domestic intimacy and educational exchange combined to kindle the literary mind of the individual while cultivating an intellectual congeniality, a productive learning, among the collective.

The reading and recitation of verse, which through tropes of literary self-awareness and allusion became poetry, called for kinds of memorization and comprehension quite distinct from what prose required. The "form and style" of Fireside Poetry featured "heavy rhyme and metre, semantic clarity, stanzaic construction, hortatory or nostalgic content," according to scholar Stephen Burt. Specifically, the genre showcased "repetitions of rhyme and meter" that came to "constitute the shape of nostalgia," of "more or less unconscious but powerful 'memories' that readers had internalized and wanted to repeat." A continuum existed between the poetry's aesthetics and popularity, its appeals on the page and the stage. A culture of recitation united the printed poems of Longfellow in the precollege classroom and the poems recited by the likes of Riley, Field, and Paul himself.[13]

People at the time embraced poems in their everyday lives. Lay genres— including worker song-poems, dialect poems, musical lyrics—drove the popularity of verse. So did its accessibility: the degree that the simplicity of rhyme, meter, and language in poems was easy to understand by the middle-class people who read, heard, or wanted to recite them. Public schools were crucial to the way people, especially as children, learned the experimental possibilities of poems; they also helped draw the boundaries within which children, in reciting dialect poems, identified with different regional communities and distinguished them from their own.[14]

The sentimental nature of Fireside Poetry could certainly have contributed to its appeal to children who encountered it, beginning in the 1880s, in the textbooks they were assigned to read in school. American poetry at the time privileged children as icons of authorship, readership, performance, and nostalgia. As shown especially in Bryant's "To a Waterfowl" (1818) and Longfellow's "A Psalm of Life" (1839), thematic overtures less to the mind than to the heart and the home and to the oppressed accompanied the schemes that children could learn to memorize. As a child, Paul himself likely learned how to read, write, and recite verse by examining the Fireside Poets. In *Oak and Ivy*, he likewise tried to lay the ground for instructing future generations of readers, young and old, to do the same with his own poems.[15]

As Paul was entering his literary prime, he and fellow American writers of his era knew that publishing literature meant two different media of publicity: print, as in periodicals and books, and performance, as in recitals before audiences. Fortunately, he possessed a gift for declamation. Terms such as "fervor" and "intensity" often described the force and feeling of how he engaged audiences. He had a marvelous voice, which one contemporary regarded as "a perfect instrument" that he "knew how to use" to excellent effect. On paper he wrote the kind of poems that complemented his verbal talent for reciting them before an audience.[16]

The recitative nature of Paul's poems, the way they were conducive to memorization and recitation, had much to do with their simplified end rhymes. Couplets had long been among the easiest to remember and recite aloud; he put that scheme, appearing in close to a third of the poems in *Oak and Ivy*, to consistent use. Even the first poem, "Ode to Ethiopia," begins with couplets (as does each of its eight stanzas). Couplets ground verse in a melodic simplicity nowhere more fascinatingly than "Lullaby," a placative song that could be hummed even by a child at an early stage of comprehension:

> Sing me, sweet, a soothing psalm,
> Holy, tender, low, and calm,
> Full of drowsy words and dreamy,
> Sleep half seen where the sides are seamy;
> Lay my head upon your breast;
>   Sing me to rest.

By correlating a letter of the alphabet with a line's end rhyme—which in the case of "Lullaby" is *aabbcc*—one could see that almost two out of every three poems in the manuscript featured the hallmark scheme of a nursery rhyme. A little more than a quarter of the book's poems have a scheme of *abcb* either as a set of lines within a stanza or as a quatrain. Likewise the form *abab* pertains to one in five poems; this is the same ratio for verses with a scheme of *aabb*. More complicated end rhymes and typography cycle through the string of poems "John Boyle O'Reilly," "Columbian Ode," and "The Meadow Lark." Here and elsewhere, Paul was not averse to experimentation and challenging standard poetics.[17]

The ease with which one can largely follow the rhyme schemes of Paul's poems belies the sophistication he developed in handling classical meter. The majority of his poems have short lines and show his mastery of the classical iamb.[18] The complex end rhymes, typography, and meter incorporated into the poems Paul wrote in formal English applied equally to those he wrote in dialect. Punctuation enabled him to manipulate the spellings of standard written words to turn them into dialect. Sometimes, written dialect could become so indecipherable that it might compromise the ability of readers to scan and comprehend the words at a normal rate. Apostrophes were a key tool in Paul's literary orthography (his printed transcription, as opposed to his public recitals) of dialect. They cropped either the start or the end of words, to approximate and, inevitably, stereotype the natural phonetics of colloquial speech peculiar to a certain region—or, more precisely, the people native to that region.

"A Banjo Song" was one of the first poems Paul printed in dialect under his own name, unlike his *Dayton Tattler* pieces published anonymously or under a pseudonym, such as "Lager Beer." Leveraging the mythical trope of Negro music, the lengthy poem, in which ballad form interlocks with a sorrowful theme, sought to re-create a slave's powerful hope that, by playing music, a

miserable world could be transcended to a world almost divine in relief and
respite, as the first two stanzas show:

> Oh, dere 's lots o' care an' trouble
> In dis world to swaller down;
> An' ol' Sorrer 's purty lively
> In her way o' gittin' roun'.
> Yet dere's times when I furgit 'em,—
> Aches an' pains an' troubles all,—
> An' it's when I take at ebenin'
> My ol' banjo f'um de wall.
>
> 'Bout de time dat night is fallin'
> An' my daily wu'k is done,
> An' above de shady hilltops
> I kin see de settin' sun;
> When de quiet, restful shadders
> Is beginnin' jes' to fall,—
> Den I take de little banjo
> F'um its place upon de wall.

The story lies beneath a presumable layer of Negro dialect, given the typically racial trope of the banjo and speaker's self-reference as a slave. The dialect spellings aside, the punctuation (excluding the apostrophes) controls the
cadence; the metrical feet remain intact, regular, predictable.[19]

"A Banjo Song"—along with "A Summer Pastoral," "Goin' Back," a section
of "James Whitcomb Riley," "My Sort o' Man," and "The Ol' Tunes"—typified
the extreme category of dialect poems. "Keep a Pluggin' Away," "The Old
Apple Tree," and "The Chronic Kicker," on the other hand, represented only
slightly colloquial examples of the genre. Dialect poems make up only a little
more than 10 percent of the fifty-three poems in *Oak and Ivy*. To excel in the
literary world, he evidently believed that, at this very moment, such poetry
was not his best foot forward.

————

Just before Christmas in 1892—almost two years to the day since his first publishing venture, the *Dayton Tattler*—*Oak and Ivy* appeared in print. On its own,
the release of five hundred copies by the Press of United Brethren Publishing

House was a newsworthy event, but publicity for the first book of poems by Dayton's prodigal son began well beforehand. Paul led the charge.

A couple of months before, close to the end of October, he reached out to one Charles Johnson. Buoyed by the rising interest in Paul in the weeks following Matthews's rave review in the *Indianapolis Journal*, Johnson contacted Paul with a wish to see more of his poetry. "Herewith I comply with your request to send you ten of my poems in manuscript," Paul humbly replied in a letter; "several of them are my earlier efforts while others are of quite late date. I hope after you have deciphered my writing you will not be wholly disappointed in the verses." But he went beyond the courtesy to make a pitch for his forthcoming book. "I am preparing to publish a book of verse about Christmas, if you could send me the names of any . . . buyers, you will greatly oblige me." To help Johnson along, he noted the first edition was priced at only one dollar, a relative bargain.[20]

Students at Paul's high school alma mater also expressed interest in his new book, doing what they could to advertise or buy it. A couple of months before *Oak and Ivy* appeared, he received a letter from the office of the *High School Times*, which listed the names of more than a dozen students who each had agreed to buy at least one copy. A December 1892 editorial in the magazine advised readers to sign up for a copy of Paul's book by dropping by the Callahan Building, where he was still working, or by contacting the paper's editor. The editorial revealed the intensity of student advocacy Paul continued to cultivate as an alumnus. His poems "have appeared in some of the widest circulating magazines and publications in the West. He will publish a volume of his poems in a short time," the editorial went on to say, "and every high school student should procure a copy of the works of one, who, two short years ago, was among us." Shortly after New Year's Day, yet another issue of *High School Times* announced the release of the book. Paul could not have hoped for a better grassroots campaign.[21]

For a poet still trying to make a name for himself, *Oak and Ivy* sold well. Within the first three days of publication more than eighty copies were in the hands of subscribers and early buyers; at least another forty more were sold over the subsequent two weeks. By this time Paul remembered the promise he had made: to pay one hundred dollars to the printer of the United Brethren Publishing House after enough of his books had sold. Now was that time. Few times in his life was he relieved to pay a debt; in this case, it meant that he had reached a milestone—that he was succeeding, not failing.[22]

Acclaim in local papers followed closely behind. A January 7, 1893, article in the *Cleveland Gazette*, subtitled "A Young Man Whose Poems Have Attracted Wide-Spread Attention and Comment," was a self-fulfilling prophecy. A "fair outline portrait," modestly detailed in black and white, "does not indicate his complexion, which is usually termed 'a dark brown skin,'" but it still provided a compelling start to a column that, although brief, opened by calling him "Master Dunbar" and demanding the reader's attention. (Paul's middle name is misspelled—one of the consistent early occasions when that happened, since "Lawrence" was more common than "Laurence," and since *Oak and Ivy* prints his full name only as "Paul Dunbar.")

The article was a biographical sketch written scrupulously enough to ingrain in the minds of readers the facts of a poet they likely had not yet heard of but who seemed destined for greatness. It recounts the perseverance of Paul's mother in raising three boys and ensuring their education; his steady matriculation across all grades; the reverence for his poetry, culminating with his honor as class poet; and the twists and turns of a fledgling career in which he placed poems in various periodicals, recited them before audiences, and finally released a book. Closing the essay are the same poems, "A Drowsy Day" and "The Ol' Tunes," that had first elevated him to notoriety in the article months earlier by James Newton Matthews and earned him recognition from James Whitcomb Riley. The fascination with *Oak and Ivy* expressed in the *Cleveland Gazette* foretold what was yet to come.[23]

Despite the growing raves over Paul's mastery of verse, the fact that he never went on to receive formal education after high school weighed heavily on him. While completing the manuscript of *Oak and Ivy*, he could only express shame to James Newton Matthews about his educational failings. Highly educated and erudite in literature, Matthews had routinely ordered books for Paul to read. One was a thesaurus. "Crabb's book of Synonyms had long been one of the desires of my heart," Paul indicates. "If there is anything in me, the fact that you have taken such pains to help me, and that others are interested in my career will spur me on to its highest cultivation." He was indebted to Matthews for being a confidant willing to listen, but also for those books that could stimulate the mind and calibrate it for the reading and writing of creative literature.[24]

Matthews was eager for Paul to notify him whenever his books arrived. Paul begins one letter doing precisely that. "As you requested, I write to let you know of the arrival of the books. They have just come, and I am charmed with them and perfectly happy." His elation turns to concentration on the actual assortment of books now in his possession. Despite the absence of John D. Quackenbos's *Illustrated History of Ancient Literature, Oriental and Classical* (1878), he was thrilled to see instead *Harper's Cyclopedia of British and American Poetry* (1882), edited by Epes Sargent, "a grand thing" and "the source of benefit and instruction as well as pleasure." Through Matthews's help, Paul was building a small library to feed his autodidactic hunger to become a major writer.[25]

In one letter, after thanking Matthews for a raft of books, Paul admitted something heartfelt: "I have always had the desire to go to college, but must confess to having little faith in the 'on flow'ry beds of ease' method," a world where classroom education is a bastion of privilege, where poems are wrought less from the toil and tribulation of the outside world than from the exchanges of ideas during tea time, as it were. If he did go to college, he would want to do so on his own terms—through perseverance and hard work, not through the privileges that young men of greater means enjoyed. "It would do me good to be able to fight my own way through a good school; but if it be denied me," he accepted, "why all I can do is to resign myself and try to secure as much of a higher education, alone, as I can." Paul's embrace of autodidacticism attested to the very resolve of his genius as well as to the purpose of his writerly ambitions.[26]

Paul's wish to go to college, along with his dismissal of its privileged comfort, resonated in his reported confession that he wished he could have studied at Harvard University under Adams Sherman Hill, a professor renowned for his scholarship on the foundations and principles of rhetoric and their applications. But higher education for African Americans was arduous in Paul's era. For those like him who had finished high school, the next step would have been a normal school, in which students bolstered their previous academic training and learned about pedagogy to join the next generation of teachers. By 1895, across the country, most philanthropically supported institutions of higher education for African Americans were normal schools (seventy-three total), not colleges (thirty-two). College was not as obvious an option as Paul made it seem.[27]

Paul's aspirations also understated the public controversy over the different kinds of higher education available to African Americans, which in the 1880s focused on industrial education: applied scientific and technological labor, such as engineering and architecture; trade labor; and manual labor, related to thrift, morality, and industry. Such education was widely promoted. The first three Republican presidents after the Civil War—Ulysses S. Grant, Rutherford B. Hayes, and James A. Garfield—endorsed the focus of African American teachers and students on a popular model of manual curriculum in industrial education at the Hampton Normal and Agricultural Institute. Hampton's course of study was established in Virginia in 1868 by Samuel Chapman Armstrong, a former Union Army lieutenant colonel who helped lead the Eighth and Ninth United States Colored Infantries and whom the presidents trusted. The explicit goal of the Hampton Institute was to train students to embrace the moral purpose of manual labor and aspire to be the next generation of teachers, who would then bequeath such an educational philosophy to students. The white patrons who engaged Paul and witnessed his talent did not relent as easily as he did on higher education; they still believed it was in his best interest, and they were willing to pay for it so that he could go.[28]

In early 1893 another positive review of *Oak and Ivy* appeared in the *Toledo Blade*. The review caught the eye of Charles A. Thatcher, an attorney in Toledo. Like others fascinated with Paul, Thatcher wrote him a letter. But more than expressing this sentiment of admiration, he wanted to learn more about the poet. At that time, Paul was traveling, riding the wave of interest in his poetry while positive word of *Oak and Ivy* continued to circulate.[29]

One place Paul visited more than once was Richmond, Indiana. In the first few months of 1893 he gave readings that, according to one report, "held his audience in delicious thrall, their delight being frequently evinced by loud and prolonged applause." Recitals of this kind earned him a letter of support from W. F. McCaughey, general secretary of Richmond's YMCA, who likewise praised him for his "entertainment . . . that was most pleasing and satisfactory." McCaughey went a step further to detail Paul's gifts—his "ease, grace of manner, and talent"— but also, regarding the poetry's content, to commend that his "dialect stories are true to nature." Affirmations of Paul's appeal ricocheted through such local newspapers as the *Richmond Independent* and buoyed him as he navigated through the city, reciting his work whenever and wherever he could.[30]

Paul could only have been further encouraged to receive a cheerful letter from Thatcher. Amid pleasantries and gratitude, Paul's letter of reply told Thatcher that he was planning to travel to Detroit, Michigan, to recite poems. Thatcher invited Paul to stop by Toledo on his way home from Richmond so that the elder gentleman could learn more about the rising poet. Paul agreed. Despite the distance Paul would have to travel—Toledo was over 180 miles from Richmond and around 50 from Dayton—in mid-April both men met. In their conversations Thatcher began to realize the depth of Paul's concern over his lack of formal higher education. At that time Thatcher himself began to identify fellow patrons who, in Toledo and elsewhere, might be attracted to the idea of funding Paul's tuition if he ever decided to attend college.[31]

Thatcher eventually cabled Paul an invitation to recite poems at Toledo's West End Club, an exclusive society of white men that met regularly and welcomed edifying lectures and entertaining recitals. Paul was probably the first African American to speak before the members of this newly formed club, a fact not lost on him when he agreed to come the evening of Wednesday, April 19, 1893. Little did he know that his presence would stand in stark relief to the subject of the lecture that another invited guest had been set to deliver.

Paul arrived at the West End Club, located in downtown Toledo on 1709 Adams Street. He was ushered into the room where he was scheduled to recite his poems. Reportedly, as he sat down, he came to learn that another man, Dr. W. C. Chapman, was slated to deliver a talk on the Negro in the South. After Dr. Chapman finished his lecture to a round of applause, Paul prepared to make his way toward the front of the room. As soon as it was announced that this poet would "favor the club with several original selections," Dr. Chapman blanched. All along he thought that he had been spreading his advocacy of white supremacy only to a roomful of fellow Anglo-Saxon men.[32]

Though Paul was infuriated, his response was measured. He stood before the room. "I shall give you one poem which I had not intended reciting when I first came here," he declared. Then he exclaimed "O Mother Race!"—the opening phrase of "Ode to Ethiopia," the first poem in *Oak and Ivy*. Recited in full, the poem was an expression of pride, both as a descendant of Africa and as an artist who could bring that diasporic kinship to poetic life. But it was also a demonstrable rejoinder to Dr. Chapman's thesis that someone like him could not achieve the heights of dignity and intellection so prized by the wider world.

Once Paul finished "Ode to Ethiopia," he went on to recite the other poems he was planning to showcase, each with a lighter touch and with a proven appeal. There was "The Rivals," a long poem, recently written, that recounts, with a clever tongue, a contest between two men over a woman's affections:

'T was three an' thirty year ago,
When I was ruther young, you know,
I had my last an' only fight
About a gal one summer night.
'T was me an' Zekel Johnson; Zeke

'N' me'd be'n spattin' 'bout a week;
Each of us tryin' his best to show
That he was Liza Jones's beau.[33]

There was "The Ol' Tunes," also in *Oak and Ivy* and favored by Riley and Matthews. And there was "Life," the closing poem in his first book that fittingly helped conclude the evening with a wise panorama of the emotional unpredictability of human experience:

A crust of bread and a corner to sleep in,
A minute to smile and an hour to weep in,
A pint of joy to a peck of trouble,
And never a laugh but the moans come double;
    And that is life!

A crust and a corner that love makes precious,
With the smile to warm and the tears to refresh us;
And joy seems sweeter when cares come after,
And a moan is the finest of foils for laughter;
    And that is life![34]

A roar of applause trailed Paul as he departed the room, from which Thatcher accompanied him with sincere gratitude and the promise that he would hear from him soon. The collective pleasure the white men showed, plus the broadening of his network of ardent supporters to include the Toledo attorney, convinced Paul that the evening was a success.

"On behalf of the members of the West End Club," Thatcher wrote two days later, thanking Paul for his Toledo recital, "all express themselves as not only greatly pleased with your composition and delivery but surprised that one of your years should produce such beautiful poems." So astounded were these gentlemen by Paul's skills—relative to his youth and, truth be told, his race— that they encouraged Thatcher to pick up where he left off: a discussion with Paul about college as his logical next step. Thatcher's letter goes on to describe an offer that a young man from small-town Dayton with literary or intellectual aspirations, especially coming from a race long denied formal education on any level, should consider without delay:

If you find that by your own efforts that you will not be able to enter college I will be one of [xxx] persons to loan you $50.00 per year during the time you may wish to spend in college. Think I can procure four others in Toledo to do the same and do not doubt but that there are five in Dayton who would be glad to join us. Let me know how you feel about such a plan. If in the future you should wish to come to Toledo again by giving me due notice [I] can make your trip even more prosperous than was the first.[35]

Paul asked James Newton Matthews for advice on what he called this "very fair" offer. If he were to accept it in the fall of that year, the offer would take effect just after his twenty-second birthday. In an April 1894 letter, Paul recounts the offer as coming "from a member of the club where I read in Toledo last year, who wishes to lend me money enough to go to college if I want to go and pay it back after I graduate." This would have been his dream come true. He was so dependent on others for the books to build his personal education library. Now he had the chance to build his own. Another offer Paul was considering at the time, equally "very fair," attracted him, too. J. L. Shearer of the Shearer Musical and Lecture Bureau of Cincinnati, Ohio, was offering him twenty-five dollars per week to travel with musicians and recite his poems. As he had done in the past, Paul turned to Matthews. "Will you advise me which to take?"[36]

Paul was not as indecisive as he let on. As much as higher education held a magnificent allure, the gravity of family was more powerful. "My mother has just recovered from a very severe attack of pneumonia." Paul was fretting that Matilda, nearly forty-nine years old, was growing increasingly frail. "I begin to feel that I must take all responsibility as to living and providing necessities off her mind; so the latter offer has attracted me very much tho' I longed for college also," Paul wrote. Time and again, it turned out, Paul would choose professional commitments over higher education. News soon came from Thatcher that potential donors dropped out, due to committing funds to other "colored" youth. Thatcher's talk with the president of Oberlin College, William Gay Ballantine, who had a distinguished record of interest in racial justice at the institution by Ohio's Lake Erie rim, only 180 miles north of Dayton, reaped minuscule dividends. Circumstances of this kind ended up discouraging Paul.[37]

As long as Paul was not a household name, he continued to struggle. To agents, editors, and publishers he was a "stranger." Close to Thanksgiving in 1894, he sent a letter to the Central Lyceum Bureau in Rochester, New York, hoping that it would provide representation and opportunities at this early stage of his career. He was put in his place. "I have long since made it a rule not to commend an artist whom I had not seen + heard," the agent replied. "If you are to be in the section of Cleveland, let me know and I will try + hear you." A month later the editorial department of his favorite periodical, the *Century Magazine* in New York City's Union Square, was even more blunt.

The magazine was willing to accept submissions that were worthy of the "Lighter Vein" department, but it was unwilling to accept any without a recommendation of the author from "some person known to us," according to the associate editor, R. U. Johnson. A note of recommendation was the rule of *Century*. Johnson did not hold back when he wrote to Paul that "you are a stranger to us" and therefore "a voucher for your good faith" was required. But he was still attracted to the young poet's potential. Extending an olive branch, he advised him to secure a note from Johnson's own cousin who also lived in Dayton, or anyone else Paul knew who could speak on his behalf.[38]

Paul did not suffer a shortage of people willing to vouch for his character or to broker relationships between him and publishers. Thatcher was one of them; his expertise in law and his express commitment to Paul's professional advancement proved crucial. As early as 1893 Thatcher was speaking with a representative at the *Toledo Bee* and negotiating Paul's delivery of an unpublished piece and his opportunity to receive feedback.

Over the course of the next year, Thatcher received a series of letters and telegrams in which Paul explained that he had accepted the twenty-five dollars for the J. L. Shearer engagement even though it did not come to pass. Paul wondered whether he had to pay back the money. He would. A contract had been formed between them, even though it was not "drawn in a formal manner," Thatcher wrote in response. From here he advised Paul on how to deal with the problem, but he also offered his services as liaison, as someone who could write on Paul's behalf about the degree to which he had to fulfill his part of the contract. He instructed Paul on how to deduct the debt from whatever earnings he would make in the near future. And he helped Paul promote his works, from his individual poems to *Oak and Ivy*, by arranging engagements for him to recite them and build his readership.[39]

Depression besieged Paul, despite the solution. He described his state of mind and soul this way; he detached his dejection from the state of his earnings. Not infrequently he apologized for being so glum. "I fear that I painted the picture too darkly," he tells Matthews, about the probability that he would lose his elevator job after complaining to a boss about his low wages. This was a sort of topic that irked him as far back as his days in high school, when he was trying to sell a newspaper to African Americans in Dayton. The darkness dissipated only when he began "to feel timidly hopeful" around Christmas in 1893, when he decided, finally, to "become practical enough to do a little prose work."[40]

In the years after *Oak and Ivy*, Paul realized the importance of attaining the highest quality of writing in his submissions to publishers. Self-deprecation usually tinged his queries about his literary merits. In late 1892, to one publisher who had informed him of the rejection of his manuscript, he mailed postage so that it could be returned but also with the request that he could revise and resubmit it. Obsequiously, he asked, "Could I make any corrections in it, so that it would stand a show of acceptance or is it hopelessly bad?" Sometimes editors went above and beyond the call of duty and commented on the errors in his poetry. In a poem he was trying to place, "Retrospect," the line "Wind fanned our fevered brows" lacked a metrical foot, warned an office editor at *The Independent* in 1895. Also, one of the poem's penultimate words, "choir," was wrongly employed as "two-syllabled." Metrical oversights such as these were not unfamiliar to any reader who scrutinized *Oak and Ivy*. Still, the editor appreciated Paul's persistence in trying to get the poem published ("this poem had been sent to our office before"). In the resubmission, "these little faults . . . showed possibly all the plainer." Even despite rejection, Paul could be heartened by a final word of encouragement: "I like the spirit and movement of the poem very much and should have been glad to use it." The literary standards were as high as the pile of manuscript submissions in the "crowded . . . poetic department," but Paul acquired both learning and motivation to hone his craft.[41]

The confidence expressed by Paul's acquaintances helped fuel his hope for a successful literary career. Most notably they came from Matthews, his confidant; but they also came from people whom he merely encountered or whose letters randomly came his way. In his first letter to Paul, Thatcher marveled at the young man's poetic gifts but also advised him almost as a mentor would. "You shall keep your work and above all things strive to preserve the modesty which you now possess," he encouraged. "You know that the attention you are receiving would turn some person's head but I don't think you will fall." Since Thatcher was neither a friend nor even an acquaintance, apologies were in order, but candor was needed, too, he felt, at such a crucial stage of Paul's literary development. "You will pardon my plain talk but it is a breaker that we all must match and I have taken the liberty to refer to it." Unsolicited advice, such as "So make it be with poor, humble, industrious Paul Dunbar," trickled in from all around. Random people wrote him letters of support. Paul's genius so inspired some men that they admitted their envy. And it so fascinated some women that they divulged their infatuation with him.[42]

———

For the second consecutive year, Paul attended the Western Association of Writers conference in 1893. He admired the "so altogether delightful" event. In attendance were only a handful of "prominent members" who read samples of their own work: Ben S. Parker, an Indiana poet; Mary Hartwell Catherwood, Ohio author of historical romances; Eugene G. Ware, Connecticut-born politician and poet known pseudonymously as Ironquill; and, again, Will Pfrimmer. The social events excited him, too—the "fishing and boating parties, music and many kindred amusements." Amid the rarefied and congenial symposia, Paul delivered a new poem, "The Old Country Paper," in "pure English," and as an "encore" "The Ol' Tunes." For a concert he read "The Rivals," "a humorous dialect sketch," along with "My Sort o' Man." In giving these readings he reached a remarkable conclusion: despite reading poems in a dialect that privately frustrated him, he reveled in being in a new world of prestige, a sort of western salon of literati: "I don't believe I ever enjoyed a week more in all my life."[43]

CHAPTER 7

The White City

I know not how to thank you for the many kindnesses which you showed me
while at Chicago. Indeed I feel that I owe the success and pleasure of my whole
summer to your instrumentality. In my gratitude I cannot say—but will try to
do—will try to be worthy of the kind of interest which you took in me, and let
it not be a vain boast when I say, that if ever I arrive at that estate in letters
which you have so kindly wished as to my destination,—if haply it should be
my lot to write some songs that posterity shall sing, the name of Douglass shall
not be forgotten in my numbers.

—PAUL LAURENCE DUNBAR TO FREDERICK DOUGLASS
(DECEMBER 30, 1893)[1]

In the months following the release of *Oak and Ivy*, a local paper, the *Dayton Herald*, invited Paul to write a couple of stories. The first was an article about Dayton's Central Branch of the National Home for Disabled Volunteer Soldiers, where his father had lived and died a little over a decade earlier. A second article, which would take more work to write, concerned the upcoming 1893 World's Columbian Exposition, or World's Fair, in Chicago, scheduled to last from spring to fall. For the latter essay he knew he should visit the city to acquire a firsthand experience of the fair.[2]

Paul had visited cities before—Indianapolis, Detroit, Toledo—but none yet with Chicago's ferment and flair. His commissioned newspaper essay entailed his self-immersion, his witness to and grasp of the nature of the exposition. He had to observe the many participants and bystanders, from the city and the broader world, coming and going and playing key roles in the story he sought to tell for his audience back home, the *Dayton Herald* readers. He knew that it would be difficult to retain his daily job as elevator boy while conducting

research, and he considered quitting. After all, the newspaper's commission of
his writing, more so than the Callahan building's commission of his time, would
benefit his long-term aspiration: to be a distinguished writer.

In deciding to quit the elevator job and go to Chicago, Paul could not anticipate how much the trip would show him what he had been missing out on
after all these years, for better or for worse. The young man born and raised
in a small Ohio town would encounter the first clues of what the world had in
store for him and his career.

———

The arrival in 1893 of the World's Columbian Exposition in Chicago commemorated the four hundredth anniversary of Christopher Columbus's arrival in the Americas. The idea for the exposition originated two decades
earlier, when the city was rebounding from a devastating fire to host the Chicago Interstate Industrial Exposition from September 25 to November 12,
1873. Located downtown, the exposition was distinguished by the Italianate
architecture of a large exhibition building: it featured just over a quarter of a
million square feet of floor space. Mostly from the Chicago area, approximately sixty thousand visitors frequented 580 businesses; the event showcased household items, the fine arts, and artifacts of natural history. The 1873
exposition inspired Chicago political leaders and residents to consider hosting a similar event on a much grander stage. Successful international expositions had appeared in Philadelphia, which celebrated the centennial of the
Declaration of Independence in 1876; and in Paris, whose world fair in 1889
set the bar of magnificence that the Chicago elite sought to achieve. The facilities, products, and people of Chicago—these could bridge American citizens
with the citizens of the wider world.[3]

The unified interest of Chicagoans in an international exposition was not
atypical in the late nineteenth century. In the four decades following Reconstruction, expositions were held in major cities across the country—
Philadelphia, Chicago, Atlanta, Nashville, Seattle—and attracted close to 100
million visitors. In 1893 close to 30 million would attend the World's Fair in
Chicago. American cities provided a wide global canvas upon which American
leaders—in politics, business, culture—could illustrate their brands and values. Fairs promoted a common experience of Americans, whose residence in
these host cities or in another state gave them leverage to declare the superiority of their local customs. The expositions were also "the timekeepers of

FIG. 7.1. Exposition grounds, World's Columbian Exposition in Chicago, 1893. (Frances Benjamin Johnston Collection, Library of Congress Prints and Photographs Division)

progress," President William McKinley once stated: the advancement of American civilization had as much to do with economic growth and techno-logical advancement as with ethnological acclaim for Anglo-Saxon progress. By the same token, such proclamations inevitably alleged the cultural inferior-ity of people descended from Africa.[4]

Historian Robert W. Rydell characterizes the World's Fair as possessing "mythopoeic grandeur." Chicago assumed the name "White City," a reference to the Court of Honor: the large white-painted temples, in neoclassical Roman and Greek style, erected around a lagoon and demarcating the main con-course. The splendor was the outcome of several years during which cultural aficionados, artists, intellectuals, educators, and the wealthy, with comparable enthusiasm, could partake in the captivating concourse of museums, galler-ies, schools, and libraries. The patronage of these institutions was deemed crucial to the social good. Prevailing over New York City, St. Louis, Philadel-phia, and Washington, D.C., in a competition to host the World's Fair, Chi-cago earned the approval of the United States House of Representatives on February 24, 1890.[5]

The World's Fair opened its doors to the public on Monday, May 1, 1893. Spanning 686 acres, the fair exhibited a 264-foot-high Ferris wheel; over sixty neoclassical buildings, some enormous; and artifacts and individuals from thirty-nine American states and eighteen nations from around the world. Located in Jackson Park, the marshlands along Lake Michigan eight miles from downtown Chicago that were converted into an actual city, it became the greatest international fair the nation had ever seen.[6]

———

Paul fretted to Matilda over heading toward the White City. Still, the novelty excited him. She encouraged him to go; he likewise tapped into his own well of courage that had brought him this far in his quest to become a professional and distinguished writer, the kind that had whispered in his ear that a breadth of literary imagination could come only after a breadth of world experience. Plus, he would not be in Chicago alone: he would stay with his half-brother Rob Murphy, who was living in the city with his wife, Electra, and their daughter, Ethel, and son, Paul, both toddlers. Rob already had a full house, including not only his family but Will, his other half-brother. To be sure, Rob's own financial ability to support the whole home was strained, given his un-even employment. Paul was reluctant to impose. The sooner he could earn enough of his own money, the better off and less complicated his life would be in finishing his assignment and being on his way.[7]

On Sunday, April 30, the day before the exposition, Paul wandered through Chicago, beholding the technological marvel of city life. "The buildings at the World's Fair are indeed a wonder in themselves," Paul wrote to James Newton Matthews a couple of days later. The surroundings so disoriented him that he had forgotten he was touring the streets on the Sabbath instead of going to church, which he had regularly done since his adolescent days in Dayton. Yes, "there was nothing to remind one of the sacredness of the day," with the din of workers milling about everywhere, without "even the sound of a chapel bell" to bring his "wandering mind back to the day."[8]

Beholding the World's Fair was antithetical to his experience of Chicago itself, a stark contrast to Dayton. Chicago, historian Jackson Lears writes, was known at the turn of the century for "shining its bright lights, attracting young moths in search of bright new selves." By the time Paul arrived there, the city had a population of over 1.2 million, a growth of 800,000 people, including American citizens and European immigrants, over the previous two decades.

With that growth came perceptions and preconceptions. Some focused on deleterious financial speculation amid economic centralization; others on the unequal societal distribution of wealth; yet others on the rise of crime. Some exaggerated these views with biased claims that the city exacerbated moral weakness. Others believed the large population increased the probability of interpersonal encounters and conflicts. Nonetheless, Chicago was the metropolitan hub of the Midwest, an urban generation of forces both centrifugal and centripetal, productive and consumptive, of numerous goods (food and equipment), technologies (the railroad), and capital resources (banks and corporations). Walking among thousands of people and hundreds of buildings, Paul realized that he had to reckon with the cutting edge of American modernity, a far cry from the province whence he came.[9]

To say that Paul found Chicago alienating in its size and density, in being unwieldy and suffocating, would be an understatement. What he dismissed as the worst elements of Chicago emerged unapologetically on the fair's first day, when he learned that close to half a million tickets were sold to those wishing to tour the grounds. "I mutely thanked my Maker that I had not gone out to be in the crush," he reflected, after he had decided to stay indoors on that inaugural day. More than the population, the city's urban modernity and urbane diversity, its cosmopolitanism, unsettled his small-town sensibilities:

> The streets were thronged with people and the street cars and elevated roads were tested to their utmost capacity. People of every color and nationality were to be seen upon the streets, flocking toward the line of march of the great procession. I looked a little while, but I was not wed to such scenes and I confess that my brain was whirling so with a sigh: "O cosmopolitan Chicago thou makest me sick."[10]

Paul was comfortable staying with Rob and Will, who were treating him "very nicely." As the spring rolled into summer, Matilda would eventually arrive to stay with them, adding an extra layer of familial warmth for Paul to brave the strange city. But he remained a fish out of water. Living out of his solitary trunk, he had only his "old black clothes" that "look shabby out here," in contrast to the garb of "all the young colored men [who] go dressed up all the time."[11]

The good pay he earned at the World's Fair somewhat offset the expenses—of course financial, but also emotional—he incurred while residing in Chicago. "My job is a soft snap. I help attend to a gentleman's toilet room," he commented in a letter to his mother just before she moved. Yet he wanted a job better than being a lavatory attendant and, prior to that, a downtown Chicago hotel waiter.

"If I can get anything better I will take it but I'll hold this one until I do." His salary was, for him, a useful $10.50 per week, part of which paid for the passbook and badge he needed for permission to access and traverse the grounds. To help ends meet, Rob also had been loaning money to him. In spite of the hardship—the high cost of "board, lodging, laundry and car fare"—Paul was always mindful of giving his mother money. (Before, while she was still in Dayton and he in Chicago, Paul wanted Matilda to keep trying to sell copies of *Oak and Ivy.* "Keep and use all money for books you sell," he wrote his mother. If she encountered an old friend, "try to sell one + so get another dollar.") Within a couple of months, in mid-July, Paul welcomed his mother with open arms to Chicago, where she could keep tabs on all three of her sons and where she was "enjoying much the sights." In the "Haitian Building" on the World's Fair grounds, Frederick Douglass had by then offered Paul a job; he was proud to earn such good money, a salary that was good for them all. Even so, he sought other opportunities for work at the fair; to wit, "doing some World Fair letters to a small syndicate of papers." These solicitations came to no avail, but at least he could work in the meantime.[12]

———

Within the first months of arriving in Chicago, Paul was rubbing elbows with some of the greatest people of his race—with classicist educator and scholar William Sanders Scarborough, author and activist Hallie Quinn Brown, anti-lynching activist and investigative journalist Ida B. Wells, and writer and suffragist Mary Church Terrell.

None was greater than Frederick Douglass. Seventy-five years of age in 1893, the Maryland-born legend had taken an extraordinarily eventful path toward his present-day statesmanship. He chronicled the first two decades of his life as a slave in three influential editions of autobiographies; just one year prior to the World's Columbian Exposition, he had added more than one hundred pages to the latest edition, *The Life and Times of Frederick Douglass,* to account for his seemingly boundless experiences across eras and nations in the postwar nineteenth century. The problem of slavery and the necessity of freedom had driven him to author his own life in book form. He was also inspired to write about social policies and politics in newspapers, which he also edited, and to orate on these issues before diverse audiences across the country and abroad.[13]

Douglass's accomplishments as a writer, editor, and orator matched the pioneering acclaim of his political leadership. In the late 1840s he was the sole

African American to attend the pro-woman Seneca Falls Convention. In 1872 he was the first such person to be chosen as a candidate to run for vice president of the United States and, in 1888, a vote on a major political party's roll for president of the United States. A year later, amid public outcry, he began serving as the United States minister to the Republic of Haiti. Shortly afterward, in 1891, he stepped down, partly fueled by his own protest against the nation's adversarial policy toward Haiti.

Douglass did not abdicate all loyalty to the Haitian government. The following year, in February 1892, he accepted an appointment to commission a pavilion representing Haiti at the Chicago World's Fair. He began working with Charles A. Preston, assistant commissioner and the son of a former minister to Haiti, to confirm the location and design of the Haitian Pavilion. Over the next year, his most significant public role as Haiti commissioner occurred during the dedication of the building on January 2, 1893. Before a congregation of 1,500 citizens in Quinn Chapel, right by the snow-laden Jackson Park fairgrounds, Douglass delivered a lecture on Haiti's "progress in the line of civilization; of her relation with the United States; of her past and present; of her probable destiny; and of the bearing of her example as a free and independent Republic, upon what may be the destiny of the African race in our own country and elsewhere." The ceremony augured the presence of Haiti at the exposition, but it further authorized Douglass's own charge, "appointed by the government of Haiti, to represent that government in all that belongs to such a mission in connection with the Exposition."[14]

By the time Paul arrived in Chicago in May 1893, Douglass was in the city on a mission. By now celebrated as the "Sage of Cedar Hill" or "Old Man Eloquent," Douglass was that storied man scarred by slavery and in battle against its racist afterlives, its remnants within a nation still blinded by this curse of history. On the highest level of political discourse and statesmanship, he was coming to the end of a long-running debate with the United States government and its more influential citizens about the relevance of Haiti's revolutionary origins—namely, its historical metaphor of the sword wielded by Toussaint L'Ouverture, a Haitian general whose life spanned the second half of the eighteenth century and who led a successful slave insurrection against French colonial rule. Now Douglass focused on dispelling the ethnocentrism of the White City and of the wider Anglo-Saxon world whose eyes lay upon it.[15] It was only a matter of time before Paul and Douglass crossed paths in Chicago. Inquisitive, the young poet desired to learn more about the fair and his status, as an African American, within it. Few could teach him about these issues better

Copyright 1892 by Small, Maynard & Company

FIG. 7.2. Frederick Douglass, 1893. (Library of Congress Prints and Photographs Division)

than the elder statesman—and Paul knew this as soon as the chance arose for him to meet Douglass.

By the end of his first month in Chicago, Paul's circle of acquaintances included Wendell Philips Dabney, a guitarist and teacher. Wendell introduced Paul to his friend, the violinist Joseph Douglass—whose grandfather was the one and only Frederick Douglass. Unsure of whether the elder Douglass knew of him, Paul asked "Joe" if he could send a word to "Mr. Douglass," as Paul called him. Could they meet in the near future? Joe replied that he would see what he could do.

Joe got back in touch with Paul. The Sage of Cedar Hill wanted to meet! The date, time, and place were set: the evening of Sunday, June 4, at the West Lawrence Avenue apartment of Samuel Laing Williams and Fannie Barrier Williams in Chicago's Sixth Ward. Husband and wife, Samuel and Fannie had been hosting Douglass since April, the month before the exposition's official start. Born in Georgia, Samuel was the first African American to graduate from the Columbian School of Law (later George Washington University); he was also a distinguished lawyer. Fannie, a native New Yorker, was an African American clubwoman and educator well known on the Chicago lecture circuit. Together, the couple headed a formidable household that more than accommodated Douglass's intellectual and activist sensibilities; conversely, his own presence stimulated their interest in civic engagement. The home was an ideal place for Douglass to meet guests who likewise shared an appreciation of enlightened and lively conversation as well as an expectation of courageous political action.[16]

Joe knocked on the door, Paul by his side. Fannie invited them in, but, as Paul later recalled, they "found the old man gone." Expecting them earlier in the evening, Douglass had left to get dinner at a nearby merchant tailor's house, where Joe and Paul proceeded to track him down. Eventually, the men found "the old man" "just finishing dinner." Pleased, almost bemused, Douglass "got up and came tottering into the room," Paul remembered. He reached out to shake Paul's hand, smiling affectionately. "And this is Paul Dunbar," the walking legend said, patting the poet on the shoulder. Over the course of the evening, the two men exchanged recitations. Paul honored a request to recite one of his dearest poems, "Ode to Ethiopia." Douglass read Paul's catchy "The Ol' Tunes," "with which he seemed delighted." As the evening came to a close, Paul gave Douglass a copy of *Oak and Ivy*. (Douglass first offered to purchase the book but soon relented and accepted the gift, stating that he planned to buy copies for others.)[17]

Later that night, Paul, so impressed, reflected on the gathering. "I am in the very highest and best society that Chicago affords," he wrote in a letter to his mother. How could such a statesman in Douglass, he wondered—a man so distinguished that during his lifetime he had met with presidents of the United States and fellow leaders from around the world—admit so readily a reverence for a "boy" almost fifty-five years his junior? "I've been knowing you for some time and you're one of my boys," Paul recalled Douglass saying. In fact, Douglass had been aware of Paul's rising stardom for "about a year" (in Paul's estimation). Dawning on Paul was the probability that this occasion, this evening with the great Douglass, had altered the course of his life and career.[18]

In the weeks after the gathering, Douglass offered Paul a job as an assistant at the Haitian Pavilion of the World's Fair. Paul accepted and helped Douglass with tasks ranging from setting up exhibits to editing the scripts that introduced them to the public. Douglass mentored the young man he so admired, and Paul learned from the elder statesman, whom he reciprocally embraced while earning some money to put into his often-empty pockets.[19]

The "old man," as Paul came to call Douglass, introduced him to the musician Will Marion Cook. A little more than three years Paul's senior, Cook was born in Washington, D.C., studied the violin at the Oberlin Conservatory in his early teenage years, and thereafter continued his studies in Berlin at the Hochschule für Musik. Cook recalled his first impression of meeting Paul at the Haitian Building. Vivid was the poet's stylistic elegance and physiognomic expression:

> [I]n his rusty black suit (in which you could see your face and figure) was a sight to behold. Of less than medium height—perfectly formed, and smooth black skin he inherited from his mother (also a beautiful black)—a brow noble in proportions—and eyes that were soft, glowing, [and] eloquent . . . toothpick shoes (Dunbar had the feet of an aristocrat). [He had a] hat, cane and gloves to match and all the trimmings. He was a mess—I mean a mess of good looking [fellow] except the mouth . . . the mouth which was ugly— uglier than mine—and that's a record. His teeth were perfect—and so white that they threw into bas-relief his glossy black skin and hair. He was a picture of the finest Kaffir type. And I don't believe any of his women ancestors had even looked at a white man much less stop to idle away a few moments.[20]

More impressive than Paul's face was the literary intellect behind it. "And he could write quicker, more beautifully and with less erasures than any body I've

FIG. 7.3. Will Marion Cook, n.d. (Schomburg
Center for Research in Black Culture)

seen," Cook remembered, as he grew more familiar with Paul's gifts. "Lyrics of
all kinds poured from his soul and pen in a coloring of beautiful melody." The
artistic attraction between the two men in Chicago would precipitate a series
of collaborations over the next several years.[21]

Douglass would become one of Paul's most ardent supporters. In the last
years of his life, Douglass memorized the biographical facts of Paul's
journey—the artistry and the poverty, the promise and the tragedy—and
relayed them to anyone and everyone willing to listen. He became one of the
first in the early 1890s even to mention Paul's name to fellow African American intellectuals, to whom he would recite from memory the young man's
stanzas from his most famous poems, like "A Drowsy Day." At times Douglass's voice would quaver, his eyes growing misty; he would despair "that a
young man with such talent as he undoubtedly possesses should be so terribly handicapped as he is." The relentless way that he would spread the news

of Paul to the world gathered momentum precisely after his grandson Joe fatefully brought them together in Chicago.[22]

Like a father embracing a son, the old man wanted to be the poet's custodian. Perhaps unwittingly, he was filling the paternal void of mentorship or, more profoundly, of love and grace that Joshua Dunbar did not or could not. That Sunday evening of their first encounter, when their time together was coming to an end, Douglass invited Paul to stay at his Washington, D.C., home: "It would do my heart good just to have you there and take care of you," he said to Paul. "I have got one fiddler there," gesturing to Joe, "and now I want a poet; it would do me good to have you up there in my old study just working away at your poetry."[23]

———

For Paul, the springtime splendor of the World's Columbian Exposition could not hide the grave consequences it implied for his race. In gaining intimate proximity to Douglass's mind and spirit, Paul accessed the inner workings of what the Haitian Pavilion meant, not only what it was supposed to do. The plight of African Americans emerged right before his eyes at the World's Fair.

When the Department of Foreign Affairs and Ethnology started planning the World's Fair in October 1890, it sent officers to various parts of the world, especially Europe and South America, with the goal of identifying the countries that would make the best exhibitions, that would be the most representative of diverse cultures, and that would be, ultimately, worthy of constructing a pavilion on the fairgrounds. Over time, outside nations proposed preliminary designs, which the exposition's architects either approved or disapproved. Nations tended to design their sections in styles more culturally distinctive and traditional than state pavilions, though both still ended up being erected alongside each other on the fairground's northern area. Buildings, villages, even miniature islands were a few of the things that the World's Fair constructed to showcase a one-stop shop of multicultural heterogeneity.[24]

Beneath that veneer was a purposeful emphasis on what essentially made an ethnic group unique, according to the Department of Foreign Affairs and Ethnology. Allegations abounded of the inherent racial superiority of Anglo-Saxon ancestry. Artifacts of high culture and technology at the fair represented the putative civilization of certain countries, such as the pavilions of the United States and those of Austria. Supposedly primitive people—the Javanese, the Egyptians, the Dahomeans—lacked civilization. A curator at the Smithsonian Institution's Bureau of American Ethnology noted that "the World's Columbian Exposition was one vast anthropological revelation." The contrast between high and primordial culture displayed on the fairgrounds played into long-standing preconceptions about human evolution. Most human species developed over time into civilized beings, it was said, but the watershed markers of this progress congregated in certain hemispheres, countries, and races, the apex evident in the West (in western Europe and North America) and in the racial trope of the Anglo-Saxon. Peoples of African descent were absent from this ethnological formula of white supremacy.[25]

Stereotypes in the exhibited Dahomean village infuriated Douglass. Associating his race with barbarity and located at the end of the Midway Plaisance, the village featured grass huts, its African American exhibitionists only half-clad. The scene provided fodder for wily journalists and cartoonists who covered the World's Fair, it seemed, only to lampoon Africans and African Americans and to reaffirm public prejudices about their racial inferiority. Douglass knew what was at stake for the "Negro" here: international fairs assumed a commanding role in reinforcing racial biases in the world.[26]

Millions of people were passing through the fair. As consumers they were exposed to a highly visible assortment of racial and ethnic groups, yet within an accessible, and quite entertaining, environment. Little room was made at the table of leadership commissioning the event to ensure that African Americans were being properly treated or shown. Douglass anticipated the necessity for such leadership, beyond whatever repute he earned as commissioner of the Haitian Pavilion. Two months before the fair officially began, his essay in the *World's Columbian Exposition Illustrated* asserted a crucial moral claim: "The presence of one of this race in a prominent position would speak more for the moral civilization of the American republic than all the domes, towers and turrets of the magnificent buildings that adorn the Exposition grounds." But that was never meant to be. The U.S. National Commission that worked with local Chicago leaders did not appoint even one African American to commission the pavilion of an American state. (After much pressure, a token school principal from St. Louis was designated an alternate.)[27]

Nor was there much room at the exposition for representative African Americans, three decades since the Emancipation Proclamation, to assert their rightful place as progressive members of American civic society. Previously, the United States had had only two world's fairs after the Civil War—the Philadelphia Centennial Exhibition in 1876 and the New Orleans World's Industrial and Cotton Exposition in 1884–1885. African Americans regarded each fair a pillar of racial progress, but they were disappointed for having to accept terms that somewhat reaffirmed their public sense of inferiority. The Colored Department at the New Orleans Exposition, for instance, sanctioned the segregation of black- from white-run exhibits. In Chicago, African Americans writing in the press and those petitioning in the city and elsewhere were concerned that such segregation replicated Jim Crow on the fairgrounds. An alternative approach could have been to use existing state exhibitions as a way of integrating whites and blacks. The racial segregation of exhibitions prevailed, as did the prejudicial exclusion of nonwhites from state exhibits. The result was the creation of a miniature Dahomean village, a primitive conflation of the African diaspora across space and time.[28]

Douglass's involvement in these debates, or at the very least his opinions on them, gave Paul a bird's-eye view of how an African American could possess an acutely and internally conflicted sense of belonging to the United States, a country that was still largely denigrating its darker-skinned citizens in the three decades after slavery. By the time Paul settled in as Douglass's assistant, the statesman was already part of a venture to release a pamphlet whose title was self-explanatory: *The Reason Why the Colored American Is Not in the World's Columbian Exposition*. Slated for a publication of twenty thousand copies on August 20, the pamphlet contained essays by legendary and rising leaders of the race: an introduction by Douglass; a concluding essay by the newspaper publisher and attorney Ferdinand Lee Barnett, the professional partner of Douglass's Chicago host, Samuel Williams; another on postemancipation African American life by Irvine Garland Penn, an educator; and two essays on class legislation and lynching by Ida B. Wells, the antilynching activist who, two years later, would go on to marry Barnett.

Paul was not personally involved, but he was close enough to the center of the media firestorm. He likely witnessed Douglass's fundraising for the pamphlet's circulation—the very appeal to the "Friends of Equal Rights." Perhaps this sympathetic group agreed with the premise of *The Reason Why the Colored American Is Not in the World's Columbian Exposition*: "the absence of colored people from participating therein will be construed to their disadvantage by the representatives of the civilized world there assembled." Controversy saddled the pamphlet's message, however, dividing the African American community into two groups. Some welcomed the public indictment of the World's Fair; others regretted that an international spotlight was now glaring on their customary mistreatment. Paul could only wonder at the gravity of the debate, of what it portended about the future of relations not only between the races but also within his own.[29]

Five days before the pamphlet's release, Paul had a front-row seat to another racial controversy. Yet again Douglass was standing at the eye of a media hurricane in his quest to establish the respect, leadership, and social uplift of African Americans at the World's Fair. This time, Paul was right there with him.

"Colored People's," "Colored American," or "Jubilee" Day, as it was alternately known, was scheduled for August 25. For one day only, the cultural accomplishments of African Americans took center stage at the World's Fair. Joe Douglass implored Grandpa Fred to support the occasion. He wanted very much to play the violin before an audience, to showcase the best of what their race had to offer. Joe, others interested in performing, like fellow violinist and friend Will Cook, and sympathetic observers believed that African Americans should participate and take full advantage of Jubilee Day. The more skeptical folks—like the pamphlet co-author Wells, who led a boycott—predicted that the day would be a recipe for disaster: that it would end up being yet another racist emblem of the World's Fair. Many writers in the white, mainstream press were utterly opposed to what would be "the last of the dark days at the fair." In the end Douglass believed that he and his race should protest within the existing structure of the World's Fair. They should not avoid it. He proceeded to prepare for the event, which had a central program scheduled for 3:00 p.m. in Festival Hall, one of the exposition's main buildings.[30]

Paul was hired to help run Jubilee Day. Little did he know what he was getting into. To Paul's surprise and to Douglass's consternation, when they arrived at the fairground, vendors were setting up stands to sell watermelons. Due to its perceived origins in tropical Africa, the fruit was caricatured in America as the staple that black slaves and their descendants loved to eat. The exposition exaggerated that myth. A show featuring Aunt Jemima, the icon reminiscent of the subservient black women characters from the century's fiction and minstrelsy shows about American domesticity, was also gearing up for a swelling crowd. Paul also saw that the boycott by the more famous invitees had real effect: Sissieretta Jones, an African American soprano of opera and popular music, decided not to show up. Nor did the African American clergy of Chicago. Paul stayed behind as Douglass left, incensed. Word had it that he was so disappointed he left the fairgrounds altogether, returning to the Williamses' residence.[31]

A reporter was snooping around the premises, in search of Douglass, for news and quotations for a humorous story. Not finding him there, he accosted Paul, peppering him with queries about the lack of parades and dancers; about the flyer printed with "No watermelon, no Negro jubilee"; about the visible watermelons themselves. Paul sought to divert his attention from the event's curious indignity to the promise of a more respectful gathering at Festival Hall in the afternoon. The reporter went on to file a piece for his newspaper's afternoon edition, not waiting for the later event; his headlines captured his verdict on the morning: "Few Colored Folks There," followed by "Negroes Apparently Not Interested."[32]

Quite different was the later event at Festival Hall. Upward of 2,500 people showed up, about two-thirds African American. Outside, the temperature at its height approached ninety degrees, with a westerly wind; the weather was generally fair, on occasion drizzling throughout the day. In an orderly fashion, the visitors assembled outside and proceeded into Festival Hall. Douglass showed up as well, despite his earlier thoughts and feelings. Paul was ready to read his poem after Douglass, so-called President of the Day, introduced his guests. The congregation settled into its seats. Douglass walked across the stage to deafening applause, with him Isabella Beecher Hooker, his guest of honor. Accompanied by her two nieces, Hooker was the sister of famed Harriet Beecher Stowe, author of the classic 1852 novel *Uncle Tom's Cabin*. Thereafter, Douglass introduced the honorary vice presidents, who were members of the clergy: Bishop Henry McNeal Turner of the African Methodist Episcopal Church and former president of Morris Brown College in Atlanta, along with Bishop Alexander Walters, also of the AME Church.[33]

Sitting there, awaiting his turn, Paul observed Jubilee Day's stark contrast. Whereas the fairground that morning focused on watermelon sales and an Aunt Jemima skit, Festival Hall was a stage for the most dignified congregation of African Americans at the World's Fair. Scintillating was the classical music played in the hall. Accompanied by Maurice Arnold Strothotte, National Conservatory of Music professor of harmony J. Arthur Freeman sang Dudley Buck's aria "The Shadows Deepen." Tenor Sidney Woodward of Boston sang a Giuseppe Verdi aria, "I due Foscari," to five encores. Desiree Plato sang Giacomo Meyerbeer's aria "Lieti Signor." Hattie Brown recited pieces of drama. Joe Douglass played a number of violin pieces, including a fantasy from *Il Trovatore* and another from Will Cook's opera, *Uncle Tom's Cabin*, a gesture to the honored guest in their midst.[34]

Douglass delivered a version of his speech "The Race Problem in America." For the first time, Paul saw up close the oratorical gift of moral suasion for which the statesman was renowned. Here, Douglass was wrestling with the meaning of Jubilee Day. He pointed out the very contrast Paul himself saw: "Apparently they want us to be represented by the music and by the civilization of Dahomey," he complained. He went on, so wrote a local reporter in attendance:

> "They have filled the Fair with the sound of barbaric music, and with sights of barbaric rites, and denied to the colored American any representation." The contrast painted as starkly as possible, Douglass exclaimed at the climax of his speech: "But stop. Look at the progress the negro has made in thirty years! We have come up out of the Dahomey unto this. Measure the negro. But not by the standard of the splendid civilization of the Caucasian. Bend down and measure him—measure him—from the depths out of which he has risen."[35]

The somber notes Douglass struck contrasted with the tender, touching classical music that had soothed and uplifted. Paul began to hear catcalls among some of the white men in the crowd. For a moment Douglass's "voice faltered," but he stood resolute, inspired. So did Paul. Varying reports of the half-hour speech indicated that Old Man Eloquent, his mane of white hair flapping, spoke in a voice by turns tremulous yet toughened, exasperated yet invigorated. Quivering, his hand clasped the speech's typewritten pages; then, after tossing them against the lectern, he plucked his glasses from his face. The day had rattled him, but the recurring slights of racism felt by generations of African Americans steeled his posture and oration, the latter of which seemed longer in effect than in reality.[36]

After Douglass finished and returned to his seat, Paul ascended the stage. He began to recite the ode—his favorite lyrical form—written for Colored American Day. For the occasion he aptly titled it "Ode to the Colored American." The poem was entrenched, of course, in memory of a Civil War, not too distant in the past, that not only affirmed the emancipation of Paul's race but also anticipated, in terms of his own father and his Union comrades, a collective legacy of military pride and generational freedom:

> And their deeds shall find a record,
> In the registry of Fame;
> For their blood has cleansed completely
> Every blot of Slavery's shame.
> So all honor and all glory
> To those noble Sons of Ham—
> The gallant colored soldiers,
> Who fought for Uncle Sam![37]

An ovation followed. When Bishop Turner announced to the audience that Paul wrote it especially for the occasion, the applause grew even louder. The following day, the praise continued. Encouraging reviews appeared of Festival Hall and of Paul's recitation in particular. He was lauded in the Chicago newspapers—the *Herald*, the *Record*, the *Tribune*, the *Inter-Ocean*, the *News*, the *Mail*. On Jubilee Day, Paul's perspective on the world and his place in it matured through his witness of Douglass's own challenges. He embraced the newfound media attention.[38]

The World's Columbian Exposition closed on October 31, 1893. By this time Paul had realized that, for all the knowledge he had acquired from his time at the fair, it was time to go home, to Dayton. Aside from handing the book to a few folks within his inner circle, like Douglass, he was not able to sell enough copies to his liking. Resigning himself to a quick departure, Paul confided to his newfound acquaintance Ida B. Wells, "I guess there is nothing for me to do, Miss Wells, but go back to Dayton and be an elevator boy again."[39]

As soon as Paul got back to Dayton, he wrote to Douglass. Penned less than a week after Christmas in 1893, the letter expressed gratitude to Douglass for helping a young poet find his way in a densely populated city and, all the while, in a promising yet unfulfilled literary career: "I know not how to thank you for the many kindnesses which you showed me while at Chicago. Indeed I feel that I owe the success and the pleasure of my whole summer to your instrumentality." Paul vowed that if he ever reached "that estate in letters," he would remain indebted to the blessing of mentorship that Douglass gave him.[40]

Paul's letter sought to reconnect with Douglass, but it was also a cry for help. "For myself I am well in body but not in mind," he lamented. Ever since Paul returned to Dayton, the lack of encouragement he had received—in his own mind—from local townspeople who resented his departure, however brief, to Chicago had finally pushed him to the breaking point. In words similar to those written exactly one week earlier, on December 23, to Matthews—"Especially since I returned from Chicago have I been bemoaning the fact that my own people were growing away from me, that they watched not for my success but for my failure, that they saw in my efforts no worth, only presumption"—Paul told Douglass that, to overcome his conditions, he needed his help:

> I have learned all too soon that the price of even meagre success is much calumny. The people in my town have never encouraged my aspirations, they have done all they could to crush me and now on my return from a

summer of hard work and honest effort I find a score of slanders afloat concern[ing] my sojourn in Chicago—as to my reception there, my social status and a dozen other petty trifles, but I did not deign to notice any of them until it came to my ears that a Dayton visitor to Chicago had returned and reported here that I was discharged from the Haitian Building, and that the course of said discharge was drunkenness and dissipation. I cannot overlook this so I thought I would write and ask you to send me a few words of refutation that I can publish in the daily papers here.[41]

The accuracy of the rumors was debatable. Nowhere did Paul, in his letters, indicate any such discharge from his job duties. But this is one of the earliest rumors that attached to him about "drunkenness and dissipation"; about the alcoholism he may have witnessed in the Tenderloin district, which was only a handful of blocks from his residence in Chicago; about the failing of behavioral self-discipline; about the frittering away of the money he was trying to earn at the World's Fair. Arguably, his presence amid the unpredictable Chicago social scene only coincided with his struggles making ends meet. No record exists that Douglass actually furnished the letter Paul was seeking. Still, the World's Fair marked the beginning of a bond between them that overlapped a host of social circles.[42]

The Dayton tales of Paul's alleged recent misfortune; his beseeching of Douglass for a letter that he could circulate to vouch for his character; his eventual turn to professional opportunities beyond where he was born and reared—all these facts partly explained the chasm of depression into which he had fallen. A woman he happened to meet around this time came to wonder about his mind and heart—about how and why they had become, in her view, so precarious.

PART TWO

A True Singer, 1893 to 1898

CHAPTER 8

Chafing at Life

I think nothing quite so sad and plaintive as your "One Life." Tell me what it is,
my friend, that saddens all your songs?

—REBEKAH BALDWIN TO PAUL LAURENCE DUNBAR
(DECEMBER 5, 1894)[1]

Aside from his mother, Matilda, Rebekah Baldwin was the woman in whom
Paul confided most in his early twenties. They met at the World's Columbian
Exposition in Chicago, possibly during his performance at Festival Hall.[2]
They exchanged letters from 1893 to 1895, when she worked as a teacher in
Washington, D.C.[3] Their relationship had all the twists and turns of a fledgling infatuation. Most of their archived correspondence comprises letters
written from Rebekah to Paul; still, quotations and references in her letters
express Paul's own voice, his own language, loud and clear. On multiple occasions the two were mutually absorbed, irrefutably intimate; on others, they
reciprocated frustrations over where their courtship stood, and whether it
could proceed. Even the infrequency of her letters to him was a matter of
debate. She was concerned that he would attribute her bouts of silence to lack
of free time; closer to the truth, schoolwork preoccupied her. She often apologized for the delays; she really could not help it. "I have had no time for
anything else," she once wrote.[4]

Letters helped Rebekah and Paul overcome the gulf of distance and time;
they also unveiled the layers of her attraction to him. She would regularly confess
her attraction to him. Looking back, in late 1893, to when they last stood face-
to-face in Chicago, she remembered vividly, "How quickly the days have sped,
since you and I stood together on the steps and bade each other goodbye!" For
her it seemed but yesterday that she sat by his side in the Haitian Pavilion,

listening to his voice "in praise or blame (more often the latter)" of her "humble" self: "Those were pleasant hours, my friend, and I shall not soon forget them."[5]

During the early part of their relationship in winter 1893, Rebekah would also go out of her way to compliment Paul, especially his distinctive "muse." Divine abstractions about his muse, she felt, attested to his literary promise. He was on the cusp of greatness! An autographed book from him would be a wonderful prize. "I should be so proud of it Paul. Why will you not send me one?" She could have bought one from him—"the cost is little"—but she did not want to. She was a fan of sentimentality. "I want you to *give* it to me—it is *a present of the volume from its author* that I crave. You will do this for me Paul will you not?" In her eyes, whether he would give a book to her meant, metaphorically, whether he would give himself to her.[6]

Of equal importance to the gift of a publication was its content, which, Rebekah felt, could also bespeak a token of Paul's love. "You say you write love stories best. I want to read some of them, that I may know your idea of what love is and how it affects the human heart," she wrote. Verse or prose, his creative writing held an allure that inspired her even more to reach out to him, to learn what he truly felt inside. Did writing literature bring happiness or woe to his fancy? "I would know the graces with which you clothe your heroines. I would know with what qualities you invest the woman who makes your hero fall down and worship at her feet." Vicarious readings and writings of literature informed her certainty that his ideal woman would find her way into some of his stories. Paul's "muse" casting Rebekah's likeness in one of his stories would have been one of the greatest compliments he could pay her, short of playing out intimacy in real life.[7]

Rebekah revered Paul for being so distinctly "poetic," while the form and content of his poetry attracted her, too. On her own time she read writers, such as the English playwright and poet Robert Browning, who had died just a handful of years before, in 1889, and whose work prompted her to ask him about the craft. Initially, she did not expect poetry to confound her. "Tell me Paul, do you not think him willfully obscure?" She wondered of Browning, most known for *Men and Women*, his two-volume collection of poems published in 1855, and for his even more ambitious twelve-book-long poem in blank verse, *The Ring and the Book*, released thirteen years later. "Should it be the aim of the poet, think you, to *puzzle* and *perplex* the *mind* rather than elevate the *soul*? It does seem to me that Mr. B[rowning] puts forth most strenuous efforts to write what no one can understand." Rebekah often turned her inquiries into self-deprecation, perhaps for the benefit of buoying Paul up, of stroking his ego. Allegations of Browning's literary complexity perhaps said more about her than about the poems themselves. She worried that she was too unintelligent to comprehend Browning's flights of fancy and depths of meaning. Her appeals to Paul's literary insight—"I shall look eagerly for your opinion"—recurred across their many exchanges as the winter turned from late 1893 into early 1894.[8]

Rebekah's replies to Paul's letters were repeatedly, and regrettably, tardy. She tended to open her letters with apologies, expecting that he might read her words with sighs and eye rolls. More likely, he did so with a calloused heart. He likely wondered at her long delay in replying to his last letter. One letter to her was so terse that she thought it wise not to test his patience any further. Defensive and formal, she delayed writing him, with the hope that the receipt of her next letter would find him in "a better and more *expansive* state of mind." But she hoped not to sustain this divisive tone; she wanted their letters to unite them. "I would not like to think, mon ami," she softened, "that this correspondence has grown irksome to you, though I confess that in *my* part of it there is little to interest or amuse you." Whenever they fell into the rut of discontentment, stepping out of it was not simple at all for her.[9]

Like couples in any rocky relationship, Paul and Rebekah could be petty. While he complained about the tardiness of her replies, she would counter that his letters had only just reached her, the delay caused by his repeated failures to place the correct postage on the envelopes. Hints of conflicts, whose salience betrayed their original triviality, caught her attention. She mostly loved his poetic letters, the aspirant, ambitious ones, "not one of those mean little scribbles like your last of which I so complained." She would then delve into the personality she deemed antithetical to their future as, at the very least, a friendly couple. "But pray, my dear Paul, what means that oath of yours to hereafter always appear before me in 'company manners'?" she reminded him. "'Twas an idle oath, mon ami for you know you couldn't always (if ever) treat *me* like company—in that cold, formal way that you always so thoroughly dislike, so unlike *our* friendship, which is so warm, so genial, so unrestrained." In contrast to moments when she relished the vivid memory of their time in each other's presence, she disdained those of opposite sentiment, like "a dull, dismal, murky day." In February, the moment was opportune "for the parting of two such friends as we—even the heavens wept that we should part so soon."[10]

————

Literature kept Paul and Rebekah together. Her proximity to him was as much her desire for their increased physical intimacy as for uniting their reading experiences. During summer 1894, on one of the hottest days of the month in

Washington, D.C., she wrote a letter feigning the worst: "I fear life for me is o'er—I am slowly fading—no melting away. Oh this awful heat!" As she inquired into Paul's own struggle with the weather, she forcefully proposed a literary union between them:

> And you, Paul!—are you keeping cool in that delightful bit of paradise you described to me as "a smile flashing through tears"? How I wish I were there too!—then we would go and sit on the bank of some shadowy stream, some cool delightful spot, one of Nature's poems—a poem made of sparkling waters, fair flowers, stately trees, waving grasses and an arch of heaven's blue, above—a poem set to music in the leaves' melodious rustle and the riffle of the stream. You would read or recite to me Paul and the music of your voice would blend with that of leaf and stream and with the Muses, hand in hand enlivened we would wander for long hours forgetful of all else.[11]

But Rebekah continued to face Paul's irascibility. Playing conciliator, she would encourage him to look at the brighter side of life and, hopefully, to pen a "nice" letter, which she believed would reflect his truer self. As they approached the midpoint of 1894, she noticed his irritability was giving way to utter detachment: that he would not write a letter at all whenever he was "feeling more *pessimistic* than usual." Over the course of his early adult life and career, his chronic depression was proving inconsolable, even in the face of her entreaties. A handful of months into his twenty-second year, he had little room for her, beyond what he would likely accord to an acquaintance.[12]

Gloom hovered over every step Paul took. Rebekah wondered, in response to his recounting of "the *dewy* lamentations of Jupiter Pluvius" besieging an early spring trip he took to Indiana to read his poems, "I wonder why the rain god grieves so copiously over all your little leaves taking?" Before long she began to connect the dots between his state of mind and the state of his career. A couple of years into their relationship, at one of the times when, in a letter, he wrote a poem that buoyed her, she ventured an observation as insightful as her previous sense that he distrusted the world. She tried to make him believe that the very society which made him skeptical was full of friends who, she imagined, grew despondent without his presence:

> Yet, Paul, notwithstanding the happiness your *letter-in-rhyme* inspired in me, there crept into it a vein of sadness, for you spoke of being *ill*. Not *very* ill, dear friend, I hope. You have been working too hard, these hot days, isn't that it? *Do* stop, and rest awhile, Paul,—I know you need it. Your friends

can not afford to have you fall ill, dear, think what an element of pleasure would go out of their lives. So you must take good care of yourself for *our* sakes—I am afraid to say for *my* sake.[13]

———

Through her letters, Rebekah was able to keep Paul abreast of news about the family of Frederick Douglass. Starting in March 1894, Rebekah was identifying herself as interlocutor when she would write, in her own letter to Paul, "Mr. Douglass was saying that he would answer your letter soon." She knew the locus of Douglass relatives that Paul probably met at the World's Fair: "I presume you met them in Chicago—Mr. Chas. Douglass and his wife. He, you know, is the son of Mr. Fred'k Douglass." Rebekah enjoyed staying at the Douglass's "nice little place on the Chesapeake." And she had the ticket to high society in Washington, D.C., which featured the Douglasses and in which she invited Paul to partake: "Perhaps you have some curiosity as to who 'we' are," she sought to clarify.[14]

How Washington, D.C., became a city where African Americans were concerned with their "social position" dated back to the Civil War. At this time, African Americans pervaded the District of Columbia as slaves. With their expedited emancipation here in April 1862 (not in 1863, which affected the rest of the slave territories), they filled the society as laborers, crucial to both the menial and commercial work being done in private or in public, ranging from the construction of buildings as historic as the White House to the selling of fruit and vegetables as street vendors. Noted for straddling both the North and the South, such that the city felt southern to northerners and northern to southerners, Washington, D.C., attracted freed slaves who came to enjoy its hybridity and stimulation.

In the immediate wake of the war, African Americans in Washington, D.C., were still prevented from high economic pursuits. They had access to unskilled occupations of lower status than many whites wanted for themselves, ranging from being waiters and bartenders to bootblacks and cooks. Still, these jobs established the promise of livelihood. During Reconstruction, businesses created or owned by African Americans approached two hundred. A black middle class rose in which the adults were acquiring property, the children excelling in the classroom, and literacy slowly but surely becoming less the exception than the norm. "The vast and wonderful revolution which has, during the last dozen years, taken place in the condition and relations of the American people is nowhere more visible, striking, and complete, than in Washington," so declared Frederick Douglass himself, probably the city's most eminent African American resident, in 1877. "The spade, the plough and the pick-axe of the Freedman have changed the face of the earth upon which the city stands." Douglass was speaking literally, regarding the manual labor of African Americans, as well as figuratively, in terms of the soil they were cultivating for their own cultural and political efflorescence in the District of Columbia.[15]

By the turn of the century, the conditions were ideal in Washington, D.C., for the emergence of an African American elite. This society was alternately called "the upper tens," "the best society," and the black or colored "four hundred," in reference to that mythical number of eminent black families. It featured signature surnames that were synonymous with prestige: the Wormleys, who were known as hoteliers; the Syphaxes and the Cooks, educators; the Terrells, judicial and activist leaders; the Grimkés, advocates of racial uplift. Members of these and other distinguished families formed and frequented exclusive social clubs, such as the Lotus Club, the Sparta Club, the Columbia Social Club, the Diamondback Club, the Manhattan Club, the Acanthus Club, the Carreno Club, the Art Club. And they established "literaries," or intellectual societies called the Eureka Literary Society, the Chautauqua Literary Scientific Circle, the Monday Night Literary Society, and the Bethel Literary and Historical Association. The African American members in these societies were exclusive in much the same way that distinguished whites excluded them from their own circles. However, both shared the elitist behavior of willfully shunning the lower class.[16]

The African American elite was known for its emphasis on etiquette as a signal of racial progress, a message communicated through local newspapers and in private. Indeed, "the treatment which will be accorded her by all will be at once felt favorably if she be well dressed," wrote lawyer and consul Archibald Grimké around this time, to his relatives about his daughter's preparation for boarding school. "If she appears at once to be a young girl of refined manners & tastes & used to the best Society, & this the general style of her dress contributes much to [prove], she will be treated quite differently [than] if her dress were indicative of a lower position in the social scale, & other associations." Rebekah likewise had decoded the norms and expectations of the elite, and she was alerting Paul that they had to fulfill them to the best of their abilities.[17]

———

Around this time Paul was leaving no doubt how much he admired Douglass. "Of Negro Journals," published in a summer 1894 issue of the *Chicago Record*,

was Paul's evaluation of the press since Douglass's initial tenure as this periodical's editor. A failsafe measure of the sophistication of a people, in Paul's
view, was the quality, or "the character and tone," of its magazines, newspapers, and journals. Journals by and about African Americans had shown, from
the era of slavery to the present, how much their race had attended to the
need for freedom. He cited *Freedom's Journal*, founded in 1827 and the first
newspaper owned and operated by African Americans, and *North Star*,
founded in 1847 by Douglass himself. As federal emancipation arrived, these
papers declared that "the head of Slavery was cut off," but in any event this
"monster" became a "Hydra." The subsequent release of like-minded papers
enabled African Americans to report and opine on their newfound conditions in the country.[18]

A founding editor of the black newspaper the *Dayton Tattler*, whose own
title was telling, Paul learned that "Negro journals" suffered from being "too
closely a chronicle of unimportant personal facts, unrelieved by the less confined interest of an editorial column." Alas, "the colored newspaper is not literary; it seldom publishes a story or poem, and a review is almost an unknown
feature." The *Dayton Tattler* tried to be self-consciously literary. In actuality,
African American writers at the turn of the century did publish extensively in
periodicals, though Paul told the truth from his own vantage point in 1894.[19]

Douglass ascertained Paul's discouragement was due to his miserable lot in
Dayton. Two letters Rebekah wrote in fall 1894 alerted Paul that Douglass had
realized this: "I saw your good friend Mr. Douglass not long ago and he told
me you had written him. He also added that he was going to write you a long
letter very soon. Have you received it yet?" Douglass had noticed that Paul was
"despondent," an appearance she had noticed, too. "Why are you so cast down
in spirit, my friend?" she asked.[20]

Paul, it turned out, had just requested a letter of recommendation from Douglass. Paul sought to leverage the statesman's influence for professional gain,
such as in his own application for a position as an English literature teacher at
the same Washington, D.C., high school where Rebekah was teaching. The cre-
dential of self-directed, independent study was a theme in Paul's anxieties over
his lack of formal education beyond secondary school. Rebekah might have
first sowed the seed when she brought the position to his attention at the outset
of the fall 1894 semester and asked, "Of what school are you a graduate?—it is
necessary that you be a graduate of some recognized school or college." Paul
was on his heels when he reached out to Douglass, whose son Charles, it so
happened, was a candidate for membership on the high school's board of trustees. "My high school studies in Language and Literature have, since my

graduation, been supplemented by much special study along those lines," Paul wrote, "and I have been somewhat successful in practical literary work." This kind of reasoning enabled Paul to assert his professional qualifications for publishing literature or being a school instructor. While making a case for the excellence of his autodidactic learning, he needed help in taking the next professional step: Paul would be thankful if Douglass—the father Frederick or the son Charles— would use any influence to assist him in getting the job. Paul leaned on Rebekah, his second means of contact with Douglass. And she knew this. To open one letter, an awkward tone of secretarial formality seeped into her affection: "I received your letter yesterday afternoon and in compliance with your request have been to see Mr. Douglass."[21]

Aside from Rebekah and Douglass, the World's Fair also happened to introduce Paul to Alexander Crummell, another legendary man at the time. Born to African American abolitionists in the spring of 1819, Crummell worked for the American Anti-Slavery Society as early as his childhood days. After graduating from high school, he headed to New Hampshire's Noyes Academy, where a mob destroyed the school to protest the enrollment of African American students. Crummell instead matriculated at New York's Oneida Institute and matured into a bona fide intellectual. Eventually, he wished to become an Episcopal minister and applied to New York's General Theological Seminary, but he was rejected due to his race. Undeterred, he sought and received his ordination in Massachusetts by 1842. From 1849 to 1853 he studied at Queens College of the University of Cambridge, where he was the first student of identifiably African ancestry to graduate from the British institution.

Armed with extensive formal education, Crummell conceived of a so-called Pan Africanism in which peoples of African descent could unite to solve problems from slavery to discrimination. After a trip to Liberia at the end of his time at Cambridge, he charged the more enlightened brethren of his race to visit and civilize Africa, as it were—namely, to convert the citizens to Christianity. Crummell resided in Africa for two decades. Upon his return to the United States, he established an independent African American church in Washington, D.C., taught at Howard University, and remained politically active.

When Paul delivered the Jubilee Day ode at the World's Fair in 1893, the occasion brought him and Crummell together. Over a year later, in September 1894, the poet finally reached out to the elder activist. Paul was resigned that Crummell may have long forgotten him. Yet he was hopeful for a glimmer of recollection as he inquired into the English literature job at Rebekah's high school. "Presuming upon this brief meeting" at the World's Fair in Chicago,

Paul wrote, "I have taken the liberty to drop you a line about a matter that concerns me very deeply, and wherein, I believe, you can greatly help me."[22]

Paul had a steep hill to climb. He was self-conscious that he was not the most qualified candidate. Given that he had not gone to college, he knew he stood at a disadvantage. Just as he had with Douglass, he tried to counteract that fact with allusions to his autodidacticism in the mold of James Newton Matthews. His high school course of study had been supplemented by "much special and earnest study along literary lines," he assured Crummell, and the appointment to this job would be a great boon to him. The professional security this job would provide—at once a stable wage and a chance for further intellectual maturation—could not be ignored. He was doing all that he could to secure attention to his file: the job for which he was applying compelled him to contact a trustee (and to identify a second one) there, the same school where Crummell was working. Now he was trying to exploit a back channel. "The purpose of this letter is to ask you to use whatever influence you may consistently employ to help me," Paul pleaded.[23]

Crummell welcomed Paul as a fellow "black man." "It is your right + privilege to address me as you have," Crummell wrote to Paul, who had closed his initial letter with what he later worried was a presumptuous tone ("I am afraid that I have presumed much in thus addressing you," Paul wrote, "but trusting to your charity to overlook the fault"). "Every true black man, especially a man of genius + character," Crummell responded, "has t[he] right to command my services." Crummell had wished to write this young man ever since the World's Fair, but at seventy-five, he was limited by the loss of vision in one eye and his church responsibilities.

Despite the inspiration to work on behalf of a "black man," Crummell was concerned that biases would hamper Paul's prospects. Crummell disclosed privately, but also with candor, that he could not give Paul much encouragement: "There are local . . . prejudices existing here . . . I fear may bar your success." On Paul's behalf Crummell promised to see and write a fellow school trustee to urge a full consideration of his job application. In the meantime, Crummell asked for a copy of *Oak and Ivy* in exchange for a copy of *Africa and America*, Crummell's book, published in 1891, a compilation of essays on the Negro problem at home and abroad.[24]

Eventually, and almost inevitably, Rebekah became the bearer of bad news. Despite his appeal to the likes of Alexander Crummell and school trustees, Paul learned from Rebekah that his application for the English literature job came too late. Douglass wanted Rebekah to console Paul. Douglass, Rebekah wrote, "bids me say that there is no *certainty* about your getting a position here." A trustee of great influence, Blanche K. Bruce of Mississippi, the first African American to serve a full term in the U.S. Senate, had broken the news to Douglass: "He has spoken with Mr. Bruce about you and that gentleman says he has filled the position." Douglass advised Paul to write to historically black institutions such as Tuskegee Institute, Wilberforce University, and those endowed by churches. Douglass could only say, through Rebekah, that Paul should not grow bitter. "Success *must* come to you," she believed.[25]

Times of such travail, Rebekah thought, brought her and Paul closer together. After a year of correspondence, she no longer merely hinted at her desire for Paul. How and what he wrote attracted her, and she explicitly revealed the depth of her feelings. Again she was indebted to him for one of his "*exquisite* letters"; they were "like some rare nose gay, the *beauty* of whose flowers dazzles" and "whose *perfume* intoxicates." Metaphors touching on sustenance and inebriation enabled her to flesh out her message. "When I read your *letters*, Paul, I *love* you." Somehow his letters kindled something in her heart that warmed it into love. But she did not want to alarm him. "*I love you only when I read your letters.*" The affection was harmless, meant not to cause him distress. "Do I love you when I *read* your letters because you love *me* when you *write* them?"[26]

Rebekah's sense of desire alternated with doubt, though. Rebekah was not ever truly sure that Paul wanted to embrace her as tightly as she did him. She was uncertain whether he liked her best when he wrote her. "I keep your letters, Paul. I could no more destroy them than I could some delicate perfume-breathing flowers. As I have said, your letters *are* flowers," she reminded him, "and I am engaged in the delightful task of making them into a bouquet, whose fragrance, I shall inhale for all time." History showed, by virtue of the archival existence of these exchanges, mostly from her to him, that he did retain her letters. All throughout their private correspondence, her love was unremitting. He alluded to that. She was moved enough to quote his own very words to her that she held so dear: "When a young man reads a young woman's letter over day after day, and sometimes three times a day, there must be something very pleasant to him in the correspondence."[27]

On a later occasion Rebekah admitted that her language, however intimate, lacked Paul's intrigue. Often she had wondered how she had kept him interested in her this long. "*You* are so versatile, so poetic, *so* interesting—*I* am so monotonous, so prosy and so dull." Anxieties so filled her that she once thought that the discrepancy in their skills as writers would push him away. She was also constantly fearful that delays in his letters to her resulted from "all sorts of things." Something she said might have "displeased" him.[28]

What Rebekah said in her letters did not bother Paul as much as the "self-ish and egotistical" practice of letter writing itself. Exchanges in this medium discomfited Paul; he wished not to show these two traits. But she felt the opposite. "I do not think it is *either* my friend—when we *write* a letter we at-tempt to *please*, we strive to *interest* and *amuse another*," she reminded him. "We do not write from selfish motives, it is not that desire to please *ourselves*, but to please *another* that actuates letter writing." If anything, the difference of opinion lay in how they perceived the need even to pen a letter. Letter writing was for her a crucial way of sidling up to him, but it was for him less about her than about how he felt about himself. In light of where he came from and, perhaps, his foreboding about the challenges he was facing in the present and may further face in the future, he did not appreciate the fulfill-ment he could promise her.[29]

In what would not be the only such request in his lifelong affection for women, Paul wanted a keepsake to remember Rebekah by. She abstained; she did not possess any. But more than that, she had a confession to make. "I have a most serious aversion to the camera—one which I can not over come suf-ficiently to have even a presentable likeness taken." Instead, she preferred to gesture to those moments when they were in each other's company, such as in a letter to him from the first days of 1895, when she could playfully imagine "the delightful evening" they had just "spent together." She used this as a chance to describe her interest in him as what a woman would enjoy in a man: "Confusion in a man's room is what every woman expects to find—and it is one of her few expectations always realized. To such confusion she never ob-jects, for nothing pleases a woman better than to 'set things to rights' as she calls it, though I fear very often the *man* thinks she set them all awry, eh Paul?" She proceeded, right after these sentences, to tell an amusing tale about what it meant for a "wee wifie" to organize her husband's disheveled room. Was Paul as vicariously willing to role-play as she?[30]

———

Rebekah was not alone in discerning the so-called *dewy* lamentations of Jupi-ter Pluvius in Paul's verse. Dating as far back as the poem "Melancholia" in his high school years, his poems long elicited concern among even the most ran-dom of readers or listeners. She once encountered a gentleman who wondered why Paul's poems, aside from those rendered in dialect, tended to contain "a melancholic strain." He could not figure out what made the poet "such a pes-simist." She, too, had frequently wondered why he tended to look on the "dark" side. Nothing quite so plaintive as his "One Life" had she encountered in his oeuvre:

Oh, I am hurt to death, my Love;
 The shafts of Fate have pierced my striving heart,
And I am sick and weary of
 The endless pain and smart.
My soul is weary of the strife,
And chafes at life, and chafes at life.

Time mocks me with fair promises;
 A blooming future grows a barren past,
Like rain my fair full-blossomed trees
 Unburden in the blast.
The harvest fails on grain and tree,
Nor comes to me, nor comes to me.

The stream that bears my hopes abreast
 Turns ever from my way its pregnant tide.
My laden boat, torn from its rest,
 Drifts to the other side.
So all my hopes are set astray,
And drift away, and drift away.

The lark sings to me at the morn,
 And near me wings her skyward-soaring flight;
But pleasure dies as soon as born,
 The owl takes up the night,
And night seems long and doubly dark;
I miss the lark, I miss the lark.

Let others labor as they may,
 I'll sing and sigh alone, and write my line.
Their fate is theirs, or grave or gay,
 And mine shall still be mine.
I know the world holds joy and glee,
But not for me,—'t is not for me.[31]

Melancholia, as Paul expressed it in literature, emerged for the world to see. "Tell me what it is, my friend, that saddens all your songs?" Rebekah asked in December 1894.[32]

A clue to Paul's depression lay in his early admission to James Newton Matthews. More than anyone else, in November 1892 the elder poet and physician witnessed a fragility within Paul's meditations on the future. Amid his many utterances on the precarious chances for publication, Paul disclosed to Matthews that he feared being proven a fraud. The publicity perturbed him; it made him both upset and nervous. "I feel like a man walking a slack rope above thousands of spectators, who knows himself an amateur and is every moment expecting to fall." The potential tragedy he saw was manifold: the intensity of a spotlight he did not yet know how to handle; the failure to attain a high literary quality in his poetry; the stumble, upon that failure, back into a crowded marketplace of writers and readers, the former elbowing one another for prominence, the latter marveling at and adjudicating the competition. Mainly to Matthews—not so much to Rebekah, later—did he turn for advice and promise. "I will be patient and try to do as you say," Paul once told Matthews.[33]

However unwitting, Paul's insensitivity to the depth of Rebekah's attraction annoyed her; he did not realize, or appreciate, that her attention to his well-being had a distinct purpose. "There need never come into your life, my friend, a time when you can no longer call me 'dear,' unless of course your *wife* objects," she speculated, "for certainly my husband, if *ever* I have one, will be too sensible to object to his wife enjoying the distinguished honor of a correspondence with 'Paul Dunbar,'—and that you should address her 'dear' would be the source of much gratification (since it would be indicative of your *friendship* for her) to a husband as sensible and appreciative as I hope mine shall be." Even if marriage were not on the horizon for her, she wished that at least they would remain close socially. That they always be friends was her earnest wish. "No sentiment is more beautiful than *friendship*," she reminded him, asserting that it would be a grave error for him to believe that a woman could be nothing but a sweetheart. She could also be a friend. Between such friendship and the ideal of love, their connection, she was gratified to know, somewhat sarcastically, at least piqued his curiosity. She was comforted that in some vague way his acquaintance with her had made him think "better of my sex," as she put it.[34]

———

Frederick Douglass died on February 20, 1895. A couple of years from his eightieth birthday, Douglass had remained an active man, but signs had begun to emerge that the end was nigh. Three years earlier, around the June 1892 Republican Convention, excessive exhaustion and the probability of heart disease weighed him down when he had been involved in the political advancement of the Republican Party, as a Haiti commissioner for the World's Columbia Exposition in Chicago, and as patron and patriarch for his circle of family, friends, and fellows in need. Five months later, a friend observed the increasing illegibility of Douglass's penmanship, along with his "ever-present cough," as a marker of his "weakened" state. During the Chicago exposition itself the following year, his "failing eyesight" and his personal sense that he was "going downhill" at once frustrated and frightened him; the quivering of his hand while delivering his speech on Colored People's Day, mere feet away from Paul's rapt face, was not reassuring either.

The final premonition of Douglass's mortality came the morning of February 20, 1895. He had been attending a rally organized by the National Council of Women, held at Metzerott Hall on Pennsylvania Avenue, in Washington, D.C. Adjacent to women's rights activists Susan B. Anthony and Anna Howard Shaw, "Douglass seemed in good health through the day among the fifty delegates, although one woman later reported that he continually rubbed his left hand as though it were 'benumbed.'" To a British delegate also in the vicinity, the statesman continued to exude an unrelenting power and energy in being "a commanding figure six feet high, a splendid head with large and well-formed features, soft, pathetic eyes, complexion of olive-brown, flowing white hair."[35]

Paul remembered the image of Douglass healthy enough to command an audience, not the one who had been grappling with his health. Nor did he witness the life of the spiritually tireless sage come to an end around 7:00 p.m. that evening. Douglass had been waiting in the front hallway of Cedar Hill with his wife, Helen, for a carriage to take them to a nearby church. Then he dropped to his knees; his body tumbled onto the floor, sprawled out. He was suffering a heart attack. Helen cried out for help. A doctor arrived shortly afterward, but it was too late. Douglass was dead.

From 9:30 a.m. to 1:30 p.m. on February 25, thousands proceeded past the open casket of Douglass's body at the Metropolitan AME Church. (A private family service had already occurred at Cedar Hill, after which the body was transported to the church.) Luminaries and the elite of the land paid their respects—judges, politicians, professors—as well as the African American children who could attend because colored schools in Washington, D.C., were closed for the day. By day's end, the casket was whisked away to New York City to be briefly honored at City Hall, and then to Rochester in upstate New York, where it was shown at City Hall and the Central Church, before it reached its final resting place at Mount Hope Cemetery, alongside the burial sites of his previous wife, Anna, and his daughter Annie.

If Paul had viewed the open casket at the Metropolitan AME Church, then he would have had an opportunity to see the statesman in person one last time. But he did not go. Rebekah, who did attend, wished he had. "I expected you to come," she wrote Paul close to a month after Douglass died, "for well I knew your great love for him, whose going has left such a gap [in] life. I thought you might even at the last moment so I secured for you a card of admission." Perhaps the visit would have been too painful for him to endure. She sensed that possibility. For Paul's benefit, Rebekah "painted" the image of Douglass's dignified body as respectfully as she could. The heartrending language could not cloak the pain she was feeling on Paul's behalf:

> I wish, dear Paul, that I could paint for you the sweet majesty of this great man as he lay within his oaken casket calmly sleeping death's still sleep. As in life, that soft silk snowy hair formed a halo of pure glory round his lofty brow, where sat enthroned all virtues, his eyes, those mirrors of a majestic intellect and unstained soul, were softly, secretly closed, his lips where fell such pearls of wisdom and of thought, met almost in a smile, and yet the firmness that they wore in life still lingered there, his stately form might well have served as a model of Hercules lain down to rest.[36]

CHAPTER 9

The Bond of a Fellow-Craft

Will you write to me soon Miss Moore? I do want to hear from you very much. Write if it is only a word or two. I feel that the bond of a fellow-craft joins us together. If I am somewhat enthusiastic over having found you or if a visionary vein peeps through the fabric of this letter, shut your eyes to it as if you had been my friend always and, like all my friends, were used to making allowances for me.

—PAUL LAURENCE DUNBAR TO ALICE RUTH MOORE
(MAY 23, 1895)[1]

In April 1895 Paul came across the photograph of a woman in the *Monthly Review*, the Boston-based "illustrated independent magazine," according to its subtitle, "devoted to the interests of the American people through the United States and the world." The contours and complexion of her skin captivated him. Not coincidentally, within many African American communities, social stature rose in proportion to the lightness of skin color. The color discrimination among shades of brown existed within these communities as an extension, however unwittingly or obliquely, of racial discrimination in the United States. Certainly, the degree of one's hue was always a matter of personal opinion: what appeared light or dark in color to one person did not necessarily seem so to another. There was a color consciousness especially among the African American elite: it reared its head in their electoral contests and political relations; their various institutions of education; their church and religious groups; their social clubs.

By the time Paul had gazed at the picture of "Miss Alice Ruth Moore of New Orleans,"[2] the aesthetics of her likeness blurred with the aesthetics of her lightness in proportion to the way that the upper classes and the so-called

FIG. 9.1. Alice Ruth Moore, circa 1895.
From G. F. Richings, *Evidences of
Progress Among Colored People*
(G. S. Ferguson, 1896).

fair-complexioned went hand in hand. "Indisputably, the overwhelming majority of aristocrats of color were mixed-bloods ranging in color from light brown or 'yellow' to virtually white," writes historian Willard B. Gatewood, in reference to the "mulattos" who supposedly descended from a racially mixed ancestry. "Their appearance was obviously an advantage in a society that placed the highest premium on white skin." Paul subscribed to this phenotypical—and, it so happened, physiognomic—doctrine as he approached Alice. (A couple of years hence, for example, he would lavish praise on her light-skinned beauty—on her becoming his "fair American Girl," whose "eyes, hair and complexion" recalled those of a "Jewess." And when he would ask for pictures of her, he hoped that they would show her adorable "little profiles," including her "dear turn-up nose.")[3]

An essay Alice would publish two decades later, on the "people of color" in her native Louisiana, pointed to the very social and class differences she perceived between light-skinned and dark-skinned people. By "common consent," after the Civil War, she wrote, the "Negro" meant "those whose complexions were noticeably dark," whereas the "mulatto" were "always a class apart, separated from and superior to the Negroes, ennobled were it only by one drop of white blood in their veins." Born and reared in New Orleans, Alice racially identified herself with African ancestry, but she also sought to understand her own embodiment of a Creole self in which the genealogical strains of Spain and France shaped the attitudes of her homeland. How she would view Paul, who was being praised not merely as a poet but as one remarkable for being so dark-skinned, so racially pure and authentically black, contributed to the drama unfolding in his vying for her attention.[4]

On April 17, 1895, Paul wrote his very first letter to Alice. Admittedly forward, he believed he had license to be so, given the craft to which both were trying to dedicate their lives. "You will pardon my boldness in addressing you, I hope, and let my interest in your work be my excuse," his letter began. "I sometimes wonder if in the rare world of art, earthly conventions need always be heeded. I am drawn to write you because we are both working along the same lines and a sketch of yours in the *Monthly Review* so interested me that I was anxious to know more of you and your work."[5]

Paul and Alice shared an interest in circulating their work in periodical venues. Since the summer of 1893, when he had been reporting on the World's Fair, he had been sending articles to the *Chicago News Record*, which was the morning edition of the *Chicago Daily News*. (The previous year, his publication of poems initiated his contributions to the paper.) He also had published an article in the *Detroit Free Press*; several poems in the "Lighter Vein" column of the distinguished *Century Magazine* and in *Kate Field's Washington*; and a story in the New York *Independent*. Meanwhile, Alice was a columnist for the *Journal of the Lodge*, published by the Colored Knights of the Pythias, a New Orleans fraternal organization of charity and benevolence.

In his first letter to Alice, Paul summarized his publishing history to prove his relentless effort at becoming a professional writer. A classic metaphor of Greek mythology helped him portray the struggles of his early career and the pessimism that gripped him. "I am a writer, one trying to struggle up the thorny path of literature," he wrote, "with the summit of Parnassus not yet in sight." Their epistles therefore could be literary in focus, to enable them to practice the craft together. "I should like to exchange opinions and work with you if you will agree," he offered. "The counsel and encouragement of one who is striving toward the same end that I am would, I know, greatly help."[6]

As an olive branch, Paul submitted for Alice's review the verses he had just finished on Douglass's passing almost two months prior. He had released the poem in Boston's *Monthly Review*, the same venue that had acquainted him with her work, just the previous month, in March. The final stanza resoundingly concluded a heartrending ode to a man of immeasurable reverence:

Oh, Douglass, thou hast passed beyond the shore,
But still thy voice is ringing o'er the gale!
Thou 'st taught thy race how high her hopes may soar
And bade her seek the heights, nor faint, nor fail.
She will not fail, she heeds thy stirring cry,
She knows thy guardian spirit will be nigh,
And rising from beneath the chast'ning rod,
She stretches out her bleeding hands to God![7]

Paul also sent Alice the latest lines of a poem that he would title "Phyllis," about Phillis Wheatley, a New World African known only to the most avid readers of his race:

Phyllis, ah, Phyllis, my life is a gray day,
Few are my years, but my griefs are not few,
Ever to youth should each day be a May-day,
Warm wind and rose-breath and diamonded dew—
Phyllis, ah, Phyllis, my life is a gray day.

Oh for the sunlight that shines on a May-day!
Only the cloud hangeth over my life.
Love that should bring me youth's happiest heyday
Brings me but seasons of sorrow and strife;
Phyllis, ah, Phyllis, my life is a gray day.

Sunshine or shadow, or gold day or gray day,
Life must be lived as our destinies rule;
Leisure or labor or work day or play day—
Feasts for the famous and fun for the fool;
Phyllis, ah, Phyllis, my life is a gray day.[8]

Unveiling these poems signaled Paul's willingness to lift the veil and expose his literary mind and creative process alike; it was an invitation to social and intellectual intimacy—with him—that would have been all the more sacred if not for the reality that he likewise deployed his poetry to court potential benefactors and belles for personal gain and pleasure.

Caveats aside, the letter was a success. Alice's interest was piqued. She received it at "a singularly inopportune moment": when a damaging fire at her family's home, located on 1924 Palmyra Street in New Orleans, partially

blinded her and burned her hand. She put Paul's letter to the side and returned to it the following week, when she could concentrate. Appealing to
her fancy, the letter contained "those dainty little verses," which had been
"ringing in my head ever since I read them," she said. After the first week of
May, Alice finally replied in full, grateful for Paul's self-introduction and—her
turn to be forward—expressing her own desire for more letters, both epistolary and literary. "I must thank you ever so much and though I don't like to
appear greedy, still if you have any more like them, please send them down
this way," she said. Alice suggested an important point about this man three
years her senior: slowly but surely Paul's published writings were launching
him into public fame, but he could flatter himself in seeking companionship
from a woman who was still a fledgling. After all, his name was familiar: she
had already encountered his poems in periodicals. "I always enjoyed them
very much," she informed him, putting his popularity and skill in perspective.
"You do a great deal of work in different lines which is fortunate for you, since
you have the entree in so many of our best papers." From a practical standpoint he was well positioned to advise her on the quality of her writing or the
opportunities available for her to get published.[9]

Paul replied to Alice from Indianapolis, where he was reciting his work and,
from the end of May through July 1895, serving as temporary editor of the
Indianapolis World while the paper's owner, Alexander Manning, was away on
vacation. Paul was buoyed to see that Alice had even responded. His celebrity
charmed her, he noticed. Pleased that she had seen his name somewhere of
relevance, he was now able to fend off the label of "a presumptuous upstart."
That she enjoyed his verses also inspired him. Well before he had read her letter, he was hopeful that she would write him back. In the meantime he researched her publishing history, noting that she was editing a women's column
in the *Journal of the Lodge*, a newspaper geared toward an African American
readership and published by the Colored Knights of Pythias in New Orleans.
"Never did I devour a woman's column with such avidity and judge with what
eagerness I now watch for it each week," he confessed.[10]

Although the initial premise of Paul's letters to Alice was to build a relationship of literary exchanges (to which she agreed), he perceived her reply as a
window to an opportunity in which he could shift the rhetorical gears of flirtation. "But let us not be literary in our letters, let us be friendly," he declared. "I
like it better, don't you; and won't you send me some of your work when or *if*
you write again." He extended yet another olive branch, this time leveraging

his reputation at the *Indianapolis World* for her benefit. He would be honored and privileged to take a copy of her first book manuscript, *Violets and Other Tales*, when out later in 1895, if she would pardon him for taking the liberty of mentioning its anticipated release in the *World* columns that week. Literature and friendship went hand in hand, in his eyes; "I feel that the bond of a fellow-craft joins us together," he ventured, optimistically.[11]

Only two days after drafting this sentence in late May, Paul followed up with a proposal. As part of his goal in making the *Indianapolis World* a strong literary weekly, he needed Alice's help—which, actually and cleverly, would redound to her own benefit if she accepted his request. "If you have any articles or poems to spare will you send them to me? While we cannot offer financial return, we will do all that we can to assist those who give us their aid. I should be delighted to run your cut and a sketch of you at *your* earliest convenience. I am interested in you and want all my western friends to know about you." Introducing her work to a wider audience was an offer she could not refuse. As a writer and editor he had special access to newspapers and offered to help her attain the success he anticipated in her life, although he issued the typical caveat—just as Crummell had expressed to him before, with respect to his Washington, D.C., high school job application—that his newfound role might be limited.[12]

Ultimately, in an early June letter, Alice agreed to send her poems to Paul, such as one titled "Love for a Day," which he would later call "beautiful," "exquisite," "rich, warm, *luxuriant,* if you will, in phrasing and glow[ing] with color." (The poem was never published, incidentally.) She also worked with Paul to secure the possible consent of Charles Alexander, editor of the Boston *Monthly Review*, to lend her halftone picture to the *Indianapolis World* for republication. The literary and professional negotiations at the outset of their relationship—his submission of poems for her sustained attention, her submission of writings with knowledge of his ability to publish them—laid the ground on which Paul and Alice built their trust as friends. For her acts of kindness in entertaining and replying to his letters, he would playfully shift his epistolary discourse ("I will close my prosiness now to drop into verse or worse") while gesturing to what was being exchanged in doing so. He loved these lyrical forms and hoped that his attempts in them would please her. "Hoping to hear from you very soon, not less in the capacity of friend than of editor," he concluded. Quite smartly, instead of sending Alice random, miscellaneously published verses, he wrote two in private. The content seemed to speak precisely about her, about what she meant to him and the prospects of their love, with her name even explicitly invoked:[13]

"A Song"

My lady-love lives far away,
And, oh my heart is sad by day,
And, oh my tears fall fast by night;
What may I do in such a plight?
    Why, miles grow few when Love is fleet,
    And Love you know hath flying feet.
    Break off thy sighs and witness this,—
    How poor a thing mere distance is.
My love knows not I love her so,
Say, would she scorn me, did she know?
How may the tale I would impart
Reach my love's ear and win her heart?
    Calm thou the tempest in thy breast;
    Who loves in silence loves the best.
    But bide thy time, she will awake,
    No night so new but moon will break.
But tho' my heart so strongly yearns,
My lady loves me not in turn.
How may I win the blest reply,
That my void heart shall satisfy?
    Love breedeth love, be thou but true,
    And soon thy love shall love thee too,
    If Fate hath meant you, heart for heart,
    There's naught may keep you twain apart.

"Song"

To Miss Alice Ruth Moore

Know you, winds that blow your course,
Down the verdant valleys
That somewhere you must, perforce
Kiss the brow of Alice?
Where her smiling face you find,

Kiss it gently, naughty wind.
Roses, waving fair and sweet,
Thru' the garden alleys,
Grow until a glory meet
For the eye of Alice.
Let the wind your off'ring bear
Of sweet perfume, faint and rare.
Lily, holding crystal dew
In your pure white chalice,
Nature kind hath fashioned you
Like the soul of Alice.
It of purest white is wrought,
Filled with gems of purest thought![14]

Eventually, Paul left the *Indianapolis World*, but not without assuring Alice that he would look out for the work of hers he had tried to place there. "The *World* will go on in my absence just as usual (a thing the world is famous for)," he said. "I am looking for your story with pleasant anticipations and hope to soon have it in hand." Even though records remain spotty as to whether she ever published as much as they both wanted, the soil was tilled for their bond to flower.[15]

———

Four months after Paul first wrote Alice, they continued their conversation in letters. At this time, he raised for discussion her first book, *Violets and Other Tales*, published in 1895 by the Monthly Review Publishing House of Boston, to which she had only alluded before, but which now he had gotten ahold of and read. The book showcased Alice's literary ambidexterity. Of the twenty-nine pieces, fifteen were short fiction; the remainder were poems. Across them certain themes recurred: love and intimacy; vulnerability, whether physical or metaphysical; human access to the divine; references to classical authors, like Gustave Flaubert, and classical literature, like Nathaniel Hawthorne's 1850 novel *The Scarlet Letter*. In select stories, such as "Anarchy Alley" and "A Carnival Jangle," Alice revealed a deep familiarity with New Orleans, her native land. In others, like "Titee" and "Little Miss Sophie," she asserted a kinship with Creole life. Though not among the most artistically mature books of Alice's era, *Violets and Other Tales* marked the start of a promising career. Unmistakable were her talent and versatility, not to mention her special knowledge of the religion and spirituality behind human connection.

Pontificating on this book enabled Paul in August to disclose even more of what were turning out to be his ulterior motives for befriending Alice. From the first time that he noticed her work, he was intrigued by her more than he had dared to say. Now that he had read the book, he was "fairly bewildered": "I have read it with delight, and my appreciation is equaled only by my surprise." Of this praise he poured out even more, again using the word "exquisite" not only to describe the fiction itself but in association with the artist's hand. "I consider your stories pieces of most exquisite art; and it is in them chiefly that I am interested." He continued to work on her behalf, moving beyond the *Indianapolis World* to showcase her work.

In early August, Paul spent five days in Toledo, where he gave a recital at the Toledo State Hospital for the Insane. There he met for the first time Henry A. Tobey, a medical doctor who served as the hospital's superintendent, and who, in later years, would become one of Paul's most dedicated patrons. At the hospital Paul recommended *Violets and Other Tales* for friends in attendance, one of whom even gave Paul money to purchase a copy. Paul enclosed the sum of fifty cents in a subsequent letter to Alice, with the proviso that she send a copy along at the earliest opportunity. He later monitored, quite politely, whether she had in fact sent the book along to his friend. Meanwhile, he would work to fulfill her own request for a mailed copy of *Oak and Ivy*.[16]

Around this time, Paul was beginning to take the liberty of expressing reservations about Alice herself or her work. After all, the critical praise he was receiving for *Oak and Ivy* distinguished him as one of the rising poets of his time, at least among the most talented. Of poetry qua poetry he was protective in commenting truthfully on *Violets and Other Tales*. "Although I liked your poems—you asked me to be honest—I was less impressed with them," he began. "They are rich in conception and imagery, but they lack that exactness of form which is one of my literary hobbies." Alice's prose did not draw Paul's ire; he was a less experienced writer of fiction and nonfiction and lacked authority in these genres. Where poetry was concerned, though, even her "exquisite" beauty could not temper the scrupulous aggression of his criticism.

Other matters irked Paul. *Violets and Other Tales* received a strong review in the July 1895 issue of the *Boston Daily Standard*, which lauded Alice's literary talent but also her favorable portrayal of independent women of the South. Paul could not tell whether Alice's skepticism (regarding the *Boston Standard* review) was "earnest or sarcasm." A tinge of jealousy crept in as he noticed her

FIG. 9.2. Dr. Henry A. Tobey, n.d. (Henry Archibald Tobey Collection, Ohio History Connection)

book's anonymous dedication: "To my friend of November 5, 1892." Paraphrasing Horatio's line from Shakespeare's play *The Tragedy of Hamlet, Prince of Denmark*, Paul demanded an explanation. "It puzzles me and forms 'a mote to trouble the mind's eye.'" Drafted in August, this is one of the first letters in which Paul's unbridled emotions, rendered through his criticism of Alice's literary work, became manifest. A clue lay in the letter's final sentence: "To-night for the first time, I believe, I am sorry that I am not handsome and wealthy—then perhaps I might not have to write a letter that concealed my thoughts!" His insecurity over his own looks and finances meant he believed he remained at a disadvantage in his courtship. Without being "handsome and wealthy," he would have to find other ways of capitalizing on the privilege of her personal attention.[17]

———

As Paul courted Alice, he faithfully corresponded with his mother, Matilda, an unrelenting activity he sustained for much of his adult life. Rarely were his letters to his mother as effusive as those he sent to his intimate female partners; nor were these letters as engaged as those to his professional acquaintances. Between mother and son, the economy of words in their letters partly had to do with her occasional need to have someone else, such as one of her sisters or her other sons, handwrite hers, due to her increasing age or ill health. Or it had to do with the illegibility of the letters she did handwrite, which "takes long experience and the grace of God to read," Paul once sighed. Each still monitored what the other was doing. As a son, he felt obligated to attend to her every concern about his well-being, while ensuring that she herself was being adequately supported as she entered her fifties by the mid-1890s and, like him, worried over her own finances. Quite often their private correspondence devolved into cold, transactional disclosures of his earnings and what expenses of hers he could afford to cover.[18]

In late summer 1895 one of Paul's earliest recorded letters recognized the temperamental nature that had made Matilda legendary in his household as a youth. For him, the mood usually took the form of impatience, such as when he would receive a card saying that she had not heard from him. Or when he would have to verify when and where he mailed letters to her. He gave her the news that one of his patrons, Tobey, wanted to advance his higher education at a storied New England institution, a desire recalling the wishes of his previous patrons. "Dr. Tobey and his friends want to lend me 400 or 500 dollars to spend a year in Boston at Harvard. I am going to take it." Records do not indicate that Paul took up the invitation; over the next couple of years, Boston—or Cambridge, more accurately—turned out to be one of the cities he scarcely visited. Yet the story of his formal education and financial support, he knew, would be one that his mother would appreciate.[19]

When Paul was not describing to Matilda the opportunities that possibly lay ahead, he was explaining why he had decided to leave others behind. Around this time he was reeling from her consternation, discernible in her epistolary "tone," over his decision to decline a guaranteed job as a clocksmith. For two reasons he turned it down. First, the clocks were too large, and he was not physically strong enough to do the work; "some of the clocks, it would take two ordinary men to wind." Though entering his early twenties, he never was a man of muscular build, a physical frailty he inherited from his father. (Five years later, after a bout of illness, he told his mother, "I now weigh 143¼, the highest yet. I don't know if father ever weighed more than that.") Second, he was expected to do all the repairing, and he did not count amongst his "educational attainments a knowledge of the mechanism of clocks." Paul's erudition lay in the history and craft of writing poetry. The life of the mind, his well-wrought tales of the heart and soul, would lead him down the path of destiny.[20]

Matilda's criticism of Paul's rejection of a manual job came from her belief that he was a spendthrift. She said that she would not spend so much money running about, as he did, and advised him to "get something steady." Being a clocksmith would at least have settled him down. The accusation surprised him. "Do you suppose that if I could get something steady, I would not take it?" he asked rhetorically. "Have you even known of my running about to any place where I did not go for the best?" Her lack of faith in his financial and professional common sense disappointed him, as did the fact that, in having his half-brother Rob transcribe these words for her, the insult was privy to someone beyond their private circle and could be disseminated even further.

The dispute aside, Paul continued to confide in Matilda—at times, petulantly—that he wished to pursue his dream of writing and reciting poetry. "I have a call to West Carrollton + Toledo again, to recite. If you deem this *too much running about*," he growled, "I will write + decline them + sit here sucking my [xxxx] + waiting for '*something steady*'." He would not relent on his dream of higher education; he waited on his patron expectantly, and there was nothing his mother could do about it. "I have made up my mind long ago to go to college, and am now waiting on Dr. Tobey's movements. If I go to Toledo I shall call upon him."[21]

In a little while Paul would learn that he could not matriculate after all, according to an unfortunate letter sent by Tobey, if he did not attend at some point in the academic year from fall 1895 through spring 1896. "But I want anything that will settle me for the winter"—words from Paul that Matilda would surely have found encouraging. "I am tired of uncertainty," he went on to say; "I must close now."[22]

Paul never did.

———

Literature was not the only form of art that stimulated Paul's mind in 1895, though it was the genre of poetry, at this point, that preoccupied his communications with Alice. Theater and music happened to be sources of inspiration as well. As early as 1891, while in high school, he had held the theatrical stage with friends who sang and recited poems. Within a couple of years, one of his most famous poems to emerge from *Oak and Ivy*, "A Banjo Song," employed a musical instrument as the trope of a slave community inspired by performance. And during the World's Fair in Chicago in 1893, he read poems on a stage that also featured some of the rising African American stars of classical music. During all these occasions, Paul came closer and closer to realizing the aesthetic and commercial appeal of music, even as he tried to prove his literary mettle reciting poems amid vocalists and instrumentalists respectively singing and playing their tunes for audiences. Given his propensity for conceiving and classifying his poems as lyrics, he was already taking artistic steps toward music and drama.

Paul began pursuing musical theater in earnest. The last decade of the nineteenth century was the right time for him to do so. During this era, musical composition, with respect to black folks songs, meant the production and presence of Antonín Dvořák. A Czech composer who became director of the National Conservatory in New York in 1892, Dvořák developed a fascination with the folk songs regularly crooned by one of his African American students, Harry Burleigh. A year later Dvořák premiered a symphony, *From the New World*, celebrating the idiomatic melodies and harmonies of the "Negro spirituals." African American musicians—like Burleigh under Dvořák, or others under Julius Eichberg, director and co-founder of the Boston Conservatory—also were enjoying newfound admission to formal schools of music, although their actual inclusions in public orchestral performances were few and far between. Just as Paul was entering his literary prime, so were cohorts of African American musicians emerging at educational institutions across the country.[23]

Formally educated African American musicians eventually began to take advantage of composing and conducting on their own terms. They not only began to compose folksongs with musical arrangements but also enfolded these compositions around poems written or published by African Americans as well as around traditional dances passed down in their communities across generations. To be sure, the transition in American entertainment from minstrelsy to vaudeville and comedies at the turn of century did not eliminate the racist portrayals of African American people and folkways. But through resilience and agency, African American musicians went on to become educators themselves and autonomously formed their own symphony orchestras in cities from Washington, D.C., to New York to Philadelphia. The prospect of these composers producing shows for Broadway went from being improbable to possible.[24]

Paul's involvement in this industry began in earnest with his relationship with Will Marion Cook. After studying in Berlin and returning to the United States, Cook became a student of Dvořák's during 1894 and 1895, although eventually he fell out of favor with the teacher. Cook's schooling was notable as much for its wide range and depth as for its instability, moving in fits and starts as he bounced from instructor to instructor, state to state, country to country. Paul and Cook developed a professional bond during the World's Fair in Chicago: both were included on the same program in which Cook performed the operatic "Uncle Tom's Cabin" and Paul read his poem "Ode to the Colored American." But their bond was also quite personal, a mutual admiration verging on collegiality, if not friendship.

In working with Cook, Paul became exposed to a network of fellow African American artists of the same generation who were seeking to build names for themselves and what they stood for as musicians and on the stage. One was Egbert "Bert" Williams, who by this time was one of the leading vaudevillian entertainers in the country. Two years younger than Paul and born in the Bahamas, he specialized in minstrel performance, singing and dancing, and comedic routines. His tour partner was George Walker, whom he had met in San Francisco in 1893. A year Paul's junior and from Kansas, Walker also had ascended the ranks by performing vaudeville and minstrel shows. Combining to become the Walker and Williams Company, the performers welcomed Cook as a major composer and conductor for their acts. Williams and Walker represented the preeminent African American duo in musical theater in New York City, if not the entire country. Williams alone tended to possess greater name recognition than Walker, but together they eclipsed the likes of Bob Cole and Billy Johnson in vaudeville and Ernest Hogan in "coon"-oriented comedy. Aside from their commercial impact, a social orbit of composers, musicians, dramatists, actors, and entertainers revolved about Williams and Walker—and included Paul.

The vicinity of West 53rd Street, between Sixth and Seventh Avenues, in New York City delineated the location of the four-story brownstone hotel owned by the charismatic James "Jimmie" L. Marshall: it generated a gravitational pull for African American guests to engage the performers who frequented Williams and Walker's nearby flat. A headquarters of sorts, this flat welcomed the likes of Burleigh; Will Accooe, a songwriter; and the Johnson brothers: Jim, a writer (whom today we call James Weldon), and Rosamond, a composer. It was located in the so-called Tenderloin district. Infamous for its spate of clubs for dancing and gambling, of cabarets and brothels, the district had over the previous couple of decades slowly but surely repelled its more upstanding residents. But not only did the area tempt the likes of those whose moral rectitude had wavered, it also invigorated those who gravitated especially toward the African American residents, proprietors, and tourists that concentrated along Sixth Avenue. The Tenderloin became known as a hub of African American artists and celebrities—writers, performers, athletes—that generated an atmosphere of "artistic innovation, theatrical energy, moral experimentation, interracial contact, and professionalism," according to historian Robert M. Dowling.[25]

The expansive section of the Tenderloin that enjoyed the society of these and other folks of the intelligentsia was nothing less than a "Negro Bohemia," which consisted of about thirty-six square blocks, the core of which was delineated by the streets running east to west from Fifth Avenue to Seventh Avenue, then from north to south from 42nd Street to 24th Street. Here, African American and Caribbean performers came together to exchange ideas, advice, and support, and to ascertain "the manner and means of raising the status of the Negro as a writer, composer, and performer in the New York theater and world of music," according to James Weldon Johnson in his 1933 autobiography, *Along This Way*. Alas, the release of more than six hundred "coon" songs in the last decade of the nineteenth century was a fact that Dunbar, Cook, and other African American performers had to reckon with as they sought to break through the racial prejudice of the marketplace.[26]

In early to mid-1895, Cook himself traveled from Washington, D.C., his home at the time, to that bohemia—for the cultural and intellectual energy, but specifically to visit Walker and Williams. He wanted to pitch them an idea for a show: a musical about the Louisiana cakewalk, a special prance recalling when slaves supposedly danced, in part, to mock the gait of their white owners, and evolving over time as a comic routine in minstrel shows. Cook wrote the act first with Walker and Williams in mind. They declined, but they passed along some helpful suggestions for Cook to consider.

When Cook returned to Washington, he reached out to Paul to see if the poet wanted to join. Paul was reluctant to take on this effort. He was struggling to manage his own personal and professional affairs. "After a long siege of persuasion," Cook would recall decades later, "I finally got Paul Laurence Dunbar to consent to write" the libretto and a few lyrics for what would be called *Clorindy, the Origin of the Cakewalk*. Living only three blocks away, Paul met up with Cook one evening, at 8:00 p.m., in the basement of his brother John's rented house on 6th Street, along the bottom edge of Howard University. The poet and the composer burned the midnight oil, drinking "two dozen bottles of beer [and] a quart of whisky." (Paul rarely turned down an occasion for recreational drink.) Plus, Cook remembered, "we took my brother's porterhouse steak, cut it up with onions and red peppers and ate it raw." Despite having only a kitchen table to write on and no musical instruments on hand to practice tunes, they finished almost all aspects of the show, from the songs to the libretto, eight hours after they started.[27]

Paul and Cook worked contractually to formalize and profit from their collaboration. With M. Whitmark and Sons, they worked on a contract stipulating that Paul and Cook would proportionally divide any future domestic and international royalties between them generated from the show's first four consecutive weeks. Paul would be entitled to 40 percent of North American sales and 27 percent of sales outside this territory; Cook would receive the remaining percentage of sales in each category. Signed on July 15, 1895, the contract anticipated the commercial and financial rewards for their creative venture.[28]

———

Over time Paul grew increasingly willing to lift the veil to show Alice the complexity of his creative process and personal side. He relayed to her the minutiae of writing that he rarely told anyone else. By the end of October 1895, he was toiling to release a second book larger than the first one he had published three years previously, *Oak and Ivy*. He was making progress; he wanted to name the new book after the poem he slated to be first therein—"Ione," a twenty-nine-verse-long poem in three sections, which began:

Ah, yes, 'tis sweet still to remember,
    Though 'twere less painful to forget;
For while my heart glows like an ember,
    Mine eyes with sorrow's drops are wet,

And, oh, my heart is aching yet.
   It is a law of mortal pain
That old wounds, long accounted well,
   Beneath the memory's potent spell,
Will wake to life and bleed again.[29]

Paul hit a snag. "The initial poem for which I want to name the volume is not yet finished, though I have many more than I can publish in one book, ready at hand." He decided that he would repurpose "a baker's dozen of the verses" from his first book; otherwise, the rest would be new. Although he had promised first to send a copy of the book to a friend in Washington, D.C., Alice was on the list to receive the next available one. Once she received it, he wanted her to tell him "frankly" what she thought. He insisted that there would not be "polite little lies or regard for petty conventions" between them. "We will speak very plainly to each other as long as we are friends."[30]

Open access cut both ways. Just as Paul showed Alice what lay behind the curtain of his creative writing, he inquired into her own progress, including the reception of *Violets and Other Tales*. He hoped that her book was successful but regretted that he was not able to do more than he had. Not only did he try to widen her audience through his networks at the *Indianapolis World*; he sought other venues to support his strategy, to little avail. He solicited the help of Charles Dennis, a supposed friend who was serving as managing editor of the *Chicago News Record*, to place his review of her book there. Bad luck scuttled this plan. Dennis abandoned the paper and left for Europe, leaving Paul empty-handed. "I had hoped to surprise you with a review of it in the *Chicago News-Record*, and for nearly three months past I have been fuming with rage that my contribution should be held over until all its timeliness had evaporated." Failing, in his view, to advance her career, he apologized. "This is the lot of the poor quill driver," he lamented.

Paul then offered up other publications—"Have you ever sent any of your stories to the *Bohemian* at Cincinnati?"—as promising opportunities. He advised on which stories in *Violets and Other Tales* Alice might consider republishing, such as the "Louisiana heart-stones." Due to her racial and regional ancestry, he believed that she could emerge as a leading writer of French and Creole local color in New Orleans. Or, due to her extended vacation time with her family in Bay St. Louis, a town on the Mississippi Gulf Coast, she could paint that experience in equally authentic fashion.

By now, Paul had come to learn in broad brushstrokes about Alice's background, which compelled him to make this recommendation. She was born in

New Orleans on July 19, 1875, the daughter of a former slave, Patricia Wright, and a seaman, Joseph Moore. Patricia was supposedly of Native American descent, and Joseph, likely a white Creole. Exceptionally intelligent, Alice was reared by her mother to be a high achiever and attended New Orleans public schools, where she showed a gift for academics and became popular, and after which she went on to attend Straight University, a historically black college founded by the American Missionary Association of the Congregational Church. With such solid educational grounding at a time when very few young men and women of African descent enjoyed higher education, she decided to commit her life to being an educator, on occasion working as a bookkeeper and stenographer, and to embark on a second career of writing short stories and poetry. With her embryonic literary career in mind, Paul applied a comprehensive view to his mentorship of her, showcasing his access to periodicals and identifying what in her personal background and literary oeuvre might prove most marketable.[31]

Incidentally, there were not many degrees of separation between them. In early December, Paul traveled to Chicago to serve as best man in the wedding of Richard B. Harrison, a dramatic reader whom Paul had met a few years earlier at the World's Fair. At the reception afterward Paul was surprised to learn that another poet recited a verse "dedicated to Alice Ruth Moore!" Whether true or not, Paul told this story to Alice to make a point: "Ye Gods! Is Alice Ruth Moore to be the theme of every tawny-skinned poet? The toast of every dark gallant?" The episode enabled him, if anything, to tout her amorous value: her ability to tickle any man's heart, not only his own.[32]

CHAPTER 10

Heroine of His Stories

I am sitting here with your picture before me and my heart is throbbing faster than my pen goes. I have kept your picture this long because I could not bear to part with it. It seemed to me, your other self and I was better for its presence. I am afraid that you will think I am foolish when I say that this "counterfeit presentment" of yourself has kept me from yielding to temptations. You cannot, and yet I believe you can understand my impulsive nature.

—PAUL LAURENCE DUNBAR TO ALICE RUTH MOORE
(OCTOBER 13, 1895)[1]

Within a couple of months after their initial exchange, the private correspondence between Paul and Alice took a decidedly flirtatious turn. In summer 1895 he requested to see more of her. "I should be more grateful than I can tell you, or than you could understand, if you would give me the photo you would spare for a cut," he inquired. A week later he asked again, in passing but with an inkling of brewing obsession: "I can write no more now for I am being bored to death," he began to conclude his letter. "I shall write again when circumstances are more favorable. Please send the photo immediately if it will not inconvenience you."[2]

Whereas Paul beseeched Alice for her photograph, after these requests he sought to blunt any reciprocal demand she might have for his own. "Please do not ask me for my photo or express any desire to know how I look," he pleaded quite self-consciously; "for I fear if you knew, our budding friendship which is to me as sweet as a full-blown rose, would be checked; because women so love beauty—and I do not blame them either—though, I have not that to offer them." Paul marveled at Alice's beauty, which captivated him when he first saw her picture in the Boston *Monthly Review* three months prior. In search of intimacy, he began to pry into her admirable life, to learn more about what she liked to do or what she could do. "Do you recite? Do you sing? Don't you dance divinely?" Even as he started to show his flirtatious hand, he respected its limits and encouraged her to halt him if he were proving too forward: "If I am impudent in asking these things don't hesitate to tell me so."[3]

Alice did not regard him as "impudent." Still addressing him as "Mr. Dunbar"— just as he was politely calling her "Miss Moore"—she dismissed his possible speculation that he had run her off. Since her school in New Orleans was closing for the summer and she had several time-consuming duties that distracted her, she had taken almost two weeks to reply to his previous letter. "Then I just laid me down and rested, indefinitely," she confided to him, "and to-day is actually the first day since last Sunday that I have aroused myself sufficiently to think." Only at this time did she reply to his letter, including "a little legend" about New Orleans for him to consider for publication in the *Indianapolis World*. Probably more important to him, she also enclosed what he had so desired: a photograph of herself. "But you must return it to me as soon as you have finished with it," she admonished him, "for I borrowed it from my mother and she'd take the next train for Indianapolis if you did not send it back." Coupled with this sense of humor about how much she or her kin would view unkindly his overextended possession of the photo, Alice sought to appease Paul with a promise that she would send him one that he could "truly own."

If at any time Alice could have closed the door to Paul in these early few months, now was the time. But she elected not to. In fact, she wanted to continue the exchange, to learn even more about him and his family, in the wake of his recent birthday the previous month, on June 27, when he turned twenty-three. "Many congratulations upon your birthday, and I hope you'll spend many, many more happy ones," she wrote. "The only thing was, that you did not tell me how many birthdays there had been before this one." Just around the corner, she disclosed, was her own birthday, on July 19. (She demurred on revealing that she would turn exactly three years his junior and therefore that, right now, she was still a teenager.) She also answered his questions. Yes, she did occasionally recite. Yes, she did dance. And, yes, she periodically did draw and sing in the chorus. She was delighted to clear up any misconceptions he might have had about her. "Now, if there are any more questions you want to ask, chip right in, and I'll answer every one, honor bright. That's the only way to get acquainted."[4]

———

During this summer, Paul was residing in Dayton but traveling across the Midwest reciting his poems. In Indiana, he traveled most notably to Eagle Lake for the Western Association of Writers convention; to Lakeside, for the Lakeside Summer Assembly and Camp Meeting; and to Indianapolis, where he was editing the *World*. During this time Alice was in New Orleans, with her family.

As Paul and Alice continued to write to each other, they began to reveal more and more insight about their private lives. Aside from routinely apologizing to each other for not having written a reply sooner, their letters were remarkable clues to their daily thoughts, feelings, and activities. Fleshing out these details, exposing themselves, brought them closer to each other. In the intermittent frequency of his letters he saw great humor. Only when actually settled—an infrequent leisure, given how busy he was—could he lift his pen to write: "In manner and periods of moving about, I am much like the Irishman's flea." In other words, "you see I am not idle." Still, Paul did secure enough time to thank Alice for the desired photograph. "I prized your picture very much and was decidedly pleased until I reached the qualifying clause in your letter," about her request that he return the photo quickly and to expect another at some undefined point in the future. Utterly unsatisfactory, that provision compelled him to vow that he would never be satisfied until he owned her photo.[5]

Despite his mastery of literary language, Paul fumbled for the words to express his yearning to see Alice for the first time, to be with her in person. Four months after his first letter to her, he had become more open about the challenges he faced in mind, body, and spirit, at once alluding to what may have been as obvious to her as it was to him, but also to the possibility of even greater future clarity. He confessed that he would sit down to write her "without knowing what in the world to say." There was much that he would like to say, much in his "'inner consciousness' that is struggling for expression, but they are things that do go and must continue to go unexpressed." From one vantage point, such words may be a startling admission for a writer creative, and gifted, with words; this elusiveness of language, however, testified less to his inability to find the right words than to his frustration with finding the right time to utter them. In response to the news that, at last, she was planning to send him a photographic keepsake, he could barely tame his emotions. Beneath the surface his feelings lay full of potential energy. He prayed that she would not regard him a fool, but his nature was enthusiastic and she had aroused it. He deplored having to wait until close to Thanksgiving for her picture.[6]

Still embracing the first photograph, Paul, overwhelmed by his heart, finally told Alice the truth. "While I do not wish to apologize for what I am about to write," he began his letter, "I do think it needs an explanation, that is if the spontaneity of emotion can be explained." Picture in hand, Paul for the first time midway through October 1895 admitted what he had been hesitant to say explicitly all along:

> I am sitting here with your picture before me and my heart is throbbing faster than my pen goes. I have kept your picture this long because I could not bear to part with it. It seemed to me, your other self and I was better for its presence. I am afraid that you will think I am foolish when I say that this "counterfeit presentment" of yourself has kept me from yielding to temptations. You cannot, and yet I believe you can understand my impulsive nature. But you *will* not understand when I tell you that I love you and have loved you since the first time that I saw your picture and read your story. I know it seems foolish and you will laugh perhaps, or perhaps grow angry; but I can explain in one sentence. You were the sudden realization of an ideal! Isn't there some hope for me? I wish you could read my heart. I love you. I love you. You bring out all the best that is in me. You are an inspiration to me. I am better and purer for having touched hands with you over all these miles.

Until this moment, Paul had been calling her "Miss Moore." Now, referring to her by her first name, he appointed her his muse. "Think of it, Alice—let me call you that just this time—before I had ever written to you, you were the heroine of one of my stories." He never granted the privilege to Rebekah, by the way; but he did here for Alice: "And since then you have inspired all my songs. I am afraid that up till now I have been much of the dilettante, but the hope of winning you will inspire me to greater & more earnest work." He confided that Alice had been crucial to his literary imagination; he mentioned "a friend to whom I sang [a couple of songs for Alice] the other day said: 'What has come into your life? . . . surely something has inspired you.'" Desperate measures he would consider if they enabled him to secure her love. She had told him to pray and he would—that God would give her to him. "I know that this letter is bold, untimely and perhaps presumptuous. But please don't let it offend you." He could not help it. Sometimes his heart would let his head write her a letter, but this time what he had to say could not hide his "real self" any longer. Here as well as in a subsequent letter he sent a few days later, he oscillated between genuine expressions of love and apology for speaking too freely about his true feelings, too hastily and without discernment.[7]

Alice did not object to the blatancy of Paul's utterances of desire and love, although he did infer that her response was not commensurate in private expression; in his view he was "dealt with in half so gentle, considerate or tactful a manner." He was thankful that she was kind, that she did not disregard him as a fool; but he did sense that he should be forgiven then and in the future, in case his true feelings for her were to spill out, and that he should not take for granted her authorship of a letter of reply "as sensible and kindly" as the one he now treasured.[8]

As 1895 turned into 1896—well after November, when Paul expected to receive the keepsake photograph of Alice—he could not hide his disappointment. The picture had not yet arrived. Had she broken her promise? Though he remained infatuated with her, his feelings were now mixed, with the first ostensible trace of anger she had ever encountered in their correspondence. Equivocation, or ambivalence, enabled him to manage the displeasure rhetorically. "The question with me in sitting down to write to you today, is shall I proceed to thank you for your last delightful letter," he wondered, "or to tell you how provoked I am that you have not sent me the photograph you promised. In short, shall I be agreeable or disagreeable?" Then came a warning shot: "Whatever my qualifications for the former are, I can be the latter with a vengeance. But I am unable to decide on any course so I go on writing at random." And write at random he did for the rest of his letter, penning recent observations of the weather and the house he lived in, but also behaving in a disoriented manner as he sat among the books stacked and strewn by his chair, "dreaming a thousand things," unable to "put these dreams down on paper." He could play the disciplined persona of gentleman. As time went on, his language betrayed the depth of his overwhelming love. Unbridled grew his pen.[9]

Traces of Paul's anger were not lost on Alice; he realized his own misconduct through her epistolary eyes. A couple of weeks after his "agreeable or disagreeable" letter, she sent him the photograph, which he adored, but without the endearing prelude that would suggest the emotional attachment he was hoping to see. "Your letter and photograph have been forwarded to me here and brought a great deal of pleasure to me," he admitted, "notwithstanding your peremptory 'order for a picture' and your merciless guying." Up until this point Alice stopped short of reciprocating the language of love to which he had first opened a window four months earlier. He only wished that, in her "slang vocabulary," she could find some expression for *"I can learn to love you"* and be able to convey it to him.[10]

No, Alice could not—at least not yet.

Then, Alice turned the tables on Paul: she wanted *his* picture. Now he began to drag his feet, his reluctance obvious and hypocritical: "About that picture,— oh yes—well it's coming, and coming soon, though you must wait till I have one made," he hemmed and hawed, stalling. "Do you want it with a full beard or smooth face? careless or sedate expression, with spectacles or without? please specify. But you really shall have it dear little friend and soon." Whether he could meet her demand as promptly as he wanted her to fulfill his own remained to be seen.[11]

In an instant Paul felt nothing less than the pressure of having self-consciously to produce a likeness of himself for someone over whose beauty he and his acquaintances raved. Eventually he came through. "Your peremptory demand for a picture has compelled me to make a hurried sitting (or standing) and I enclose to you the result," he relented. "Don't look at it too closely or you will find that I am standing in a crooked position." At the same time, to offset the possible implication of his unattractiveness, he gestured to a photographer of one Studio Parisienne in Dayton. Of her he spoke in a way portending his flirtatious affinity for women. "The photographer-ess is a friend of mine and we were joking and cutting up at the time. She is such a charming woman that any man would be willing to go wrong for her." Afterward, Alice thanked him with a tinge of reassurance over the quality of the photograph, of his own beauty, or of both; but she did not relieve him of his culpable tardiness in meeting her demand. "Your picture is very good and I am quite pleased with you for sending it along," she retorted, "though you *did* have to be quarreled at to get it."[12]

Paul wanted to hear more from Alice, in terms not just of the frequency of her letters but also their length. Their brevity marked what he viewed to be Alice's "abject self-sacrifice." The text was a metaphor of her personhood: he desired to see more of her—or, precisely, since they had not met yet, to read more of her writing so that he could gain a more intimate impression of her, of how much she was willing to divulge. "Don't curb your powers of expression as you have been doing; don't harness down your voluminous vocabulary;

don't bridle your careening wit—don't!" he exclaimed, before veering from formal to informal discourse and intonation. "'Some p'n might bus'!' *I want to hear from you.* I don't want a note. I want a letter and if you can't write me a letter you just try again!" Alice had pointed out that she had to "quarrel" with Paul to get his photograph, but her assertion only excited him carnally. "I am in a beastly mood tonight and want to quarrel with someone and as you are at the safest distance for the encounter, I take this opportunity of throwing my venom at you." In his playful take on human instinct, he wanted her to agree that they go out "just itching for a fracas," even though for the time being this was relegated only to their correspondence. His letters, his language, burst at the seams of epistolary decorum.

Paul's feigned antagonism was also a passive-aggressive expression of disappointment that Alice proactively refused to see him for the first time in late spring of 1896. She was moving her family from New Orleans to 55 Jerome Street in West Medford, Massachusetts, and he wondered whether she would detour through Dayton, where he was residing. Without warning, he thought aloud of this abstract possibility, yet with certain "people" in mind. "Wonder if people on their way from New Orleans to Boston couldn't pass through Dayton some way—my geography don't tell me and I thought perhaps you could," he speculated. "It would be lovely if some folks could and would so as to brighten the heart of certain other folks." Alice did not travel to Dayton; their first in-person encounter would continue to be deferred.[13]

Slowly but surely, the ice was breaking. Alice eased Paul into the company of her family. She invited him to the upcoming wedding of her sister, Leila Moore, to one James Young. For that Paul was grateful, although this time he had to decline, citing his need to stay in the Midwest—he had to return to his prior vacation spot of the summer resort in Lakeside, Ohio, and visit his half-brothers, Robert and William, in Chicago. Once again, he requested that she send him more photographs. If she went east this summer she probably would have some more photos taken; and if she did, he wanted her to send him one. "I cannot have too many of my little southern songbird," he said. Just as eagerly as he made this demand, he once again, half-jokingly, alluded to another woman who seemingly piqued his affection and reaffirmed his market value, just in case Alice neglected it. "I feel too like being kissed and so I am going to hurry through the closing lines of this letter and go to see the prettiest, sweetest, daintiest little girl who lives on Bruce Street. (There are no other pretty, dainty or sweet girls on that street, hence the superlatives.) She will kiss me, but oh how I wish it were you." Trying to goad Alice into yelling "Paul!"—as he then impersonated her scolding him—he awaited her quarrelsome rejoinder. Her subsequent taciturnity tantalized him.[14]

———

Paul's release of his second book of poems, *Majors and Minors*—copyrighted in 1895 but actually not appearing until early 1896—marked the beginning of what would become his hallmark strategy as a professional writer: in any one book, to reprint verbatim or with small revisions the texts he had previously circulated in periodicals or books. The three poems in *Majors and Minors* he first published in periodicals included "Columbian Ode" in the *Chicago Daily News*, "Curtain" in *Century Magazine*, and "The Ol' Tunes" in the *Indianapolis Journal*. The eleven poems he had already featured in *Oak and Ivy* were "A Banjo Song," "A Drowsy Day," "Columbian Ode," "Hymn," "Life," "Ode to Ethiopia," "Sunset," "The Meadow Lark," "The Ol' Tunes," "The Seeding," and "Sparrow." Plus, in contrast to *Oak and Ivy*, which included only four dialect poems out of fifty-six total, *Majors and Minors* indicated Paul's more self-conscious effort to feature more of them—six times as many—in a book of ninety-four total. In the closing section of the new book, in fact, he clustered them beneath the subtitle "Humor and Dialect."

Paul's first two books offered a glimpse into his evolving sense of how to market and distribute his dialect poems. Unapologetically, he stretched the boundaries of commercial expectations for literary originality. Reviewers scarcely caught on to his economical method of maximizing the exposure of certain poems: initial publication of an individual poem in a periodical or edited collection; its syndication; its reprint in a first book; its subsequent reprint in a second book; and, in between these moments, his multiple recitations of it in speaking engagements. For each occasion he would receive compensation, maximizing his professional earnings as much as possible for any one piece of literature.

Alice's opinion on *Majors and Minors* meant more to Paul than anyone else's, perhaps. He had already begun to open his soul to her, his literary imagination and creative process, in the individual poems and the book he had sent her way to enjoy as a friend and critic. Into one of her epistles she incorporated her analysis, and he was piqued by both its praise and its warning that, perhaps, their relationship was hurtling too quickly beyond the realm of platonic friendship into someplace too serious, if too romantic. "Your opening sentence speaks of my book as 'conquering,'" Paul wrote her, during the first few weeks of 1896; "I wish that the word meant as much in regard to you as I want it to mean." He wished that he could assuage her resistance to the progress of their relationship, but he knew she was not ready. Gently, she told him that there remained one topic "which is to be tabooed" between them. He tried to respect her wishes and maintain discretion. More and more Paul tried to insinuate his desire for her through multiple threads of their exchanges. At the very least, their conversations about literature and the profession, and particularly about her own thoughts and feelings regarding his poetry, were slowly but surely bringing them closer together.[15]

As Paul tried to impress on Alice that they both were coexisting within overlapping literary and social circles, he cited evidence of his own access to even higher echelons of literary celebrity. In late January 1896 he had "a most delightful chat" with George Washington Cable. As an expert on literary dialect, Paul knew Cable's writing well. By this time Cable was a little over fifty years old, a legendary popular writer of southern local color. Touring the country and reciting his stories, a couple of days earlier in January he had passed through Dayton, where one of Paul's friends, Charlotte Conover, introduced the two men to each other after the reading. Paul relayed to Alice his pleasure in talking to the legend. "I found him delightful—he said some very surprising and encouraging things and invited me to contribute to a new magazine which he has bought and is to edit." Beforehand, Conover had given a copy of *Majors and Minors* to Cable, who liked the book so much he invited Paul to contribute poems to *The Letter*, a periodical Cable was slated to edit. (Paul would publish "Theology" in the summer 1896 issue.) As much as Paul's letters were strategically worded to court Alice, at bottom he always was and would be a writer fascinated by the wisdom and creativity of colleagues he would come across in the profession. Preoccupations of this kind inevitably crept into his letters; self-aware, he wondered aloud if they detracted from his appeal. He feared that he was dull, but he could not help it: "my heart is so thoroughly in my work that at times I can talk of nothing else." If one of those moods possessed Paul any evening, Alice would hear little from him during that time.[16]

———

"What on earth are you writing now? Anything?"[17]

By the start of summer 1896, Paul and Alice had been writing letters to each other for close to a year. Until now they had been exchanging poetry and fiction, the byproducts of inspiration and creativity. But there were occasions when the flame of imagination went unkindled, when they struggled to put pen to paper and bring their ideas to life. For him to inquire in these terms about her creative process was not anomalous; it was yet another occasion for him to share a private side of himself. For some time now he had been "mentally stagnant," but "a couple of poems wrote themselves." The *Century* had just recently accepted another poem of his, "Discovered," for the June issue.[18]

"What am I writing now?" Alice replied. "An occasional article for the *Age*," a New York–based newspaper for African American readers to which she had been contributing. More than that, "an occasional sketch for myself, some very vile French translation, and letters, that's all." Like Paul, she was ambitious and preoccupied with whether she was productively using whatever spare time she possessed. She fretted that she was wasting time, opportunity, everything else. The perception of "how hopelessly, helplessly lazy" she was made her "weep." She was hyperbolic in conveying to him how her lack of discipline had as much to do with the restlessness of her body as with the distractions of her mind: "I'll commit suicide for very despair some of these days if I don't find myself improving in the manner of work. It's not mental stagnation with me, it's simple physical disability to sit long enough at my desk to write anything more lengthy than a letter." Despite the unhappiness, that she was willing to pen letters to him on a regular basis implied the equivalent worth between her desire to communicate with him and her desperation to write literature. Even if she were not willing yet to enunciate that their bond was more than platonic, at least it grew stronger with each letter.[19]

The letters came to represent developmental stages of Paul and Alice's friendship. As with her inability to sit for long periods at her desk to write anything lengthier than a letter, both grew increasingly conscious of how meaningful their private correspondence had become, of how epistolary letters and *belles lettres* could intersect in space and time. In late summer he realized his state of affairs, which forced him to apologize to her. "My table is littered with papers and pens, and photographs. There are some late magazines, some good books, a box of excellent cigars a soothing drink at hand and a sea-breeze in my face,—what more could a man ask!" The life of pleasure came at a price. The thought startled him that he had not yet answered her last letter. Seeking forgiveness, he regretted that he could not write a line even to the friends he revered most deeply. By this time, Paul and Alice had expected to see each other's letters in the mail at least twice a month, if not more. Anything less frequent prompted each henceforth to apologize for failing to read or reply to the other's letter quickly enough. To the apology he would add a layer of flattery: she had become one of the friends he most revered.[20]

Paul at times exploited this insecurity to open, yet again, an intentionally exacting conversation on the nature of their relationship, given his deep-seated love. After an apology for failing to reply sooner, he counteracted with even more flattery Alice's doubtful allegation that his remorse was overstated. "So you are in doubt as to whether I owe you a letter or not," he started, "well, you just remain in that delectable state for I am sure I shall not enlighten you." He put on the table the platonic threshold of friendship; he toyed with the prospect of how close their relationship was to it. "You might care enough for me even platonically to keep trace of my letters. But I pardon you everything. How could I do otherwise when you write so charmingly to ask it?"[21]

CHAPTER 11

A True Singer

A true singer of the people, white or black, it makes no difference, has been found.

—*NEW YORK TIMES* ADVERTISING BLURB FOR PAUL LAURENCE
DUNBAR'S *LYRICS OF LOWLY LIFE* (1896)[1]

Early on in their relationship, Paul was quite open with Alice about the issue of race. In April 1895, in one of their earliest exchanges, he stated that he was regularly producing three to four short stories a month for the *Chicago News Record*—stories dating back to the June 1892 issues that featured the poems "The Old Fashioned Way" (a reprint, with a different title, of "The Ol' Tunes," published in *Indianapolis Journal* earlier in the summer) and "A Summer Pastoral." He remarked that he was hopeful not only for himself but also for "the future of our race in literature," presuming that they shared at least this view on the same racial and political side of the color line. (He once hailed Alice "one fair American Girl," but their shared sense of racial belonging was rarely in question.) He did not want to presume too much, however, but rather to learn her ideas on literature and dialect, on their ancestral American writers of race in literature—the main issues he was grappling with as poet and performer alike.

To this end Paul articulated the conundrum he, as a modern American writer of African descent, faced: did he have an obligation to recover the folklore that he and his fellow "Afro-American" authors had heard as children and adults and that had been, fairly or not, invigorating the commercial success of past and present white writers? He posed the issue to Alice:

I want to know whether or not you believe in preserving by Afro-American—I don't like the word—writers those quaint old tales and songs of our fathers which have made the fame of Joel Chandler Harris, Thomas Nelson Page, Ruth McEnery Stuart and others! Or whether you like so many others think we should ignore the past and all its capital literary materials.[2]

Alice answered with a series of philosophical agreements. Paul had long been concerned with readers and audiences not realizing the literary sophistication of his use of dialect. Similarly, she believed that no one should be prohibited from writing in dialect if one so wanted, for creative purposes. "Well, I frankly believe in everyone following his bent," she said. "If it be so that one has a special aptitude for dialect work, why it is only right that dialect work should be made a specialty." Yet Alice took her opinion even further. Paul had been worried that, due to his African ancestry, he was being pigeonholed into writing and reciting dialect; the complexity of this literary tongue was being reduced to mainstream racial stereotypes against his will. She condemned this media maltreatment. "I don't see the necessity of cramming and forcing oneself into that plane because one is a Negro or a Southerner."[3]

Finally, Paul had long held the opinion that recalled his own words from the defunct *Dayton Tattler* of 1890: that publications should "give us a variety and cease feeding your weary readers on an unbroken diet of the race problem." Likewise, Alice objected to the preconception that African American literature had to bear not only the form of supposedly ethnic or racial dialect but also the content of racial politics. "Now as to getting away from one's race—well, I haven't much liking for those writers that wedge the Negro problem and social equality and long dissertation on the Negro in general into their stories. It is too much like a quinine pill in jelly. I hope I'm not treading on your corns."[4]

Alice then stated a literary philosophy that Paul likewise had held dear: "Somehow when I start a story I always think of my folk characters as simple human beings, not as types or a race or an idea." Paul's curiosity over her spunk was palpable. In reply, he borrowed her own humorous, though presumptuous, metaphorical language about his toilsome feet: "No dear Miss Moore, you did not tread on my corns in expressing your opinion on Negro Literature," he assured her. "I too believe that a story is a story and try to make my characters 'real live people.' But I believe that characters in fiction should be what men and women are in real life,—the embodiment of principle or idea." Paul and Alice embraced a common language about the role and goals of the African American writer and about the nature and meaning of race in literature. To this shared decree he would periodically adhere in his subsequent writings of poetry and fiction.[5]

From this point onward, Paul was quite comfortable talking with Alice about what it meant to be the rare, celebrated "colored" man in the largely white world of American letters. In summer 1895, for example, he wrote her from Eagle Lake, Indiana, where he was attending the meeting of the Western Association of Writers. He was asked to discourse on the topic "One Point in the Ethics of the Short Story Writing" and to read from an unpublished story of his, "The Luck of Lazy Lang." Upon arrival he recognized the meeting's racial exclusivity but was not dismayed. Instead, he enjoyed the privilege of being embraced by colleagues with interests as eclectic as his own: "although I am the only colored member, I am not allowed to feel it. It is boating, fishing, music, poetry and general literature in pleasantly varied layers." By now he had grown accustomed to standing as the lone colored man on the mainstream stage of American letters. In this setting, despite and because of this fate, he had learned how to thrive.[6]

Just as Paul could confide in Alice his solitary experience in the white world, he could share with her his resentment toward the doctrine of racial uplift. His first letter to her disavowed "Afro-American" with the curt phrase "I don't like the word." Later he elaborated his rejection of the term, but twice, parenthetically, reiterating the venom he held for it. Indeed, from May until August 1895 he edited the *Indianapolis World*, a minor newspaper serving a mostly African American readership; but unlike his *Dayton Tattler*, which served a similar readership but intended to avoid overstating stories of racial politics and black folklore, the *World* represented a brand that published no shortage of them. "I am a good deal disgusted with my little taste of *Afro-American* (I hate the word) Journalism," he said. "(I hate the word Afro-American; it is a barbaric and clumsy affectation.)"

What irked Paul was not so much the hyphenation's implicit nod that the African descendant in the United States was becoming modern. More cynically, the term "Afro-American" signaled a pretentious celebration of racial and national selves that did more to hail the African descendant's difference from being an American rather than affirming an identity with it. He was not sure he wanted to buy into a word that distinguished him as part of a self-conscious class of New Negroes quite removed from benighted slaves or their undereducated children. "But it is heavy and highsounding and sonorous," he complained, "so your educated Negro who by the way loves show, loves the word and rolls it as a sweet morsel over his tongue."[7]

Paul found in Alice a person to whom he could disclose how much he was wrestling with the images of himself both in the mirror and in the public, both as a writer in search of an independent voice and as an intellectual overcome by the collective voice of his "Afro-American" community. However, even as he contested the assumptions of that community, instincts cultivated from childhood to manhood told him that he felt a responsibility to recover his folkloric past, a topic that attracted Paul and Alice to each other.

Time and again during the courtship, Paul returned to folklore as a touchstone of his budding companionship with Alice. He would gesture to her heritage in New Orleans and her "commendable" effort in her "determination to contest Cable for his laurels," for his designation as the preeminent Louisiana local-color writer. But Paul also regarded her the "interpreter" of not so much the "*New* Orleans" but the "*old* Orleans." "I long to see the old town, to roam about its streets, to plant foot in its historic places and to see some of the old creole houses, if any now remain," he said. A sense of obligation to an authentic, folkloric past united how they imagined the world and why they wrote literature. And for this reason—not only the fact that both were widely read—they regularly chatted about a core set of American writers of folklore, to the extent that they could talk quite good-naturedly about being "Joel Chandler Harrised, so Geo. W. Cabled, so Frank L. Stantoned," in creative inspiration.[8]

———

The issue of *Harper's Weekly* released on June 27, 1896, was historic for Paul because it was historic for the magazine itself. A photograph of William McKinley of Ohio, Republican candidate for president of the United States, appeared on the issue's cover after the magazine had endorsed him in the wake of the Republican National Convention, held in St. Louis, Missouri, from June 16 to June 18. All the articles on the convention were frontloaded, focusing on the virtues of McKinley and his running mate—the vice presidential nominee Garret A. Hobart of New Jersey—as well as on the "sound-money victory," an equally compelling storyline about the successful Republican promotion of the gold standard for the country's monetary system. The perfect electoral storm conspired to attract more readers to a single issue of *Harper's Weekly* than probably ever before. The staple column inside, "Life and Letters," in which the so-called dean of American letters reviewed Paul's second book, *Majors and Minors*, happened to introduce the Dayton poet to his largest ever readership.[9]

THE REPUBLICAN NATIONAL CONVENTION, ST. LOUIS.

HARPER'S WEEKLY

JOURNAL OF CIVILIZATION

Vol. XL.—No. 2062.
Copyright, 1896, by Harper & Brothers.
All Rights Reserved.

NEW YORK, SATURDAY, JUNE 27, 1896.

TEN CENTS A COPY.
FOUR DOLLARS A YEAR.

WILLIAM McKINLEY, REPUBLICAN CANDIDATE FOR PRESIDENT.

ENGRAVED BY E. SCHLADITZ FROM A COPYRIGHTED PHOTOGRAPH BY COURTNEY, CANTON, OHIO, APRIL, 1896.—[SEE PAGE 628.]

FIG. 11.1. *Harper's Weekly*, June 27, 1896. The issue featured coverage of the St. Louis Republican National Convention and William Dean Howells's review of Paul Laurence Dunbar's *Majors and Minors*.

Born in Martinsville, Ohio, on March 1, 1837, that reviewer, William Dean Howells, was the second of eight children. His father, William Cooper Howells, was a dedicated Free-Soiler who printed Ohio newspapers and edited the *Hamilton (Ohio) Intelligencer*. After he quit this paper, the family moved to Eureka Mills, an experimental self-sufficient commune. William was thirteen at this time and had just suffered from a bout of cholera. Within a year he followed in his father's footsteps and started working full-time as a printer, but he also immersed himself in reading and writing literature. He once had aspired to be a poet; yet he also understood, given his father's profession, that literature was both a business and an art. By 1852, his father had secretly published one of William's poems in the *Ohio State Journal*. A literary career was launched, even as, over the next couple of years, William struggled with ill health, including hypochondria.

Howells began to make a name for himself through the regular writing of columns, reviews, poems, and stories; through the publication of his biography of Abraham Lincoln; and through the expansion of his literary circle to include such luminaries as Ralph Waldo Emerson, Henry Thoreau, and Nathaniel Hawthorne. Howells met his future wife, Elinor Mead, in 1860; they were married at the American embassy in Paris two years later. Upon their return to America, Howells continued to ply his trade: at the *Atlantic Monthly* he ascended the professional ranks, as assistant editor from 1866 to 1871 and then as editor from 1871 to 1881; he became a writer of columns such as "Editor's Study" from 1886 to 1892 and "Life and Letters" starting in 1895. These roles cemented his notoriety as the dean of American letters, a nickname he embraced not merely because it punned on his middle name. The renowned literary historian Van Wyck Brooks would later remark that "Howells was perhaps the only critic in the history of American literature who has been able to create reputations by a single review."[10]

Howells's sensitivity to social politics, not only literary aesthetics, opened his eyes to the travails of America. Two decades after the Civil War, he was roiled by circumstances ranging from the possibilities of socialism, inspiring him to edit for a brief period *Cosmopolitan* magazine with socialist entrepreneur John Brisben Walker; to the May 4, 1886, bombing and shooting of labor activists (who were protesting for an eight-hour workday and against police violence) at Haymarket Square in Chicago, which incited him to pen a public letter demanding clemency for the convicted anarchists and to envision analogous incidents in *A Hazard of Good Fortunes*, which he published in 1889. By the century's last decade, Howells's most famous works were the novels

FIG. 11.2. William Dean Howells, circa 1900. (William Dean Howells Collection, Ohio History Connection)

A Modern Instance (1882); *The Rise of Silas Lapham* (1885); *A Hazard of Good Fortunes*; and *An Imperative Duty*, released in 1891, the same year he published *Criticism and Fiction*, a classic treatise on the genealogy of realism in Western literature.

With this storied background, no wonder Howells held career-long relationships with American writers such as Mark Twain, Henry James, Stephen

Crane, Frank Norris, and, of African descent, Charles W. Chesnutt. Now it was Paul's turn to grasp that the "effect" he "felt" was his induction into a sacred society, touched by the dean. The wide circulation of the Republican Convention issue of *Harper's Weekly* enabled Howells to reach readers beyond the regular audience of his columns or the magazine in general. Undoubtedly, these conditions put Howells in the best position to sway the expectations of readers about Paul and his poetry, amplifying his voice even beyond his current influence as a critic who enjoyed one of the loudest media microphones.[11]

To lure the readers into his column, Howells invited them to imagine when he first laid hands on Paul's book. In the early summer in Toledo, Ohio, James A. Herne, an American actor and playwright, had been directing and performing *Shore Acres*, a three-act play that had been running for four years. The play centered on the conflict between two brothers, both New England farmers, whose differing personalities—one generous and humble, the other selfish and stubborn—led them toward the deviating paths of economic success or ruin. While he was staying at a hotel, the clerk told him that someone had left a gift for him: *Majors and Minors*, by Paul Laurence Dunbar. Herne read the book and found the poems "wonderful." Coincidentally, he happened to have been well acquainted with one William Howells. So the story went that a preeminent dramatist had sent along a prodigious poet's new book to the most influential literary critic in the country.

Behind the scenes, Paul had played a crucial role in the events turning out this very way. He had just seen and enjoyed *Shore Acres* and proceeded to track Herne down at his local hotel. Although Herne did not reply to Paul while *Shore Acres* was playing in Toledo, he did do so later, when it was running in Detroit. "While at Toledo a copy of your poems was left at my hotel by a Mr. Childs," Herne wrote, in reference to the clerk; "I tried very hard to find Mr. Childs to learn more of you. Your poems are wonderful. I shall acquaint William Dean Howells and other literary people with them. They are new to me and may be new to them." True to his word, Herne passed *Majors and Minors* on to Howells, who decided to review it in *Harper's Weekly*.[12]

As *Majors and Minors* approached publication, Paul had already released about twenty poems in individual periodicals, mostly in the *Indianapolis Journal*, Chicago newspapers, and *Century Magazine*. For his second book, he compiled his oeuvre of original and reprinted poems into the most coherent and compelling example of his literary talents. Still, his book was "new" to both Herne and Howells not because it resonated with the genres of British

Romantic and American local-color poetry. Given Herne's familiarity with American literature and Howells's specialty in classic and contemporary Western literature alike, Paul's dexterity in this area did not excite their aesthetic imagination. Rather, the frontispiece of *Majors and Minors* made the book seem new: an image of Paul, at age eighteen, peering back at the reader. So compelling did Howells regard the image that, for the benefit of his readers, he described it in great detail, illustrating Paul's phenotype and physiognomy: "the face of a young negro, with the race traits strangely accented: the black skin, the woolly hair, the thick outrolling lips and the mild, soft eyes of the pure African type." Howells alienated Paul. Someone like Howells, a white man, "cannot be very sure, ever, about the age of those people," of the darker-skinned races of the world; and he knew that this poet, during slavery, "would have been worth, apart from his literary gift, twelve or fifteen hundred dollars, under the hammer." Only after reading the book did Howells perceive Paul in a special light: the text arrived at a time when Paul's "race has not hitherto made its mark in art."[13]

The section "Humor and Dialect" most attracted Howells. Folk humor and dialect, he implied, defined the entertainment of African American culture and proved most aesthetically pleasing—and realistic—on the literary page. This was not the realism of the largely white and middle-class Anglo-American novelists such as Howells himself alongside Henry James, Stephen Crane, and Edith Wharton, his contemporary acquaintances. Rather, the realism of *Majors and Minors* was more analogous to that in the works of African American and Jewish American writers—groups of ethnic minorities who held a precarious place in the canon of American literature. For Dunbar and the likes of Chesnutt and of Abraham Cahan, a Jewish American whom Howells also knew, only when their stories illustrated scenes—or, in the case of poetry, when their verses also conveyed songs—that conjured memories or visions of authentic folklore did they achieve realism. American writers faced different commercial expectations depending on which side of the color line the public perceived they stood. Where Paul stood was unquestionable, thanks in part to his image in *Majors and Minors*. His purported racial purity authenticated his dialect writing in ways inapplicable to lighter-skinned African American authors of ostensibly mixed racial ancestry.[14]

The pitfall to Howells's acclaim was its turn to the mythical caricatures of minstrelsy to describe Paul's phenotype and physiognomy, the language of which seeped into his assessment of the poetry: "Majors and Minors," the first and largest section of the book, was the moment when Paul was "least himself," or when he was least the "pure African type." Playing up the dialect's racial

FIG. 11.3. Frontispiece of *Majors and Minors* (1895). (Paul Laurence Dunbar Collection, Ohio History Connection)

authenticity while playing down its local-color, regional character, Howells lauded Paul's racial and regional sensitivity: "He calls his little book Majors and Minors; the majors being in our American English, and the Minors being in dialect, the dialect the middle-south negroes and the middle-south whites; for the poet's ear has been quick for the accent of his neighbors as well as for that of his kindred." This praise belied how quickly Howells sought to make the dialect a racial hallmark rather than a regional one, to regard Paul as more African than American, to dismiss as more anomalous than the norm his formal English poems in the section "Majors and Minors."[15]

To underscore the link of the poem's racial authenticity to the poet's racial purity, Howells created an analogy between Paul and Robert Burns, the late eighteenth-century Scottish poet. Like Paul an autodidact, Burns had achieved a literary command of dialect from his childhood engagement with orally transmitted folk songs and folktales; and with his 1786 publication of *Poems, Chiefly in the Scottish Dialect*, he cemented his stature as the premier Scottish dialect and realist poet of his country in the late eighteenth century. One should read "Burns when he was most Burns, when he was most Scotch, when he was most peasant," Howells believed, just as one should read Paul because he was "the first man of his color to study his race objectively, to analyze it to himself, and then to represent it in art as he felt it to be: to represent it humorously, yet tenderly, and above all so faithfully that we know the portrait to be undeniably like."[16]

Best exemplifying such poetry in *Majors and Minors* were those poems that Howells laboriously transcribed—and, through ellipses, abbreviated— himself in the review. The first was "Conscience and Remorse," in which he found "the proofs of honest thinking and true feeling," "the record of experience, whose genuineness the reader can test by his own":

"Goodbye," I said to my conscience—
    "Goodbye for aye and aye,"
And I put her hands off harshly,
    And turned my face away,
And conscience smitten sorely
    Returned not from that day.

But a time came when my spirit
    Grew weary of its pace;
And I cried: "Come back, my conscience,
    I long to see thy face."
But conscience cried: "I cannot,
    Remorse sits in my place."

There was "The Party" (mistitled by Howells as "The Pahty"), about a party attended by African Americans from local plantations, which "will perhaps suffice to show what vistas into the simple, sensuous, joyous nature of [the black] race Mr. Dunbar's work opens." The poem began:

Dey had a gread big pahty down to Tom's de othah night;
Was I dah? You bet! I nevah in my life see sich a sight;
All de folks f'om fou' plantations was invited, an' dey come,
Dey come troopin' thick ez chillun when dey heahs a fife an' drum.

Evahbody dressed dere fines'—Heish yo' mouf an' git away,
Ain't seen no sich fancy dressin' sence las' quah'tly meetin' day;
Gals all dressed in silks an' satins, not a wrinkle ner a crease,
Eyes a-battin' teeth a-shinin' haih breshed back ez slick ez grease;
Sku'ts all tucked an' puffed an' ruffled, evah blessed seam an' stitch;
Ef you'd seen 'em wif deir mustus, couldn't swahed to which was which.

"When de Co'n Pone's Hot" was the next poem Howells included, on the blessing of freshly cooked cornbread, and resonant with a "rich, humorous sense," "without excluding a fond sympathy." Its first stanza read:

Dey is times in life when Nature
    Seems to slip a cog an' go,
Jes' a-rattlin' down creation,
    Lak an ocean's overflow;
When de worl' jes' stahts a-spinnin'
    Lak a picaninny's top,
An' yo' cup o' joy is brimmin'
    'Twell it seems about to slop,
An' you feel jes' lak a racah,
    Dat is trainin' fu' to trot
When yo' mammy says de blessin'
    An' de co'n pone's hot.

Howells then exhibited "When Malindy Sings," regarding one woman's overwhelming vocal talent, a poem "purely and intensely black . . . in its feeling." The poem began:

G'way an' quit dat noise, Miss Lucy—
    Put dat music book away;
What's de use to keep on tryin'?
    Ef you practice twell you're gray,
You cain't sta't no notes a-flyin'
    Lak de ones dat rants an' rings
F'om de kitchen to de big woods
    When Malindy sings. . . .

Ain't you nevah heerd Malindy?
    Blessed soul, take up de cross!
Look heah, ain't you jokin' honey?

Well, you don't know whut you los'.
Y'ought to heah dat gal a-wa'blin',
Robins, la'ks, an' all dem things,
Heish dey moufs an' hides dey faces
When Malindy sings.

The concluding poem, which was not as long as the entirety of the previous two, was "Accountability," about the significance of human individuality and destiny, a "black piece" of "fine irony and neat satire":

Folks ain't got no right to censuah othah folks about dey habits;
Him dat giv' de squir'ls de bushtails made de bobtails fu' de rabbits.
Him dat built de gread big mountains hollered out de little valleys,
Him dat made de streets an' driveways was n't shamed to make
de alleys.

We is all constructed diff'ent, d'ain't no two of us de same;
We cain't he'p ouah likes an' dislikes, ef we'se bad we ain't to blame.
Ef we'se good, we need n't show off, case you bet it ain't ouah doin'
We gits into su'ttain channels dat we jes' cain't he'p pu'suin'.

But we all fits into places dat no othah ones could fill,
An' we does the things we has to, big er little, good er ill.
John cain't tek de place o' Henry, Su an' Sally ain't alike;
Bass ain't nuthin' like a suckah, chub ain't nuthin' like a pike.

W'en you come to t'ink about it, how it's all planned out it's splendid.
Nothin's done er evah happens, 'dout hit's somefin' dat's intended;
Don't keer whut you does, you has to, an' hit sholy beats de dickens,—
Viney, go put on de kittle, I got one o' mastah's chickens.

The transcription of these poems, whose nearly 1,400 words constitute about half of the text typed for the review, proved Howells's dedication to showcasing for readers as much of Paul's poetry as the space of his column "Life and Letters" permitted. (Howells also mentions, but does not transcribe, another poem, "The Deserted Plantation," a postbellum account of abandoned slave territory.)

In the end, *Majors and Minors* validated Howells's hyperbolic claims about the canonical adolescence of African American literature. Howells unwittingly echoed W. H. A. Moore's essay in the July 5, 1890, issue of *New York Age*. Lamenting "the void in our literature," Moore wondered whether a poet would yet emerge to represent "an indication of the character" or "the capacity of a people" of African descent in the West. The black race, he regretted, "has not given to English literature a great poet. No one of his kind has, up to this day, lent influence to the literature of his time, save Phillis Wheatley." Moore expressed the hope that "every fragment, every whispering of his benighted muse [would be] scanned with eager and curious interest in the hope that there may be found the gathered breathings of a true singer."[17]

Six years after Moore wrote these words, Howells proclaimed that Paul emerged as the "true singer" that the world had been looking for. Howells declared that, before *Majors and Minors*, the African "race has not hitherto made its mark in his art." He—and Moore, for that matter—neglected to mention that, in both America and abroad, several writers of African descent were already notable, albeit not regularly mentioned in the mainstream press: Phillis Wheatley and George Moses Horton at the turn of the nineteenth century; William Wells Brown and Frederick Douglass in the mid-nineteenth century; Albery Allson Whitman, James M. Whitfield, Chesnutt, and Frances Ellen Watkins Harper in the latter part of the century; and, regarding those abroad, France's Alexandre Dumas (*père* and *fils*) and Russia's Aleksander Pushkin of the early nineteenth century. Wheatley, Horton, Whitman, Whitfield, and Harper published volumes of poetry; African American contemporaries such as James Edwin Campbell, Daniel Webster Davis, and J. Mord Allen wrote the kind of dialect poems appearing in the "Humor and Dialect" section of *Majors and Minors*. None of these writers had reached the esteem worthy of Howells's recognition. The de facto stature Paul had attained came from Howells's blessing.[18]

Praise from the dean of American letters could only be a boon to a literary career, especially, in Paul's case, the career of a poet whom audiences and readers applauded as much for his racial accomplishment as for his creativity. Joseph Seamon Cotter Sr., prized as the first great Kentucky-born African American poet and playwright, wrote Paul in early July, right after the media excitement, with advice. "Mr. W. D. Howells has done you a great and just favor," Cotter noted. "Profit by it." Paul's proximity in the magazine to Ohio governor and Republican nominee McKinley did not go unnoticed for its financial potential. "You and Gov. McKinley are close together in *Harper's*. Do you see the point?" Cotter asked. "If he is made President, get your friends to speak for you. It may bring you a position in Washington worth $1000 or $1200 a year." Cotter wondered, then, if Paul could identify a mainstream publisher, such as one in New York, for his next book. "By all means, arrange and give some readings in New England," he advised. Time was of the essence. "If Howells hears you read he will say some things that will mean thousands in your pocket. Don't wait for an invitation. Go to New York and be your own manager." The current hurdle Paul faced was his relative obscurity. Counterbalancing Howells's praise in his essay was the admission that Cotter inferred: "Howells in his article says you are unknown to him."[19]

Merely a few days after reading Cotter's letter, Paul reached out to Howells. Paul admired the elder statesman of literary criticism. Yet Paul recognized that he had to write a letter similar to his previous correspondence, in 1892, with such patrons as James Newton Matthews. Then and now, Paul strategically embraced an older white man who praised his poetry but also turned out to be the foremost member of the literati. "I have seen your article in *Harper's* and felt its effect," Paul began. "That I have not written you sooner is neither the result of willful neglect or lack of gratitude. It has taken time for me to recover from the shock of delightful surprise." At times Paul's flattery verged on excessive, such as when he disclosed that his emotions had been too much for him to bear. "I could not thank you without 'gushing' and I did not want to 'gush.'" Still, Paul wanted to grab Howells's attention at least to convey, not without Cotter's prodding, that he understood how much his life would be altered hereafter.

In his letter to Howells, Paul conceded his minuscule status in the literary world. "You yourself do not know what you have done for me. I feel much as a poor, insignificant, helpless boy would feel to suddenly find himself knighted. I can tell you nothing about myself because there is nothing to tell. My whole life has been simple, obscure and uneventful. I have written my little pieces and sometimes recited them, but it seemed hardly by my volition." That Paul, in his mind, had potentially ascended to literary royalty scared him in two ways: first, he must be even more "careful," more rigorous, in artistry and intellection while writing his poems; second, and above all, Howells may have been more patronizing than just. Paul thanked Howells for his "more than kindness," as well as Herne, who passed along his complimentary copy of *Majors and Minors*.[20]

Within the next month Paul further followed Cotter's advice and sought a publisher in New York City. In the late summer he traveled there, enjoying the environs, arranging recitations of his poems, and spending time with Paul Shivell, a fellow Dayton poet. (He also wished to spend time with Ernest Blumenschein, a friend from high school who was now a magazine illustrator, but he was not around.) He successfully sought out and obtained the services of

FIG. 11.4. Paul with Brand Whitlock, mayor of Toledo, Ohio, outside the home of Major James Pond, Paul's literary agent, in 1896. (Paul Laurence Dunbar Collection, Ohio History Connection)

James Burton Pond. A former Union Army officer and winner of the Medal of Honor, earning him the moniker "Major," Pond was quite well known for being the literary agent of Mark Twain and social reformer and speaker Henry Ward Beecher, the brother of famed novelist Harriet Beecher Stowe. He had heard Paul recite poems for the Lyceum Theatre Lecture Bureau on the afternoon of Tuesday, September 8, 1896, in New York City, and the performance convinced him to take the young man on as a client.[21]

Word spread that Paul and Major Pond had united forces. A little more than a month after the *Harper's Weekly* review, Howells wrote to Ripley Hitchcock, D. Appleton & Company's literary editor and adviser, that "Major Pond is going to platform young Dunbar next winter, and I believe a book of entirely *black* verse from him would succeed." Patting himself on the shoulder, Howells concluded, regarding his *Harper's* review: "My notice raised such interest."[22]

Despite the racial pigeonholing of his poetry, Paul was proud to affiliate with Major Pond. (A letter from Paul to Alice in late 1896 even appeared on

Major Pond's office stationery.) With an agent in his employ, around that time he dispatched a new letter across town to Howells at his home in Far Rockaway, Long Island. For his generosity he thanked him again but remained ever self-deprecating, afraid that his notoriety of late would liken his life story to Aesop's sixth-century fable "The Ass in the Lion's Skin." Paul was comfortable revealing some of himself to Howells, as he was to other confidants in his family, that his physical health tended to fluctuate. He had borrowed Howells's coat (during an engagement in New York City, arranged by Major Pond) and returned it to him, at his home across town, in Far Rockaway. Paul contracted a cold; he hoped that Howells was more fortunate and that his note would find him and his family well.[23]

A couple of days after Paul wrote his letter, Howells replied. Touched by Paul's goodwill, he thanked the poet for returning the coat "safely and promptly." Then his words took a compassionate turn: "I am very sorry to learn that it did not save you from taking cold." Howells and his family delighted in Paul's infectious personality and talent in New York City. "May it cover, hereafter, as good and gifted a man as when you wore it," Howells said; he also reiterated that he would root for Paul, to observe his "fortunes with the cordial interest of friends."[24]

By the fall season, Paul and Howells had developed more than a merely courteous or collegial relationship; it was, at least ostensibly, one of mutual admiration. In age, race, and profession they differed; on the date of the *Harper's* review, which also happened to be Paul's birthday, the black poet turned twenty-four, while the white critic had just turned fifty-nine a few months before. But their backgrounds were not any more antithetical than was Paul's from the backgrounds of his past white patrons. The lives of Paul and Howells were united by the groundbreaking *Harper's* review of *Majors and Minors,* and by their common pursuit and recognition of literary excellence, whether as an artist or a critic.

Over the course of their epistolary exchanges their bond grew. Writing from Dayton in September 1896, Paul wrote Howells to reiterate his appreciation of their first meeting face-to-face. He had retained many pleasant memories of New York and the kindness he received there. "There are many people whom I have to thank for favors shown and none more than yourself," Paul told Howells. Opportunities to collaborate now were in store.[25]

When Paul contacted Howells at this time, he realized the commercial promise of the introduction. "Not the least source of my gratitude, by any means, is your excellent introduction to my new book," he said. "It was no little thing for you to introduce a book of verse by an obscure black writer and I believe that I fully appreciate the nobility of your act." He reiterated the power that Howells's words had had over his life and reaffirmed the truth behind his stardom. His affairs had materially changed for the better, entirely through Howells's "agency," or perhaps through the newfound professional connections he now had to the likes of Major Pond. More accurately, he was alluding to the "nobility" of Howells's "act," to his generous willingness to extol a son of former slaves.[26]

In more private conversations, however, Paul condemned Howells's perception that race conditioned the excellence of literature. In a slight—among several to recur across his letters—Paul wrote Alice in September that he was on the verge of answering a letter from Howells when the arrival of hers distracted him. Gladdened, he made an admission: "after reading your words Howells and all his tribe were forgotten." This reference, whether to whites or esteemed critics, suggested that, either racially or professionally, their "tribe" was a group to which he did not belong. In her warmth he took refuge. "I immediately changed my paper and opened this note to you."[27]

Despite Paul's reservations over what the newfound acclaim connoted, he benefited from the advocacy of Howells, a distinguished man who genuinely worked in ways seen and unseen to circulate the name of Paul Laurence Dunbar. In early 1897, when Howells was one month from his sixtieth birthday, he deemed Paul, albeit only in his mid-twenties, his "friend." Howells admired Paul's talent and demonstrated humility to want to help him. "Allow me to present my friend, Mr. Paul Dunbar, the first of his race to put his race into poetry," Howells wrote in a letter to David Douglas, his publisher in Edinburgh, Scotland. "I hope he will show you his book, and let it say for his worth the things that he is too modest to say for himself."[28]

Like a pass to secret society, Paul agreed to follow Howells's instruction and hand-deliver his letter to Douglas in the United Kingdom, where Major Pond also advised the young man to tour and build his reputation. Paul thus arranged an itinerary to begin next year, on February 6, 1897, when he could depart from New York City.

———

Regularly, Paul enclosed in letters to his mother whatever bits of money he earned and could afford to pass on. He usually combined news of his rise in prominence with the money he could share with her. As the year 1896 proceeded with highlights of his critical acclaim and professional milestones, he delighted over his success and his increasing commercial demand. "The very wealthy people are very much interested in me and are willing to pay fifty cents admission," he wrote. He was not "very flush" yet, but he enclosed two dollars to help her out. A day after writing this letter, he wrote another, relishing even more his financial boon, this time with the republication of *Majors and Minors*. He was to receive two hundred dollars immediately and a royalty of 15 percent on the first ten thousand copies. "How is this for high?" he boasted.[29]

Financial aspiration and social ambition were constant, overlapping story-lines in Paul's letters to Matilda. In a fall 1896 visit to Washington, D.C., he marveled at African American high society. He was honored to mingle among its members; how they embraced him was unlike anything he had ever experienced in his hometown. "The people have proved very hospitable here," he told Matilda, "and I have had the good fortune to fall in with the very cream. You can't imagine how they seem to appreciate me here. It is so different from Dayton."

Aside from spending time (without Alice's knowledge, of course) with "dear Rebekah" Baldwin (so "divine," in his eyes) and the widow and son of the late Frederick Douglass (Helen Pitts and Lewis Douglass), Paul's professional career seemed headed in the right direction. Major Pond had scheduled to "work for" him once the presidential election of 1896 concluded. Even his trip to Washington, D.C., signaled his rising celebrity. "I especially enjoyed the scenery thro' Virginia as I could look out on it from a luxurious coach all the way and did not once have to take a 'Jim Crow' car," he wrote his mother in fall 1896.[30]

Paul wrote this mere months after the landmark case *Plessy v. Ferguson* was settled by the Supreme Court of the United States. About half a decade earlier, in 1890, the New Orleans Comité des Citoyens persuaded a local African American citizen, Homer Plessy, to act as a test case to challenge a newly created law that segregated the public spaces of train cars by race. Though born both a free man and an "octoroon" (putatively having only one-eighth African ancestry, or having white ancestors except for one African-descended great-grandparent), Louisiana law required that he sit in the "colored" railway cars. In June 1892, to test the legality of racial segregation, Plessy purchased a first-class train ticket and boarded a whites-only car. The train company had been informed in advance of both Plessy's racial background and his intent to challenge the law. He was asked to leave and arrested when he refused to do so. During his state trial, his lawyers argued that the separate-car law was in violation of both the Thirteenth and Fourteenth Amendments, but the judge ruled in favor of the state's right to segregate by race.

Over time the case underwent judicial review and ultimately was considered by the U.S. Supreme Court in April 1896. Before the highest court, prominent African American writer Albion W. Tourgée both submitted a brief and provided oral testimony on Plessy's behalf, arguing that the law of separate cars automatically implied the inferiority of blacks to whites. An overwhelming majority of justices (seven out of nine) nonetheless ruled that "separate but equal" public facilities were constitutional, and racial segregation, therefore, was legal.

For a literary artist on the rise like Paul, despite his obvious African ancestry, Jim Crow was becoming an increasingly abstract, if not alien, concept. He was entering a chapter of remarkable privilege in his life. Most men who shared his dark skin color, but were not as celebrated, were consigned for the next half-century to the plight of interstate travel in which their racial inferiority was both official and public. Paul's fortune was not trivial in this regard.

———

Close to a year and a half after they had begun writing to each other, in fall 1896 Paul and Alice reached a crossroads. Without having yet met face-to-face, should their bond remain platonic, or should it grow more into a serious relationship, with an eye toward marriage? In raising the prospect of mere friendship, she frustrated him. Now, it dawned on him, the promise of love may not have been mutual all along; their infatuation may not have been anything more than asymmetrical, a flirtation flowing in only one direction—from him to her. "Do *I* believe in Platonic friendship. That is hardly the question. In reading your last letter I see when you propose such a friendship between us," he fretted, "have you forgotten so soon?" He then resorted to gender stereotyping her words as typical of her: "How delightfully inconsistent you are; but that's the woman of it you know. Well, you new women *are* women after all."[31]

In future letters Paul now began to hammer home his view that Alice underwent extreme emotional oscillations. Mooring herself to a union with him, he argued, was exactly what she needed, a rescue from her unstable immaturity. In his view, she had been a "sadly deceived and mistreated, little girl," and what she needed above all was a "champion." She needed salvation; she was "in bondage" and must be "emancipated." She wanted to be loved and coddled, but not by an immediate or extended relative. "I really don't suppose that there is a man in Boston with enough warmth about him to treat you as you should be treated."

Once again Paul offered up himself as the solution to her ills. Though in Ohio, he promised to provide what no Bostonian gentleman could. Almost a year to the day after he first admitted his love for her, he articulated his desire even more explicitly and passionately:

> If I were there, I should simply take you up in my arms, fold you to my breast and kiss you until you forgot all your woes (either in anger or plea-sure, more likely the former.) Then I should sit down and hold your hand (or play with your fingers) and let you talk to me, and what better balm does a woman need for all the ills & wounds of life than just to be allowed to unburden her heart to some sympathetic and attentive listener. I should be so gentle and good to you that you couldn't forbear forgiving me all my shortcomings even to the silliness of this letter.

Paul rebutted Alice's proposal of a platonic relationship. No longer was he in the mood for lollygagging. "Now isn't this enough of this?" he pleaded.[32]

A few months after rejecting Alice's proposal of a platonic relationship, on February 5, 1897, Paul finally made the proposal he himself had long wanted. The previous day, another storm was predicted to head toward New York City, but this report was deemed premature and revised to call for fair weather, al-beit just below freezing. That night, at a gathering organized for him by their common acquaintance, author, activist, and educator Victoria Earle Matthews, Paul was scheduled to meet Alice in person for the very first time.

Both Alice and Paul had come to deeply respect Matthews. Matthews had launched her literary career in the early 1880s, using a series of names to pub-lish her work. She also worked as a subreporter for several mainstream news-papers and also as a correspondent for African American–oriented publications; her columns ranged in topic from managing a household to national politics. Her most famous work by this time was *Aunt Lindy: A Story Founded on Real Life,* published in 1889, an autobiographical fiction about postbellum racial politics. Yet she was equally well known for her creation of political and intel-lectual clubs for African Americans, such as founding the Woman's Loyal Union in 1892; helping journalist and activist Ida B. Wells, Paul's previous ac-quaintance in Chicago, publish her accounts of lynching in the South; and aiding in the establishment of the National Association of Colored Women.

Both Alice and Matthews had come to befriend each other, especially in their collaboration in the White Rose Mission, a settlement house with social clubs for women, recreational events for mothers, and classes for children.

In the "warm room in the old house" Matthews owned on 9 Murray Street in New York City, she arranged for Paul and Alice to meet. When the couple encountered each other, a "soft crimson light" cast across "the flower face of the girl" that he realized belonged to her. For years he had been yearning to see in person what he had only obsessed over in print. At last, they looked into each other's eyes, their bodies within arm's reach. He asked for her hand in marriage. She relented. They kissed. This act meant that he had "won" a promise from her that they would always be committed to each other.[33]

That night, parting ways ached Paul's heart; he watched Alice fade from view. He weakened. A lump formed in his throat. "Oh my darling how I love you, don't trifle with me now, for Cupid's shaft has gone too deep. I have your violets yet and I feel a little tremulous at the heart as I kiss and kiss their withered petals," he would later reminisce of that moment.[34]

The following day Paul was set to travel to England. Upon his departure, the snow was predicted to arrive and, with the rise in temperature, turn into rain.

CHAPTER 12

England as Seen by a Black Man

I am entirely white! My French waiter takes off his cap when I come up the steps, and my blooming rosy-cheeked English maid kisses me as if I were the handsomest man on earth.

—PAUL LAURENCE DUNBAR TO MATILDA DUNBAR
(FEBRUARY 28, 1897)[1]

One critic says a thing and the rest hasten to say the same thing, in many instances using the identical words. I see now very clearly that Mr. Howells has done me irrevocable harm in the dictum he laid down regarding my dialect verse. I am afraid that it will even influence English criticism, although what notices I have had here have shown a different trend.

—PAUL LAURENCE DUNBAR TO DR. F_____
(MARCH 15, 1897)[2]

On Saturday, February 6, 1897, Paul departed from New York City, destined for Liverpool, on the SS (screw steamer) *Umbria*. Leaving behind a city where a storm was fast approaching, he looked forward to a potentially wondrous tour of England. Paul was in high demand as a speaker. Before his scheduled trip to England, fans in that country were already recruiting him to recite his more popular, audience-pleasing poems. Edwin H. Keen, who remarked that Americans were raving over the stories about Scottish life by British author Ian Maclaren (the pseudonym of Free Church of Scotland minister John Watson), teased Paul with a request for recompense on his English side of the Atlantic. "Come pay us back by reading 'The Deserted Plantation' and 'The Delinquent' as only their author can read them."[3]

The *Umbria* bore the Royal Mail Service acronym, like other Victorian ships, and the RMS insignia (a crown) for the world to see. Built in 1884, it was among the largest liners in service, with regular travel between New York City and Boston in America and (by way of Queensland) Liverpool in Europe. With two huge funnels, three big steel masts, and an enormous hull on the outside, with luxurious accoutrements on deck and inside, the SS *Umbria* was Victorian sailing at its best and most reliable.

Paul was one of about thirty passengers in "Second Cabin" captained by Thomas Dutton and staffed by a surgeon, purser, and chief steward.[4] A delightful eight-hundred-foot promenade gave passengers a view of the undulating seascape. Entrances to separate saloons for men and women, and to the captain's room, were on deck, overshadowed by a lookout bridge for officers and a house for the steersman. A flying bridge hovered even higher above the deck. So robust and accommodating were the facilities on the SS *Umbria* that in the event of war, the government could deploy it as an armed cruiser. Aside from its architectural attributes, the ship was a remarkable voyager. As early as 1892 it could travel across the Atlantic at an approximate speed of 19½ knots and in an average of six to six and a half days, depending on weather conditions and sea turbulence.[5]

Paul was not entirely built for overseas travel. "I have proved a somewhat better sailor than I anticipated," he wrote to Alice on Wednesday, his fifth day out, "although I have been somewhat sick. The passage has been very rough though we have not had a real live gale as [of] yet." But he said he enjoyed the journey, which afforded him time to realize what he had left behind. "At night I love to stand on deck and through the rifts in the clouds watch the swimming moon and the friendly following stars," he confessed; and the experience was drawing him ever closer to Alice, in direct, and ironic, proportion to his increasing nautical distance from her: "I think of you, by night and by day, and I long for you my darling."[6]

Even though his marital destiny was secure, and his journey across the Atlantic exciting, the physical separation from Alice pained him. For him to wait even this long without writing her was hard, but the circumstances compelled him, "for a rolling ship gathers no letters." Little time had passed before he started to grow nervous. He needed reaffirmation of her promise to marry him, to join his mother, Matilda, as the only women in his private life. He thought of her and his mother as the "guardian angels" whose "kindly spirits" were guiding him safely over the Atlantic Ocean or the metaphorical "seas" of life. "Will you, too, keep me in mind, dear, and remember the promise you have made me, the one on which I shall live through all the coming days?" he wrote.

The promise would sustain him, he believed, as would the lasting image of her in his mind's eye. After only five days on the SS *Umbria* and with almost another week to go before landing in Liverpool on February 17, Paul's longing for Alice was more intense than ever.[7]

Despite their engagement, Paul could not shed entirely his old habits of flirtation. Two weeks after Alice had agreed to marry him, he wrote her to describe the women he was encountering in England: "The girls here are not only mildly seductive but aggressive," he said. Perhaps a psychological tactic of persuasion, he followed this observation with a wish that they were already married. "You could keep me out of a deal of mischief and share a great many pleasures with me," he believed. To Paul, Alice's presence in his life was helping him mature. His reluctance to mail her a photo of himself telegraphed his ongoing insecurity about his own physical, particularly youthful, appearance. While alone in England, his anxious self-awareness reappeared. "I would give 150 down today for a mustache and an older look," he hoped. The literati knew him there by name, but people invariably said, "[I]s *this* Mr. Dunbar, why I thought you were a much older man." If Alice had accompanied him abroad, Paul thought, she could have improved his profile: "Now if you were with me, you might do the talking while I lounged around and looked wise." He could barely wait to return. Once his tour ended, he could return promptly—so that they could marry soon thereafter. Her letters would be crucial to his self-confidence but also to reaffirming her love for him. "Oh darling, darling life of my life! Write to me very soon and if you do really care for me let me know it," he pleaded. Within weeks Alice did write Paul a letter, which he was grateful to receive.[8]

Paul's allusion to flirting with attractive women noticeably ruffled Alice. Working to mitigate her displeasure, he repeated his belief that no woman could ever come between them. She enraptured him, and he yielded himself fully. "I would rather be your captive than another woman's king," he wrote to reassure her. Though separated by an ocean, their bond retained a core of faith: "You have made life a new thing to me—a precious and sacred trust."[9] Still, Paul knew that Alice likely believed they moved too fast in agreeing to be engaged. They had met in person only once, after all; moreover, she hinted that she regretted having kissed him when he took her hand. Perish the thought, he retorted. The pace had been ideal; the engagement came right on time. "You did wrong to kiss me?" he asked. "But darling you could not have helped it. This love of ours was predestined." Always he clung to the belief that they were fated to be together. But he had to prove that he would be "true and pure."[10]

Throughout his six-month stint in England, Paul wrote Alice over and again that he hoped her love for him would not wane as a consequence of their distance or the youth of their engagement: "But what am I that I should have your love? Can I hold it? Will it last?" By day and by night, these were questions he asked himself. If only he had not left behind all his pictures in Chicago, including Alice's, which at least would have represented what he called a "counterfeit presentiment." He asked her to send him another shortly. The request anticipated his subsequent deliberation over whether he could send for Alice (and his mother) to come to England and hold the wedding there. An English wedding was only a dream—its logistical barriers were too high to overcome—but his thoughts about it signaled his unhappiness at their current separation.[11]

Alice in turn likewise wondered whether Paul's own love for her would wane—whether he would grow bored. "Tired of you, darling! sweetheart of mine, how can you ask it?" he exclaimed, in response. "Instead of growing tired of you, my love seems to grow stronger day by day, and I yearn for you more and more." So preoccupied was he with her that he claimed he saw her in others. After one of his April recitals, Paul wrote Alice about one of the accompanying musicians: "The little violinist is a Jewess with eyes, hair and complexion that reminded me so much of you that I felt like hugging her for your sake." Surely the incident, as he described it, attested to his undying infatuation with Alice. Equally and unfortunately, it also revealed that he continued to gaze at attractive women nearby.[12]

———

During the early period of Paul's engagement to Alice, he spoke loosely and unapologetically about social differences and his peculiar place in the world of race relations. Now one month after their private engagement, he related to her his newfound experiences in another land. His literary tour was well underway, even before he stepped foot in Liverpool: he recited poems while still sailing on the SS *Umbria* ("Recited on the boat this [Thursday] night . . ."). In the country itself, he spoke in venues ranging from churches to exclusive members-only clubs.[13]

In one visit to a place of worship, Paul linked up with Quaker poet William Kitching, who thanked him for his "attendance of our meeting for worship" and his "interesting recitations," an occasion that inspired Kitching himself to reach out to Paul and suggest exchanging their respective verses, whether published or in progress.[14]

Writing to Alice from a residence at 16 Imperial Mansions on London's Oxford Street, Paul also described his experience at the Savage Club, one of the most exclusive gentlemen's clubs in London, where he recited his work as part of the after-dinner entertainment. As an African American, he marveled at how far he had come; he was now in rarefied air. "I was an honored guest and held a unique position as the representative of a whole race," he boasted. "I took my turn with the rest, and—dear is this egotism?—was received with wonderful enthusiasm."[15]

Paul took pride in being a bona fide representative of his race; he also appreciated other race men who exemplified "the effect of the higher education upon the pure Negro." Realizing how much being a racial spokesman and a literary celebrity were intertwined both at home and abroad, he was more than willing to take his fiancée along for the epistolary ride.[16]

———

By and by, Paul grew restless in London. Snow and rain fell relentlessly; the temperature hovered around freezing; and his first impression of England was overcast, muggy, and wet. Worse than the uninspiring weather was the presence of a man who turned out to be a thorn in Paul's side: Henry Francis Downing.

Born in New York and twice Paul's age, Downing in the early 1870s had served in the United States Navy; was appointed in the late 1880s as U.S. consul to West Africa; and in the early 1890s came to run the United States African News Company, a news service that had on its roster luminaries ranging from Frederick Douglass and Booker T. Washington to Ida B. Wells and William Scarborough. (A while back, when Downing passed through Dayton, they happened to meet for the first time.) Coincidentally, in 1897 both were in London. Downing was there settling down with family.[17]

One Saturday morning in late February, the two men ran into each other. Each happened to be passing by the National Gallery in Trafalgar Square, near Low's Agency, the management firm located on Northumberland Avenue that Paul had been visiting quite often since his arrival in England. Paul was walking alone; Downing was strolling with his wife. When Paul and Downing saw each other, they "rushed into each other's arms," as Downing recalled three decades later; "and perhaps we engaged kisses after the manner of the French."[18]

In their chat, Paul confided that he was "down on his luck." Just that morning, he had had a falling out with Edith Pond, who was in England as well and had been working on her father's (Major Pond's) behalf, but who, in Paul's view, was not as invested in his career as he wished. When Paul embarked on his tour of England, he had already developed experience in reciting his literary writings for a variety of audiences and occasions, from Jubilee Day at the World's Columbian Exposition in Chicago to a local home in Ohio. Now, in spring 1897, both the management of Edith Pond and the sales agency of Keith, Prowse, and Company expected to capitalize on Paul's versatility—on his reputation for being a coveted "Negro poet-reader," a moniker he would come to bear over the course of his career.[19]

Downing also came to learn that the beleaguered poet's housing conditions were deplorable, in no way conducive to inspiration or enlightenment; and they only depressed his enthusiasm for the region, where snow, sleet, and snow continued to fall unabated beneath persistently overcast skies. As far as Downing could tell, Pond "had housed him in a small and poorly furnished garret through whose soot-covered windows he could view nothing but chimney-pots belching forth black, thick smoke." (Downing's sepulchral image was not so dissimilar from what Paul himself described in a letter to his mother in March: "Out of my window I look upon a row of London roofs, a street where people are passing to and fro on their way to church and above all a great patch of dark gray sky. The bells are ringing, London's numerous chimes and an inexpressible sadness creeps over me. Like a sad nun telling her beads my mind will go back one by one over the more than three thousand miles that are between me and all I hold dear, and I begin to wonder how long this exile must last. It is as if some hoary old ancestor of mine had neglected or violated the home love and I was doing penance for his sin.") Just as bad, Pond provided him "very little, if any, of John Bull's coin of the realm."[20] Paul's misery compelled Downing to invite him to stay at his home. Paul accepted and was so buoyed by the favor that he gleefully wrote his mother about the salvation of running into Downing. "It was none other than our old friend Dip or in other words the Hon. Henry F. Downing, looking like a prince, married to a white woman and looking at ease." Over the course of their time together, Paul welcomed the idea of Downing's management of his London speaking engagements. Ultimately, he hired Downing for the job.[21]

In Downing's garden, Paul loved to gather dandelions, which he fried with bacon chunks. On one occasion in the garden, with Downing looking on, a housekeeper escorted into the garden "a light-brown young colored gentleman modest in his demeanor," wearing "a frock-tail coat over wide and baggy trousers," with "a sort of Sarah Gamp umbrella" in one hand, and "a wide-rimmed felt hat peculiar to heroes of the 'Wild and Wooly West'" in the other. Paul, in the "new knicker suit of clothes" he had borrowed from his newfound host, observed the visitor. Not until both heard the young man speak—"his low, soft voice, all music"—did they realize that he was special.

The stranger was Samuel Coleridge-Taylor. Born in Holborn, London, to an English mother and a Creole father from Sierra Leone, he had never known his father, who had returned to his home country before his son was born. Samuel was named after his mother's favorite writer, the Romantic poet and philosopher Samuel Taylor Coleridge. Eventually the boy studied violin and composition at the Royal College of Music. After graduation he taught music and conducted the orchestra at the Croydon Conservatoire. By the time Coleridge-Taylor met Paul, his compositions had earned him renown at home and abroad. Three years Paul's junior, the musician was a celebrity in his own right and drawn to the poet after he read the caption "Nigger Poet and Actor" in an article published in a local London newspaper. It is unclear whether Coleridge-Taylor was seeking Paul out specifically; nonetheless, the composer wondered whether the poet would grant him permission to set his poems to music.

Paul had deep interest in "Negro music," in the African heritage of slave songs, and he believed that these songs resonated with an artistry, a beauty, that should be celebrated. Three years before he had said as much in an interview with the *Chicago Record*. Now he was intrigued by this self-styled Anglo-African composer who likewise not only admired this heritage but sought through his training to bring racial thought and spirit to bear on classical music.[22]

At least where the potential collaboration was concerned, Downing's influence served its purpose. As an international consul, his experience played into his ability to secure "the immediate patronage of His Excellency John Hay," so headlined the printed program. (In early May, Hay began his role as U.S. ambassador to the United Kingdom, and he agreed to support the joint recital featuring the African American poet and the Anglo-African musician. Days after the recital, Paul reciprocated the gesture by sending Hay a complimentary copy of the English edition of what would become his third book of poetry, which Hay acknowledged.)[23] The recital was held at the central London venue of the Salle Erard on Great Marlborough Street. Scheduled for Wednesday, June 2, 1897, at 3:00 p.m., the event was set to include Paul's "selections" from and readings of his "poetical works," and Coleridge-Taylor's "vocal and instrumental compositions," with assistance from violinist Marie Motto and singers Helen Jaxon, a soprano, and Gregory Hast, a tenor.[24]

FIG. 12.1. Samuel Coleridge-Taylor, circa 1905. (Library of Congress Prints and Photographs Division)

Since the scheduled event initially did not garner sufficient reservations, the program was delayed a few days, to Saturday, June 5. Paul enjoyed these warmer days of England—in this month, the temperature reached as high as ninety degrees. Despite the regular thunderstorms and frequent clouds and rain, this recital was the bright spot, or climax, of his international trip thus far.

The "happiest" poems Paul read, according to a reviewer in *The Times*, a London newspaper, "were those conceived in a humorous vein," although the critic found his "admirable" recital afflicted by his "enunciation," which required "improvement in the matter of clearness." The clash of English snobbery and American Midwestern vernacular aside, when Paul recited his famous poem "The Party"—the same one that so moved William Howells in his review of *Majors and Minors*—the American minister, biographer, and former abolitionist Moncure D. Conway "laughed and laughed loudly," tears trickling down his cheeks. Paul's acquaintance Alexander Crummell, who happened to be sitting beside Conway, guffawed. That oddity was not enough to overshadow the overall pleasure that, according to *The Times*, the "eminent musical critics," "many of the titled and untitled gentry," and the "leading members" of the American Colony in London shared at quite possibly "one of the great events of the London musical season of 1897." More people in the audience were familiar with Coleridge-Taylor than with Paul. The contrast in stature worked to Paul's benefit. The poet basked in the musician's glow.[25]

Alas, the initial enthusiasm with which Paul had embraced Downing gave way to dread. Eventually, he realized the low bar that he should have accorded Downing's managerial expertise and ethics. By the time early June arrived, he was grumbling that Downing was demanding too much of his earnings. "I made 17 guineas Saturday at a recital and was positively robbed of them by an unprincipled scoundrel," Paul grumbled in a letter sent back home, to Alice. At this rate he seemed predestined to have a miserable time in England. "The jubilee is killing everything—that and two poor managers are my bane," he said, in reference to Downing and Pond.[26]

Indeed, upon Paul's arrival in England in February, residents there were paying more attention to Queen Victoria's diamond jubilee than to anything else. In September 1896 Victoria, as queen of the United Kingdom of Great Britain and Ireland, technically became the longest-ruling monarch in English history. Nine months later her reign was celebrated by a diamond jubilee, in celebration of the sixtieth anniversary of her accession to the throne. Dubbed a "Festival of the British Empire," festivities highlighted the empire's expanse across the British colonies, or what Colonial Secretary Joseph Chamberlain metaphorically called its "crown jewels." State dinners were frequent at her home in Buckingham Palace. London was awash with color and draped in Union Jacks. Fewer opportunities than normal therefore existed for Paul to recite his work and earn money. The jubilee's royal extravaganza so preoccupied the public that one person remarked to Paul that, "for engagement & pressure of business," it "would make even some of you 'go ahead' Americans 'sick up.'"[27]

————

In the months leading up to his trip to England, Paul had been thinking about his third book of poems. In coming to conceive of his verses as lyrics—a form that also applied to a number of the verses in his first two books, *Oak and Ivy* and *Majors and Minors*—he was selecting one of the most common forms of poetry ever written, read, and performed in the West. The lyric was a "natural" form of poetry, alongside the narrative and the dramatic, as Johann Wolfgang von Goethe stated in 1891; together, those three represented the main genres by which poems could be classified. Of course, the variety of poems penned across Western history—such as odes and elegies, ballads and hymns—made this triangular depiction debatable. Yet the distinctive accessibility of the lyric to lovers of poetry around the world made indubitable its stature as a literary tradition.[28]

The lyric had certain notable qualities. First, its personal expression of thought and feeling was paramount. Second, across history the lyric came to be associated with the speech of rituals and recitation; it could encase the symbols, the language, of seers and kings, of oracularity; it imbibed the realities of the outside world and conveyed a vision of such palpability through a singular consciousness. Third, the lyric referred to music. Rooted etymologically in the ancient Greek word *lyra* or, more familiarly, *lyre*, the lyric in Paul's day implied a modern sense of song. Scholar James William Johnson states that the lyric represented music, "basing its meter and rhyme on the regular measure of the song," or "to approximate the tonal variation of a chant or intonation." From ancient Greece to the final decades of the nineteenth century, scores of poets produced self-consciously melodic verses to distinguish their legacies as writers and, in some cases, as performers if they recited them.[29]

The lyric turned out to be a staple of Paul's work. For example, the word "lyrics" would anchor the title of four out of the fourteen books of poems he published over his career. He also consistently described his poems as "lyrics" whenever he sent drafts of them to Alice. "Since I cannot at this time write you a long letter, I will send you a couple of little lyrics that I have lately written," he once wrote her, three weeks before his birthday in 1895, as he worked on the manuscript for *Majors and Minors*. "Your beautiful name lends itself so readily to verse that I have taken the liberty to use it in one of the songs and dedicate the same to you." To conclude the letter, he noted, "I will close my prosiness now to drop into verse or worse. I love these lyrical forms and I hope that my attempts in them will please you." Later that month, he again remarked to her in a letter, "I have just finished a little lyrical bit in seventy-two lines, entitled 'When Malindy Sings.' It rather strikes my fancy and I shall add it to my repertoire for recitation." A handful of months later, regarding another poem, "Ione," he indicated to her that he was willing to experiment with the form, turning it into a hybrid. The poem was, for Paul, "a lyric narrative and is to be somewhat long. You seem somehow to be woven into the fabric of it, but that is true of all my work now." The interchange between "lyrics" and "songs" in Paul's letters to Alice correlated with how often he called his various poems songs in his books. Even if the poems went by other titles, their forms were not so dissimilar.[30]

In drafting his third book of poems, which would include "Ione," Paul was pleased with his progress, despite the challenges created by his manager, Edith Pond, who decided to abandon Paul for Paris during the jubilee and left Paul with unpaid bills. Since he had secured a contract with a publisher, he was thinking he might as well leave England and return home, to Alice. "I may take it into my head to get up and come home," he wrote. "It would be inglorious but it would be independence. Then too, I have placed my book with a publisher on excellent terms so I don't much care." Chapman & Hall was set to publish this new book in England by the middle of April 1897. He promised to send her a copy, but his tight schedule repeatedly delayed him.[31]

Beyond Alice, Paul spread the word to his professional acquaintances. Upon the book's publication he informed William Howells, his most ardent supporter, back in the States. He also reached out to R. W. Gilder of *Century*, to whom Paul reported not only the fact of its release but some insight into his apprehension about the new book. "I am trembling for what English critics will say of it." He had received word that it would likely receive a "kindly reception," but he was not sure yet.[32]

———

Touring England could not quell the anxiety Paul felt upon the release of his third book, which he titled *Lyrics of Lowly Life*. He was still reconciling himself to Howells's notion that he was "the first of his race to put his race into poetry," despite all the creative ways he felt he was advancing the lyrical form. In March 1897 he had written one of his more honest letters opining on Howells's praise, including the ironic possibility that it had cost and catapulted his career in equal measure. To an acquaintance Paul wrote about "the utter hollowness of most of American book criticism." Reviewers made him alternately smirk and snarl, and he pointed to the herd mentality of literary criticism: the way that one book review, positive or negative, could spark self-replicating series of subsequent reviews, each perpetuating true or false impressions of the original critic. This phenomenon had worked in his favor only several months earlier, when book reviewers echoed Howells's praise for the dialect poetry in *Majors and Minors*.

Yet this phenomenon had also been a curse. Paul felt that such praise put him in a cage, denying his complexity as a writer and a man. "One critic says a thing and the rest hasten to say the same thing, in many instances using the identical words," he bemoaned. "I see now very clearly that Mr. Howells has done me irrevocable harm in the dictum he laid down regarding my dialect verse."[33] Paul saw the dean of American letters as an emblem of "intelligent people" who were "unable to differentiate dialect as a philological branch from the burlesque of negro minstrelsy."[34] Howells was not so naïve as to regard Paul's dialect poetry as burlesque or its intention to replicate the language of minstrelsy. Still, this white critic could not resist being swept up with the commercial wave of public appreciation for the supposed realism and authenticity of the dark-skinned Dayton poet.

England did not exactly mimic the racial climate of literary criticism Paul had borne back home, in America. Broken, at least for now, was the cycle of language expressed by critics on how he was "the first of his race to put his race into poetry." But he was still worried: he was afraid that Howells would influence criticism even in England. His grief over the past and what the future could hold depressed him in the present.[35]

Such concerns, however, did not keep Paul from celebrating professional success. He had just secured a publisher, Dodd, Mead, and Company, to release his first novel, which he was trying to write while touring England. To Alice he bragged that the publisher's president, Frank H. Dodd, was in London, interested in him. Dodd was "anxious," Paul wrote, about his progress on the novel and wanted him to come home promptly. Paul also had interest from other publishers, including John Lane in England and D. Appleton & Company in the United States. The commercial attraction to Paul's first work in a genre, which he had not even finished writing yet, showed how powerfully—and, again, ironically—the dean of American letters had anointed his career as a poet. Publishers sought almost anything Paul was willing to write.[36]

Paul continued to cultivate his bond with Howells. If on March 15, 1897, he was bemoaning Howells's "irrevocable harm" to his reputation, merely six weeks later, on April 26, he struck an obsequious note in a letter to the same authoritative gentleman: "I have been long promising myself the pleasure of writing to you. But I have forborne for lack of something really interesting to say, nor even now is this disability removed." Paul apologized for not yet having had the chance to visit Edinburgh to deliver Howells's letter to David Douglas. In the meantime, his career was advancing with the English edition of *Lyrics of Lowly Life.*

For the majority of *Lyrics of Lowly Life,* Paul compiled the poems he previously showcased in *Oak and Ivy* and *Majors and Minors.* Paul's third book included 104 poems, only ten of which were new.[37] Closer in structure to his first book than to his second, the third book also does not separate the poems in dialect from those in formal English. Rather, it presents about one dialect poem per six poems, seasoning the book more evenly and thoroughly than he had before. *Lyrics of Lowly Life* opened with a double sign of racial and textual authenticity: a photograph of Paul dressed in a debonair tuxedo, his hair parted down the center, his face bespectacled with sophisticated thin-rimmed glasses; and beneath the image was a copy of his flowing signature, legible enough to confirm the proper spelling of his middle name, "Laurence," almost as a corrective to any and all previous misspellings.

Following this paratext was Howells's preface, which welcomed readers first by introducing Paul's father, an African American man who had "escaped from slavery in Kentucky to freedom in Canada." This former slave, Howells wrote, had a son in Dayton, who "grew up with such chances and mischances for mental training as everywhere befall the children of the poor." Despite these circumstances, the son had come to learn from a father who "taught himself to read, loved chiefly to read history," and from a mother who shared a "passion for literature, with a special love of poetry." *Lyrics of Lowly Life* was the latest outcome of this incredible saga.[38]

Howells's introduction to *Lyrics of Lowly Life* differed from his *Harper's* review of *Majors and Minors* in one crucial respect: the white critic had now come to know the private life of the black poet who, like him, was an Ohio native but who lived in a community racially segregated from his own. Otherwise the two essays were similar, exclaiming that Paul was "the only man of

FIG. 12.2. Frontispiece of *Lyrics of Lowly Life* (1898).

pure African blood and of American civilization to feel the negro life aesthetically and express it lyrically." A blessing and a curse, this description comprised a clear, succinct gauge of the racial and aesthetic value of Paul's work,
but it also foreshadowed the language to which he would feel shackled for the
near future.[39]

Positive reviews of *Lyrics of Lowly Life* abounded on both sides of the Atlantic. "I have just had a letter from my English publisher saying that the reviews of my book are many and *favorable*," Paul wrote to Alice. "He sends
them, and if they are what he calls favorable I don't know where the *un* would
come in." And he was pleased to know that he was able to earn a reasonable
royalty of $250 from the book sales, which would remain steady well into the
next year.[40]

Despite the good news, Paul apprised Howells at the end of April of his
misery in England. His arrival in the winter-to-spring off-season meant that
he could recite his literature only in clubs and "hotel smoking concerts"

between vaudeville dancing girls and variety show clowns, and at the behest of Ms. Pond, who, Paul felt, had been treating him in the worst way, and who wanted him, rather than reading poems, "to *tell vulgar stories!*" Paul protested, which had led to their falling out months earlier, and prompting her to flee to Paris and leave unpaid his boarding bill. "She has scrupled at nothing to repress and annoy me, but I shall not come home without accomplishing something to keep from being marked a 'failure.'" Dodd, the publisher, loaned Paul money to help him get through hard times, but Ms. Pond was ruining his enjoyment of England.

Paul also confided in Howells his insecurity about writing a novel for the first time. Still, the manuscript was coming along. "Although I distrust my ability very much, I am hard at work upon a novel and have made some progress with it," Paul wrote. The English press had been generally kind to him, but he wondered what they would say about his future work, since they were "so conservative here." He knew if he could make it in England and America with his novel, if he could continue his professional success and earn enough money from his writings, then he could give up recitals. "I have had my fill of readings and managers. If I can make my living by my pen I will not use my voice," he wrote. This is one of the only instances when Paul admitted that he preferred the written to the spoken word. Public performance was too strenuous for him.[41]

As Paul was settling in England, to the degree that he could comfortably do so amid his activities writing and reciting his work, the quest toward writing his first novel began to clarify. First, there had been multiple bidders. "Mr. Dodd my publisher was here," Paul wrote in reference to Frank H. Dodd, the president of Dodd, Mead and Company; however, "I have promised the book to another firm John Lane in England and Appleton in America." Yet Paul seemed to be leaning toward Dodd; Dodd's anticipation was palpable. "He is very anxious about the novel I am writing (this is secret) and wanted me to come home."[42]

During the third and fourth weeks of July, Paul stayed at Askew House, the Quaker home of the Impey family. The gray stone edifice located in Street, a village in the county of Somerset, 135 miles from London, had belonged to the Impey family since the 1880s. Paul marveled at the "old house," with its views of "magnificent leaves and flowers and fields as far as I can see."[43]

From 1888 through 1895, Catherine Impey had edited and published *Anti-Caste*, the activist journal that agitated against racism. She had collaborated with Ida B. Wells, whom Paul had encountered during his days in Chicago, during Wells's antilynching tour across England. Catherine and her sister,

FIG. 12.3. Paul with friends in England, 1897. (Paul Laurence Dunbar Collection, Ohio History Connection)

Ellen, were known for their hospitality to friends and family who happened to be passing through England.[44]

For the benefit of the Impeys and their social circle, on Thursday, July 15, Paul held a recital attended by more than a hundred people. He also toured Wells, eight miles north of Street; and Bristol, twenty-two miles farther away. He visited the exotic limestone cliffs of Cheddar Gorge, fifteen miles north of Street, in the Mendip Hills, as well as the nearby hill of Glastonbury Tor. Amid these excursions he found time to work on his novel.[45]

When Paul left the Impeys' house, he left a poem in the guest book that expressed his gratitude:

> When days were dark & life seemed drear,
> Dear friends, you kindly asked me here
> I thought the year had passed its prime;
> But woke to find it summer-time.
>
> . . .
>
> One thinks that days of summer pass
> Like fleeting forms before a glass;
> 'Tis false: your house shall prove it yet,
> For here, indeed, the Summer's set!

Staying with the Impeys fueled Paul's sense that, overall, he had been treated quite well by those whom he would regard as his "friends" in England. "I have been truly blessed with friends who are wonderfully kind to me," especially those belonging to the Quaker community.[46]

"My novel grows apace," Paul wrote Alice, "though I can hardly call that a novel which is merely the putting together of a half dozen abstract characters and letting them work out their destiny along the commonplace lines suggested by their natures and environments. It has some plot, but little incident and incident seems to be the thing nowadays."[47]

Alice did her best to placate Paul as he plowed ahead. "Write me soon," she closed one letter. "How is the novel coming on?" Shortly afterward, she signed "with tenderest love." As spring turned to summer, Paul confessed to Alice, "My novel also still moves on apace, but I have my doubts about it as it entirely lacks incident. I *may* finish it however." On Independence Day, he wrote, "Still the novel grows." He finished it by the end of July and wrote of his relief, "just lazing around among the trees and flowers."[48]

During Paul's courtship of Alice, he had worked to project success and confidence. Now, during their engagement, he disclosed his professional insecurity. "I am so far from being cheerful that I cannot, for the life of me write a cheerful letter," he confessed to Alice. "I am thinking sadly and deeply." That

Paul was not so handsome and wealthy, that his success as a creative writer could turn out to be negligible, prompted him, perhaps subconsciously, to solicit the reaffirmation of Alice's love for him. "Alice could you still love me and would you wed me if I returned home a failure?" he asked. "If instead of a laurel to wear I should come back with a grief to share darling would you share it?" Oscillating between bouts of anxiety and indications of success became part and parcel of Paul's letters to Alice. More than anyone else, she could steady him during his routine speculations over whether he had enough talent to prolong what had so far been a promising career.[49]

Paul in turn tried to instill confidence in Alice whenever her own insecurities and problems arose. Just as he had before, he tried to instruct her on venues where she should publish her writing, again leveraging his own prior access and success. "Dear I want you to try the *Ladies' Home Journal* with some of your work," he urged. His poem "My Thought—And Hers?" was slated for the May issue. For the work they paid quite well. Poems such as "When the Old Man Smokes" and "Dat Chrismus on de Ol' Plantation" would end up in the offing for Easter and Christmas, he told her. "I believe that something brief of the work of colored women might prove an entering wedge for you," he suggested. "I am so proud of you and have such perfect faith in your work that I think everyone else should know and appreciate it." As writers with evidence of success in the professional world, Paul and Alice admirably rallied to each other's aid when the other needed it most. "Remember dearie that I consider you mine already, that your fights are my fights, that I am with you right or wrong," he stressed.[50]

———

After Paul began exchanging letters with Alice in spring 1895, he ended his private correspondence with Rebekah. By the middle of 1897, while in London, he confessed to his mother that he might have been too abrupt in detaching himself from her and that she might have represented the destructive nature of his past philandering. "Rebekah does not write to me any more," he wrote, "and I do not hear from or write to any of the other victims."[51]

———

As Paul toured England, he encountered a predicament through which only Alice could help him. "People are writing about this and that appearing in the

American papers concerning me," he said, yet he had seen none of it. He asked her to send any newspaper articles about him she came across, and also asked for her assistance in burnishing his public image.

Aside from the concern about his notoriety in America, Paul continued to relay to Alice his increasing fame in England. His time abroad was turning out to be so successful that she worried he would not want to return home. Given her engagement to him, she further worried that she would have to comply with every imagined wish of his to continue to revel in his celebrity abroad. He sought to allay her fears by pointing out that English life was not perfect. "So you think that my heart has gone out to things English," he wrote. "Well, darling, there are some things that I like about England but not everything; and then I did not mean for you to live here *always*. I thought you might enjoy living here for a while." No longer would he stir her anxieties, he promised; they would talk no more of it. If nothing hampered him, he would return home in a year and he asked where she preferred to live. His marital life with her would depend on his professional success as a writer. "I am planning and planning for our future," he said. "If I am successful here, I want to marry you soon after I get back. If I am unsuccessful, I will release you." By mid-June 1897, the American media, in reporting that Paul's tour in England had been a failure, contradicted Paul's perception of his own experience in England. The American papers were correct insofar as he was not making a fortune, partly a consequence of the jubilee. Thankfully, Alice, Paul's "own little girl," was courageous enough to defend him if needed, but he regretted that she had to do so alone in their country.[52]

Namely, while so far away from the epicenter of controversy, Paul could not adroitly counteract the rumor that he broke off his contract with Edith Pond, as opposed to his belief that she had left him behind. He had little choice but to part ways; both were incessantly at odds. By midsummer, she had decided to tour Europe on her own without him. And to make ends meet and continue his mission of building his name, he secured opportunities and commissions for recitals without her, of which she would eventually catch wind. His ultimate disagreement with her claim that she was entitled to a portion of his earnings fueled the leak of their contractual dispute and severance.

Paul was defiant. "What the papers say about my breaking the contract, I do not care a fig about," he wrote, "for when the truth is known about this woman here, I shall be exonerated from all blame." Sure, he was earning only meager sums from his recitations. But the currency of social capital, of earning esteem in elite society, redeemed him: "But if the extension of my reading public, if social recognition, if being compared favorably with Douglass at a banquet of the finest club in London, if getting into the hearts and homes of good and intellectual people is success, then I have succeeded beyond my wildest expectations." He could almost argue that his race did not obstruct his progress—at least not in England. "Miss Pond, white as she is cannot stick her nose where I go," he boasted. "This is not egotism, dear but I wish to reassure you." Overall, Paul's letters to Alice sought to allay her trepidation about marrying an embattled African American man constantly in a defensive posture against the journalists and pundits back home.[53]

In the meantime, Paul continued to reveal his innermost thoughts and feelings to the other woman in his life: his mother, Matilda. Londoners were "very nice" to him, he began one letter to her, and he was quite optimistic about the success of his tour. He regarded himself the most interviewed man in London, the best local papers having sent reporters his way. Beyond this, his elevated stature had racial implications, in light of the company he now was keeping. "Did I tell you that I was at tea with Henry M. Stanley?" he asked Matilda, referring to the Welsh American journalist and explorer Sir Henry Morton Stanley, notorious for his two-volume *Through the Dark Continent*, an 1878 treatise marked by its imperialist and racist ethnography of Africa. "I am entirely white! My French waiter takes off his cap when I come up the steps, and my blooming rosy-cheeked English maid kisses me as if I were the handsomest man on earth." The dignity he enjoyed among the men and women he visited or encountered in London was comparable to what any respectable white gentlemen would have expected. Paul's encounters lacked the indignity he anticipated as a "Negro" man, of dark skin color, in America. In England, his dark skin color did not impede his admission to the more rarefied precincts of English society. Race was not an obstacle to joy.[54]

Access to high society had its consequences: Paul could not afford all its costs. "My expenses here are necessarily high on account of my social position + the duties it entails," he told his mother. Earning close to £20 per recital (or, after adjusting for inflation, equivalent to a little more than £2,619, or $3,400, today) was not enough to cover all the expenses of London life (its pleasures and necessities alike); of lending money, he revealed in a letter, to the likes of Alexander Crummell; of the losses incurred by the bad luck of recital hosts, such as Henry Downing, taking a share of his earnings. For these reasons he could not send his mother as much as he would like. "I am so sorry that I must again disappoint you as to money," he apologized, but he remained optimistic that better times were ahead. "I have not given up the ship by any means," Paul assured Matilda. "I shall try to stay until after the Jubilee is over (June 22nd) and see what I can do then," hoping that more recital opportunities would fill the festivity's void. Until then, high society would continue to tickle his ego, though he privately made clear his preference for pounds and pence over pride. The pleasantries of native gentry and ladies and clergymen were secondary to his refrains: "what I want so badly is money," and "I am tired of waiting and could be making more at the watering places in America."[55]

Central to Paul's financial dilemma was Edith Pond, who turned out to be a recurring, and irritating, theme in his letters back home. As he did before Alice, he took the liberty of lambasting Ms. Pond before Matilda. From his standpoint, her managerial neglect and incompetence were robbing him of the funds he could have sent his mother: "She is like the dog in the manger. She can't do any thing herself and won't let any body else do any thing." After five months in London he had earned hardly any money from his public readings, fueling speculation in America that his London tour was an utter failure. Minimal earnings and declining savings, coupled with a need to restore his reputation, were compelling him to consider returning home earlier than expected. "If things continue as they are I shall leave Ms. Pond again and this time come home," he admitted, "although I hear that the American papers are saying that my trip is a failure." Still, he remained hopeful. "As far as money is concerned it is, but I have made a reputation here and gained a following that will help me in the long run."[56] Aside from himself, he needed enough money to support Matilda: "to supply you with all you need, while I am trying to get on my feet," he wrote.[57]

Paul expressed a sigh of relief when the jubilee eventually ended. The removal of this nationwide distraction helped spur in England the sales of his new publications and the demand for his recitations, both of which had been commercially depressed by the festivities.[58]

———

A letter Paul wrote to Alice in early May 1897, when he was comfortable enough to address her as "Little Wife to Be," began more ominously than usual: "I feel like coming to the confessional this morning." He detailed the transgression: "I hope you are not acting as badly as I am. Dear little girl, I am flirting horribly." He sought to put a positive spin on his behavior: "You would laugh to see it, though; it is all so innocent. I am flirting for the fun of it, and not for value received." He portrayed his flirtation as a thrill, not as a prelude to misconduct, and he even encouraged her to follow suit. Perhaps he wanted to alleviate the guilt that inevitably came with the confession: "I do not prove false to you in thought or deed, but nevertheless I am having a good time, and I want you to get out of your seclusion and do the same. I am not going to be jealous of you because I am sure that you will be as true as I am trying to be." Despite the countless times Paul declared love for Alice, his confession to being a flirt, their ensuing debates over this fact, her admonitions, his repentance—these would emerge as prominent patterns in their relationship.[59]

Another pattern involved Alice's bouts of silence. Not infrequently she attributed the silence to her work: "But really I have been busy, up to my eyes in work of all sorts, and treating all of my correspondents shabbily, even my lover-like Paul."[60] Yet Paul's ability to recognize that he might have misbehaved made him suspect an ulterior motive in Alice's occasional silence: "And are you still too busy to find time to write to your forlorn lover?" he asked in a letter postmarked only a couple of days after her claim of being "busy." (The distance the letters had to travel indicates in this instance that perhaps they got their wires crossed.) "Particularly am I yearning just now for the sight of one fair American Girl who starts two letters to her absent lover and stops both of them in the middle," he started in a sort of metaletter—that is, a letter on the nature of Alice's letters and what the silences within and between them portended. When he first read her "missives," he became angry and picked up his pen to write her at once, but he laid it down again and kissed the envelope, for her "dear hands had touched it and that was much." Yet he complained further, wondering on what she was going to educate him. "What on earth have I done now? Pray proceed with your lecture and so relieve this killing suspense." To wit: "Write me soon again love and liven me up a bit. Your letters grow too few." (He would repeatedly complain that she was sending him "mere perfunctory epistles.")[61]

Within days Alice sent Paul a letter that buoyed him, not least of which because it included a photograph of her. For the next five weeks Paul clutched that picture; it held him over until July 31, the date he would sail back to America. The final month of his time in England was, at last, the opposite of the overall dreariness he had grown accustomed to: the weather was mostly fair and dry, the temperature comfortably settled in the upper sixties, the sunshine brighter than the average. Ironically, at the time of his departure, the outside conditions were most enjoyable.

Each night on the ship back to America—travel he could afford, his delinquent bills behind him, thanks to the generosity of Henry Tobey, who cabled funds over—Paul meandered to and fro across the vessel.[62] He watched "its wake when the electric sparks were flashing like a legion of rings in the white turmoil of hell." At "the friendly following stars" he stared. In either case, he wondered how speedily Alice and he could reunite, how soon he could see her in person for only the second time, after the nearly seven-month journey.[63]

———

Upon his return from England, Paul deplored the media demand for his writings about his time in England. But he was weakened by his desire and need for money; his willpower wavered as he tried to withstand the sensationalist overtures of the media. "I am still in the 'impression' business for the sake of my financial health and the satisfaction of the yellow journals," he wrote one friend in early August, right after his return to New York City. "This rush for London impressions seems to me a very disgusting thing and I am only sorry that I am not in a position to resist the demands made upon me."[64]

In response to the American media demand to learn of his experiences abroad, Paul wrote two reflective essays, both published in 1897: "Some London Impressions" appeared in April in the *Chicago Record*, while "England as Seen by a Black Man" came out in September in the *Independent*. England made such a profound impression on him that he presented a philosophy of life by which African Americans should abide if they sought to live happily in the world. What struck him most about England was the subordination of individualism to "pure family life," in which "the good of the whole is the primal thing, and how all work together harmoniously for the best ends." Freedom lay in the attitude he appreciated in the "British subject's contentment with his lot in life":

It is rather, a stolid, common-sense philosophy of life which says: "Let me enjoy whatever of pleasure comes to me and make the best of the inevitable sorrows." It says: "I will love my children and do the best I can to raise them to a better condition; but if I cannot leave them any other heritage, I will not leave them one of discontent and unrest." Our peasantry, if such the laboring blacks may be called, in condition is much like that of England; but in realization and acceptance of their lot, how different. The novel message of freedom has been blown into their ears with such a ringing blast that the din has for the moment confused them.

Paul advised "black men" especially to stop "beating their heads against the impregnable wall of adverse circumstances" and "cease to fret away their little lives in unavailing effort." Living abroad clarified this ethos for him; he advised his readers to do the same, to "cool in their blood the fever-heat of strife."[65] On its surface, "England as Seen by a Black Man" sought to relate an American writer's observations of the facts of English life. More deeply, it captured the optimism Paul felt after an international journey. The inspiring prospect of marrying Alice introduced him to the possibility of starting his own family. Merged with these ideas was a coherent and cogent philosophical expression of views he shared with Booker T. Washington. "I want this for the blacks because I want them to be happy," he concluded. Paul would not always hew to this line of thinking, but this was where he stood midway through 1897.[66]

CHAPTER 13

East Coast Strivings

I am going out this morning to attend to business as soon as I can get away.
I will either telegraph or write as soon as I know anything. I shall stay here
about five days or a week and then go back to New York with my novel. I am
working on the New York Journal now, doing a series of stories for them and
other things. I shall come [west] of course but shall not stay long as the money
seems to be in the east. My hands are more full than I can tell you, and it may
not be a bad thing for me if this [xxxxx] does not pan out.

—PAUL LAURENCE DUNBAR TO MATILDA DUNBAR
(SEPTEMBER 27, 1897)[1]

Writing from New York City in early August 1897, Paul assured his mother,
Matilda, that he had arrived from England safe and sound, generally in good
health, and that he could resume sending her money. But he also told her his
professional responsibilities required him to spend more time on the East
Coast, in New York City and Washington, D.C. He could not travel to Chicago,
where his half-brothers Rob and Will lived and took care of their mother while
he was abroad. Business would force him to remain about two or three weeks
longer. Only his attachment to his mother could draw him back to the Midwest, he said. "If it were not for seeing you I should not leave here at all, as all
my business lies in this part of the country now"—to wit, "the money seems
to be in the east." Paul enclosed in each letter a check or some cash amounting
to, on average, fifteen to twenty dollars.[2]

For reasons of money and marketplace, Paul had no plans to leave the East
Coast. His agent, Major Pond, worked out of his office in New York City, and
settling there had a second benefit: Alice had moved there earlier in the year,
in February, to teach in Public School 83 in Brooklyn. Located on 1634 Dean

Street in a neighborhood called Weeksville, it was one of Brooklyn's first racially integrated schools. During the summer months of 1897, however, she spent time with her family in West Medford, Massachusetts. Sometimes he considered trailing her to Massachusetts, but he resisted, for he needed to earn a living. In the time Paul had between writing newspaper essays on his tour of England and letters to the acquaintances he met abroad, he continued to correspond with Alice whenever they were apart for substantial periods. He reiterated matters as profound as his love for her and, for instance, those as irritating as the brief theft and fortunate recovery of his typewriter from his 129 West 30th Street apartment in Manhattan.[3]

By August, Paul was regularly addressing Alice as "My Dear Little Wife to Be," but their engagement remained a secret.[4] Alice believed they should take their time in announcing their engagement and setting a wedding date. Despite his impatience, Paul came to agree with her that they should not marry for another two or three years: "However much we love each other, we are both young and can afford to wait," he wrote. "I await with anxiety nevertheless the answer from your mother." Before he left for England seven months earlier, he had not yet asked Alice's mother, Patricia Moore, for her daughter's hand. Only now did he write for permission. He hoped that Mrs. Moore would forgive the delay of news and approve of him as the right husband for Alice.

In September, Paul unselfconsciously—and unwisely—concluded his letter to Alice about her mother with an allusion to another woman who returned to his life. "I have seen my friend Rebekah," he admitted; "I think I had best not tell her of our engagement just yet." Whatever his reasons for mentioning Rebekah, Alice was unsettled.[5] A couple of weeks after his letter about Mrs. Moore, she responded. In coordination, Alice sent her mother her own letter; in a postscript she asked her mother: "Why did you not answer Mr. Dunbar's letter? He is waiting to hear from you—so am I, mama dear." Alice elevated the prospect of marriage above all. "She will cry when she reads that," Alice knew, "and I hate to cause mama tears—but then sweetheart I love you very much."

Resolute in love, Alice wrote these words after a tempestuous night in which she and Paul almost broke up over his flirtatious ways. "I never loved you before so deeply, never felt so near to you in heart and soul as I do now," she wrote. "Perhaps it is because we came so near to parting last night. I was firm at first, dear, but when I saw that awful vista of gray years before me, I wavered; and when I saw your tears, oh, Paul, I could have put my arms about you and sobbed with you." During their quarrel she had come around to the view that Paul had first broached in his letters from England: they were destined to be together. In an instant the idea came over her that love like theirs was made to survive under all conditions; that it was not she who had its "ordering and disposal—but a Diviner power." She needed assurance, however: "Paul, you will be true to me? You will not let man or woman come between us? You will be strong for my sake, resisting evil and temptation because you know I am praying for you?" His careless or unwitting mentions of other women raised the specter of infidelity, despite the sincerity of her love for him and the frequency with which she was signing her private letters to him, "Your Little Wife to Be."[6]

In the wake of their dispute, Paul told Alice that he "was a *little* bit blue." Yet he understood that he needed to overcome his short-term temptations for the long-term trust he had to build with Alice. In his heart he knew that any "sacrifice of inclination" was for her sake and for their future happiness. How forlorn he would have been if they had separated, he said, and how pleased he was that their bond could grow stronger—as it would, through the push and pull of wills and the strain of conflict and cease-fire.[7]

———

Finances weighed on Paul and Alice during their engagement. Among their discussions of writing and publishing opportunities, they also discussed fears and disagreements about making ends meet. An early clue to Paul's own preoccupation with finances came in the fall, right after his return from England. From the Manhattan port he traveled to 33 Poplar Street in Brooklyn, the home of Victoria Earle Matthews, where Alice was staying. He had hoped to surprise Alice, but moments before he arrived she had left for her relatives in West Medford, Massachusetts. He considered following her but changed his mind. "I feel like starting right on for Boston today, but this is nonsense," he wrote to Alice. "We cannot live on love so I must stay here and make something that we can live on."[8] A month later, in September, Paul wrote to Alice from Washington, D.C., where he was visiting friends, including Henry F. Baker and Lewis Douglass, Frederick's son.[9]

September 27, 1897, was the date when Paul would learn whether he had won a coveted job. Incidentally, two months earlier, in the middle of July, he had received an uplifting letter from "Colonel" Robert Green Ingersoll. An influential Civil War veteran and attorney from New York, and revered by American poets as esteemed as Walt Whitman, Ingersoll revealed in his letter that a remarkable new era in the history of the Library of Congress had just begun:

> My Dear Dunbar,
>
> The other day John Russell Young was appointed librarian at Washington. I know Mr. Young well and it may be that I could induce him to give you a place. I will try. It seems to me that the President would like to recognize your ability—in some way. I will see—if the library fails—what can be done in that direction. Do not become disheartened. You have already succeeded. Be true to yourself—you have genius and that is enough. Better crusts and rags with genius than feasts and robes without. Be true to the "inward light." I will write Mr. Young today (July 5th).
>   Hoping that you are well and hopeful, I remain
>
> > *Yours Always*
> > *R. G. Ingersoll.*[10]

By the time Paul received this letter, Ingersoll's admiration for him was well established. Ingersoll was an acquaintance of Henry Tobey, who had sent the colonel a copy of *Majors and Minors*. "I do not profess to be literary, but I think probably have ordinary human feeling and common sense, and I would like you to read over the poems I have marked, and which I think unusual," Tobey wrote in April 1896. "If after reading them you feel the same way, it would be a great consolation to Mr. Dunbar in his poverty and obscurity if you would write a letter of commendation." Eventually, Ingersoll did write back— enthusiastically. "Some of them are really wonderful—full of poetry and philosophy," he said; "I am astonished at their depth and subtlety. Dunbar is a thinker." Convinced as well that the poet was "a genius," Ingersoll asked, "Now, I ask what can be done for him? I would like to help." Ingersoll's reverence for Paul informed his latest intrigue in assisting Paul's application for a position in the Library of Congress.[11]

Ingersoll kept his word. On July 5, he sent a letter to John Russell Young, just appointed the seventh Librarian of Congress, on Paul's behalf. Ingersoll had already been in touch with Young, congratulating him on winning the librarianship, and he used this initial contact to request a favor. He summarized Paul's story: his parents' enslavement, his public schooling, and the literary promise of *Majors and Minors*, whose "poems are wonderful," "show great thought and great subjects," "are intense, subtle, passionate and poetic," and "are filled with touches of pathos—of joy—or real humor." He then made his request: "Dunbar is now in England. He is coming home. He, of course, is poor. He is crazy to read—to be in the company of books. Could you give this young fellow a place in the Library?" When Paul returned to America, he also wrote to Young, hoping "to call upon you with the letter of our common friend, Colonel Ingersoll."[12]

In 1897 President McKinley had appointed Young Librarian of Congress precisely because his predecessor, Ainsworth Rand Spofford, according to the *Library Journal*, was not "able to keep in touch with the modern developments of library organization and practice," when the library needed to fulfill its "manifest destiny" of becoming "in name as it is in fact the national library." The former managing editor of Horace Greeley's *Tribune* and a later contributor to the *New York Herald*, Young was an eventual companion to a previous president, Ulysses S. Grant, who ended up floating his name to McKinley.[13]

In his new role as head of the library, Young was poised to open its new building on November 1, with the permission to increase the staffing from 42 to 108, to be distributed among such areas as the Reading Room, Copyright Office, Law Library, Periodical Department, Cataloging Department, Music Department, Manuscripts Department, Art Gallery, and Hall of Charts and Maps. The library's call for workers attracted thousands of applications for junior positions that paid on average sixty dollars per month, while Young personally sought out the best candidates for the more senior administrative roles. The growth of the Library of Congress at the outset of Young's tenure made Paul hopeful that Ingersoll's intervention on his behalf would succeed.[14]

Initially, Ingersoll's letter did not inspire Paul's optimism. When he wrote to his mother about it, he remarked as if schooled well by repeated rejections from editors and publishers. "This letter is good but don't hope too much from it," he wrote. "We have been disappointed as often."[15]

Fortunately for Paul, in the end his pessimism was unwarranted. Paul did win a job as "Assistant Librarian." Not only did he have a legitimate post in the magisterial Library of Congress, the concentration of such distinguished men on his literary potential and professional progress revealed the high regard this young man, born from slaves, was beginning to enjoy in the halls of the United States government.

———

Paul could not help but grow increasingly cynical about his loss of literary innocence as he continued to bite the apple of commercial knowledge. "When one is just over the first flush of youthful dreaming, how sordid and cynical and commercial we grow," he wrote to a close friend as he approached the autumn of 1897. "It reminds me of a very devilish devil, consciously contemplating: 'what a devil of a devil I am!' But I think it is the condition of the atmosphere that has made me think about devils."[16]

Financial concerns indeed motivated Paul, while living in New York, to write a series of what he called "Tenderloin stories." Appearing in four consecutive September and October issues of *New York Journal*, they were set in poor districts and whetted the appetite of readers who liked supposedly authentic "darkey dialect." Each of the stories—"Bus Jinkins Up Nawth," "Yellow Jack's Game of Craps," "How George Johnson Won Out," and "The Hoodooing of Mr. Bill Simms"—was subtitled as a "Sketch of Real Darkey Life in New York." He wrote to Alice, "If you look in today's *Journal* you will see and disapprove of the first of my Tenderloin stories, but go on disapproving dear."[17]

Certainly, as Paul was writing his Tenderloin stories, he was surfing a movement of literary bohemianism that had been cresting in the nineteenth century. Henri Murger's playful illustration of Parisian vagabondage in his 1851 book of stories *Scènes de la Vie de Bohème* pioneered the redemption of unorthodox society and culture, both in Europe and in America, as a worthy literary subject. Ranging from Walt Whitman and Henry Clapp Jr. in 1850s New York City to Mark Twain and Charles Warren Stoddard in 1860s San Francisco, California, bohemianism inspired the fancy of writers who would interact with one another, form intellectual clubs, and experiment with themes about the defiance of social conventions.[18] The international fame of Giacomo Puccini's 1896 opera *La Bohème* was not mere happenstance, given its explicit nod to Murger's book, and given its implicit essence and expression of a modern generation of artists. This fame was the backdrop to Paul's new venture in short fiction.

Alice expressed disgust for Tenderloin districts and the prospect of Paul's literary exploitation of New York's for commercial gain. He responded, "I am getting money for it, that means help toward a cozy nest for my little singing bird."[19] The stories manifested what he had explained in a poem that first appeared in *Majors and Minors*, "We Wear the Mask." Assuming the form of the three-stanza rondeau with the *rentrement* of performance, the poem described a "mask" of rhetorical doubleness: a grin could be at once a smile and a grimace; a lie could conceal and reveal. And a writer like Paul, through mental fortitude and literary strategy, could turn the condescending expectations of white audiences about what he, an African American, could and should write about to his advantage. In this respect, the poem does not have explicit

markers of African American experiences, but the autobiographical undertones expressed by Paul's own life authenticate the stanzas with potential racial
implications:

> We wear the mask that grins and lies,
> It hides our cheeks and shades our eyes,—
> This debt we pay to human guile;
> With torn and bleeding hearts we smile
> And mouth with myriad subtleties,
>
> Why should the world be over-wise.
> In counting all our tears and sighs?
> Nay, let them only see us, while
> We wear the mask.
>
> We smile, but oh great Christ, our cries
> To thee from tortured souls arise.
> We sing, but oh the clay is vile
> Beneath our feet, and long the mile,
> But let the world dream otherwise,
> We wear the mask![20]

Alice implored Paul to stop writing Tenderloin stories. For his sake, she
relayed an urgent, though confidential, plea: "*don't, don't* write any more such
truck as you've been putting in the *Journal*. Now this is between us as between
husband and wife." To the world she would emphasize her support of his work
("To everyone else I champion your taste"), but privately she cautioned him:
"It is not fair to prostitute your art for 'filthy lucre,' is it?" She did not want to
marry a literary pimp who shamefully sacrificed the quality of his stories for
financial gain.[21]

Paul knew that the *Journal* work was far below his literary standards. But as
much as he wanted to comply with Alice's request, the financial allure was irresistible. "I will quit if you wish me to," he wrote, "but it is hard to give up the
money those little sketches bring." For a story, the *Journal* would pay him fifteen to twenty dollars to begin with—but he needed more. "Fifteen dollars a
week is so much less than thirty and looks particularly small when a man wants
to marry soon," he said. Until he felt more comfortable with his regular earnings, he had little choice, in his mind, but to write in this popular vein.[22]

Finances also dictated Paul's selection of professional opportunities outside
of publication and public speaking. In October, Claflin University, a

historically black institution in Orangeburg, South Carolina, offered him a position as a professor of literature, rhetoric, and elocution. He asked Alice's opinion on the compensation. "They have written to ask what I will come for," he informed her. "The letter was held in New York three weeks, but I answered to day setting my price at $1,000." Paul knew it well as "one of the largest of the colored schools"—established in 1869 by William Claflin, a white philanthropist in support of "Negro" education—but Alice had never heard of it. Afterward, Paul began to wonder whether he had set his asking price too high, but he soon received a letter inviting him to meet with the university president, Dr. Lewis M. Dunton, in Washington, D.C.[23] Bad luck denied Paul the opportunity. Not only did Paul fall ill and fail to meet with Dunton in person; the messenger he instructed to relay word of his illness likewise failed to complete the errand.[24]

———

Paul soon grew restless over keeping the secret. "I am so proud of you my darling that I am anxious for every one to know about our engagement," he wrote. "I have told the man from whom I expected to hear the meanest things, but he only exclaimed, 'They say she's a sugah-lady, Jesus! but won't you two make a hot train—Alice Ruth Moore and Paul Dunbar!'" He told another friend about their plans, who ribbed Paul: "My friend Baker is astounded and delighted at the arrangement but he asks 'where on earth did she get her taste?' I don't care, sweetheart, I believe that you love me and know that I love you with my very heart of hearts."[25]

By mid-October, the news of Paul and Alice's engagement had spread beyond their inner circle. Alice wrote to Paul, "Dear, when I think of the awful responsibility and gravity of the situation it makes me tremble." She was not yet sure that she could trust him "absolutely, positively, unconditionally." She needed more evidence that he had been, and would forever be, truly faithful. And they had yet to hear from either his own mother or her own, granting them their blessing to wed. After eight months, the engagement remained less than ideal because already it was appearing more indefinite than he initially thought.[26]

Paul was grappling with a complicated life as a rising celebrity. Media desired to take photographs of him and his mother; he learned that extended family, like his maternal uncle Robert N. Burton and Elizabeth Burton (Robert's wife, whom Paul called his aunt), "even want to get my little den of a work

FIG. 13.1. Paul at Berean Baptist Church, Washington, D.C., November 14, 1897.
(Ohio Historical Society)

room before the camera," he complained. Past friends had turned into enemies; past enemies attempted to become friends. Dayton no longer resembled
what he left behind. Alice, he believed, could guide him as he reckoned with
his increasing literary notoriety in a changing world.[27]

———

Yet Paul struggled to meet the moral standards that Alice had been expecting.
Multiple times in the past, such as during his time in England, he had hinted at
how much women, whether friends or strangers, tempted him to flirt with them.

He was getting close to misconduct. By late 1897 he also began to acknowledge more openly the temptation that had long afflicted his father: alcohol.

As early as the antebellum era, the problem of alcoholism had attracted the reformist attention of temperance societies, which encouraged drunkards to sign pledges to stay sober, but also to share their stories within a supportive, therapeutic environment. By the end of the Civil War, social reformers and physicians alike were coming to new medical understandings of habitual drunkenness. States developed medical institutions and revised laws to redress public drunkenness. By the late nineteenth century, close to twenty recorded Alcoholics Mutual Aid Groups had sprouted across the country: some focusing on sobriety through medical treatment; others through religious conversion; yet others through financial incentives; and some through encouragement of moderation rather than abstinence. The alcoholic came to be diagnosed as diseased. Doctors debated whether genetic inheritance or the plight of free will was the culprit.

Doctors at this time commonly prescribed alcohol as medicine for a variety of physical ailments and illnesses. Paul likewise would come to ensure that liquor was always on hand to help him cope with his struggles, physical and mental. He owned a hollow wooden cane, close to three feet tall, that, with the help of a brass ornamental cap that could be screwed on or off, concealed a long, cylindrical flask he could slide out to swig whisky, for example. (He owned typical canes as popular accessories, too.) He suffered from iatrogenic dependence, a side effect in which medical treatment caused his illness. If he subjected himself to medical analysis, a verdict at that time could very well have been an atavistic indictment of his own father, Joshua, a habitual drunkard. (In 1891 Indiana physicians went so far as to claim, notoriously, that habitual drunks should not be allowed to marry or procreate, and by implication should be sterilized, so as not to infect others.) Whether a form of self-medication or a genetic consequence, Paul's addiction to liquor was nothing less than a temptation he had to fight to overcome.[28]

"I am trying to live just as you would have me live," he promised Alice in a July 1897 letter. "Liquor seldom passes my lips, and I am striving hard against other temptations that are strongly accosting me." Stress rendered even more unbearable being the object of a rumor mill, of being laughed at, regarding the ongoing delay of his marriage. Folks within their social circle were gossiping about their approaching marriage, and he was being ridiculed over it.[29] Relatives and acquaintances began to weigh in on the news. Alice received a letter from her sister, Leila Young, and permitted Paul to read it. The letter congratulated Alice, although Paul also thought it questioned the wisdom of her decision. With deep-felt appreciation, he received support from his benefactor Tobey. Reactions to the news were largely positive, although some of Alice's friends expressed outright resistance to the idea of their marriage.[30]

Paul and Alice above all awaited final word from their mothers. "You have never told me yet what your mother thought of the affair," she worried. "Is she pleased? Does she mind? Do you think she will like me?" Matilda, in Paul's portrayal to Alice, longed for the day when the couple would be settled together so that his mind would be at rest; she could not stand his raving about Alice much longer. Mrs. Moore, by contrast, said she never received Paul's letter. "It is just what I expected," Alice wrote. "Mama didn't get the letter and sis didn't see it either. Some one else did, read and destroyed it." She asked Paul to write Mrs. Moore another letter, which she would enfold in her own, to ensure that Mrs. Moore received it. Securing Mrs. Moore's blessing was crucial. Alice was quite anxious to have her mother sanction their love. Within a week, Paul enclosed his letter to her mother, but his impatience ran high.[31]

"Talk about being blue—well blue is no name for it." Paul had no other way to describe the "missive" Alice's mother sent her daughter in response, cautioning against a hasty marriage. Paul was at a loss: "What shall we do darling? Is our dream to be wrecked entire?" he asked Alice. Mrs. Moore's refusal to bless their engagement compounded the skepticism expressed by some of Paul's Washington D.C. friends, who likewise believed that the couple should wait. But Paul refused to imagine that he and Alice would go unmarried past May 1898. They had already gone nine months engaged without a wedding date in sight.[32]

———

Given Paul's preference and need to stay on the East Coast, Matilda had to help manage some of his personal affairs—such as his house on 140 Zeigler Street, in Dayton—while he was living in Washington, D.C. She wished that he would fund its renovation, but his financial duress constrained him. As they approached Thanksgiving in 1897, he explained the problem to her. "I have received your several letters about the house. All I can say is, go as easy as you can, I am not a millionaire," he wrote, exasperated. The rent of twenty dollars per month he had to pay for his Washington, D.C. residence—a house at 1934 Fourth Street NW, in LeDroit Park, a neighborhood located a ten-minute walk southeast of Howard University—among other monthly expenses, restricted the amount he could send to Matilda. "But of course the house must be fixed," he wrote. "Find out how much it will take to send what things we need and send them to me as soon as I send the money." He assured her that he did not need extra furnishings, "as my house has all the modern improvements."[33]

Paul and Alice discussed the kind of home they should live in after their wedding, and the cost. Their opinions diverged. Paul realized that he was not earning enough to meet her expectations of the life they should have as an intellectual couple with access to some of the more exclusive circles of African American society in Washington, D.C. "I have come to see how far from great even an income of $1500 or $1600 is." Regarding the possible insufficiency of the house, he further joked: "Don't you think that we might squeeze along with a six room house at first until I have a chance to grow some?" For the time being he begged that they lower their expectations, such as the size of the house they should purchase, until he could pull in more revenue from his writings and recitals.[34]

The quarrel over the "six room house" did not abate. Paul decided that instead of selling his Dayton house he would rent it out, although it needed costly repairs. "I want you so badly and I want you so soon that it seems almost like treason to reason about it," he said, "but if reason did not cool us now it would freeze us hereafter. However dear if you can stand a six room house such as most of my Washington friends who make more money than I do occupy, why should we not marry soon?" He believed that Alice's quest for a standard of living that was expensive but, in her view, appropriate to their social stature ignored the reality that his richer friends of Washington, D.C., were or would be quite content with the living conditions he had been proposing to her.

Paul implored Alice to consider a more modest way of life. After all, such a way of life satisfied him, even though he was at that time the more financially successful and celebrated author. In a tone increasingly defensive and antagonistic, he argued that it would be irrational to live more luxuriously than those who earned more than he did. As they quarreled over the meaning of the six-room house, he suggested a house at 1934 Fourth Street NW where they could live as husband and wife. Alice agreed in November to examine the property, and Matilda would visit in early December to help him settle in.[35]

———

Paul thought he had finished writing his first novel by the end of July 1897, while in England. But it turned out he had more—and more, and more—to write. Now it was the fall, and he was back in New York. The manuscript continued to swell. "I have just finished typing more than two thousand words on the ever present novel," he complained to Alice. "I wish it were done and in the hands of the publisher." More than the evidence of literary accomplishment, publishing the novel would bring him one step closer toward a public union with his fiancée. "I am hoping much that its acceptance will be the means of hastening our nuptial day for which I so dearly long when I dare tell the world that you are mine all mine," he wrote. No novel, no money—no marriage. "Everything that keeps us apart seems to loom up hugely on my horizon," he explained. "The days drag themselves away. The dollars come in all too slowly and not a finishing line will come to that blessed novel."[36]

Just as finances influenced Paul's decisions on what kind of literature to write, where to publish it, and how Alice critiqued its quality and purpose, they also dictated how soon the couple could hold their wedding. The year 1897 was coming to an end, and he was growing restless. "I wonder if there is any possible show of our marrying in December?" he asked Alice. "Do you think so? Every thing, you know, depends upon the coming in of the cash. How I wish it would hustle in, for I want you with me darling soon, soon, soon."[37]

Since his return from England, Paul was turning into nothing less than an admitted literary hustler, the pimp of poetry and fiction Alice had admonished him to avoid becoming. In his view, his decision to write and publish especially for commercial purposes served the greater, long-term good. Not only did he apply this rationale to his authorship of individual poems and short stories, which he could promptly produce and place for publication, but he also viewed his long-form prose—namely, his first novel—in this way, again at the potential expense of creative choices. He had just finished the last chapter of the novel and admitted that its ending was something to be desired. "I have finished the last chapter of my novel and it is indeed very flat," he told her, less an expression of triumph than of resignation. "I am sure that it ruins the ending." But his pursuit of more money to wed Alice took greater priority than his endeavor to write a legendary story of high quality. "But if they will just hand me over some cash to hasten the happy day I shall be satisfied."[38]

Finances determined Paul's strategy for publishing the novel. While he ultimately planned to release his first novel as a book, his plan initially to release it in serial form would bring him the financial security he needed to marry Alice. "Let me know how much money you want," he wrote to her, "and I will work my fingers off but you shall have it."[39] The novel marked the time, as early as the fall of 1896, when Paul was thinking of trying to showcase his literary versatility beyond poetry. To the point of exhaustion, he had been trying to meet the market demand for his poems. "I am worked to death and totally tired out mentally and physically," he once wrote Alice, while trying to "fill a couple of orders" for such magazines as the New York *Independent* and *Ladies' Home Journal*. A novel was a welcome change. He had promised one for D. Appleton & Company, a "novel which I fear will never be written." Initially, the path was not yet clear how he would complete it; nor was he yet certain of the quality he could achieve.[40] Less than a week after he wrote these desperate words, however, Dodd, Mead and Company accepted the novel, as well as the idea of releasing it serially, "giving me all the clear gain," he smiled. "Ain't it bully if they are able to do it."[41] By the middle of December 1897, Paul learned that *Lippincott's Magazine* had accepted the novel for serialization. For this particular release Paul received $350, in addition to the advance that he had already received. "This makes $750 for the book before a line is printed," he wrote Alice during his spare time at the Library of Congress. "I hope it will be a success."[42]

Established in 1868, *Lippincott's Monthly Magazine: A Popular Journal of General Literature, Science, and Politics* was located in Philadelphia and published by J. B. Lippincott Company. The authors and critics who appeared in its pages ranged from Anna Katherine Green and Stephen Crane to Oscar Wilde and Arthur Conan Doyle.[43] Paul could possibly become the first African American writer to contribute regularly to the magazine. Here, he could abandon the Negro dialect styles and themes for which he had become celebrated and revel in the magazine's reputation for fostering "comparative freedom from staleness and familiar routine," as one reporter had stated almost three decades earlier.[44]

Just before Christmas, a squabble ensued between the publishers of Dodd, Mead and *Lippincott's*. "Dodd wants the latter to sign a contract promising not to get out a special edition of his magazine when my novel comes out," he informed Alice, flattered by the spectacle of two famous publishers battling over the rights to his work. "Lippincott refuses and the fight proceeds while I look on." A week into the New Year, the dispute was resolved: *Lippincott's* would release the novel first and Dodd, Mead second, but *Lippincott's* wanted more lead time ahead of its release as a book to ensure that sales of the magazine issues would not be impinged on. Dodd, Mead wanted Paul to decide.[45]

Paul was torn. "If I decide for [*Lippincott's*] I lose the friendship of Dodd," he wrote. "If I decide for Dodd, I lose $350.00 and a big opening," he added. "I have no one with whom to advise. I am discouraged & worried to death," he wrote. "I wish God had let me die before the canker-worm of ambition began eating at my heart."[46]

———

As eager as Paul was to marry, while he lived in Washington, D.C., he remained friendly with his old flame, Rebekah Baldwin. For better or for worse, he did not hesitate to tell his fiancée that, on occasion, he would see his old girlfriend. When Paul was awaiting word on whether he had won the job at the Library of Congress, for example, he wrote to Alice: "I am hoping for the best issue on tomorrow. I have seen my friend Rebekah and she is also hopeful." But he was reluctant to disclose to Rebekah the even more momentous news: whether Alice's mother approved of their planned marriage. "I think I had best not tell her of our engagement just yet."[47] He took pleasure, even while engaged to Alice, in the friendship he reignited with Rebekah and in enjoying three women in his life. In an 1897 letter to his mother he wrote, in consecutive sentences, "Alice is back at work in the Brooklyn schools and doing nicely"; "I have seen Rebekah and she is as good and charming as ever"; and, to Matilda, "Write me soon."[48]

Always concerned about Paul's weakness for drink and dalliance, Alice questioned his decision to spend time with an old flame. He claimed that Rebekah kept him out of trouble. From a winter gathering, "I came away at once & sober," Paul assured Alice. "I go out to very little. If I go there is talk. If I stay in, they say I am out some where with a white woman, so I shall just let them talk. It is just for this reason that I am so much with Miss ___." Alice did not like Paul's writing about Rebekah. Defensive, he promised his fiancée that his former girlfriend was not "a nigger," which in their shared racist parlance meant that she was not racially inferior, and that she hated the gossipers as much as he did. As a member of the Washington, D.C., elite, Rebekah, he argued, was worthy of his time and Alice's trust. Alice remained skeptical.[49]

CHAPTER 14

The Way Is Dark

I pity you, oh how I pity you, but what avail has my pity? I pray for you, but what might can my prayers have when I, the wicked one, brought it all on you myself. If I were brave enough or coward enough I would do the only honorable thing a man can do in such a case, but while I am not afraid to die, I am afraid to take my own life.

—PAUL LAURENCE DUNBAR TO ALICE RUTH MOORE
(NOVEMBER 26, 1897)[1]

About a week before Thanksgiving in 1897, Paul admitted to Alice that he had been behaving like an alcoholic. On a recent trip to recite poems in Philadelphia, his excessive drinking and inebriation stunned attendees, including Will Lewis, who witnessed the incident and likely reported it to Alice, his friend. Paul did not lie about it, but he also portrayed the event as a success. "I was very drunk at Philadelphia, but made a great hit," he wrote to Alice. "I went alone to a white hotel and filled up on champagne."[2] Far worse, during a subsequent visit to Alice in New York, alcohol fueled another kind of temptation for Paul. While with her he became drunk again, and then they had a pivotal physical encounter. Sometime afterward, when he had returned to Washington, D.C., to return to work at the Library of Congress, he reflected on what he had done.[3] In the language of decorum and reticence of the Victorian era, he confessed to Alice in a letter that he had "dishonored" her.[4]

Paul's admitted misconduct, his suggestions that Alice had not granted consent and that he had violated her, was tantamount to rape, although the societal odds were stacked against her to prove this. They were in an intense private relationship in which they were engaged to be married; however, his chronic oscillations between sobriety and inebriation complicated the impression that their bond was healthy. For her to allege rape meant that she would have had to bear a burden of proof that was suffocating for women in her situation: being in a relationship with a man with whom, despite their secrecy, evidence had pointed to her being in love—and vice versa. Moral depravity, a condition publicly condemned even more than the criminality of a rapist, stigmatized women alleged to have partaken in sexual activity outside of wedlock.[5] Not only were wives denied "the right to withhold consent" in the late nineteenth century, according to scholar Estelle B. Freedman, but it also followed that "having had sexual relations, or even having a reputation for impurity, strongly disadvantaged women" who claimed that they had withheld consent in sexual activity. Marriage—and, by extension, engagement to be married—exerted "categorical restrictions" on what women could say, do, or achieve if they wished to allege that they were raped. Alice was in this bind. In the short term, only her silence could represent her reaction to Paul's apologies, to his inadequate gestures of repentance in lieu of the commensurate justice that she was helpless to exact.[6]

In mid-November, Paul wrote to Alice again: "My feelings this morning have been a strange admixture of remorse & exultation," he confessed. "I know that I done wrong, very wrong. My course has been weak and brutal. I have dishonored you and I cannot forgive myself for it." He knew he had violated her. "I have no plea to make, no excuse." He apologized. "My heart bleeds for what I have done. Forgive my darling and love me." But he also expressed "exultation," suggesting that his transgression represented an act of enhanced intimacy: "Dear, while I feel myself a scoundrel, do you know that I feel infinitely nearer to you?"[7]

Mere hours after writing these words, Paul wrote again to Alice. This time his remorse was more fulsome. He could not shake the memory of what he had done. "The letter I wrote you at the library today did not seem to say half that was in my heart," he began. "I want to pour out my whole soul to you and let you know how entirely it is yours. I have been very greatly depressed since my return from New York. I have grieved for my escapades while there." Guilt lay heavily on his heart; he feared that his misbehavior would incur a divine penalty: "Only God knows how I have suffered in the last two days, how I am still suffering and, too, how I deserve to suffer." Admitting to his "weakness" of moral character, he called himself a "maudlin, reeling drunken libertine," praying that his love "condone" him. "I want you in my arms again when I am sober," he added. He suggested Thanksgiving, just days away, as the perfect holiday on which he hoped she would "consent to a civil marriage."[8]

Alice was not willing to talk about marriage. Given the nature of Paul's letters to her, one could ascertain that he was realizing the full magnitude of his misconduct. Her injuries were not only emotional and mental, they were physical as well. "Do you mean to say that I in my bestial lust have so hurt and injured you—my God—my God," he wrote. "Alice, my darling I wish I had died before it happened." He noticed that, in her letter, she had modified her signature, and realized that he had imperiled their engagement: "Dearest—I hardly dare call you by any endearing name, brute that I am—you did not sign your self 'Little Wife to Be' as usual. Does that mean that you can or will never be mine?" he asked. "Alice I could not stand the thought of it." Contrary to his wish, she did not want him to visit her in New York. She could not bear to see him.

Ironically, Paul came to understand that, despite his initial plans, he probably could not bear to be face-to-face with Alice either. ("I think it would drive me mad," he said.) She needed consolation and convalescence. ("But you will be better, dear. God will not let you suffer long for this sin of which I was the sole author.") He assured her that he would always provide for her. ("Whether you get well or whether you are invalid for life, you are mine and I shall always love you and take care of you. . . . Spare no expense. It will be my right to pay your bills.") He tried to encourage her recovery. ("Keep your mental state strong dear and get well.") He promised to change his behavior. ("I will never drink again, so help me God!") Sounding like a quack, he even sought, graphically, to explain that his inebriation saved her from accidental impregnation. ("One thing, dear, be easy about, you are not with child. I was too *drunk* for flow. I might have told you before but I was ashamed even half-drunk as I was of my own bestiality.") To prove the depth of his faithfulness, he was preparing now, close to eleven months after their engagement, to mail her an engagement ring—which he did. (In all their months together since his marriage proposal, he had yet to buy one, although he had given her a secondhand friendship ring.) Within mere days he found the perfect ring, with a ruby stone on top to represent love, and glittering diamonds on either side.[9]

Guilt, depression, and thoughts of suicide gripped Paul. Images of Alice "lying there bandaged and bruised and sore" haunted him. His remorse reached a turning point. The gravity of her condition was now crushing *him*. "I have been criminally careless and a brute besides," he wrote. He wavered between his own commitments to life and death. "If I were brave enough or coward enough I would do the only honorable thing a man can do in such a case, but while I am not afraid to die, I am afraid to take my own life."

Wrestling with these thoughts and feelings, Paul closed his letter with the request that Alice send him all her medical bills so that he could pay them. He enclosed a piece of "hypocritical irony"—a poem that he had just written and had an eye for publishing down the road:

Lead gently, Lord, and slow,
For oh, my steps are weak,
And ever as I go,
Some soothing sentence speak;

That I may turn my face
Through doubt's obscurity
Toward thine abiding place,
E'en tho' I cannot see.

For lo, the way is dark;
Through mist and cloud I grope,
Save for that fitful spark,
The little flame of hope.

Lead gently, Lord, and slow,
For fear that I may fall;
I know not where to go
Unless I hear thy call.

My fainting soul doth yearn
For thy green hills afar;
So let thy mercy burn—
My greater, guiding star![10]

Days after Thanksgiving, word was beginning to circulate about Alice's health. She was on leave from her job as schoolteacher, a job she enjoyed. Friends were bound to learn that she was dealing with some serious ailment. Rumors were swirling as far away as Washington, D.C., where Paul was working and acquaintances inquiring. "I have told those who ask me here that you have nervous prostration," Paul wrote her, so "everyone sympathizes with you very much." Repeatedly he implored her to forgive him and accept his love—to marry him, still.

The silence on Alice's end was deafening and disconcerting. She was unwilling even to write Paul a letter of reply, to indicate whether she forgave him or even to jot "just a line or two" on whether she received and liked the ring he had just sent. By the time she did reply—a few days later, on December 1—she continued to express shock that he would do "that" to her, that he would make her suffer so "bodily," that she would be his "poor bruised, broken, tortured wife." For much of November she could not return to work, a reality that at once disturbed him, due to guilt, yet also delighted him, due to his long-standing opposition to her working there. As his wife, she should stay home. He believed he would earn the money for them to live on.[11]

Paul told Alice he was glad to be "suffering for my folly, suffering bitterly and constantly, now," for his mistreatment of her. "Every time I feel a pang it thrills me because I seem to feel that I am some way paying you back in kind pang for pang, for all that I have caused you." But it turned out that he, too, would suffer physically as well as emotionally: he had contracted gonorrhea. Symptoms of gonorrhea, a disease spread through sexual contact, appeared within six days of infection. Treatment at the time included doses of mercury or, more popularly, silver nitrate—at least until Protargol emerged in 1897 as the drug of choice. As uncomfortable as Paul's physical symptoms were, they paled in comparison to those Alice suffered from both his physical "dishonoring" of her and his inability fully to comprehend her suffering.[12]

Paul was able to secure some kind of medicine from Dan Williams, his friend who was also a physician; but Williams had to depart for Chicago, leaving behind only a small dose as Paul's symptoms worsened. In disclosing to Alice his own illness, as well as his abstention from drinking despite a "very strong" temptation, he tried to empathize with her plight.[13]

Alice rarely wrote Paul during this contentious time. More than two weeks after the incident, she had yet to promise either to visit him in Washington, D.C., or to allow him to visit her in Brooklyn. He wondered whether she hated him or were too sick to write. "Suspense you know is worse than a painful certainty," he reminded her the first week of December. "Won't you write to me at once and ease my mind?" If she could not write to him, he wished at the very least that someone else could write on her behalf.[14]

To Paul's relief, he finally received a letter later during the first week of December in which Alice referred to herself, once again, as "Little Wife to Be." She still wanted to marry him, contrary to his mounting fear that she had moved on. "I was afraid that you had thrown me over for good and all and I was very miserable," he wrote. Now he wanted to rectify as much as he could. He remained committed to paying her medical bills. (For instance, he enclosed ten dollars in a letter.) He planned to devote as much of his earning power as he could toward eliminating the financial debt.[15]

Paul's reputation had not yet recovered from his recent drunken behavior in Philadelphia. The news of that event had reverberated across their social circles. For Alice's sake, he tried to dispel the rumor that, in addition to being drunk, he "soiled" himself. That was untrue. "I dressed at the hall dressing room in all clean linen, but had to send a nigger out for a standing collar because mine were all lay-downs." He reiterated that he was not fully inebriated because he was nothing but "excessively polite" and "exceedingly exuberant" in his recitation. By the way, his reading "brought the house down."

Paul's recklessness embittered Alice's mother, who had learned of the drunken episode. "I don't quite see what people can tell her to my discredit," he wrote. He proceeded to defend himself, to assure Alice that staying with him would not taint her own reputation. "Few people know of my fondness for women, and while my drinking is known or guessed by more, few have ever seen me under the influence," he said. "But you know I am bound to be talked about. Ostracism might ensue upon your marrying me, but I hardly believe it." He cared little that he was not as acceptable or distinguished as some of Alice's Boston-area male friends, for example. He was confident that their mutual love would win out, though he asked whether family and friends were gossiping about his "escapades."[16]

As the bond between Paul and Alice healed, he worked to renew her trust in him. He so bared his heart, he so repented, that he seemed almost to depress her as she read his letters. Exposing his soul was crucial. He believed that she would never trust him again; that she was growing farther and farther away from him; that she was ashamed of and despised him. In spite of his history of misbehavior, to a degree she felt as though she were holding him back, like an albatross. He rebutted that notion. But over time it became the emotional leverage he exploited to reel her back in. Never did he want to be released from her. "But I do feel depressed and hopeless, when I view my situation." He came clean about his mistakes despite his promise to change his ways and avoid temptation. "As for going to a party drunk," he confessed, "I have been to only one since coming here, and to that I went with Joe Douglass perfectly sober." Better than being alone and drunk, he figured, was enjoying the company of a sober friend—in this case, Frederick Douglass's grandson—who could keep him safe.[17]

Alice came around and finally responded to Paul's entreaties. After all that he had done, *she*, ironically, was relieved that he continued to desire her and that their marriage was back on track. "Your letter of this morning made me so happy until I sat right down and woman like cried from pure joy," she wrote one week before Christmas. "It was so much like the old times, like my Paul—I felt that you loved me still."[18]

————

Each time the engagement of Paul and Alice attained a semblance of normalcy, an oddity undermined it. Now that they were back on speaking terms, he revealed that a ring he had given her (different from the ring he had sent her around Thanksgiving, which was brand-new, purchased only for her) had belonged to his previous admirer, Rebekah Baldwin. He should not have passed it along, he said, and beseeched Alice to cooperate in returning it to him. "One thing, dearie, won't you return Miss Baldwin's ring at once," he begged. "She wants it, and is quite angry with me." He added, "I have not told her that you have it because I promised not to let any other girl wear it. But, then you are different, because you are mine and I am yours—so you can wear any thing that I have, even to the trousers when we get married." Paul had not yet been quite forthcoming to Alice about the outstanding social contract he had with Rebekah or, in turn, about the fact that he had not been honest to Rebekah about how his deep commitment to Alice had superseded this contract.[19]

Closer to Christmas, Paul was pleased that Alice was not upset. ("I have your letter and am happy because you are not angry with me," he said. "I always open your letters so fearfully and it makes me glad to find you in good spirits.") But he still tried to pry Rebekah's ring loose while reaffirming Alice's commitment to the new engagement ring. "I want you to be a good careful girl when you go down to Boston," he wrote, referring to a holiday trip she was taking to her family in West Medford. "I don't need to warn you to let nothing slip. Take up for me good and strong and *wear your ring on the right finger.* By 'right' I mean 'proper.' Tell me if you are going to do this." Alice's placing of the ring on her "right" finger—or the correct one, on the left hand—would declare her impending marriage to him. Later, he wrote, "I hope you had a joyous Christmas, and that the shadow of approaching fate did not so seriously dampen the ardor of your family that they could not enjoy your presence." As a postscript to his best wishes, he prodded, "Dear, won't you please send me Rebekah's ring?"[20]

Alice responded by reveling in the admiration she had received all around at the news of her engagement: "I am besieged, overwhelmed with congratulations and love from my girl friends." She did not mention Rebekah's ring, only the new engagement ring she wore: "I don't say anything but laugh and show my ring."[21]

Paul was relieved that Alice, "having such a nice time" with friends, sounded like her old self again. He replied that his holidays had been quiet until he reunited with an old flame (*not* Rebekah) with whom he "chased around a little" into the evening. By now many in their social circles knew of the engagement— not always to his delight, though. "It's thrust down my throat at every turn I make," he said, regarding the indiscretion of acquaintances. "People hint and rhapsodize, joke or moralize about it." Despite the increasingly widespread news, he confessed to his chronic moral weakness without Alice's presence by his side. "I shall be so glad dear when you can come to me and keep a watchful eye over all my tendencies to naughtiness, so people won't be kept busy running to you with stories of my unexampled wickedness," he wrote. "You must get very tired of it." He started to sign his prenuptial letters, "Your Devoted Husband."[22]

Alice took notice of Paul's dalliances with Rebekah. "So you and Rebekah are friends again?" she inquired. "That's good, only don't be *too* friendly, dear." She then described a lengthy discussion with her sister, Leila, who relented to the idea of her marriage to Paul and whose husband, James Young, was looking forward to meeting him. Her mother, Patricia Moore, had not yet given her blessing, but Leila's approval "rules the roost." Getting married would require more than the support of the Moores, Alice reminded Paul. He had to do his part. "Oh, Paul, if you will only be a good boy for me, we shall be so happy," she pleaded. "I want to, I *must* have a *long* talk with you. You *must* come to N.Y. *very* soon, won't you?" The geographical distance was a symbol of their emotional separation. With all eyes on them now, she needed him within arm's length: to hammer out the wedding plans, but also to strengthen his moral self-discipline. At every turn she hoped that he was "being strong and true during these holiday times," that he was enjoying himself "without giving way to 'Bacchus' temptations,'" an allusion to the fawning women of Greco-Roman mythology who gravitated to Dionysus, the Roman god of wine. She wanted his "assurance," which he later would provide, that he would no longer succumb "to Bacchus nor to Venus either, though the temptation to both has been strong."[23]

———

In December, the financial desperation that led Paul to accept a full-time job at the Library of Congress and, in his spare time, to travel and recite his literature was taking its toll. Finite was his well of energy. Writing in haste one afternoon from the library, Paul said he barely had time to draft a letter for

Alice to read. "I am greatly depressed without exactly knowing why. I am very tired physically & mentally and spiritually." Amid recitals in four cities during the week of December 13, he worked each day at the Library of Congress from 9:00 a.m. to 4:00 p.m.—his usual hours—then traveled to his engagements. He was in Baltimore, Maryland, Monday night; scheduled to visit Wilmington, Delaware, the following evening; and had to look ahead to dates in Philadelphia Thursday night and Washington, D.C., Friday evening. Reciting his work did not invigorate him the same way it did during his tour of England. His reading in Baltimore the previous night was a success, but it did not excite him. Few things did anymore.

"I am only weary, weary, and I wish to God the fight was over and I were where I could rest always," Paul confessed. Compounding these pressures was the peculiar condition of being a writer wrestling with the expectations of readers and audiences, respectively—with the stereotypes governing their prejudice of him and his race. The next scheduled recital—in Wilmington, North Carolina—was likely to prolong his misery. "Only it seems now there is no more light & in this mood I must go to Wilmington tonight to play the buffoon for a lot of grinning Negroes whom I hate." Even as he was a distinguished gentleman of letters, the caricature of the buffoon, even in the eyes of members of his own race, was never too far from his persona.[24]

The cost "physically & mentally and spiritually" Paul was incurring discouraged him from accepting an invitation to deliver two more readings in Wilmington. "My head is so dizzy now I can scarcely write. I am glad the day is nearly over," he would write Alice afterward, upon his return to Washington, D.C. Traveling farther to see her in person certainly would help assuage his misery. But the fragility of his finances, which deterred him from spending money on the train fare from Washington to New York City, perpetuated the fragility of his mind, heart, and spirit. Frugality remained crucial as 1897 turned into 1898; "but the time cannot, must not be long until I see you."[25]

Alice wanted Paul to come to New York City for another reason. Delaying their efforts to get married was the obligation she had to herself and her friends to earn certification to teach in New York. He was already resistant to her employment as a teacher in Brooklyn, so she knew that he might not have the most sympathetic ear; but her educational and professional advancement meant a lot to her, and he knew that. On New Year's Day, 1898, she relayed to him that she was willing to get married as early as that month of January— which is what he had wanted all along, an expedited wedding—in exchange for keeping the news secret until she received her certificates. His cooperation, she told him, would help improve the conditions of their future life together. She wished their home to have "the highest possible position, the respect and admiration of all the powers that be. . . . We owe it to ourselves to create and maintain an unquestioned, looked-up-to social position. Don't you think so? And so much depends upon your attitude now."[26]

Alice proposed an attractive deal to Paul. "If you will say yes" to the agreement, she offered, "come up to New York when you can—and I will be really yours." He accepted the offer, with one condition: "Darling I will come up to New York this month and marry you if you will agree that I may bring my mother," he said, a clue that even marriage would not come between him and Matilda. Next, he tried to allay Alice's fear that their own social standing in Washington, D.C., was compromised. Though his life currently was "unexceptional," he wanted to become rich and promised that Alice's life would be "happy and care-free." To console her further, he contended that everyone wanted word of when he planned to bring her to town. "Even Rebekah says she wants to love you & I know she will," he remarked, peculiarly, "while I am sure you will like her aristocratic manners and her brilliancy." His engagement to Alice, and the word-of-mouth about it among friends and family, was working well in diverting him from those ethical or moral hazards by which he could be led astray.[27]

Alice was elated that Paul agreed to her plan. Even so, she had to verify Paul's loyalty and his understanding of the gravity of marriage—of doing "the deed," in her words. Three months since his sexual violation of her, she continued to enclose in her letters medical bills for him to pay. To mitigate her embarrassment before John W. Parrish, the doctor who had been treating her injury, she asked Paul to append to the check a statement that they were already married, implying that her injury was not premarital, to protect Alice's reputation. (Paul did affix a note.)[28]

Traces of the past dictated the way Paul and Alice pivoted toward the future. "Why will you not send Rebekah's ring, dear?" he asked. Alice was not willing to comply with Rebekah's wish. "Why don't I send Rebekah's ring?" she asked. "I don't know. It looks so much better on my finger than I imagine it looked on hers, I suppose is the only reason." While it is not clear whether Alice wore Rebekah's ring in addition to or instead of her new engagement ring from Paul, the quibbling marked the territories at stake among the three of them. At the very least, Alice, as his fiancée, implied that whatever he possessed would soon belong to her. Alice's assertive response led Paul to apologize for his own irritable and petty tone.[29]

Paul would not let the matter drop without having the last word—that is, without his hallmark indiscretion. "You conceited little minx, you," he wrote; "I don't know about that ring looking better on your hand than Rebekah's. She has the most beautiful hands in the world—speaking generally of course."[30] By the end of January both moved on from the matter. In subsequent months they exchanged frequent letters about their genuine love for each other, their plans to visit each other as much as their schedules allowed, and their mutual anticipation of being husband and wife.

————

In early 1898 Paul learned that a woman working as a librarian at Howard University had married and tendered her resignation. The renowned university was about three miles from the Library of Congress and merely a quarter of a mile from his rented home on 1934 Fourth Street NW. He thought the job would be ideal for Alice. She had extensive experience reading and writing literature, and she could garner recommendations from local acquaintances or colleagues in New York City. "I know Gilder and others in New York would recommend and push you," he said, referring to his colleague Richard Watson Gilder, editor of the *Century* magazine and a prominent authority in the New York social and intellectual circles overlapping her own. "I know that I am selfish to be always planning to have you near me," he said, "but there are times when it seems that I must have you, when a few minutes and a few steps will take me to your side for help, counsel, sympathy and inspiration."[31]

Ever since they became engaged almost a year earlier, expenses continued to delay Paul's ability—their ability—to hold the kind of wedding Alice wanted. "Dear, do let us talk plain business," Paul wrote to her. "I want to marry you at once very much," but the "wedding is totally impossible for months to come." He thought that holding the event where Alice's family lived—closer to her in New York City than to him in Washington, D.C.—would have been too expensive. He did not mean to whine, but he wanted her to realize the state of his financial affairs. From the Library of Congress he earned a salary of $60 per month (equivalent to about $1,870 today) coupled with scattered revenues from literary publishing, most prominently an upcoming February royalty payment of close to four times this amount for *Lyrics of Lowly Life*.[32]

Paul proceeded to list his expenses for Alice. To her alone he had paid $85 since Thanksgiving to cover her medical bills, to which there had yet to be an end in sight; he paid more than that for the furniture in their Washington, D.C., home; and $125 in the taxes, assessments, and repairs incurred by the property. He had to pay rent for the Washington home. He had overworked himself to keep ahead of his obligations since he had been there. He apologized for taking such an analytical turn in his letter, which "cannot indicate all the current of longing love and yearning for you that underlies these ugly, discouraging facts, so I will come to you as soon as possible when we can talk it over."[33]

Alice did not begrudge the financial specificity of Paul's letter, but she worried that the pressure he put on himself to be a breadwinner compromised his mental and physical health. "I hate to think of you slaving so. Don't," she implored. "If you break down and become all ill what will I do? Cry my eyes out?" She envisioned a wedding in 1899, not 1898, thus extending their engagement to two years.

While Paul sought to earn as much money as he could to expedite the wedding, Alice was willing to wait longer and avoid the financial pressure. She was confident in their bond as it stood. "Don't be blue, nothing is going to part us, but yourself," she assured him. "I can wait years if you will. Have faith and trust in me. I am yours through all time."[34] Alice encouraged Paul to be patient and more selective in his professional opportunities: she argued that the rise of his literary celebrity would coincide with the decline of his financial desperation.

For example, Josephine St. Pierre Ruffin, an African American suffragist and publisher of *Woman's Era*, the first newspaper by and for African American women, had recently invited Paul to Boston to read at the Woman's Era Club. Both the club and the paper would draw a large audience with his help. Critical of Ruffin's motives, Alice suggested to Paul that the invitation was not worth his time and effort. He should develop the proper wisdom to overcome the financial angst guiding his professional decision-making: "You are a good drawing-card and would fill the house," Alice wrote. "Good. Well, why cannot she be honest and say, 'Mr. Dunbar, will you help us,' instead of masking under a guise of helping *you*, and introducing *you* to the people who will help *you* in your 'literary career.'" She did not dispute that Boston was "anxious" for his recital, but she issued a warning: "better that you forfeit the golden privilege of 'meeting the literati of New England,' than go under such auspices. You are young, dear, with a career before you, that, thank God, isn't begging to be helped along at such a rate." In light of the number of books, articles, and public recitals Paul had produced by this time, he could be selective. "The time has passed for you to grasp at *anything* for the sake of being seen," she concluded. "You can afford to be dignified and wait for the right moment."[35]

———

Late in January, Paul became sick. He could barely muster the energy to write Alice on the letterhead of the Library of Congress, where he had now been working for close to four months. But he did—and was glad he did so. "I have been trying to write to you all morning but haven't had spirit enough," he said. "I am still a miserable sick boy, though your two dear letters this morning were like medicine to me." Reading her prose enabled him to cope with having fallen "violently ill," whereupon he went straight to bed the previous night.[36]

This was not the first time Paul had relayed to Alice recurrences of ill health. For months he had written to her about ailments ranging from gonorrhea, which he had explained before, to cerebrospinal meningitis. Also known as meningococcal disease, after Austrian bacteriologist Anton Weichselbaum's recent discovery of meningococcus in 1887, cerebrospinal meningitis was an inflammation of the membranes of the spinal cord and brain. Paul's symptoms included a high fever and severe stiffness or aches in the head and neck. He was vulnerable to confusion, vomiting, sensitivity to light and noise. It was a chronic medical condition often fatal due to its impact on the brain and blood circulation by way of viral or bacterial infection. Fortunately, he, like most infected, recovered within ten days.

A year and a half earlier, while touring London, Paul had been sick for days with similar symptoms and mentioned that he would first need to recover, to be "well enough to wield the pen," before he could reply. Months later, in August, shortly after his return from England, he fell ill again, this time hardly able to hold his head up. Closer to Thanksgiving he came down with sickness again; he had been so ill he had to postpone work at the library. And right after inflicting a sexual injury on Alice, he had contracted gonorrhea, "suffering bodily."[37]

By the time Paul was writing to Alice in the early months of 1898, such poor health had been a regular theme in their letters, and it continued with his current contraction of meningitis. Alice wondered whether his harrowing and debilitating physical symptoms had resulted from his withdrawal from excessive drinking. But he believed quite the opposite: drinking could be the antidote to his current suffering. "No, dear, I don't think my sickness comes from not drinking," he corrected, "but I do believe a good deal of my weakness does—no don't laugh." He disclosed his strategy for coping with physical pain:

"I drank some yesterday and am going to continue to take a little stimulant in the house behind closed doors."[38]

Privy to Paul's private life, Alice could see that he was still battling the temptations that he promised he would conquer in proving his marital worth. He was struggling to break free of the alcoholism that had beset his father, Joshua, along with so many other men of the nineteenth century: namely, the mythical story of the promising young man whose moral weakness made him succumb to drinking, which distracted him from family and economic goals in life, and which potentially required the principled hand of a woman, such as a wife. The shame that Paul sometimes felt about his own condition seeped into his understanding of his illnesses and thereby into his letters to Alice.[39]

Eventually, Paul would feel better, albeit his "head and eyes" would not appear "very steady." Poor health would continue to impair his productivity as a creative writer and public performer.[40]

————

As much as Paul was strapped for money in Washington, D.C., Alice's life was not so different. In February, her employer unexpectedly shifted her monthly payday from the first of the month to the fifteenth. Worse, one day her purse was stolen: she lost her cash and had to replace her keys, pencils, and tickets to her gymnasium, the Young Women's Christian Association, the Teachers' Association, and the Women's Era Club.

In a letter Alice drafted to Paul on the first of February, when she discovered she would have to wait another two weeks for her pay, she worried that the month's first two weeks would be the worst of her life financially. "I cried to-day until it seemed I was going to sob my heart out," she revealed. "One of the teachers loaned me carfare and I came home and sat down helplessly." She turned to her fiancé for help. "Paul, will you lend me enough carfare to last until the 15th?" she asked. She promised to reimburse him after her pay on February 15, but she was penniless in the interim. Saddened and ashamed, Alice was reluctant to ask fellow schoolteachers or her friend Victoria Earle Matthews.[41]

In short order Paul sought to console Alice. "Why are you afraid to write to your own husband for any thing you want?" he asked. "Don't you know that it makes him only too happy to do whatever will please you? You are a poor abused little girl and it's mean for people to steal from you—that's what it is." Alice's moment of weakness enabled Paul to communicate strength, to bolster his case that they needed each other now more than ever, that their impending marriage should alleviate any guilt she might feel in asking him for money. "But we aren't going to talk about borrowing from our husband, now are we? It's a pity if a husband hasn't a right to pay his wife's carfare for a week or two." As a married couple—which they technically were not, yet—what was his would belong to her, and vice versa.[42]

———

By now, so comfortable were Paul and Alice in each other's epistolary company that they used stereotypical and even racist language as easily as any other discourse as they talked about what it meant to be an African American. Apparently, Paul cared little how impolitic were his references to fellow men and women of African descent. More than once he expressed to her his distaste for certain members of his race by calling them "niggers." He did not hold back classifying his own work in discriminatory fashion either. For a possible collection he had in mind, Paul once told Alice that he wrote "Dely":

> Jes' lak toddy wahms you thoo'
>   Sets yo' haid a reelin',
> Meks you ovah good and new,
>   Dat's de way I's feelin'.
> Seems to me hit's summah time,
>   Dough hit's wintah reely,
> I's a feelin' jes' dat prime—
>   An' huh name is Dely.

This first stanza captured how "Dely" was "a darkey dialect love-poem," one that could "balance the effect" of a sonnet he was planning on drafting later in the afternoon.[43]

Alice's tongue could be even sharper than Paul's. To him she openly admitted that she disliked working under "Negro women" or that, on one occasion, she teased a "new 'nigger' head of dept. crazy" who had an inflated sense of self. Once she referred to the husband in a constituent family of the White Rose Mission as "a shiftless, dirty Negro." When she started teaching at a new school, Public School 66, in the Brownsville neighborhood of Brooklyn, she remarked on the population of "Polish Jew kids" and not "a single darky anywhere for miles." Close to this time, when Paul was preparing to visit her in Brooklyn, she wrote to demand that he stay in "first-class *white* hostelries." "Then you will be away from the—well niggers," she wrote. Despite their mutual affiliation with largely African American families and communities, they were, in private, willing and able to entertain and reiterate racial stereotypes as disrespectful and disparaging as those perpetuated by racists on the other side of the color line.[44]

Alice tried to lift Paul's spirits about his creative or intellectual abilities as a writer beyond race. As much as he held the increasing privilege of enjoying exclusive circles of cultural celebrities, he could not always sustain his self-confidence there; nor did he always hold his own work in the highest esteem. Regularly, she sent words of support to counteract his belief that he was a middling writer seeking to make a living by his pen. "You are not mediocre, and I will not let you be content."[45]

Alice went on to tell Paul of a private talk she had with Richard Watson Gilder, editor of the *Century Magazine*, one of his favorites. Gilder said, according to Alice: "Mr. Dunbar is a *literary* man, not a *colored literary* man, but one about whom there is no question." In line with their shared resistance to being merely "Afro-American" writers, Alice encouraged Paul to view himself as a racially transcendent man of letters. To be otherwise—such as a man primarily colored, secondarily literary—would more tellingly signify mediocrity, in her view. Bearing the reputation of African ancestry was a detriment to cultural prestige, a perspective that she held dear and communicated to him, with the hope that he would aim higher, to study as he worked, to read and render the world with literary exactitude and excellence.[46]

Alice never hesitated to stress to Paul that, despite how demeaning her words may be about fellow members of his race, she tried to protect his reputation in spite of them. When she advised Paul that he should stay only at "first-class *white* hostelries," she had an important reason, as brusque as it likely sounded: she thought more of his reputation than even he did. "I want you to be dignified, reserved, difficult to access. You cheapen yourself too often by being too friendly with inferior folks, and your wifie doesn't want it. You will be better appreciated if you are more reserved. See?" Central to her plan in molding him in the months ahead of their marriage was to subject him to moral rigor, ensuring that he did not succumb to the temptations of infidelity and inebriation, especially. Yet she also wished to shape him into a beacon of dignity and prosperity as a member of a race less than a century removed from its federal emancipation from bondage. Paul belonged to the rising class of New Negroes who displayed cultural refinement, intellectual sophistication, and political advancement. But he would be a cause célèbre even within this rarefied group. Alice sought to ingrain in him that he should seek to shape his reputation as much as she wanted him to.[47]

CHAPTER 15

The Wizard of Tuskegee

Born of Southern parents from whom he had learned many of the
superstitions and traditions of the South, Howard Dokesbury himself had
never before been below Mason Dixon's line. But with a confidence born of
youth and a consciousness of personal power, he had started South with the
idea that he knew the people with whom he had to deal, and was equipped
with the proper weapons to cope with their shortcomings.

—PAUL LAURENCE DUNBAR, "THE ORDEAL AT MT. HOPE,"
FOLKS FROM DIXIE (1898)[1]

Paul's deep, philosophical preoccupation with the so-called Wizard of Tuskegee, Booker T. Washington, began in 1898, even though they first corresponded
about two years before, in summer 1896, right after Howells's review of *Majors
and Minors*. By that earlier time, the story of Washington's personal life and
political rise was nothing less than extraordinary.

Born enslaved in southwestern Virginia five years before the Civil War,
Booker Taliaferro Washington lived a stratified ancestry: his biological father
was a white man with whom he interacted little and who likely was his mother's
master; and he borrowed his stepfather's first name to serve as his own. Raised
in poverty, he worked in the salt furnaces and coal mines of West Virginia
throughout his childhood, an education in physical toil that predicted his
eventual commitment to manual and industrial training. He attended formal
school at night. In 1872 he walked two hundred miles to the Hampton Institute
in eastern Virginia, seeking to advance his education. In the early days of Reconstruction, Hampton was founded under the auspices of the American Missionary Association to educate African Americans and Native Americans.
There he was introduced to Samuel Chapman Armstrong, a Union Army

general who believed that industrial education best prepared former slaves economically for the postbellum world.

At Hampton, with Armstrong as his mentor, Washington worked as a janitor to pay his room and board, and ultimately graduated with honors three years after he arrived. Though he briefly attended Wayland Seminary in Washington, D.C., by the late 1870s he had returned to serve on the faculty at Hampton. His life underwent a momentous change when General Armstrong recommended that he become the leader of a new normal school, modeled on Hampton, in Tuskegee, Alabama. Washington founded the school in 1881. At the outset, it consisted merely of a barn; a plot of land; and a small amount of money to pay for teachers, books, and equipment—modest resources that would slowly but inevitably grow to become a campus with dormitories, classrooms, libraries, and an endowment exceeding a million dollars by the turn of the century.

The school originated from a promise made by a former slaveowner to a former slave. Lewis Adams was a formally uneducated but literate and talented leader of an African American community in Macon County, Alabama, who had assisted Wilbur F. Foster, a former Confederate colonel and candidate for reelection to the state senate of Alabama, to secure African American votes. In exchange for his help, Adams asked Foster to help him establish an educational institution in Alabama for African Americans. Foster fulfilled his pledge by securing the passage of legislation to fund a "Negro Normal School in Tuskegee." When asked for his recommendation for the leader of what would be called the Normal School for Colored Teachers at Tuskegee, General Samuel C. Armstrong, the head of Virginia's Hampton Institute, proposed Washington.

Officially, the school was founded on July 4, 1881. Originally housed in a tiny church but later moved to the vacant grounds of a former plantation, the school received only two thousand dollars for teachers' salaries. Students, led by Washington, built the school from the ground up. He modeled its curriculum after Hampton Institute's industrial education and changed its name to the Tuskegee Normal and Industrial Institute—known informally as Tuskegee Institute. Under his leadership, the curriculum stressed not only individual self-reliance but also labor in and knowledge of practical trades. In effect, the institute downplayed the liberal arts education of historically white peer institutions, even as it proved progressive in employing a predominantly African American faculty for the purposes of encouraging and exemplifying racial leadership. In 1892 Alabama's state legislature granted Tuskegee Institute the autonomy and authority to act independent of the state, further solidifying Washington's presence there as its main principal.

To build Tuskegee, Washington courted white patrons of considerable wealth to donate to the institution. In doing so he espoused laissez-faire capitalism and a system of cultural and economic values of racial uplift that eschewed calls among African Americans for political agitation or even absolute racial integration. His declaration in his September 1895 speech at the Cotton States and International Exposition that in "all things that are purely social we can be as separate as the fingers yet one as the hand in all things essential to mutual progress" struck a tone of assurance for his largely white southern audience.[2] But these words infuriated not a few African American leaders, especially civil rights activist and educator W. E. B. Du Bois, who bemoaned not only Washington's intentional or perceived condoning of racial segregation but also his delaying of economic and intellectual progress in the emphasis on industrial training. Washington's public model of racial uplift, it was argued, discounted the systemic role racism played in creating a permanent class of disfranchised former slaves and their children.

Despite the controversy, Tuskegee grew to be an institutional metaphor of the educational and political machine—as it was called, a Tuskegee machine—that advanced Washington's conservative philosophies of industrial and economic education for African Americans. When on June 24, 1896, he became the first African American to receive an honorary degree from Harvard University, his stature as the leading African American educator and politician of his time was cemented merely nine months after he leapt onto the national stage in Atlanta.

As he was approaching the height of his political powers, Washington sent Paul a congratulatory letter a few days after Howells's famous review of *Majors and Minors*. The poet was touched that the renowned educator took the time to write him. "Dear Sir," Paul began his letter of reply; "Yours of late date received with great pleasure. I thank you for your words of encouragement and congratulation." Going further, Paul suggested that he, the lowly poet, and Washington, the lauded politician, had much in common. "I think that you for one can thoroughly understand what all this means to me after a long and hard fight. I have gotten nothing without working for it and have contested every bit of the ground over which I have passed."[3]

Albeit respectful in direct communication with Washington, a month and a half later Paul signaled that, in private, the Tuskegee machine was unsettling. Among the first indications of his discomfort occurred when Paul had given Alice a fresh copy of *Majors and Minors* and wrote in the flyleaf a small verse that she had regarded as mortifying for its flirtatious air. She revealed to him

FIG. 15.1. Booker T. Washington, circa 1895. (Library of Congress Prints and Photographs Division)

that she could not show anyone the flyleaf's inscription, which she likened to a song of infatuation:

Jan. 3, 1896
With the compliments of the author to Miss Alice Ruth Moore.
Oft in the darkness of hearts and lives
Comes song that brings joy and light,
As out of the depths of cypress groves

The mockingbird sings at night
Paul Laurence Dunbar

"By the way what nonsense did I write on the fly-leaf of your book that you were ashamed to show it to Mrs. Washington?" Paul asked.[4]

By "Mrs. Washington," Paul meant Margaret James Murray, Washington's third wife. (His first was Fannie N. Smith, who died after they had a child together; and his second was Olivia A. Davidson, who also died after they had two children.) As one of ten children of an interracial sharecropping couple, Murray lived with a foster family of Quakers after her father's death. This progressive background in racial politics, coupled with a love of reading and a record of academic excellence, led her ultimately to Fisk University, where she and Washington began their courtship in 1890. Washington married her three years later; although they did not have children of their own, she helped raise his three children. She went on to serve as assistant principal at Tuskegee, created the Tuskegee Women's Club, founded several country schools, and co-founded the National Association of Colored Women.

With her deep interest in the role of labor in the moral elevation of African Americans, Mrs. Washington had a profound involvement in her husband's approaches to racial education and economics. Their shared decorum explained the response by Mrs. Washington that Paul found so surprising and that further biased Alice's own reading of the flyleaf. Quarreling over the inscription in *Majors and Minors*, Paul and Alice were on opposite sides of the question about the nature of their relationship. He grew emboldened, however, and used his published poetry to broadcast his love. Worried, she was unwilling to permit him to insinuate on her behalf in public what had yet to be confirmed as true between them in private.[5] Equally important, he objected to the suggestion that contact with his words might have defiled Mrs. Washington's reputation as much as it supposedly had done so to Alice herself. "Won't you tell me? *Profane hands*? Mrs. Washington's might not have been profane hands; but if she looked upon reading the book as you do, she might have grown profane afterward." This would be only the first of several reactions by Paul to the doctrine of racial uplift, to the belief in the perfectible social and moral character of his race, that almost always coalesced around the name of Booker T. Washington.[6]

Paul was no less a public figure than Washington, albeit not as politically powerful. As a measure of Paul's stature, in the spring of 1897 Alexander Crummell, one of his dearest acquaintances, was planning to establish a society of African American writers and scholars called the American Negro Academy.

Crummell invited Paul to join, along with Presbyterian minister Francis James Grimké; Reverend A. P. Miller; inventor John Lee Love; educator W. B. Hayson; and John Wesley Cromwell, founder of the Bethel Literary and Historical Association, a learned society. Cromwell happened to be a public defender of Washington's policy that industrial education and economic progress went hand in hand for the Negro. Cromwell also happened to be Washington's confidant. As 1896 turned into 1897, Cromwell informed Washington of this upcoming meeting, reserved for "the perfection of the organization," and extended the invitation, which Grimké suggested be passed on to the Tuskegee leader. Paul was one of the core gentlemen who organized the academy, which laid the groundwork for the two minds to meet.[7]

Over time, Paul began to focus on the industrial and economic philosophies of that storied educator whose work the poet had long observed and read from afar. In early 1898, as he worked at the Library of Congress, Paul wrote Alice about how Washington remained a source of controversy in their personal life but also in his own mind. "We have a disagreement too about Booker T.," he said. "Do you know that he came nearer converting me in his *Independent* article than ever before?" Washington had just serialized an article across the late January and early February issues of the New York *Independent*. Titled "Industrial Training for the Negro," it was a defense of the industrial training that he had been touting for some time. He argued that the "object and value" of this education continued to be "misunderstood," and the "differences" that had grown "out of unequal opportunities in the past," especially due to slavery, likewise continued to be underacknowledged. Contrary to what the African American intelligentsia likely thought, slavery enabled "the Southern white man to do business with the Negro"—"every large slave plantation in the South was, in a limited sense, an industrial school." To educate African Americans in the classical languages of Greek and Latin, to focus on their "mental development" for professions, rather than on the skills of artisanship (such as carpentry, plastering, masonry, and so forth), deprived them of their chance to have equal, competitive footing with the whites who were advancing in industrial areas.[8]

Paul experimented with such ideas—and with the iconic meaning of Washington himself—in his fiction. "A story which I was writing called 'The Ordeal at Mt. Hope' also took the bit into its teeth and made the strongest plea for Booker T. that has yet been made to me," he confided to Alice. Set in the postbellum rural South, "The Ordeal at Mt. Hope" follows the efforts of an African American reverend to transform a town called Mt. Hope, particularly by uplifting its African American residents. It is a tale of the challenges an

alternately ambitious and jaded leader faces in counteracting what he per-
ceives to be "the accumulated evil of years of bondage" that had stunted the
moral, cultural, and economic development of his race. By the end, the story
pivots on the town's thematic title and elucidates the practical means by which
his people could overcome the poverty of character and resources and aspire
toward a promising future. Literature enabled Paul to grapple with Washington, whose proclamations had considerable implications for the higher education of their race as well as for how the Dayton author, however tentatively,
could tackle this topic in print.[9]

Alice encouraged Paul to enter the public debate over higher education. An
avid reader herself, she provided him a list of articles he should examine to
deepen his knowledge of the opposing viewpoints. In addition to Washington's
Independent articles, she advised that he read relevant ones in the *New York Age*,
Southern Workman, and especially *Atlantic Monthly*, which featured an essay by
John Stephens Durham. In "The Labor Unions and the Negro," Durham described the way that labor organizations, with their history of racial exclusion,
had undermined the advancement of African Americans as industrial workers.
Industrial labor had been a noted pathway of African Americans from the menial jobs of farmhands and great-house servants to the more skilled work of
being a blacksmith, carpenter, caulker, and stevedore. Denying menial laborers
the "civilizing contact with the other classes," Durham argued, only stunted
the desire of African Americans to learn trades in the short term while imped-
ing the uplifting of the race in the long term. Whether "Hampton, Tuskegee,
and other trade schools of the South" could stave off this ongoing racial discrimination against African American laborers had yet to be seen.[10]

At the outset, Alice was more empathetic than Paul to arguments for industrial education. As a Brooklyn schoolteacher, her curriculum included "Manual Training Class," supported by Washington himself, and she hoped Paul
would not object.[11] She wanted to further acquaint him with Washington, in
fact. On Saturday, February 12, 1898, the Armstrong Association—named after
General Armstrong—was holding an annual celebration at New York City's
Madison Square Garden. All signs pointed to a grand event. Not only would
Grover Cleveland, the former president of the United States, serve as master of
ceremony, but Washington himself would be the keynote speaker. By that time,
Alice happened to be on familiar terms with Margaret Murray, Washington's
current wife, and she planned to fortify the social bond of the husbands, despite
their potential differences in political philosophy. Alice painted the brightest
face on the situation; she wanted Paul to take her. "I am very anxious to go, and

I want to introduce you to Mr. W. He is a very good friend of yours." Paul responded, "[W]e must talk it over when I am with you." In the end they did attend the event, spending time with Washington himself over the weekend.[12]

Alice was clearly, and willingly, in the social circle of Margaret and Booker T. Washington; the question remained whether Paul wanted to come along. On Sunday, a woman in Paul and Alice's company called Washington an example of "the present" of the race, which Paul took to mean that he himself represented "the feeling"—or the metaphysical dimension, as opposed to a current political leader—of the race. Mortified, Paul left the party. "Dear, it was more than I could bear, almost, to have you go from me," Alice revealed to him later. "I stayed upstairs a bit—to recover my composure, then went down again. As soon as Mr. B. T. W. left I went to bed." Paul took exception to the idea that Washington, a glib speaker of political prose, was eclipsing his own well-wrought poetry. "I have enough self-esteem to deem myself as much a poet of the present as Mr. Washington," he declared, "and sufficient respect for him to believe that I slaved no more for the future than he." In background and struggle, he argued, the two men were not as different as the world viewed them to be.[13]

Alice sought to defend her friend, while figuratively slapping Paul on the wrist, by suggesting that she had frequently deployed that dichotomy in conversation. "By calling B. T. W. the present, and you the feeling, she says that he represents the present or known condition, while you mark the beginning of a new era, a future condition knowing no——. I suppose you understand. You mustn't be so hasty and impulsive dear little boy." Alice tried to redeem Washington in Paul's eyes. She and Washington had an extended conversation about him, whose reputation for drinking preceded him. "Mr. D. has been fearfully misrepresented," Washington confided to her. "I've heard so many tales about him being such a hard drinker and so dissipated. I don't believe a word of it." Alice was thrilled to hear him claim that he could discern "a hard drinker at a glance." He confirmed her sense that Paul "had been leading an exemplary life for *at least* three or four months." Alice sought to assuage Paul's concern that any competition existed between the educator and the poet. Quite the opposite, she said: Washington so defended and admired Paul that true friendship between them only made sense.[14]

———

Paul remained friendly with Howells after his glowing review of *Majors and Minors* in *Harper's Weekly* and his guest introduction to *Lyrics of Lowly Life*. In spring 1898 he sent Howells a copy of a new book he had published, with a note: "Won't you accept the accompanying little collection of my short stories. I cannot ask you to read it; but I hope you will read my novel which appears in the May *Lippincott's*."[15]

Paul reminded Howells of how thankful he remained for the older man's help in making him a cause célèbre: "I am trying to take advantage of the start your kindness gave and still, all goes fairly well." In future years he would still try to find ways of seeing Howells in New York, to continue gathering advice and sustaining their friendship.[16] In the meantime, a few weeks into the following year, Paul revealed good news to Alice about a different project. "Mr. Dodd is very anxious for a new volume of poems," he wrote, "but I am going to edit my next very carefully." He had received respectable acclaim for his book *Lyrics of Lowly Life* two years earlier; this time, he sought to elevate the quality. "I want it to show in the pure English poems improvement over the Lyrics' which, by the way, is still selling steadily," he told Alice. Despite his attention to the "pure English poems," he knew the dialect poems remained the true reason behind the political appeal of *Lyrics of Lowly Life* to most readers. On their quality "I cannot improve," he said, resigning himself to a truth: "I shall write nothing better than 'When Malindy Sings,' 'A Coquette Conquered' & 'Signs of the Times,'" three of the more memorable poems in dialect showcased in *Lyrics of Lowly Life*.[17]

"Will the new volume of poems have new ones in it?" Alice asked. "The book of verses will be entirely new," Paul assured her, "gleaned from my magazine pieces and other unpublished things." More important than the manuscript's originality would be the bond it represented for them both: it would occasion a chance to converse on their mutual love for poetry, but not before they formalized their union. "But you will know all about it, for I expect your hands to help me prepare it for the printer. We will be one before that time," Paul told Alice.[18]

Paul's oeuvre was growing. In addition to the novel and the book of poems, by mid-February he was publishing the book of short stories that he had mentioned and sent a copy of to Howells. Before, he had released stories in individual magazines: in 1890, his first few in the *Dayton Tattler*; the following year, a couple through A. N. Kellogg's Newspaper Company; in 1895, another in the *Independent*; and in the fall of 1897, the sketches of "real darkey life in New York" in the *New York Journal*. A branching out of sorts, in 1898 he released his stories in a host of magazines—*Cosmopolitan*, *Outlook*, *Current Literature*, and *New York Journal*. Just as he compiled many of the individually released poems into books, previously published stories also ended up in book form, this time through the publishing muscle of Dodd, Mead.

Now, with the full encouragement of Frank H. Dodd—in charge of Dodd, Mead and Company—Paul was taking the bold step of publishing fiction about folks he had long known in his family and communities. To render the stories vivid, Edward Windsor Kemble, renowned for illustrating the first edition of Mark Twain's 1884 novel *Adventures of Huckleberry Finn*, was enlisted to illustrate the book of short stories. Not only did Paul use Kemble's help, he wrote Alice for hers. "I enclose the names of the stories and want you to try and choose a name for the book," he requested. In his letter he listed all the stories to be included.[19] Figuring out a title for this book was a struggle. "I still think 'The Ordeal at Mt. Hope & Other Stories' a good title don't you?" Alice asked him in one letter.[20]

Paul settled on the title *Folks from Dixie*, scheduled for release in the following month but delayed until April. Featuring twelve tales—the first of which was "The Ordeal at Mt. Hope," a fictionalization of the leadership of Booker T. Washington and the book's highlight—the collection concentrated on the rural South and plantation settings and themes. With a few taking place during the period before the Civil War, the stories indulged in the caricatures of African Americans that white readers in his era had grown accustomed to seeing in literature, but Paul embedded in these stories the social criticism born from his deeply held political views.

Paul was unsure what sort of critical reception *Folks from Dixie* would receive. He mailed a copy of it to Paul Revere Reynolds, who beforehand had taken on the writer as a client. (Reynolds, who founded the first literary agency in the country in 1893, managed the contracts of some of the most prominent American and British authors of the time.) "I do not know what its chances for selling are as it is in all dialect," he wrote, even though his poetry in dialect had received favorable reviews.[21]

The release of a book (and, in this case, fiction) entirely in dialect was new commercial territory for him; and, at this early point, writing a book full of dialect had not yet become a profitable literary enterprise. "Dodd has sent me as my royalty a beggarly $178—all from the *Lyrics*," he wrote Alice, in reference to his publisher. Yet "after telling me that *Folks from Dixie* had earned over the $499 advanced, he now says it hasn't yet earned that," he grumbled. "He sold an edition of 500 copies to London & gave me $20 from it. What do you think of that?"[22]

Reviews of *Folks from Dixie* in major periodicals like the *New York Times* and *The Nation*, and lesser-known ones like *Outlook* and *Bookman*, cited Paul's success in capturing the relevant details of racial life—on both sides of the color line—particularly those in the South. Reviewers said he excelled in revealing "the inner life of the American Negro," which he treated with "truth and sympathy," and served as a model heretofore unachieved by an African American author.[23]

With the publication of multiple books of poems and short stories, and with a novel potentially right behind, Paul's versatile career was now in full swing.

PART THREE

The Downward Way, 1898 to 1906

CHAPTER 16

The Wedding of Plebeians

I did not intend to write this, but as I view the matter calmly and outside the intoxicating influence of your presence, my bitterness grows.

We have disappointed every one. Many looked forward to our marriage with pleasure, and it should have been an event. Instead, we sneaked away & married like a pair of criminals or two plebeians with the fear of disgrace hanging over them.

—PAUL LAURENCE DUNBAR TO ALICE RUTH MOORE
(MARCH 8, 1898)[1]

The day finally came. Paul and Alice married on March 6, 1898, in New York City. He was twenty-five; she, twenty-two. Despite the previous thought of holding it in Medford, the wedding ceremony was modest and private—against the backdrop of the city—overseen by William B. Derrick, bishop of the African Methodist Episcopal Church, with Joseph Derrick and J. H. Henderson as witnesses.[2]

By the time of the wedding, Paul was a bona fide celebrity, fueling Alice's impression—shared by the public and even, grudgingly, her new husband—that he was "a conceited donkey." He told her that he was tired of being "bored and lionized" as well as "looked upon" by his "new friends" as "a ladies' man."[3]

Paul's flirtatious nature always threatened their engagement. Four days prior to their wedding, while in New York City, his poor judgment struck again: he became a self-described "thoughtless scoundrel" when he ran into Maud Shannon, yet another "old flame." Embarrassed, he told Alice about it: "Well, while all was innocent between us, I gave her a lot of taffy and she has taken it all in and been telling people about it." He described Shannon's manipulative nature, as though by tarnishing her name he could exonerate his own. Shannon, a seamstress, proceeded to circulate to acquaintances a letter he had written: an invitation for her to come down to Washington, D.C., to complete his mother's sewing of her own personal dress. Paul sought to intercept any false rumor of infidelity emanating from this circumstance within days of their wedding.[4]

Begging forgiveness, Paul maintained to Alice that although he had flirted with Shannon, he had not done "an illicit act" or "uttered an impure word." As late in their engagement as she learned of this misconduct, it was not enough to discourage Alice from marrying Paul.[5] They married in the spring, but Alice had been calling Paul her husband as early as New Year's Day. The month before their wedding, he communicated his gratitude—and relief—that a year earlier she had "promised to try to learn to love" him. "Oh my darling you have kept your promise haven't you," he wrote. "You have learned to love me." He admitted that her love had elevated him "higher and higher," "even out of the mud," now in the position of "even lightly touching the subject like one unpurified laying sacrilegious hands upon what is most sacred." Marrying Alice was not only a formal consummation of his love and devotion, which they were also informally expressing to each other while, between letters, spending much time together on weekends. The wedding represented a propitious road out of the valley of temptation in which he had been salaciously mired.[6]

In the days after their wedding, Paul marveled at the gravity of what they had just done. "We have taken a very bold, rash step whose only vindication will be our entire happiness and well-being," he wrote. But the wedding's aftermath sowed seeds of discontent that would grow in the months ahead. The couple disagreed over who was sacrificing the most in familial relationships so that they could be together. He was mindful that parents may generally be reluctant to release a child to another person through marriage, but he was also concerned that Alice was overstating her own claims of familial pain. "You argue that sacrifice you made; but then your mother had seen *one* of her children married"—namely, Leila, Alice's sister. He resented that although their marriage was a dream come true, they still had to write letters to each other: for the meantime, due to professional obligations, he continued to live in Washington, D.C., and she in New York City.

The clandestine nature of the wedding came to embitter Paul, contradicting his earlier wish, for financial reasons, to avoid the expense of a large wedding. "We have disappointed every one," he complained, his words almost rising to a scolding. Many of their friends anticipated that they would marry with pomp and circumstance. Instead, they "sneaked away & married like a pair of criminals or two plebeians with the fear of disgrace hanging over them." The consequence of their actions included denial of her mother's fore-knowledge of the wedding. He thought she had better write or let him write Mrs. Moore before the news reached her from elsewhere. Before it was too late, he had to use common sense to rein in his love and anticipate the controversy that could ensue.[7]

Paul pressed Alice at least to send out the announcement cards immediately. Each card read:

Paul Laurence Dunbar
Alice Ruth Moore
Married
Sunday, March sixth,
eighteen hundred and ninety eight.
New York.

At Home
Thursdays after May first,
1934 Fourth Street, N.W.,
Washington[8]

This notice differed from the more detailed letter that Paul planned to draft to send to Alice's mother, but Alice had not given him her approval to do so. Alice was routinely sensitive to their "*social* position," explaining why she preferred a secret wedding. But it was ironically and precisely the ongoing secrecy that was endangering this position, and he sought to obviate the hazard. He believed Alice remained vulnerable to the pressures inflicted by her mother and sister, and that, despite relenting to the marriage, she would always be vulnerable to the sense that he only pretended to love her and that he disgraced her. Only with the wider dissemination of the news could Paul avert her possible feeling of buyer's remorse.[9]

Fortunately for Paul, Alice had no such sentiment. She had come to believe that a private wedding best enabled her as quickly and irrefutably as possible to become his wife—her practical desire at this point. "Perhaps time will show that I was right," she wrote, although she recognized that Paul must be "angry, disgusted," with her for preferring privacy over publicity. A week afterward, she implored him, "Dear, please don't say anything more to others about our marriage, and don't feel meanly about it." No longer did she want his letters of admonition or recrimination; rather, she wanted once again to see some of his "long, sweet loverlike letters" such as those he sent during their courtship and engagement. Conciliatory, she signed her letters to him as his "devoted wife."[10]

Paul assured Alice that he had not told anyone of their marriage. In mid-March he was ill with tonsillitis, pharyngitis, and an ailing eye that strained to focus. The throat problems hindered his ability to work at the library for much of the month; in the mornings his eyes needed to be sponged open. For days, during daylight, he bided his time resting on a sofa by a window. Still, he mustered the strength to write Alice regularly from Washington, D.C. He told only a few acquaintances, such as his friend and physician Daniel Williams and his other friend Ella Smith, of his marriage. Neither Rebekah Baldwin nor the chief clerk at the library knew. The prospect of informing people beyond an inner circle so worried Alice that she told Paul of her "nervous strain and anxiety," her hands "shaking like aspen leaves," her throat burning and her whole body aching "from sheer nervousness," her entire being trapped in the "business of suffering." Eventually he soothed her somatic symptoms. He praised her for being "the bravest little woman in the world and the sweetest," "bold enough to take arms against a sea of troubles and by opposing end them." To an extent they were growing increasingly prideful, if rebellious, in being the so-called Mr. and Mrs. Browning of the race—their own inside reference to the analogous predicament of Robert Browning and Elizabeth Barrett, two Victorian poets who married despite their frustration with social mores and their disapproving parents. Paul and Alice likewise embraced each other in this way.[11]

Bothersome, though, was the inevitable geographical distance of 250 miles separating Paul and Alice, forcing them to spend substantial time apart despite being husband and wife. For him she prayed nightly, plagued with guilt over the prospect that, while she was at work in New York City or traveling to family in Medford and New Orleans, he might be confined to his home in Washington, D.C., with the help of a nurse during his multiple illnesses. Despite his condition, his mind was coherent enough to realize her absence and to miss her affection. "I am feeling pretty 'warm' this morning because I dreamed about you all last night—dreamed things that were sweetly naughty—real husbandly things in which there were twin beds but only *one* of them came in for use," he wrote. Enjoying the liberation of marriage, he asked, "Well you're my wife, can't I say this to you?" He could. Epistolary intimacy was a proxy for physical intimacy while they lived apart.[12]

For the first three months of 1898 Paul resented their "enforced separation"—namely, her refusal to live with him in Washington, D.C., until she finished the academic year as a New York City schoolteacher. The separation convinced her that she needed to keep their marriage a secret until she fulfilled her professional duty. His continued accommodation of her wish put him in a precarious spot. To Alice's plea of "Love & Ethics" Paul responded that the concepts of "love" and "ethics" may "never react well in double harness." Palpable was his frustration. Like a caged bird, beating its wings against marital regulations, he despised living under "responsibility & restraint" without either "comforts or privileges." In the face of her repeated accusation that he was selfish, he refused to accept living in this "anomalous situation."[13] (Yet he continued to underestimate how the marriage estranged her from her own mother and sister: the mother, Patricia Moore, lamented to Alice in a letter, "I am not angry at all about your marriage. I am heartily glad of it—only I would have liked to have given you away.")[14]

At last, Alice presented a plan to resolve their dispute: she offered to resign from her position on April 1—a Friday, the last day of the workweek—with the idea that Paul would come for her the following Wednesday. The only catch was financial. Since her salary for March would not be disbursed until mid-May or June 1, she needed him to send her enough money (sixty dollars) to cover her remaining expenses between her date of resignation and the date of disbursement. An unabashedly practical request, "a cold transaction," in her words, this was the collateral price he would have to pay to expedite their permanent reunion. She promised to reimburse him.

Yet Alice had mixed feelings about moving in with Paul. If he were willing to scold her in letters, would he not also be willing to scold her in person? "But, dear heart, you have thoroughly frightened me about going *home*," she wrote. She issued a plea. "Paul, don't quarrel with me. I can't quarrel and make up and be the same. Something in me dies every time. I hate to speak crossly to anyone. I am ridiculously tender-hearted and sensitive. Slight words and looks hurt me for days, though I may laugh it away apparently. Won't you try to remember this dear, and not be sarcastic or cross with me."[15]

Alice had been under stress since their wedding, frightened by her own financial insecurity, her chronic physical ailments since Paul's premarital assault, her tension with family in Medford, her dustups with him. Further, she struggled with the notion that her desire to live apart from her husband and complete her schoolwork was reprehensible in his eyes. The prospect of living with Paul brought all these issues to a head. But with her assent that they move in together came a resolve that surely appeased him: she was willing to start sending out the cards announcing their marriage. She wanted three hundred to send to relatives and acquaintances in New Orleans and the Boston area; he would take care of sending cards to those in Washington, D.C., and Dayton.[16]

Still, Alice expressed painful thoughts and feelings in multiple letters at this time. She contested the idea that she alone preferred the secret wedding, when, according to letters she dredged up for his review, Paul had written that he wanted precisely this: "Passage after passage urging a quiet wedding, a civil ceremony, a marriage to take place at once—tc. tc. *ad infinitum*. Passage after passage begging for the protecting *knowledge* of a tie between us." She also could not bring herself yet to submit her letter of resignation from her teaching job; "every minute I felt something deeper and deeper in my soul against my husband who could reproach me so," she admitted, at once feeling "supersensitive" and "nervous." At this point she issued Paul an unanticipated ultimatum: "You have told me that you regret the marriage. Let it be annulled then."[17]

Paul could only counter Alice by suggesting that their misunderstandings resulted from their living in different parts of the country. Sensing that they were growing apart, he pointed to the role this geographical distance played in their miscommunication, not to the disproportionate, unfair blame he was placing on her. "Sometimes, the very intensity of my desire to have you here makes me seem hard," he wrote. "Alice, darling, we don't understand each other yet, but let us not grow further apart. We will understand each other better when we are together." He even adopted her self-description as appropriate to his own: they were "two highly strung, supersensitive young cranks." Alice's troubled letter, coupled with another Paul received from her sister, Leila, "entirely melted" him. He appreciated that he deserved culpability for the secrecy of their wedding. He sought to make amends by assuring her that, "through this hush of selfishness & hardness" down in his heart, he loved and worshipped her, and that she was "bound up in the warp and woof" of his life.[18]

Alice responded favorably to Paul's apology, although she disliked, as she stated in her letter to him, "the bossy epistles" he had been writing her of late. She also informed him that opinion had changed somewhat in her family. Although the secret ceremony denied her mother, Patricia, the privilege of formally giving her daughter away, the couple received their blessing in the end. Alice quoted the evidence: "My good wishes for both of my children. May God bless both of you. Best love to my dear boy. Tell him I am proud to have such a son. God will bless him if he takes care of you." And Alice's sister, Leila, came around as well: "My letter to you did not contain a single word against Mr. D. as I do not make it a practise to say things about *any member of my family*, especially when one is loved by the other as you love him."[19]

With these signs of reconciliation, Alice felt more comfortable wrapping up her affairs in New York City and settling down with Paul in Washington, D.C. Cards announcing their wedding began to circulate the first week of April. She looked forward to a life with her husband without the need for corresponding across state lines. Writing on Sunday, April 10, Alice was relieved. "I am going to write you every day if possible this week until Friday—then no more letters! Oh, Paul!"[20] Exactly one week after she wrote these words, Alice, with the new public surname of Moore Dunbar, arrived in Washington, D.C. Paul picked her up from the train station. In a carriage that conveyed them home, they sang a melody they knew well, "Last Night."[21]

———

"A little one act musical farce of Will Cook and mine is to be put on next week by the Oriental America Co.," Paul divulged to Alice in spring 1898, regarding *Clorindy*. Despite being a "farce," a word that revealed his true opinion on the show's occasional crudity, he looked forward to reaping immediate commercial rewards and longer-term financial benefits. "If it is a success, it will mean more work in that line."[22]

Paul's letter was the outcome of Cook's hustle, in the first half of 1898, to gather support for the show. Around this time, Bert Williams and George Walker happened to be passing through Washington, D.C., as part of the traveling theater led by Richard Hyde and Louis Behman, and they reunited with Cook to hear the more developed version of the act they first heard him present to them in New York City. Impressed, Walker and Williams encouraged Cook to travel back to New York City and connect with Isidore Witmark, the head of Marcus Whitmark and Sons, the sheet music publisher and legal firm named after the founding father.

One Saturday afternoon in Witmark's office on 37th Street, Cook, a novice pianist, struggled through a piano rendition of *Clorindy* before the boss. Cutting him off after forty minutes, Witmark expressed skepticism that anyone, let alone a mainstream audience on Broadway, would want "to listen to Negroes singing Negro opera." Cook persisted. From across town he rounded up African American performers and taught them bits and pieces of the songs. He convinced Ernest Hogan, a notorious African American comedian and author of the hit song "All Coons Look Alike to Me," to lead the show, since Williams and Walker could not abandon the Hyde and Behman show while it continued to tour the East Coast.[23]

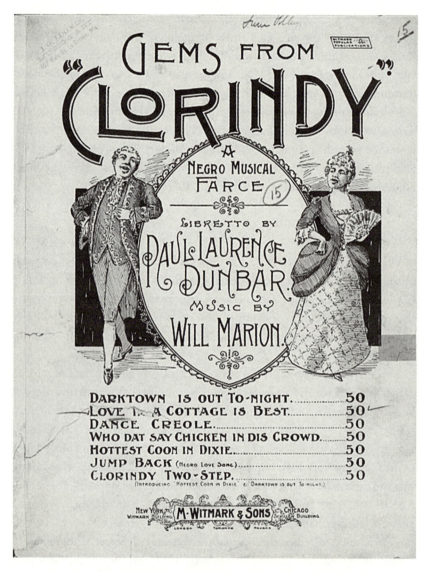

FIG. 16.1. Advertisement of *Clorindy* in *Harper's Weekly* (1898).

After fits and starts, including a rain cancellation of the originally scheduled Tuesday, June 28, date, Cook conducted the magnificent midnight preview of *Clorindy* exactly one week later at the famous Casino Roof Garden, located atop Casino Theater on Broadway and 39th Street. The packed venue of over eight hundred people marveled at the performers. Many in the audience had proceeded there after a show downstairs in Casino Theatre had just concluded.

Hogan had excised one piece of dialogue Paul had written for the one-hour operetta, but he enhanced and made a main attraction one of the Dayton poet's undeleted lyrics, "Hottest Coon," which complemented the others that were likewise tinged with racial flair: "Darktown Is Out Tonight, Jump Back," "Love in a Cottage Is Best," and "Who Dat Say Chicken in Dis Crowd?" For much of the summer the show ran with Hogan and Abbie Mitchell, later to be replaced by Williams and Walker. *Clorindy* turned out to be the first musical with a full African American cast to appear on Broadway.[24]

During the summer, whether Paul was earning what he deserved from *Clorindy*, based on his contractual agreement with Cook, was a source of concern between him and Alice. She ran into Cook, and the surprise encounter raised her hackles. In a profane way, she distrusted him when he recognized her: "He started as though he had seen a ghost. Honestly, the nigger looked scared. He asked where you were," she recalled. "Now, in my opinion, money has been made on that cake walk, and since your name is used so muchly, your plain duty is to find out where do you come in. I shall go to the music stores tomorrow and see if the songs are on sale."[25]

Eventually, Paul grew tired of the uncertainty over getting his due from his collaboration with Cook. By the end of the summer, during a visit to New York, he had had enough with *Clorindy* and another show they had worked on together, *The Cannibal King*. "There was nothing to do in New York except to turn over my right in *Clorindy* to Will Cook & to sell *The Cannibal King* outright which I did," he told Alice. "Two hundred cash & two hundred more on production. I am glad to get out of it." Paul revealed to Alice that, by the first week of September, he had "got nothing as yet" from his share in the *Clorindy* royalties, "except a contract for a ten days option to try it for four hundred dollars." At least in selling the rights to *The Cannibal King*, for which Jim Johnson would write the lyrics and Bob Cole the libretto, he "got two hundred down & contract for 200 more on production or 200 forfeit if it is not produced." Finally, he was pleased. "Thank you ma'am I got my truth."[26]

The commercial and financial complications aside, Paul and Cook were a formidable team in musical theater. They expanded *Clorindy* into *Senegambian Carnival*, which was more a variety show than a one-act performance, and it opened August 29 at the Boston Theatre, starring Williams as a rich man and Walker as a potential thief of his fortunes. Paul and Cook expounded on *Senegambian Carnival* and created another show, *A Lucky Coon*, a vaudeville comedy revolving about the same characters played by Williams and Walker and opening in New York. Other joint projects that year included *Hottest Coon in*

Dixie, Jump Back (Negro Love Song), and *Who Dat Say Chicken in Dis Crowd?* In the world of musical theater, yes, Paul knew how to write a hit.[27]

———

In theme and tone, Alice persisted in her hope that Paul would walk the straight and narrow moral path. Too embedded in her psyche was his refrain about his incessant temptations—women and liquor. She issued him disciplinary reminders. "Dearie, I do hope you're going to be a *good* boy. You will be won't you?" she asked. She did not want to think of him ever carelessly misbehaving while lacking self-reflection. "You've been my own good, true Paul, let me think of you being so always, won't you?" She could only pray that he took her prodding to heart.[28]

In the early part of married life, Paul continued to oscillate dramatically between health and illness. Routinely suffering colds, he took any kind of medication that would help him feel better. At times he would act and write skittishly from the excessive dose of quinine he took in the mornings. From the ground bark of cinchona trees, quinine helped his muscles relax; it arrested his shivering and stemmed his diarrhea. Seeing Alice or writing her letters usually buoyed his spirit and distracted him from what was becoming a regular struggle; yet the recurrence of his sicknesses at once troubled and exasperated her. "I am sorry dearie, that you are not well," she wrote him. "What is the trouble now? Another cold. Do take care of yourself." Over time he would learn to consult his friend Dr. Tobey on remedies.[29]

Married six months, Paul and Alice's relationship had room for growth. More often than not, personal opinions on race attracted them to each other; on rare occasions these opinions formed wedges of dispute. One of their worst arguments—particularly over Paul's brooding, quarrelsome, almost mentally unstable nature—concerned a festering wound in their relationship: his long-standing disregard of her own racial heritage.

The births and lives of their parents represented separate trajectories. Paul's father and mother were former slaves in Kentucky who, respectively, by way of flight and manumission, of service in the Civil War and an arduous journey across the Ohio River, settled in the African American community of Dayton, Ohio. The contrasting legacies of the Dunbars and the Moores, Alice felt, did not merely fuel Paul's resentment, but an undercurrent fault line of race, embedded in questions of genealogy and heritage, divided them. "Dearest—dearest—I hate to write this—How often, oh how pitifully often, when scarce meaning it, perhaps, you have thrust my parentage in my face," she started to exclaim, laying out the issue for them both to examine clearly:

> Won't you let me love New Orleans as you love Dayton? Won't you let me love home-folks as you love your friends of high school days? Won't you respect my traditions as I respect yours? Won't you let me speak enthusiastically of my friends as you speak enthusiastically of yours? Won't you let me cherish girlhood memories as I hear you cherishing yours? Won't you think kindly of those girls I care for as I think kindly of the boys you like? Won't you let me speak of old things dear to me—or must I be silent?

How their respective families emerged in the postslavery world, how they predestined the way that Paul and Alice came to meet, appreciate, and love each other, offered a clue to what might tear them asunder. Paul, in Alice's view, felt insecure about the value of his own past as opposed to hers, he favored his own creation of family and the social networks of Dayton over hers of New Orleans, and he came to advance his own doctrines of cultural and racial memory at the expense of hers. So complicated was this dispute that, although neither was out of town, Alice preferred to articulate her stance on paper, as part of her broader disquisition on how incompatible they may actually be.[30]

From afar, Paul kept a steady eye on a man fourteen years his senior, Charles Waddell Chesnutt.

With roots in Fayetteville, North Carolina, in the free African American community of his parents, Chesnutt was a prodigious, though isolated, young man who found an ally in the principal of the Howard Normal School. After the principal hired him to teach there, Chesnutt became assistant principal of the State Colored Normal School in Fayetteville for African American schoolteachers. He married a fellow teacher, Susan Perry, and set his sights northward, settling in Cleveland, Ohio. In 1885 he sold his first short story, "Uncle Peter's House," while he worked as a stenographer and studied law. A couple of years later, short stories appeared in such popular magazines as *Family Fiction, Tid-Bits,* and *Puck.* Local color and realism blended in his fiction. By 1887, when "The Goophered Grapevine" became the first piece of fiction published by an African American in the *Atlantic Monthly,* Chesnutt had adapted to his multiple occupations as legal stenographer, author, cultural critic, and father. That same year he passed the Ohio bar examination with the highest grade in

FIG. 16.2. Charles Waddell Chesnutt, n.d. (Cleveland Public Library, Fine Arts and Special Collections Department)

his group. He was a literary artist and intellectual on the rise, and the books of short stories and novels he would publish in subsequent years reaffirmed his promise.

Paul turned to Alice to speculate on Chesnutt's progress, both as a professional writer and as a measure of his own success. "Didn't I tell you there was something behind those paragraphs in Chesnutt?" Paul rhetorically asked. Under a separate cover, James MacArthur, an adviser to the publisher Dodd, Mead and editor of the *Bookman* magazine, apprised Paul that Walter Hines Page, an American journalist, "inspired" Chesnutt's creative writing. Through such influence, Chesnutt had lucked into a commercial break, according to MacArthur. "He writes me again today that Houghton, Mifflin & Co. are to bring out a collection of 'Conjure stories' of his," Paul added, "and that he *is* at work upon a novel."

Paul revealed to Alice the depth of his frustration. Shackled to the tedium of cataloging at the Library of Congress, he feared that Chesnutt would beat him to the punch. The library was assigning him the task of rearranging a slew of books, because a co-worker had severely mixed them up. Library work was threatening to slow down his literary work. "The work with the counting would take me six good months and at night I should be too tired to do anything literary." Paul's fear of Chesnutt's star eclipsing his own was a window to the anxiety he was trying to keep at bay, but also to how he was turning to Alice for help. Grabbing the helm of the literary world, of being the elite even among the rarefied of his race, appealed to him most. In Chesnutt he saw a genuine threat. "As long as the Negro literary field held me above I could afford to take it pretty easily, but now that another Richmond has come on—a Richmond so worthy of my mettle, too,—'a horse, a horse!'" Paul's offhand allusion to Shakespeare's 1592 play *Richard III*, in which the title character says, "I think there be six Richmonds in the field," captured the true literary competition he sensed at the time. Years after this exchange with Alice, Paul could never truly conquer the insecurity and competition he felt whenever he encountered Chesnutt's name or fame.[31]

Fortunately for Paul, he finally had a published first novel under his belt, which he titled *The Uncalled*. It appeared in its entirety in the May 1898 issue of *Lippincott's Monthly Magazine* and thereafter, in September, in book form from Dodd, Mead. Avoiding the traditional cast and vernacular of African Americans commercially expected of an African American author, the novel tells the story of Frederick Brent, whose early life reflected similarities with the turbulent household of Paul's own youth with his parents, Joshua and Matilda.

Initially, Fred accepts the belief of residents of his Midwestern hometown of Dexter that a strict Methodist upbringing and a formal education could uplift him from the indignity of his birth to an impoverished housewife and an abusive drunk. After he deals with his parents' divorce and subsequent tragedies, including his mother's death and his father's abandonment, one Miss Hester Prime—a probable allusion to the protagonist, Hester Prynne, in Nathaniel Hawthorne's 1850 novel *The Scarlet Letter*—takes Fred in and rears him with a disciplinarian's hand. Miss Prime hopes to turn her ward into a preacher at the local Methodist church, but, after completing his divinity studies, Fred cannot survive the community's insincerity and moral hypocrisy. He flees for Cincinnati.

In the new city, Fred encounters the same societal crises, such as poverty and drunkenness, he faced at home and tries to escape. In a sense he remains in a mental and emotional deathmatch with predestination. But a reunion with his father, Tom, marks a turning point. Not only has his father turned his life around, but he has now made it his life's goal to advise others to avoid his mistakes. Tom moves back to the hometown of Dexter but rapidly falls ill. In a descent toward death he begs his son for forgiveness. In response, Fred vows ethical and spiritual self-improvement. He finds happiness in a loving bond with a woman uncoincidentally named Alice, who not only helps him to detach himself from the past but also to propel him toward an optimistic future.

The release of *The Uncalled* was timely for both literary and personal reasons. At this moment in history, American writers were anticipating or even demonstrating what the American writer Stephen Crane was noticing: "a change in the literary pulse of the country within the last four months." Crane uttered these words in 1894, one year after he published *Maggie: A Girl of the Streets*, a salacious novella about a young girl who grapples with the urban destitution of New York City. Howells did not disagree with Crane; in response, the dean of American letters opined: "What you say is true. I have seen it coming. . . . I suppose we shall have to wait."[32]

Frank Norris, a contemporary, played a key role in this American literary movement—alongside Crane and Hamlin Garland, it turned out—that indicted the genteel predisposition characterizing Howellsian realism and, for example, the fiction of elders Henry James and Edith Wharton, which touted the generational privileges of familial aristocracy and cultural refinement. Norris published an essay in 1896 that, in redeeming the influential work of French novelist Émile Zola (which contradicted such literary gentility), raged against "the real Realism." "We ourselves are Mr. Howells's characters," Norris wrote, "so long as we are well behaved and ordinary and bourgeois, so long as we are not adventurous or not rich or not unconventional." Norris would say, in another essay five years later, that literature should instead explore "the unplumbed depths of the human heart, and the mystery of sex, and the problems of life, and the black, unsearched penetralia of the soul of man."[33] Norris's philosophical musings on a new literary space for writers seeking to investigate the more unseemly dimensions of human life identified the gray areas of cultural, moral, and economic complexity typifying the drama of life "among the lower—almost the lowest—classes; those who have been thrust or wrenched from the ranks, who are falling by the roadway."[34]

Norris articulated the genre of naturalism as it emerged among his contemporaries, including Paul Laurence Dunbar, who likewise conceived of fiction in this way—namely, how literary characters could embody the demise of individualism in the face of hereditary and environmental determinism, and therefore how they could lack control over the strong forces, internal or external, that cause a visceral human effect. The Uncalled was Paul's first major literary foray into naturalism; it would not be his last (his fourth novel, The Sport of the Gods, published in 1902, would be). And it would permeate his intellectual observations of human life, whether white or black, in fiction or in nonfiction.

The arrival of Paul's first novel was also a remarkable personal accomplishment, however. He and Alice were both relieved to see the novel in print at last. "I forgot to congratulate you upon the adjudication of the differences between Dodd & Mead and Lippincott," Alice wrote. "It is very good and I am proud and happy therefore. How fortunate for us both is your great, good luck." The Uncalled was the first book by Paul dedicated to Alice. Emblazoned on a flyleaf with "Dedicated to MY WIFE," this was the first opportunity he had within a book to declare to his readers that he was betrothed. But it also was his first prideful chance to assign to her a spot in his publications that he had reserved only for those most distinguished in his life. On the flyleaves of his first three books, Oak and Ivy, Majors and Minors, and Lyrics of Lowly Life, were heartfelt dedications to his mother; and on his next two, Folks from Dixie and Poems of Cabin and Field, were dedications to his friends Henry A. Tobey and Bishop Henry C. Potter. With the ink barely dry on his marriage certificate, Paul regarded his first novel a timely beginning to what he believed would be a long series of gestures to a woman whom he had craved and, according to their marital vows, from whom only death could part him.[35]

Paul was not yet certain how his first novel would be received, but he was curious to learn of the public comparisons already being made between it and other contemporary novels. A preliminary sense among readers was that *The Uncalled* resembled *The Damnation of Theron Ware*. Similarly focused on American provincialism and religious life, this other novel appeared in England in 1896; it bore the title *Illumination* and was written by Harold Frederic, likewise an American author. The comparison would compel him to buy the book as soon as he returned to the United States from England.[36]

When the reviews did arrive, they noted that Paul's novel boded well for African American authors, showing that they could escape "the safe shelter" of their putative "specialty"—namely, "the occasional peculiarities of their own people"—and depict "the spirit of humanity." *The Uncalled* attracted attention from newspapers around the country, from the *New York Times* to the *Indianapolis Journal*; the "graphic and vivid" nature of the story, its "force and vigor," proved that his first novel could turn out to be a remarkable accomplishment, that he could have a professional future in the realm of fiction, not only poetry.[37]

Paul was not fully satisfied with this outcome, however. Just as the novel constantly swelled while he was writing it over several months, looking back he wished he could have revised it. "Even now, though I have, revised and revised it, there are many things about it that I would change if I had the chance," he wrote to an acquaintance. Thankfully, he did earn money on it. Toward that end he was fulfilled.[38]

———

While Paul and Alice lived together as a married couple, newfound circumstances were enhancing their love but also, in certain ways, making it more volatile. Sometimes they could resolve their differences in the privacy of their home. Sometimes they could not. Disputes occasionally spilled out into public view, among strangers and acquaintances, and into letters, a consolatory medium of choice even when their close, interpersonal proximity did not require it.

Most troublesome were discords that strained the marriage. Summer 1898 marked the period, for example, when Alice started to be more openly critical of Paul's attachment to his mother. When Alice had to return to Brooklyn briefly and leave Paul behind with his mother in Washington, D.C., Alice fretted over her own seemingly diminished importance. "I hope you and mother will have a taste of your old happy life while I am gone. When you wish me back, dear, tell me, and I will come," she sulked. "You know that I love you. I am not angry, only hurt, hurt terribly. It is of no use for me to say I am sorry that I have come into your life and wrecked it so—I have done it, and I alone am to blame. If I could atone I would." The exchange came out of an argument with a recurring theme: whether their marriage was a case of fortune or misfortune. Given that Alice traveled frequently between New York and Massachusetts, word of her impending departure only irked him. Almost always he disclosed his angst, in this case even to his mother. To this Alice could only seek reconciliation; she hoped Matilda was not angry at her. "I kissed her good-bye. I am sorry you both misunderstand my motives and feelings so." By contrast, Alice made sure to inform Paul that, in her mind, her relatives could not supersede him. "After all one's mama and sister and old-time friends can't take the place of one's own hubbins," she remarked.[39]

Recurring marital arguments distressed them. By summer's end, Paul would look forward to their reunion in Washington, D.C., after Alice had spent some time in New York City. "I shall be so glad when we are to-gether again in our own little nest. I shall be glad too of the little time we spend to-gether there by the sea; but I want that to be short so that I can get you away to myself." Concern over their sniping at each other tempered his enthusiasm: "Then, dear I do hope there won't be any little spats or bickerings. I have been thinking it all over, and I am going to try to be too big to quarrel over petty things with you." Only by "loving kindness" could Paul strengthen Alice's love, not by quibbling.[40]

Yet Paul could not help himself, and Alice noticed. Quite often, especially whenever they were apart for a brief period, she wondered whether he enjoyed her company as much as he had before. In autumn she wrote him and posed the question directly. "Do you really want me back?" she asked. "I am lonely and want you too, dearest, but what's the use? We would not be together twelve hours before I would irritate you and make you despise me, and cause you to magnify my human weaknesses into unpardonable sins." In her view, he subjected her to the kind of scrutiny that made her feel insecure and unworthy as a wife, at the same time distracting the couple from the glaring flaws of petulance and pettiness in his own character. He condemned her. ("I am faulty and frail, and so far from your ideal," she sighed.) He lambasted her. ("I only irritate and anger you, and hinder you in your work—even why I try to help and think I am helping," she went on.) And he destroyed her self-confidence. ("I have tried so hard, so hard, and it all is unavailing. I suppose I am utterly unfit, and it's no use. I am beginning to think you don't love me now, for how can you love a woman who persistently does the wrong thing, and destroys your ideals and hurts your work?") Marriage was not heaven; it was hell. For baring her soul so honestly, she later apologized.[41]

Disputes sometimes threatened to become public. To Paul's consternation, the epistolary fault lines that formed between him and Alice over the years and remerged in the home they shared caused audible domestic earthquakes. In one of their more consequential exchanges, in early September, he was "very lonesome & desperate & broody." He blamed her for his disconsolation. Sometimes he thought he never wanted to see her again. He thought she "ruined" him. What irked him most was her behavior. Fury, in turn, gripped her so much that she apparently could not help herself; the implications boded poorly for their future reputation as a married couple and for his own as a celebrity. "The night you lay on the bed & yelled like a Comanche is reported even as far as Cincinnati and people all believe that I beat you," he said.[42]

Word was spreading that Paul was a violent man. Rumor was solidifying into fact, despite his belief to the contrary. "I was told down there that you were yelling away like an Indian and that I kept on pounding you," he reported. "While another person,—an old friend told me to treat my wife better. When I think of it and the reputation I am bearing because you chose to scream in anger, I grow both bitter and desperate." Between the genuine discontent brewing in their marriage and the conflagration of hearsay spreading beyond his control, Paul grew more incensed as he wrote to her about the episode. To save face he cut his letter short, his rage growing as he wrote: "I do not mean to be hard; but I am hurt, hurt! so I will close before more will come—"[43]

The morning after writing this letter, Paul inflicted on Alice a "scolding." As during his earlier relationship with Rebekah, he ran emotionally hot and cold. Within a span of mere sentences or paragraphs, he alternately expressed his love for her and a sense of resignation to his unfortunate condition. He disclosed that he was hurt but that he still loved her. He followed with dissatisfaction about their home: "The very house oppresses me." Yet he wanted her by his side, and he wanted confirmation that she desired the same thing.[44]

Alice responded to Paul, enclosing the letter she first intended to send him—which was even more indignant. She was reaching the limit of her ability to withstand his cantankerous behavior, his refusal even to try to manage his brooding tendencies and use common sense. In perfect proportion, she was also imagining her withdrawal from their relationship, from their very marriage: "Suppose I decide to remain away altogether, for fear of constant bickerings and quarrels? Would either of us be happier?"[45]

To guarantee her return, Alice wanted him to promise that he would fulfill four codes of conduct. First, he had to let bygones be bygones, without the brooding and harping on their conflicts that should now be a distant memory. Second, he had to control his tongue and temper, restraining his relentless stream of insults. Third, he had to permit her to occupy her respectable dual roles as "the housewife and head." Fourth, he had to help make their home "a little Paradise," not as oppressive as they, for different reasons, both saw it.[46]

Concluding this list of promises, Alice issued Paul an ultimatum that included the potential diagnosis and prognosis if he strayed from fulfilling his part:

> I warn you that any evidence on your part toward brooding, blues, morbidity, theatrical posing, nonsensical introspection and sensation-studying that I see, I shall regard as sheer morbid nonsense, preceding from an unhealthy mental and physical condition—and shall treat it as such. I shall regard you as an unfortunate, unhealthy, uncontrolled child, to be humored a little, pitied a great deal, and dealt sternly with at the right time. I do not propose to have two lives wrecked.[47]

In the second letter enclosed—which was just over one thousand words, whereas the covering letter was about half that length—her mood was more pessimistic, her tone less conciliatory. She feared that, despite being married, they were not yet "confidential friends." When he derided her as "silly" and "hysterical," she was afraid to be vulnerable, to confide in him her innermost thoughts and feelings, given the probable consequences. Paul reacted to Alice's "silly twaddle" in predictable ways. Along with an attitude of derision, he grew, in her words, "angry," "intolerant," "scornful," and "noisy." If he understood her, he did so conditionally: "sometimes your 'understanding' takes the form of ascribing the lowest motive to my words and actions." Remarkably, she wrote her letter while they were living together in Washington, D.C. She had to interrupt this secondary letter with premonition and anticipation, a double sense likewise symptomatic of a marriage that, slowly but surely, was ripping her apart: "There, you have just come in. I must stop. Do not be angry with me, heart's own. I love you, love you and I want to be truly one with you."[48]

After Paul read these letters, Alice told him in person that it would be best for them to remain separated a while. She stayed away from Washington, D.C., for close to two weeks. Despite his pleas for her return, she traveled northeast to family and friends in New England and New York City, beyond his reach. "Your begging for me to come home awakened every fiber of my being," she wrote. "You don't know, you don't know how I've wanted to fly to you, but

I simply steeled myself to stay because I really believe we'll be so glad to see each other we *can't* spat." She truly hoped that her absence would make his heart grow fonder.[49]

Paul and Alice reunited by the end of September, but not before he punished her with "cruel silence." He refused to send any letters to her during their period apart. In letter after letter she sent him, she expressively writhed in emotional pain; she reiterated her deep love for him. But she did not withhold calling out another truth over and again: he was cruel.[50]

CHAPTER 17

Our New Madness

I note what you say in regard to Dunbar's article. I am very sorry that he has suffered himself to fly off in this way, not because it will do Tuskegee or the cause of industrial education any harm but I regret to see a man discuss something about which he knows nothing. In matters of poetry and fiction Dunbar is a master; in matters of industrial education and the development of the Negro race he is a novice.

—BOOKER T. WASHINGTON TO EMMETT JAY SCOTT
(AUGUST 23, 1898)[1]

By fall 1898, Paul was fed up with the political movement for industrial education, led by Booker T. Washington—their friendship, which Alice was trying to cultivate, be damned. In an essay entitled "Our New Madness," published in the August issue of the *Independent*, Paul registered his skepticism toward the "feverish delight" across the country with the industrial education of African Americans. The essay formed a public wedge between them. The public excitement over Washington's advocacy for the training of "the hand and the head" tended to focus more on the former than the latter. Given that the experience and expertise of African Americans with manual labor had been well proven ever since the days of slavery, their promise in the intellectual realm, where there existed "all appreciation for the beauty of art, science, and literature," continued to go unrecognized. Paul lamented that there had not yet "in the history of the country, risen a single intellectual black man whose pretentions have not been sneered at, laughed at, and then lamely wondered at."[2]

In this context Paul criticized the Wizard of Tuskegee. No one should question "the ability and honesty of purpose" of Washington, he said, whom he regarded an "earnest man." But Paul regretted that Washington's influence was turning out to be counterproductive. "I do fear that this earnest man is not doing either himself or his race full justice in his public utterances," Paul wrote. Washington "says we must have industrial training, and the world quotes him (in detached paragraphs) as saying that we must not have anything else." More preferable would be if the media and whites—along with African Americans themselves, even—tempered the craze for industrial education with "a right idea of the just proportion in life of industry, commerce, art, science, and letters, of materialism and idealism, of utilitarianism and beauty!" The exclamation highlighted the bafflement, but also the urgency, with which Paul implored his fellow citizens to correct their thinking.[3]

"Our New Madness" did not go unnoticed by Washington, who not only read it but received letters from colleagues who did so as well. Less than a week after the essay appeared, Emmett Jay Scott, special managerial and philanthropic adviser at Tuskegee, wrote Washington to express reservations about Paul's wisdom. Washington concurred, likewise mystified and saddened by what he saw as reckless indiscretion, yet also stalwart in defense of "the cause." "I am very sorry that he has suffered himself to fly off in this way," Washington wrote Scott, "not because it will do Tuskegee or the cause of industrial education any harm but I regret to see a man discuss something about which he knows nothing." Washington never confused Paul's domains of expertise. "In matters of poetry and fiction Dunbar is a master; in matters of industrial education and the development of the Negro race he is a novice," he wrote. Washington never made these private views public, but he took solace in knowing that one Timothy Thomas Fortune would work on his behalf to address his concern.[4]

Born into slavery in Marianna, Florida, in 1856, Fortune initially attended the first local school for African Americans, started after the Civil War, but transferred to Stanton High School for Negroes when his family moved over two hundred miles within the state to Jacksonville. He developed political acumen from his father, a Reconstruction-era state politician; he also cultivated an expertise in editing and communications after he started working as an apprentice printer at a newspaper and as a page in the state senate. He witnessed the Ku Klux Klan perpetrate violence firsthand, which further drove him to hone what would become a lifelong joint interest in politics and journalism. Despite being mostly self-taught, in 1875 he enrolled at Howard University and majored in journalism. (He quit school after only two semesters.) He then worked at the *People's Advocate*, a Washington, D.C., newspaper, got married and had a child, then moved with his family back to Florida to take up a teaching position, only eventually to return with them to New York City to advance his newspaper career. In 1881 he established the *New York Age*, a newspaper catering to the concerns of the African American community and quickly becoming the most influential periodical of its time in the United States, commissioning African American writers of prominence ranging from Victoria Earle Matthews to Ida B. Wells.

With the cultural and political winds at his back, Fortune founded the pioneering National Afro-American League in 1887. Eleven years later, he published *The Kind of Education the Afro-American Most Needs*, which helped popularize "Afro-American" in the public lexicon. Beyond his professional chops, Fortune was even being compared to Paul Laurence Dunbar on the question of who was the race's premier poet. Whereas the *Colored American* regarded Fortune "the leading poet of the race," Kansas's *Leavenworth Herald*, in an October 1894 issue, disagreed: "He *is not* the leading poet of the race. It must be remembered that Mr. Paul Laurence Dunbar of Dayton, O., is not dead."[5] Fortune not only had the charge by Washington to reply, but the editor and the poet were compeers perhaps destined to be antagonists. "Mr. Fortune I think is going to answer him," Washington wrote Scott.[6]

So antagonistic was Paul's essay that even more prominent folks in Washington's circle, including African American inventor and botanist George Washington Carver, chimed in. Carver encouraged the Tuskegee leader to stay the course. "Mr. Washington I hope you will not let any such articles similar to that of Paul L. Dunbar give you a moment's uneasiness but simply stimulate you to press on," Carver wrote. "You have the only true solution to this great race problem. It is only ignorance *mostly* and a bit of prejudice that prompts such articles." A claim that ignorance beset Paul as he wrote "Our New Madness" was unlikely at this time; but the notion that a bit of prejudice laced his words was probable.[7]

With their dispute now public, Washington decided to extend Paul an olive branch to squelch the controversy. Warren F. Kellogg, publisher of *New England Magazine*, wanted to convene a meeting in Boston "in the interest of Tuskegee," including Washington, Paul, and W. E. B. Du Bois. A brilliant thinker who was only four years Paul's senior, Du Bois had emerged as one of the foremost educational and political leaders of Paul's time. Born thirty years earlier in Great Barrington, Massachusetts, Du Bois honed his intellectual craft studying at Fisk and, in his late teenage years, teaching in rural Tennessee and witnessing the poverty of African American life. He graduated from Fisk and went on to Harvard. His greatest influences came from philosophers William James and George Santayana, and accordingly he finished his undergraduate degree with a concentration in philosophy. He progressed toward a doctorate at Harvard, with an educational detour at the University of Berlin, focusing on sociology and economics. After receiving his PhD in 1895, he would publish books on topics ranging from the African slave trade to the social science of African Americans living in Philadelphia. Few people of the black intelligentsia knew or published as much rigorous scholarship as Du Bois did.[8]

Paul was somewhat tickled that, a few weeks after his essay appeared in the *Independent*, he heard from Washington himself, inviting the poet to share the stage with the educator and the social scientist: "Well I had a call this morning from Booker T. Washington, a gentleman from Tuskegee whom you probably know," Paul informed Alice. A proposed date for the event was a few months down the road, sometime in early December.[9]

Instead of allowing Washington's notoriety to preoccupy him, Paul wondered about the purpose of the event. Speculation filled his mind. "*Now what is their game*? Is it to destroy any future power Du Bois and I may have by bringing us before the public in the character of speakers for the very institution whose founder's utterances we cannot subscribe to? Am I too sagacious?" Dunbar had gone on the public record to rebut Washington. Now, the staged optics of these two men in conversation, shoulder to shoulder, threatened to obscure their political and philosophical differences. Paul could not shake that imagery; "looking at the matter either synthetically or analytically, the same result appears to me," he revealed in a letter to Alice. He also had cast a curious eye on Washington's opportunism. "Mr. W. tells me that there will be a great audience of wealthy New Englanders there and that it will be a great advantage to me to go and that he can fix it with Mr. Young," who was Paul's superintendent at the Library of Congress. Paul was no stranger to patronage, and the reality of Washington's influence, whether among the wealthy elite or Paul's own boss at the Library of Congress, was undeniable.[10]

Due to Paul's need for money, he was tempted to turn Washington down. He crafted an excuse more principled and polite than a flat rejection. "As it looks now, unless I am able to get a leave until the first of the year, I shall not be able to go to Boston with you," he apologized in a letter delayed by yet another illness. "I am now at home sick, and have been for two weeks past." But he left the door ajar: if Washington could wield his influence over his boss, John Russell Young, the Librarian of Congress, and secure a waiver, then Paul would be in a better position to entertain the invitation.[11]

The Library of Congress was turning out to be too inhospitable to Paul's well-being. Weeks of scorching weather in June and July of 1898 had so heated

FIG. 17.1. The Thomas Jefferson Building of the Library of Congress, Washington, D.C., circa 1897. (Library of Congress Prints and Photographs Division)

the library's metal shelves that he had come to compare the facility to a penitentiary from which he wished to escape. Not even his abiding love of books could mitigate the summer dread of work. Two decades later, Alice would recall that "the iron grilling of the book stacks" were analogous to "prison bars in more senses than one." No longer could he endure these conditions; his string of illnesses only complicated his tenure there.[12]

In late October, Paul issued an appeal to Young. "As you know I have been ill for two weeks past, and away from the library," he wrote in almost the same words as his private correspondence with Washington. "I was there today, and tried to resume my duty, but found myself unable to do so." Still, he put on a good face. "I like my work, and do not want to resign, but find myself completely broken down both in health and spirits." He wondered whether Young would be compassionate enough to grant him a leave of absence, even without pay, until the start of the following year, so that he could make a full recovery. To blunt the edge of his request, he added a postscript in which he inquired if Young would like to receive a copy of *The Uncalled*.[13]

Young was understanding. "I am sorry to hear of your continued illness and hope it presages a speedy recovery," he wrote. He reminded Paul that, under the law, at most he could grant a leave of sixty days, from November 1, 1898, to January 1, 1899. But he was willing to permit him to return to work thereafter. He welcomed the gift of the novel, but more important was the restoration of Paul's health: "my only wish being that you shall return in the best form."[14] Paul did not improve; participating in the Boston event was now at risk. To "recuperate shattered energies" he was compelled to take those two months of sick leave seriously. "Of course after being so long away from work, I could not conscientiously ask for even a day until my annual leave in August. I should not wish to take more time, even were it offered." Such unfortunate circumstances were conspiring to keep the educator and the poet apart. Neither could agree on an occasion to disagree in public, even if they wanted to.[15]

———

Wilmington was at one time a bona fide utopia. In the last decade of the nineteenth century, it was the largest city in North Carolina; it was also the home of approximately fourteen thousand African Americans, who constituted the majority of the population there. Given that many of them were successful entrepreneurs and skilled professional workers, they exemplified the ideal outcome of racial uplift. Business and political leaders emerged from the community, and they successfully leveraged their economic and electoral power at the ballot box, either on their own Republican platform or in the "Fusion" coalition with poor white farmers. Known as the Populists, these farmers shared the opposition of African Americans to the conservative platform of the Confederacy-decorated Democratic Party, albeit for slightly different reasons. The Democratic platform advanced corporate capitalism, which failed to address Populist labor concerns during the decade's economic depression. At the same time, African Americans could negotiate to promote a political vision for equitable enfranchisement and equal rights across the color line.

White resentment started exploding in the city amid the sharp increase in successful African Americans, such as their evident proliferation in businesses or the perception of their unfair acquisition of privileges, including their general payment of less than 7 percent of the city's overall property taxes. (The latter, ironically, was due to the hardship they faced in being denied access to financial capital and land ownership by whites themselves.) Social and economic frustration, coupled with the undying racial animosity that continued to inform media campaigns and the mythology of hypersexual blacks raping white women, galvanized the Democratic and Populist constituencies under the racist auspices of white supremacy. African Americans could only be on the defensive in this age of Redemption.

After an intimidating series of white political rallies and conventions, newspaper editorials, as well as public threats and fearmongering, on November 10, 1898, whites were resolved to overturn what they perceived to be "Negro Rule." Behind hyperbolic accusations of African American noncompliance and instigations, about two thousand whites, almost all men, led a coup d'état in Wilmington, overtaking the local police, rampaging through neighborhoods, and massacring hundreds of African Americans. Thousands of African American survivors fled, unlikely to return to a city where their electoral and economic power had disintegrated. Whites dealt with only a few injuries, despite the frenetic media storyline of a "race riot." Any hope for peaceable and equitable race relations fell to a "nadir," a historical term for the horrifying series of race massacres and lynchings, numbering in the thousands, that occurred in the United States at the turn of the twentieth century. The Wilmington tragedy was just one example of this phenomenon, which lasted roughly from the end of Reconstruction to World War I.[16]

The massacre in Wilmington so provoked Paul that weeks later, in December, he published an essay, "The Race Question Discussed," with a local paper he was familiar with, the *Toledo Journal*. The injustice that occurred in North Carolina was an affront to citizens not only there but across the country, he argued, for the "race spirit in the United States is not local but general." General media coverage was demoralizing him. Some reporters congratulated "the murderers of Wilmington," he wrote, and chronicled "the armed resistance of the community to the Negroes in the exercise of those powers and privileges which are the glory of the country for which the colored men fought." Paul pointed out that African Americans enlisted in the Union Army to rescue a nation being torn asunder over the matter of slavery, only for this class of people—his own race—to be reviled and killed by the very same white citizens whose livelihood was preserved or restored after the Civil War. For all to see, he listed those contradictions while impersonating such hypocritical white attitudes: "Negroes, you may fight for us, but you may not vote for us. You may prove a strong bulwark when the bullets are flying, but you must stand from the line when the ballots are in the air. You may be heroes in war, but you must be cravens in peace."[17]

The tone and theme here differed from those in the essay Paul had published a little more than a year earlier, "England as Seen by a Black Man," in which he implored African Americans to be more satisfied with their lot. The Wilmington riots compelled him to warn that many African Americans had already enjoyed the taste of freedom and agency through their heroic efforts as soldiers during the Civil War, that they would not regress to the disfranchisement imposed on them in previous generations. Violence by whites against blacks would never be the answer to their need to acclimate to this new world. The virtues of "calmness, justice, breadth and manliness" should characterize "a great nation," and they should supersede any disagreement that may exist between the races.[18]

Notably, as incensed as Paul was over the Wilmington tragedy, he stopped short of encouraging racial retaliation. Conciliation remained his preferred rhetoric. Such "catastrophes as the Southern riots, terrible though they be, are but incidents in his [the Negro's] growth, which is inevitable." That is to say, regardless of the event, whether a calamity or a celebration of interracial contact, racial progress was on the horizon for the Negro.[19]

If dismay fell upon Paul as he reflected on how racial uplift, in Wilmington, could be undermined from without, it did the same as he considered how this doctrine, in northern cities, could be undercut from within. Seeing firsthand the influx of African Americans to the Tenderloin fueled his writing of "The Negroes of the Tenderloin," a manifesto he published in the *Columbus Dispatch* six days before Christmas in 1898. "One looks at the crowds of idle, shiftless Negroes that throng these districts," he sighed, "and the question must arise, what is to be done with them, what is to be done for them, if they are to be prevented from inoculating our civilization with the poison of their lives?" The city infected his race with an inclination toward moral turpitude and criminal behavior, he believed. The damage was done not only to the migrants themselves but to their children, who would inherit and grow into "the misdeeds of the Tenderloin."[20]

Full of sorrow, Paul could only pity his race for "flocking" to a city in the North "to lose so much and to gain so little," when these "ignorant and irresponsible Negroes" would have been better off remaining in the South, where their failings would not be so blatantly obvious—where they could retain their "purity, simplicity, and the joy of life." While Paul did not foresee many solutions, he advised his fellow "better-class Negro" to uplift not only themselves but those African American "denizens of the Tenderloin," else the debasement would corrupt all.[21]

———

The accumulating disenchantment between Paul and Alice that had prompted her, in fall 1898, to impose a marital separation of two weeks remained painfully strong five months later. In anguish, she wrote him her most powerful letters—by turns lyrical and metaphorical, emotional and spiritual, in self-exploration. She pled for wisdom: why, as husband and wife, were their conversations consistently devolving into acrimony?

Suffering from bronchitis, Alice's respiratory challenges gave word and image to her problems of verbal articulation. In her letters to Paul, at best she could only stitch together lengthy, involved paragraphs with typography ("xxx xxx"), owing any sense of rhetorical and thematic flow to the power of emotional undercurrents. "Do you know what it is to have a something within you crying for utterance," she began, "beating the bars of its prison, begging to be let out and you cannot give it freedom?" Like a caged bird, her own spirit was stifled; she possessed an "original soul struggling for utterance," for a freedom that would only inspire their marriage. But she likened their bond to an "opium devotee," planning "great deeds in his stupor and wakes only to weakness and nausea." She could only grope for a solution, but the darkness of her life with Paul continued to obscure her vision, to render elusive her attainment of joy.[22]

Again Alice hinted at Paul's maltreatment of her confidence. "If only we could realize what we are doing when in a moment of anger or jest we refer slightingly to some heart confidence from one we love," she explained. "It is like crushing a violet within a ruthless hand." Throughout her letter she imagined "winding paths," various tropes of nature punctuating the journey of life, that she wished they could explore together, to learn more about each other. Never had they wandered together in its depths, whereupon they would have known each other better. Until then, Alice figured that she and Paul remained strangers. Twists and turns of logic and language led her to craft excessively archaic, stylized proverbs that captured her disorientation. They had not yet found each other, so to speak. Even in the physical presence of each other, they were apart in emotion and spirit: "Thou dost not appear even when your body's arms are closest about me and your body's lips are whispering the tenderest secrets within my ear."[23]

Ironically, their cohabitation in Washington, D.C., widened the gulf between them. If more friendly and respectful, they were intimate in private correspondence. The decorum of the written word kept at bay the firestorm that more routinely emerged from the disputes they waged in person. The tendency to write sassy letters to each other was becoming equally routine. Fewer and farther between were the expressions of unconditional love that had marked their letters of courtship and engagement.[24]

Frustration was settling in. Wrestling with his literary writing, Paul realized that his struggles had much to do with his time apart from Alice. "The getting together of my work for the book of verse goes steadily on,—and what a hopeless, shapeless mass it is!" he reasoned. "I wish you were here to help me." But he thought their distance remained in her best interest; his local weather was insufferable. "I positively believe that you could not stand Washington now. It is so dreadfully, cruelly hot. The women who come back to the library from their vacations are having to leave again." Presumably, Alice would have done the same had she worked alongside her spouse in the Library of Congress.[25]

———

Paul was taking full advantage of having previously published individual poems in magazines and newspapers. By 1899, his rate of such publications had multiplied remarkably. In the three years since *Majors and Minors* appeared, he was publishing on average twenty poems per year, an amount almost equaling the entire set of poems he had published between 1888, the approximate start of his career as a published poet, and 1896, when he appeared on the national scene as a professional writer. *Century Magazine* remained his top choice, his poems appearing in it more frequently than in any other periodical; he accrued fame as he circulated multiple poems in each of the reputable venues of the era, including *Current Literature, Bookman, Ladies' Home Journal, Washington, D.C. Times,* and *Critic;* and he was starting to gain a foothold for the first time in the *New York Times, The Nation,* and the papers of the largest cities like Boston and New York.

Paul's fourth book of poetry, which he came to title *Lyrics of the Hearthside* and once again dedicated to Alice, was a remarkable feat. Not only was it the most robust of the books of poetry he had published thus far; it was the longest, with 109 poems, five more than *Lyrics of Lowly Life,* the longest of his previous books of poems. But his new book was mostly new. Save for the reprinting of one poem, "My Sort o' Man," which first appeared in *Oak and Ivy,* his new book gathered up his best and freshest poems. And just as he had in *Majors and Minors*, he cordoned off the dialect poems at the end of the book—a little more than thirty poems, explicitly marked in this collection, as were the closing twenty-four poems of *Majors and Minors* that had the subtitle "Humor and Dialect." Signaling the strength and versatility of his literary powers for all the world to see, *Lyrics of the Hearthside* consummated Paul's professional stature with an impressive scale of literary compilation and commercial circulation. Releasing merely one or a couple of poems in obscure or even noteworthy periodicals simply could not grant him the hallmark of distinction that a book would.

The criticism of *Lyrics of the Hearthside* resembled what Paul's earlier books of poetry had garnered. All of the books divided their poems in dialect from those in formal English; the consequence was felt in the almost uniform way that reviewers implored him to stick to penning dialect. Together, the reviewers contended that readers likely would favor the dialect of the slave or the regional bumpkin over the high, though unfortunately "imitative," language of the Romantics. "There is no reason why a Negro poet should not write good English, but, after all, it is to Mr. Dunbar's dialect verse that the reader will turn with the expectation of finding the work which has the most individuality to it," wrote one reviewer. "Dunbar writes well in grammatical English, but his best work is still in Negro dialect," admonished another. "As in his former volumes," sighed yet one more critic, "Mr. Dunbar is at his best in his dialect verse, because in this verse he is dealing with the things he knows first at hand. His other work, although often very good, is sometimes conventional and secondary." Evidently, the book was not good enough to quell the skepticism newspaper critics, mostly white, expressed whenever they encountered his experimentation across linguistic genres of poetry.[26]

———

Only a few days before Christmas in 1898 did Paul feel healthy enough to reconsider Washington's invitation to attend the Boston event on Tuskegee. Now Paul was able to go. He just needed to know the details in advance. Washington's silence on the matter (he did not send along any letters about it) stoked Paul's impatience. His desire to share the stage with Washington grew. "I have had other offers for dates, but I cannot arrange my course until I know what you are going to do," he wrote. "I should be glad if you would inform me as soon as possible."[27]

Now was Paul's turn to extend an olive branch, if not a quid pro quo, regarding Tuskegee's Eighth Annual Negro Farmer's Conference. "I have been asked to write up your Negro Conference in February, and would be glad if you could give me any special facilities for so doing. I think it would make a very interesting article, and not be entirely unprofitable to the school itself." In public and private alike, Paul previously had been unequivocal in expressing his disappointment over the rise of so-called Negro industrial education. At the turn of 1899, however, he was ready to scratch Washington's back, as Washington had scratched his own by using his influence to obtain him a sabbatical from his job at the Library of Congress. (After the time away, Paul resigned from the job.) If Washington could help arrange his accommodations, Paul could offer a favorable report on the upcoming conference in Tuskegee.[28]

Washington fulfilled Paul's request, offering to provide transportation to the conference. At last accepting the invitation, Paul made yet another request: he had been approached by a syndicate to write an article ahead of the conference. "May I ask you if you have on hand any data or matter pertaining to the conference, its subject and so forth, with any photographs that would make an interesting article?" he asked Washington. A couple of days after this letter Paul wrote a second one, this time revealing that the *Philadelphia Press* also wanted him to contribute a 2,500-word article on the conference. "If my transportation can be made for two I will take Mrs. Dunbar along to Tuskegee, as she knows something of this sort of work and can be of great assistance to me," he wrote, apologizing for how high he was piling his letters of need onto Washington's desk.[29]

Paul sought security in Washington's collaboration, seeking to mitigate the tension between them that he had created with "Our New Madness." Writing laudatory pieces about Tuskegee could be a solution. In his essay "The Tuskegee Meeting," published in the *Providence Telegram* that February, Paul extolled that "men may disagree with some of Mr. Washington's ideas, and some thinkers do, but they cannot withhold their admiration for his energy, industry, and singleness of purpose."[30]

A week into February, Paul wrote Washington that he had received reports on the conference but awaited other items, such as the declaration and photographs. He assured Washington that he would arrive at Tuskegee by the twentieth of the month: "I shall do what I can to make the articles helpful to Tuskegee, as well as to the race in general."[31] Paul arranged to leave Washington, D.C., on February 16 to get there on time. (Unfortunately, Alice could not join him, as originally planned, due to her sister's illness.) Now, the Tuskegee leader had an alliance with a writer whom he had once dismissed as a "novice" on the education and evolution of the Negro.

———

In the years since Paul first emerged on the international scene as the preeminent African American poet of his time, the nature and implications of his success had perfectly crystallized in his mind. Whether printing his literary works in newspapers, collections, or books, or reciting them before private and public audiences, his theory of portraying in literature the individuals, language, and activities of African American society was fully derived. Now he was experienced enough to explain it.

In mid-February 1899, an entertaining show in celebration of Hampton Institute was held at the Waldorf-Astoria Hotel, a captivating German Renaissance building with a magnificent ballroom, at the corner of Fifth Avenue and 34th Street in New York City. "One by one came in the cheerful black faces of Hampton students," reported the *New York Commercial*. A snowstorm delayed the event's start, but once it began, a series of performers entertained all night: a quartet sang folk songs and spirituals; Henry Thacker Burleigh crooned baritone solos; Charles Winter Woods, a Tuskegee educator and actor, read literary pieces; Paul himself recited poems.[32]

As the evening came to a close, Paul and the other performers congregated by a window, watching the snow fall. A reporter for the *New York Commercial* approached Paul with a question that cut to the heart of his travails in the literary marketplace.

"In the poetry written by Negroes, which is the quality that will most appear, something native and African and in every way different from the verse of the Anglo-Saxons, or something that is not unlike what is written by white people?"

"My dear sir," Paul answered, "the predominating power of the African race is lyric. In that I should expect the writers of my people to excel. But, broadly speaking, their poetry will not be exotic or differ much from that of the whites."

The reporter proved unrelenting in projecting the racial stereotypes with which Paul had been long familiar.

"But surely, the tremendous facts of race and origin—" said the reporter, pursuing the line of thought.

"You forget that for two hundred and fifty years the environment of the Negro has been American, in every respect the same as that of all other Americans," Paul replied.

The reporter objected. "Isn't there a certain tropic warmth, a cast of temperament that belongs of right to the African race, and should not that element make its lyric expression, if it is to be genuine, a thing apart?"

"Ah, what you speak of is going to be a loss. It is inevitable. We must write like the white men. I do not mean imitate them; but our life is now the same," Paul said. "I hope you are not one of those who would hold the negro down to a certain kind of poetry—dialect and concerning only scenes on plantations in the south."

Reflecting on Paul's concern, the reporter later recorded in his article: "This appeared to be a sore point, and the questioner at once truthfully denied having any such desire."

Given that slaves and their descendants had over multiple centuries cohabited in the Americas with their enslavers and their progeny, Paul believed that human differences attributable to race were subordinate to the interpersonal similarities that evolved from a shared national culture. The reporter's line of thinking opened a wound still fresh in Paul's memory, about the "irrevocable harm" Howells had inflicted on his career almost three years earlier in *Harper's Weekly*. Even the reporter, mired in his own prejudices, detected Paul's insuppressible sensitivity to the matter.

The conversation took a turn with the participation of Charles Winter Wood, when Paul began to ponder the traditional and newer genres of poetry to which he and other African American writers were likely to gravitate:

"There are great questions in my mind regarding the forms of poetry," Paul began. "Do you think it is possible now to invent a new form? Have the old ones completely exhausted the possible supply? Then, I wonder if the negro will ever reach dramatic poetry."

"Edwin Booth once said to me," Wood responded, "that he considered that the negro should make the greatest actor in the world—because he had the most soul."

"I don't think that," Paul said. "The black man's soul is lyric, not dramatic. We may expect songs from the soul of the negro, but hardly much dramatic power, either in writing or in acting."

The reporter concluded the interview with an inquiry into the tradition of writers to which Paul belonged. "Is there a large school of negro poets?"

"Haven't you read McClellan?" Paul asked. "Then there's Moore, Corrothers, Whitman, who has just finished an epic called *The Rape of Florida*. It appears to me, also, that that is not negro poetry only which is written by negroes, but all that is written by whites who have received their inspiration from negro life."

The races have acted and reacted on each other. The white man who, as a child, was suckled at the breast of a black mammy has received the strongest influence of his life, perhaps, from the African race. Why, the white people in the south talk like us—they have imported many of our words into the language—and you know they act like us."

"Which one of the current writers of negro stories best represents the race?" the reporter wondered.

"Joel Chandler Harris shows the most intimate sympathy—Mrs. Stuart, too." Paul said.

"You omit the one who is perhaps most popular."

"You mean Page? Yes, I left him out with intention. His attitude is condescending, always," Paul declared.

The names Paul cited were the accomplished African American poets of his time—George Marion McClellan, James David Corrothers, Albery Allson Whitman, and his wife, Alice. (Of these, Paul owned the books of McClellan and Whitman—respectively, *Poems*, published in 1895, and *Twasinta's Seminoles; or, Rape of Florida*, in 1885—in his personal library. Of course, he already knew Alice's poetry by heart.) Yet Paul's reply also revealed how widely he defined this tradition of "negro poetry" to include poems "written by whites." Despite their Anglo-Saxon ancestry, white writers could also lay claim to portraying his race in authentic ways, given how racially intermixed was American culture.

Paul drew distinctions between the white writers he was willing to regard as literary relatives and those he was not. Ruth McEnery Stuart, who hailed from Alice's own backyard in New Orleans, elicited Paul's admiration; and Harris was a Midwestern legend who inspired Paul early on. But Thomas Nelson Page was not attractive at all. Diplomatic geniality, which the Dayton poet was yet learning to master, steered him away from criticizing that elder statesman from Virginia. But the *Commercial* reporter's query left him little wiggle room, and Paul also was not the kind to lie about matters such as these.

———

Paul arrived in Tuskegee on time—on Monday, February 20. Previously, Tuskegee Institute was only an abstract idea. Now, it was a concrete reality, with the remarkable history that included but also preceded Washington, and Paul was now standing on its campus. For ground as hallowed as this, he knew that for the weary there would be little rest. The first thing he learned when he arrived was that he would have to recite his literature the same night. And he did. He could not reject the itinerary, not after Washington had paid for his transportation to Alabama. Exhausted, he recited only four poems, then retreated to the guest residence of Charles Wood, a Tuskegee faculty member and the delightful fellow he befriended in New York, where both were reading their works in the Lincoln Day program in support of Hampton Institute in Virginia.

After the event, Paul could only stew over his self-inflicted predicament in the heart of the Deep South. Lamentably, "the trick the Washingtons did last night I thought very shabby," he complained. "They asked me to dinner, finally, by note & did not ask my host. Of course, I could not refuse without causing feeling on their side, this is not policy."

That evening Washington cornered Paul, who had to relent somewhat on the industrial education of the Negro. Once the poet arrived in the clutches of the Wizard of Tuskegee, there was not any escape. Washington watched him closer than ever and on the last night, he forced a discussion upon Paul at his house. "Well, he retired from the field after awhile," Paul wrote Alice, "after having confess[ed] that every argument he had advanced had been met." Paul reached a likely irrevocable conclusion, at once a compliment and a condescension: "*He is slick,*—pardon me I meant with a capital (S)."[33]

Paul was relieved to leave Tuskegee intact. "Mr. Washington after making me recite four times in three days didn't give me a cent for it, only paying up my expenses of $55.10." The Tuskegee community enjoyed the privilege of listening to his multiple recitals—performances that, in total, represented a recompense, if not also a repentance, for his public denigration of the institution and its leader a couple of months earlier in "Our New Madness." The visit deepened Paul's insight into a world of which he no longer wished to be a part—a world in which, although remarkable for its cultural and political value to his race at that time, he would have contracted his own new madness, given his reservations about Washington's ethos, had he not fled at the soonest chance. Paul's hagiographical essay on the conference eventually appeared in the March 5 issue of *Philadelphia Press*.[34]

Paul's ingratiation to Washington continued to contrast starkly with the agitation with which he discussed Tuskegee in his letters to Alice. On the same day that his *Philadelphia Press* article appeared, Paul wrote to Washington, enclosing copies of two articles—the first from *Philadelphia Press*, the other from an "International Literary" syndicate—with the sincere hope that they would please him. Clearly, Paul subordinated his philosophical differences to his appeals to Washington's ego.[35]

From this point onward, Paul held his vocal reservations at bay while hitching his wagon to the Tuskegee leader, aware that doing so was a lucrative enterprise.

Horace Bumstead, the president of Atlanta University, had asked Paul if he were willing to appear alongside W. E. B. Du Bois in several cities near Boston during March. Paul was excited. Merely a day after sending along his articles to Washington, he wrote Alice that new opportunities lay on the horizon. "You know they are asking me to read for Atlanta on the 19th," he wrote, "and I have promised on condition that Mr. Washington consents to the deal. This with the probable repetition of our reading at Cambridge"—the rescheduled Boston-area event, where both were supposed to speak, for the benefit of Tuskegee—"will make three and a very snug sum I hope."

Before Washington had a chance to be invited, he caught wind of Paul's tour with Du Bois. In a letter to Bumstead, Washington suggested that this tour would detract from his own major Tuskegee fundraising event at Boston's Hollis Street Theater, scheduled for March 21. Washington invited Paul and Du Bois to share the stage with him during his own event, a diplomatic and clever gesture. Du Bois asserted the life of the mind over the vocation of the hands in racial uplift, but Washington would much rather accommodate this difference of opinion rather than permit the professor from Atlanta University to upstage him. As for Paul, money talked: Washington reimbursed the poet once again for his rail fare and expenses, in the amount of $133.[36]

The event at Boston's Hollis Street Theater was the first time the three luminaries had shared a stage. Paul especially gravitated to Washington's speech, "The Influence of Object-Lessons in the Solution of the Race Problem," a staple message of uplift. First, Washington set the scene: in the wake of the Civil War and the emancipation and departure of slaves from the South, a former white slaveowner in the heart of the Black Belt watched his plantation fall into disrepair. So dependent had he and his family been on slave labor that this condition "had deprived him and his offspring of the benefit of technical and industrial training, and worst of all had unconsciously led them to see in labor drudgery and degradations instead of beauty, dignity, and civilizing power." Washington went on to claim that slavery and its aftermath had inflicted two kinds of racial damage. A "temporary" wrong had been done to African Americans, yet an "eternal" psychological and emotional damage had been wrought upon "those committing the crimes." Before a grand audience, Washington was soliciting listeners for money to fund Tuskegee's accommodationist mission to help "in lightening the burdens" of not "one race but two," "to put that spirit into men that will make them forget race and color in efforts to lift up an unfortunate brother."[37]

Previously, Paul had criticized some of these views in "Our New Madness," but on this occasion he marveled at their oratorical force. While Washington continued to exhaust himself at his home institution managing the faculty, students, and staff on campus as well as the folks in the local community, he still fulfilled an obligation to be the public leader nonpareil who could speak representatively, and convincingly, about the future of his race. Paul watched Washington and Du Bois excel in raising funds and captivating an audience. He basked in their glow. Washington's campaign target was $150,000. Du Bois earned a considerable sum for his own efforts. Paul lined his own pockets as well. To boot, he and Du Bois received the loudest applause of the evening, while Washington's hoarse voice and sickly guise dampened his own effect.[38]

Paul was more than willing to keep his future calendar open, ensuring that his recitals would not conflict with the occasions he and Washington, if not also Du Bois, could once again share the stage.

———

As Paul considered the kind of book to publish next, he received a boost from an institution Washington held dear: Hampton Institute. The same school that Washington had revered for the legacy of General Armstrong, who had established Hampton's original curriculum along with industrial education and its employment of African Americans, also had asserted a mission that inspired Paul's creative and commercial strategies. And that mission found expression in the Hampton Institute Camera Club.

Founded on October 21, 1893, the Hampton Camera Club was initially chartered as Kiquotan Kamera Klub, a name alluding to the Pamunkey Native American town in Virginia where Hampton Institute was situated. During the last decade of the century, the club was born when the technological innovation known as the Kodak camera was making photography more accessible to mainstream consumers. Cameras and their lenses were growing more sophisticated, more precise, in rendering and representing the three-dimensionality of the real world. Packing more and more of the innovations into a smaller package, the cameras also were more portable, evolving to encourage and excite photographers of all skill levels to embark on newfound documentations of American life. Now, they could record scenes of human experience, circulate them with greater ease, and experiment with the medium. The Hampton Camera Club rode this tide of public interest.

The circumstances of Hampton Institute shaped the ethos of its camera club. The membership consisted of sixteen Hampton faculty, including Mary Alice Armstrong, the widow of founder General Armstrong, who died only months before the club's creation. Amateur photographers, the members tended to be artistic or intellectual in their teaching of art, their editing of the institution's official journal, *Southern Workman*, and their photographing of folklore. The camera club was established only one month before the folklore society, but almost all of its members were white, consistent with the predominant racial demographic of Hampton's faculty. The club sought to engage any and all amateur, but aspiring, fans or practitioners of photography. Well organized in its bylaws of membership, benefits, meeting procedures, and professional education, the camera club emerged as a remarkable structure to cultivate the expertise of Hampton in photography.[39]

Folklore was a key subject for the Hampton Camera Club. Hampton Institute had broadcast its interest through its founding of the folklore society one month after the inception of the camera club, which likewise indicated that its members viewed photographs as a medium through which "the study of typical Negro life" could be conducted. Although the club photographed a variety of settings without human subjects, ranging from buildings to landscapes, its consistent emphasis on African American lives became the graphic extension of *Southern Workman*, which also regularly discoursed on the topic. Intentionally or not, the camera club coordinated its thinking and efforts with the folklore society, which featured an overlap of members. The club provided a host of images of African American life that multiple offices of Hampton Institute could borrow to articulate its educational mission.

The camera club, folklore society, and *Southern Workman* together represented three distinct legs of an institutional stool. The groups revolved around the historical preoccupation of the Hampton Institute with the advancement of African American society. The eventual inclusion of African American members, starting with Robert Russa Moton and Allen Washington, further exemplified how progressive the camera club was relative to comparable photography clubs across the country, but also even on Hampton's campus itself, which contained remnants of de facto racial segregation.[40]

The Hampton Camera Club thus turned out to be fertile ground for a series of coincidences that pulled Paul into its orbit. First, his publisher of choice so far—Dodd, Mead and Company—enjoyed deep roots at Hampton. Charles L.

Mead and Amzi Dodd were Hampton trustees from 1881 to 1899 and from 1886 to 1896, respectively. Charles's sons Frank and Edward were Paul's editors and in regular correspondence with Hollis Burke Frissell, the Hampton chaplain who in 1893 succeeded General Armstrong as Hampton's president. Frissell's wife, Julia, was also the daughter of Amzi Dodd, one of the founders of the camera club. These coincidences positioned Dodd, Mead to become the book publisher most prominent to the inner circle of Hampton leadership and influence.[41]

Almost inevitably, the Hampton Camera Club and Paul crossed paths, first by virtue of his increasing personal association with Hampton Institute. Aside from Paul's fraught admiration of Hampton's storied pupil in Booker T. Washington, the two main women in Paul's life held a significant connection to Hampton. The Brooklyn-based mission where Alice had been teaching manual education happened to have been partially backed by the finances of Robert Ogden, an early donor to and eventual trustee of Hampton. And Paul's mother, Matilda, vacationed at the school in the summer of 1899. ("I quite approve of your idea of going to Hampton, for all the summer or as much of it as you care to spend there," Paul wrote Matilda on June 22 of that year. "The board is very reasonable, and I will send you a check whenever you let me know what you want.")[42]

For years Paul also had a relationship with Frissell, who sought to cultivate the poet's affiliation with Hampton and improve the institution's brand of racial uplift. A longtime supporter of elevating the race, Paul was quite open to the engagement. "By all means use my name," he wrote Frissell in fall 1897, "I am interested in this work for uplifting of my race & shall be glad to do whatever lies within my power to help it along."[43]

Paul's desire to "help" Hampton consisted in the sentiment he expressed to Alice the following year, when it became more obvious that Frissell was imploring him to work more often for Hampton's benefit. Back in January 1898, Frissell had inquired for the first time whether Paul would deliver lectures at the meetings of the New York Armstrong Association, where he could explain "what has been done in literature by members of the colored race." Not only would the poet be welcome before the association, but he would be embraced as well at Hampton, where colleagues were "very proud" of his achievements. Out of generosity, Paul was accepting invitations to speak for Hampton for free or at below his market rate. (At this time, he wrote Alice, "I see a chance to *help* Hampton by reading in New York.") But he had his limits and preferred to avoid setting a precedent at his financial expense for other institutions.

("Here is another letter from Boston. I don't know who they are or how to answer it. Received one offer this morning of $25.00 a week and expenses to go on the road. Will I go? Nit!")[44]

Southern Workman played a key role in cementing Paul's association with Hampton. Like many periodicals across the country, it reviewed *Lyrics of Lowly Life* in its April 1897 issue, commending the book's poems for representing the extraordinary accomplishment of an author descended from slaves. Perhaps to return the favor, Paul published several poems in *Southern Workman*, appealing to the journal and, more broadly, Hampton's interest in African American folklore.[45]

Unsurprisingly, the camera club gravitated to one of the poems that helped put Paul on the national map: "The Deserted Plantation." Encapsulated well in its first few stanzas, the poem presented the iconography of a southern plantation abandoned in the wake of the Emancipation Proclamation, with the dilapidation of the farmland, the quietude of the main house, and the absence of the slaves. Georgic in form and theme, the poem expounds pessimistically on the modern burden and suffering African Americans faced as manual laborers—without the guarantee of civic redemption, such as recognized citizenship and elective franchise, popularized by racial uplift—in post-Reconstruction America:[46]

> Oh, de grubbin-hoe's a rustin' in de co'nah,
>   An' de plow's a tumblin' down in de fiel'—
> While de whippo'will's a wailin' lak a mou'nah
>   When his stubbo'n hawt is tryin' ha'd to yiel'.
>
> In de furrers wha' de co'n was allus wavin',
>   Now de weeds is growin' green an' rank an' tall;
> An de swallers roun' de whole place is a bravin'
>   Lak dey thought their folks had allus owned it all.
>
> An' de big house stan's all quiet lak an' solemn,
>   Not a blessed soul in pa'lor, po'ch er lawn;
> Not a guest, ner not a ca'iage lef' to haul 'em,
>   Fu' de ones dat tu'ned de latch-string out air gone.
>
> An' de banjo's voice is silent in de qua'ters,
>   D'ain't a hymn ner co'n-song ringin' in de ah;
> But de murmur of a branch's passin' waters
>   Is de only soun' dat breks de stillness da.

Wha's de da'kies, dem dat used to be a dancin'
    Ebry night befo' de ole cabin do'?
Wha's de chillun, dem dat used to be a prancin',
    Er a rollin' in de san' er on de flo'?[47]

"The Deserted Plantation" emerged as a perfect project for the Hampton Camera Club. In late spring of 1898, according to the minutes of a club meeting, members discussed the project of providing photographs for the poem. Over the course of several months—or by January of the following year—the club decided on a more expansive project in collaboration with Paul and Dodd, Mead and Company. Contrary to the initial plan of focusing only on "The Deserted Plantation," members agreed that "several other poems of Dunbar's be published with it, and the book illustrated by the club." For the compensation of one hundred dollars, the Hampton Camera Club embarked on what would be the first of a series of books of poetry, compiled by Paul and his publisher, on African American experiences in postbellum America, starting with *Poems of Cabin and Field*.[48]

Published in late 1899, *Poems of Cabin and Field* was a thin book. It contained only eight poems, of the type the camera club and Hampton Institute preferred, in the dialect readers knew all too well. Paul chose all eight poems from his previously published books (*Oak and Ivy, Majors and Minors, Lyrics of Lowly Life*, and *Lyrics of the Hearthside*).[49] Paul understood that publishers, critics, and fans most admired his poems in dialect, which for them represented the authentic language of the Negro. He knew that the photographs provided by the camera club—coupled with decorations by Alice Morse—would make *Poems of Cabin and Field*, essentially a book of old poems, feel new. He retained some creative control over the selection of the photographs but accepted that the images relayed more vividly than his verses alone the stark realism of African American life. The marriage of poetic words and photographic images sought to stimulate ideas in readers, who also became spectators, sympathetic toward the varieties of black folklore. For readers encountering the poems for the first time, the juxtaposition of verses with photographs was instantly powerful. For those reading the poems once again, the visual images refreshed the meanings of the words and invited closer rereadings.[50]

Paul also understood that, for critics, whether he published brand-new or reprinted dialect poems mattered little. Reviewers rarely, if ever, delved below the vernacular surface of race to understand poetic intricacies. Readers of *Poems of Cabin and Field* were taken by the palpable racial realism of verse and

An' de banjo's voice is silent in de qua'ters,

D' ain't a hymn ner co'n-song ringin' in de air;

But de murmur of a branch's passin' waters

Is de only soun' dat breks de stillness dere.

19

FIG. 17.2. Sample decorated page and photograph from "The Deserted Plantation," in *Poems of Cabin and Field* (1899).

FIG. 17.2. (*continued*)

illustration, if the raves of book reviewers may be regarded as a measure. Published in the weeks between Thanksgiving and Christmas, *Poems of Cabin and Field* became, according to critics, "one of the handsomest holiday books of the season," a work of art in which "verse melts the reader's heart with its soft, pathetic music," with language "exclusively in the fascinating and childlike vernacular of the southern Afro-American."[51]

Poems of Cabin and Field comprised the best or most popular dialect poems that Paul had originally released in periodicals or previous books. The genre to which the book belonged (photographically illustrated poems) was popular during the second half of the nineteenth century, featuring *Idylls of the King*, published between 1859 and 1885 by Alfred, Lord Tennyson and illustrated by Julia Margaret Cameron, alongside *Love Lyrics*, published in 1899 by Paul's idol James Whitcomb Riley and illustrated by William B. Dyer. The images created by the Hampton Camera Club brought more attention to some of Paul's most popular dialect poems: he remarked to his agent, Paul Reynolds, that the illustrations were "magnificent, all being taken from life in the South." Giving the readers, and the inspired Hampton Camera Club, what they all wanted, Paul Laurence Dunbar was rewarded for his efforts. The camera club reaped dividends as well.[52]

CHAPTER 18

Still a Sick Man

I shall get out of doors, when I am in Colorado. That is the only thing for the lungs. I shall ride all the time.

—PAUL LAURENCE DUNBAR, *TOPEKA (KANSAS) PLAINDEALER*
(SEPTEMBER 22, 1899)[1]

I did not think he would live six months. If he pulls through the winter I shall be surprised.

—TIMOTHY THOMAS FORTUNE TO BOOKER T. WASHINGTON
(SEPTEMBER 23, 1899)[2]

In the nineteenth century, more people died from tuberculosis in the United States than from any other illness, and in Europe the disease was responsible for roughly one in four deaths. In the seven decades prior to Paul's birth, 20 percent of deaths in the country resulted from this disease, whose symptoms tended to be chronic, their diagnoses delayed, but whose afflictions did not discriminate by race or age, class or region. First it went by the name of consumption in 1839, when it was discovered by German physician J. L. Schönlein; the name referred to the way the rapidly spreading and fatal disease could consume the whole body. At the time, doctors regarded it as mostly hereditary and by no means contagious. Not until 1882, when Robert Koch happened upon the tubercle bacillus in sputum, did the disease's communicable danger become clear. And not until a few years later did sanatoriums begin to proliferate, with the hope that the disease could be cured.

Tuberculosis was not easy to diagnose. Its early symptoms of cough, general fatigue, and inflammation of the lungs resembled those of the common cold, and many people who were infected did not become ill for months or even years after initial exposure. By the end of the century, it was typical for physicians to prescribe alcohol as an oral remedy. Alcoholism was the collateral damage, incurring recidivism, especially among those who sought to quit the liquor bottle in the first place.

This turned out to be Paul's fate. It was not atypical for bouts of sickness to interfere with his literary tours, although he strove to keep the symptoms at bay. ("While I am not very well in health all goes well with me," he wrote to his mother during the summer months of 1897 in England. "I have caught a cold and it has settled in my throat to some extent.") However, in late spring 1899, Paul contracted an illness so severe that it bore the symptoms of tuberculosis and received public coverage (albeit as pneumonia or consumption).[3]

In May 1899 Paul was scheduled to give a reading in Albany, New York. He had been looking forward to it, because he had traveled there before and enjoyed the visit. Indeed, from November 28 through December 9 of the previous year, he had gone there as part of his recital tour. Coincidentally, Winifred Edgerton Merrill, an Albany clubwoman (who also happened to be, in 1886, the first American woman to earn a doctorate in mathematics), invited him to give a recital at a meeting of the "Fortnightly Club" of which she was a member. In reply, Alice said she hoped that he would regale her with his tales of his adventures while there: "Write to me, dear, and tell me about the good times in Albany." Paul stayed at the Hotel Kenmore and recited poems on December 8 at the Fortnightly Club. The audience included luminaries ranging from socialites and religious and political leaders to Melville Dewey, librarian and founder of the so-called Dewey System of decimal-based cataloging of library books. Before proceeding on to the rest of his regional tour, Paul telegrammed Alice through Western Union to affirm the success of his trip. "All right now off for Toledo Albany good," he said.[4]

Paul had nothing but fond memories of Albany when he prepared to return there five months later—until he fell sick and had to deal with the aftermath. Newspapers broke the news. "Paul Laurence Dunbar Ill," read one headline in the *New York Tribune*. Stating that "the Afro-American poet" was "seriously ill with pneumonia," the article indicated that he "came last Saturday [on April 29] to fill engagements here [in New York City] and in Albany," and was "taken ill almost upon his arrival and under the advice of a physician went to bed," developing such "acute pneumonia" that "his wife, who was in Washington, was sent for." As a consequence, Paul "has been compelled to cancel all

engagements." In the days following this report, smaller newspapers regurgi-
tated or embellished the story.[5]

From all around letters came in. Friends and acquaintances who had read
the newspaper stories reached out to extend best wishes to Paul. "I was so
grieved to see in the papers that you were very ill with pneumonia," wrote
Roger Clark, whom Paul had befriended during his tour of England (and who
continued to live there, in Somersetshire), "and can only hope that newspaper
accounts are, in accordance with all tradition, exaggerating!"[6]

A week into May, Paul was feeling better. "Paul is doing well + the doctor is
very proud," Alice wrote Paul's mother. The illness still exacted a professional
price: he could not fulfill his upcoming obligations for his reading tour, which
included another visit to Albany.[7]

Constituents of Albany were not pleased. Between May and November, a
volatile exchange erupted between Paul and the National Afro-American
Council, a civil rights organization. John Edward Bruce, a council officer in
Albany, was a primary player. Despite Bruce's hearing of reports that the poet
was "so near death's door that he could hear the creaking of the hinges," the
officer said that he would have been "satisfied with the payment of the amount
advanced for transportation." He sent word to Paul that he expected this
reimbursement to be "settled." Yet Paul took offense at the expression and
nature of this request. He accused Bruce of having appointed a lawyer to
"hound" Alice during his illness, and of having "designs" on accessing his
"bank account." Bruce denied that he would ever submit a mortally ill man
to such "persecution."[8]

Paul also entered into an equivalent dispute with Francis Zaccheus Santiago
Peregrino, an émigré from Ghana, by way of England, living in Albany and
working as the publisher of the *Fortnightly Spectator*. Peregrino sought to defend himself and his colleague Bruce from Paul's vitriol. "Sir, patience having
ceased to be a virtue, I have been compelled very reluctantly to take some
notice of your treatment of myself and Mr. Bruce," Peregrino wrote. "I can but
add that justice to us dictates that the thing shall not cease and this is our
preliminary step, unless some steps are taken to set us right."[9] Within days of
this letter, Paul communicated with the most powerful person in whose backyard this kerfuffle was occurring: Theodore Roosevelt.

Certainly, it was remarkable that the poet would even consider requesting
help from someone like Roosevelt, who lived in the rarefied air of American
culture and politics, and was presently serving as governor of New York.[10] On

FIG. 18.1. Theodore Roosevelt, circa 1906. (Library of Congress Prints and Photographs Division)

November 1 Roosevelt received Paul's letter of concern, claiming that he was being unfairly, and perhaps even illegally, treated. Roosevelt sympathized with Paul's plea. "I have just received yours of the 1st. inst," he wrote. "This is the first I have heard of this matter. From what you say I should judge that you had been simply blackmailed."[11] The governor offered himself as the poet's protector. "If any attack is made upon you, of course I shall defend you," he promised. He sought to wash away the poor taste the exchanges with Bruce and Peregrino had left in Paul's mouth. In fact, "if you come to Albany again," Roosevelt assured, "let me know and I will take the matter of the reception to you into my own hands—at any rate, to the extent of seeing that thoroughly reputable people take hold of you."[12]

The subsequent anger expressed by Peregrino unsettled Paul no longer. "Sir," Peregrino wrote Paul, "your insolent behavior is perfectly on a par with a man who would accept by seeking money for his fare from Washington to New York, then fail to keep his appointment." No matter. With the newfound shield of a governor who was on a trajectory toward an even higher office of American politics, the poet could let Peregrino's threats roll off his shoulders as he himself aspired to a higher stature among American writers.[13] In the meantime, Paul had to get healthy.

Matilda was gravely concerned. Paul enlisted an acquaintance named Sallie Brown to inform Matilda of his condition. Brown did not take for granted the bond between the mother and her son. "Paul has talked so much to me about his dear Mother that I really feel as if I knew you," Brown wrote Matilda. "You his Mother are so dear to him I have never seen so tender an affection between Mother and son as exists between Paul and you." At its worst, she said, the pneumonia was a "crisis," but now it had passed. "And the Dr. says [he] is doing nicely. At no time of his illness has he been in real danger, but as you know Paul is very frail." Paul had always been slight in build, prone to brief but worrisome colds and other ailments. This occasion was no different. His vulnerabilities made any attack on his health more severe than usual. Yet Brown's letter was meant to assure, not alarm, Matilda; "if at any time I had thought his Mother was needed at his bedside," she wrote, "I should have at once sent you word and I would do so now." The doctor recommended that Paul have complete rest for six months, well into the autumn. Brown would keep Matilda abreast of developments.[14]

As much as Matilda worried over Paul's illnesses, she also complained that he did not write her as promptly as he used to. "Will you ever get done complaining?" he asked. Given that he was "*still* a sick man," he told his mother that

Alice had to handle most of his private correspondence, so Matilda should be grateful that she received any letters from him at all, since his doctor had ordered him not to write or even dictate. He was improving slowly, but until he reached full health, he said, his letters would remain uneven in penmanship, punctuality, and vivacity. ("Alice is writing to-day in my place," he began one midsummer letter.)[15]

While sick, Paul enjoyed the intermittent company of his childhood friend, Will "Bud" Burns, who was just a few years removed from medical school in Western Reserve University (which today goes by the name of Case Western Reserve University) in Cleveland, Ohio, and who all the while had assumed the role of Paul's ad hoc, private physician. With Bud he could relax with a cigar and dream of drinking beer. At the very least, Bud helped convince Paul later that month to travel to the "beautiful" Catskill Mountains of New York, the backdrop to the community of Brodhead's Bridge in Ulster County, to recover for three months. (Paul loved to fish. He would come to own a special bamboo and brass fishing rod, symbolizing his investment in what would become one of his favorite hobbies. He also loved to compete in the sport of fishing. On one occasion in the Catskills, he caught the most: he snagged five; Bud, two; and Alice, who accompanied them, one.) Exploring the mountains of New York was therapeutic.[16]

Still, Paul's well-being fluctuated between sickness and health. Excessive coughing resulted in chest aches. In letters to his mother, though, he focused more on her welfare. "I hope that you are nice and getting along nicely now as every time I think you are not, it worries me a great deal," he wrote. "I have dreamed about you every night since I have been here." Between the two, the adoration had always been mutual.[17]

———

Whenever Paul had the strength to do so, he enjoyed touring New York City, especially the Tenderloin. He happened to visit a theater in which two companies with African American actors and actresses were rehearsing. A man in attendance recalled vividly the arrival of the Dayton poet, who was now "at the height of his fame":

> When he walked into the hall, those who knew him rushed to welcome him; among those who did not know him personally there were awed

whispers. But it did not appear that celebrity had puffed him up; he did not meet the homage that was being shown him with anything but friendly and hearty response. There was no hint of vainglory in his bearing. He sat quiet and unassuming while the rehearsal proceeded.

The man scrutinized Paul's likeness: "He was then twenty-seven years old, of medium height and slight of figure. His black, intelligent face was grave, almost sad, except when he smiled or laughed."[18]

That man who produced this acute description was James Weldon Johnson. He was born in Jacksonville, Florida, in 1871, the second of three children in a middle-class household. He graduated from Jacksonville's largest predominantly African American grammar school and enrolled in 1887 at Atlanta University. He was an excellent student. After college, he returned to Jacksonville to become principal of his former grammar school; he served from 1894 until 1901. During this time he founded and edited a newspaper, the *Daily American*; and, in 1898, he became the first African American lawyer admitted to the bar in Florida's Duval County. An aspiring poet, Johnson watched Paul enter the hall and remembered that they had met five years earlier, when the Dayton poet was yet unheralded. Now, "notwithstanding this lack of ostentation" as Paul settled into the theater, "there was on him the hallmark of distinction."[19]

For years Paul enjoyed exuding sartorial elegance. In pictures of his public appearances, his outfits were neat and fashionable, classic in cut and conservative in dark colors, whether striped or not. He frequently wore a gentlemanly three-piece suit of conventional length or, on occasion, a traditional frock coat extending past his thighs; a handsomely black, six-inch top hat (which he preserved in a hatbox at home); and black, size eleven dress boots.

For Johnson, a poet on the rise, their reunion was fortuitous. He marveled at Paul's public demeanor. "He had an innate courtliness of manner," Johnson noticed, "his speech was unaffectedly polished and brilliant." Moreover, Johnson admired the person and persona of this literary artist. He recounted that Paul "carried himself with that dignity of humility which never fails to produce a sense of the presence of greatness."

In the final weeks of summer, as Johnson prepared to return to Jacksonville, he and Paul spent extended time together. A bond formed between the two. Johnson stated, "I was drawn to him and he to me." Just before Johnson left town, he received from Paul a gift: an inscribed copy of *Lyrics of Lowly Life*. "It

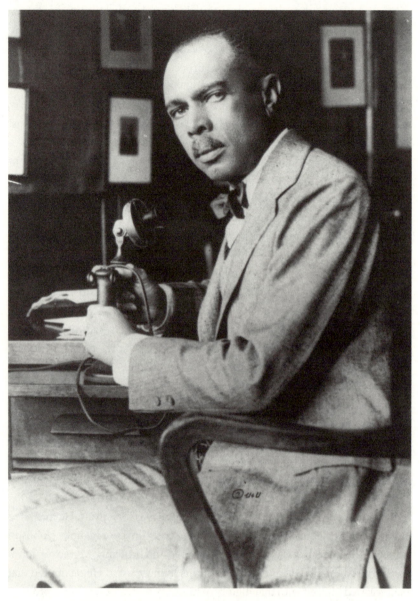

FIG. 18.2. James Weldon Johnson, circa 1900. (Library of Congress Prints and
Photographs Division, Visual Materials from the National Association for the
Advancement of Colored People [NAACP] Records)

FIG. 18.3. Paul with his mother, Matilda, circa 1896. (Watkins-Lehman Family Collection audiovisual series, Ohio History Connection)

is one of my most treasured books," Johnson would reflect in the autobiography he published more than three decades later.[20]

———

"Mr. Dunbar has gone to Denver for his health."[21]

So stated the *Topeka Plaindealer*, which caught up with Paul just before he traveled there. He was scheduled to arrive in Colorado by way of Omaha on September 12, 1899. "He is ill with consumption, one lung being very badly affected, and is going to try the mountain air in the hope that it will be beneficial." Optimism fueled his desire to travel to Colorado. The region, he believed, was the key to his survival, if only because the outdoors brought pleasure to all his sensibilities, not only relief from his respiratory ailments. "I shall get out of doors, when I am in Colorado," he anticipated. "That is the only thing for the lungs. I shall ride all the time." Paul's imagination of equestrian freedom

FIG. 18.4. Paul and Alice Dunbar en route to Colorado, 1899. (The Mark E. Mitchell Collection of African American History)

gave way to the reality that his sickness imprisoned him. "He spoke hoarsely and but little at a time, so ill has he been," the newspaper article noted.[22]

Medical science in Paul's time helped guide how people understood tuberculosis, for better or for worse. Contrary to empirical truth, the more privileged circles of society regarded themselves as less vulnerable to the illness than the lower and immigrant classes. Public health experts tried to raise awareness about the disease. As one leading expert, Sigard Adolphus Knopf, explained at the time, the key to avoiding infection was to "strive to be as much as possible in the open air, drink plenty of pure, clean water, keep early hours, live as regular a life as possible, avoid the saloon, and never take to alcoholic beverages."[23]

Some took this advice to mean that where they lived, not only how they lived, could help them avoid tuberculosis. One doctor, Henry I. Bowditch, concluded in 1862 that the "damp soil" of Massachusetts "bred consumption," while "health seekers" before and after that time looked for "their cures in the American southwestern plateau, in the mountains and deserts of Colorado, New Mexico, Arizona, and California." Edenic myths of the American West as an environment to heal and sustain the body, to invigorate the soul, had long persisted in the nineteenth century. The myths laid the fertile ground in which stories of tubercular recovery took root.[24]

Mark Twain described it best in his 1872 travel book, *Roughing It*: "I know a man who went there to die but he made a failure of it. He was a skeleton when he came and could barely stand." Yet Twain went on to say that, three months later, the man "was sleeping out of doors regularly, eating all he could hold, three times a day, and chasing game over mountains three thousand feet high for recreation. And he was a skeleton no longer, but weighed part of a ton. This is no fancy sketch but the truth." The key line, after all this, was the fact that the man's "disease was consumption." Twain captured the spirit and language of an age. Ease of railroad travel across the continent enabled throngs of people to explore the West on their own, to learn whether the climatological promise of better health could bode well for themselves, too.[25]

Paul was nothing less than a health seeker. By the time he visited Colorado, one out of every three migrants went there looking for better health. It was one of a handful of states—along with California, New Mexico, Texas, and Arizona—renowned among sick migrants for their enticingly "dry and arid plateau," "a salutary climate, where they could follow a health-giving routine," according to historian Sheila M. Rothman. Seventy miles south of Denver, Colorado Springs especially attracted migrants as the fountain of health. Reverend Edward Tenney, a self-described former victim of consumption, published in 1880 a best-selling book, *Colorado and Homes in the New West*, seeking to instill "hope to thousands of invalids" coming from those "eastern states." Two decades later, Paul was just that kind of person.[26]

Paul decamped to Harman, a town just outside of Denver. Fair weather welcomed him. Easterly winds were gentle. For days the temperature averaged around eighty degrees, and the mean relative humidity, 25 percent. Rain was rare. Paul purchased and learned to ride a horse named Old Sukey, to which he grew attached. He wrote a poem about their bond:

Want to trade me, do you, mistah? Oh, well, now, I reckon not.
W'y you could n't buy my Sukey fu' a thousan' on de spot.
    Dat ol' mare o' mine?
Yes, huh coat ah long an' shaggy, an' she ain't no shakes to see;
Dat's a ring-bone yes, you right, suh, an' she got a on'ry knee,
But dey ain't no use in talkin', she de only hoss fu' me,
    Dat ol' mare o' mine.[27]

In Harman, Paul moved into "a dainty little house, pleasant and sunny," in which his living room and home office merged into a rustic alcove of serenity and privacy, with a semicircular stone fireplace and, to its side, a firewood pile

FIG. 18.5. Paul Laurence Dunbar on horseback, circa 1900. (Paul Laurence Dunbar Collection, Ohio History Connection)

in a log holder.[28] Heritage plates and a picture of a horse, not unlike Old Sukey, adorned the walls, alongside shelves of books key to his reading and writing. A home away from home, the house comforted him; and for this residence he had purchased enough souvenirs later to adorn his permanent place in Washington, D.C. He also bought a buggy to transport himself, and potentially others, around the neighborhood. With Alice and Matilda, both of whom accompanied him to Colorado, he planned to stay until he regained full health and could resume his professional life. "I have not been very well, you know," he told a *Denver Post* reporter when he first arrived, "but I come with great faith in the invigorating properties of Colorado air."[29] Aside from the hospitable weather, Paul also enjoyed the introduction made by one medical doctor, his friend Henry A. Tobey, to another, Jeremiah Thomas Eskridge, who could monitor his health in the weeks and months ahead.[30]

Despite Paul's physical limitations, he continued to hone his craft. The fatigue of illness and travel was slowly giving way toward physical rejuvenation, as long as he remained "prudent" by imposing a regular schedule of rest amid daylong activities. His mind remained active. The scenery stimulated him. He found Colorado's "great rolling illimitable plains, and bleak mountains standing up like hoary sentinels guarding the land" thrilling, as he wrote to his agent in New York, Edward F. Arnold. In Denver he also detected an existential tension, a fatalism, that intrigued him; it was a city "where so many hopes are blighted, where so many dreams come true, where so many fortunes go up and so many lives go down," he wrote Arnold; and it was a city "over which nature broods with mystic calm, and through which humanity struggles with hot strenuous life."[31]

In Colorado, Paul arrived as a celebrity: reporters swarmed him, and their newspapers sought to commission essays by him on his newfound experiences in the region. A couple of years earlier, he encountered a media frenzy for his singular perspectives on being an African American in the unfamiliar territory of England. Now, the prospect of his residence in and travels through Colorado was likewise a compelling media storyline. "Only one thing—or really, several things in one—have bothered me—the reporters," he wrote Henry Tobey in early September 1899. "The Denver Post wishes to pay my expenses if I will travel slowly over the state and give occasionally my impressions of it."[32]

As curiosities filled Paul's mind, as his life in the region shaped his sensibilities, he relented in exercising his imagination and submitting himself to local interviews and imparting his discoveries. In reflective tones, on topics ranging from the city to his career to race, he spoke with more mainstream periodicals such as the Denver Post (which, incidentally, had known of his arrival and inquired if he were willing to be a correspondent, but he declined, offering instead a handful of poems and articles), the Plaindealer, the Denver Republican, the Rocky Mountain News, and lesser-known papers such as the Denver Statesman, an African American weekly.

Conversing with the periodicals gave Paul a direct hand in writing his own story, which verged on self-mythmaking. "Dunbar's presence in this city was known to the colored population almost as soon as he arrived," so announced the Plaindealer. "He is their literary idol and they have done homage to him."

Paul confided that he would write "some short stories" and "occasional verse" for the *Saturday Evening Post,* and he attested to his recent prolific streak. "I have written more verse, however, sick than ever before," he claimed, but he wished to be careful that what he was producing would be his best work. "I have a fear of writing now something that I should not be satisfied with in a short time. I feel that I am growing—maturing—rapidly, and I wish to hold back my verse for a little while until I am sure of myself."[33]

Overall, the response of readers to the new slate of literature that Paul was publishing was positive. The scintillating dawn he witnessed daily in Denver inspired him to capture this experience in a poem:

> Golden glow of the morning
>   Over the snowcapped heights,
> Not a cloud between; and the wondrous scene
>   Sets all my griefs to rights.
>
> For rage seems poor and petty
>   In sight of the sun-kissed peaks,
> And I have no care for the pain we bear
>   Nor the tears that dew our cheeks.
>
> Life seems broader and deeper
>   For the breadth and the height I see;
> Though I love the main, yet the rolling plain
>   And the snow-capped hills for me!
>
> So, here I sit all a-wonder
>   By the morning silence held,
> And, gazing high at the hills and sky,
>   Clasp hands with the Gods of eld![34]

Autobiography could also be found in essays he wrote for local newspapers. For the *Denver Evening Post,* he published "The Carnival Is on in Denver," in which he expressed genuine surprise at the distinctive gaiety he encountered in "the city of folly." Qualities intrinsic to its "greatness" included the ability of its citizens, despite the strain of labor and the bustle of "commercial enterprises," to swell into the "great good-humored crowds" of a carnival, accumulating along and across the streets without conflict or shame. To a degree he regarded the spirit "very Southern" in how "light-hearted" the people turned out to be. Contrary to the impression that they descended from or, in fact, were actually those "who were delving in mines, laying steel tracks across the prairies, and tearing with rude hands life and wealth from the reluctant soil," the carnival elicited a spirit akin to what one would find abroad in the joy of Provence and the love of Italy, or at home in the festivity of New Orleans. No longer would he look at "the man with the hoe" the same way again.[35]

There were a number of allusions to the South in "The Carnival Is on in Denver," such as in the notions that the city's carnivalesque fun "all seems very Southern," or that its population evinced "the glamour of a warm Southern spirit." Remarkably, this theme—of the distinctive origin, nature, problems, and trends of African American life—likewise permeated the short essays and fiction he wrote at this time. In the first few weeks of September, he released his widened perspective on race relations in "Home, the Solution of the Negro Problem" in the *Denver Republican*, and "Solution of Negro Problem Seen from Two Sides" in the Denver *Rocky Mountain News Sunday Magazine*. He also published "The Hapless Southern Negro," in which he encourages African Americans to migrate not to the North but to the West. In the realm of fiction, he released "A Council of State," about competing interest groups at an African American political convention, in an early October issue of the *Denver Post*. And he ruminated on two potential future novels: one called "Copperheads of the Civil War," and a second that was a bona fide western, his upcoming winter project, if he remained healthy enough.[36]

In short order, word started circulating among the elite that Paul was in town. Booker T. Washington, a previous partner on the lecture circuit, mentioned the news in passing in a letter to Timothy Thomas Fortune. In the letter, the Tuskegee leader alleged the jealousy held by American Missionary Association secretaries, whose sentiment fueled an article appearing in a mid-September issue of the *Washington Post* designed "to do anything to break my influence," he thought. Washington decided to convene a meeting in the next month and a half with the secretaries to address their concerns. To close the otherwise petulant epistle, Washington ventured, "I hear that Dunbar is in a bad fix and has gone to Colorado."[37]

Fortune replied, first of all, with empathy for Washington's protest over the American Missionary Association. Both men shared the supportive view of industrial education as the driver of the economic progress of the Negro, so Fortune was inclined to pass along the *Post* article and monitor the aftermath. "I will watch the influence of the *Post* article," he assured Washington, "but the damage of it will be done with those who sustain our education work and are never heard of in the public prints."[38]

Amid their mutual encouragement during the never-ending controversy over the Tuskegee machine, Fortune corroborated Washington's report on Dunbar's poor health and therapeutic self-exile: "I too understand that Dunbar is in a bad way and has gone to Colorado Springs." Like Washington, Fortune was acquainted with Paul, but for this information he had witnessed and anticipated the future severity of the poet's poor health. "When I last saw him he declared that he would not go near Colorado, so I judge him from his going that he is in worse shape than when I saw him last." Then Fortune dropped the bombshell that few would prognosticate for such a young man: "I did not think he would live six months. If he pulls through the winter I shall be surprised." He did not anticipate that the Dayton poet would even reach his twenty-eighth birthday.[39]

Washington was so worried about this news that, when he scheduled a trip to Denver early the following year (he came and left in late January), mainly to deliver a lecture in Colorado Springs, he sent Paul a letter about his visit. Paul was thrilled to receive the letter and wrote back to Washington, who was staying at the Brown Palace Hotel, that he would be willing to greet him on his arrival in the city and, if a couple of hours were available, drive him to the house where he was staying and catch up there. The separation of time, space, and political opinion—not so much age, although Washington was a little over a decade and a half older than Paul—undermined too much the possibility that the men could grow close. Still, any communication from Washington continued to have a remarkable effect on Paul, who tended to drop whatever he was doing, or planned to do, to accommodate interaction or partnership with the Tuskegee leader.[40]

Two major occasions marked Paul's reverence for Washington. The first occurred in late September, after Washington had delivered a lecture, "Solving the Negro Problem," at the Central Presbyterian Church. Both men, along with Charles S. Thomas, governor of Colorado, were featured in a banquet later that evening at the Arapahoe Café. For the occasion, Paul had written a speech in which he recounted his first impressions while visiting Tuskegee only eleven months earlier. At the speech's climax, he admitted that this experience had dispelled the skepticism he first held in assessing "the worth of Mr. Washington's work":

For a long time, we have heard of this man of Tuskegee, and for a long time we have been told great things of the work he has done away down there in the Black Belt of the South, where our own people, our brothers and sisters and their children have so little opportunity for development along the best lines. But hear what we may, from whatever source we may, we can know nothing of the great work that is being done there, until we have been and seen for ourselves. Then our cry will be that of the Queen of Sheba in coming to the court of Solomon, "The half has never been told!"

I can never forget my first visit to Tuskegee. I went there a skeptic; I came away a convert. I went there questioning; I came away wondering. Before me lay no longer a theory, but facts in the case; facts in broad acres, wide fields, bricks and stone, and a thousand bright advancing young men and women, who said indeed, what that boy years ago had said in words, "We are rising."[41]

The second instance of Paul's admiration for Washington occurred a couple of days after this speech. Paul and a host of other accomplished men gathered in the home of Joseph D. D. Rivers, graduate of Hampton Institute, proprietor of the weekly *Colorado Statesman*, and executive board member of the Denver Colored Civic Association. At the reception was an "assemblage" that "was probably as notable a collection of colored people as ever sat down at one time, and spoke well of the achievements of the race in the last thirty years," according to a late January 1900 issue of the *Denver Post*. Washington was "nothing less than a man of preeminence, whose color was a secondary consideration," "in the class of Frederick Douglass, and above popular prejudice." Just as he had been gracing the city with his presence, Washington was gracing the house with it as well.

Washington was seated at the head of the dinner table, with Paul to his left. The other men in attendance included the physician and politician Paul Edward Spratlin, attorney Joseph H. Stuart, lawyer and city auditor's clerk Edwin H. Hackley, and the socialites Samuel H. Hobson and Wharton D. Phillips. The talk was "exceedingly interesting," according to the *Denver Post*, "sparkling with bright sayings and apropos quotations from the best English literature, showing a degree of reading and observation not often met with." The overarching theme of the banquet—"without a dissenting voice"—was the assumption that Washington had broadcast in his legendary, if not also notorious, speech five years earlier at the Cotton States and International Exposition in Atlanta: "Southern people were the most friendly to colored people, understood their nature and affections better and were more willing to assist them than any class of people."[42]

Months after Paul arrived in Denver, he was now well enough to do speaking engagements. In late January, the local papers reported his upcoming readings of his works at the local Trinity Methodist Episcopal Church. (He would read his poetry again there in mid-March, and he would also read that month at Temple Theater in Colorado Springs.) By this time, he was a man of myth. Part of it began in late September 1899, when the *Plaindealer* printed a quotation that Paul "wanted to go to Harvard" and study under Adams Sherman Hill, Boylston Professor of Rhetoric and Oratory, and that he "was not unknown there, for many of his Dayton friends were in the old college and told of his work so often that he was known there by reputation before W. D. Howells introduced him to New York and his first volume of verse was published."[43]

In March of the following year, the *Colorado Springs Gazette* picked up the Harvard thread. In a promotional sketch on his upcoming reading at Temple Theater, we learned that "Mr. Dunbar is a graduate of Harvard College and one of the most refined and cultured of his race." Evidently false was the first part of that statement, although many fans and his peers could corroborate the second part. An earlier night, "the celebrated poet" was "accorded an enthusiastic ovation last evening in the YMCA building," where the audience was "completely captivated" and "added hundreds of ardent admirers in his circle of friends." Back from illness, once again he was a poet to behold.[44]

Paul's speaking engagements at churches in Denver and Colorado Springs signified his early resumption of professional travel. For a span of six weeks during the spring he crisscrossed the country, through the Midwest to as far away as the East Coast, and back to Colorado, where Alice and Matilda had been staying. By the end of March, they had moved southward, from Denver to Colorado Springs, where they would reside for close to two months.

In retrospect, Paul was grateful for having spent as long as he had among the Rocky Mountains. He projected the care he received onto Denver: the city "took me into her arms," he noted at the time in a magazine titled *Health.*

> Through a long golden autumn, the most beautiful I have ever seen, she nursed me like a gentle mother, and I lay on her breast drinking her pure air like a child its mother's milk. New life glowed within me. New strength throbbed in my limbs. The future that had been so dark brightened. I awoke in the mornings to look out upon the mountains with joy in life again.[45]

It was time to go. Reflecting back, Paul came to realize, "I was so far from my publishers and my situation was a very lonely and isolated one," relative to the "very congenial and delightful circle of friends" he enjoyed in Washington, D.C.[46] In mid-May, everyone packed up and prepared to travel back home near Le Droit Park.

Ultimately, Paul enjoyed the companionship of Matilda and Alice as he rested in Colorado, but the time there was not without familial discord. Louder and louder grew the rumor that he drank excessively; "there were times when he was not sober for days," Alice would later recall. Consequently, their "whole married life was far from happy." He was no longer the man who had swept Alice off her feet and convinced her to marry him, who had a lyrical way with words in poems that expressed love in language familiar and attractive to her, who had attended to her basic needs as any faithful husband would do for his wife (insofar as he was capable of being faithful).

As a "heavy drinker," Alice remembered, Paul turned out to become "a different man altogether, brutal, in fact." The abuse that he inflicted on her was by this time "an open secret, common gossip" among their friends in the circles of Washington, D.C. Even worse, as they traveled together, mere strangers came to witness his hostility. Alas, this reality characterized their sojourn: "people in Denver, Colorado, where we went after he had contracted tuberculosis, would bear me out in this statement"—namely, that their marriage was "part of the time a cat and dog existence."[47]

Peculiarly, the climate that had enabled Paul to recover—the overall cooler weather and thinner air of Colorado's altitude—caused a proportionate decline in his mother's health. Even as the advice of medical authorities suggested that he rest in Colorado longer, he made curing Matilda's illness his priority. Later, she would regard his decision to return east as yet another example of his "sacrifice" of his own life for hers. Never would she forget this act of generosity, his utter devotion to her, even at the expense of others, including Alice.[48]

———

Paul shopped his second novel to more than one publisher. In one instance, he encountered skepticism about the viability of the manuscript in its initially slim state. "As you know, under ordinary circumstances we can only report that 29,000 words is hardly enough to make a book of," H. W. Laurie, an acquisition editor at Doubleday & McClure, confirmed. Still, there was potential in bringing out the book in a series of "short novels" that would be "very nicely gotten up, bound in cloth, to be sold at 50 cents," provided that Paul also granted the publisher the right of first refusal on his "next long novel." This proposition turned out to be unacceptable to Paul. Though the manuscript retained its word count over time, ultimately he decided not to part ways with Dodd,

Mead, the publisher with which he had built a professional relationship and would continue to do so in future years.[49]

First released by Dodd, Mead in 1900, *The Love of Landry* tried to be a romance; it takes place in the familiar setting of Colorado. As with his first novel, *The Uncalled,* Paul revealed autobiographical clues in the development of main characters, although with the predictable tweaking of facts: Mildred, the invalid recuperating in the mountains; and Landry, a free spirit. The objections of Mildred's relatives to Landry recalled those of Alice's to Paul a few years earlier. Against the backdrop of family drama, the novel illuminates the social tensions resulting from class differences and the moral corruptibility of the city. Unlike the plantation books of poetry and short stories, *The Love of Landry*, like *The Uncalled*, avoids the casting of African Americans as the protagonists, and it captures once again Paul's willingness to experiment in ways that white readers and reviewers were not expecting.

Criticism of *The Love of Landry* reiterated the standard of racial authenticity by which Paul's work continued to be judged. Worse, it was a cage from which escape remained impossible. Puzzlement described the initial reaction of some critics, who believed he had betrayed his literary and racial calling to depict African American life. Paul would have done "much better to stick to his own line," wrote one reviewer. Since he had not, the novel was not "a specimen of his best work," and experimenting with a "province which is not his own" potentially set his work up for even greater failure than the boilerplate "darkey" tales and verses by which he had come to be known. However, Paul's testing of new boundaries—writing what one critic called "a white man's novel" (i.e., with whites, not blacks, as the main characters)—amused reviewers. The novel turned out to be pretty "clever": it was "a fairly well written tale of the average type of ephemeral work," "pretty," "prettily told," "a very engaging and cleverly written story," an "exceedingly clever little story," as the critics variously characterized it. Inside the accolades of this sort, though, were impressions that the novel was superficial, lacking the realism that had distinguished his fiction and poetry on the Negro. Paul could be applauded for depicting whites with "a spirit of fair minded restraint and impartiality," so wrote the *New York Tribune*. Yet the very fact that he "has not chosen the characters for his story from among his own people," according to the *Houston Post*, "may in part account for their lack of originality." Betwixt and between the respective criteria for literary art created by blacks and whites, Paul could not win. Either way, he was damned.[50]

While recovering from tuberculosis in Colorado, Paul had not only been working on *The Love of Landry*, but he had also been revising twenty short stories for publication in *The Strength of Gideon and Other Stories*. Including a handful of stories he had released earlier in periodicals, this new collection came out with Dodd, Mead once again. As in the case of his previous book of short stories, *Folks from Dixie*, *The Strength of Gideon* is set in the antebellum era, but this time the settings range from the rural South to the urban North. Even as Paul continued to adopt discourse and images that arguably tapped into the stereotypes of African American plantation life, he used humor and irony to insinuate his skepticism of societal progress toward racial justice for African Americans.

The reviews of *The Strength of Gideon and Other Stories* spanned from the amused to the dismayed. By most accounts, Paul impressed with his ability to pen stories about the "humor and pathos," as it was put by the *Washington Post*, of African American life; or in depicting "the fidelity and unrestrained humor of which this exponent of the characteristics of his race is capable," as noted by the *New York Journal*. Other periodicals, such as the *Boston Transcript*, disregarded some stories as "quite crude and trivial." Even the same newspaper, such as the *New York Times*, positively echoed the praise of Paul's "humor and pathos" in March 1900, only to circle back in another review two months later, in May, and admit that some of these same stories were "weak and pointless." All in all, Paul's latest book only reaffirmed the critical impression that he could achieve a realistic portrayal of "the character, feeling, and sentiment of the southern darkey." While that quality elevated the book to mainstream entertainment, it had little chance of breaking the distinctive ceiling of *belles lettres*. Literary excellence may not have always been Paul's ultimate goal, like commercial viability, but any criticism of his books' aesthetic failings still stung his pride.[51]

CHAPTER 19

A Sac of Bitter Sarcasm

He was the Dunbar of the courtly manners, polished speech, and modest behavior that I had marked; but, as lovable as he was with people he liked, I learned that under this polite tongue there was a sac of bitter sarcasm that he spat out on people he did not like, and often used in his own defense.

—JAMES WELDON JOHNSON, *ALONG THIS WAY* (1933)[1]

The address of Charles Dudley Warner on higher education disappointed Paul more than any other speech he had ever encountered. By 1900, Warner was a renowned editor of magazines such as the *Hartford Press* and *Harper's*; a prominent author of books on traveling throughout the United States and Europe; a fellow satirist in his co-authorship, with Mark Twain, of *The Gilded Age: A Tale of Today*, a revealing 1873 novel about the corruption of postwar American politics and corporate capitalism; as well as the president of such distinguished organizations as the National Institute of Arts and Letters and, most recently, the American Social Science Association. For the general meeting of the latter association in Washington, D.C., during the second week of May, Warner headlined a series of speakers on the issue of social progress. As president, Warner arranged to deliver "The Education of the Negro," but since he could not attend, a colleague, Reverend Dr. Joseph Anderson of Yale University, read the address on his behalf. So consequential was the address that on May 8, 1900, the *New York Times* published an article about its conclusion to the meeting's first day. Not only did the article borrow the title of Warner's speech as its own; it also included the controversial subtitle, "In It He Declares That Present Plan for Higher Culture of the Race Is Wrong," followed by long excerpts in which the association's president made this case.[2]

Premised on the myth that innate physiological and psychological traits differentiated people of African descent from those of Anglo-Saxon ancestry, Warren's address argued that an emphasis on the higher education of a putatively inferior race like the Negro was politically wrongheaded and financially wasteful. To grant African Americans greater access to electoral franchise, such as the ballot box, they had to improve their literacy. But the societal allocation of resources to the higher education of African Americans, rather than a more rudimentary level of primary education, for example, was an impractical fulfillment of their personal wish to assert their equality with whites. This allocation also rested on an unrealistic belief that African Americans could evolve at a rate faster than what, in Warner's view, the world history of human civilizations otherwise proved. Aside from the exceptional accomplishments of the likes of Booker T. Washington, whom Warner recognized by name as "the ablest and most clear-sighted leader the negro race has ever had," overall he believed the race had devolved in sophistication and morality—and he cited New Orleans as the perfect example. "This is not saying that the higher education is responsible for the present condition of the negro," he clarified. "I only say that we have been disappointed in our extravagant expectations of what this education could do for a race undeveloped, and so wanting in certain elements of character, and that the millions of money devoted to it might have been much better applied."[3]

One month after "The Education of the Negro" was delivered before the American Social Science Association, Paul published a rebuttal in the June 10, 1900, issue of the *Philadelphia Times*. With the title "Is Higher Education for the Negro Hopeless?" he faced squarely the implications that listeners of the address—and, as it circulated more widely in the press, its readers—likely drew from it. In the opening sentences he wasted no time in calling Warner out by name and questioning his credibility: "It is a matter of some surprise to me that the articles by Charles Dudley Warner on the education of the Negro should have attracted so much attention, for it is so evidently the work of one who speaks without authority. It might appropriately be called an essay, founded upon observation of the South from a car window." Paul's rejoinder might be viewed as a companion piece to "Our New Madness," in which he bemoaned the public overemphasis on the manual or industrial education of the Negro, a line of rhetoric that Warner perpetuated in his own admiration of Washington and his conclusion that the "only visible solution is for the negro to become an integral and an intelligent part of the industrial community." Paul had never seen higher education deter African Americans from labor; he also took to task the misleading depiction of New Orleans, a place and a community he had known personally through Alice, and where, unlike Warner, he had "the good fortune to know also some of the Negro officials" and had "found them men of high intelligence, clean morality, and undisputed ability."[4]

Unmistakable was the potential impact of "The Education of the Negro." Before a wide audience, the president of the American Social Science Association had pronounced the cultural and intellectual inferiority of African Americans, based on information ranging from ignorant personal anecdotes to suspect data on "Negro criminality" that looked at their great numbers in prisons rather than at the excessive law enforcement apprehending and prosecuting them at disproportionately high rates. "Statistics may prove anything, but in this case especially they are inadequate," Paul countered. "Mr. Warner's ill-advised article has done the Negro, who has looked to him as a friend, unutterable harm, more harm really than he knows." Echoes existed between this observation and Paul's own reflection on the "irrevocable harm" Howells had inflicted on his own career. In both cases, the media amplified pronouncements made by an influential—and, in subtle ways, benevolent—white man, whose perpetuation of racial stereotypes and discrimination ultimately denigrated the subject he was initially seeking to uplift for the world to see.[5]

In the years since Paul had published "Our New Madness" castigating industrial learning for the Negro, he had over and again demonstrated in person to Washington that he had come around to appreciating this educational and economic philosophy of racial uplift, especially in light of the more extreme, if racist, views of Warner. By the fall of 1900, Paul had come to convey his support in print, not only explicitly in content but in form as well.

In early August, Paul sent to Robert Underwood Johnson, editor of the *Century*, a sonnet he dedicated to Washington. For years, at least since 1894, Paul had been corresponding with Johnson, with the hope that he could place his work there, one of his favorite magazines. In the past, the exchanges had been frosty. Johnson had written "you are a stranger to us" in one of his first letters to Paul, and "no[t] one of them takes us by the throat," in reference to his submitted poems. Paul expressed gratitude, closing his own letters with such phrases as "many thanks for your continued kindness."[6] Despite the sense that Paul may have developed that he had built some capital with Johnson, this latest exchange, or lack thereof, concerned him. He inquired with Johnson directly. "I sent you the sonnet to Booker T. Washington of which you spoke to me, and received it back with the usual printed slip." Worried that he had suffered the rejection that countless lesser-known, aspiring poets received after submitting their work to the *Century*, Paul sought a workaround. "I was in doubt as to whether or not you had seen it. Will you let me know if you saw it? If not, I will be glad to send it to you personally."[7]

Evidently, the direct appeal did not matter. The poem appeared instead in the October issue of *New England Magazine*, with the unmistakable title "Booker T. Washington," an explicit reverence for this "peer of princes," this "master spirit," renowned for his relentless, "rugged force":

> The word is writ that he who runs may read.
> What is the passing breath of earthly fame?
> But to snatch glory from the hands of blame,—
> That is to be, to live, to strive indeed.
> A poor Virginia cabin gave the seed,
> And from its dark and lowly door there came
> A peer of princes in the world's acclaim,
> A master spirit for the nation's need.
> Strong, silent, purposeful beyond his kind,
> The mark of rugged force on brow and lip,
> Straight on he goes, nor turns to look behind
> Where hot the hounds come baying at his hip;
> With one idea foremost in his mind,
> Like the keen prow of some on-forging ship.[8]

Paul sent a copy to Washington himself, who was nothing less than effusively grateful in response, perhaps his most effusive to date. "I thank you very sincerely for sending me a copy of the *New England Magazine* and more heartily for the poem which you were kind enough to dedicate to me," he wrote. With a November reprint of the poem in the periodical *Outlook*, which Washington also noted with thanks, Paul's latest effort in verse was effectively eclipsing the essay that had initially polarized him from Washington in the public eye.[9] As his thoughts evolved more and more from the original publication of "Our New Madness," he had grown more sympathetic to the rationale behind promoting industrial education. "Give the negro, I should say, thorough industrial training," he told an interviewer, "and, if any among them are able to get above this, let them do it."[10]

———

On Sunday, August 19, 1900, Paul filed a report with a local police department in New York City. He said that he had been drugged and robbed. Now, he was angry. This was a luckless end to a week that, for him and others in the city, had proven to be quite distressing. On Friday night, he had been trying to placate friends and acquaintances who had been embroiled in the worst disturbance Harlem had faced in recent memory. The "riots," as the media called them over the second half of August, had exploded only a couple of days earlier, on Wednesday and Thursday, drawing the broader attention of the city and the country to a series of racial tensions that had long been simmering.

By 1900, the African American population in New York City had been growing rapidly in size and vibrancy, but also in complexity. Close to twenty-five thousand African Americans were living in the city in 1890, and their numbers would nearly quadruple in size over the next two decades. Beginning, and especially, in the 1880s, their influx into the region from the South, the very early phase of what would be called the Great Migration toward the North and the West, compounded the cultural differences and discrimination between southerners and northerners but also the racial prejudice and segregation that existed between blacks and whites. Condescension tinged the language of African Americans in the North, some of whom regarded the southerners as "the low element of our race," as "the class who own a lot of dirty rags and dogs and crowds of children," according to letters to the editor that appeared in the New York Times in summer 1900. Alienation was the policy of restaurants, theaters, hotels, and saloons in which white owners and workers increasingly refused to accommodate the scores of African Americans, whether native to the area or from elsewhere, settling down in their midst.[11]

The crowding of African Americans not only in the Tenderloin but also in the neighborhood of Harlem, in upper Manhattan, fueled the bohemian culture for which these places had come to be known. But these also demarcated the loci of potential antagonisms between African Americans and the local white and Irish immigrant populations. Each group tried to secure the unskilled jobs in the city, leading to intense rivalries that existed beneath the surface of their social or economic interactions. Not only did skirmishes between African American and Irish residents regularly make the news in the 1890s; as urban historian Gilbert Osofsky explains, the Tenderloin circa 1900 was constantly under threat to "explode into serious violence with little provocation."[12]

By the middle of August, a heat wave was suffocating the city: the temperature regularly exceeded an excruciating ninety degrees. The unbearable atmosphere was almost a perfect symbol of the oppressive circumstances under which a street altercation could escalate to an explosive level of interracial unrest. Arthur Harris, an African American man in his early twenties, decided the evening of Sunday, August 12, to step out of his residence at 241 West

41st Street to purchase cigars and then while away some time at a nearby saloon called McBride's. For about a year he had been living with May Enoch, also African American, whom he had alternately called his "woman" and "wife." As Sunday night turned into the wee hours of Monday morning, she thought her man had been out of the house long enough, and it was time for him to come back.

At two in the morning, Enoch proceeded to McBride's and ended up waiting on the corner of 41st Street and Eighth Avenue. While there she was approached by a plainclothes white police officer, Robert Thorpe, who perceived her to be "soliciting," or offering herself up for prostitution. Without granting her much of an opportunity to clear up the misunderstanding, he tried to apprehend her for misconduct. Harris happened to encounter the two grappling each other, at which time he confronted the officer. A verbal dispute between the two men turned immediately into a fight in which the officer hit Harris multiple times on his head with a club and pummeled him with his fists. Harris pulled out a penknife, its blade a couple of inches in length, and sliced the officer's torso twice. As the officer reeled from his wounds, the couple fled, the woman back to her residence, the man farther away, eventually to Washington, D.C. A crowd swelled around the bleeding officer, who was quickly taken to nearby Roosevelt Hospital on 58th Street and Ninth Avenue. Within seven hours of his arrival, Thorpe died of the "post-operative shock, septic pneumonia, septic peritonitis, and hemorrhage" resulting from the wounds he suffered in the chest and stomach. In the meantime, despite the efforts of Harris to cover up his involvement in the incident, Enoch was soon located. Under arrest and pressure, she identified her beau as the assailant. Thereafter Harris was arrested and brought back to New York twelve days after the incident.[13]

For the week and a half between the perceived killing of a white police officer by a black man and the arrest of the assailant in Washington, D.C., whites in New York City thirsted for justice. A twenty-six-year-old man engaged to be married, Thorpe was depicted in city newspapers as a victim who had been trying to fulfill his police duty in cleaning the streets of criminal activity. The officer fell at the hands of "negro men and women, who rescued the woman prisoner whom Thorpe was taking to the police station," announced the New York Times the day of his death. Thorpe's funeral, which would be "the largest ever given to a policeman," up to the point, was scheduled for Thursday, August 16.[14]

Early clues that the interracial calm would be destroyed arrived the morning of Wednesday, August 15. W. H. Cooper, an African American man on his way from his West 41st Street residence to the Eighth Avenue post office, came across a group of white men and boys who, he overheard, were scheming to seek vengeance for Thorpe's death. "We are going to get back at the niggers tonight," said one. "Is that true? Is there going to be a riot tonight?" asked another. "Yes," was the reply. That evening, as a throng of whites, including sixty officers from the 37th Precinct, gathered outside Thorpe's residence on West 49th Street to express their condolences ahead of the funeral, fury was poised to erupt.[15]

And it did. That very night, Spencer Walters, a black man, and Thomas Healy, a white man, got into a fight close to the memorial event. A white mob formed to attack Walters, and the "riot" that had been predicted in the morning finally came to pass. As the *New York Daily Tribune* reported the next day: "If there had been a carefully arranged plot and this had been the agreed signal, the outbreak could not have been more spontaneous." As part of the so-called Nigger Chase, white mobs abducted African Americans from the Eighth Avenue electric cars. White police officers refused to intervene in public episodes of white-on-black crime. Whites scoured saloons and hotels for blacks to beat down. Certain African Americans fled the vicinity, while others sought to shelter in place. Even though a thunderstorm in the early morning of August 16 quelled some activity, daily clashes continued for well over a month after the riot's outbreak.[16]

By the time Friday came, the world of revelry to which Paul had been accustomed in New York City was being turned upside down. He tried to do something about it. For the early part of Friday night, he worked "to pacify the negroes who had been agitated about the West side riots." Eventually he grew "very tired" doing so, according to a news report on his activities. Around midnight he decided to return to his lodging on Ninth Avenue. He encountered an African American gentleman named William Ricks, who advised him to come along for a drink in Joe Walcott's saloon at 111 West 31st Street and not to travel home by way of West 37th Street, which he believed to be too dangerous. Not one to turn down an invitation to a saloon at this point in his life, Paul agreed.[17]

Then Paul's night took a turn for the worse. The hours after his meeting with Ricks vanished from his mind; he only remembered waking up fifteen hours later, during Saturday afternoon. An African American family discovered him sleeping on the top floor of a 210 West 30th Street building. Disoriented, Paul also realized that prized assets on his person were missing: his $450 diamond ring, his gold watch, and forty dollars in cash. He concluded that the gentleman who last engaged him likely was also his robber, and that he was given a "knocker-out" to put him to sleep.[18]

Clerks listened to Paul when he filed his report with the local police department, but more so because of his celebrity, not so much because they were
sympathetic to his quest for justice. Only days after the outbreak of the riots,
African Americans were inundating police departments across the city with
claims that they had suffered physical violence at the hands of whites, whom
the police themselves were negligent in arresting. Allegations arose of collusion
between white mobs and police against blacks: that crowds of whites had been
attacking any black person in sight without repercussion; that police had consistently been in the presence of such misconduct and failed to intervene; and
even that, at police stations, certain officers piled on with their own assaults
against black victims. The minimal compilation of injuries suffered by blacks
across the police precincts corroborated local newspaper headlines alleging
racist police brutality.[19]

Paul earned his own sensational headline alongside media accounts of the
riot. In the few weeks after he filed the report, newspapers used vivid language
to characterize his plight: he was a "Negro poet" "trying to pacify men of his
race" but then was "drugged," "doped," or, worse, "drugged and robbed," fell
"into evil hands," or suffered "a poet's hard luck," and "los[t] his valuables," including "jewelry and money," to "a New Yorker." Although the details in the
news story grew more specific over time, the essence, and its assumptions, remained the same—that an internationally revered African American poet from
outside the region arrived as a Good Samaritan to calm down agitated African
American New Yorkers, only to be preyed upon by a thief belonging to this
group. The stories cast Paul in a positive light. Onto those of his race, the racial
stereotype of incivility and criminality again cast its shadow. As the *Kalamazoo
Gazette* observed from afar, "That story about Paul Lawrence Dunbar, the negro
poet, having been drugged and robbed in New York is undoubtedly colored."
Also, when the time came for Paul to press charges, the historical record is
ambiguous as to whether he actually wanted to do so. Resulting in no demonstrable evidence aside from Paul's story itself, the allegation may have been a
ruse to cover up his recurring weakness for the saloon and to protect his name.[20]

The New York City race riots and their aftermath, their circumstances and
conclusions, left a deep impression on Paul as he entered autumn. The conflict
rendered clear in his mind's eye the city's challenges for African American
migrants from the South; the tensions governing contact between blacks and
whites; the strain of southerners as they tried to comply with the norms of
northern culture; the class divisions afflicting the cohesion of society; and,
more subjectively, the moral failings of urban commercialism and communities.

In the months ahead, these themes would form the scaffolding for his literary imagination.

―――――

Half a year later, in spring 1901, Paul took up an invitation from James Weldon Johnson to visit Jacksonville, Florida, to deliver a public reading. Paul affectionately called him "Jim," and his brother Rosamond, "Rosy." Both Johnson brothers asked Paul to stay with them as long as he wished. The visit lasted six weeks, a defining moment in how Paul elucidated his personal views on poetry and in how his legacy as a poet of dialect would subsequently be written.

By March 21, Paul had arrived in Jacksonville. The southward trip was pleasant, "altho it was broken by large and copious coughing," he said to Alice in a letter. (Nightly he would request a bedtime snack of a salted raw onion, a bottle of beer, and a bowl of ochre soup, the quackery he employed in his ongoing battle with tuberculosis.) He spent much time chatting in passing with Victoria Earle Matthews, who also happened to be in the area. Paul avoided other acquaintances, however, such as the "irritating, crass and disgusting" J. Douglass Wetmore, a Jacksonville lawyer whom he and Alice knew from Washington, D.C. In Florida, Wetmore was behaving too "outrageously" for Paul's taste. No shortage of distractions existed to agitate Paul, who believed his goal was mainly to recite his poems.[21]

Paul was in Jacksonville at Johnson's behest—for better or for worse. As time went on, it became clear that the sense of camaraderie was one-sided, asymmetrical. Johnson recalled the friendship he and Paul had developed ever since their substantial time together in New York City in fall 1899. The invitation of Paul to Jacksonville "was more than professional," as Johnson would later put it. Paul was somewhat resigned to his condition, sounding as if he were suffering from claustrophobic misery and undergoing a struggle both metaphorical and medical. "It still rains and I am closed up in the house with Jim and his father," he wrote Alice. "It is thundering so that the very windows rattle but the air is soft and warm."[22]

Aside from Jim, Paul was flanked by Rosy, a trained composer and pianist, as well as by the father, James Johnson; the mother, née Helen Louise Dillet; and the maternal grandmother, Mary Barton. In the town of LaVilla, a Jacksonville neighborhood, on a large lot located at the corner of Lee and Houston Streets, James Johnson bought a five-room frame house and lived there with his wife. There, in 1871, Jim was born. By the end of the century, a more modern house was built, replacing the old one. In this new house, in 1899, Jim and Rosy collaborated to write the hymn that would become legendary for African American churches and communities, "Lift Every Voice and Sing." And it was here that Paul was invited to stay.[23]

Alas, the creative promise of the LaVilla house was lost on Paul, who complained almost his whole time there. Rosy interfered with Paul's creative process. "If I want to write Rosamond plays his opera to me and I should be impolite not to listen." To Paul, Rosy was "a consummate old bore" who "maintains his right to hold the floor at all times," "talks incessantly and after the manner of his kind is forever looking around for applause like a spoiled child that has been taught to show off its sweetness or a spot dog that must exploit its tricks." The mother fretted over Paul's health, especially whenever he decided to go outside. And there was the grandmother, who, whenever he ascended the stairs, would call him into her "sick room" and talk with him about his "soul."[24]

So cramped did Paul feel at the Johnsons that, one day, even though the rain poured—"It is raining here and the sand is drinking in the water," he said—he was "going out pretty soon in spite of the rain." The weather perfectly captured his wry humor about the state itself. "They have made a mistake in naming Florida. Instead of the Land of Flowers it should be the 'Land of Showers,'" he laughed. "It is raining again and is gloomy & muggy and cheerless, and I—oh I am very blue." The incessant downpour mirrored the effect of being encircled. "You know my horror of being endlessly entertained and talked to,—well that is just what I find at the Johnsons'."[25] Paul's aggravation at either the political world or his personal circumstances was not going to abate any time soon.

Whereas Paul disregarded his encounters with the Johnsons as fruitless annoyances worthy of comedy, Jim wanted to learn more about his guest's poetics. In the months before Paul's visit to Jacksonville, Johnson had an epiphany: that poetry written in supposedly Negro dialect was a relic of minstrelsy. "I got a sudden realization of the artificiality of conventionalized Negro poetry," Johnson would write decades later, "of its exaggerated geniality, childish optimism, forced comicality, and mawkish sentiment; of its imitation as an instrument of expression to but two emotions, pathos and humor, thereby making every poem either only sad or only funny." Paul's sophistication and dexterity as a poet enabled him to "cut away much of what was coarse and 'niggerish,'" to provide "a deeper tenderness, a higher polish, a more delicate finish," in Johnson's view. Still, the star poet from Dayton could not unmoor dialect poetry from the history of minstrel stereotypes. "I saw that not even

Dunbar had been able to break the mold in which dialect poetry had, long before him, been set by representations made of the Negro on the minstrel stage." The demands of the commercial marketplace, of an audience that was "a section of the white American reading public," forced Paul to cater only to certain preconceptions about the Negro. Only the degree to which he could appeal to this prejudice, to fulfill the expectations of readers for racial caricatures, determined how acceptable and profitable his poetry would be.[26]

Johnson brought these views to bear on his discussions with Paul in Jacksonville, but not as an antagonist. "Paul and I didn't clash," he remembered; "I recognized his genius, and in a measure regarded myself as his disciple." Rather, he did so as a matter of personal development, of voicing his "doubts regarding the further possibilities of stereotyped dialect." Johnson wondered whether Paul, given his past success with dialect poetry, would turn out to be less doubtful about its future. Would not Paul seek to encourage Johnson to advance experimentation with this genre?

No. A tone of resignation instead laced Paul's reply. "You know, of course, that I didn't start as a dialect poet," Paul began. "I simply came to the conclusion that I could write it as well, if not better, than anybody else I knew of, and that by doing so I could gain a hearing." But he bemoaned the fateful choice he made at the outset of his career. Ever since, he had been reeling from the consequences. "I gained the hearing, and now they don't want me to write anything but dialect." Johnson heard in these words nothing less than "self-reproach," an admission that now it was too late for Paul to turn the tide, even though he was only twenty-eight years old, presumably with decades of a career ahead of him. Both men eventually agreed that "the public still demanded dialect poetry, but that as a medium, especially for the Negro poet, it was narrow and limited." For Paul, the rationale behind his part in the agreement was long rooted in his desire, his need, to earn as much money as he could to support his livelihood. He stayed on this path toward solvency, even at the expense of the principles he privately shared with Johnson.[27]

For many evenings, when the two poets neither went out nor received visitors, they sat, smoked, and talked poetics, with Rosy playing and singing in the background. At times they would cease their talk; they listened only to the music. Jim believed that is what both men wanted; Paul thought, instead, he "should be impolite not to listen."[28]

By the end of Paul's visit, he and Jim Johnson agreed to disagree on a number of issues. One was the worth of Walt Whitman, the accomplished poet, journalist, and essayist who had died only recently, in the spring of 1892.

Reading Whitman's 1855 book of poetry, *Leaves of Grass,* in fact, spurred Johnson's epiphany on the minstrel limits of Negro dialect. But when Johnson presented his Whitman-inspired verse, Paul read the lines and looked at him "with a queer smile," and said, "I don't like them, and I don't see what you are driving at." Johnson proceeded to read him his favorite verses in *Leaves of Grass.* Perhaps behind that "queer smile" was Paul's resignation to his "horror of being endlessly entertained and talked to," the words he at the time wrote to Alice, marking, as he said to her, "the first time that I have written you without people about talking to me."[29]

Johnson did not have access to these very words, nor to information about the depth of Paul's discomfort at his house and among his family. But after spending many hours of social and intellectual intimacy with Paul, Johnson discovered the person behind the persona of "the Dunbar of the courtly manners, polished speech, and modest behavior." Clairvoyantly, Johnson learned that under Paul's "polite tongue there was a sac of bitter sarcasm that he spat out on people he did not like, and often used in his own defense." Only some people in Paul's life knew this side all too well.[30]

In late March, Paul wrote Alice a letter about a remarkable opportunity he had encountered that had little, if anything, to do with his professional aspirations in literature or his financial angst as a married man. Knowing that he would spend consecutive parts of March and April in Jacksonville reading his poetry, he realized that this could be an invitation he could not turn down: the chance to be made a Master Mason. The $12.50 application fee was affordable, only half of what he would have had to pay if he had tried to apply in Washington, D.C. Why undergo an initiation later in that city, when for half the price he could do so now in Jacksonville? He learned that he could have his membership subsequently transferred to Washington, D.C. He needed to know Alice's thoughts. "What do you say, write at once or wire," he urged.[31]

So began one of the more obscure journeys of Paul's life: his initiation into becoming a Freemason. The news first began as a secret. Three days after informing Alice of the opportunity, he wrote another letter that explicitly instructed her to keep word of his application confidential. "Don't tell any body there about my masonic business," he requested, "because I want to surprise them all."[32]

Paul was a student of history and knew that being a Mason would be more than just a feather in his cap; it would be an induction into a storied franchise of African American men. The Freemasons were a distinguished organization dating back to their founding in the new republic in the late eighteenth century.

Since then, Freemasonry had transcended generations, uniting men as "brothers, citizens, and cosmopolitans"—that is, including those "of all nations, tongues, kindreds, and languages," according to scholars Peter P. Hinks and Stephen Kantrowitz.[33]

For African American Freemasons, the genealogy traced back to Prince Hall, a previously enslaved leatherworker, who led fellow Masons of African descent in 1777 to charter African Lodge No. 459 in Boston. This pioneering group of fifteen began the long history of African American Masons seeking recognition from majority-white lodges within local regions and across the country. Well after Hall's death in 1807, African Lodge No. 459 continued to encourage benevolence and fellowship, charity and evangelism, deep-seated aspiration for racial freedom and equality among its Masons and those with whom they came into contact. In the face of slavery and social policies and practices of racism, these doctrines of universal brotherhood and citizenship threaded together the generations of African Americans who would claim membership in the Freemason lodges that were sprouting up across nineteenth-century America.

By the time Paul was considering the initiation, an eminent line of African American men had been Freemasons. By turns literary writers, intellectuals, and activists, Prince Hall, John Marrant, Richard Allen, and Martin Delany, among others, worked to give Freemasonry the cultural prestige and political force that the Dayton poet found attractive. The organization already was a context for cultivating the political promise and networking that African Americans needed as they transitioned from slavery to freedom. And it had already served as the society from which African Americans such as Hiram Revels, U.S. senator from Mississippi and the first African American to serve in Congress, and John Mercer Langston, U.S. representative from Virginia and the first dean of Howard University's law school, emerged to organize communities and win elections to political office during the era of Reconstruction.

By 1900, approximately fifty thousand African Americans belonged to various societies of Freemasons, including, most notably, his nemesis-turn-comrade Booker T. Washington. These societies represented "a place where men simultaneously declared their commitments to dignified, bourgeois respectability and to a militant tradition of protest and resistance." But it also was, according to Hinks and Kantrowitz, "a school for leadership and a vehicle for collective expression outside the channels of formal politics." Straddling both formal and informal kinds of political activity, African American Freemasonry was something that Paul wanted to be a part of.[34]

As much as Paul wanted to keep his Masonic aspirations a secret, Alice noticed something afoot in Washington, D.C., even while he was in Jacksonville. In her first letter of reply about his desire to become a Mason, she recounted her struggle in locating a free library near their home where she could borrow books. So frustrated was she that she complained even to her gynecologist, who pitied her and recommended that she visit the local Masonic library on Third and E Streets. She had not heard of this library before; she went there to learn more about it. "The librarian, a very polite young man, told me that the library was only for relatives of Masons or Masons, or for someone who was recommended very highly." Once Alice relayed her own full name and her gynecologist's ("Dr. Parsons"), she gained special access, not only because of the latter's name but because of Paul's surname. Alice relayed the ensuing exchange with the librarian: "I think the librarian must be a close reader of yours. He asked if you were a Mason and if you thought of joining. I said that I thought probably you did."[35] Right after telling this story, Paul's opportunity preoccupied Alice. She was full of anticipation. "I wonder if you are going to be a Mason to-night," she speculated, in a letter she wrote to him the following afternoon.[36]

The initiation was not easy. About thirty men convened "to organize a lodge of young men, and in honor of Paul, name it the Paul Laurence Dunbar Lodge." Jim, who accompanied Paul to partake in the initiation, later recorded the experience in a memoir. For one night all were initiated and "carried through the first three degrees of Masonry," a source of great misery for them all, Johnson recalled: "The Negro Masons of that day in Jacksonville were a horny-handed set. The Odd Fellows lodgers were made up of white collar workers, but the Masonic lodges were recruited largely from the stevedores, hod carriers, lumber mill and brickyard hands and the like. The initiation was rough, and lasted all night." So grueling were the activities that a fellow was rendered lame for a series of weeks after landing on the floor upon being thrown into a blanket.[37]

Though physically and mentally wasted after the initiation, Paul got in. "Well dear, at last I am a mason and a pretty sore and tired one at that, but glad to be through it," he wrote Alice, five days after his initial letter to her about it. Electing to join in Jacksonville rather than in Washington, D.C., turned out to be a wise move. His pure literary celebrity inoculated him from the hazing's severest parts; the bar for disqualifying his candidacy turned out to be higher than most. "They would have killed me in Washington, but a certain awe of my mysterious greatness made them handle me less roughly than the others and my name was a certain protection," he confessed.[38]

Alice expressed enthusiasm about the positive news she received, although her concern with the elitism of an unfamiliar organization tempered her emotion. "Well, you are a Mason now and quite a great man, I suppose," she reckoned. Playfully taking a dig at the ritualism of the Masonic rite of passage, she patted him on the shoulder but admonished him as a wife would. "I hope you rode the goat and climbed the greased pole with sufficient dignity and that you won't be so dreadfully stuck up, when you come home."[39]

The stature Alice would begin to enjoy as the wife of a Mason was not lost on her. Now she was an adjunct to an exclusive fraternity. With other wives in the same situation, by default she belonged to a spousal sorority. "I suppose I am a Mason's wife now and can hold my head up with the rest of the 'sisters,'" she said. He wished to rein in any publicity about his newfound status. She promised not to say a word about his initiation. "Being a Mrs. Mason I must learn to keep a secret. N'est-ce pas?" The question captured at once her affirmation of the required complicity but also her discomfort with the paradox of social privilege and the individual captivity intrinsic to it.[40]

Contrary to Alice's mixed feelings, Paul enjoyed being a Mason. Despite the application fee (the "$12.50 I gave to be a mason cut me down some"), he implied that the Jacksonville trip gave a wonderful boost to his sartorial self-esteem and professional potential. Each and every week he had his suits pressed so that he could keep up with "the hot pace these southern gents set." Other formal accoutrements were required. "Do you think I had better get my masonic pin before I get home or shall I wait?" he asked Alice. Stroking Paul's ego, she agreed that he should. "Yes, get your Masonic pin so you can come home in all your glory," she smiled.[41]

Close to a couple of weeks later, Alice reiterated her awe, which appeared to grow in sincerity over time. "I am so tickled over your masonship. Really, I shall have to bow down to you when you come home." She began to realize the significance of his induction when she imagined its potential elevation of his social standing in Washington, D.C. "I should like to see Mr. Terrell's face when you display your pin and give him the grip." Paul Laurence Dunbar, the Mason, would stand eye to eye with Robert Heberton Terrell, the first African American D.C. justice of the peace and the husband of famed civil rights activist Mary Church Terrell. Of equal importance, being a Mason lifted Paul's self-confidence in the wake of identifiable periods when it had been fluctuating wildly or hitting rock bottom, as a consequence of his challenges as a professional writer and as a husband.[42]

Paul tried to perceive the glass as half full when he received his Masonic pin, but, alas, it failed to meet his expectations. "My pin is awful," declared a curt postscript to his early April letter. He also criticized the misbehavior of fellow Masons. In his mind, they infected him not only with despicable temptations but with illness. "I have been feeling quite good; but was out late to lodge last night and my cough is back and my throat bad again," he complained. "What do you suppose those nigger masons have done?"[43]

Nonetheless, Paul's grousing gave way to the honor he was granted in Jacksonville: having a Masonic lodge named after him. "They have named the new lodge, now the finest in the state of Florida, the Paul Laurence Dunbar Lodge, No. 1. F & A.M. Whew!" he exclaimed. "It will take much to get the swelling out of my head when I get back to Washington." The endowment reminded him of how much Freemasonry was poised to elevate his standing within the African American community, both there and at home. Indeed, word did begin to circulate in and around Washington, D.C., that Paul had been initiated and had a lodge named after him, to the fascination of their friends and acquaintances.[44]

———

As much as Paul was trying to hone his poetry and poetics, he still was trying to make a name for himself as a novelist. His third novel, *The Fanatics* (1901), initially had the makings of commercial success with Dodd, Mead. "I am delighted with the Fanatics and I do hope that it is going to sell," he wrote Alice in the spring.[45] Previously, the novel had the working title of "Copperheads of the Civil War," a constant refrain that referred to the Democrats ("Copperheads") who wished for the Union to reconcile with the Confederates and avert the violence of the Civil War. ("Copperheads only talk, they never fight, ha, ha," says Tom Waters, a protagonist in the novel who enlists in the Union Army and eventually dies in battle.)[46] *The Fanatics*, like previous fiction, delved into the rich historical context of his own family's life for storylines. The novel is less about the military minutiae of the Civil War itself than about the practical division of society into ideological camps, not infrequently at the expense of reason. We see that the war not only antagonized regions of the country but also tore asunder families and communities—husbands from wives, parents from children, sibling from sibling, friends and acquaintances from one another. The nearly fanatical devotion of northerners and southerners to the racial and political causes of their own respective side blinded each group to a crucial fact, as Tom's father, Bradford Waters, an elder of one of the featured families in the novel, cautioned: "we must all remember that war brings more tears than smiles, and makes more widows than wives."[47] That folksy maxim summed up the fate of Paul's own mother, Matilda, when she never saw her first husband again after he departed to serve the Union Army. Consequently, for a time she had to contend with raising her first two sons as a single mother.

The Fanatics takes place on the eve of the Civil War (in the spring of 1861) and in the imaginary city of Dorbury, Ohio, the outer geographical limit of freedom for slaves. Slavery is the blight on the conscience of the nation, of which Dorbury serves as microcosm. Love supersedes military duty in the cases of three families: the Waters, who, upon mourning a death in the family, are presented with an opportunity to put aside internal political differences; the Van Dorens, in which a family member loses an arm to save a beloved; and the Stewarts, who shun one of their own, Walter Stewart, for joining the Union fight, but later welcome him home as a hero after he risks his life for a future wife. Only at this point in his oeuvre of novels, however, did Paul portray the life of an ex-slave in a substantial way. In a scene reminiscent, but also a reimagination, of the racial unrest and violence in Wilmington, North Carolina, in 1898, an anonymous ex-slave (who happens to belong to a refugee African American family that just arrived in Dorbury) murders an abhorrent drunk and remarkably drives away a cowardly white lynch mob. Succeeding in confronting those who wish to resuscitate slavery by way of racial segregation, this young man, as scholar Jennifer Hughes puts it, performs "a heroic act," one "due to a commitment to the protection of loved ones rather than to pure fanatical principle." The man is an allegory of Paul's "carefully-crafted, subversive revaluation of African American valor and retaliation," ensconced in a novel ostensibly focused on the destinies of three white families and their fanatical impulses.[48]

Once again, the response of the critics tempered any elation Paul might have experienced over the novel's sales. Only informational notices were circulated early on. The reviews were minimal—one from the *Kansas City Star* and another from the *New York Times*—and less than glowing. They described Paul as someone who was closer to the end than to the outset of his literary prime. "They are both almost eulogistic while the Times is very discriminatory and good," Paul noticed, sensitive to the failings of his product. "They make my heart warm. They both hit on the first chapter in the book." He sent them along to Alice, so that she could "enjoy them" herself. In the meantime, he would continue to keep an eye out for the reviews, which instilled ongoing anxiety. "I am very much afraid for it," he would later write, when he asked her if she herself encountered any in print.[49]

With yet another novel that stretched the boundaries of what Paul—or any African American, for that matter—could achieve as a writer, the reviewers of

The Fanatics at least conceded that his literary versatility had to be taken more seriously. The critics had to acknowledge, in Paul's most complex work of fiction to date, his dexterous thematic handling of the Civil War and the alliances and conflicts that formed during this calamity. One critic regarded the novel "doubtless his best work in fiction," while another said it "fully demonstrates the author's right to serious consideration." Still, the negative commentary that afflicted his prior publications persisted. To reviewers, the novel was shallow; it was "a very pretty story of reconciliation and harmony," for example, or "not profound as a character study. All there is of it is upon the surface." As at other moments in Paul's professional career, the pigeonhole of race could not be avoided. "Abundantly endowed with the primitive intuition, the music and poetry of the Negro," wrote one reviewer, "it is only at brief intervals that this intuition appeals to the Negro fascination for the occult and exaggeration of the mysterious and gruesome." In a stereotypical way, *The Fanatics* retained Paul's canonical self-imprint, if only this time modulated somewhat by the equally stereotypical perception of his race's temperament and predilections.[50]

Paul regarded *The Fanatics* a failure. In the fall he thanked an acquaintance for the kind words about it ("I am glad to have you say nice things about *The Fanatics*"). In his expressed gratitude, he lifted the curtain slightly to expose the depth of his hope for success after all the recent challenges of his life. "You do not know how my hopes were planted in that book and it has utterly disappointed me," he confessed. Worse than the novel's mixed reception was his realization that it was the very best he could do, and his best simply was not good enough. In a sense, "it went very lame upon me," like an injured limb, he wrote, and "discouragement has taken hold upon me."[51]

CHAPTER 20

Old Habits Die Hard

I want to suggest that you have Dunbar come to New York Monday morning
early or Sunday evening for the reason that I find that he is still keeping up in a
greater or less degree his old habit of drinking.

—EMMETT JAY SCOTT TO BOOKER T. WASHINGTON
(MARCH 13, 1901)[1]

By the spring of 1901, Paul's long letters to Alice were relics of the past. Close
to age thirty, he clipped their individual lengths, the consequence of his battles
with poor health over the previous several months. The reading he had delivered in Jacksonville on March 21 "was a great success," applauded by "eight
hundred enthusiastic people white and black," but he was regularly paying the
price for his strenuous workload. "Of course I am sick this morning and coughing horribly," a symptom that would afflict him for days, grow to become almost insufferable pain beneath his shoulder blades, precipitate weight loss,
and partly cause his depression while in Florida for March and April.[2]

As time went on, Paul's public and private efforts exhausted him. To recite
his poems, he would have to draw upon the same well of energy that had fueled his ability to write. He was unable to write more than a few sentences at
a time. "I am feeling badly," he wrote to Alice, "but am going to be out in the
street to-day and stay in the Sunshine all I can. Everyone is so good to me
down here and I have fallen in love with the people. I may stay here the full
month after all, as I am to give two more readings in this city." A far cry from
his initial annoyance at the Johnson family, Paul was equally inspired to enjoy
the warm weather and sunlight, to get better in Florida, and imagined staying
longer than he once thought, even as doing so meant that he would live away
from his wife.[3]

Paul still closed some of his letters with paragraphs of emotional attachment, as brief as they were. In one he wrote: "Give my love to ma and take whole piles of kisses for yourself. The time cannot pass too fast that will bring me back to you." In another, even punctuation was sacrificed: "With a thousand kisses & Love to ma." Alice likewise sought to advance their marriage to realms of greater commitment. To the letters Paul had written in March, Alice reciprocated with love, doting, and, of course, spousal surveillance. "Well, here goes for a great hug and snuggle and lovings. Ma sends love. Take care of yourself, darling, don't get any more cold. Have you found out about your medicine? Don't forget your emulsion and get rid of that cough." For the first time she gestured to a particular wonder she had been having about growing their family: "Why don't we have babies? I want a little boy who can wear little clothes like his papa, raglan and little shirts and collars."[4]

By this and other measures, Paul and Alice's marriage seemed to be improving. Now three years since the moment they had reunited in Washington, D.C., when their life in the same residence together closed the chapter of their long-distance marriage, she was nostalgic. In spring 1901 she wrote him an optimistic letter reflecting on what they had accomplished ever since. "So we have really only been married three years to-day, and what years they have been, too. Years of sorrow and years of joy and pain and gladness all intertwined like a many hued garland. I am glad that I am yours. I wish you were here to-day so that I might kiss you full and sweet upon the lips and tell you so." Whenever they avoided arguing over the past, over the demons of their disputes, their marriage was golden. Spoiled by their shared punctuality, each spouse expressed sincere frustration whenever a letter from the other did not arrive on time—such as when one did not arrive every single day. Both felt this way, despite the remarkable fact that each had drafted and mailed a letter to the other, however long or short, one out of every two or three days, whenever a cluster of exchanges did exist. Any longer gap in epistolary frequency portended meanings as powerful as those communicated by the words in the letters themselves.[5]

Alice monitored literary news about Paul just as closely as he had, consistent with her broader endeavor to protect his reputational standing in American society. In April 1901 she came across "Three Negro Poets," an article by John Livingston Wright, published in the *Colored American Magazine*. For understandable reasons, the essay bothered her, because it, like the trend of other contemporary articles, consigned her husband to the familiar cage of dialect literature. Despite more than a century of writing to the contrary, Wright wrote that only in the early twentieth century had African Americans achieved the ability to portray themselves in literature with a folkloric and authentic realism as skillfully as "the white man." As in the case of James Whitcomb Riley, whites had for too long served as "the depicter and the mimic." Paul as well as fellow African American dialect poets James Corrothers and Daniel Webster Davis—respectively, authors of *The Snapping of the Bow* (1901) and *'Weh Down Souf* (1897)—"are three young men of African blood who have arisen to paint in faithful imagery the life of the black man as he lives in America today," and are "the first of the Negro blood to attain in the realm of poetry a footing which entitles them to first consideration." With the standard allusion to Howells's famous anointing of Paul's poetry, Wright claimed that Paul's "best work and his reputation depend mainly upon his dialect verses," which "won his first success, and in which he has maintained and enhanced his literary standing." The message was that Paul's ideal creative writing was in dialect, a genre to which he should stick to ensure his future commercial success.[6]

Alice was incensed. "It is sickening and I feel like writing the writer of the article and telling him what I think of him and his article," she vented. She despised the article's implication that readers should embrace dialect as racially authentic and as the best aesthetic signature of literature written by African Americans. This view echoed what white critics in mainstream magazines and newspapers had been saying for years about Paul's work, yet Alice used the occasion to profane what the *Colored American Magazine* stood for: "Telling you to 'stick to dialect'! Now if that isn't presumptuous in a nigger magazine I'd just like to know!" She said she would send him the article, just so that he could see how reprehensible it was, but not before taking one last swipe at the magazine's title: "I send you the nigger American."[7]

Almost a week to the day after Alice wrote her grievance, Paul replied from Tuskegee, where he had been visiting. He sent word that he would deliver three papers, the second of which he would title, tellingly, "The Negro in Literature."[8] Gradually, he began to share the distrust she had previously expressed to him of "inferior folks," including African Americans, that could by association "cheapen" him. He likewise scorned and objectified them. Whenever they behaved in reprehensible ways, he uttered a phrase that implied his race could not surprise him any longer: "Niggers will be niggers."[9]

For a while Paul and Alice saw eye to eye on a host of racial and literary matters, but in April their marriage entered a precipitous decline. Paul's demons returned—namely, the temptation of women. He brought it to Alice's attention once again. Writing from Tuskegee, he declared that he was at a loss without

FIG. 20.1. Paul with friends and his mother, Matilda, at rear, n.d. (Paul Laurence Dunbar Collection, Ohio History Connection)

her. "Oh how I miss you, your love and help and our own home." But he also confessed that his eye had been wandering while in Jacksonville. Using their inside language—of whether he was being a "good boy" or "bad boy"—he indicated that his behavior had inched up to the line of what she would have deemed unacceptable. "Dear heart, I have not been a bad boy down here," Paul assured Alice, "but I have been—well, let us say rather flirty and I am afraid three or four women in Jax like me a little more than is convenient, but fortunately none of them is unattached—three being engaged and one married." Evidently, that Paul himself was not "unattached" played a role in his self-discipline not to flirt too much, not to be "naughty" as Alice would be wont to put it. But his emphasis on the personal circumstances of the fond Jacksonville women, as opposed to his own willpower, was not easily dismissible.[10]

When Alice read this letter, she entertained the humor latent in Paul's confession and drafted a reply two days later. "So you haven't been naughty," she cornered him, skeptical of where he drew the line, "only a little flirty, Eh?" She teased him for how readily he was "meaning to confess," as she would state in

FIG. 20.2. Paul with a friend outside of Dayton home, circa 1905. (Paul Laurence Dunbar Collection, Ohio History Connection)

feigned dialect: "'Menan' to 'fess already? All right out with it, what's next. You must have had a sweet old time with all those women, and all mortgaged property. Seems to me it must have been a mortgaged property convention. Be sure to prepare a full account by the time you get home." She jousted with him over the likelihood that whatever he was admitting to in print, his words may have been understating his ethical transgressions. A cross-examination upon his return almost a week after his departure would evince the full scale of his crimes and misdemeanors.[11]

———

Word about Paul's inebriation did not abate within the circle of Booker T. Washington. During the spring, Emmett Jay Scott, Tuskegee Institute's executive secretary, recommended that the political leader might need to come to the poet's rescue. "I want to suggest that you have Dunbar come to New York

Monday morning early or Sunday evening for the reason that I find that he is still keeping up in a greater or less degree his old habit of drinking," Scott wrote. In other words, Paul should arrive in New York after—neither just before nor during—the weekend, when presumably he was most vulnerable to social drinking. Washington was staying at the Grand Union Hotel that month and scheduled to speak alongside Paul. But with Paul's feeble grip on sobriety, Scott sought to protect Washington by raising his awareness of the problem. "It would be very unfortunate if he should reach you not in the proper condition." He would go on to relate the recent story that Paul was invited to participate in the entertainment of a Chicago church, but he showed up drunk. Consequently, "the church paper roasted him unmercifully for coming to them in such condition that he could not read."[12]

Washington replied to Scott with the news that he planned to invite Paul again to Tuskegee to perform—"to come when I please," as Paul later wrote to Alice—and that the poet needed careful management. "I want him taken good care of," Washington ordered. "Give him a room somewhere where he will be comfortable." After all, whenever Washington invited him to the school, he arranged a laborious schedule that required his multiple contacts with the Alabama community. "I want him to read to the students several times, and perhaps he might do some work with one or two of the classes in literature while there." Washington expected that Paul be sober, with his wits about him, to fulfill these obligations and be in residence for ten whole days. Paul tried to reduce his time there.[13]

Paul had reason to cut his visit short. Traveling in the Jim Crow car agitated him, first of all; he "was on the train all day and an awful trip it was," given that it had "no sleeper and about half a dozen changes." Humbled, or humiliated, by the transportation, upon his arrival he was as overwhelmed by the expectations of this visit as he was by those when he had visited Tuskegee a little over two years prior. Just as Washington foretold Scott, Paul conveyed to Alice his institutional imprisonment. "They want me to lecture here to the literature classes but I hardly think I shall do it as I am anxious to get home." And he was asked to stay longer than ten days. "Think, they want me to stay a month," he wailed. "I wouldn't if I could." At least he was fortunate to have plenty of writing to draw upon, such as his essay "The Negro in Literature," a copy of which he wanted her to send him soon, so that he could draft a lecture.

To make his predicament worse, Paul was inherently unwell, frighteningly so: "Don't worry when I tell you that in gagging today, I had quite a flow of blood. Where it came from I don't know." While at Tuskegee he would eat hardly at all, putting him at odds with the Washingtons, who had arranged a series of dinners. For these he could only pretend to eat. The instability of Paul's health and the unpredictability of his working and living conditions were dialectically related; each made the other worse. He was fed up. "These dinners are stupid affairs and I don't want to be bothered," he complained.[14]

Paul suffered a penalty for his noncompliance. When he declined dinner one evening, a painfully early breakfast was scheduled for the following morning: a solitary meal he had to endure with the ever-garrulous Mrs. Washington. Though she proved to be gracious, the episode enlightened him. "More and more the shams of life impress and oppress," he moralized to Alice, "but that is because I am older and day to day know more of human deceit." He might have come to appreciate Washington the leader, but he was respecting less and less Washington the man.[15]

The longer Paul stayed at Tuskegee, the more visceral was his disapproval of it, despite the instances, the most recent while in Colorado, when he seemed to applaud the institute's virtues. "I believe my disgust with Tuskegee has never been more keen than now," he realized. Deplorable were his living conditions, and he witnessed the discharge of two women teachers "for using buckets and setting them in the hall-way," rather than "sh—ting on the floor of the hall." Against the backdrop of these inconveniences, Washington's right-hand man, Emmett Jay Scott, unsurprisingly proposed a professional opportunity for Paul to consider. "During a fourteen mile drive yesterday afternoon, the adroit Mr. Scott managed as best he could to draw me out as to whether I would accept the position of literature teacher here," he began. "I have seen this all along, and knew that matters were tending that way." For close to two hours, Scott tried to convince Paul to accept the offer. Washington lamented the absence of a "literary department" at Tuskegee. Paul, if hired, could help establish the department while potentially imbuing the institution with "a stronger tone" of academic seriousness.

The inquiry tugged at Paul's heartstrings. Dating back to more than six years earlier, when he spoke of Tobey and his colleagues potentially lending him about five hundred dollars to study for a year at Harvard, he had wished for greater involvement with higher education. Whereas this premise had been based on his enrollment as a student, prior to his professional ascent as a writer, the current scenario proposed that he serve as "a mere adjunct of Tuskegee and Washington." Paul was insulted. "Then Mr. Scott, bullied & stammered & I smoked blissfully & silently on," he smiled. "He knows as much now as when he started." (A smoker, Paul collected for pleasure a variety of

ornately carved wooden pipes, embossed cigars, and accompanying cases.)
Both men recognized that Washington's prominence would always eclipse
Paul's reputation. The poet refused to give any ground, offended that the educator sent his henchman to do his dirty work. "Whenever Mr. W. sees fit to
come at me with a square question instead of sending his minion to skirmish,
he will get a square answer." Washington had to say more than just "it would
be a good thing to have Mr. D. here oftener," after marveling at the local chapel's overflowing sanctuary of students where Paul was reciting his work.[16]

Equally eventful was the following day. Paul attended a claustrophobic gathering of luminaries: it included Tuskegee philanthropist and trustee Robert
Curtis Ogden, Coadjutor Bishop William Neilson McVickar of Rhode Island,
publisher Frank Nelson Doubleday, and the wife of Rufus Wills Cobb, a former
governor of Alabama. Paul "escaped," but only into the arms of Washington elsewhere. For Alice, Paul recalled their startling exchange, begun by Washington:

"Where have you been?" he said, "I've been looking for you."
"I knew it, and I've been lying low."
Then he struck his hands together, "I've just thought of something, I wish
    you could write a poem for the dedication and read it this afternoon."

Paul scrambled into town and purchased twelve bottles of beer to drink.
Inspired, he wrote "On the Dedication of Dorothy Hall (Tuskegee, Ala.,
April 22, 1901)" within two hours, the only time allotted:

Not to the midnight of the gloomy past,
    Do we revert to-day; we look upon
The golden present and the future vast
    Whose vistas show us visions of the dawn.

Nor shall the sorrows of departed years
    The sweetness of our tranquil souls annoy,
The sunshine of our hopes dispels the tears,
    And clears our eyes to see this later joy.

Not ever in the years that God hath given
    Have we gone friendless down the thorny way,
Always the clouds of pregnant black were riven
    By flashes from His own eternal day.

The women of a race should be its pride;
    We glory in the strength our mothers had,

We glory that this strength was not denied
    To labor bravely, nobly, and be glad.

God give to these within this temple here,
    Clear vision of the dignity of toil,
That virtue in them may its blossoms rear
    Unspotted, fragrant, from the lowly soil.

God bless the givers for their noble deed,
    Shine on them with the mercy of Thy face,
Who come with open hearts to help and speed
    The striving women of a struggling race.[17]

Later, Paul encountered Washington and handed him the poem. After reading it, Washington applauded the effort and asked, "How *did* you do it?" Both men shared a laugh.[18]

Washington did not keep the information to himself. "At the meeting I got an ovation and when I got through, he got up and announced how it had been done & the audience went wild." This was a rousing conclusion to what otherwise had been a nettlesome visit. "Mr. W. is elated & altogether I am a hero." The readings and lectures had excited a base of fans, and his classes were full.[19]

————

In spring 1901 Paul received two special pieces of mail. The first document appointed him to the rank of colonel for the inaugural parade of William McKinley, who had been elected to his second term as president. With the familiar face of John Hay, who had ascended from U.S. ambassador to the United Kingdom to secretary of state in 1898 within McKinley's cabinet, Paul continued to benefit from recognition at multiple levels of government. Scheduled for March 4, the inauguration would represent his most public affirmation. The second document further distinguished Paul: it assigned him the role of aide to the Third Civic Division. Upon reflection, the prospect of riding on a horse during the parade discouraged him, so self-conscious was he of appearing a novice. He was tempted to decline the prestigious invitation. Only at Alice and Matilda's behest did he change his mind and consent to go.[20]

This was not the first time Paul's clout in the halls of government referred to his literary stature. Ever aspiring to reinforce his own political network of influence, Paul not only commanded the ear of Washington but had proactively sought out the explicit protection of Theodore Roosevelt when he was governor of New York. Since that time, Roosevelt had gone on, in 1900, to finish his service as governor, so that he could campaign on the Republican ticket as vice president, while McKinley vied for the presidency. The McKinley–Roosevelt ticket won the 1900 election. Within the span of one year, in September 1901, McKinley was assassinated, and Roosevelt automatically became president, the youngest ever to hold this office. Now, the governor who had once sought to assure Paul that he would be shielded from New York debt collectors was henceforth the most powerful man in the world.

Paul had a direct line of communication to Roosevelt, as indicated by the case of Dr. Austin Maurice Curtis in fall 1901. Curtis belonged to a social circle that included Paul and extended from Chicago to Washington, D.C. Four years Paul's senior, Curtis was by the 1890s well distinguished: he had earned a baccalaureate degree from Lincoln University in Pennsylvania and a medical doctorate from Northwestern University in Evanston, Illinois. Afterward he embarked on a career as a practicing surgeon in Chicago, where he was appointed in 1896 as the first African American physician to work in the city's Cook County Hospital. Two years later, he became surgeon-in-chief of Freedmen's Hospital in Washington, D.C. He would have a corresponding appointment as a faculty member in the Department of Surgery at Howard University.[21]

Paul's social circles possibly overlapped with those of Curtis. Paul likewise lived in Chicago in 1893 during the World's Columbian Exposition and in the late 1890s in Washington, D.C. In both cities, the poet and the physician belonged to the tightly knit, exclusive circles of African American professionals and intellectuals. But the more direct link pointed to Dr. Daniel Hale Williams. Right after medical school, from 1891 to 1894, Curtis studied under Williams as a surgical intern at Chicago's Provident Hospital. Williams and Curtis were close.

While Paul lived in Washington, D.C., in spring 1894, he was close friends with Charles Mitchell, who was working at the office of the Freedom Manufacturing Company. In a letter to Paul, Mitchell remarked that he was looking forward to a potential opportunity with Williams. "I am expecting a position at the Freedman's Hospital under Dr. Williams and if I can get it Dunbar, I want you to come down in the fall and spend a month or more with me." Through this link, Paul came to know of Williams and regard him as his "physician and friend," sometimes depending on him for medicine to get through his recurring bouts of illness. So close did Paul grow to Williams that, when he secretly married Alice, his physician was one of the few people he told.

Paul and Alice thereby came to be good friends with Curtis and his wife, Namoyoka Gertrude. In the last couple of months of 1897, the Dunbars and the Curtises regularly spent time together in Washington, D.C.[22]

Hence, when Paul heard that Curtis had abruptly retired from the Freedmen's Hospital, he wanted to know why. An extension of the Freedmen's Bureau, the Freedmen's Hospital was established in 1862 in Washington, D.C., where it would have a long-standing connection with the medical faculty and the campus of Howard University, chartered five years later. When the bureau was dissolved in 1872, the hospital came under the administrative remit of the United States Department of the Interior. To obtain the answer he needed on Curtis's retirement, Paul decided that he would contact not Ethan A. Hitchcock, secretary of the interior, but rather Hitchcock's superior, the person he was familiar with: President Theodore Roosevelt.

With Paul's letter in hand, Roosevelt wrote to Hitchcock on October 1, 1901. "Paul Laurence Dunbar is a man for whom I have a high regard on account of his literary ability," he declared. "Would you look into this case, and report to me?" Hitchcock conducted an investigation and relayed the outcome to George B. Cortelyou, secretary to the president, who went on to write a letter to Paul a week later. "Referring to your recent letter in regard to the case of Dr. Curtis, I find upon inquiry that after a very careful investigation the Secretary of the Interior concluded that the interest of the public service, in connection with the administration of the affairs of the Freedmen's Hospital, necessitated Dr. Curtis' retirement; and accordingly Dr. William A. Warfield has been appointed to succeed him." Warfield studied medicine at Howard University and, starting in 1894, interned at the Freedmen's Hospital. Like Curtis, he trained under Williams to be a surgeon. Given the pedigree of his academic training, Warfield was a logical choice to succeed Curtis.[23]

During his appeal to Roosevelt, Paul swung by the White House and left behind one of his books as a token of his appreciation. William Loeb Jr., assistant secretary to the president, transmitted Roosevelt's gratitude. But he also reaffirmed the poet's direct access to the president. "I am directed by the President to thank you cordially for the book you left at the White House for him," Loeb wrote, "and to say that the next time you call he desires you to be sure and see him." Word of President Roosevelt's open-door policy was likely music to Paul's ears.[24]

Luckily for Paul, the support from Roosevelt he came to enjoy was hidden from the public. A few weeks after Roosevelt courteously launched an investigation into Curtis's retirement, the president would do something that roused the ire of many opponents, and even supporters, from around the country. "Roosevelt Dines a Darkey," so ran one newspaper headline; "Roosevelt Proposes to Coddle the Sons of Ham," so said another.[25]

To wit, on October 16, 1901, the president of the United States invited Paul's companion Booker T. Washington to dinner at the White House when he heard that the Tuskegee leader was in town. Washington accepted, and that evening he dined with Roosevelt and his wife, Edith. Roosevelt's worldview, both personal and shaped by his family, was that the Negro race, as a whole, were inferior to whites in the short term, a consequence of the still rather brief period that they had been emancipated from slavery and enfranchised as a political class. Contrary to mainstream belief, he did envision in the long term their collective advancement as part of American civilization. Until then, he admired and embraced only those very few African American men he came into contact with and permitted into his inner circle. Roosevelt's invitation anointed Washington the first African American ever to be a dinner guest at the White House. Two weeks prior to this controversial event, the record shows, Paul likewise had a standing invitation to see the president.

In light of the media firestorm that swirled after the fateful dinner with Washington, Roosevelt came to regret that his decision was politically negligent. In spite of that, he believed that his "action was absolutely proper," that "the only wise and honorable and Christian thing to do is to treat each black man and each white man strictly on his merits as a man." Through this lens, Roosevelt came to appreciate Paul. For the handful of years that they corresponded, the president proved to be an unwavering guardian of what was in the poet's best interest.[26] The record would show that, over the course of their lives, Roosevelt, in his own words, eventually "had the pleasure of meeting Mr. Dunbar once or twice," and did so because he was "a great admirer of his poetry and his prose."[27]

———

Word continued to circulate of Paul's alcoholism, but also of his poor influence. Once again, Booker T. Washington heard about it. By late 1901, Washington had known this rumor well; to a degree he had seen it firsthand during Paul's last trip to Tuskegee, where the poet downed bottles of beer to pen verse for students and philanthropists. Perhaps by inviting Paul onto the lecture circuit with him—by keeping him nearby—Washington thought he could help keep a close eye and steady hand over his life.

Nine months earlier, the Tuskegee executive secretary, Emmett Jay Scott, had beseeched Washington to come to Paul's rescue in this very way. Paul's alcoholism was spiraling out of control. Now, in the first week of December, Edward Elder Cooper, *Indianapolis Freeman* publisher, corroborated this story and told Washington that Paul and Timothy Thomas Fortune went hand in hand. Their misbehavior was evident for the world to see. In Washington, D.C., the meeting site of the Bethel Literary and Historical Association, Fortune "and Paul Laurence Dunbar got on a 'holy terror' last Wednesday and continued it up until just before the meeting." Fortune embarrassed himself; he "came in late and in no condition to speak. He had lost or mis-laid his manuscript and made an offhand talk in a rambling way very similar to the one he had made at the Business League last August in Chicago."[28]

Another colleague, a realtor named Whitefield McKinlay, reported this incident to Washington. In his view of the "revolting" "spectacle" of Fortune, people at the Bethel meeting "tried to sober him up so that he could be in condition to read his paper, but took him off with the result that he could not read his paper but he was incoherent." Cooper reiterated McKinlay's point. "Don't say anything about the Fortune matter for I really blame Paul Laurence Dunbar rather than Fortune," he said. "Fortune is bright and witty and entertaining and when two live spirits get together they are apt to do most anything."[29]

Neither Cooper nor McKinlay went as far as Scott in advising Washington to rescue Paul from himself. McKinlay took the opposite tack: he sought to rescue the Tuskegee leader from mischievous socialites like Paul. The affair did "confirm what I have stated to you," McKinlay asserted to Washington, "that for the race whose hopes are centered in you—you must diplomatically cut loose from these fellows and that at once." Alarming was the fact that several prominent men were now questioning the judgment behind Washington's association with drunkards.[30]

Despite the letters Washington received that either insinuated or insisted that he dissociate himself from Paul, no one could mistake the Dayton poet's talent. Paul could still serve Tuskegee well. Midway through December, Washington asked Paul to compose a song for the institute. He had already seen him succeed in crafting fine verse on short notice; the song should turn out to be fantastic on advance notice, the logic went. Paul agreed to do it, but he regarded the circumstances as unfavorable: "while I do not quite understand how much of the surroundings and object of the school you want put into the song, I will try it, and let you see the result as soon as possible."[31]

To craft a Tuskegee school song with an air of distinction, Paul turned to the song of another institution whose prestige was unquestionable at that time: Harvard University. By this time, Harvard was one of a handful that had earned the moniker of being a "real university," the others being Johns Hopkins University, Cornell University, Massachusetts's Clark University, and Columbia University. Harvard's stature was further cemented in 1900 when it headlined the Association of American Universities, which the presidents of fourteen distinguished institutions chartered to great notoriety. Founded in Cambridge, Massachusetts, 264 years earlier, Harvard, like the five other Ivy League schools initially included in this association, was a well-oiled educational and corporate machine renowned for its institutional maturity and academic excellence. Philanthropic wealth and intellectual energy orbited it. Synonymous with the highest standards of the great modern American university, Harvard was a leader in building its private endowment, touting a visionary and enterprising president, cultivating and celebrating expert professors, breaking ground in classroom and experiential pedagogy, expanding the professional possibilities of its curriculum, and maintaining the classical architecture of its campus facilities.[32]

By the time Paul was researching Harvard, it had become a "distinctly American institution," or American education at its best. That the World's Columbian Exposition, which he had thoroughly toured, had featured Harvard eight years earlier, in 1893, came as no surprise. Perceived there as "America's foremost educational institution," Harvard's "sprawling" exhibit occupied over 4,500 square feet of "charts, graphs, laboratory specimens, and photographs," proving that the Ivy League institution was nothing less than an "educational miracle."[33] Settling on Harvard made sense for someone like Washington, who had earned his honorary degree there only half a decade before and, incidentally, was still seeking the ideal institutional model for Tuskegee.

Paul also had a long-standing personal fascination with Harvard. A couple of years earlier, in an interview with a local newspaper reporter during his recovery period in Denver, he had admitted, "There are two things I have wanted in my life, and wanted badly, that I could not have." One of them was "College," and Harvard in particular: "I wanted to go to Harvard and study under A. S. Hill. That was my great ambition." He was referring to Adams Sherman Hill, Harvard Law class of 1855 and, since 1876, Boylston Professor of Rhetoric and Oratory at the university. Hill was admired for his writings on the principles of rhetoric and composition. Paul even knew his own course of study if he were under Hill's tutelage. "I studied Hill's rhetoric and I wanted to study

English under the man who wrote it." Alas, given that he never inherited a base of wealth and had to support his own livelihood as a writer, he never pursued that dream. Penning a song for Tuskegee, by way of Harvard, gave him a chance to immerse himself in that dream, at least for a little while.[34]

Paul discovered that Harvard's official school song was "Fair Harvard." This, too, was perfect for what he sought to accomplish. Reverend Samuel Gilman, a graduate of Harvard in 1811 and a tutor there from 1817 to 1819, wrote it in Fay House. (Within a century this house would belong to Radcliffe College, the unit of Harvard devoted to the education of women.) Harvard officials unveiled the "ode" during the university's centennial celebration on September 8, 1836. At the heart of the order of services, the song was bookended on the program between the opening prayer by Reverend Ezra Ripley and, on the other hand, a "discourse" by Josiah Quincy, the institution's president. The melody was reminiscent of what one scholar from long ago, W. H. Grattan Flood, had called "the old Irish air" of poet and songwriter Tom Moore's 1810 lyric, "Believe me, if all these endearing young charms." For a legendary university, "Fair Harvard" appealed to students, faculty, and alumni loyal to an institutional "Parent," "the nurse of our souls," by which their "manhood" could achieve shape, their minds "freedom to think":

> Fair Harvard! Thy sons to thy Jubilee throng,
>   And with blessings surrender thee o'er,
> By these festival-rites, from the Age that is past,
>   To the Age that is waiting before.
> O Relic and Type of our ancestors' worth,
>   That hast long kept their memory warm!
> First flower of their wilderness! Star of their night,
>   Calm rising through change and through storm!
>
> To thy bowers we were led in the bloom of our youth,
>   From the home of our free-roving years,
> When our fathers had warned, and our mothers had prayed
>   And our sisters had blest, through their tears.
> *Thou* then wert our Parent,—the nurse of our souls,—
>   We were moulded to manhood by thee,
> Till, freighted with treasure-thoughts, friendships, and hopes,
>   Thou didst launch us on Destiny's sea.
>
> When, as pilgrims, we come to revisit thy halls,
>   To what kindlings the season gives birth!

Thy shades are more soothing, thy sunlight more dear,
   Than descend on less privileged earth:
For the Good and the Great, in their beautiful prime,
   Through thy precincts have musingly trod,
As they girded their spirits, or deepened the streams
   That make glad the fair City of God.

Farewell! Be thy destinies onward and bright!
   To thy children the lesson still give,
With freedom to think, and with patience to bear,
   And for Right ever bravely to live.
Let not moss-covered Error moor *thee* at its side,
   As the world on Truth's current glides by;
Be the herald of Light, and the bearer of Love,
   Till the stock of the Puritans die.[35]

Three weeks to the day that he last wrote Washington, Paul replied with good news. "I am sending you herewith the school song, embodying, as near as I could, the object and distinction of Tuskegee." To impress Washington with the song's thoughtful context and text, he disclosed the inspiration. "It is sung in the same line as 'Fair Harvard' and may be sung to that tune." The gravity of the song was not lost on Paul; he was "hoping" that it would "please" Washington. After all, the song was nothing less than a ringing endorsement.[36]

The Tuskegee leader was not pleased, it turned out. He wrote Paul to express his disappointment. Two weeks after sending Washington the song, Paul replied in a tone more defensive and disgruntled. At stake was his own reputation. In their previous, more contentious days, Washington had conceded that in "matters of poetry and fiction Dunbar is a master." Now, was he skeptical? When the song came to focus on Tuskegee itself, Washington objected to its form and theme. "I have your letter and note your objections to the song," Paul grumbled.

First, Washington objected to the song's very first line: "Tuskegee, thou pride of the swift and growing South." He was concerned that the emphasis on the incomplete progress of the South would interfere with the song's timeless quality. The line should express with greater confidence the assumption that the South would achieve full maturation as a regional home for the Negro. This critique was "not well taken" by Paul, who argued that the song captured the evolving nature of the South at the turn of 1902, an accurate depiction that should not preclude the song's resonance. The song's value lay in its representation of a moment in time. Indeed, "a song is judged not by the hundred years that it lives but from the time at which it was written," and the phrasing "only indicated what the South has been, and will contrast with what it may achieve or any failure it may make." Paul sought to leave open the possibilities that the South could "grow" in either direction, toward the distinction of success or one of "failure."[37]

Second, the song had included a line referring to the "industrial idea" of Tuskegee. Washington objected to this overstatement of the institution's mission in terms of the cold language of public controversy enveloping it. He implied that he wanted it portrayed as yet another aspiring and holistic institution of higher education. The concern puzzled Paul, but he relented. "As to emphasizing the industrial idea, I have done merely what the school itself has done," he assured, "but I will make this concession of changing the fourth line of the third stanza into 'Worth of our minds and our hands.'" The symbolism of minds and hands captured the jointly intellectual and manual nature that Washington asserted on behalf of Tuskegee, but Paul complained about this editorial tweak ("it is not easy to sing").[38]

Finally, Washington objected to the song's neglect of the Holy Bible. Christian undertones had long accompanied his statements on racial education and economics. As a young boy, Washington was as acquainted with Sunday school, refusing to play outside on the Sabbath, as he was with regular school. By ten years of age, he and his family were attending the African Zion Baptist Church in Tinkersville, West Virginia. At Hampton, he envisioned himself developing into a preacher; he committed himself to "pious reading" of the Bible and paying close attention to the spiritual education he was receiving from the Presbyterian, Congregationalist, and Unitarian teachers. In his early twenties he even spent a year, by some accounts slightly less, at Wayland Seminary in Washington, D.C., which did not resolve entirely the increasing tension he felt between his skepticism of organized religion and his personal submission to Christian principles of living.[39]

Never would Paul be confused with a man who aspired toward Christian behavioral self-discipline. He refused to abide Washington's scriptural taste. "The Bible I cannot bring in," Paul said flatly. His reasons referred less to his own heathenism—although it could never be completely off the table—than to the undue burden that scripture would impose on the delicacies of poetry. "The exigencies of verse will hardly allow a paraphrase of it." Paul likened biblical language as ill-fitting for verse as "an auctioneer's list."[40]

Paul closed his letter with yet another allusion to "Fair Harvard." For understandable reasons having to do with Harvard's sense of security, "Fair Harvard" was demonstrably less self-conscious about putting the university's best foot forward to the world. Harvard's privilege was long-standing; its promise, self-evident. Paul took for granted that this difference of institutional legacy, relevance, and prospect had as much to do with the color line as with anything else. Even so, the concerns of Washington as a founder and builder of Tuskegee did not prompt Paul to alter the song further. They did not and could not fully see eye to eye. "I believe if you will look over 'Fair Harvard' you will note that they have not given their curriculum in the song or a list of the geological formation[s] of the country around the school," Paul snapped.[41]

In the end, Washington accepted the song. Three weeks later, the *Tuskegee Student*, the school newspaper, published a final version of it:

Tuskegee, thou pride of the swift and growing South
   We pay thee our homage to-day;
For the worth of thy teaching, the joy of thy care,
   And the good we have known 'neath thy sway.
Oh, long striving mother of diligent sons,
   And of daughters, whose strength is their pride,
We will love thee forever, and ever shall walk
   Thro' the oncoming years at thy side.

Thy hand we have held up the difficult steeps,
   When painful and slow was the pace,
And onward and upward, we've labored with thee
   For the glory of God and our race.
The fields smile to greet us, the forests are glad,
   The ring of the anvil and hoe
Have a music as thrilling and sweet as a harp
   Which thou taught us to hear and to know.

Oh, Mother Tuskegee, though shinest to-day
   As a gem in the fairest of lands;
Thou gavest the Heav'n-blessed power to see
   The worth of our minds and our hands.
We thank thee, we bless thee, we pray for thee years
   Imploring with grateful accord,
Full fruit for thy striving, time longer to strive,
   Sweet love and true labor's reward.[42]

One week after it was published, Washington sent a check for twenty-five dollars to Paul, who, of course, accepted the money.[43]

CHAPTER 21

The Downward Way

The names that I have thought of for *The Sport of the Gods* are,
> *The Jest of Fate*
> *The Downward Way*
> *The Weakest of These*
> *When the Gods Laugh*

—PAUL LAURENCE DUNBAR TO PAUL REYNOLDS
(JANUARY 25, 1902)[1]

Over the last several months of 1901, Paul experimented with publishing a brand of short stories analogous to the poems in formal English that reviewers and readers had been slow to embrace. From August through December he released these stories under the title of "Ohio Pastorals" in *Lippincott's*, which had first published *The Uncalled*. The "Ohio Pastorals" comprised five short stories that appeared in consecutive months: "The Mortification of the Flesh," "The Independence of Silas Bollender," "The White Counterpane," "The Minority Committee," and "The Visiting of Mother Danbury." Neither the protagonists nor the settings of the stories were defined in the explicitly racial and cultural terms of his popular plantation fiction and poems. Rather, they were local-color stories about an Ohio village. The first two stories described two friends residing in the small town and wrestling with the issues of marriage, women, individuality, and provincialism. The third focused on a mother's attempt to cope with the possible loss of her son, whom she had struggled to raise and support, to another woman of comparable fortitude. The fourth dealt with the intergenerational conflict between older and younger townspeople over whether and how to modernize a church service. Finally, the fifth story looked at two grandmothers disagreeing over how to care for their ill grand-child, who eventually died. Characters made cameo appearances across the five stories, which could possibly form a novella if Paul sought to further co-here the stories as a book.

Lest anyone forget that Paul also plied his trade in poetry, a little more than a year after the release of *Poems of Cabin and Field*, he worked with Dodd, Mead in yet another collaboration with the Hampton Institute Camera Club on an illustrated book of poems. The camera club was keen on the idea, al-though it preferred greater compensation than the hundred dollars it earned with that first book. After negotiation, the fee was raised by seventy-five dol-lars, and the club was satisfied to begin work on the second in a series of pho-tographically illustrated books of poetry, although this time, instead of Alice Morse, with Margaret Armstrong (no relation to founder General Armstrong) as page decorator. Paul titled the new book *Candle-Lightin' Time*.[2]

Candle-Lightin' Time was for the most part a new book of dialect poems. The exceptions included the first poem, "Dinah Kneading Dough," which happened not to be in the standard styling of dialect, and the two poems "At Candle-Lightin' Time" and "Song of Summer," reprinted from Paul's previous books *Lyrics of the Hearthside* and *Lyrics of Lowly Life*, respectively. Other-wise, *Candle-Lightin' Time* shared the qualities of its illustrated predecessor, *Poems of Cabin and Field*, in being thin (the prior book had only eight poems, and this one only nine) but also in doubling down on presenting dialect poems as the window to a photographic realism of African American life and race relations.

A review of *Candle-Lightin' Time* in the December 1901 issue of *Southern Workman* captured well the irrepressible public admiration for Dunbar's use of dialect: "we are especially glad that he has since devoted himself entirely to dialect writing—especially in his verse," the reviewer wrote. "It's not that he can't do the other thing"—that is, write poems in formal English—"but that his white brother can't do this; at any rate not anything like so well." Other reviewers echoed this satisfaction. Never should Paul, in another example, be "tempted away from the homely, familiar path of poetry which he walks with assured tread," admonished one satisfied reviewer.[3]

Equally compelling were the photographs that accompanied the poetry. Pictures and verses together enabled Paul to paint once again a multidimen-sional portrait of African American life. The written word imbued the real-world images of African Americans with poetic language. In turn, these images layered material, visible realities onto the vernacular style and themes communicated by poetic language. The power of the illustrations offset the literary deficiencies of *Candle-Lightin' Time*, which, although not among his best work, all the same had the promise of being among his most memorable.

Paul let the world know how far his commercial fortune had taken him in life. This reality fueled the gist of his essay "Negro Society in Washington," which circulated in the *Saturday Evening Post* a couple of weeks before Christmas in 1901. The article extended the observations on African American life in the District of Columbia that he had recorded and published a year earlier in "Negro Life in Washington." In that earlier essay (published in the January 13, 1900, issue of *Harper's Weekly*), he had laid out less a coherent argument than a string of observations, with the core claim that "negro life in Washington is a promise rather than a fulfillment." He told the story of "the old black mammy," attracted to the city for its status as "the Mecca for colored people, where lay all their hopes of protection, of freedom, and of advancement," only to continue navigating the streets in the same fashion in which she arrived: "penniless, trundling her baby-carriage, a historic but pathetic figure." For Paul, "the pleasure and importance" of African American life in Washington struck him as overrated in its dignity and drama. But the commercial enterprises and the individuals with degrees in higher education abounding within the city demonstrated that "it is worthy of note for the really excellent things which are promised."[4]

The subsequent essay, "Negro Society in Washington," was a more "intimate" perspective on what he and fellow African Americans in elite circles "dignify by the name of society." He looked at the exclusive insularity of such society; the interpersonal tension between and among cliques; the divide between this class and the lower economic classes, such as domestic laborers; and the cultural vibrancy—the dances, the literature, the music—for which African American high society came to be known. No region in the country could claim to have as omnipresent a "Colored Sassiety" as Washington, D.C. Coteries of people with academic degrees from the Ivy League and other prominent institutions of higher learning populated the city. So meritorious and accomplished were his Washington, D.C., folks that "you will not find any particular racial stamp" upon their "pleasure-making," as in the case of an opera that a musical society presented, or of various social teas featuring discourses on the nature and criticism of art. More than anything else, when taken together, Paul's two articles on these socialites turned out to be self-serving: they publicized the exclusive circles to which he had now ascended.[5]

———

In contrast to the previous three novels, Paul dedicated the entire storyline of his fourth to African American life and the North, although he would likewise devote it to the genre of literary naturalism that had characterized his first novel, *The Uncalled*, which depicts how environmental forces can threaten individual agency. Indeed, the new novel considers the themes of corruption, hypocrisy, and duplicity; at the same time, it defies the popular genre of plantation fiction to which his readers were accustomed in their encounters with African American characters in short stories and novels. In sophisticated, nuanced ways, Paul illustrates the personal choices, local circumstances, and nationwide realities of racism, migration, and the rampant criminalization of African American behavior at the turn of the century.

In the new novel, we learn that Berry Hamilton, an honest and caring former slave, is falsely accused of stealing. Despite this allegation, he has faith that his old master, Maurice Oakley, aware of his history of integrity, would trust him. But when Oakley falsely convicts Hamilton and sends him to jail to save his own brother, who also happens to be the real thief, the community shuns Hamilton and his family. The remaining Hamiltons—the wife, Fannie, and the two children, Joe and Kitty—move to the urban North. Not unlike the realities of the Tenderloin district of New York City that Paul himself had experienced and even enjoyed in years past, the city seduces the children, who symbolize the younger generation of African Americans declining in moral character. Eventually, a diligent reporter proves that the father is in fact innocent, triggering his release. Be that as it may, Berry Hamilton cannot restore the dignity of his reputation. Ultimately, he and his wife move back to the Oakley plantation, where his former master has gone insane. Hand in hand, the couple overhear shrieks of madness and, in a sense, wait for the gods to finish their cruel sport.

In fall 1900 Paul had sent this 40,000-word story to Paul Reynolds to vet the quality. *Lippincott's* had commissioned it, and he was less than certain whether it was strong enough for them to publish it. "I am not sure, however, whether they will accept it or not," he admitted, "and this copy I will send you to look over and give me your opinion whether there is any chance of its serial or book publication in England." The exercise of trying to get published was never easy for Paul. But he was prolific and relentless, a combination he leveraged whenever he could to increase his chances. Whereas Paul had written to Reynolds only a couple of times beforehand (with submissions of *Folks from Dixie* and *The Uncalled* for his commercial assessment), in the year 1900 alone he corresponded with him close to twenty times; and the following year, more than twice that amount, with consecutive letters at times separated by only a couple of days. Indefatigable was Paul's persistence in trying to get his work placed in the right venue and at the right price.[6] Plus, given that, in his view, his "voice has failed," he had started giving fewer and fewer poetry recitals to earn income. "Yes, I find that my pen yields me a support," he would soon tell an interviewer, with a tinge of resignation.[7]

Until the middle of summer 1901, Paul was mulling how he could maximize his new novel's sales. As in the case of his previous novel, *The Fanatics*, he initially had high hopes, but he wanted to ensure the pricing model enabled him to earn money on both the front and back ends of the novel's commercial life. "What I should prefer to do would be to follow the plan that has been followed by Dodd, Mead and Co," he wrote Reynolds. "Get an advance of four or five hundred dollars, four hundred being the former figure from them, and then a royalty of fifteen percent." Quite a more experienced negotiator than he had been before, his tone of self-assurance expressed a wisdom in securing what was in the best interest of the product, and he expected Reynolds to communicate his wishes to the publisher with comparable persuasiveness.[8]

By summer's end, however, the degree of Paul's inexperience emerged. Only copyright, the way that an author could establish exclusive legal right as literary creator and owner, could ensure his claim to revenue. He was in a bind. "I find myself in somewhat of a mix-up with Messrs. Dodd, Mead and Co," he told Reynolds. "They have learned through Jarrold and Sons of London" that the right of the novel had been "offered to them, and forgetting their former terms to let the novel go to *Lippincott's*, want to arrange for its publication." Paul had been loyal to Dodd, Mead, and they in turn had been instrumental to his literary success. Working with the publisher under these circumstances made him uncomfortable, and he preferred not to burn the professional bridge. He had been dragging his feet. "I shall have to make an immediate answer to their letter which is now a week old," he wrote Reynolds, whom he wanted to investigate a solution. Dodd, Mead agreed to publish the book the following year, in the spring.[9]

Once again, when the matter of Paul's publication arrangement with Dodd, Mead, arose, he was hands-on. The book contract for the novel a "good deal puzzled" him. Not only did Reynolds send only one copy to him, rather than two—which customarily would include one for him to keep for his own records, the other to return to his agent, signed—but oddities riddled the text. "Section 3 says that the copyright shall be vested in the publisher. This has not been done before," he worried. The royalty schema also bothered him. "Neither do I understand part of the matter written in nor the counting of thirteen copies as twelve in the reckoning of royalties. The whole agreement is very puzzling to me, and I am unwilling to sign it without further elucidation." Paul was adamant that the contract disempowered him. Dodd, Mead initially even wished to retain the authority to release the book "at any time." Paul regarded that stipulation as unfair, given that the language was written to impute the copyright to the publisher, not to him. He refused to move forward until the contract was improved.[10]

Paul was willing to alter the title if doing so would attract readers. He proposed four titles that captured the storyline's fatalism: *The Jest of Fate, The Downward Way, The Weakest of These,* and *When the Gods Laugh.* "If these names do not suit ask them to choose a title of their own." None suited. As 1902 progressed, *The Sport of the Gods* became the title of choice.[11]

For all the critical appreciation Paul earned for the literary progress he had made in *The Fanatics,* by most accounts *The Sport of the Gods* signaled his crowning achievement as a novelist. Disparate reviewers achieved almost telepathic agreement that it was "a novel of the new Negro," or of racial uplift: the book "takes up the Negro where Harriet Beecher Stowe left him in slavery" and seeks "to awaken interest in his own people." Paul restricts *The Sport of the Gods* to the arena of African American life that previous readers of *The Uncalled* and *The Fanatics* bemoaned that he had left behind, but in doing so he struck a balance. Not only had he transcended the popular genre of so-called southern darkey dialect into which his fiction, as well as his verse, had often been cast. Apparently, he had taken strides in attaining a quality of creative writing that hitherto had eluded his grasp or that, in retrospect, he had been wrongfully denied. "This is by far the strongest and best fiction from a pen noted for its humor and pathos," raved one critic. Further, the novel "shows that this author can write good prose as well as excellent poetry," noted another. One went so far as to proclaim that the novel "has strength, vigor, timelessness and above all a suggestive purpose that lifts it above its class." Finally, Paul had garnered the praise for which he had so longed.[12]

By the time *The Sport of the Gods* was released, Paul had achieved a stature that foretold the proverbial crisis that came with his being an intellectual leading the masses. With each publication of an essay about the social divide between the upper and lower classes of African Americans, not unrelated to his personal observations on racial uplift and the privileges of elite circles, Paul's tone and theme grew ever more elitist. The condescending tenor of "England as Seen by a Black Man," "Negro Society in Washington," and "Negro Life in Washington" reached its rhetorical crescendo in "The Negro as an Individual." Published in a fall issue of the *Chicago Tribune* and in the same year as *The Sport of the Gods*, this latest article identified "a positive lesson for a race that has in the years of its freedom been attempting to lift its masses to a level of a people with a couple of thousand years the start of them": the "exaltation of the individual," "the bringing out of the few bright lights among us, and they are few, to cast some gleam into the darkness that surrounds the masses."[13]

Evidence of the progress of Paul's race, in other words, should not focus on the multitude of those who are struggling and stumbling through life. Rather, the handful of those "who walk with calmer steps near to the heights" represent the "value of individual success." In a story he then told about why certain white boys were willing play with a certain black boy, he pointed out that the latter was "colored," not "a nigger." Paul left unchecked the way this logic denigrated other, less acceptable black boys while sanctioning the language of white supremacy. Most important was how exceptional character and accomplishment could distinguish the individual among the masses and dignify that person as a synecdoche of racial progress. Paul was disclosing a truth he applied to himself and other African American leaders in society like him: to be among "the few bright particular stars which may be held up as beacons for the whole race."[14]

———

Temptations returned. A couple of weeks into 1902, in Charleston, South Carolina, Paul wrote Alice that, perhaps, he indeed had been a bad boy. Calling himself "Yours Lonely," he admitted to having gotten "in somewhere about two o'clock this morning." Six and a half hours later, he woke up to have coffee in bed, only to return to "his infant slumbers," later awaking only thirty minutes before noon. Not only did his tardy return home exhaust him; questionable conduct, just short of sin, sapped his energies. First, he was gambling. "The occasion of my staying out was a man's card party where I was impolite enough to 'clean up' at euchre." Over the next couple of days he looked forward to attending a reception for him but also to even more gambling, "a card party" on Friday night.

Compounding Paul's temptation to gamble—and, presumably, during this activity, to drink until inebriation—was the temptation of women. As before, he blamed his behavior on the women, not on his own indiscretion. "As usual, I am being much petted, spoiled and bewomaned," he told Alice, "though the princip[al] woman is old & motherly, & the rest are not dangerous. They sit calmly at the table & discuss what they call my perfect form, my hands or my feet and I have to look like a rock." Once again, he expected her to tolerate his tales of lust during their time apart. Whether he truly delighted in regaling Alice about being desired to make her jealous, or simply was transparently disclosing the full range of his conduct, good or ill, little evidence showed that he self-consciously assessed and addressed the long-term impact of his words and acts of indiscretion on her and their marriage.[15]

The first hint of concern, possibly of guilt, was Paul's protest one day after his confession that Alice did not reply to him promptly enough. "What is the matter that you do not write to me? You must be having a very good time that you cannot drop me even a card." He couched his complaint with a threat that he would partake once again in questionable activity. "If I do not get a letter by this afternoon's mail, I shall go out and have a time just for spite." A couple of days later, he followed up with yet another subtle jab at her anxieties: "Try to keep well, dear, and be a good girl for I am being a disgustingly good boy. I really feel like a seraph and when the fourteen girls file past me looking at me with silent awe I *know* that I am almost an angel."[16]

———

"Dunbar went home and tried to kill his wife."[17]

Two months after colleagues wrote Booker T. Washington about the alcoholic misconduct of Paul and Timothy Thomas Fortune during the Bethel Literary and Historical Association meeting in Washington, D.C., Fortune reached out to Washington himself. He wrote not about this incident—which presumably was too shameful a story to admit. Rather, he verified the rumor that, among the two, Paul was truly the bad boy, and his misdeeds at other times supported this conclusion. He alleged that Paul's attempt to murder his wife on one fateful night was one of them. The record showed that the day cited in Fortune's allegation coincided with the letter Paul wrote to Alice, postmarked Thursday, January 30, 1902, effecting their separation.[18]

"He left Washington on the 12 o'clock train," Fortune recounted, "and had not been heard from when I left Washington Thursday morning."[19]

Word began to circulate that Paul and Alice were no longer together, but also that the gravity of this separation portended an irreconcilability unlike ever before. "You will be seriously shocked to hear that Mrs. Dunbar and I are now living apart," he wrote one acquaintance, "and the beautiful home I had in Washington is now a thing of the past." His letter subordinated any culpability he might have had for the split. At her expense, he sought to protect his own reputation.[20]

Alice, while still living in Washington, D.C. (but now temporarily at 327 Elm Street NW), wrote to his mother, Matilda, trying to set the record straight. Through the grapevine, Alice, to her dismay, learned that "Paul had said disgraceful things about me down at a saloon on the Avenue, I cried and said nothing, for I was so shocked. Then I got a lot of letters from people in New York, and folks here brought me a lot of stuff that Paul had said about me." Alice complained further: "So you see how much talk and nigger mess I have to contend with." Eventually, she would move away from Washington, D.C., and settle down in Wilmington, Delaware. Working as a schoolteacher, she would resume the career in educating students she had loved and left behind. She would leave behind the "nigger mess," a term she used repeatedly in her letter to Matilda to describe the hearsay that was making even more stifling the social circle she and Paul once shared.[21]

Rumors had long been swirling that theirs was a tempestuous marriage in which Paul abused Alice. One story alleged that he had beaten her years ago, when they had sojourned together in the Catskills. Another accused him of slapping her during the subsequent period of his recuperation in Colorado. And more emerged later from witnesses to his battery of her while the couple lived in Washington, D.C. The latest incident would not have "seriously shocked" anyone familiar with the two. Rather, such people would have expected it if they were also willing to assume that, at some point, she was not going to accept his abuse anymore. To an acquaintance in common, Paul claimed that Alice's recent action to part ways with him contradicted what he believed to be her longtime acquiescence in the abuse—"that he had slapped me in Denver and I didn't seem to mind it then, and he wondered why I minded it now," Alice revealed to Matilda. Matilda knew all too well, based on her own life with her deceased former husband, Joshua, close to three decades earlier, what it meant to leave a tumultuous marriage behind. One could only imagine her thoughts about the reality that her son now bore an even more striking resemblance to his father—and, for that matter, her daughter-in-law

to herself—in succumbing to the vices of alcoholism, violence, and recalci-
trance and dooming his marriage.[22]

A handful of years later, Alice would reflect on that fateful night and disclose why she had had enough. From her perspective, the moral failings of
body, mind, and spirit that she had first noticed in Paul at the outset of their
relationship, which she resented and had been grappling to exorcise from him,
reared themselves once again and pushed her to the breaking point: "He came
home one night in a beastly condition. I went to him to help him to bed—and
he behaved disgracefully. He left that night, and I was ill for weeks with peritonitis brought on by his kicks." As Alice dealt with her ailment—an inflammation to her peritoneum, linked to the rupture of an abdominal organ—her
marriage to Paul came to an end. "I never saw him again after that night."[23]

The beating Alice suffered was not only the acute violence of that night. It
was the accumulation of abuse that she had endured for years and that had
solidified her resolve never to take him back. "I was genuinely afraid of him,
and disgusted too, for this was only a culmination of the misery of four bitter
years." The "memory" of the "happy days"—of his charm, his companionship,
his collaboration, his genius, his dedication of poems to her, his expressed
love—was not powerful enough to overcome the nightmare that was her
marriage.[24]

Despite the conflicting perspectives on what exactly transpired between
Paul and Alice on that fateful night in January 1902, the repercussions were
clear and definitive. In letters he sent her right afterward, he refrained from
calling himself "Hubbins" or addressing her "Dear Heart" or "My Dear Wifel-
ing," the nicknames he used in his previous two letters and whose numerous
permutations dotted his hundreds of letters during their nearly four years of
marriage. Now cold and callous, he wrote her from his new residence on 227
West 33rd Street in New York City, having left her behind at their previous
residence of 321 Spruce Street NW, Washington, D.C. The separation was both
physical and formalized in a January 30 letter, whose language resembled what
one presumably would find in a letter of eviction:

Mrs. Alice Moore Dunbar,

Kindly send to this address what ever clothing, underwear socks
[e]tc[.] you can pack easily. You may pay the rent for this month
as it will take some time for you to adjust matters & leave the
house.

Take what ever of the things you want except ma's, turn them
into cash and store the rest in my name. Store my books, of
course. Separate yours, and take them with you.

Send my things at once.

Paul Laurence Dunbar.[25]

"He is a high class brute," Fortune tried to ingrain in Washington's mind.
So outrageous was Paul's conduct that Fortune was unwilling to commit it to
paper. "I will tell you what led up to it when we meet. His family has left his
home, on the advice of friends, but I do not know their address. I am sorry,
for them, as they are helpless." (Paul had evicted Alice from their D.C. house,
in fact.) Almost a week later, Fortune followed up and addressed Washington's concern with the terse line: "The whole Dunbar business is disgusting
and pathetic."[26]

———

In the couple of years after separating from Alice, Paul's direct engagements
with Booker T. Washington declined, except for two major occasions. In late
spring 1903 he sought to introduce Washington, who happened to be traveling
to Toledo, to his longtime supporter Henry Tobey and to "the most prominent
colored man in town and the most active worker in the State," Charles A. Cottrill.[27] Second, he asked Washington for biographical information so that he
could complete his article on "Representative Negroes"—a request that came
around the same time, also in the first half of 1903, and began a similar exchange with W. E. B. Du Bois about the same project.[28]

James Pott and Company, a religious publisher based in New York, reached
out to Paul early in the year to inquire whether he would be interested in contributing an article to a collection of essays edited by Booker T. Washington
and authored by the leading African American figures of the era. In response,
Paul referred them to Du Bois as a potential contributor. In a side letter to Du
Bois, however, he also could not help but admit, regarding his own main
source of appeal, "they have not mentioned money" in this project. Du Bois
replied that he was "suspicious" of the "scheme" of J. Pott and Co., which, he
felt, was requesting a contribution from each person "as tho' all the rest had
consented." He preferred to "have nothing to do with the matter unless it takes
more definite and tangible shape."[29]

In the meantime, Du Bois was working to launch in the spring a small monthly magazine and trying to secure Paul's assent to be a founding contributor. For this magazine he also reached out around the same time to Charles W. Chesnutt, among others, as he sought to establish an outlet for the "Talented Tenth" that could overcome Washington's stranglehold over the national press about the central role industrial education should play in racial progress. Thus, Du Bois wished to broadcast his own circle of leadership by announcing in the first issue, to begin with, "the cooperation of Mr. Paul Laurence Dunbar." "May I use your name?" Du Bois asked. (Eventually, Du Bois would publish a short-lived periodical called *Moon*, but much later, in 1906.)[30]

After seeking to allay Du Bois's suspicion about J. Pott—"I have had another letter from them also, I think they seem to be in earnest," Paul said—he thereupon requested Du Bois's biographical information for an essay he was working on about representative African American leadership. Coincidentally, both men happened to be working intensively on the same set of topics, at the same time, and even within the same venues. They contributed to what would become *The Negro Problem: A Series of Articles by Representative American Negroes of To-day*, released by J. Pott later in the year. The collection included a variety of essays on contemporary African American experiences, including by Washington (the editor) on industrial education, Du Bois on the intelligentsia, Chesnutt on disfranchisement, constitutional legal expert Wilford Horace Smith on the law, educator Hightower Theodore Kealing on (racial) nature versus (cultural) nurture, T. Thomas Fortune on the perspectival relativism of national experiences, and Paul himself on "representative American Negroes." Elsewhere, in the July 1903 issue of *Booklover's Magazine*, Paul wrote the biographical sketch for Du Bois's essay, "Possibilities of the Negro: The Advance Guard of the Race."[31]

All in all, Paul sought to explain the meaning of racial representation in the United States while also contributing to the media campaigns of both Washington and Du Bois, the premier African American leaders whose ideological divisions would flare up even more once Du Bois's manifesto of essays, *The Souls of Black Folk*, hit the shelves that same year.

———

Close to three months after Paul and Alice's separation, his frustration spilled over into his letter to Matilda. His mother had been asking Alice if she knew of his whereabouts, and evidently she claimed that she did not. That news mortified him. For quite a while Alice had been rebuffing his entreaties for communication. "Alice is such a liar," he said. "Does she pretend not to know where I am, when she is *forwarding* all my mail to me *every day*?" The wedge between Paul and Alice divided her from Matilda.[32]

Nine months after their separation, on the eve of Thanksgiving in 1902, Paul finally reached out to Alice. He wrote her a letter. But the lapse of time apart and the callus that had grown around their hearts impeded his effort. "I don't know how to write to you," he began, after tiptoeing toward her with the address of "Little Girl." "For so long a time there has been in my heart something uncompromisingly hard against you. But I know now that love is above everything and I have just found out what you have gone through." In their time apart Paul had both carried out an eviction and insulted Alice's own mother. No longer a "sickly supplicant" and now "sober," he wrote a letter that came as close to an apology as possible. He never said sorry; instead, he said "I love you." He hoped that these three words would suffice. "That is all, Wifelums. Is it enough—?"[33]

CHAPTER 22

Waiting in Loafing-Holt

This is the last letter I shall write you. I have done every thing to amend my faults, and you have kept a brutal silence. That is quite as you pleased. You have shown my letters and my telegrams, and yet, girl of my heart, I love you. Once more I ask you to come back to me and the future shall make up for a past that was not altogether unhappy.

—PAUL LAURENCE DUNBAR TO ALICE RUTH MOORE
(JUNE 14, 1903)[1]

As Paul's personal life devolved into uncertainty, his professional life flowered. By 1902, he had been shuttling between Washington, D.C., and New York City for two years as his collaborations with Will Marion Cook developed.[2]

With Paul writing the lyrics and Cook composing the music, they had been a productive team. In 1899 they created *Uncle Eph's Christmas*, a show that ran during the holiday season that year at Boston Music Hall. The following year they conceived of *Jes Lak White Folks*, which opened at New York City's Cherry Blossom Theater during the summer, and they co-wrote *Down de Lover's Lane*. And 1901 was one of their most prolific years together, completing *Cannibal King, Czar of Dixie Land, Hot Foot*, and *Possum Am de Best Meat After All*. Some shows never saw the light of day; others rolled out with considerable fanfare. Regardless, each man creatively inspired the other. Paul's success in musical theater helped ease the pain of his failure to place his own dramatic pieces, such as *Herrick, an Imaginative Comedy in Three Acts*, an English comedy of manners that a publisher once called "literature but inactable."[3]

In 1902 Paul and Cook created their most significant show since the Broadway appearance of *Clorindy*. The genesis came not solely from them but from their longtime partners in performance, Bert Williams and George Walker.

About a decade earlier, Williams and Walker had been invigorated by interacting with Dahomeans during their tour through a Midwinter Fair in San Francisco. Since then, Williams had been a voracious reader of atlases and literature about the West African country and the broader African continent. His sensitivity to the misperceptions of Dahomey provoked him to think whether he could rescue "Africans out of the realm of ethnology" and resituate them "into a more meaningful and personal sense of ancestry," according to scholar Camille Forbes. He sought to correct the image of Africans on the stage. This was where Paul and Cook came in.[4]

With a production cost of fifteen thousand dollars, the musical settled on a plot satirizing the antebellum mission of white colonizers to repatriate free New World Africans and their descendants back to Africa. Paul wrote a host of songs to capture the gist: with Edward P. Moran, he wrote "Evah Dahkey Is a King," but he also penned "On Emancipation Day," "Good Evenin'," "Returned," and "Hurrah for Captain Kidd." The musical was titled *In Dahomey*.

In Dahomey premiered in Stamford, Connecticut, in September 1902. Over the next few months it played in the East Coast cities of Boston and Philadelphia and then the Midwestern cities of Chicago, Cleveland, St. Louis, Kansas City, and Minneapolis. At the end of this run, on February 18, 1903, it finally opened on Broadway and ran for a remarkable fifty-three performances. Starting in April, the show appeared abroad, in London's Shaftesbury Theatre, for a span of ten months. Some critics expressed concern that the show did not advance the cause of racial uplift. As one critic in *New York Age* wrote, the "stage is the medium by means of which ideas—whether true or false—are disseminated; where many opinions are molded. The stage will be one of the principal factors in ultimately placing the negro before the public in his true and proper light." Such words were all too familiar to Paul, who knew the specter of racial authenticity surrounding his dialect poems.[5]

The initial appearance on Broadway legitimated not only *In Dahomey* but the performers and writers involved in it. "And Broadway (as any good surveyor can tell you), is the centre of the universe," Walker once reflected. "And in that centre is a smaller centre. And we're in it." That center included Paul. Just as *Clorindy* was historic for being the first Broadway musical (albeit with only one act) with an all African American cast, *In Dahomey* broke new ground for being the first full-length Broadway musical to be both written and performed by African Americans.[6]

The poet from Dayton lent a hand to both feats. Paul's commercial success in both the high culture of literature (poetry, fiction, and essay) and popular culture

FIG. 22.1. Bert Williams and George Walker, *In Dahomey*, with words by
Paul Laurence Dunbar and music by Will Marion Cook (1902).
(Schomburg Center for Research in Black Culture)

(vaudeville lyrics and theater) made him the most ambidextrous professional African American writer at the turn of the century. He became both "the prince of 'coon' song writers" and "the foremost colored literary man of the age."[7]

———

While Alice continued to give Paul the silent treatment, he kept at work and published *Lyrics of Love and Laughter*, which turned out to be as astounding a book of poems, in terms of overall length and freshness, as its slightly longer predecessor, *Lyrics of the Hearthside*. Dedicated to the Impeys, whom he had visited during his tour of England, *Lyrics of Love and Laughter* topped over one hundred poems and was almost entirely new. Attentive readers of his books would notice only a handful of poems that had appeared in prior books; the reprinted poems all came from *Candle-Lightin' Time*.[8] But there was a stark difference in this iteration of what may be called Paul's *Lyrics* series of books: exactly half of the 102 poems in the book were in his customary styling of dialect. In no other prior book of poetry that contained both poems in dialect and those in formal English did he reserve so much space for the former. From the standpoint of his literary choices, the nearly all-dialect poetry books of *Poems of Cabin and Field* and *Candle-Lightin' Time* marked the turning point when he decided to more prolifically meet the market demand for his dialect literature.

As in the cases of Paul's previous books of poetry in which he segregated the poems in dialect from those in formal English, reviewers diagnosed the split personality of *Lyrics of Love and Laughter*. The genre of verse they preferred went without saying. "When Mr. Dunbar drops the dialect and writes in our English idiom the result is disappointing," sighed one reviewer, but the book was redeemed when he went on to say that the formal English poems were "certainly not inferior to the average product of the poets of the present day." Regardless, the reviewer's designation of the "English idiom" as "our" highlighted the fence that Paul could not hurdle: it separated him from the claim to a language into which he had been born, and which, over time, he had come to master more convincingly than even the elder, experienced, and mostly white critics who tended to dismiss him with each book he released.[9]

———

Buried deep inside *Lyrics of Love and Laughter* was Paul's clever attempt to communicate with Alice, given that his letters to her were going unacknowledged.

"The Debt" expressed his regret over the price he continued to pay for what he believed to be his single day of transgression—although, closer to the truth, that day marked the culmination of unremitting violence:

> This is the debt I pay
> Just for one riotous day,
> Years of regret and grief,
> Sorrow without relief.
> Pay it I will to the end—
> Until the grave, my friend,
> Gives me a true release—
> Gives me the clasp of peace.
> Slight was the thing I bought,
> Small was the debt I thought,
> Poor was the loan at best—
> God! but the interest![10]

By mid-1903, Alice was "free" of Paul. By public accounts they were no longer married, although legally they were not divorced. At a loss for words and also aware of his severe disadvantage, he still tried to reach out to her. "I hardly know how to begin writing to you," he started. "It has been so long since I could call you 'little girl.'" He thought deeply about her; he desired her, but he also recognized that she may wish to remain apart: "your freedom is too sweet to give up," he reckoned. He realized how far their reputation had fallen after he met a woman—a friend of Alice's sister, Leila, in Salem, Massachusetts—who knew that they were separated and "sent love and sympathy to the deserted wife!" Staying briefly at 221 West Newton Street in Newton, Massachusetts, near Alice's family in Medford, and possibly thinking that his proximity could ease their reunion, Paul implored: "My God, how I felt, Alice, there must be some plane upon which we can come together. I have been a coward and a dastard but I love you, may I call you wifelums again? Won't you meet me some where and talk it over?" Just as he had during the years of their engagement, he warned her to resist her friends' influence. But she refused to meet with him. Silence was her repeated response to his multiple requests, whether he happened to be residing nearby her family's residence in Massachusetts or her own in Wilmington, Delaware.[11]

Writing almost two weeks before his thirty-first birthday, Paul declared that he had had enough of Alice's silence. She had refused even to communicate with him since their separation a year and a half ago. "This is the last letter

I shall write you," he promised. "I have done every thing to amend my faults, and you have kept a brutal silence. That is quite as you pleased." He beseeched her one last time to return to him—as his wife. "Once more I ask you to come back to me and the future shall make up for a past that was not altogether unhappy." Without her, he was not the same man; she was crucial to his sense of self-fulfillment. He wished to be whole again, hand in hand with her. But he indicated that he refused to wait forever. He would give her a week.[12] Unfortunately for him, yet another birthday elapsed without a word from her.

———

From the early summer after Paul's estrangement from Alice, he had been spending time in Chicago with his mother, Matilda, on 3209 Dearborn Street.[13] In June, he fell into sickness again, with a serious bout of pneumonia, which was reported widely in the news. In due course he decided to move back to Dayton, briefly staying at 118 Sycamore Street, with the hope of settling down someplace more permanently and reconnecting with his roots and friends. In fall 1903 Paul came across a house located in Dayton's West Side, on 219 North Summit Street, at the intersection of Summit and Edison Streets.

The charming two-story Victorian brick house was a public emblem of middle-class status in the turn-of-the-century Midwest. The lot was legendary. Close to a century prior, in July 1807, William King originally purchased the land, with the actual deed sealed by Thomas Jefferson, the nation's third president.[14] Over time, construction bifurcated the land into two lots. Built circa 1887 by the businessman and developer Samuel Chadwick, an eastward-facing house emerged along the easternmost edge of the northern lot, defined by Summit Street; it sold for $330 on January 1, 1894. Nine months later, the entire lot sold for $2,000, including the house and the adjacent southern lot beside it, where a barn was eventually erected along the latter's westernmost edge, next to an alleyway. Since its initial construction, the house indeed had changed owners' hands multiple times and undergone renovations by the time Paul saw it up for sale by the Miami Loan and Building Association.[15]

There was much to enjoy about the design of the land and the house. Sitting lengthwise on its narrow lot, the house was roughly nineteen feet wide and fifty-six feet long; the barn had a smaller footprint, about thirty-two feet wide by twenty feet long. Around and between them were convenient walkways and a patio. Plus, close to three-quarters of an acre of lawn was open for play on the barn's lot. Distinguishing the house's exterior were a roof with

FIG. 22.2. Home of Paul Laurence Dunbar, 219 North Summit Street, Dayton, Ohio, circa 1900. (Ohio History Connection Properties File)

interlocking asphalt shingles and slate shingles for the gable infill; walls bricked in stretcher / running bond; and a foundation of rock-faced plain ashlar (with a rock-faced water table).

The house itself had undergone a few novel renovations prior to Paul's arrival. The rear porch was converted into a modern kitchen and bathroom; the original kitchen, which at first abutted the pre-renovated porch, was transformed into an office. Otherwise, the house was relatively unchanged since its construction a decade earlier. On the left-hand side of the house's face, one ascended the stone steps and crossed the wood decking to the Eastlake-style front door. Upon entering, one walked into the middle of the living room. To the right was the front parlor with a fireplace; to the left was the dining room. Passing through the dining room led one into the office and, beyond that, the rear kitchen. Diagonally across the room was the bathroom, which also marked the vestibule for a walkway down to the basement, which was spanned by three dark rooms—the first for the laundry, the next one for the furnace, and the third for coal.

On the second floor, one diagonally crossed the living room to the stairwell against the house's northern wall, leading up to four spacious areas. Toward the front of the house was the first and largest area—the study, which came with its own closet. Along the southern side of the house were three contiguous bedrooms, each diminishing in size: the first and largest was adjacent to the study, but with only one door it had the greatest privacy; the second bedroom was connected by a doorway to the third; and at this doorway was a tiny stairwell to an attic, where another guest room was possible. The house was roomy, to say the least.

The barn was an attractive bonus to the property. A roof of asbestos shingles covered it, and it was made entirely of wood (except for the concrete foundation). Aside from the typical large spaces on the first floor for horses and their troughs, upon entry a small stairwell led one upstairs to a cozy square room, ten feet by ten feet, that could serve if needed as a second study. It could be a delightfully meditative space if one wished to spend time away from the main house but remain on the property, perhaps amid the silence or the neighs of horses.

After touring the lot, Paul realized that he had to have it. He put down a deposit. Before long it was his, with a purchase price of $4,100. When the deed was formalized in June 1904 with Matilda's name, they became the fourteenth set of owners of the lot in its century-long history.[16]

The Dayton home turned out to be a resting place for Paul's weakening body. (To try and maintain some fitness during his life of largely sedentary work and physical frailty, he owned a five-pound dumbbell for arm exercises.) The house was the perfect place for his personal library, for the many books sustaining his mind. The books spanned the gamut of his interests as a writer and intellectual. They arrived by way of a host of people, ranging from the famous to the obscure, from random authors and fans to acquaintances intimate and distant. They included not only his own books but also those that once belonged to Alice, particularly the ones emphasizing schooling and pedagogy. Other books belonged to his mother, Matilda, who also resided in the home. Books were scattered across the house—in the sitting room with the fireplace; on shelves in the bedrooms; and, of course, in the glass-front bookcase, on the wooden bookshelf, on and inside the desk, and inside the closet of his second-floor study, which he had come to call Loafing-Holt.[17]

In his 1905 book *Lyrics of Sunshine and Shadow*, Paul included a poem, "At Loafing-Holt," which conveyed the physical and spiritual respite his study, "this sylvan, cool retreat," afforded. The poem opens:

Since I left the city's heat
For this sylvan, cool retreat,
High upon the hill-side here
Where the air is clean and clear,
I have lost the urban ways.[18]

Paul had accumulated a "who's who" of political authors in his library. He had collected the writings of Booker T. Washington, all rendering crystal clear the Tuskegee leader's controversial modern vision of racial uplift. He also owned the two 1904 volumes of addresses and state papers given him by Theodore Roosevelt. Washington and Roosevelt also happened to personally inscribe these books to him, with their compliments.

A series of books were given and inscribed by Paul's literary friends. There was *Driftwood*, the 1890 book of poems by Will Pfrimmer, sent to him "with good wishes." There was *Tempe Vale and Other Poems*, an 1888 collection by James Newton Matthews, provided "with the admiration and esteem of his friend." Also, a slew of books he kept as gifts from authors who inscribed expressions of their respect for his work. During his life he was a magnet for personalized editions from fellow rising or accomplished poets, men and women: Mary Berri Chapman, M. A. Merritt Cramer, Caroline "Danske" Dandridge, Andrew Downing, Euretta A. Hoyles, Edward Maslin Hulme, Elizabeth Bryant Johnston, Benjamin Franklin Leggett, William J. Lloyd, James Ephraim McGirt, Carrie Blake Morgan, Benjamin S. Parker, James Carleton Young (also known as Arcadius Yonge). He also possessed such editions from writers of fiction and nonfiction, including H. S. Cunningham, Oliver Davie, Mifflin Wistar Gibbs, Samuel M. Jones, and Horace Judson Rollin.

Thumbing through the books brought Paul much peace of mind in his peaceful home.

Mine are calm and tranquil days,
Sloping lawns of green are mine,
Clustered treasures of the vine;
Long forgotten plants I know,
Where the best wild berries grow,
Where the greens and grasses sprout,
When the elders blossom out.

Young's 1903 "fairy tale," *Fantasma*, captured the tenor and praise of writers who sent their books to Paul. "To the genial and brilliant poet Mr. Paul

Laurence Dunbar, who has added glory to his race and the literature of his country with the homage and admiration of James Carleton Young." Some acquaintances who were not authors sent him books anyway. Publisher Frank H. Dodd sent his regards in Hamilton Wright Mabie's *In a Forest of Arden* (published by Dodd, Mead in 1899). Victoria Earle Matthews signed a copy of Ralph Waldo Emerson's 1847 *Poems*. And Major James Burton Pond signed a copy of Henry Ward Beecher's 1887 *A Summer in England*, the lectures and sermons Beecher delivered in England in the summer of 1886—and edited by Major Pond himself.

The bulk of Paul's library featured books that had stood, or seemed bound to stand, the test of time. At the very least, they were popular during his own time. These were the books he could read again and again, over the course of the day.

> Now I am grown weather-wise
> With the love of winds and skies.
> Mine the song whose soft refrain
> Is the sigh of summer rain.
> Seek you where the woods are cool,
> Would you know the shady pool
> Where, throughout the lazy day,
> Speckled beauties drowse or play?

Ever since his secondary education, Paul had gravitated to classical literature; unsurprisingly, he possessed editions of Virgil's *Aeneid* along with manuals of Greek and Roman mythology; the translated orations of Cicero and of *The Rubaiyat of Omar Khayyam*; not to mention John Bunyan's 1678 *Pilgrim's Progress*. He was a collector of the best poetry from both sides of the Atlantic. His American poets were headlined by the various writings of James Whitcomb Riley, followed by Oliver Wendell Holmes Sr. and James Russell Lowell; while his English poets were William Shakespeare, Robert Burns, Alfred, Lord Tennyson, John Keats, and George Herbert.

Paul's writers of short fiction and the novel likewise spanned the West. Among the Americans, Washington Irving was a favorite, with multiple copies of his books; then there were Nathaniel Hawthorne, Edith Wharton, Frank Norris, Stephen Crane, Ruth McEnery Stuart. Regarding the writers from Europe, he owned quite a few books by Rudyard Kipling, Émile Zola, Alexandre Dumas (*père*), and Arthur Conan Doyle rounded out the list. Finally, he possessed more books by the Scottish philosopher Thomas Carlyle than by any

other author. He also owned books by the Scottish historical novelist Sir Walter Scott (his autobiography), English philosopher Herbert Spencer, and his
very own William Dean Howells (*Italian Journeys*, an 1867 book on being an
American consul in Venice).

> Would you find in rest or peace
> Sorrow's permanent release?—
> Leave the city, grim and gray,
> Come with me, ah, come away.

Paul owned a considerable library of books by or about African Americans.
Above all, he had several books by Booker T. Washington, all released in 1900:
A New Negro for a New Century, Sowing and Reaping, and *The Future of the
American Negro.* Frederick Douglass had inscribed an 1893 edition of his third
autobiography, *The Life and Times of Frederick Douglass* (first published in 1881,
then revised in an 1892 reprint), "to his dear young poet friend," "a man of
whom I hope great things." A formidable literary contemporary of his,
Charles W. Chesnutt, held a spot on his shelves with the books of 1899, *The
Conjure Woman* and *The Wife of His Youth.* Paul also owned *Imperium in Imperio,* the 1899 novel of a lesser-known contemporary, Sutton Griggs. There were
the books of his African American acquaintances, such as Alexander Crummell's 1891 publication of "addresses and discourses," *Africa and America,* and
Victoria Earle Matthews's 1893 "story founded on real life," *Aunt Lindy.* There
were the volumes by African American poets of the nineteenth century:
George Marion McClellan, Albery Allson Whitman, Frances Ellen Watkins
Harper, Joseph Seamon Cotter Sr., Aaron Belford Thompson. Interspersed
among this literature were remarkable histories of African American life—
books on the African Methodist Episcopal Church; the American Sons of
Protection for unfairly taxed African American citizens in Dayton; legislative
documents or conference proceedings on the politics of race relations in
North Carolina and South Carolina; and African American soldiers of the
Civil War.

> Do you fear the winter chill,
> Deeps of snow upon the hill?
> 'Tis a mantle, kind and warm,
> Shielding tender shoots from harm.

Beyond his evident erudition in Western literature and history, Paul's library veered into topics that presumably transcended the poet's natural base

of literary knowledge—truth be told, the autodidactic knowledge of a poor Dayton poet born to former slaves. One book was a background in natural philosophy. Another focused on the American copyright enactments from the late eighteenth century to the turn of the twentieth. A third book exhibited the history of "oriental and classical" ancient literature. Another recorded the life of Frederick the Great, the mid-eighteenth-century king of Prussia. And several more covered, respectively, the mental philosophy of intellect, sensibilities, and willpower; the natural history of caves; and the latest dietetic and medicinal approaches to disease.

The swath of these books likely overlapped with Alice's own. Technical and rudimentary textbooks attended to English grammar, elocution, and rhyming; algebra and arithmetic; on learning music and rhyming; the lexicon of foreign languages; and the taking of entrance examinations for schools to train teachers. (Some books contained Alice's own notations of the place and time of her work as a teacher, in Brooklyn in 1897.) If not Alice's, then these books possibly could have been those that Paul accumulated along the way in his own primary and secondary education, and afterward his autodidactic learning of literature and language. (One book, Joseph Ray and Eli T. Tappan's 1868 *Treatise on Geometry and Trigonometry*, bore Paul's own inscription "Central High School," with his marginalia throughout.)

Do you dread the ice-clad streams,—
They are mirrors for your dreams.
Here's a rouse, when summer's past
To the raging winter's blast.
Let him roar and let him rout,
We are armored for the bout.
How the logs are glowing, see!
Who sings louder, they or he?
Could the city be more gay?
Burn your bridges! Come away!

Centered on the floor of Loafing-Holt was a handwoven Navajo blanket, serving as a rug, with large horizontal sawtooth diamonds of gray, red, brown, and orange triangles against a red background; he purchased it in April 1900, during his convalescence in Colorado. On a wall hung his framed Central High School diploma. Individually framed portraits of friends and acquaintances, such as fellow writers and artists of his time, congested the top of his walnut desk and of his doored bookcases, between and among colorful mugs, wineglasses, teacups, trinkets, figurines, and personal artifacts. A Morris chair enabled him to recline in solitary reflection, his hand not infrequently balancing a cherished pipe among his fingers. A green tufted daybed, which doubled as extra storage underneath, lay a few feet away and was comfortable for napping or resting. He also took solace in his black and gold metal Remington (Standard Typewriter No. 6), which he used on the desks in his study or his bedroom for composing literature but also for writing letters of correspondence. And Matilda could stay nearby, in a smaller though well-furnished bedroom on the same floor.

———

Paul's career in giving literary recitals was coming to an end. Sickness slowly robbed him of the energy he needed to persevere in this business. "Paul Laurence Dunbar Cannot Come," read one *Kansas City Star* headline in fall 1902; word trickled in that he was "ill in New York and cannot fill his engagement," with the hope that the "entertainment probably will be held later."[19] Uneven health of this kind relegated him to a mostly sedentary life. No place enabled him to read and write with greater peace of mind and spirit than Loafing-Holt, especially when his health was failing him. In a letter to an acquaintance, he admitted: "I have indeed been very ill and am glad to be here at home where good nursing and good air ought to do me good."[20]

Separate from trying to sustain the life of the mind, Paul whiled his time away consuming large quantities of alcohol. Dozens of bottles of beer, rye, gin, and burgundy were purchased less for their mythical properties in healing ailments than for helping him fulfill his longtime addiction to alcohol. Accordingly, his funds declined. To his mother he conceded, in fall 1903, "I haven't got $50.00 to my name," and he had fallen behind on paying utilities bills. Deteriorating health meant that recitations and producing more books were not on the near horizon for him. Making ends meet was proving tougher and tougher.[21]

As a public intellectual, however, Paul's irritability with the world did not wane. Of all the essays he published over his career, the one printed in the *New York Times* one week after Independence Day in 1903 was, although brief, the boldest, if the most scathing, critique of racism he had ever inflicted on America. The "fine irony" he laid out in "The Fourth of July and Race Outrages" recalled the address delivered by Frederick Douglass a little more than half a century earlier, "What to the Slave Is the Fourth of July?" on July 5, 1852, before the

DUNBAR & DOUGLASS.

The Greatest Recital of the Season

PAUL LAURENCE
DUNBAR

THE WORLD'S

Greatest Author,
Poet and
Dialect Writer.

JOSEPH H.
DOUGLASS

LEADING

Violin Soloist of the
Colored Race.

Mr. Douglass will lead Foreman's
Celebrated Orchestra.

Under Management Thos. G. Hammond.

PAUL LAURENCE DUNBAR.

FITZGERALD'S AUDITORIUM,

Kentucky Avenue, above Atlantic,

Tuesday Evening, July 9th, 1901.

FIG. 22.3. Advertisement for Paul's recital with Joseph Douglass in Atlantic City, New Jersey, 1901. (Paul Laurence Dunbar Papers, Ohio History Connection)

Rochester Ladies' Anti-Slavery Society in Rochester, New York. Decades apart, both the orator and the poet indicted the hypocrisy of those who admired the constitutional legacy of the holiday but who then trampled upon its extension to people abducted by force from Africa or of African descent born in the United States. At the apex of his address, Douglass proclaimed:

FIG. 22.4. Paul giving a recital at the National Cash Register Company, Dayton, Ohio, January 6, 1903. (NCR Archive at Dayton History)

Standing with God and the crushed and bleeding slave on this occasion, I will, in the name of humanity which is outraged, in the name of liberty which is fettered, in the name of the Constitution and the Bible which are disregarded and trampled upon, dare to call in question and to denounce, with all the emphasis I can command, everything that serves to perpetuate slavery—the great sin and shame of America![22]

With comparable rhetorical flourish and fervor, Paul incorporated the same points of reference in Douglass's address to confront mainstream readers, likewise at the climax of his editorial:

A new and more dastardly slavery there has arisen to replace the old. For the sake of reenslaving the Negro, the Constitution has been trampled under feet, the rights of man have been laughed out of court, and the justice of God has been made a jest and we celebrate.

The fury flowing out of Paul's pen was equivalent to his temper incited by the numerous murders of African Americans in Wilmington nearly a decade earlier and expressed in his essay "The Race Question Discussed." Not just in the South but in the North as well, slavery had been reincarnated as a phantasmagoria of racial prejudice, discrimination, and terror against African Americans—in the form of beatings, murders, lynchings, burnings, and disfranchisement. In contrast to the din of celebration in public was the silence of prayer in "private closets," where those in desperation kneel "with hands upraised and bleeding hearts," beseeching "out to God, if there still lives a God, 'How long, O God, How long?'" The religious skepticism that had permeated Paul's writings was bluntest here; he could not help it. He reserved his spiritual empathy for those who appealed to divine intervention because, it appeared, all else had failed on earth.[23]

As politically vitriolic as Paul may have been in his nonfiction, his fiction and poetry were far less so, despite their emphasis on African American life. Three years after *The Strength of Gideon and Other Stories*, during which time he had published individual stories in magazines and newspapers, Paul released his third collection of stories. Published again by Dodd, Mead and Company in 1903, *In Old Plantation Days*, as he came to call it, in title and content played up what he did best: portray the lives and language of African Americans. The book contained twenty-five stories, nearly all set on the plantation of Stuart Mordaunt. The stories cover the gamut, such as conjure, the banter between masters and slaves, music, the bond between men and women during slavery, as well as the church and folk religion.

The coverage of *In Old Plantation Days* barely amounted to three reviews; still, they attested to Paul's unmistakable skill in painting African American life for all to enjoy. One reviewer even extolled the book as superior to what Thomas Nelson Page, an acclaimed predecessor, had once written. "These are good stories, such as tend to the encouragement of good feelings between races—black and white," one wrote. "Dr. Thomas Nelson Page himself does not make 'ol Marse' and 'ol Miss' more admirable nor exalt higher in the slave the qualities of faithfulness and good humor." Paul stood in rare company, more for the conciliatory type of Negro he depicted than for the excellence of the prose he wrote. And he would take little consolation from the fact that the literary typology and aesthetics of the Negro went hand in hand. The "plantation" elevated the extrinsic aesthetics of *In Old Plantation Days*, even as this theme also ensured the intrinsic derogation of his writing to the lowest levels of literature.[24]

In 1903, *When Malindy Sings* stood in stark contrast to the other book of poetry Paul also released, *Lyrics of Love and Laughter*. Whereas exactly half of the latter book was in dialect, all of *When Malindy Sings* is in this genre. More than that, it proceeded in lockstep with *Poems of Cabin and Field* and *Candle-Lightin' Time*. Once again it included photographs by the Hampton Institute Camera Club, with decorations by Margaret Armstrong, to enhance the effect of the poems, and vice versa, in revealing African American life. (The compensation for the club rose to two hundred dollars, in light of their lasting commitment and good work.) Half of the twenty poems in *When Malindy Sings* he had released before in *Lyrics of Love and Laughter*. Appearing as far back as *Majors and Minors* and *Lyrics of Lowly Life*, the popular "When Malindy Sings" inspired the title of Paul's eighth book of poetry.[25]

Given that *When Malindy Sings* contained only poems in dialect, critics unsurprisingly rewarded Paul with praise. Ultimately, the collection exhibited "the same delightful vein which won Mr. Dunbar so enviable a reputation as a poet of his own people." The book did not exemplify as much versatility on Paul's part as other books of his, such as those that ranged across a more diverse range of linguistic and formal genres. Even so, the absence of negative reviews marked *When Malindy Sings* as one of his more successful books, critically speaking.[26]

———

Paul broke his promise that he would not write Alice again. He made yet another appeal. "Dear Heart, if ever we come to an understanding, it will be now, for I am perfectly with you as I have been all day," he wrote gently. He tried to guarantee what she had wanted: that he would not obsess over past problems but cherish the brighter occasions when they most loved one another. "All day I have talked of you and recalled not the bitter, but the pleasant times we had together and they were many. I am starved for you Trix," he said, uttering his nickname for her, peeling away any callousness that might have been lingering in his address, trying to rekindle what they once had. He was virtually on his knees. "Oh my darling remember just the better part and give me just a word," he begged. "Hasn't the mistake gone on long enough?"[27]

Alice did not reply. Paul fully resigned himself to his separation from her forever. She had not communicated with him for close to three years. With this in mind and a sense of resignation, he sought to collect whatever range of personal items of his that she still happened to possess. To begin this process he enlisted Marie E. Denier, a secretary he had hired while living and working in Dayton. On Paul's behalf, in November 1904 she wrote Alice a letter requesting the return of his possessions. "You will do a great kindness by sending some little personal trifles which are dear to Mr. Dunbar's heart—his walking sticks—one of which he won when but a boy, and the Ridpath's history of the world, with the standard dictionary, which you will be good enough to give him."²⁸

When Alice did not reply, Denier followed up. Not only did she again urge Alice on behalf of Paul to comply with his wishes, but she indicated that their exchange could take a divisive, legal turn. "Mr. Dunbar begs to reiterate his demand for certain things sent for within the past week, and to add to it, his portfolio and first scrap book containing Riley's letter," Denier said in reference to correspondence from James Whitcomb Riley. "These must be sent or his attorney will be authorized to take due action to bring them."²⁹

———

Paul lay at death's door. "Poet Paul Dunbar Dying" read the headline of local newspapers as early as fall 1904. "For five weeks he has been confined to his bed the greater portion of the time at his home," one article stated in the *Cleveland Plain Dealer.* "Consumption is taking his life." It hypothesized ominously:

> It is probable that the voice of the singer Paul Laurence Dunbar, whose writings in prose and poetry have given him a distinguished name as the poet laureate of the race, will be hushed by death before many days.³⁰

Medical experts had urged him to find a better climate, with clearer air and warmer weather. "I have indeed been very ill and am glad to be here at home where good nursing and good air ought to do me good," Paul wrote an acquaintance in October, "but I fear that I am not going to be allowed a chance to stay, as the doctors are crying California, California, even as before they cried Colorado."³¹

The following month, as Paul's health declined, his friends and acquaintances grew more despondent. They implored him to return to Colorado to convalesce—and he was taking their advice seriously. "I was very glad to get your letter or shall I call it a note, and your plea 'Go back to Colorado,' strikes me very near the bull's eye," he wrote to Edwin H. Hackley, once an editor of the *Denver Statesman.* "I am thinking of going back, but I have transportation to California and it would not be by way of Denver." In the end, Paul would never go back to the West Coast.³²

Over the next year, Paul confided his poor health to the most consequential person in the country and, in late 1905, finally received a response. "I am touched that you should write to me from your sick bed," wrote Theodore

Roosevelt, who was especially touched to receive a gift in Paul's letter, and wished to exchange it, in kind, with his own: "I appreciate the poem. As a token of my regard, will you accept the accompanying two volumes of my speeches?" Paul did, and shelved them in Loafing-Holt.[33]

What compelled Roosevelt to give his books—the first two volumes of *Presidential Addresses and State Papers of Theodore Roosevelt*—was a poem that Paul sent along as a sign of reassurance that at least this person, one who had enjoyed unwavering support ever since the president was governor of New York, was still rooting for him.[34]

> There's a mighty sound a-comin'
> From the East, and there's a hummin'
>   And a bummin' from the bosom of the West,
> While the North has given tongue
> And the South will be among
>   Those who holler that our Roosevelt is best.
>
> We have heard of him in battle
> And amid the roar and rattle
>   When the foeman fled like cattle to their stalls;
> We have seen him staunch and grim
> When the only battle hymn
>   Was the shrieking of the Spanish mauser balls.
>
> Product of a worthy sireling,
> Fearless, honest, brave, and untiring—
>   In the forefront of the firing there he stands;
> And we're not afraid to show
> That we all revere him so
>   To dissentients of our own and other lands.
>
> Now the fight is on in earnest,
> And we care not if the sternest
>   Of encounters try our valor or the quality of him,
> For they're few who stoop to fear
> As the glorious day draws near
>   For you'll find him hell to handle when he gets in fightin' trim.[35]

Roosevelt wrote his letter six days before the nation went to the polls to decide whether he should be reelected, on the Republican platform, as president of the United States, or the Democratic Party's nominee, Alton Brooks Parker, a conservative judge, would be elected.

Perhaps more important, Roosevelt wrote it two days before he revealed to the world that he was in the fight of his political life: he had issued a thousand-word press statement through the White House. Biographer Edmund Morris claimed that "[o]ld time journalists had to look back to the 1880s for a political utterance that packed more force." He railed against Parker's accusations during his late October and early November speaking tours that George B. Cortelyou had ascended the administration ranks from secretary to the president to the first secretary of commerce and labor in perfect proportion—again, allegedly—to Roosevelt's "precise intent of dunning captains of industry" to demand their financial support. Parker threatened to leak confidential information from the Bureau of Corporations with damning proof of his claims that, in essence, the Republican National Committee colluded with Roosevelt to extort huge campaign donations from corporations. The White House press release, with the claim that the "statements made by Mr. Parker are unqualifiedly and atrociously false," sought to contain the October surprise, which was on the verge of devastating Roosevelt's reelection prospects.[36]

Behind the scenes, Paul reached out with a poem that encouraged the president amid the political controversy. Likely a jab at Parker and his ilk, Paul assured him that support existed all across the country, despite the opposition: "[t]hat we all revere him so / [t]o dissentients of our own and other lands." This politician was a fighter, and this poet was likewise willing to fight on his behalf.[37]

Roosevelt succeeded in his reelection bid. Saturday, March 4, 1905, was the date set for thousands to converge on the Capitol and the surrounding ten acres to witness him take his second oath of office. Though a couple of weeks remained for him to attend the festivity, Paul anticipated visiting the Capitol and preparing for the arrival of visitors. "A couple of girlfriends of mine from Dayton are coming on to Washington to inauguration," he wrote a friend, as he sought to find accommodations for them. For places to stay there were slim pickings, he knew; the best he could do was reach around for friends and acquaintances residing in a city he had once for several years called home.[38]

Inauguration day was cold. All attendees braced against the wind chill. Even for the president, "a blustering wind tore at his hair and speech cards as he stepped forward to address the crowd," "his silk pince-nez ribbon slapping the side of his face," even as he spoke for only a handful of minutes. Afterward, in the early afternoon, folks congregated toward the easternmost part of Pennsylvania Avenue.

The parade was the most diverse ever. Fellow African American Republicans milled among the Rough Riders and Harvard alumni, Native Americans and Grand Army veterans, in a marvelous parade that lasted well over three hours. Presiding over all was Roosevelt, who reportedly "stood alone in the constant wind, waving his tall hat, bowing, clapping, and laughing."[39]

As a memento of this day, Paul kept a postcard of the inauguration. Published by Washington, D.C.'s P. J. Plant, captioned "President Roosevelt Taking the Oath of Office," the postcard featured a photograph of the exact moment Roosevelt was taking his second oath of office, his hand on the Bible as he was sworn in by Melville W. Fuller, chief justice of the Supreme Court, with men in military regalia in the foreground and a full crowd, standing shoulder to shoulder, behind them. A memorable day, for both Paul and the nation.[40]

———

Except for short spells, Paul could barely write new literature. In 1904 he released what would be his very last collection of short stories. Abandoning the plantation setting of previous collections, the sixteen stories of *The Heart of Happy Hollow* center on the complex, multidimensional humanity of African Americans in a city called "Happy Hollow." *The Heart of Happy Hollow* turned out to be proof that Paul kept "to his own people whose nature he knows so well," according to one reviewer. "Just in proportion as these stories stick with the Negro and the Negro quarter they are good stories," opined another. In this sense of adhering to the script, Paul showed the world why, at the turn of 1905, he was the "foremost Negro author in America." Rare were the superlatives pointing to the universalism of his stories that focused on African Americans. "If these little stories go for anything it is to show that the same heart beats in man's breast whether his skin is black or white," wondered one critic. While at the time it applied to stories about and casting whites, this praise was a rare assessment of those about and casting blacks. For all the angst the commercial marketplace and critical commentary incited in Paul, the application of his stories to all races, even when concerned with a race long debased, was a welcome shot across the bow of public opinion.[41]

Then came *Li'l' Gal*, of which a little less than a third of its poems were new.[42] The rest had appeared in previous books, some as early as *Majors and Minors*. And *Li'l' Gal* appeared as the fourth in the series of Paul's illustrated books, the previous being *Poems of Cabin and Field*, *Candle-Lightin' Time*, and *When Malindy Sings*. If anything, the book marked the emergence of Leigh

Richmond Miner, a member of the Hampton Camera Club since 1900, as the primary photographer for Paul, along with Margaret Armstrong's ongoing contribution as page decorator. Miner helped rescue the project when Dodd, Mead asked in April 1904 for a completely illustrated book within three months, a timetable faster than the previous requests and than what the club was capable of meeting under normal circumstances. The book was finished by the end of the year, and a review in *Southern Workman* applauded the work: "All show sympathetic understanding of Negro character and a decided artistic sense not surprising when one knows that the illustrator was for a number of years the art teacher at Hampton Institute."[43]

Though *Li'l' Gal* did not attract as many reviews as each of Paul's previous books of poetry garnered on average, the ones it did receive were uniformly approbative. One again, he excelled in penning verse that was "the natural expression of the Negro race in its least exalted aspects," according to one critic. Despite his attempts to be taken seriously as a writer of literature, his value remained in this supposedly authentic access to a "race," which he reproduced as "the poetry and inherent romance of the African spirit." By the end of 1904, this reputation had proven unshakable for him.[44]

Lyrics of Sunshine and Shadow would be Paul's final effort to integrate in book form poems in dialect and formal English. With close to eighty poems in total, a little more than three-fourths were new; here, he made a good-faith effort to return to the versatility and originality that had characterized the earlier books of poems in his oeuvre. It stood apart from the other books of dialect poems he published in 1905 and 1906, *Howdy, Honey, Howdy* and *Joggin' Erlong*, which stayed more in keeping with the genre of slimmer books, featuring both poems and photographs, that he had been releasing with regularity.

During a period of failing health, the last two books of poems Paul would publish in his lifetime, *Howdy, Honey, Howdy* and *Joggin' Erlong*, shared an important quality that enabled him to leverage his name and extensive oeuvre of published poetry: almost all of the poems had been printed before. In a career during which he published close to seven hundred poems across fourteen books, 35 percent of these poems first appeared in one or more previous books. (This percentage does not include the individual poems he first published in newspapers, magazines, or edited collections, which would have created an even larger pool of poems already publicly consumed.) The last two books contained nothing but reprinted poems—except for a new one, "Sling Along," in *Joggin' Erlong*—and the included photographs were once again provided by Leigh Richmond Miner of the Hampton Camera Club. The images represented

African American life in the ways that readers and reviewers had come to expect from Paul's volumes of illustrated poetry.[45]

Reviews of these final books differed negligibly from those of Paul's earlier books featuring dialect verse: the "spirit" of his race glowed through the poetry. As one of the final books Paul would publish, *Joggin' Erlong* elicited the kind of reviews that characterized much of the fate of his writings. For one reviewer, the "volume will add nothing to the laurels won by the young Negro poet," so unremarkable was it as a work of literature. Nevertheless, it reaffirmed the popular genre that at once launched and limited his career, as another review unwittingly, but so aptly, stated: "The humor and tenderness of the darky characters and rhythmical quality of the verse are always a source of delight." To readers and tastemakers, they certainly were "a source of delight." To Paul they were a source of damnation.[46]

For what would be the last book dedication of his life, Paul paid tribute to an obscure man. After the consecutive—and, it turned out, the only—dedications to Alice in *The Uncalled* and *Lyrics of the Hearthside*, he had been gesturing mostly to friends he had come across over his career. There was William Cooke Daniels, in commemoration of whose death he inscribed thanks in *The Love of Landry*; Captain Charles B. Stivers, a teacher from his youth and later a good friend who merited recognition in *The Strength of Gideon and Other Stories*; Miss Catherine Impey, whose hospitality in England he remembered upon completing *Lyrics of Love and Laughter*; and admirers like Edwin Henry Keen, George Horace Lorimer, Ezra M. Kuhns, and Charlotte Reeve Conover, who respectively earned tributes in *The Fanatics*, *In Old Plantation Days*, *The Heart of Happy Hollow*, and *Lyrics of Sunshine and Shadow*. However, the last dedication, for *Joggin' Erlong*, went to William L. Blocher. Formerly of the United Brethren Publishing House, Blocher, in Paul's words, "aided me financially in the publication of my first book *Oak and Ivy*." At a time when human mortality was increasingly preoccupying him, Paul recognized publicly the foreman perhaps most crucial to launching his career in selling books. Across the twenty books of poetry, short stories, and novels he published over thirteen years, he recognized, his family aside, only those friends who substantively influenced his life and literature for the better.[47]

Despite being only in his early thirties, ill health, which rendered more onerous the task of literary writing, convinced him, rather fatalistically, that his career was over. At times he mustered up a self-deprecating sense of humor as a salve for his literary ego. "Don't ask me as to the value of verse writing as a financial proposition," he said to Reginald W. Kauffman, associate editor of the *Saturday Evening Post*, in early October 1905. "I have been contemplating for a long while the institution of a pension committee for ancient and decayed verse writers." Paul spun this punch line after a curt response, punctuated by his legendary dialect, to Kauffman's request for his "winter's work": "they ain't goin' to be no work."[48]

———

For three years Paul had been intermittently but severely ill. For the last year of his life, he was critically ill. He could not survive any longer, even as he continued the activities requiring only modest energy, like trying to read, write, and converse with family and friends. Perhaps if only he had returned to Denver. A handful of years earlier, he had recovered there, among the Rocky Mountains, enjoying one of the more remarkable periods of rejuvenation in his life. In his closing days he acknowledged that doctors were trying "to force me back to Denver." But he was disconsolate; he accepted the inevitable. "I am ill and discouraged, and don't care much what happens." He rejected overtures—such as those from his friend Edwin Henry Hackley, an African American playwright, poet, and attorney based in Colorado—to return west. Paul was destined to die where he was born and raised.[49]

Indeed, around 3:30 p.m. on Friday, February 9, 1906, Paul died at his home. The outside weather was clear, although snow was forming near Lake Erie and the northeastern part of Ohio. In Dayton the temperature was well below freezing, making travel throughout the city and the broader region more uncomfortable than usual. A cold front was passing through.

Paul defied the odds, living longer than the initial predictions of his death ventured by local newspapers. Until the very end his mind was alert. According to Matilda, who sat by his side, his last words quoted Psalm 23:4 of the Bible: "Yea, though I walk through the valley of the shadow of death, I—" He repeated the phrase over and again, until his voice dropped to silence. A handful of months shy of his thirty-fourth birthday, his life had come to an end.[50]

Paul's struggles with tuberculosis resembled what most relatives and doctors encountered trying to rehabilitate the sick. Remission came and went, spanning his final years. "Lives were lived in the shadow of the disease," writes medical historian Sheila M. Rothman. Fortunately for him, he did not die while away from home, which turned out to be a common fate for the sick. Congregating in his home, family and friends encircled him with the genuine love or respect that one would expect for a man who, despite his imperfections, grew to be so legendary and honorable that witnessing his last days alive was itself sacred.[51]

Three days later, on Monday, February 12, a series of private and public ceremonies were scheduled to commemorate Paul's death. Despite the high northwest winds of a cold wave passing through outside, the first gathering was held at 9:00 a.m., when his body lay in an open casket at the North Summit Street residence. A couple of hours later, a funeral service was held at the AME Church on Dayton's Eaker Street, where he had been a member since his early teenage years. "During that time hundreds of friends and admirers from all stations of life of both races called and in silent sorrow passed the bier of the dead," reported the *Cleveland Gazette* about the event's solemnity. A "handsome steel gray of the couch pattern," the casket was positioned in the front parlor, with "floral designs surrounding it," one being lilies and lilacs from his idol James Whitcomb Riley, the other roses from his high school alma mater. Pallbearers came from an inner circle of friends and acquaintances. Ezra Kuhns, Dr. Walter L. Kline, and Harry Eckl were high school classmates; Charles Higgins, Edward Deaton, and Adam Hickman gave Paul company in the last months of his life.

At the church, a host of men commemorated Paul's life and career. A reverend read a hymn to open the services, followed by another who led a prayer. A quartet convened in front of the sanctuary and sang "Lead, Kindly Light." Other performers crooned "Far Away," "The Holy City," and "Only Remembered by What We Have Done." Another reverend recited scripture. An obituary was read. A funeral sermon was preached. Another address was given. Henry Tobey, Paul's longtime friend, who worked as a doctor at the State Hospital of Toledo, spoke a few words of his own. Then he read a eulogy provided by the Toledo mayor, Brand Whitlock, who also was Paul's close acquaintance. Mindful that the day of the funeral was also the anniversary of Abraham Lincoln's birthday, Whitlock declared that Paul was "a poet of his own people, and he was this; he expressed his own race—its hum, its kindliness, its fancy, its love of grace and melody; he expressed, too, its great suffering." Going further, in moving eloquence, Whitlock sought to cast the deceased in a wider frame of analysis and recognition:

But without the least disparagement, I think I can say that Paul's range and appeal were wider than those of any other of his race; if they had not been, he would not have been a poet. For the true poet is universal as is the love he incarnates in himself, and Paul's best poetry has this quality of universality. . . .

There was nothing foreign in Paul's poetry, nothing imported, nothing imitated; it was all original, native and indigenous. Thus he becomes the poet, not of his own race alone—I wish I could make people see this—but the poet of you and of me and of all the men everywhere.[52]

The casket then was opened at the church for a final view. This would be the last memorial service in which Paul's body was present for public view. But it would mark the first of several such services, held around the country, in honor of his life and work.[53]

———

Alice did not attend any of that day's funeral services, but she was devastated nonetheless. For years she and Paul had been separated; she had avoided direct communication with him, despite his relentless efforts. Still, she took the news hard.

Five days after his death, Alice wrote to Bud Burns, the longtime friend with whom Paul had reunited when he returned to Dayton. Ever since their time as classmates at Central High School, Paul and Bud had been close friends, corresponding on matters ranging from shared acquaintances and the delights of women to scheduling time together. One went on to become a preeminent poet; the other, the first licensed African American doctor in their hometown. Both men reveled in their respective successes as working professionals.[54]

When Alice learned that Paul had died—and unwilling to write to Matilda, with whom her relationship had frayed during the marital separation—she sent Bud, whom she had long admired, neither condolences nor compassion. Instead, she expressed disappointment—in him. Bud had "promised" to contact her when Paul's end was near, she reiterated, but he had failed to do so:

> I have just been reading over an old letter of yours dated September 1904 wherein you promised me that whenever Paul's illness reached a stage that was truly serious you would let me know. I read it over because I wondered if I had been mistaken or had forgotten what you said; but I was not.
>
> I had rather relied upon you, feeling that you would surely be good enough to send me word when Paul was really ill. So many conflicting rumors and reports were in constant circulation about him that it was hard to tell what to believe. In one letter I would hear that he was ill; in another day there would be a denial from his own pen of anything more serious than a slight cold.

Knowing our home life as you did and realizing how I felt towards Paul you can imagine how I felt when I opened a paper on the car last Saturday morning. Oh, I thought you might have spared me that shock.

I have waited each day hoping that you or some kind-hearted soul in Dayton would write me some little line; or send a paper or say, even a post-card that he was buried somewhere. I know you all think I was wrong—of course, you have a right to your opinion—but do you think I have merited such a cruel course from *all* of you?

Do you know that I would have come to Dayton by the first train had you or anyone telegraphed me to come before he passed away? Do you know I would have liked to look on his face before he was laid away? I may be cruel and heartless as you all doubtless think—of course I have my side—but there is one thing I shall go to my grave unforgetful of—that at the last I was of so small account in Paul's life that not one of you remembered to say to me—He is dead.

I did not intend to write or make a sign, since I had been so served, but when your letter fell from a pigeon-hole in my desk a short while ago, all the pent-up despair of the last few days rushed out for expression. I am sorry that you, whom I had depended upon, failed me at the last.[55]

Alice evidently did not know that just over a year after she had read the "old letter," on November 19, 1905, Bud himself had died of typhoid fever, at the age of thirty-two. In mere months, without his longtime friend's inspiration, Paul's descent was rapid and, it turned out, as inevitable as the local media made it seem.

———

The weather was yet too unforgiving to bury him at Dayton's Woodland Cemetery. During the cold front of February, the cemetery's soil was impenetrably solid. Until further notice, on cemetery grounds he remained in a receiving vault.

At last, the burial date arrived on April 16, 1906. The land had warmed up, the soil loosened and softened just enough for digging.

Paul's final resting place turned out to be adjacent to the main entrance of the cemetery, at the intersection of Woodland Avenue and Brown Street, by the chapel. Unlike the obscure grounds of Potter's Field—located on the cemetery's opposite side, contiguous with Stewart Street, where his deceased sister, Elizabeth, had been laid to rest—the grave of Paul Laurence Dunbar was prominent to passersby, its visible location a symbol of the stature he had attained in Dayton, if not the country.[56]

EPILOGUE

In a letter dated February 24, 1906, Dodd, Mead and Company replied to W. E. B. Du Bois's inquiry into whether it would be interested in publishing a bibliography of Paul Laurence Dunbar's writings. Dunbar had just passed away two weeks earlier, and the longtime publisher of his works was best positioned, one could argue, to commemorate the deceased poet in this way. The publisher regretfully declined. A single, unequivocal sentence said it all: "We are sorry to say that we have no such bibliography made up of Mr. Dunbar's works nor do we believe that a life of him would sell sufficiently well to warrant its publication."[1]

Dodd, Mead would change its mind in short order, although it would never compile and issue that comprehensive bibliography. (One would have to wait until 1975 for Eugene W. Metcalf Jr.'s *Paul Laurence Dunbar: A Bibliography*.) The publisher came to realize that the market demand existed for a reprinting of Dunbar's major works. In 1907 it released *The Life and Works of Paul Laurence Dunbar*, a book edited by Lida Keck Wiggins, Dunbar's first major biographer, and featuring as its introduction a reprint of the essay that William Dean Howells had written to open Dunbar's third book, *Lyrics of Lowly Life* (1896). Not only does the book contain what was at that time, in its own words, the most "complete" biography of Dunbar ever written, a section entitled "The Life of Paul Laurence Dunbar," according to its detailed subtitle, the book also reprints Dunbar's "complete poetical works, his best short stories, and numerous anecdotes." *The Life and Works of Paul Laurence Dunbar* laid the foundation for how general readers and specialized scholars ever since would understand and debate Dunbar's life, literature, and legacy.

We have come a long way since then. Indeed, the year 2022 marks the 150th anniversary of Paul Laurence Dunbar's birth.[2] Over the past century and especially more recently, scholarship has unearthed new details about or writings by Dunbar, shedding fresh light on his complex life and protean artistry; and with an eye on the anniversary, I anticipate even more archival discoveries and public awareness of all things Dunbar.[3]

As I wrote this biography, I myself encountered obscure or published writings by Dunbar and innumerable trivia about him and others within his social circle, and wondered whether this information altered our grasp of him in any fundamental way and deserved more attention on my part. In some instances, this new information turned out to be the ephemeral minutiae of people, artifacts, activities, and events that come and go each day, week, month, or year in anyone's life—a stray note from or encounter with a stranger here, a scrap of verses there, and so on. In other instances, this information did come to signify something greater, something I considered worth talking about at some length. Carefully selecting and telling the best stories that deepen our sense of Dunbar the man, that put his life and literature in their proper perspective, capture the standard challenge faced by any biographer of a subject who has been so widely renowned and well researched for over a century. Due to the historical distance between the turn of the twentieth century and today, some factual details about Dunbar's life still elude even the most scrupulous investigations. "Biography has to explain and examine the evidence," according to Leon Edel, award-winning author of the definitive five-volume *Life of Henry James*. "The story is told brushstroke by brushstroke like a painter, and the biographer often has to say he simply doesn't know—he cannot fill in the gaps. There's so much that can never be known, whereas the omniscient novelist can be—well, omniscient, something impossible in biography."[4]

For a family, like Dunbar's, belonging to the African diaspora, this fateful impossibility of historiographical or biographical omniscience is especially true. Slavery has eliminated or, at the very least, compromised the historical and biographical archives of Africans and their descendants in the New World America of the seventeenth century and afterward. This is why narratives penned during the nineteenth century by current or former slaves, or transcribed by amanuenses on their behalf if they were illiterate, have been so critical to restoring such archives. Slave narratives, according to scholar John Ernest, "represent a body of writing and testimony that was designed to speak for the many, to represent the unspeakable, and to account for the experience of enslaved and nominally free communities."[5]

For studies of America in the long nineteenth century, the discrete fields of intellectual history and social history have demarcated two separate approaches to researching and recovering African American experiences. Intellectual history, on one hand, has implied, among many things, a "top down" documentation relying heavily on stories told by courageous, eloquent, and typically literate slaves. Over time, these stories established a genealogy of

ideas likely reproduced, consumed, and restricted to a relatively "elite" intellectual class. Calling slaves "elite" may seem distastefully at odds with the
historical derogation they had suffered during their actual bondage. But how
else, for example, should we term Frederick Douglass's basking in the glory
of the Executive Mansion on March 4, 1865, the date of Abraham Lincoln's
inauguration as sixteenth president of the United States? In the third edition
of his autobiography, published in 1892, Douglass claimed that "[he] had for
some time looked upon [himself] as a man, but now in this multitude of the
elite of the land, [he] felt [himself] a man among men."[6] Social history, on
the other hand, seeks to illuminate the "non-elite" populations neglected by
intellectual history, to identify those social, cultural, and political patterns of
behavior that unlock the agency and aspirations of a subaltern class of people.
The founding of such academic journals as *History Workshop Journal* and
Social History in 1976, in addition to the 1977–78 commission by the American
Historical Association of essays for the 1980 volume *The Past Before Us: Contemporary Historical Writing in the United States*, instituted the discourse of
social history for scholars.[7]

The systemic puzzle especially borne by the study of nineteenth-century
African American subjects, therefore, can compound the standard biographer's challenge of distinguishing between what is knowable versus what
is not. At times, there may be a methodological need to bridge intellectual
history with social history on behalf of illuminating the recesses of African
American biography and historiography.

Telling the story of Dunbar's life in terms of his parents, Joshua and Matilda,
for example, requires defining the life of a modern creative writer in light of
the lives of those, as slaves, once regarded as premodern, incapable of creativity, and disqualified from participating in the culture and polity of representative democracy. When Thomas Jefferson claimed in his 1787 *Notes on the State
of Virginia* that the poems of "Phyllis Whately [*sic*]" are "below the dignity of
criticism," and that the literature of Ignatius Sancho, a fellow black writer of
Wheatley's generation, also lacks "reason and taste" and, "in the course of its
vagaries, leaves a tract of thought as incoherent and eccentric as is the course
of a meteor through the sky," he was connecting literary aesthetics to political
philosophy: reason and imagination were prerequisite to the induction of any
society of individuals into the early American polity. This thesis disqualified
the African diaspora from American emancipation and citizenship, not merely
from the canon of American literature.[8] For all their lives, Joshua and Matilda
Dunbar evidently never attained the exceptionally high degree of literacy and

literariness of their son, but their own lives, once obscure, have been collaterally spotlighted within the encompassing glow of his literary celebrity.

Dunbar never wrote a memoir focused on special moments in his life; nor did he write a wide-ranging autobiography about his whole life. Nor, finally, do we have evidence that he kept a diary, although he did keep a cryptic journal of miscellanea.[9] Certain canonical African American writers of the nineteenth century and early twentieth century, including Olaudah Equiano, Harriet Jacobs, William Wells Brown, Frederick Douglass, Booker T. Washington, and W. E. B. Du Bois, did write and publish personal narratives or had legacies buoyed by the posthumous publication of original or revised editions of these narratives. Unlike these writers, Dunbar did not employ the autobiographical word to help orchestrate his public relations and self-representation. (A diary, if published, could have substituted for a standard autobiographical narrative, but it likely would not have been as conscientiously rhetorical or public facing in trying to shape the opinion of readers, since the readership presumably was imagined to be the private self.) Consequently, bridging biographical gaps within his family, or those gaps from Dunbar's family to previous generations, required corroborating and correcting information based on his literary writings, contemporaneous accounts of his life by individuals and the media, and his letters of correspondence.

For this book, I analyzed and refer to close to one thousand pertinent letters, along with additional materials from scrapbooks, held in the Paul Laurence Dunbar Papers of the Ohio Historical Society, in addition to the papers of his contemporaries held in other archives and special collections. Microfilmed across nine rolls, the Dunbar Papers include about ten thousand items dated between 1873 and 1936. The papers include the full collection owned by the Ohio Historical Society; the papers of Alice Dunbar-Nelson, provided by her niece, Pauline A. Young; and the private correspondence between Dunbar and James Newton Matthews, donated by the heir Courtland Matthews. The Dunbar Papers also include photocopies from special collections held at twelve academic libraries or research institutions.[10]

By accounting for previously published letters by, to, and about Dunbar, I was able to document the psychological and emotional ebbs and flows of his courtship of, marriage to, and separation from Alice Dunbar-Nelson. I was also able to trace his personal relationships with extended family and friends during his youth; with critics and patrons, intellectuals and politicians; and with the professional acquaintances of editors and publishers. Mindful of the historical forces that shaped him, I consulted, where possible, previous biographies of Dunbar, or scholarship with extensive biographical information, in which actual sources and information are verifiable, including the work of Lida Keck Wiggins, Rubie Boyd, Benjamin Brawley, Virginia Cunningham, Addison Gayle Jr., Eugene Wesley Metcalf Jr., Felton O. Best, and Eleanor Alexander.[11] I also traced the cameo appearances of not only Dunbar but also members of his social networks in the recent biographies of his contemporaries, including the brothers Orville and Wilbur Wright, Theodore Roosevelt, Frederick Douglass, Booker T. Washington, Ida B. Wells, and W. E. B. Du Bois.[12]

A remarkable detriment to previous biographical overviews of Dunbar's life, however, is their reliance on unverifiable myths that have accumulated in the century or so after his death. (However, the earliest biographies, which sometimes rely on hearsay—such as those of Lida Keck Wiggins, Benjamin Brawley, and Rubie Boyd—benefit from the proximity of their authors with Dunbar's actual relatives and acquaintances, if not also with the subject himself right before his death.)[13] To strengthen the factual and bibliographical rigor of the stories I have told about Dunbar's life, I consulted and cited as much as possible his actual private letters of correspondence, even if doing so forced me in this book to downplay or diverge from the more compelling or sensational hearsay in Dunbar lore.[14] In the meantime, I also sought to reconcile conflicting data or testimonies I had encountered as unresolved or discrepant in previous biographical accounts of Dunbar. For example, I sought to achieve greater accuracy on the date of Joshua Dunbar's birth, which I have narrowed to the window of early to mid-1816. Similar to the problem of birthdates of other slaves during his time, Joshua's has been compromised by slavery's destruction of the archives, or the demographic blind spot slavery wrought through the census, in which slaves were only tallied or enumerated without names.

Given how prolific Dunbar was in publishing and reciting literature during the last decade and a half of his life, choosing the individual poems, songs, essays, and examples of fiction worth examining or showcasing is a difficult task. An enumeration of the output and range of his writings and performances illustrates this point. By the release of his twelfth book of poetry—that is, not including his thirteenth, *Howdy, Honey, Howdy* (1905),[15] and fourteenth, *Joggin' Erlong* (1906), both of which included mostly reprints of poems released earlier—he had already published over 400 individual poems in newspapers across the country, resulting from the exponential growth of his circulation and syndication of poems after his career as a published poet began circa 1888. By the outset of 1897, he had published over thirty poems; by 1899, over seventy; by 1901, over 230; by 1903, over 350; and by 1906, about 400—the last few years of his life showing the toll of poor health on his literary productivity and commercial activity. (All in all, he published about 435 brand-new poems across his fourteen books of poetry, if one sifts out the reprinted poems that these books accumulated as his career progressed.) Still, the wide geography of his literary circulation was unparalleled by any other African American writer of his time. He placed poems in local, regional, and national newspapers and magazines that appeared across swaths of the Midwest, along the opposite coastlines of the United States, and in England (especially during his months there in 1897 and in years afterward). As the most accurate measure of his commercial footprint, Dunbar's publications of poems across his career exceeded those of any other genre (such as fiction, nonfiction, and drama) in which he experimented. That he also published in these other genres while performing in recitals, staging librettos, and giving speeches further attests to the commercial scale of his energetic literary writing.

By the time Dunbar traveled to England, which marks the high point of his literary celebrity, he had begun to curate a portfolio of poems and even some fiction to recite before enthusiastic audiences. Whether in America or abroad, for his recitals he paid visits to various denominational churches; to historically black schools; to homes for elderly colored women; to theaters; to the conferences of literary, historical, or political associations. Not infrequently, his lyrics were buttressed by the musical accompaniment of fellow African American artists, including violinist Joseph H. Douglass, vocalist Lola Johnson, and pianist Beatrice Warwick. His attraction of large audiences in Newark, Rhode Island; Washington, D.C.; and Norfolk, Virginia, among other venues in the United States, were newsworthy, comparable to how the very advertisements of his readings amounted to hyperbolic celebrations of his historic arrival. An African American writer of his stature came only "once in a life time," according to one ad; his show was destined to be "the greatest recital of the season," given by the era's "greatest author, poet, and dialect writer," said another. For a long time his stardom as a reciter was commensurate with his stardom as a writer.[16]

The lyric, of course, should be regarded as the true bread and butter of Dunbar's versification, as the traditional form of poetry with which he felt most comfortable experimenting over his career, a fact so obviously telegraphed by its appearance in the titles of four (or nearly a third) of his books of poetry, *Lyrics of Lowly Life* (1896), *Lyrics of the Hearthside* (1899), *Lyrics of*

Love and Laughter (1903), and *Lyrics of Sunshine and Shadow* (1905). Yet, like many renowned poets of his time, he also interwove grand poetic forms and themes through his verses. At times he was strict, such as in his canonical use of the sonnet ("To Dr. James Newton Matthews" and "Harriet Beecher Stowe"), rondeaux ("We Wear the Mask" and "Not They Who Soar"), and ballad ("A Border Ballad" and "The Haunted Oak"), among other forms.[17] He was not shy about alerting his acquaintances to his dalliances with such poetic forms. In late 1893 he shared with an early patron, James Newton Matthews, a "couple of Rondeaux," the poems "Not They Who Soar" and "'Twixt Smile and Tear." A handful of years later, in an early 1898 letter, he said to Alice, his "Dear Little Lady-Bird," "I had already written two little bits for you and to you, a sonnet and a Rondeau," referring, respectively, to "Sunset" and, once again, the rondeau "Not They Who Soar."[18]

More often than not—indeed, in countless cases, worthy of comprehensive and rigorous scholarly analysis in the future—Dunbar took liberties with traditional rhyme schemes, experimenting with or straying from them for the purposes of literary expression, social commentary, or both. Margaret Ronda, for instance, has shown that the "georgic" resonances of poems in Dunbar's *Lyrics of Lowly Life* (1896) capture "his most incisive thinking about the hardships of African American life in the post-Reconstruction era," insofar as these poems focus, albeit rather pessimistically, on the burden and suffering of African American labor without the hope of civic redemption, such as recognized citizenship.[19]

Dunbar also leaned on the ballad, which served multiple purposes for him. On one hand, the ballad was a specific genre shared by the Fireside Poets, including John Greenleaf Whittier, Oliver Wendell Holmes, William Cullen Bryant, Henry Wadsworth Longfellow, and James Russell Lowell, with whom one can readily associate Dunbar, beginning with his archetypal *Oak and Ivy*. On the other hand, as Virginia Jackson has shown, the ballad also enabled Dunbar to tell the story of Reconstruction's aftermath. The poem "The Haunted Oak," in Jackson's words, is one example of how his "work marked a key moment in the creation of poetry's modern life form," which was "forged in the intimate relation between post-romantic fictions of poetic address, late-nineteenth century ideas of the ballad, and the racism that continues to haunt American poetics from root to branch."[20] Against the backdrop of this biography, my hope is that the hundreds of poems Dunbar wrote in the wake of Reconstruction attract in the future a rich, widened perspective on his versatility as a literary intellectual and artist.

Despite the plethora of poems Dunbar published across his career, it remained a temptation in this biography for me to showcase—or, literally, to reprint at length—poems that are widely regarded as longtime public favorites. (Truth be told, mine is the classic rondeau, "We Wear the Mask.") From a more cynical perspective, I suppose, there could be a more collective desire to highlight those poems by which audiences over the decades, then and now, sensationalized him as the "poet laureate of his race," a melodramatic title that had overshadowed Dunbar's career during his lifetime and continued to do so even after his death, although seminal works of scholarship, published especially within the past fifty years, have been chipping away at this caricature.[21] These poems tend to reify his reputation as an African American writer of dialect literature; of literature depicting themes of race relations or African American life especially; or all of the above. Of course, one cannot ignore the fact that many poems, librettos, essays, and fictions (whether short stories or novels) in his oeuvre complied with this description. Across his life, the poem Dunbar recited most frequently before public audiences was "The Party," the same poem that so inspired William Dean Howells that, in his influential and widely quoted *Harper's Weekly* book review, he lauded it and other dialect poems in *Majors and Minors*, a book that turned out to be a fountain of other poems Dunbar recited on a regular basis, including "The Poet and His Song," "When Malindy Sings," and "When de Co'n Pone's Hot." I have excerpted and discussed these poems in the biography.

However, to focus only on these kinds of poems—or on such fiction as "Mt. Pisgah's Christmas 'Possum," from Dunbar's 1898 collection of short stories *Folks from Dixie*, also a staple of his recitals—would neglect how evenly balanced his oeuvre actually was between this overt aspiration toward racial realism and evident attempts to avoid it. For his recitals, he performed some poems noteworthy for their racial subtlety, for example.[22] By keeping a widened perspective on the generic diversity of Dunbar's creative writings, and therefore his versatility as an intellectual and artist, I have sought to highlight the literature he wrote whose value—whether formal or thematic, aesthetic or autobiographical—had gone underappreciated in previous biographies, histories, and criticism of Dunbar. I have paid attention to the extensive array of poems he wrote in formal English—not unlike "Sympathy," in the epigraph of this book's introduction—which have hardly been a centerpiece of Dunbar scholarship to date. More than this, I have pinpointed the literature in which we can discern autobiographical resonances, according to the facts of letters of correspondence or those from historical circumstances, and by which we can narrate either his personal ideas, his response to important moments in his life, or his friendships and acquaintances with others.

Taking such a comprehensive view of his writings positions us to evaluate not only those works Dunbar actually released in print or in recitals, but also those he did not, such as texts that have remained buried in archives of private correspondence or literary ephemera. In their raw state, these texts have yet to achieve literary refinement, much less canonical status. Conducting this wide-ranging kind of research and recovery hews closely to the analytical and narrative conventions of the comprehensive biography. In seeking to harness vast amounts of personal and public information about Dunbar, I have necessarily decided, in keeping with these conventions, to be highly selective and synoptic in any close reading of his literature. The more academic and sustained kinds of close readings that one could apply to this literature—indeed, the kinds I myself have conducted in my own previous books of literary history and criticism—may be found in the informative scholarship I cite in endnotes. In these pages, I have applied such a reading only to Dunbar's first book, *Oak and Ivy* (1893), mainly because it contains the archetypal forms and themes identifiable in the poems he wrote later in his career.

A closing word must be said about Alice Dunbar-Nelson.[23] Given that a standard biography usually ends with the death of its main subject, I likewise conclude Dunbar's story in 1906, shortly after his death. Consequently, I cover only a portion of Dunbar-Nelson's life and writings; more precisely, the couple's irreparable and decisive separation four years earlier, in 1902, marks the narrative moment when her actual presence recedes in my biography. This narratorial decision of mine does not suggest at all that her independent life without Dunbar turned out to be insignificant or uncompelling. Far from it. In fact, she flourished as a working professional and a political activist, and her private life and personality evolved in such remarkable and complex ways that I wish briefly to explain here what this information means on its own terms and what it may imply for a future writing of the comprehensive biography she herself has long deserved.

After separating from Paul Laurence Dunbar in 1902, Alice Dunbar (as she was then called) moved to Wilmington, Delaware, where she lived for the next three decades. From 1902 to 1920 she taught at Howard High School, one of two historically black secondary schools in Delaware; over the next two years she co-edited and co-published the *Wilmington Advocate*, an African American political newspaper. Simultaneous with and after these activities, she organized suffrage campaigns and political action committees and maintained her literary career as a poet, publishing verses in edited collections during Harlem's New Negro Renaissance of the 1920s and 1930s.

Her experiences of love and passion also evolved in special ways. She married two men, Arthur Callis from 1910 to 1916 and then Robert J. Nelson, with whom she edited and published the *Wilmington Advocate*, from 1916 to 1935. But she also enjoyed an intimate lesbian relationship with fellow journalist and activist Fay Jackson Robinson during her marriage to Nelson. Dunbar-Nelson's bisexual expressions of sensuality, desire, and pleasure complicate the staid portrait of herself only as Dunbar's widow or as a woman defined generally by her heterosexual marriages. In the words of her own diary, Dunbar-Nelson remarked that "love and beautiful love has been mine from many men, but the great passion of at least four or five whose love for me transcended that for other women—and what more can any woman want?"[24]

Amid Dunbar-Nelson's flights of ecstasy came bouts of psychological and emotional instability. Insecurity and depression, frustration with finances, and ailments characterize many sections of her diaries and hearken back to the storylines I have documented in her private correspondence with Dunbar. She lived an eventful life, lasting almost twice as long as Dunbar's; she died in 1935, just two months after her sixtieth birthday. Though three decades old, the excellent scholarship of Akasha Gloria Hull and, most recently, Tara T. Green have provided so far the widest and deepest perspective on the life of Alice Dunbar-Nelson beyond her marriage to Paul Laurence Dunbar.[25]

A few confidential thoughts and feelings Dunbar-Nelson had about her life during and after her marriage to Dunbar are transcribed in the diary she started on July 29, 1921. After Dunbar-Nelson's death, Pauline A. Young, her niece, owned this manuscript along with a host of other writings, published and unpublished, that the University of Delaware would later acquire and microfilm as part of the Paul Laurence Dunbar Papers of the Ohio Historical Society. Eventually, Young collaborated with Hull, who received permission to publish the diary in 1984. Through Hull's meticulous review of the archive and the release of Dunbar-Nelson's diary, we see a more nuanced portrait of Dunbar-Nelson. More than ever before, she comes across as vibrantly intellectual and unwaveringly political; as uniquely sensual and unapologetically bisexual; as a distinctive public leader but also a staunch defender and representative of Dunbar's literary work and legacy.

Regarding this last point, Dunbar-Nelson's contradictions should not be understated. Although Dunbar's life and legacy have tended to cast a shadow over her own, while alive she nonetheless devoted herself to warding off disrespectful inquiries into her private life with him and critiquing those who misinterpreted, mischaracterized, or downplayed his literary success and social impact.[26] In public and private, she also admired his mindfulness of contemporaneous political activism and his resistance to racial prejudice. A 1921 advertisement said that she delivered "a series of lectures throughout the country in the endeavor to awaken literary consciousness in her race by showing them the serious side of the literature of her late husband." Eight years later, on the other hand, she bemoaned in her diary, as Dunbar did in his own letters to her, the existence of audiences "who would want to hear dialect Dunbar [his poetry written in 'Negro dialect'] at the end" of her lectures. "Makes me sick," Dunbar-Nelson wrote to herself.[27]

The complexity and longevity of Dunbar-Nelson's social impact have attracted in recent decades a growing academic interest in reassessing the extent that her life may represent a window to African American women's writing at the turn of the twentieth century. I personally experienced this scholarly energy when, on April 29, 2017, I attended the Nineteenth-Century American Women Writers Study Group, hosted by the University of Delaware Library and the Department of English at the University of Delaware, which devoted the entire conference to giving Dunbar-Nelson the attention she deserved. A number of the conference attendees had contributed to an equally remarkable special issue of *Legacy: A Journal of American Woman Writers* published the year prior, entitled "Recovering Alice Dunbar-Nelson for the Twenty-First Century."[28] At long last and without a doubt, Dunbar-Nelson is being recovered despite and because of the long shadow cast by her first husband more than a century ago.

As exciting as this scholarly momentum may be for recovering Dunbar-Nelson's life and work, only the portion of it overlapping the years of her time with Dunbar—between 1895 and 1902—bears the greatest relevance in this biography to illustrate the social, intellectual, and private dimensions of their lives together, including the more strained, tempestuous, and violent moments she survived. (I similarly limit my coverage of the lives of certain members of Dunbar's immediate family, such as his mother and half-brothers, all of whom likewise at some point drifted away from his daily life and outlived him.)

Enough evidence does exist for us to conclude that Dunbar's maltreatment of his wife was objectionable, and that the scholarly consensus arguing for a recovery of her life, literature, and legacy is absolutely right. Dunbar-Nelson's struggles and suffering during her intimate years with Dunbar warranted an unvarnished telling in this book precisely because this is a story that she herself tried to tell. In August 1906, half a year after Dunbar's death, Dunbar-Nelson wrote a letter of such personal self-revelation to Lida Keck Wiggins. In this letter, Dunbar-Nelson disclosed the domestic abuse she weathered under a husband whom, she confirmed, we would now call an alcoholic, or who demonstrated what she once called "a beastly condition."[29] A later scholar, Eugene Metcalf Jr., revealed that Wiggins's hagiographic impulses had suppressed this unsettling story, whereas, more recently, Eleanor Alexander and Tara T. Green have examined the nature and context of Dunbar-Nelson's allegations. Mindful of this information, I likewise sought to account properly for the harrowing stories of Dunbar's irresponsibility and misconduct alongside the canonical stories of his intellectual acumen, professional activities, public celebrity, and racial leadership. Both sides coexisted in the same man.

Fortunately, we have arrived at the moment when multiple studies and biographies of Alice Dunbar-Nelson are appearing in print. This body of scholarship, we expect, would retread the footsteps of Akasha Gloria Hull, yet also chart new paths of archival research and discovery. It would chronicle the world where Dunbar-Nelson lived or wanted to live, the literature she wrote or wanted to write, during the first two decades of her life, before she even read the first words about or from Paul Laurence Dunbar. It would document her life and literature both within and beyond his reach during their seven years together. It would describe her new adventures and challenges as a teacher, writer, activist, lover, clubwoman, and public speaker during the three decades after they parted ways. And it would show how and why she embodied the roles of region, gender, sexuality, class, and racial politics in the identities and innovations of ambitious African American women writers of her era.

I hope that this new scholarship would tell at least these stories and much, much more. I further hope that, despite and because of its inevitable defects, this biography of mine would prove useful to the ongoing and necessary recovery of Alice Dunbar-Nelson for current and future generations.

ACKNOWLEDGMENTS

The literature and legacy of Paul Laurence Dunbar have intrigued me for most of my academic career. I have taught Dunbar to generations of students in universities, and published articles and book chapters about him for scholars as well. But in 2008 I embarked on a new journey: I decided to write a comprehensive and accessible biography of his life. I planned to examine his oeuvre from the widest possible angle, while accounting for the robust debates that fellow scholars had been holding about his work. I also sought to delve into the private realms of his mind and heart. I wished to grasp even more what drove or distracted him, what delighted or disappointed him, what assuaged or angered him, what energized or enervated him—indeed, what made him, ironically, at once an ordinary man and an extraordinary, prodigious talent.

Biography enabled me to achieve these goals. As a flexible genre rooted in storytelling and scholarship alike, it helped me articulate how a complex and, at times, conflicting set of human traits could produce one of the greatest literary minds ever to descend from slaves in the United States. A century and a half since his birth, Dunbar's literature continues to enlighten and captivate diverse audiences around the world. My hope is that telling the story of his innermost thoughts and feelings—of those interior forces that guided his literary pen, his professional choices, and his sense of self amid the sweep of history—could enlighten and captivate readers as well.

My efforts to develop the ideas and language about Dunbar's life faced the inevitable difficulties of biographical research and writing. I needed to track down and interpret the private correspondence that belonged to him or to others who wrote about him; to sift through and correlate the verifiable observations of family, friends, acquaintances, fans, and bystanders; to splice together historical maps of Dayton, Ohio, so that I could, for example, trace the multiple residential moves of his family and, accordingly, his own complicated walks to and from school as a boy; to size up and distinguish the actual clothes he wore as a budding star; to survey and inspect the artifacts, furniture, typewriter, books, and bookshelves he bought for the Dayton home in which he lived for the final years of his life—I could go on and on. Research of this kind always fueled my intellectual exhilaration, yet it just as often could be arduous, prolonged, circuitous, and devoid of any meaningful conclusions.

Fortunately, many individuals, scholarly communities, and academic or cultural institutions generously helped me overcome these challenges to complete this biography. To begin with, I received a Walter Jackson Bate Fellowship from the Radcliffe Institute for Advanced Study at Harvard University in 2010 and a fellowship from the American Council of Learned Societies in 2014. Both sources of funding permitted me to secure time away from classroom teaching and administrative service to conduct research and writing at crucial stages of the project.

A series of outstanding conferences focused especially on Dunbar or Alice Dunbar-Nelson informed my work immensely. "The Paul Laurence Dunbar Centennial Conference," the first major conference of this kind I attended in my career, was held at Stanford University on March 10–11, 2006, and turned out to be both a celebration of Dunbar and, at that time, the first substantive reassessment of his literature, life, and legacy in more than three decades. The primary organizers of this conference have been longtime mentors and colleagues of mine: Shelley Fisher Fishkin, Arnold Rampersad, Gavin Jones, Meta DuEwa Jones, and Richard Yarborough. The conference participants were also insightful and collegial: Elizabeth Alexander, Marcellus Blount, David Bradley, Joanne Braxton, Michael Cohen, Michele Elam, Joanne Gabbin, Adrian Gaskins, Donna Akiba Harper, Jennifer Hughes, Jennifer James, Blair L. M. Kelley, Thomas Leuchtenmüller, Xilao Li, John Lower, William J. Maxwell, Deborah McDowell, Elizabeth McHenry, James Miller, Harryette Mullen, Aldon Lynn Nielsen, Nadia Nurhussein, Yolanda Pierce, Lauri Ramey, Greg Robinson, Lillian Robinson, Wilfred Samuels, Ray Sapirstein, Reynolds Scott-Childress, Amritjit Singh, James Smethurst, Jennifer Terry, Nicole Waligoria-Davis, Kenneth W. Warren, Cary Wintz, and Loretta Woodard.

My participation in a portion of "Paul Laurence Dunbar and American Literary History," a monthlong National Endowment for the Humanities Summer Institute held in July 2015, enabled me to work closely with Becki Trivison, project director of the Ohio History Connection, and Professor Thomas Lewis Morgan of the University of Dayton, the institute's lead faculty member. I also enjoyed the collegiality and insight of the other faculty and researchers who participated, including Nadia Nurhussein, Andreá N. Williams, Ray Sapirstein, and Herbert Martin, as well as the summer scholars who enrolled in the program.

On April 29, 2017, I attended a conference on Alice Dunbar-Nelson convened by the Nineteenth-Century American Women Writers Study Group, hosted by the University of Delaware Library and the Department of English at the University of Delaware. I express gratitude to the following colleagues for their involvement in planning the conference, attending it, or conversing about Dunbar-Nelson's life, literature, and legacy: Kate Adams, Faith Barrett, Denise Burgher, Verdie Culbreath, Anna Mae Duane, Eve Dunbar, Jesse Ryan Erickson, John Ernest, Brigitte Fielder, Pier Gabrielle Foreman, Ellen Garvey, Susan Harris, Rebecca Lipperini, Brandi Locke, Jean Lutes, Laura Mielke, Cristanne Miller, Shirley Moody-Turner, Timothy Murray, Nadia Nurhussein, Jean Pfaelzer, Jennifer Putzi, Rose R. Robinson, Carol Rudisell, Karen Sanchez-Eppler, Bethany Schneider, John Senchyne, Curtis Small, Karen Woods Weierman, Angela Winand, Nazera Wright, and Sandra Zagarell.

While a fellow at the Radcliffe Institute during academic year 2010–2011, I held remarkable discussions with a host of gifted and collegial fellows with whom, in some instances, I have remained in touch afterward: Daphne Brooks, above all, as well as Angela Ards, Nancy E. Hill, Anna Maria Hong, Evan Horowitz, Erica Caple James, Walter Johnson, Shankar Raman, and Barbara Weinstein. Susan Reed served as my talented undergraduate research assistant during my fellowship.

I wrote a large portion of the manuscript while a professor in the Department of English and the Program in African American Studies at Boston University. My English Department colleagues there were brilliant, convivial, and encouraging—most notably, Amy Appleford, Joseph Bizup, Laurence Breiner, Julia Brown, William Carroll, Robert Chodat, Bonnie Costello, Anna Henchman, William Howell, Ha Jin, Karl Kirchwey, Laura Korobkin, Sanjay Krishnan, Maurice S. Lee, Christopher Martin, John T. Matthews, Susan Mizruchi, Erin Murphy, Anita Patterson, Robert Pinsky, Carrie Preston, Michael Prince, Joseph Rezek, John Paul Riquelme, Charles Rzepka, James Siemon, Kate Snodgrass, and James Winn. My colleagues in the Program in African American Studies at the time—Linda Heywood, John Thornton, Mary Anne Boelcskevy, Alison Blakely, and Patricia Hills—also supported my work. Other supportive colleagues at Boston University at the time included Ann Cudd, Jeffrey Henderson, Patricia Johnson, Virginia S. Sapiro, and Stan Sclaroff. Finally, Kerri Greenidge, John Barnard, and Megan Dawley were at the time outstanding doctoral students who served as my main research assistants over the years, while Abhishek Seth was my tireless undergraduate research assistant.

Subsequently, I finished writing the manuscript while a professor at New York University, where colleagues in the Department of English were sources of inspiration and insight, particularly Thomas Augst, Una Chaudhuri, Patrick Deer, Carolyn Dinshaw, Lisa Gitelman, Phillip Brian Harper, Wendy Anne Lee, Elizabeth McHenry, Sonya Posmentier, and Bryan Waterman. In the Office of the Dean of the College of Arts and Science, Amelia Byrnes and Tayllor Johnson provided key support as I managed late drafts of the manuscript. Katherine E. Fleming, Georgina Dopico, Matthew S. Santirocco, and Catharine R. Stimpson were among my dearest colleagues and confidants who supported me as I sought to finish this biography while serving as an academic dean.

The following organizations, institutions, and scholarly communities invited me to deliver lectures, which occasioned crucial feedback for my work on Dunbar: the Hutchins Center for African and African American Research at Harvard; the Department of English at New York University; the Madame C. J. Walker / Frederick Douglass Fourth Annual Symposium at Indiana University–Purdue University in Indianapolis; the American Literature and Culture Seminar at Harvard's Mahindra Humanities Center; the Department of English and the Center for the Study of Race and Ethnicity in America at Brown University; the W. E. B. Du Bois Department of Afro-American Studies at the University of Massachusetts, Amherst; the English Department Colloquium at Stanford University; the Americanist Colloquium for the Departments of English and African American Studies at Yale University; and the Radcliffe Institute for Advanced Study at Harvard.

Parts of my research required that I visit various libraries and archives. The staff at the Library of Congress, Wesleyan University Library, and Harvard Map Collection helped me establish information about Dunbar's historical context and contemporaries. I took trips to Dunbar's hometown of Dayton, where a plethora of facilities granted me firsthand access to his possessions or to materials about his life. The staff of the Dayton Aviation Heritage National Historical Park, which administers the Wright-Dunbar Interpretive Center, generously and kindly addressed my inquiries and assisted me. The staff at the Paul Laurence Dunbar House, where I met and marveled at the wondrous storytelling of Dayton historian LaVerne Sci, were excellent guides through this historic site, which contained fascinating artifacts and paraphernalia for my review. The staff of the Dayton National Cemetery, where Joshua Dunbar is buried, and of the Woodland Cemetery and Arboretum in Dayton, where Paul Laurence Dunbar, the Wright brothers, and their respective family members are buried, provided crucial information about how these cemeteries and the location of these particular plots have evolved over time. I appreciate the colleagues of the Ohio History Center in Columbus, Ohio, for introducing me to archives of Dunbar's materials as well.

In addition to those mentioned above, I have discussed Dunbar in detail with the following colleagues: GerShun Avilez, Shanna Benjamin, Nicholas Bromell, Glenda Carpio, Helena de Groot, Brad Evans, Christopher Freeburg, Jacqueline Goldsby, Philip Gould, Douglas Jones, Judith Yaross Lee, Keith Leonard, Britt Rusert, Gary Scharnhorst, Joseph Slade, Cheryl A. Wall, and Ivy Wilson. I apologize to any colleagues whom I have forgotten to mention here.

A handful of scholars have had the greatest impact on my thinking and writing of this biography—colleagues with whom I have spoken about Dunbar or this biography in a variety of ways and at great length, whether with respect to the strategic narrative arc of the story, the art and science of biography writing, or the factual discrepancies surrounding Dunbar's life.

Early on in my career, about half a decade before I seriously began working on this biography, Shelley Fisher Fishkin inspired me with her prescience in recovering Dunbar and sharpening our discourse about him in the scholarly field. Joanne Braxton, also a longtime leader in the scholarly recovery of Dunbar, personally engaged and inspired me to pursue the project at a time when it still existed at an embryonic stage of development. When I began mapping out the twists and turns of Dunbar's life and of his parents, I spoke at length with Arnold Rampersad, a former professor of mine and masterful biographer who explained to me the nuances of depicting the life of a legendary author. I spent time over lunch with David Levering Lewis and David Mayers, which enabled me to tap Lewis's extensive knowledge about biographical research. While I lived in the Boston area, I cherished my regular breakfasts in Cambridge with John Stauffer, whose erudition about race and American intellectual thought in the nineteenth century, along with his own experience in writing about the joint lives of Frederick Douglass and Abraham Lincoln, guided my own portraiture of an individual against the canvas of history. Henry Louis Gates, Jr. has long kept an eye on my progress in writing this book and provided sage instruction over the past decade.

My longtime friend and collaborator Thomas Lewis Morgan provided unrivaled camaraderie as I worked on the biography. When we first met in a café in Buffalo, New York, we were meant to talk about all things Dunbar, and have done for the two decades since. Over the years, I have enjoyed working with him to recover and reevaluate Dunbar's work, as well as spending countless hours talking with him about the minutiae of Dunbar's life and literature.

Wendy Strothman agreed to be my literary agent at a time when this biography was barely a book proposal. Her faith in this project helped sustain my effort in completing it.

Ever since this biography was contracted by Princeton University Press in 2010, notes about it, I presume, have passed across the desks of multiple acquisition editors. Of all of them, I must reserve my greatest praise and gratitude for Anne Savarese, the press's executive editor for books about literature. Anne always paid attention to my progress on the manuscript, both before and during the Covid-19 pandemic. Her gentle prodding and clear-eyed focus on the completion milestones were crucial as I was fulfilling my substantial academic responsibilities as a department chair and academic dean across multiple universities. Her careful stewardship of the editorial process, her promptness, and her wisdom have been a godsend. The anonymous peer reviewers solicited by the press provided incisive comments and critiques of the manuscript. And the final leg of the manuscript's production depended on the experienced oversight of Ellen Foos and the editorial acumen of Daniel Simon.

My parents and brothers have been my tireless advocates. Almost every month since I started writing the biography more than a decade ago, my father would ask me "How's Dunbar?" almost whenever I spoke with him. I am glad to have reached this day to reply, at last, "Dunbar's done." And I will always cherish the warm embrace and encouragement of the Boynton family.

My wonderful children, Nyla, Noah, and Nadia, always considerately accommodated me when they saw me working on this book. They continue to motivate me to be a strong, resilient father in the face of all challenges in life.

Last but never least, Renée Boynton-Jarrett has been the bedrock of my life and family. When I first came across Dunbar's curious first novel as an undergraduate at Princeton University, she was my classmate there, lovingly by my side. And as I completed the final sentences of this book, she never wavered in being my unrelenting champion. My great regret is that I so immersed myself in this biography that an eavesdropper could reasonably have mistaken Paul Laurence Dunbar as an actual person who lived in our household. But Renée never failed to anchor me to the real world of our family's wonderful life. She inspired me to be bold, to try to achieve something great, in writing this biography, as much for my personal and intellectual growth as for telling a remarkable story to the world. Doubtless this book suffers from imperfections, but I pray that our journey toward its completion was at least scenic, adventurous, and gratifying.

Gene Andrew Jarrett
Montclair, New Jersey
July 2021

NOTES

Acronyms

Paul Laurence Dunbar	PLD
Alice Ruth Moore (or Alice Dunbar)	ARM
Matilda Dunbar	MD
Rebekah Baldwin	RB
James Newton Matthews	JNM
William Dean Howells	WDH
Frederick Douglass	FD
Booker T. Washington	BTW

The letters of correspondence and archival sources are drawn from:

Paul Laurence Dunbar Papers (MSS 114 and MSS 659), Ohio Historical Society, Columbus, Ohio

Eugene Wesley Metcalf Jr., "The Letters of Paul and Alice Dunbar: A Private History" (PhD diss., University of California, Irvine, 1973)

The Papers of Wilbur and Orville Wright, Volume 2: 1906–1948, ed. Marvin W. McFarland (New York: McGraw-Hill, 1953)

Booker T. Washington Papers, Volume 2: 1860–1889, ed. Louis Harlan et al. (Urbana: University of Illinois Press, 1972)

Booker T. Washington Papers, Volume 3: 1889–1895, ed. Louis Harlan et al. (Urbana: University of Illinois Press, 1974)

Booker T. Washington Papers, Volume 4: 1895–1898, ed. Louis Harlan et al. (Urbana: University of Illinois Press, 1975)

Booker T. Washington Papers, Volume 5: 1899–1900, ed. Louis Harlan et al. (Urbana: University of Illinois Press, 1976)

Booker T. Washington Papers, Volume 6: 1901–1902, ed. Louis Harlan et al. (Urbana: University of Illinois Press, 1977)

Booker T. Washington Papers, Volume 8: 1904–1906, ed. Louis Harlan et al. (Urbana: University of Illinois Press, 1979)

In a quotation "[xxx]" means that a word in a handwritten letter was too illegible to transcribe.

Paul Laurence Dunbar, "Sympathy"

1. Paul Laurence Dunbar, *Lyrics of the Hearthside* (New York: Dodd, Mead, 1899), 40–41.

Introduction

1. In this biography, I follow a narratorial convention of referring to the main subjects by their first names to establish interpersonal and intimate proximity with the reader; in the case of Paul Laurence Dunbar and Alice Dunbar-Nelson, whose surnames are similar, referring to their first names also helps mitigate potential confusion. Thus, I will refer to Paul Laurence Dunbar and Alice Ruth Moore as Paul and Alice, respectively. In the epilogue, where I discuss methodological and scholarly concerns, I follow the academic convention and refer to them by their appropriate surnames.

2. After the unofficial separation of Alice and Paul in 1902, there is no evidence that either formally filed the documentation for divorce. For an explanation of the viability of divorce during the era, see Eleanor Alexander, *Lyrics of Sunshine and Shadow: The Courtship and Marriage of Paul Laurence Dunbar and Alice Ruth Moore* (New York: Plume, 2004), 148–154.

3. Alice changed her public surname from "Dunbar" to "Dunbar-Nelson" two years later, in 1916, when she married Robert J. Nelson. Today, Dunbar-Nelson is a common choice among scholars.

4. Alice Moore Dunbar, "The Poet and His Song," *A.M.E. Review* 31.2 (October 1914); reprinted in *The Dunbar Speaker and Entertainer*, ed. Alice Moore Dunbar-Nelson (New York: G. K. Hall, 1996), 323–324. Close to his death, the syndicated language said: "It is probable that the voice of the singer Paul Laurence Dunbar, whose writings in prose and poetry have given him a distinguished name as the poet laureate of the race, will be hushed by death before many days" ("Poet Paul Dunbar Dying," *Cleveland Plain Dealer* [September 21, 1904]: 10).

5. Note that the poems Alice describes were not Paul's most famous poems, to which critics readily gravitated in newspaper reviews or which audiences regularly heard during his recitals; rather, they were ones that meant most to her illustration of his mind and character. These poems include "Merry Autumn" in *Oak and Ivy* (1893); "The Seedling," "Preparation," "Delinquent," and "Discovered" in *Lyrics of Lowly Life* (1896), of which "Preparation" and "Delinquent" are also in *Majors and Minors* (1895); "Love's Apotheosis," "Lover's Lane," and "Sympathy" in *Lyrics of the Hearthside* (1899); "Song of Summer" in *Candle-Lightin' Time* (1901); "Keep a Song Up on De Way In," "Ballade," "The Memory of Martha," "Two Little Boots," "To a Violet Found on All Saint's Day," "The Monks Walk," "The Murdered Lover," "The Love's Castle," "Weltschmertz," "My Lady of Castle Grand," and "In the Tents of Akbar" in *Lyrics of Love and Laughter* (1903); and "Lost Dream" and "Forest Greeting" in *Lyrics of Sunshine and Shadow* (1905).

6. Dunbar, "The Poet and His Song," 332. Transcribed in the epigraph to my introduction, "Sympathy" in *Lyrics of the Hearthside* is not the same as the poem "Sympathy," which is briefer and different, appearing six years earlier in his first book, *Oak and Ivy*.

7. In late November 1897, a regular reader of the *New York Tribune* wrote its editor about an occasion when he visited Paul one day. "Climbing four short flights of stairs in the north stack of the library, I found my poet, seated humbly at a desk, busily engaged on some special work in connection with his present position. As I approached he arose and with a kindly greeting offered me his chair, the only one, I saw on that deck." The visitor inquired as to whether Paul was blind. Paul readily dispelled what he called a "strange" rumor (though, ironically, Paul did recite his poems to blind audiences in the Library of Congress). Afterward, he commiserated with the visitor about a poem he wrote that was inspired by his visit, in 1896, to Toledo, Ohio,

Asylum for the Insane. Anglican vicar John Henry Newman's hymn "Lead, Kindly Light" was played at Paul's request just before his recital, and he was swayed to pen "A Hymn," a poem subtitled "After reading, 'Lead, Kindly Light,'" which he would eventually release in *Lyrics of the Hearthside* (1899). The extent to which Paul told this story to the visitor "in a simple, unaffected way," a "sincere speech, aided by a very musical voice and the entire absence of pose or pretention on his part, stamped him, to my mind as the true poet and lover of his art." DKB to the editor of the *New York Tribune* (November 25, 1897) quoted in *The Selected Literary Letters of Paul Laurence Dunbar*, ed. Cynthia C. Murillo and Jennifer M. Nader (Tuscaloosa: University of Alabama Press, 2021), 98–99.

8. Maya Angelou regularly recited Dunbar's "Sympathy" from memory in interviews. An exemplary one appears in *Paul Laurence Dunbar: Beyond the Mask*, produced by Frederick Lewis and Joseph Slade (Athens: Ohio University Press, 2018), DVD, 1:08:36.

9. An excellent snapshot of the Gilded Age may be found in Alan Trachtenberg, *The Incorporation of America: Culture and Society in the Gilded Age* (New York: Hill and Wang, 1982, 2007). "Gilded Age" was coined after the title of a satirical novel by Mark Twain and Charles Dudley Warner on postbellum corporate and political corruption, *The Gilded Age: A Tale of Today* (1873).

10. William Dean Howells, "The Man of Letters as a Man of Business," in *Literature and Life* (New York: Harper and Brothers, 1902), 1–2. The essay was originally published in *Scribner's Magazine* 14 (1893): 429.

11. Paul Laurence Dunbar, "The Poet," in *Lyrics of Love and Laughter* (New York: Dodd, Mead, 1903), 82.

12. According to the International Bibliography of the Modern Language Association, Dunbar was the primary subject of an article, book, or dissertation thirty-five times during the 1970s, the decade that marked the rise of Black Studies and modern academic approaches to African American literature. (As a point of comparison, only five such publications appeared from the turn of the twentieth century to 1970.) After a decline of publications to nineteen and fifteen in the 1980s and 1990s, respectively, there was a jump to sixty-eight publications about Dunbar in the first decade of the twenty-first century, a blip coinciding with the centenary of Dunbar's death in 2006. From 2010 to 2020 we had seen more than fifty publications. Please note that these numbers do not even include the times when Dunbar was mentioned in passing by scholars, or when he was a topic in scholarship not deemed literary or academic enough for inclusion in MLA Bibliography.

13. Reconstruction lasted from 1865, the end of the Civil War, to 1877, when southern Democrats conceded the U.S. presidency to Republican Rutherford B. Hayes in exchange for pulling federal troops from southern territories. During Reconstruction, federal forces were deployed to enforce such a federal rebuilding and reforming of the South that newly emancipated African Americans could lay claim to the constitutional franchise of citizenship and freedom.

14. Eric Foner, *Reconstruction: America's Unfinished Revolution, 1863–1877* (New York: Harper and Row, 1988), 233. For more information about broad definitions of equality, the constitutional notion of republicanism, and the analogies between the American Revolution and Radical Reconstruction, see Foner 231–234, 276–278.

15. Foner, *Reconstruction*, 581.

16. Foner, *Reconstruction*, 569, 597; Nell Irvin Painter, *Standing at Armageddon: A Grassroots History of the Progressive Era* (New York: W. W. Norton, 1987), 8; Jackson Lears, *Rebirth of a*

Nation: The Making of Modern America, 1877–1920 (New York: Harper Perennial, 2010), 96, 126, 130.

17. Painter, *Standing at Armageddon*, 5.

18. Recent scholarly books on Reconstruction include *Reconstructions: New Perspectives on Postbellum United States*, ed. Thomas Brown (New York: Oxford University Press, 2008); Philip Dray, *Capitol Men: The Epic Story of Reconstruction through the Lives of the First Black Congressmen* (New York: Mariner Books, 2010); Douglas R. Egerton, *The Wars of Reconstruction: The Brief, Violent History of America's Most Progressive Era* (New York: Bloomsbury Press, 2014); and Henry Louis Gates, Jr., *Stony the Road: Reconstruction, White Supremacy, and the Rise of Jim Crow* (New York: Penguin Press, 2019).

19. In fall 2018 the journal *American Literary History* released a special issue titled "Reenvisioning Reconstruction." In Gordon Hutner's main introduction to the issue, he recognizes that, within the past decade as well, the field of literary studies has seen "[a] nucleus of scholars . . . revisiting the period [of Reconstruction] and committing a great deal of industry and intelligence toward uncovering its critical exigencies in ways previous generations of Americanists had missed" (Hutner, "Reenvisioning Reconstruction: An Introduction," *American Literary History* 30.3 [Fall 2018]: 403). Reconstruction has been widened beyond the remit only of an "occupied South" to encompass a more global imaginary of racial ideology and material production to include the Caribbean, South America, Europe, and Africa. The essays in *American Literary History* demonstrate a corrective or an expansion of our sense of Reconstruction.

20. Margaret Ronda, "'Work and Wait Unwearying': Dunbar's Georgics," *PMLA* 127.4 (October 2012): 870.

21. Dunbar, *Lyrics of the Hearthside*, 96.

Chapter 1. Broken Country

1. Paul Laurence Dunbar, "The Colored Soldiers," in *Majors and Minors* (Toledo, OH: Hadley & Hadley, 1896), 40.

2. Paul Laurence Dunbar Papers (MSS 114 and MSS 659), Ohio Historical Society, Columbus, OH, Roll 4, Frames 559–560.

3. This could have happened only between 1877 and 1882, when he was between the ages of five and ten, the only years when Joshua lived with the family. Also, no evidence exists—no letters of correspondence written by Joshua or by others referring to him—that he could read or write at all.

4. Benjamin Brawley, *Paul Laurence Dunbar: Poet of His People* (Chapel Hill: University of North Carolina Press, 1936), 13; Gossie Harold Hudson, "A Biography of Paul Laurence Dunbar" (PhD diss., Ohio State University, 1970), 31.

5. Quotes in Boyd, "An Appreciation of Paul Laurence Dunbar," 24; Hudson, "A Biography of Paul Laurence Dunbar," 24, 25, quote on 26 (*Dayton Daily*).

6. Joshua Dunbar's Civil War enlistment application, transcribed by a clerk in Massachusetts, erred in recording his birthplace as Garrett County. His pronunciation of "Garrard County" likely resembled the tongue of a native Kentuckian, but the near homonym of "Garrett" (*ghɛ/ət*) and "Garrard" (*ghaer/əd*) betrayed the differences in their spelling and meaning. (Respectively, in Garrard [*ghaer/əd*] and Garrett [*ghɛ/ət*], the phonemes ə [the unaccented *a* in *alone* and

e in *system*] and ε [*ar* in *dare*] and the syllables əd and ət sounded nearly identical. See Robert M. Rennick, *Kentucky Place Names* [Lexington: University Press of Kentucky, 1984], xiv, xxiv.) In antebellum Kentucky, only Garrard could have been Joshua's birthplace. When Joshua was born, sometime between 1816 and 1823, Garrett County didn't yet exist in Kentucky. Moreover, only when he twice enlisted in the Civil War did his own words, presumably, on his birth appear in print. In 1863, when he signed up for the Company F of the Colored Fifty-fifth Regiment of Massachusetts Volunteer Infantry, he was listed as forty years old, meaning that he was born in 1823. In 1864, when he joined the Company F Fifth Regiment Massachusetts Colored Cavalry, he was listed as forty-two years old, meaning that he was born in 1822. But his birthdate comes into sharper relief by the end of his life, ironically. The 1880 U.S. Census (which was actually written for Joshua's residential street on June 12, 1880) lists him as sixty-four. Later, when he enrolled in the National Home of Disabled Volunteer Soldiers in Dayton, Ohio, he did so on February 4, 1882, at the age of sixty-five. For these two circumstances to be true, Joshua had to have been born sometime on or between February 5 and June 12, 1816. I believe that these latter parameters represent to date the most rigorous ones for ascertaining his age.

7. John E. Kleber, *The Kentucky Encyclopedia* (Lexington: University Press of Kentucky, 1992), 202–204. Also see William E. Ellis et al., *Madison County: 200 Years in Retrospect* (Richmond: Madison County Historical Society, 1985), 21–46.

8. Slaves born in America tended to assume the surname of their first masters. See Herbert H. Gutman, "Somebody Knew My Name," in *The Black Family in Slavery and Freedom* (New York: Pantheon Books, 1976), 230–256; the quotation appears on 232.

9. Garrard County's slave population rose from 1,359 in 1800 to 3,590 in 1860, but the demographic absence of slaves in the official population records downplayed their actual numbers. Note that the total number of slaves includes both "blacks" and "mulattoes." In *Specters of the Atlantic: Finance Capital, Slavery, and the Philosophy of History* (Durham: Duke University Press, 2005), Ian Baucom characterizes the violence of property status as "the violence of becoming a 'type'" and describes the contents of a merchant vessel in September 1781, called the *Zong*, that journeyed from Liverpool, England, to the Caribbean, and from which the captain ordered 133 slaves to be tossed overboard so that the vessel's owners could file an insurance claim for lost cargo (11).

10. Robert William Fogel and Stanley L. Engerman, *Time on the Cross: The Economics of American Negro Slavery* (New York: W. W. Norton, 1974), 38–56; W. E. B. Du Bois, ed., *The Negro Artisan* (Atlanta: Atlanta University Press, 1902), 13–20.

11. Bob Arnbeck, *Through a Fiery Trial: Building Washington, 1790–1800* (Lanham, MD: Madison Books, 1991), 2, 525, 537, 541; Peter Nicholson, *The Mechanics Companion* (Philadelphia: John Locken, 1842), vii.

12. Lore has it that Joshua taught himself to read: see Virginia Cunningham, *Paul Laurence Dunbar and His Song* (New York: Dodd, Mead, 1953), 5; and Felton O. Best, *Crossing the Color Line: A Biography of Paul Laurence Dunbar, 1872–1906* (Dubuque, IA: Kendall/Hunt, 1996), 11.

13. Brown's writings—memoirs, historical scholarship, a novel, and a play—were widely read. Born in November 1814 in the city of Lexington, Brown was also hired away to work and endured slavery's horrors when Mr. John Colburn, a keeper of a Missouri hotel, "a more inveterate hater of the negro," hired him, and when Mr. Walker, a steamboat carrier of a gang of slaves, also known as a "negro speculator" or "soul-driver," employed him as a "a good hand to take care of slaves." By contrast, Elijah P. Lovejoy was "a very good man" to Brown. A publisher and editor

of a newspaper in St. Louis, Elijah was "decidedly the best master." He exposed Brown to the world of literacy that, through the words he read, enhanced his life and, through those he later wrote and left behind, enhanced his legacy. William Wells Brown, *Narrative of William W. Brown, An American Slave* (London: C. Gilpin, 1849), 24, 39–40.

14. Born in May 1815, Bibb once wrote that being "hired out to labor for various persons, eight or ten years in succession," defined his perspective on slavery. As a child, Bibb did not realize his degraded state when he was first separated from his mother. Once the wife of his master, Mr. White, died, Bibb learned that Harriet, Mr. White's daughter and Bibb's former playmate, unabashedly took control of Bibb's life, assuming legal ownership of his mother and his siblings as well. "It was then my sorrows and sufferings commenced," he recalled. "It was then I first commenced seeing and feeling that I was a wretched slave, compelled to work under the lash without wages and often, without clothes to hide my nakedness." Henry Bibb, *Narrative of the Life and Adventures of Henry Bibb, an American Slave, Written by Himself* (New York: n.p., 1849), 14–15. (The mother is called "half white" on 7, and the long quotation, "I had long thought . . . ," appears on 31. The word "sufferings" is on the title page.)

15. Far less legendary than Brown and Bibb, Clarke, born in March 1815, held impressions of slavery no less jaded than his enslaved contemporaries. For better or for worse, Clarke gained a reputation for artisanship. From splitting rails and burning coals to peddling grass seed, Clarke's skills made him at once valuable and risky in Kentucky. When Clarke was auctioned for sale after his master's death, no bids were placed. Fear mounted in his mind: "I had had too many privileges—had been permitted to trade for myself and go over the state—in short, to use their phrase, I was a 'spoilt nigger.'" Defiant words such as Clarke's captured the unique struggle of slave artisans for freedom. Lewis Garrard Clarke and Milton Clarke, *Narratives of the Sufferings of Lewis and Milton Clarke, Sons of a Soldier of the Revolution, During a Captivity of More than Twenty Years among the Slaveholders of Kentucky, One of the So-Called Christian States of North America* (Boston: Bela Marsh, 1846), 30–31.

16. See section 7 of William Littell and Jacob Swigert, *A Digest of the Statute Law of Kentucky: Being a Collection of All the Acts of the General Assembly, of a Public and Permanent Nature, from the Commencement of the Government to May Session 1822* (Frankfort: Kendall and Russell, 1822), 2:1151.

17. Du Bois, *The Negro Artisan*, 14; John Hope Franklin and Loren Schweninger, *Runaway Slaves: Rebels on the Plantation* (New York: Oxford University Press, 1999), 4, 33–36.

18. Published first in the August 1899 issue of the *New England Magazine*, the story, titled "The Ingrate," reappeared the following year in his second collection of stories, *The Strength of Gideon and Other Stories*.

19. Michael A. Chaney, *Fugitive Vision: Slave Image and Black Identity in Antebellum Narrative* (Bloomington: Indiana University Press, 2008), 180.

20. Brown, *Narrative of William W. Brown*, 40, 93–94.

21. Franklin and Schweninger, *Runaway Slaves*, 117, 134, 136, 140.

22. Comparatively, Brown escaped around 1842, at the age of twenty-eight; Bibb in 1838, at twenty-three; Clarke in 1841, at twenty-seven. (The average age of slaves fleeing Kentucky plantations during this decade was twenty-five.) See J. Blaine Hudson, *Fugitive Slaves and the Underground Railroad in the Kentucky Borderland* (Jefferson, NC: McFarland, 2002), 35.

23. Certificate of Death for Matilda Dunbar, February 24, 1934, File No. 11804, State of Ohio Board of Health (copy in author's possession).

24. Rubie Boyd, "An Appreciation of Paul Laurence Dunbar" (typescript, circa 1935), vii; 3, 6–7 (for statement on Matilda's Native American features); 110 for statement that grandmother is Rebecca Porter (or "Aunt Becca Porter), who is the only grandmother recognized in Dunbar lore; and vii for siblings. The 1850 slave schedule had demographic information about the slaves: there were four adult slaves, a man aged forty-six and females aged forty-six, forty, and twenty.

25. Boyd, "An Appreciation of Paul Laurence Dunbar," 100.

26. Matilda quoted in Boyd, "An Appreciation of Paul Laurence Dunbar," 99.

27. Jacqueline Jones, *Labor of Love, Labor of Sorrow: Black Women, Work, and the Family, from Slavery to the Present* (New York: Basic Books, 1985, 2010), 32.

28. Boyd, "An Appreciation of Paul Laurence Dunbar," 100; "David Glass (1780–1857)," Find a Grave, http://www.findagrave.com/cgi-bin/fg.cgi?page=gr&GRid=102204528.

29. Cunningham, *Paul Laurence Dunbar and His Song*, 15–16.

30. Boyd, "An Appreciation of Paul Laurence Dunbar," 100. We now have reconciled the biographical information about Matilda's early life, as stated in Alexander, *Lyrics of Sunshine and Shadow*, 19, 26; Best, *Crossing the Color Line*, 10–11; Cunningham, *Paul Laurence Dunbar and His Song*, 16–18; Benjamin Brawley, *Paul Laurence Dunbar: Poet of His People* (Port Washington, NY: Kennikat, 1967), 12; Addison Gayle Jr., *Oak and Ivy: A Biography of Paul Laurence Dunbar* (Garden City, NY: Doubleday, 1971), 8; and Lida Keck Wiggins, *The Life and Works of Paul Laurence Dunbar* (New York: Dodd, Mead, 1907), 25.

31. Quote from Jones, *Labor of Love, Labor of Sorrow*, 11.

32. Information about work in the house from Jones, *Labor of Love, Labor of Sorrow*, 14, 22, 23, 27, 30.

33. For work in the field, see ibid., 15, 16, 17, 22, 24.

34. "Colonel Robert White" is brought up in Boyd's 1933 interview with Matilda Dunbar, but there is no verification of such a person in Civil War records that accords with the interview's locus of information; there is only a distant reference in these records to a Robert White in Virginia, but no connection can be confirmed. Boyd quotes Matilda as saying, "It is from that [exchange between Colonel White and Mrs. Timewell] that I estimate my age. The Bible in which my birth was recorded was burned" (Boyd, "An Appreciation of Paul Laurence Dunbar," 101).

35. Boyd, "An Appreciation of Paul Laurence Dunbar," 102; called "Tillie" on 103.

36. See James H. Rodabaugh, "The Negro in Ohio," *Journal of Negro History* 31.1 (January 1946): 13, for the Negro population at the time of statehood and where they came from.

37. Stephen Middleton, *Black Laws: Race and the Legal Process in Early Ohio* (Athens: Ohio University Press, 2005), 15.

38. See ibid., 19, for the cultural and political ideals of early Ohio; and certificate quoted on 63.

39. According to Middleton, the justices of the Ohio Supreme Court, in *State v. Farr* (1841), "were sympathetic to the abolitionist argument that free soil made free men under certain circumstances," even regarding slaves transported through the state by slaveholders (*Black Laws*, 177–178). Newspapers regarded this as a precedent and momentous case for the freedom of all slaves in transit within state lines.

40. Hubert G. H. Wilhelm, "Settlement and Selected Landscape Imprints in the Ohio Valley," in *Always a River: The Ohio River and the American Experience*, ed. Robert L. Reid (Bloomington: Indiana University Press, 1991), 72–73.

41. Daniel Drake, *A Systematic Treatise, Historical, Etiological and Practical, on the Principal Diseases of the Interior Valley of North America* (Cincinnati: W. B. Smith, 1850), 221.

42. Darrel E. Nigham, "River of Opportunity: Economic Consequences of the Ohio," in *Always a River*, ed. Reid, 144; John A. Jakle, *Images of the Ohio Valley: A Historical Geography of Travel, 1740 to 1860* (New York: Oxford University Press, 1977), 26, 50; Franklin and Schweninger, *Runaway Slaves*, 158.

43. For the modes of transportation on the river, ranging from rafts, flatboats, and steamships, see Hubert G. H. Wilhelm, "Settlement and Selected Landscape Imprints in the Ohio Valley," and Michael Allen, "The Ohio River: Artery of Movement," in *Always a River*, ed. Reid.

44. For crossing points into free states north of Kentucky, see Mary Ellen Snodgrass, *The Underground Railroad: An Encyclopedia of People, Places, and Operations* (Armonk, NY: M. E. Sharpe, 2008), xxxix, and Hudson, *Fugitive Slaves*, 16, 25–27, 35, 105. For the movement of settlers, see Wilhelm, "Settlement and Selected Landscape Imprints," 74. Out of the eighty-eight total counties in 1850 Ohio, the free African American settlements were located in Mercer, Darke, Butler, Shelby, Miami, Montgomery, Warren, Clermont, Logan, Champaign, Clark, Green, Clinton, Highland, Pike, Scioto, Erie, Licking, Fairfield, Hocking, Vinton, Jackson, Lawrence, Cuyahoga, Muskingum, Jefferson, and Belmont.

45. The 1850 census recorded 210,981 slaves living in Kentucky. Slaveholders reported only 96 runaways among them (in comparison to the manumission of 152), for a ratio of about 0.05 percent. For the rarity of fugitive slaves, see Marion Brunson Lucas, *From Slavery to Segregation, 1760–1891*, vol. 1 of *A History of Blacks in Kentucky* (Frankfort: Kentucky Historical Society, 2017), 62, 342n33; Franklin and Schweninger, *Runaway Slaves*, 116, 367n49. For the exact statistics, see J. D. B. DeBow, *Statistical View of the United States* (Washington, D.C.: A. O. P. Nicholson, 1854), 64, 82.

46. Snodgrass, *The Underground Railroad*, xxxix; Hudson, *Fugitive Slaves*, 65.

47. Thomas Wheeler, *Troy: The Nineteenth Century* (Troy, OH: Troy Historical Society, 1970), 38–39, 41, 58, 69.

48. Ibid., 46, 47, 81, 91.

49. In 1838 the funds Henry Bibb earned at an Ohio hotel by working as a porter and blacking boots paid for his departure to Canada. Being "much better skilled in running away" and having learned to make the right "calculation to avoid detection" improved Bibb's chances of staying out of harm's way (Bibb, *Narrative of the Life and Adventures of Henry Bibb*, 14–17, 110–111, 170). In 1841 Lewis Garrard Clarke likewise fled from Kentucky, through Ohio, into British North America, but with fiery words about divine retribution for the slave's lack of compensation: "'Woe unto him that useth his neighbor's service without wages.' Woe unto him that buildeth his house by iniquity, 'for the stone shall cry out of the wall, and the beam out of the timber shall answer it.' 'Behold the hire of the laborers who have reaped down your fields, which is of you kept back by fraud, crieth; and the cries of them which have reaped are entered into the ears of the Lord of Sabaoth. Ye have lived in pleasure on the earth, and been wanton; ye have nourished your hearts, as in a day of slaughter'" (Clarke and Clarke, *Narratives of the Sufferings of Lewis and Milton Clarke*, 75). Finally, William Wells Brown once wrote, "It is well known, that a great number of fugitives make their escape to Canada, by way of Cleaveland." He went on to say, "while on the lake, I always made arrangement to carry them on the boat to Buffalo or Detroit, and thus effect their escape to the 'promised land.'" Around 1842, Brown assisted some

seventy fugitive travelers, later to reunite with them in Malden, a village in Canada, to share in their journey toward freedom. Stories such as these likely capture Joshua's own desire for the "promised land" (Brown, *Narrative of William W. Brown*, 109).

50. Robin W. Winks, *The Blacks in Canada: A History* (Montreal: McGill-Queen's University Press, 1971), 153.

51. For the Ohio and Ontario crossing points, see Snodgrass, *The Underground Railroad*, xxxviii; for what American fugitive slaves encountered in Canada, see Winks, *The Blacks in Canada*, 144.

52. Winks, *The Blacks in Canada*, 155–156.

53. Ibid., 144, 148–149, 248.

54. Lucas, *From Slavery to Segregation*, 80; Winks, *The Blacks in Canada*, 149–152.

55. Winks, *The Blacks in Canada*, 143–149, 168, 236–237.

56. Boyd, "An Appreciation of Paul Laurence Dunbar" (typescript, circa 1935), 105. There are competing accounts of Murphy's first name. Boyd remarks, after noting in his 1933 interview with Matilda that, perhaps with "a slip of the tongue," she called "R. Weeks Murphy" by a first name of "Wilson": "The Adjutant General's Office at Washington reports that it has no record of a volunteer of either such name from any county in Kentucky" (105). My own research supports this conclusion. However, in Cunningham, *Paul Laurence Dunbar and His Song*, 18, we see confirmation that Matilda called her husband "Willis." The account in Cunningham, *Paul Laurence Dunbar and His Song*, 16, says that whether Mr. Murphy purchased Matilda as a wife for his slave Willis cannot be verified. Finally, A. W. Drury, in *History of the City of Dayton and Montgomery County, Ohio* (Chicago-Dayton: S. J. Clarke, 1909), calls him "Wilson Murphy" (210). I will call him Wilson, given the record of Matilda's reference to that name and to Drury's authoritative, scholarly reference to it as well; given the reference to him in an obituary ("Poet's Mother Dies," *Cincinnati [Ohio] Enquirer* [February 25, 1934]: 19), which states: "Mrs. Dunbar was born in Fayette County, Kentucky, near Shelbyville. She was first married to Wilson W. Murphy"; and given that Willis could conceivably be a nickname for Wilson. Discrepancy exists between the *Cincinnati Enquirer* (Louisville) and Boyd's interview of Matilda ("at Marse Jack Venable's" estate in Lexington) about the location of their marriage in Kentucky, in which case I have leaned toward the accuracy of the authentic interview.

57. William A. Dobak, *Freedom by the Sword: The U.S. Colored Troops, 1862–1867* (Washington, D.C.: U.S. Army Center of Military History, 2011), 9.

58. The statistic on the enlistment of African American men from the Confederate states is in Jacqueline Jones, *Labor of Love, Labor of Sorrow*, 49.

59. Ibid., 47–48.

60. For more information about the role of the Civil War as an accomplice of revolution and its impact on slavery, the South, and the North, see Foner, *Reconstruction*, 3–18.

61. For the origin, history, and topography of Readville, Massachusetts, see William A. Mowry, *Hyde Park Historical Record* (Hyde Park, MA: Hyde Park Historical Society, 1908). For the location and meaning of Readville, see Luis F. Emilio, *History of the Fifty-fourth Regiment of Massachusetts Volunteer Infantry, 1863–1865* (Boston: Boston Book Company, 1891), 19. Andrew quoted in Donald Yacovone, "Liberty or Death: The Fifty-fourth Massachusetts Regiment," in *A Voice of Thunder: A Black Soldier's Civil War*, ed. Yacovone (Urbana and Chicago: University of Illinois Press, 1998), 29. See John D. Warner Jr., "Crossed Sabres: The History of the

5th Massachusetts Volunteer Cavalry" (PhD diss., Boston College, 1997), 76–77, for a description of the camp's facilities.

62. Yacovone, "Liberty or Death," 29–32; quotation on 28.

63. Emilio, *History of the Fifty-fourth Regiment*, 21.

64. According to Charles Fox, *Record of the Service of the Fifty-fifth Regiment of Massachusetts Volunteer Infantry* (Cambridge: Press of John Wilson and Son, 1868), 247, men had been slaves, which could mean either those who were born slaves or were born free and abducted into slavery.

65. Compiled Service Record, Joshua Dunbar, Private, Fifty-fifth Massachusetts Colored Infantry, U.S. Colored Troops Military Service Records, 1861–1865, microfilm publication M1801. Duplicated in Paul Laurence Dunbar Papers, Roll 2. See Fox, *Record of the Service of the Fifty-fifth Regiment*, 110, for the soldiers' average age and 112 for the range of their occupations; see Emilio, *History of the Fifty-fourth Regiment*, 24, for the small fraction of slaves and the light complexion of the men.

66. See Fox, *Record of the Service of the Fifty-fifth Regiment*, 112, for the birthplaces of soldiers.

67. Boyd, "An Appreciation of Paul Laurence Dunbar," viii.

68. Quoted in ibid., 109.

69. Cunningham, *Paul Laurence Dunbar and His Song*, 18.

70. Boyd, "An Appreciation of Paul Laurence Dunbar," 110–111.

71. See Boyd, "An Appreciation of Paul Laurence Dunbar," 110, for Matilda's quotation. See Jones, *Labor of Love, Labor of Sorrow*, 32, for the normative perceptions of the nuclear family in the slave community.

72. Jones, *Labor of Love, Labor of Sorrow*, 19, 35.

73. Quotations in Boyd, "An Appreciation of Paul Laurence Dunbar," 108.

74. Keith P. Wilson, *Campfires of Freedom: The Camp Life of Black Soldiers during the Civil War* (Kent, OH: Kent State University Press, 2002), 6.

75. *Supplement to the Official Records of the Union and Confederate Armies, Volume 77, Serial No. 89*, ed. Janet B. Hewett (Wilmington, NC: Broadfoot, 1998), 271; Fox, *Record of the Service of the Fifty-fifth Regiment*, 11.

76. Hewett, *Supplement to the Official Records*, 278.

77. Fox, *Record of the Service of the Fifty-fifth Regiment*, 11.

78. Gooding quoted in Richard M. Reid, introduction to *Practicing Medicine in a Black Regiment*, ed. Reid (Amherst: University of Massachusetts Press, 2010), 24. See Eric T. Dean, *Shook over Hell: Post-Traumatic Stress, Vietnam, and the Civil War* (Cambridge, MA: Harvard University Press, 1997), 46–48, on walking as the primary means of travel.

79. Quoted in Yacovone, "Liberty or Death," 47.

80. Compiled Service Record, Joshua Dunbar, Private, Fifty-fifth Massachusetts Colored Infantry.

81. Ibid.

82. Statistic in Fox, *Record of the Service of the Fifty-fifth Regiment*, 111, for wounds received in action; Emilio, *History of the Fifty-fourth Regiment*, 23, for sickness and mortality of soldiers at Readville. See Dean, *Shook over Hell*, 51–54, for the problem of disease and the haunting of death affecting all soldiers.

83. See Wilson, *Campfires of Freedom*, 51, for protests by the Fifty-fourth and Fifty-fifth Massachusetts Regiments on compensation inequity; and 27, for the issue of unequal pay among soldiers.

84. Compiled Service Record, Joshua Dunbar, Private, Fifty-fifth Massachusetts Colored Infantry.

85. D. W. Johnson and Company mentioned in Joshua's discharge paperwork; the time of Johnson setting up as a sutler stated in Wilbert Luck, *Journey to Honey Hill: The Fifty-fifth Massachusetts Regiment's (Colored) Journey South to Fight the Civil War that Toppled the Institution of Slavery* (Washington, D.C.: Wiluk Press, 1976), 56. General information about sutlers in Wilson, *Campfires of Freedom*, 6, 63–64; also see 64 about drinking being a major problem in the regiments (at Readville, in particular).

86. Hewett, *Supplement to the Official Records*, 279.

87. Warner, "Crossed Sabres," 75.

88. Enlisted on January 9, 1864 (some sheets say May 9, but this is incorrect, because he must be enlisted before he can be part of the muster-in roll). See Compiled Service Record, Joshua Dunbar, Private, 5th Massachusetts Regiment of Cavalry, U.S. Colored Troops Military Service Records, 1861–1865, microfilm publication M1817. Duplicated in Paul Laurence Dunbar Papers, Roll 2.

89. See Warner, "Crossed Sabres," 45–62, for publicity of authorization and recruitment interest of cavalry. For the structure and size of the cavalry company, see Warner, "Crossed Sabres," 51–52, 212–213, 240.

90. Weather indicated in Warner, "Crossed Sabres," 74–75. Physical characteristics in Compiled Service Record, Joshua Dunbar, Private, 5th Massachusetts Regiment of Cavalry.

91. Cunningham, *Paul Laurence Dunbar and His Song*, 18.

92. Warner, "Crossed Sabres," 213–217, on horses and firearms.

93. Bowditch quoted in Warner, "Crossed Sabres," 291.

94. Hewett, *Supplement to the Official Records*, 163. For minute details about the activities, tactics, and travels of the Fifth Massachusetts in relation to surrounding regiments, black and white, of the Union Army from the Fifth's departure from Massachusetts in May 1864 until its final settlement in Texas in June 1865, see Warner, "Crossed Sabres," 230 en passim. See Warner, "Crossed Sabres," 429–430, for the mustering out in Texas.

95. Drury, *History of the City of Dayton*, 210.

96. Stanton quoted in Warner, "Crossed Sabres," 61. While Warner may be right that "Stanton was extremely reluctant to have blacks commissioned" and that the glass ceiling they encountered was a controversial issue in the newspaper media, he is incorrect when he goes on to say that "no black men in the Fifth Massachusetts Volunteer Cavalry became officers" (61). The record shows that Joshua ascended to the rank of officer. See Compiled Service Record, Joshua Dunbar, Private, 5th Massachusetts Regiment of Cavalry.

97. For more information about the multiple distinctions between officers and enlisted men, see Wilson, *Campfires of Freedom*, 11, 44–45. For an example of an elder enlistee being ideally suited for promotion, see Yacovone, "Liberty or Death," 33–34.

98. Compiled Service Record, Joshua Dunbar, Private, 5th Massachusetts Regiment of Cavalry. For a colored Union soldier to be paid late, if at all, was not unusual. Nor was it unusual for this

soldier to be deprived of a pension. Joshua would suffer both indignities; and about two decades after his death, his future wife, Matilda, and son, Paul, would bear this consequence as well.

99. For the statistical breakdown of Ohio's rise in African American population, see David A. Gerber, *Black Ohio and the Color Line, 1860–1915* (Urbana: University of Illinois Press, 1976), 26–27.

100. See Gerber, *Black Ohio*, 27–46; Middleton, *Black Laws*, 76; and Joe William Trotter Jr., *River Jordan: African American Urban Life in the Ohio Valley* (Lexington: University Press of Kentucky, 1998), 24–26, 30, 37–40, 46–48.

101. James H. Rodabaugh, "The Negro in Ohio," *Journal of Negro History* 31.1 (January 1946): 14–15; Middleton, *Black Laws*, 47–51, 56, 108, 115.

102. Drury, *History of the City of Dayton*, 166; Rodabaugh, "The Negro in Ohio," 18; and Middleton, *Black Laws*, 70.

103. Boyd, "An Appreciation of Paul Laurence Dunbar," 19–20, 111.

104. Ibid., 62.

105. Ibid., 47–48, describes the allure of the Union during the war; the pull on families; and how the Union provided opportunity and incentive for slaves to leave their masters.

106. In 1866 an agent from the United States Bureau of Refugees, Freedmen, and Abandoned Lands (or Freedmen's Bureau) expressed awe at the number of African American women electing to leave field labor to work within the home: these women, he wrote, were "as nearly idle as it is possible for them to be, pretending to spin—knit or something that really amounts to nothing" (quoted in ibid., 43).

107. Boyd, "An Appreciation of Paul Laurence Dunbar," 20.

108. Jones, *Labor of Love, Labor of Sorrow*, 54.

109. Ibid., 70, 73.

110. Elizabeth A. Regosin and Donald R. Shaffer, ed., *Voices of Emancipation: Understanding Slavery, the Civil War, and Reconstruction through the U.S. Pension Bureau Files* (New York: New York University Press, 2008), 106. There are conflicting statements by previous biographers as to where Robert Murphy, Paul Laurence Dunbar, and Elizabeth Florence Dunbar were born. Based on my research, it may be the case that Robert and Elizabeth were born in the house on 47 Howard Street, owned by Matilda's mother, Elizabeth, and Paul on 311 Howard Street, owned by her grandmother Rebecca.

111. James Marten, *Sing Not War: The Lives of Union and Confederate Veterans in Gilded Age America* (Chapel Hill: University of North Carolina Press, 2011), 34, 49, quotations on 51–52.

112. Ibid., 50.

113. Ibid., 55–56, 76–77.

114. Stuart McConnell, *Glorious Contentment: The Grand Army of the Republic, 1865–1900* (Chapel Hill: University of North Carolina Press), 23.

115. Wheeler, *Troy*, 47, 55, 78; the quotation about churchgoers supporting the Union appears on 91.

Chapter 2. Broken Home

1. Matilda Dunbar quoted in Boyd, "An Appreciation of Paul Laurence Dunbar," 14. Boyd's interview of Matilda Dunbar occurred in 1933 (2).

2. Ibid., 12–13.

3. For information about the location of the birthplace, see Alexander, *Lyrics of Sunshine and Shadow*, 17.

4. The January 12, 1917, transcription of the marriage record spells Matilda's maiden name as "Murphey." This is likely a misspelling.

5. Matilda interview quotations in Boyd, "An Appreciation of Paul Laurence Dunbar," 12.

6. Ibid.

7. Foner, *Reconstruction*, 87.

8. Jones, *Labor of Love, Labor of Sorrow*, 62.

9. Quoted in Boyd, "An Appreciation of Paul Laurence Dunbar," 14, which introduces this long quotation with the line, "The delusion of the second marriage, Mother Dunbar was unable to explain further than to say . . ."

10. Ibid., 19–20.

11. By the time of Elizabeth's birth, doctors had long been able to identify the kidney as the culprit for *idropsis*—the Latin term, since the fourteenth century, for classifying the peculiar suffusion of interstitial cavities beneath the flesh. By the late nineteenth century, it had assumed the name Bright's Disease, which sought even more to clarify the disease's pathology. (Modern medicine later termed it edema.) Nephrology was not yet sophisticated enough to pinpoint the actual causes of dropsy, much less the ways of remedying them fully. Uncorroborated ancient myths persisted into the early twentieth century that inebriety accompanied dropsy. One could well imagine that dropsy's inheritability—its genetic transmission from parent to child—was worthy of speculation. (Joshua's alcoholism, for example, probably wouldn't have been negligible if he were still around the house.) See Steven J. Peitzman, *Dropsy, Dialysis, Transplant: A Short History of Failing Kidneys* (Baltimore: Johns Hopkins University Press, 2007), chapters 1 and 2.

12. Jones, *Labor of Love, Labor of Sorrow*, 107.

13. Mary McCarty, "Dunbar Family Together," *Dayton Daily News* (February 12, 2006): B1.

14. Matilda quoted in Hudson, "A Biography of Paul Laurence Dunbar," 29–30.

15. Marten, *Sing Not War*, quotation on 101.

16. The post-traumatic stress of Civil War veterans proved toxic when coupled with alcohol. Bad enough, according to James Marten, was that many of them "fought with family members and old friends, slept poorly, and experienced flashbacks" (*Sing Not War*, 103). Worse still was the belief that this behavior justified their turn to alcohol (or to other drugs, like narcotics), which likely caused or worsened a serious predisposition: violence "directed against civilians who have not yet shared the prolonged liminality of war," as Stuart McConnell stated (*Glorious Contentment*, 23).

17. Quoted in Boyd, "An Appreciation of Paul Laurence Dunbar," 21–24.

18. Paul Laurence Dunbar Papers, Roll 4, Frames 559–560.

19. Ibid.

20. Michael Shinagel, "A Note on the Text," in *Robinson Crusoe: A Norton Critical Edition*, ed. Shinagel (New York: W. W. Norton, 1993), 221; Karen Sanchez-Eppler, "Over a Century of Shipwrecks: American Child Readers and Robinson Crusoe," in *The Materials of Exchange between Britain and North East America, 1750–1900*, ed. Daniel Maudlin and Robin Peel (New York: Routledge, 2013), 117, 141.

21. Shawn Thomson, *The Fortress of American Solitude: Robinson Crusoe and Antebellum Culture* (Madison and Teaneck: Farleigh Dickson University Press, 2009), 137; Sanchez-Eppler, "Over a Century of Shipwrecks," 118–120, 123.

22. Thomas Babbington Macaulay, "[On Defoe]," in *Robinson Crusoe: A Norton Critical Edition*, ed. Michael Shinagel (New York: W. W. Norton, 1993), 273.

23. Thomson, *The Fortress of American Solitude*, 142. Daniel Defoe, *Robinson Crusoe: A Norton Critical Edition*, ed. Michael Shinagel (New York: W. W. Norton, 1993), 4. Quote from Defoe: Daniel Defoe, "Serious Observations," in *Robinson Crusoe: A Norton Critical Edition*, ed. Michael Shinagel (New York: W. W. Norton, 1993), 245.

24. Cunningham, *Paul Laurence Dunbar and His Song*, 17.

25. Jones, *Labor of Love, Labor of Sorrow*, 58; Foner, *Reconstruction*, 88. Quote in Alexander, *Lyrics of Sunshine and Shadow*, 18.

26. Petition for Divorce, Matilda Dunbar to Joshua Dunbar, September 23, 1876, Montgomery County, Ohio, Office of the Clerk of the Court of Common Pleas. Copy in author's possession. Duplicated in Paul Laurence Dunbar Papers, Roll 2.

27. Regosin and Shaffer, *Voices of Emancipation*, 118, on slave marriages; and see 139, 141, 148 on formal versus informal marriages after slavery.

28. Boyd, "An Appreciation of Paul Laurence Dunbar," 16.

29. Paul Laurence Dunbar Papers, Roll 4, Frames 559–560.

30. Thomson, *The Fortress of American Solitude*, 141; Barbara Hochman, *"Uncle Tom's Cabin" and the Reading Revolution* (Amherst: University of Massachusetts Press, 2011), 107.

31. Hochman, *"Uncle Tom's Cabin,"* 104–105, 129.

32. Harriet Beecher Stowe, *Uncle Tom's Cabin: A Norton Critical Edition*, ed. Elizabeth Ammons (New York: W. W. Norton, 1993), xiii.

33. Paul Laurence Dunbar Papers, Roll 4, Frames 559–560.

34. Stowe, *Uncle Tom's Cabin*, xiii.

35. Paul Laurence Dunbar Papers, Roll 4, Frames 559–560.

36. Stowe, *Uncle Tom's Cabin*, xiii.

37. Boyd, "An Appreciation of Paul Laurence Dunbar," 15–17.

38. Ibid.

39. Jones, *Labor of Love, Labor of Sorrow*, 110–111.

40. Ibid., 109.

41. Foner, *Reconstruction*, 593.

42. Whites wielded vitriol and violence against African Americans, whose franchise also suffered constitutional rollbacks by politicians, lawyers, and judges. The South sought belated capitalist retribution against the North. Aligning these actions with the decline of Reconstruction and the rise of Redemption was the doctrine of Anglo-Saxon superiority. Historian Jackson Lears notes that "there was something profoundly different about the racism of the late nineteenth century—it was more self-conscious, more systematic, more determined to assert scientific legitimacy. The whole concept of race," he goes on to say, "never more than the flimsiest of cultural constructions, acquired unprecedented biological authority during the decades between Reconstruction and World War I." The empirical certainty and putative objectivity afforded by the idea of race explained the overt racism of moral outrage, cultural denigration, social eruptions, and political disfranchisement elicited by actual or imagined contact between

the races or the terrifyingly fluid identity among them. Racial science, in counteracting or correcting such fluidity, gave meaning to the subtle racism of segregation. Emotional and psychological pain was meted out as African Americans were quarantined, in multiple senses of the word. See Lears, *Rebirth of a Nation*, 93.

43. Robert W. Steele, "Historical Sketch of the Schools of Dayton," in *Historical Sketches of Public Schools in Cities, Villages, and Townships of the State of Ohio* (Ohio State Centennial Educational Committee, 1876), 10.

44. Paul, his mother, and his half-brothers moved a little more than a mile in the northwestern direction from Magnolia Street to 116 Sycamore Street (Joshua's old residence, vacated when he moved to the Central Branch of the National Home for Disabled Volunteer Soldiers in Dayton), from which they moved over half a mile southeast to 121 Short Wilkinson.

45. Gerber, *Black Ohio*, 98.

46. Leonard Ernest Erickson, "The Color Line in Ohio Public Schools, 1829–1890" (PhD diss., Ohio State University, 1959), 245–246.

47. Cunningham, *Paul Laurence Dunbar and His Song*, 11.

48. Observer quotation on Boyd, "An Appreciation of Paul Laurence Dunbar," 24. Dunbar quotation from Paul Laurence Dunbar Papers, Roll 4, Frames 559–560.

49. If the circumstance occurred by age six, then Paul may have meant the electrical streetcar lines of East Fifth Street, for he did not have to cross railroad tracks to school until he was closer to ten years old, when he had to trek from Short Wilkinson, his residence at the time, to Tenth District School, which were separated by railroad tracks near Union Station.

50. Dunbar quotation in Paul Laurence Dunbar Papers, Roll 4, Frames 559–560.

51. Best, *Crossing the Color Line*, 18n30. Dunbar quotation from Paul Laurence Dunbar Papers, Roll 4, Frames 559–560.

52. Paul Laurence Dunbar, *Oak and Ivy* (Dayton, OH: Press of the United Brethren Publishing House, 1893), 10–11.

53. Joshua's residences spanned Sycamore Street, East Fourth Street, Baxter Street, West Fourth Street, and the Central Branch, although obviously they stretched across a greater region, with the place on West Fourth Street (in the Fifth Ward) half a mile to the west of the Miami River—while Matilda and the sons were on the river's other side—and the Central Branch another two miles farther west.

54. 1880 U.S. Census, Dayton, Montgomery County, population schedule, enumeration district 152, ward 3, p. 48, dwelling 481, family 519, Joshua Dunbar, Paul Dunbar; microfilm publication T9, roll 1051.

55. Dialogue from Boyd, "An Appreciation of Paul Laurence Dunbar," 15–17.

56. Ibid., 16–17.

57. Initially, the institution contained the word "Asylum" in place of "Home." In due time, the board of managers relented in the face of outcry by the public and the Civil War veterans themselves. Public relations had to contend with the images that asylums conjured up: a hospital to which the mentally insane were banished, in which mentally volatile patients were monitored, from which civilians sought protection. Records of veterans falling into this category did exist, demonstrating syndromes of traumatic stress in the wake of the war. But the way that public anxieties turned individual stories into rampant myths about the incivility, the poverty, the criminality of insane veterans had to stop. In the first weeks of 1873, the board of managers

converted the language of the institution from "asylum" to "home," to play up, in the Victorian middle-class sense, the entitlement of veterans to residential and medical accommodation. Since the board of managers comprised men either belonging or sympathetic to Radical Republicanism, the National Home furthered Reconstruction's priority of central government over the individual states and their citizens.

58. Patrick J. Kelly, *Creating a National Home: Building the Veterans' Welfare State, 1860–1900* (Cambridge, MA: Harvard University Press, 1997), 4, 94.

59. Kelly, *Creating a National Home,* 111, 161.

60. Maria Barrett Butler, "The National Home for Disabled Volunteer Soldiers," *Harper's Magazine* 73 (October 1886): 7–8.

61. Kelly, *Creating a National Home,* 115, 119, 122, 146, 161, 187; Butler, "The National Home for Disabled Volunteer Soldiers," 7.

62. The racial conciliation partly trickled down from Benjamin Butler. Elected as president of the National Home in 1866, Butler created policies that stemmed from his racial politics. In his role as general in the Union Army, he organized colored regiments and commissioned the officers in them. Afterward, during his service (from 1867 to 1875) as Republican congressman in the US House of Representatives for Massachusetts, he authored the Ku Klux Klan Act of 1871 and co-authored the Civil Rights Act of 1875. (The first act treated the paramilitary actions of the Ku Klux Klan as potentially federal offenses, hewing to the Republican endeavor to bolster the Fourteenth Amendment; the second act ensured the equal treatment of all American citizens in public spaces. Butler crafted both acts with protection of the African American franchise in mind.) He parlayed his legislative expertise into his National Home presidency, which he held until 1879. At the Central Branch, he implemented the equal treatment of African Americans, a policy that persisted during Joshua's time there, even while racial segregation at the facility presumed the racial inferiority of colored veterans. Ibid., 83–84, 98–99, 124, 163, 225n30.

63. Ibid., 140–141. Quote from Marten, *Sing Not War,* 106.

64. Kelly, *Creating a National Home,* 130, 142, 165, 177; see Alexander, *Lyrics of Sunshine and Shadow,* 19, for the pension amount.

65. Boyd, "An Appreciation of Paul Laurence Dunbar," 21.

66. Erickson, "The Color Line in Ohio Public Schools," 247.

67. Ibid., 284–296.

68. Jill Norgren, *Belva Lockwood: The Woman Who Would Be President* (New York: New York University Press, 2007), 108.

69. That contract had only recently (on July 4, 1884) been authorized by the commissioner of pensions, the secretary of the interior, and Congress, which standardized the language of agreement and regulated the legal fees for pension claims. (The United States Senate and House of Representatives mandated that "[n]o agent or attorney or other person shall demand or receive any other compensation for his services in prosecuting a claim for pension or bounty land than such as the Commissioner of Pensions shall direct to be paid to him, not exceeding $25.")

70. There was a cap of ten dollars on the fee Joshua could have incurred in the event that new disabilities arising after the original "invalid" "claim for pension" warranted any more remediation.

71. B. A. Lockwood, March 20, 1885; Paul Laurence Dunbar Papers, Roll 2, pages 3, 7–8, 10–11.

72. Kelly, *Creating a National Home*, 4.

73. Marten, *Sing Not War*, 208–209.

74. Boyd, "An Appreciation of Paul Laurence Dunbar," 17.

75. Paul quotation in Best, *Crossing the Color Line*, 17.

76. Kelly, *Creating a National Home*, 148–149.

Chapter 3. Public Schooling

1. Paul Laurence Dunbar, "Keep A Pluggin' Away," in *Oak and Ivy*, 8.

2. Joseph Watras, *Politics, Race, and Schools: Racial Integration, 1954–1994* (New York: Garland, 1997), 85. Location of an intermediate school, Fourth-district schoolhouse, mentioned in Steele, "Historical Sketch of the Schools of Dayton," 16.

3. Steele, "Historical Sketch of the Schools of Dayton," 16.

4. Paul Laurence Dunbar Papers, Roll 4, Frame 572.

5. Davison M. Douglas, "The Limits of Law in Accomplishing Racial Change: School Segregation in the Pre-*Brown* North," *UCLA Law Review* 44.3 (1997): 84, 92–94.

6. Erickson, "The Color Line in Ohio Public Schools," 287. For more information about the self-interested response of African American teachers to racial desegregation, see Douglas, "The Limits of Law," 109–111.

7. Paul Laurence Dunbar Papers, Roll 4, Frame 572.

8. Best, *Crossing the Color Line*, 22. For the reference to Dunbar's poetry performances at intermediate school afternoon assemblies and his nickname "deacon," see *Paul Laurence Dunbar: Beyond the Mask*, produced by Frederick Lewis and Joseph Slade, 0:12:50 to 0:13:02.

9. Steele, "Historical Sketch of the Schools of Dayton," 12. Central High School was established in 1850.

10. Drury, *History of the City of Dayton*, 453.

11. Steele, "Historical Sketch of the Schools of Dayton," 17.

12. Edward A. Krug, *The Shaping of the American High School* (New York: Harper and Row, 1964), 4–5, 11, 13–14.

13. Evidence partially includes the class of 1890 photograph shown in this chapter, but it also includes the data of the Dayton population between the ages of fifteen and nineteen years old in the census year of 1890; for this information, see *Report on Population of the United States at the Eleventh Census, 1890* (New York: Norman Ross, 1994), 119. For the total number of "colored persons" attending school during this year, see 180.

14. Patton quoted in Caroline Winterer, *The Culture of Classicism: Ancient Greece and Rome in American Intellectual Life, 1780–1910* (Baltimore: Johns Hopkins University Press, 2002), 78.

15. Ranging from Henry Simmons Frieze to William Watson Goodwin, the first generation of American scholars was born between circa 1820 and 1835 and internationally prominent. The next generation, trained by the previous one, born between circa 1850 and 1870, likewise attained eminence, and spanned Thomas Day Seymour to John Adams Scott. These and other professors set the terms by which classical education embraced historicism and served as the foundation for the elitism of liberal culture (ibid., 112).

16. Ibid., 101–102.

17. Steele, "Historical Sketch of the Schools of Dayton," 12.

18. For information about Matilda's finances, see Hudson, "A Biography of Paul Laurence Dunbar," 26–27; Cunningham, *Paul Laurence Dunbar and His Song*, 13.

19. Paul Laurence Dunbar Papers, Roll 2, page 4: inquiry by Paul into father's pension (November 4, 1887); Paul Laurence Dunbar Papers, Roll 2, page 5: paperwork on father's pension for Paul (November 25, 1887).

20. Erickson, "The Color Line in Ohio Public Schools," 419; Watras, *Politics, Race, and Schools*, 84.

21. Frederick Douglass, "Mixed Schools," in *Reconstruction and After*, vol. 4 of *The Life and Writings of Frederick Douglass*, ed. Philip S. Foner (New York: International Publishers, 1955), 289.

22. Erickson, "The Color Line in Ohio Public Schools," 295–296, 380.

23. Douglas, "The Limits of Law," 78n11.

24. Paul Laurence Dunbar Papers, Roll 4, Frames 559–560.

25. Ibid., pages 124 en passim.

26. Winterer, *The Culture of Classicism*, 1.

27. Ibid., 35.

28. Eric Ashley Hairston, *The Ebony Column: Classics, Civilization, and the African American Reclamation of the West* (Knoxville: University of Tennessee Press, 2013), 5.

29. William W. Cook and James Tatum, *African American Writers and Classical Tradition* (Chicago: University of Chicago Press, 2010), 3, 93–102; Hairston, *The Ebony Column*, 20–21.

30. For Bishop Wright's involvement in Joshua and Matilda's wedding, see Boyd, "An Appreciation of Paul Laurence Dunbar," 12. For information about Reverend William McKee, see volume 1 of S. S. Scranton, *History of Mercer County, Ohio, and Representative Citizens* (Chicago: Biographical Publishing, 1907). For Milton Wright's settling in Dayton and the principles of the United Brethren Church, see Tom Crouch, *The Bishop's Boys: A Life of Wilbur and Orville Wright* (New York: W. W. Norton, 1989), 19, 27–30, 44–45. A brief but incisive portrait of Wright also appears in William A. Shuey, *Manual of the United Brethren Publishing House: Historical and Descriptive* (Dayton, OH: United Brethren Publishing House, 1893), 296.

31. Crouch, *The Bishop's Boys*, 40–41.

32. The mother, Susan, returned to West Dayton, too, with the ten-year-old daughter, Katherine, in tow. And the other sons, Lorin and Reuchlin, aged twenty-two and twenty-three in 1884, were already residing in Dayton upon the core family's return (ibid., 52–66).

33. Ibid., 30–31.

Chapter 4. The Tattler

1. Paul Laurence Dunbar, "Salutatory," *Dayton Tattler* 1.1 (December 13, 1890): 2.

2. Poem printed in Tom Crouch, *The Bishop's Boys: A Life of Wilbur and Orville Wright* (New York: W. W. Norton, 1989), 101. Letter quoted from Orville Wright to Edward Johnson, January 2, 1934, in *The Papers of Wilbur and Orville Wright, Volume 2: 1906–1948*, ed. Marvin W. McFarland (New York: McGraw-Hill, 1953), 1162.

3. Frank Luther Mott, *A History of American Magazines, 1885–1905* (Cambridge: Harvard University Press, 1957), 94; Osman Castle Hooper, *History of Ohio Journalism, 1793–1933* (Columbus: Spahr and Glenn, 1933), 114–115.

4. Mott, *A History of American Magazines, 1885–1905*, 4: 10–11.

5. PLD to Mr. Faber, June 9, 1890. For reference to Dunbar's presidency in the Philomathean Club, see *Paul Laurence Dunbar: Beyond the Mask*, produced by Frederick Lewis and Joseph Slade, 0:14:26.

6. Crouch, *The Bishop's Boys*, 43–51, also describes Milton's editing of *The Religious Telescope*.

7. Crouch, *The Bishop's Boys*, 63–65, 94.

8. Crouch, *The Bishop's Boys*, 77–78, 94–95.

9. E. Chambers, *Cyclopedia: or, An Universal Dictionary of Arts and Sciences* (London: James and John Knapton et al., 1728), 2: 873–879, describes the antiquity of printing.

10. For information about the rudiments and economic risks of the printing business, see Richard-Gabriel Rummonds, *Nineteenth-Century Printing Practices and the Iron Handpress, with Selected Readings* (New Castle and London: Oak Knoll Press and the British Library, 2004), 1: 9, 41, 101–102, 211–212, 365–389, 447, 2: 485, 761, 813; Crouch, *The Bishop's Boys*, 94–95.

11. Crouch, *The Bishop's Boys*, 96–97.

12. One learns of Dunbar's illness in the January 1889 and December 1889 issues of the *High School Times*, which listed him for a time as class of 1890 and as an assistant editor but later, starting in the October 1890 issue, listed him as class of 1891 and editor-in-chief. I thank Thomas Morgan for alerting me to these chronological details.

13. Charles Johanningsmeier, *Fiction and the American Literary Marketplace* (New York: Cambridge University Press, 1997), 18.

14. Quoted from *Dayton Tattler* 1.2 (December 20, 1890): 1.

15. Quoted from *Dayton Tattler* 1.1 (December 13, 1890): 3.

16. Mott, *A History of American Magazines*, 4:10–11. Statistic in Johanningsmeier, *Fiction and the American Literary Marketplace*, 17–18.

17. Dunbar, "Salutatory," 2.

18. Ibid.

19. Mott, *A History of American Magazines*, 4: 214.

20. Paul Laurence Dunbar, "[Editorial]," *Dayton Tattler* 1.2 (December 20, 1890): 2.

21. "Air Ships Soon to Fly," *Dayton Tattler* 1.3 (December 27, 1890): 1.

22. Paul Laurence Dunbar, "Oh, No," *Dayton Tattler* 1.1 (December 13, 1890): 3; "Christmas Carol," *Dayton Tattler* 1.2 (December 20, 1890): 3; and, under the pseudonym of John S. Grey, *Dayton Tattler* 1.3 (December 27, 1890): 3.

23. Paul Laurence Dunbar (under the pseudonym of Pffenberger Deutzelheim), *Dayton Tattler* 1.1 (December 13, 1890): 4.

24. "Everyone can give us some aid": Paul Laurence Dunbar, "Salutatory," *Dayton Tattler* 1.1 (December 13, 1890): 2; Paul Laurence Dunbar, "The Language We Speak," *Dayton Tattler* 1.3 (December 27, 1890): 2.

25. Laurel Brake, "The Advantage of Fiction: The Novel and the 'Success' of the Victorian Periodical," in *A Return to the Common Reader: Print Culture and the Novel, 1850–1900*, ed. Beth Palmer and Adelene Buckland (New York: Routledge, 2016), 12.

26. Paul Laurence Dunbar, "The Gambler's Wife," *Dayton Tattler* 1.3 (December 27, 1890): 3.

27. Paul Laurence Dunbar, "Melancholia," *High School Times* (April 1891): 3–4.

Chapter 5. A Superior Gift

1. James Whitcomb Riley to PLD, November 27, 1892.

2. Brawley, *Paul Laurence Dunbar*; Best, *Crossing the Color Line*, 33.

3. The "opera house" mentioned in Cunningham, *Paul Laurence Dunbar and His Song*, 67. Hudson, "A Biography of Paul Laurence Dunbar," 49, cites *Dayton Daily Journal* (June 27, 1892) for location at "Becket House on Monday and a banquet on Friday." JNM to PLD, October 2, 1892, describes the scene.

4. Cunningham, *Paul Laurence Dunbar and His Song*, 55, for reference to the job. Alexander, *Lyrics of Sunshine and Shadow*, 33, describes that Rob gets married and moves to Chicago in 1887. Ibid., 43, describes Paul's physical dimensions.

5. Joseph J. Korom Jr., *The American Skyscraper, 1850–1940: A Celebration of Height* (Boston: Branden Books, 2008), 321.

6. Lee E. Gray, *From Ascending Rooms to Express Elevators: A History of the Passenger Elevator in the Nineteenth Century* (Mobile, AL: Elevator World, 2002), 241–242, 258.

7. PLD to JNM, July 26, 1892.

8. PLD to JNM, October 12, 1892.

9. In her 1907 study of "some Dayton saints and prophets," namely the "men who put into the town of Dayton the best work and thought of which they were capable," Charlotte Reeve Conover noted Paul's exceptional behavior under those working conditions, inaugurating the story that would describe his perseverance against all odds: "In 1891–92, the patrons of a certain dress-making establishment, in one of our public buildings, noticed that the elevator boy was always reading. This is not, in itself, remarkable. The yellow literature of the day finds its widest field among the employed boys in town-town offices. But this elevator boy was reading Tennyson and Shakespeare, and he was black. In the dim light that came down the shaft, with his hands at work on the ropes, and the throb of the engine in his ears, he was feeding his soul" (Conover, "Paul Laurence Dunbar," in *Some Dayton Saints and Prophets* [Dayton, OH: United Brethren Publishing House, 1907], 179–180); Cunningham, *Paul Laurence Dunbar and His Song*, 56–57.

10. Cunningham, *Paul Laurence Dunbar and His Song*, 55, 86.

11. PLD to Editors, American Press Association, August 31, 1892.

12. Gavin Jones, *Strange Talk: The Politics of Dialect Literature in Gilded Age America* (Berkeley: University of California Press, 1999), 1.

13. Nadia Nurhussein, *Rhetorics of Literacy: The Cultivation of American Dialect Poetry* (Columbus: Ohio State University Press, 2013), 3, 13, 35.

14. Ibid., 2, 4, 11, 20, 30.

15. Ibid., 91.

16. Brawley, *Paul Laurence Dunbar*, 18; Cunningham, *Paul Laurence Dunbar and His Song*, 59.

17. Johanningsmeier, *Fiction and the American Literary Marketplace*, 34–35.

18. A. N. Kellogg Newspaper Co. to PLD, December 19, 1891.

19. Johanningsmeier, *Fiction and the American Literary Marketplace*, 1–4; Eugene W. Metcalf Jr., *Paul Laurence Dunbar: A Bibliography* (Metuchen, NJ: Scarecrow, 1975), 76.

20. Put another way, the syndicated readyprint provided by Kellogg to newspapers reached 1.7 million weekly readers by 1875 and an estimated 4.7 million by 1900. Johanningsmeier, *Fiction and the American Literary Marketplace*, 5, 37–40.

21. The building was no longer located on the corner of West Fourth and South Wilkinson Streets; it moved a little more than half a mile northeast, to the corner of North Main Street and Monument Avenue.

22. Paul Laurence Dunbar, "The Old High School and the New," in *The Collected Poems of Paul Laurence Dunbar*, ed. Joanne M. Braxton (Charlottesville: University Press of Virginia, 1993), 301–302.

23. Best, *Crossing the Color Line*, 38.

24. Paul Laurence Dunbar, "Welcome Address to the Western Association of Writers," in *Oak and Ivy*, 25.

25. George Berkeley, "On the Prospect of Planting Arts and Learning in America," in *Poems of Places: America, New England*, ed. Henry Wadsworth Longfellow (Boston and New York: Houghton Mifflin, 1879), 27.

26. Brawley, *Paul Laurence Dunbar*, 21; Cunningham, *Paul Laurence Dunbar and His Song*, 68.

27. James Newton Matthews, "A Negro Poet," *Indianapolis Journal*, October 2, 1892: 16.

28. PLD to JNM, October 12, 1892.

29. David Dowling, *Capital Letters: Authorship in the Antebellum Literary Market* (Iowa City: University of Iowa Press, 2009), 2, 6–7, 10–11.

30. Dowling, *Capital Letters*, 3.

31. PLD to JNM, July 26, 1892; PLD to JNM, October 12, 1892; PLD to JNM, October 19, 1892; PLD to JNM, February 7, 1893.

32. Francesca Sawaya, *The Difficult Art of Giving: Patronage, Philanthropy, and the American Literary Market* (Philadelphia: University of Pennsylvania Press, 2014), 134–140.

33. PLD to JNM, July 26, 1892; PLD to JNM, October 12, 1892; PLD to JNM, October 19, 1892.

34. PLD to JNM, October 12, 1892; PLD to JNM, October 19, 1892.

35. PLD to JNM, December 23, 1893; PLD to JNM, April 30, 1894.

36. PLD to JNM, July 26, 1892.

37. PLD to JNM, October 12, 1892.

38. PLD to JNM, December 23, 1893.

39. PLD to JNM, October 18, 1892; PLD to JNM, November 4, 1892; PLD to JNM, November 16, 1892.

40. PLD to JNM, November 29, 1892.

41. Charles A. Thatcher to PLD, April 21, 1893; PLD to JNM, December 12, 1893.

42. PLD to JNM, October 19, 1892.

43. Nurhussein, *Rhetorics of Literacy*, 13–14, 33, 38–39.

44. James Whitcomb Riley to PLD, November 27, 1892.

45. Cunningham, *Paul Laurence Dunbar and His Song*, 76; Crouch, *The Bishop's Boys*, 100, 104–106.

46. Cunningham, *Paul Laurence Dunbar and His Song*, 78.

47. Ibid., 80–82.

Chapter 6. Career Choices

1. Paul Laurence Dunbar, "A Career," in *Oak and Ivy*, 47.

2. Eavan Boland and Mark Strand, "The Ode," in *The Making of a Poem: A Norton Anthology of Poetic Forms*, ed. Boland and Strand (New York: W. W. Norton, 2001), 240.

3. James H. Justus, "The Fireside Poets: Hearthside Values and the Language of Care," in *Nineteenth-Century American Poetry*, ed. A. Robert Lee (Totowa, NJ: Vision Press, 1985), 147, on Wordsworth and the Fireside Poets; Dunbar, "Whittier," in *Oak and Ivy*, 31.

4. Elizabeth Renker, "The 'Twilight of the Poets' in the Era of American Realism, 1875–1900," in *The Cambridge Companion to Nineteenth-Century American Poetry*, ed. Kerry Larson (Cambridge: Cambridge University Press, 2011), 136, 142.

5. Dunbar, *Oak and Ivy*, 5, 59.

6. Littell and Swigert, *Digest of the Statute Law of Kentucky*, 2: 1149–1150.

7. Waiving an owner's obligation to document transferring slaves as personal property required statutory oversight:

> "Sec. 28. All negro, mulatto, or Indian slaves, in all courts of judicature and other places within this commonwealth, shall be held, taken and adjudged to be real estate, and shall descend to the heirs and widows of persons departing this life, as lands in and by an act of the general assembly entitled, "an act directing the course of descents."
>
> "Sec. 29. *Provided.* That all such slaves shall be liable to the payment of debts, and may be taken by execution for that end, as other chattels or personal estate may be.
>
> "Sec. 30. *Provided, also.* That no such slave shall be liable to be escheated by reason of the decease of the proprietor for the same without lawful heirs; but all such slaves shall, in that case, be accounted for and go as chattels and other estates personal.
>
> "Sec. 31: No person selling or alienating any such slave otherwise than by gift, marriage settlement, deed of trust, or mortgage, shall be obliged to cause such sale or alienation to be recorded."

Littell and Swigert, *Digest of the Statute Law of Kentucky*, 2: 1155–1156.

8. Andrew Fede, *People Without Right: An Interpretation of the Fundamentals of the Law of Slavery in the U.S. South* (New York: Garland, 1992), 221.

9. Stephen Burt, "When Poets Ruled the School," *American Literary History* 20.3 (Fall 2008): 512; Justus, "The Fireside Poets," 151–152.

10. Dunbar, *Oak and Ivy*, 6, 30; Kleber, *The Kentucky Encyclopedia*, 809.

11. Burt, "When Poets Ruled the School," 509; Angela Sorby, *Schoolroom Poets: Childhood, Performance, and the Place of American Poetry, 1865–1917* (Lebanon, NH: University of New Hampshire Press, 2005), xii, xxxviii.

12. Dunbar, *Oak and Ivy*, 28.

13. Burt, "When Poets Ruled the School," 510; Sorby, *Schoolroom Poets*, xlii, 186.

14. Sorby, *Schoolroom Poets*, xii, xvi, xxxvii, 185.

15. Sorby, *Schoolroom Poets*, xxi–xxii, xxvii; Justus, "The Fireside Poets," 148.

16. Quoted in Best, *Crossing the Color Line*, 99.

17. Burt, "When Poets Ruled the School," 518; Dunbar, *Oak and Ivy*, 23.

18. Iambic tetrameter arrives early in the book, in "A Drowsy Day" ("The air is dark, the sky is gray / The misty shadows come and go") and "The Sparrow" ("A little bird, with plumage brown, / Beside my window flutters down"). "Keep a Pluggin' Away" ("I've a humble little motto / That is homely, though it's true,—") indicated his skill with the trochee, the iamb's converse. A handful of poems were more complex. In "An Easter Ode," most lines contain two initial trochaic feet and a final cretic foot ("Heeding not the children's wail, / Fathers droop and mothers fail"). The lines of "Columbian Ode" are not only pentameters but begin with a

spondee, followed by four iambs. Greater scrutiny reveals that, as a consequence of either experimentation or, more likely, neglect, a line or two within a poem sometimes strayed from the form that evidently seemed to be the governing structure. Still, the metrical versatility of Paul's new poems was an achievement. Over the years, as some of these poems reappeared in later volumes, he continued to tweak the words, to refine the punctuation and syntax, in his pursuit of perfection. See Dunbar, *Oak and Ivy*, 7–10, 50.

19. Ibid., 20.

20. Metcalf, *Paul Laurence Dunbar*, 6; PLD to Chas. A. Johnson, October 24, 1892.

21. [People Willing to Buy Dunbar's Book] to PLD, October 28, 1892.

22. For sales of *Oak and Ivy*, see Cunningham, *Paul Laurence Dunbar and His Song*, 84.

23. "A Young Man Whose Poems Have Attracted Wide-Spread Attention and Comment," *Cleveland Gazette*, January 7, 1893: 1.

24. PLD to JNM, November 23, 1892.

25. PLD to JNM, November 29, 1892.

26. PLD to JNM, November 23, 1892; Nurhussein, *Rhetorics of Literacy*, 122.

27. Best, *Crossing the Color Line*, 37.

28. James D. Anderson, *The Education of Blacks in the South, 1860–1935* (Chapel Hill: University of North Carolina Press, 1988), 33–34, 66–72.

29. Best, *Crossing the Color Line*, 47; Brawley, *Paul Laurence Dunbar*, 30; Cunningham, *Paul Laurence Dunbar and His Song*, 87.

30. Cunningham, *Paul Laurence Dunbar and His Song*, 86–87.

31. Brawley, *Paul Laurence Dunbar*, 30–31; Best, *Crossing the Color Line*, 47.

32. Brawley, *Paul Laurence Dunbar*, 31; Best, *Crossing the Color Line*, 48.

33. Paul Laurence Dunbar, *Majors and Minors* (Toledo, OH: Hadley & Hadley, 1896), 134–135; Cunningham, *Paul Laurence Dunbar and His Song*, 90.

34. Dunbar, *Oak and Ivy*, 45; Cunningham, *Paul Laurence Dunbar and His Song*, 89.

35. Charles A. Thatcher to PLD, April 21, 1893.

36. PLD to JNM, April 30, 1894.

37. PLD to JNM, April 30, 1894; Charles A. Thatcher to PLD, December 1, 1894.

38. S. B. Hershey to PLD, November 15, 1894; R. U. Johnson to PLD, December 8, 1894; RB to PLD, January 19, 1895.

39. Charles A. Thatcher to PLD, April 21, 1893; Richard Lew Dawson to PLD, October 5, 1894; Charles A. Thatcher to PLD, December 1, 1894; Charles A. Thatcher to PLD, December 9, 1894. For examples of Thatcher arranging engagements for Paul to read his work, see Charles A. Thatcher to PLD, December 12, 1894; and Charles A. Thatcher to PLD, February 4, 1895.

40. PLD to JNM, November 16, 1892; PLD to JNM, December 12, 1893.

41. PLD to C. C. Hunt, American Press Association, September 13, 1892; Office Editor of the *Independent* to PLD, February 15, 1895.

42. Charles A. Thatcher to PLD, April 21, 1893; Mrs. _____ to PLD, _____ 10, 1894. For expressed words of support, see L. C. Abbott to PLD, May 18, 1894. For men inspired by and envious of Dunbar's genius, see J. Edwin Campbell to PLD, April 8, 1894. For women attracted to Dunbar and his poetry, see Eugenia Griffin to PLD, March 7, 1892; and "Cad" Bayless to PLD, February 16, 1894.

43. PLD to JNM, August 12, 1893.

Chapter 7. The White City

1. PLD to FD, December 30, 1893.

2. Cunningham, *Paul Laurence Dunbar and His Song*, 92.

3. John E. Findling, *Chicago's Great World Fairs* (New York: Manchester University Press, 1994), 3–6.

4. McKinley quotation in Robert W. Rydell, *All the World's a Fair* (Chicago: University of Chicago Press, 1987), 152; Findling, *Chicago's Great World Fairs*, 30.

5. Rydell, *All the World's a Fair*, 4; Lears, *Rebirth of a Nation*, 167.

6. Findling, *Chicago's Great World Fairs*, 5–7, 10–15, 19–20.

7. Cunningham, *Paul Laurence Dunbar and His Song*, 92–93; Alexander, *Lyrics of Sunshine and Shadow*, 29.

8. PLD to JNM, May 2, 1893.

9. Lears, *Rebirth of a Nation*, 89, quotations on 135–136; Findling, *Chicago's Great World Fairs*, 5.

10. PLD to JNM, May 2, 1893.

11. PLD to MD, May 4, 1893; Alexander, *Lyrics of Sunshine and Shadow*, 29.

12. PLD to JNM, May 2, 1893; PLD to MD, May 4, 1893; PLD to JNM, July 17, 1893; PLD to JNM, August 12, 1893. For the reference to Dunbar's work as a downtown Chicago hotel waiter, see *Paul Laurence Dunbar: Beyond the Mask*, produced by Frederick Lewis and Joseph Slade, 0:31:15.

13. William S. McFeely, *Frederick Douglass* (New York: W. W. Norton, 1991), 360; Cunningham, *Paul Laurence Dunbar and His Song*, 100; Best, *Crossing the Color Line*, 51.

14. Frederick Douglass, "[Speech of Frederick Douglass at Haitian Pavilion Dedication Ceremonies at Chicago World Fair, 1893]" (Chicago: Haitian Pavilion of World Fair, 1893): www .canadahaitiaction.ca/sites/default/files/Douglass%201893.pdf; McFeely, *Frederick Douglass*, 359, 366.

15. The descriptions of Douglass as "Sage of Cedar Hill," in reference to his 1878 purchase of a house in Anacostia in the southeast part of Washington, D.C., or "Old Man Eloquent," in an 1883 newspaper reference to one of his moving speeches, can be found in David W. Blight, *Frederick Douglass: Prophet of Freedom* (New York: Simon & Schuster, 2018).

16. McFeely, *Frederick Douglass* 366.

17. PLD to MD, June 6, 1893.

18. Ibid.

19. Quoted in Cunningham, *Paul Laurence Dunbar and His Song*, 97; Best, *Crossing the Color Line*, 50.

20. Cook quoted in Marva Griffin Carter, *Swing Along: The Musical Life of Will Marion Cook* (New York: Oxford University Press, 2008), 38; also on 38, a reference to Frederick Douglass's introduction of Cook to Dunbar.

21. Cook quoted in Carter, *Swing Along*, 38.

22. Mary Church Terrell recalled this occasion of Douglass's meditation on Paul in her memoir. See Mary Church Terrell, *A Colored Woman in a White World* (Washington, D.C.: Ransdell, 1940), 111.

23. PLD to MD, June 6, 1893.

24. Findling, *Chicago's Great World Fairs*, 26.

25. Findling, *Chicago's Great World Fairs*, 27–28; quote in McFeely, *Frederick Douglass*, 368.

26. McFeely, *Frederick Douglass*, 368; Rydell, *All the World's a Fair*, xxxiii.

27. Quote in Rydell, *All the World's a Fair*, xxiv; Rydell, *All the World's a Fair*, xvi.

28. Rydell, *All the World's a Fair*, xix, xv–xviii.

29. Quote in Rydell, *All the World's a Fair*, xxv; for more information about the pamphlet, see xiii–xxx.

30. McFeely, *Frederick Douglass*, 370; quote in Rydell, *All the World's a Fair*, xxxi.

31. Paula J. Giddings, *Ida: A Sword among Lions: Ida B. Wells and the Campaign against Lynching* (New York: Amistad, 2008), 276; *The Cambridge World History of Food*, ed. Kenneth F. Kiple and Kriemhild Coneè Ornelas (Cambridge: Cambridge University Press, 2000), 2: 1813.

32. Cunningham, *Paul Laurence Dunbar and His Song*, 102.

33. Rydell, *All the World's a Fair*, xxxi; Cunningham, *Paul Laurence Dunbar and His Song*, 102.

34. "Appeal of Douglass," *Chicago Tribune* (August 26, 1893): 3; Maurice Peress, *Dvořák to Duke Ellington: A Conductor Explores America's Music and Its African American Roots* (New York: Oxford University Press, 2008), 208n8.

35. "Appeal of Douglass," *Chicago Tribune* (August 26, 1893): 3.

36. Cunningham, *Paul Laurence Dunbar and His Song*, 103; McFeely, *Frederick Douglass*, 371; Blight, *Frederick Douglass*, 736.

37. Paul Laurence Dunbar, "The Colored Soldiers," in *Majors and Minors*, 40.

38. Cunningham, *Paul Laurence Dunbar and His Song*, 104.

39. Ida B. Wells, *Crusade for Justice: The Autobiography of Ida B. Wells* (Chicago: University of Chicago Press, 1991), 118.

40. PLD to FD, December 30, 1893.

41. Ibid.

42. Cunningham, *Paul Laurence Dunbar and His Song*, 107.

Chapter 8. Chafing at Life

1. RB to PLD, December 5, 1894.

2. *Paul Laurence Dunbar: Beyond the Mask*, produced by Frederick Lewis and Joseph Slade, 0:35:17.

3. See Cunningham, *Paul Laurence Dunbar and His Song* (New York: Dodd, Mead, 1953), 100, for Dunbar's meeting of Rebekah Baldwin.

4. RB to PLD, September 24, 1893.

5. Ibid.

6. RB to PLD, December 3, 1893. Quite often, Rebekah concluded her letters in reference to it: "And now, oh gifted son of the Muses, to their divine inspiration I again commend thee!" Or: "I now commend you to your muse." Or: "I commend thee to kind Fortune and thy Muse divine." Or: "You would read or recite to me Paul and the music of your voice would blend with that of leaf and stream and with the Muses, hand in hand enliv[e]ned we would wander for long hours forgetful of all else." Or, finally: "May Ganymede feed thee on the nectar and ambrosia of the gods, and may the muses quench thy thirst with libations from those sacred founts whence gush poetic inspiration." Respectively, see RB to PLD, December 3, 1893; RB to PLD, January 30, 1894; RB to PLD, February 12, 1894; RB to PLD, June 23, 1894; RB to PLD, July 18, 1894.

7. RB to PLD, December 3, 1893; RB to PLD, February 13, 1895.

8. RB to PLD, January 30, 1894.

9. Ibid.

10. RB to PLD, February 12, 1894; ibid.

11. RB to PLD, June 23, 1894.

12. RB to PLD, July 18, 1894.

13. RB to PLD, February 18, 1894; RB to PLD, August 3, 1894.

14. Charles Mitchell to PLD, March 17, 1894; RB to PLD, June 23, 1894; RB to PLD, August 3, 1894.

15. Douglass quoted in Robert Harrison, *Washington during Civil War and Reconstruction: Race and Radicalism* (Cambridge: Cambridge University Press, 2011), 311.

16. For the alternate names of the black elite, see Willard B. Gatewood, *Aristocrats of Color: The Black Elite, 1880–1920* (Fayetteville: University of Arkansas Press, 2000), xi. For information about these families, clubs, and societies, see Jacqueline M. Moore, *Leading the Race: The Transformation of the Black Elite in the Nation's Capital, 1880–1920* (Charlottesville: University of Virginia Press, 1999), 10–16.

17. Archibald Grimké quoted in Moore, *Leading the Race*, 13.

18. Paul Laurence Dunbar, *The Sport of the Gods and Other Essential Writings*, ed. Shelley Fisher Fishkin and David Bradley (New York: Modern Library, 2010), 247.

19. Dunbar, *The Sport of the Gods and Other Essential Writings*, 248. For the topic of African Americans who published literature in black periodicals, see Abby Arthur Johnson and Ronald Maberry Johnson, *Propaganda and Aesthetics: The Literary Politics of Afro-American Magazines in the Twentieth Century* (Amherst: University of Massachusetts Press, 1979).

20. RB to PLD, September 4, 1894.

21. RB to PLD, September 4, 1894; PLD to FD, September 4, 1894.

22. PLD to Alexander Crummell, September 9, 1894.

23. Ibid.

24. PLD to Alexander Crummell, September 9, 1894; Alexander Crummell to PLD, September 12, 1894.

25. PLD to FD, September 7, 1894; RB to PLD, September 15, 1894.

26. RB to PLD, October 7, 1894.

27. RB to PLD, October 7, 1894; RB to PLD, October 27, 1894. For other examples of her expressions of love and friendship, see RB to PLD, September 24, 1893; RB to PLD, December 13, 1894; RB to PLD, January 19, 1895; RB to PLD, February 13, 1895.

28. RB to PLD, October 7, 1894; RB to PLD, October 27, 1894.

29. RB to PLD, November 18, 1894.

30. RB to PLD, November 18, 1894; RB to PLD, February 13, 1895.

31. *Collected Poems of Paul Laurence Dunbar*, ed. Braxton, 72; RB to PLD, November 18, 1894.

32. RB to PLD, December 5, 1894.

33. PLD to JNM, November 16, 1892.

34. RB to PLD, December 13, 1894.

35. Blight, *Frederick Douglass*, 718, 727, 733, 736. British delegate quoted in McFeely, *Frederick Douglass*, 381.

36. RB to PLD, March 3, 1895.

Chapter 9. The Bond of a Fellow-Craft

1. PLD to ARM, May 23, 1895.

2. *Paul Laurence Dunbar: Beyond the Mask*, produced by Frederick Lewis and Joseph Slade, 0:40:21.

3. Gatewood, *Aristocrats of Color*, 157. For the quotation, "The little violinist is a Jewess with eyes, hair and complexion that reminded me so much of you that I felt like hugging her for your sake," see PLD to ARM, April 23, 1897. For the quotation, "Particularly am I yearning just now for the sight of one fair American Girl who starts two letters to her absent lover and stops both of them in the middle," see PLD to ARM, June 10, 1897. See PLD to ARM, January 28, 1898, for the phrase "turn-up nose."

4. Alexander, *Lyrics of Sunshine and Shadow*, discusses this division of skin color in African American communities at the turn of the century on 46–47; Alice on the "people of color" in Louisiana quoted on 62; Alice's discussion of Creole identity on 66–73. The original publication of the essay was "People of Color in Louisiana," *Journal of Negro History* 1.4 (October 1916).

5. PLD to ARM, April 17, 1895.

6. Ibid.

7. Paul Laurence Dunbar, "Frederick Douglass," in *Majors and Minors*, 19.

8. Dunbar, "Phyllis," in *Majors and Minors*, 70.

9. ARM to PLD, May 7, 1895.

10. PLD to ARM, May 23, 1895.

11. Ibid.

12. PLD to ARM, May 25, 1895. Regarding Paul's limited power at the *Indianapolis World*: "It remains to be seen whether my connection with the *World* shall last or amount to anything. I can only try; however I thank you for your kind wishes and your promise of aid" (PLD to ARM, June 6, 1895).

13. PLD to ARM, June 13, 1895.

14. PLD to ARM, June 6, 1895. The first poem would take the name "A Lyric" in Dunbar, *Majors and Minors*, 69; and the second "Alice" in Dunbar, *Lyrics of Lowly Life* (New York: Dodd, Mead, 1896). I have preserved the punctuation and structure of the original verses, as they appeared in the correspondence; he later modified them for the publications.

15. PLD to ARM, June 25, 1895.

16. PLD to ARM, August 14, 1895; PLD to ARM, September 21, 1895. Regarding staying on top of Alice's obligation: "Mrs. Lottie Jackson writes me that she has not yet received her book and I want to know if I gave you the right town Bay City, Mich.? I did not give you her street address as the former usually reaches her. If the book has been lost in the mails, let me know at once please & I shall take in buying another to replace" (PLD to ARM, September 21, 1895).

17. PLD to ARM, August 14, 1895.

18. About Matilda's poor handwriting, PLD to ARM, February 27, 1898. For Dunbar's admission that Alice had to pen his letters, due to fatigue or ill health, see PLD to MD, June 17, 1899.

19. PLD to MD, August 18, 1895.

20. PLD to MD, September 21, 1895. PLD to MD, August 9, 1900, regarding his weight and the weight of his father.

21. PLD to MD, September 21, 1895.

22. PLD to MD, n.d. (circa September 30, 1895).

23. Eileen Southern, *The Music of Black Americans: A History* (New York and London: W. W. Norton, 1997), 266–267.

24. For the compositional opportunities of African American musicians, see Southern, *The Music of Black Americans*, 268; for the transition from minstrelsy to vaudeville, see 298–299; for the possibility of African Americans on Broadway, see 303.

25. Robert M. Dowling, "A Marginal Man in Black Bohemia: James Weldon Johnson in the New York Tenderloin," in *Post-Bellum, Pre-Harlem: African American Literature and Culture, 1977–1919* (New York: New York University Press, 2006), 118.

26. Camille F. Forbes, *Introducing Bert Williams: Burnt Cork, Broadway, and the Story of America's First Black Star* (New York: Basic Civitas Books, 2008), and Carter, *Swing Along*. Williams and Walker's flat was located on 127 and 129 West 53rd Street; see Jonathan Daigle, "Paul Laurence Dunbar and the Marshall Circle: Racial Representation from Blackface to Black Naturalism," *African American Review* 43.4 (Winter 2009): 633–654; James Weldon Johnson, *Along This Way: The Autobiography of James Weldon Johnson* (New York: Viking Press, 1933), 172–173. Gilbert Osofsky conceived of the Tenderloin as being an even larger area, from 20th to 53rd Streets, and west of Sixth Avenue to the waterfront; see Osofsky, "Race Riot, 1900: A Study of Ethnic Literature," *Journal of Negro Education* 32.1 (Winter 1963): 17.

27. Will Marion Cook, "Clorindy, the Origin of the Cakewalk," *Theatre Arts* (September 1947): 61–65.

28. Carter, *Swing Along*, 152n6.

29. Dunbar, *Majors and Minors*, 7.

30. PLD to ARM, October 28, 1895; PLD to ARM, December 29, 1895.

31. PLD to ARM, October 28, 1895. Linda Wagner-Martin and Cathy N. Davidson, "Alice Ruth Moore Dunbar-Nelson," *The Oxford Book of Women's Writing in the United States*, ed. Wagner-Martin and Davidson (New York: Oxford University Press, 1995), 21.

32. PLD to MD, February 28, 1897.

Chapter 10. Heroine of His Stories

1. PLD to ARM, October 13, 1895.

2. PLD to ARM, June 6, 1895; PLD to ARM, June 13, 1895.

3. PLD to ARM, June 25, 1895.

4. ARM to PLD, July 6, 1895.

5. PLD to ARM, July 9, 1895.

6. PLD to ARM, August 14, 1895.

7. PLD to ARM, October 13, 1895; PLD to ARM, between October 13 and October 28, 1895.

8. PLD to ARM, October 28, 1895.

9. PLD to ARM, February 16, 1896.

10. PLD to ARM, March 6, 1896.

11. Ibid.; PLD to ARM, March 23, 1896.

12. PLD to ARM, April 19, 1896; ARM to PLD, April 28, 1896. Paul showed Alice's picture to others: "I have been showing your picture to a poet friend of mine—up until the present an Amherst man but a future Harvardian—and he,—well I won't tell you what he says, but he agrees with me and I can say nothing but nice things of you" (PLD to ARM, August 2, 1896).

On another occasion, friends remarked of Alice: "Alice Ruth Moore has *glorious* eyes" (PLD to ARM, August 16, 1896).

13. PLD to ARM, May 4, 1896.

14. PLD to ARM, June 4, 1896; PLD to ARM, August 16, 1896.

15. PLD to ARM, January 27, 1896.

16. Ibid.

17. PLD to ARM, April 19, 1896.

18. Ibid.

19. ARM to PLD, April 28, 1896.

20. PLD to ARM, August 2, 1896.

21. PLD to ARM, September 19, 1896.

Chapter 11. A True Singer

1. [Advertisement for *Lyrics of Lowly Life*], *New York Tribune* (February 10, 1897): 8.

2. PLD to ARM, April 17, 1895. See PLD to ARM, June 10, 1897, for Dunbar's reference to Alice as "one fair American Girl."

3. ARM to PLD, May 7, 1895.

4. Paul Laurence Dunbar, "[Editorial]" *Dayton Tattler* 1.2 (December 20, 1890): 2; ARM to PLD, May 7, 1895.

5. ARM to PLD, May 7, 1895; PLD to ARM, May 23, 1895.

6. PLD to ARM, July 9, 1895.

7. PLD to ARM, August 14, 1895.

8. PLD to ARM, February 16, 1896; PLD to ARM, March 23, 1896.

9. [Anonymous Author], "The Sound-Money Victory," *Harper's Weekly* (June 27, 1896): 626.

10. Van Wyck Brooks, *The Confident Years, 1885–1915* (New York: Dutton, 1952), 142n.

11. Susan Goodman and Carl Dawson, *William Dean Howells: A Writer's Life* (Berkeley: University of California Press, 2005).

12. PLD to James A. Herne, undated, quoted in *Selected Literary Letters*, ed. Murillo and Nader, 80.

13. William Dean Howells, "Life and Letters," *Harper's Weekly* 40 (June 27, 1896): 630.

14. See Elizabeth Ammons, "Expanding the Canon of American Realism," in *Documents of American Realism and Naturalism*, ed. Donald Pizer (Carbondale and Edwardsville: Southern Illinois University Press, 1998), 442. This is not to say, however, that an African American writer such as Chesnutt did not regard himself as a racial insider. See Joseph R. McElrath, "W. D. Howells and Race: Charles W. Chesnutt's Disappointment of the Dean," *Nineteenth-Century Literature* 51 (1997): 493, which discusses Chesnutt's unpublished essays, "An Inside View of the Negro Question" and "The Negro's Answer to the Negro Question," along with Howells's praise of Chesnutt's racial insiderness in the essay, "Mr. Charles W. Chesnutt's Stories" (1900). Chesnutt, however, was reluctant to disclose his racial identity at the outset of his career.

15. Gene Andrew Jarrett, *Deans and Truants: Race and Realism in African American Literature* (Philadelphia: University of Pennsylvania Press, 2007), chapter 1.

16. The excerpts of the poems in Howells, "Life and Letters," are taken from Paul Laurence Dunbar, *Majors and Minors*, 44, 89, 111, 138, 120.

17. Moore quoted in Henry Louis Gates, Jr., *The Signifying Monkey: A Theory of African-American Literary Criticism* (New York: Oxford University Press, 1988), 175.

18. Eugene W. Metcalf Jr. lists nearly sixty articles published in over forty different newspapers and magazines between the years of 1892, when Dunbar first attracted interest by reading poems at the Western Association of Writers in Dayton, Ohio, and 1906, when he passed away. See Metcalf, *Paul Laurence Dunbar*, 106–112. These critics often emphasize Dunbar's literary accomplishments in light of the review of *Majors and Minors*; his other books of poetry, songs, and fiction; his lectures across the nation and abroad; and other biographical information shedding light on the privileges and troubles the poet experienced due to his African ancestry.

19. Joseph S. Cotter to PLD, July 9, 1896.

20. PLD to WDH, July 13, 1896.

21. *Paul Laurence Dunbar: Beyond the Mask*, produced by Frederick Lewis and Joseph Slade, 0:54:00.

22. WDH to Ripley Hitchcock, July 29, 1896. The letter is located in the Rare Book and Manuscript Library, Columbia University, New York City.

23. PLD to ARM, August 2, 1896; PLD to WDH, August 21, 1896.

24. WDH to PLD, August 23, 1896.

25. PLD to WDH, September 19, 1896.

26. Ibid.

27. PLD to ARM, September 19, 1896.

28. WDH to Mr. David Douglas, February 4, 1897.

29. PLD to MD, August 25, 1896; PLD to MD, August 26, 1896.

30. PLD to MD, October 15, 1896.

31. PLD to ARM, September 19, 1896.

32. PLD to ARM, October 15, 1896.

33. PLD to ARM, February 4, 1898.

34. PLD to ARM, February 10, 1897.

Chapter 12. England as Seen by a Black Man

1. PLD to MD, February 28, 1897.

2. PLD to Dr. F____, March 15, 1897. It is possible that this person is one Dr. Fisher: "I had a little book from my friend Dr. Fisher of Hoboken [New Jersey] . . ." (PLD to ARM, March 23, 1898).

3. Edwin H. Keen to PLD, undated, quoted in *Selected Literary Letters*, ed. Murillo and Nader, 83.

4. Paul Laurence Dunbar Papers, Roll 3.

5. Edward Keble Chatterton, *Steamships and Their Story* (London: Cassel, 1910), 158–161.

6. PLD to ARM, February 10, 1897.

7. Ibid.

8. PLD to ARM, February 20, 1897. In response to her reply to his wish for more letters from Alice, Paul said: "Someday, when I can hold you in my arms and punctuate every sentence with a kiss and an embrace I may be able to tell you how happy your letter has made me. Happy and yet unhappy from the very strength of my longing to be with you, a longing not to be satisfied it seems to so distant a day" (PLD to ARM, March 7, 1897). Later, he states: "Your letters have

been such a help and stimulant to me that I cannot sufficiently thank you for them. I look for one in every American mail and am greatly disappointed when they do not come" (PLD to ARM, March 26, 1897 [postmark]).

9. PLD to ARM, March 7, 1897.

10. Ibid.

11. PLD to ARM, March 26, 1897; PLD to ARM, April 23, 1897.

12. PLD to ARM, April 23, 1897.

13. PLD to MD, February 10, 1897.

14. William Kitching to PLD, April 21, 1897, quoted in *Selected Literary Letters*, ed. Murillo and Nader, 93–94.

15. PLD to ARM, March 7, 1897.

16. Paul's appreciation of fellow race men appears in his letter to Alice on the death of Alexander Crummell: "I suppose that even down there in benighted Boston you have heard of the death of my old friend Dr. Crummell. I just received a letter from him when I got home from Medford and never got a chance to answer it. We have lost the most brilliant example of the effect of the higher education upon the pure Negro. I grieve both as a friend and as a member of his race" (PLD to ARM, September 12, 1898).

17. Jeffrey Green, *Samuel Coleridge-Taylor* (New York: Routledge, 2011), 41.

18. Henry F. Downing, "Samuel Coleridge Taylor," *The Messenger* (September 1926): 267.

19. For Dunbar's recitals from 1893 to 1897, see Paul Laurence Dunbar Papers, Roll 3.

20. Downing, "Samuel Coleridge Taylor," 267; PLD to ARM, March 26, 1897.

21. Quoted from *The Paul Laurence Dunbar Reader*, ed. Jay Martin and Gossie H. Hudson (New York: Dodd, Mead, 1975), 439.

22. For background on Dunbar regarding music and the *Chicago Record*, see Caroline Bressey, *Empire, Race and the Politics of Anti-Caste* (London: Bloomsbury Academic, 2015), 232.

23. John Hay to PLD, June 18, 1897.

24. Downing, "Samuel Coleridge Taylor," 267.

25. Downing, "Samuel Coleridge Taylor," 267; "[On Coleridge-Taylor / Dunbar Performance]," *The Times* (London, England), Monday, June 7, 1897: 9.

26. PLD to ARM, June 10, 1897.

27. Unknown to PLD, June 28, 1897, quoted in *Selected Literary Letters*, ed. Murillo and Nader, 96.

28. Virginia Jackson and Yopie Prins, introduction to *The Lyric Theory Reader: A Critical Anthology*, ed. Jackson and Prins (Baltimore: Johns Hopkins University Press, 2014), 3.

29. James William Johnson, "Lyric," in *Princeton Encyclopedia of Poetry and Poetics*, ed. Alex Preminger (Princeton: Princeton University Press, 1965), 461–462. My definition of the lyric leaves untouched the fascinating debate among scholars about its development as a genre before and after the turn of the twentieth century. Jonathan Culler has incisively identified the difference between the singular, self-expressive form of the lyric in the nineteenth century and the development of this form into an impersonation of speech around the middle of the twentieth. He encourages critics to avoid flattening such distinctions in our discussions of the lyric. Likewise, Virginia Jackson points to how the lyric was construed in remarkable ways by modern literary criticism, which elevated it to a quintessential genre of poetry through the retrospection of modernity. For the correspondence between such scholars and their delineation of a field of scholarly debate, see Jonathan Culler, *Theory of the Lyric* (Cambridge, MA: Harvard University Press,

2017), especially 83–85; Virginia Jackson, *Dickinson's Misery: A Theory of Lyric Reading* (Princeton: Princeton University Press, 2005), 8; and Jackson and Prins, *The Lyric Theory Reader*, 2.

30. The titles of the four books with "lyrics" in the title are *Lyrics of Lowly Life* (New York: Dodd, Mead, 1896); *Lyrics of the Hearthside* (New York: Dodd, Mead, 1899); *Lyrics of Love and Laughter* (New York: Dodd, Mead, 1903); and *Lyrics of Sunshine and Shadow* (New York: Dodd, Mead, 1905). Poems with the word include "A Lyric" in *Majors and Minors* and "Lyrics of Love and Sorrow" in *Lyrics of Love and Laughter*. For Dunbar's references to his own lyrics, see PLD to ARM, June 6, 1895; PLD to ARM, June 25, 1895; PLD to ARM, October 28, 1895. The poem "When Malindy Sings" would first appear in *Majors and Minors*, and "Ione" in *Lyrics of Lowly Life*. Four "songs" appear in *Oak and Ivy*, and six in *Majors and Minors*. All total, he called forty-eight poems "songs" (some reprinted) across all the books published in his career.

31. PLD to ARM, March 16, 1897; PLD to ARM, March 26, 1897 (postmark); PLD to ARM, July 4, 1897.

32. PLD to WDH, April 26, 1897; PLD to R. W. Gilder, June 1, 1897.

33. PLD to Dr. F_____, March 15, 1897.

34. PLD to Mrs. Helen Douglass, October 22, 1896.

35. PLD to Dr. F_____, March 15, 1897.

36. PLD to ARM, April 23, 1897.

37. The new poems were "A Coquette Conquered," "Discovered," "Longing," "Religion," "Song of Summer," "Spring Song," "The Lawyers' Way," "The Path," "To Louise," and "Two Songs."

38. William Dean Howells, introduction to *Lyrics of Lowly Life*, by Paul Laurence Dunbar (New York: Dodd, Mead, 1896), xiv.

39. Howells, *Lyrics of Lowly* Life, xvi.

40. PLD to ARM, January 5, 1898; PLD to ARM, January 12, 1898.

41. PLD to WDH, April 26, 1897.

42. PLD to ARM, April 23, 1897.

43. PLD to MD, July 20, 1897, quoted in *Selected Literary Letters*, ed. Murillo and Nader, 96–97.

44. Bressey, *Empire, Race and the Politics of Anti-Caste*, 7, 231–232.

45. Ibid., 235.

46. PLD to MD, July 20, 1897, quoted in *Selected Literary Letters*, ed. Murillo and Nader, 96.

47. PLD to ARM, May 4, 1896.

48. ARM to PLD, June 19, 1897; PLD to ARM, June 22, 1897; PLD to ARM, July 4, 1897; PLD to ARM, July 20, 1897.

49. PLD to ARM, March 16, 1897; PLD to ARM, March 26, 1897. Dunbar's insecurities would persist even after his marriage to Alice. Six months into it, she was still trying to console him as she had before: "Your lovely letter has just come and it brought tears to my eyes. Dear, if I could at this minute spread wings and fly to you I would. I feel mean and guilty to have left my husband when he seems to need me most. You must not despair or say that *everything* you've touched lately has failed for it has not" (ARM to PLD, August 6, 1898).

50. PLD to ARM, March 26, 1897; PLD to ARM, May 14, 1897.

51. PLD to MD, June 22, 1897. Around this time we saw such letters from Rebekah as RB to PLD, July 1, 1895, and RB to PLD, July 10, 1895.

52. PLD to ARM, May 14, 1897.

53. PLD to ARM, June 22, 1897.

54. PLD to MD, February 28, 1897.

55. PLD to MD, June 14, 1897. See PLD to MD, July 31, 1897, regarding loaning money to Crummell.

56. PLD to MD, June 22, 1897.

57. PLD to MD, circa June 1897; PLD to MD, July 20, 1897.

58. PLD to MD, July 20, 1897, quoted in *Selected Literary Letters*, ed. Murillo and Nader, 97.

59. PLD to ARM, May 11, 1897.

60. ARM to PLD, June 8, 1897.

61. PLD to ARM, June 10, 1897. Dunbar once complained about the infrequency of Alice's letters: "Don't you think that sometime you might sit down and write me a letter, a real live letter when you are not in a hurry for bed or for church? I am not reproaching you for I know that you are a very busy person; but I do so want to feel your heart throb through your letters, and not have them seem as they have lately mere perfunctory epistles" (PLD to ARM, July 4, 1897). In turn, Alice complained that, even though he replied promptly, his occasional evasiveness was as reprehensible as her unpunctuality: "First—you don't *answer* my letters—Oh, yes, I know you write punctually enough and your letters are sweet and kissable, but you don't *answer* my letters—so!" (ARM to PLD, October 21, 1897).

62. *Paul Laurence Dunbar: Beyond the Mask*, produced by Frederick Lewis and Joseph Slade, 1:03:28.

63. PLD to ARM, June 22, 1897; PLD to ARM, August 21, 1897.

64. PLD to Dr. Fisher, August 7, 1897, quoted in *Selected Literary Letters*, ed. Murillo and Nader, 98.

65. Dunbar, *The Sport of the Gods and Other Essential Writings*, 255. For Washington's opinions, see Booker T. Washington, *The Future of the American Negro* (Boston: Small, Maynard, 1902), 131–132. In his 1901 autobiography *Up from Slavery*, Washington disparages, by associating them, the intellectual and political byproducts of Reconstruction: "During the whole of the Reconstruction period two ideas were constantly agitating the minds of the coloured people, or, at least, the minds of a large part of the race. One of these was the craze for Greek and Latin learning, and the other was a desire to hold office" (80); see Washington, *Up from Slavery* (New York: Penguin, 1986).

66. Dunbar, *The Sport of the Gods and Other Essential Writings*, 255.

Chapter 13. East Coast Strivings

1. PLD to MD, August 8, 1897; PLD to MD, September 27, 1897.

2. Ibid.

3. PLD to ARM, August 15, 1897; PLD to ARM, August 21, 1897.

4. PLD to ARM, August 29, 1897.

5. PLD to ARM, September 26, 1897.

6. ARM to PLD, October 6, 1897.

7. PLD to ARM, October 7, 1897. Alice's concern with Paul's flirtatious ways persisted across a host of conversations. In reference to "Dolores," Alice asked, "Did you kiss Delores good-bye? Tell the truth, dear." Paul responded, "I did *not* kiss Dolores goodbye. I felt for the first time that

it would be treason to you, so I only shook hands with her." All the while Paul sought to reassure Alice of his faithfulness: "Will I be true to you? Yes, dear, true and loyal." Respectively, ARM to PLD, October 6, 1897; PLD to ARM, October 8, 1897.

8. PLD to ARM, August 15, 1897.

9. He was sending and receiving mail either from 609 F Street NW, the business address of his friend Henry F. Baker, or from 2348 6th Street NW, a home address, where he would often hang out with his friend Lewis, Frederick Douglass's son.

10. Letter from Robert Ingersoll to Paul Laurence Dunbar transcribed in PLD to MD, July 20, 1897. Reverence expressed by Whitman, according to *Intimate with Walt: Selections from Whitman's Conversations with Horace Traubel*, ed. Gary Schmidgall (Iowa City: University of Iowa Press, 2001), 81.

11. H. A. Tobey quoted in Wiggins, *The Life and Works of Paul Laurence Dunbar*, 55–56. Robert Ingersoll to Tobey, April 1896, quoted in *Selected Literary Letters*, ed. Murillo and Nader, 81.

12. R. G. Ingersoll to John Russell Young, July 5, 1897; PLD to John Russell Young, September 3, 1897; transcribed in Peter Armenti, "The Caged Bird Sings: Paul Laurence Dunbar at the Library of Congress" (June 27, 2013): https://blogs.loc.gov/catbird/2013/06/the-caged-bird-sings-paul-laurence-dunbar-at-the-library-of-congress.

13. *Library Journal*, quoted in Charles A. Goodrum and Helen W. Dalrymple, *The Library of Congress* (Boulder, Colorado: Westview Press, 1982), 29.

14. Goodrum and Dalrymple, *The Library of Congress*, 27–31.

15. Robert Ingersoll to PLD enclosed in PLD to MD, July 20, 1897, quoted in *Selected Literary Letters*, ed. Murillo and Nader, 97.

16. PLD to Dr. Fisher, August 7, 1897, quoted in ibid., 98.

17. PLD to ARM, September 26, 1897.

18. Ben Tarnoff, *The Bohemians: Mark Twain and the San Francisco Writers Who Reinvented American Literature* (New York: Penguin Books, 2014), 53–56.

19. Ibid. Alice wanted Paul to avoid the Tenderloin at all costs. In February 1898 she wrote about the itinerary of Paul's upcoming travel to New York City, asking him to steer clear of a certain neighborhood and particular bars: "Now I don't want you to go anywhere in the neighborhood of the 'Tenderloin' to stop. 'Don't want' sounds preem[p]tory, but it's my deepest heart feeling. It's time, dearest, you were taking some decently dignified stand in the world and cutting loose from that gang of the Albany Clubs that drags you down; and causes us both unhappiness" (ARM to PLD, February 8, 1898).

20. Paul Laurence Dunbar, "We Wear the Mask," in *Majors and Minors*, 21.

21. ARM to PLD, October 21, 1897.

22. PLD to ARM, October 24, 1897.

23. PLD to ARM, October 29, 1897; PLD to ARM, November 2, 1897.

24. PLD to ARM, November 7, 1897.

25. PLD to ARM, October 8, 1897.

26. ARM to PLD, October 10, 1897.

27. PLD to ARM, October 11, 1897. Dunbar proposed the month of December; PLD to ARM, October 29, 1897.

28. *Alcohol and Drugs in North America: A Historical Encyclopedia*, ed. David M. Fahey and Jon S. Miller (New York: ABC-CLIO, 2013); Sarah W. Tracy, *Alcoholism in America: From Reconstruction to Prohibition* (Baltimore: Johns Hopkins University Press, 2009).

29. PLD to ARM, October 24, 1897.

30. PLD to ARM, October 15, 1897. An explicit rebuke came from Alice's friend Julia Lewis, to which Paul replied: "I do not, in the least mind what Julia says. I believe that you are going to marry me. I trust you and am happy in my trust. As it is, I do not half like Julia" (PLD to ARM, November 2, 1897).

31. PLD to ARM, October 15, 1897; ARM to PLD, October 24, 1897. Regarding the letter to Mrs. Moore: "I am scared to death, but I enclose this second letter to your mother. God grant that it brings a favorable answer" (PLD to ARM, October 29, 1897).

32. PLD to ARM, November 7, 1897.

33. PLD to MD, November 9, 1897.

34. PLD to ARM, October 7, 1897.

35. PLD to ARM, October 11, 1897; PLD to ARM, November 29, 1897.

36. PLD to ARM, August 21, 1897; PLD to ARM, October 24, 1897; PLD to ARM, October 29, 1897.

37. PLD to ARM, October 29, 1897.

38. PLD to ARM, November 2, 1897.

39. PLD to ARM, December 7, 1897.

40. PLD to ARM, September 19, 1896.

41. PLD to ARM, November 9, 1897.

42. PLD to ARM, December 11, 1897.

43. For more information about the establishment of *Lippincott's* in the late nineteenth century, see Mott, *A History of American Magazines*, 4: 396–401.

44. Ibid. *Nation* reporter quoted in 1873, in Mott, *A History of American Magazines*, 4: 399. For Paul's fulfillment of the request from the *Lippincott's* editor, see Cunningham, *Paul Laurence Dunbar and His Song*, 222.

45. PLD to ARM, December 21, 1897; PLD to ARM, January 4, 1898; PLD to ARM, January 5, 1898.

46. PLD to ARM, January 5, 1898.

47. PLD to ARM, September 26, 1897.

48. PLD to MD, September 27, 1897.

49. PLD to ARM, December 16, 1897.

Chapter 14. The Way Is Dark

1. PLD to ARM, November 26, 1897.

2. PLD to ARM, November 19, 1897. Alice indicated that Will Lewis was there in a later letter: "That Philadelphia yarn is muchly around here. My good friend and lawyer, Will Lewis, was in Phila. that night and saw you Oh!!!!" (ARM to PLD, December 29, 1897).

3. Paul was an attendant responsible for shelving and retrieving items from the mathematics, medicine, and natural sciences collections, located within the closed stacks; he started working there on September 30, 1897. See "Art and Literature," *The Record-Union* [Sacramento, California] (March 13, 1898): 9; https://chroniclingamerica.loc.gov/lccn/sn82015104/1898-03-13/ed-1/seq-9/?loclr=blogpoe.

4. PLD to ARM, November 19, 1897.

5. Alexander, *Lyrics of Sunshine and Shadow*, 131. For the historical unpopularity of premarital sex, see Bernard I. Murstein, *Love, Sex, and Marriage through the Ages* (New York: Springer, 1974), 429.

6. Estelle B. Freedman, *Redefining Rape: Sexual Violence in the Era of Suffrage and Segregation* (Cambridge, MA: Harvard University Press, 2013), 4–5.

7. PLD to ARM, November 19, 1897.

8. Ibid.

9. PLD to ARM, November 22, 1897; PLD to ARM, November 25, 1897.

10. Paul Laurence Dunbar, "A Hymn," in *Lyrics of the Hearthside*, 28–29.

11. PLD to ARM, November 29, 1897; PLD to ARM, December 1, 1897.

12. PLD to ARM, December 2, 1897. Dunbar confessed to having this illness when he wrote Alice: "I didn't know about the G—until last week and then I began treatment at once" (PLD to ARM, December 7, 1897).

13. PLD to ARM, December 1, 1897; PLD to ARM, December 2, 1897.

14. PLD to ARM, December 6, 1897.

15. PLD to ARM, December 7, 1897; ibid.

16. Ibid. Paul asked Alice: "Have you heard any more from your mama and your sister Leila? Have they or any one else regaled you with the spicy narrative of my escapades? After all I'm an infernally obliging fellow to give dear feminine humanity, which loves to gossip—something to gossip about" (PLD to ARM, December 19, 1897).

17. PLD to ARM, December 16, 1897; ibid.

18. ARM to PLD, December 18, 1897.

19. PLD to ARM, December 19, 1897.

20. PLD to ARM, December 21, 1897; PLD to ARM, December 27, 1897.

21. ARM to PLD, December 29, 1897.

22. PLD to ARM, December 29, 1897.

23. ARM to PLD, December 31, 1897; ARM to PLD, January 1, 1898; PLD to ARM, January 3, 1898.

24. PLD to ARM, December 14, 1897.

25. PLD to ARM, December 15, 1897; PLD to ARM, January 5, 1898.

26. ARM to PLD, January 1, 1898. Paul encountered a person who accused Alice of being a flirt: "I was told yesterday that you did not love me—that you were a flirt and I was not the first man for whom you had conceived an enthusiasm. I swore you did love me and registered a vow of eternal faith in you. Then saith the woman, 'I wish I could see her with you. I could tell if she loved you.' Then goeth this same woman unto my mother and try to poison her mind saying you and I will be unhappy together etc ad nauseum" (PLD to ARM, January 2, 1898).

27. ARM to PLD, January 1, 1898; PLD to ARM, January 3, 1898.

28. ARM to PLD, January 4, 1898; PLD to ARM, January 5, 1898.

29. PLD to ARM, January 5, 1898; ARM to PLD, January 7, 1898; PLD to ARM, January 8, 1898.

30. PLD to ARM, January 10, 1898.

31. PLD to ARM, January 19, 1898.

32. PLD to ARM, January 5, 1898.

33. PLD to ARM, January 5, 1898. A refrain from Alice was her inquiry into whether Paul paid the medical bills of Dr. John W. Parrish, who was treating her for her injury: "Have you attended to Dr. Parrish's bill yet? I hate to ask you about [it] but you know I must," she asked him,

in typical fashion (ARM to PLD, January 22, 1898). Paul replied to Alice's concern about the medical expense: "Don't worry about the doctor, dear. I have not paid him this week because I am so soon to see you and you must help me compose the letter to him or go on and compose it yourself and I will copy it" (PLD to ARM, February 9, 1898). Part of the concern was that Paul and Alice were trying to mitigate Dr. Parrish's potential suspicion and her embarrassment that she was abused under any untoward (such as premarital) circumstances. Ultimately, Paul did begin paying the doctor, accompanied initially by a letter, in mid-February (PLD to ARM, February 15, 1898).

34. ARM to PLD, January 7, 1898.

35. ARM to PLD, January 24, 1898.

36. PLD to ARM, January 31, 1898.

37. PLD to ARM, April 10, 1896; PLD to ARM, April 23, 1897; PLD to ARM, August 21, 1897; PLD to ARM, November 7, 1897; PLD to ARM, December 1, 1897.

38. PLD to ARM, January 31, 1898; PLD to ARM, February 2, 1898.

39. For the "drunken narrative" of the nineteenth century, see Elaine Frantz Parsons, *Manhood Lost: Fallen Drunkards and Redeeming Women in the Nineteenth-Century United States* (Baltimore: Johns Hopkins University Press, 2009), 3–4.

40. Paul and Alice discussed his great illness (suffering from cerebrospinal meningitis), which prevented him from writing letters to her promptly, in the last weeks of February, just before their wedding. See PLD to ARM, February 25, 1898, and ARM to PLD, February 27, 1898.

41. ARM to PLD, February 1, 1898. For background information about the White Rose Mission, see Shawn Anthony Christian, "'Upon the Young People of Our Race, by Our Own Literature': Alice Dunbar-Nelson's 'Negro Literature for Negro Pupils,'" *Legacy: A Journal of American Women Writers* 33.2 (2016): 270–271.

42. PLD to ARM, February 3, 1898.

43. "Dely" is included in Dunbar, *Lyrics of the Hearthside*, 187. Regarding the lower-class African Americans, Paul once wrote to Alice: "Yes, I was drunk at Philadelphia but don't believe any of the reports you hear. That matter about my being soiled is all a lie. I dressed at the hall dressing room in all clean linen, but had to send a nigger out for a standing collar because mine were all lay-downs." Regarding the despicable upper-class African American Bostonians who wanted Alice to marry someone upstanding, Paul wrote her: "For the Boston fools who are mad because you won't marry [Frank] Stewart or [George Washington] Forbes, I don't care a damn and the rest of the niggers if let alone will come home draggin' their tails behind them" (PLD to ARM, December 7, 1897). Regarding the poem "Dely": "I am going to try my hand at a bit of a sonnet this afternoon. I wrote a darkey dialect love-poem yesterday called 'Dely,' so I want to balance the effect" (PLD to ARM, January 28, 1898).

44. ARM to PLD, February 8, 1898. Alice likewise used this language; to Paul she once wrote, regarding her reading of "Anner Lizer's Stumblin' Block" in his book of 1898, *Folks from Dixie*: "After ~~laughing~~ crying over your letter I laughed over your story. It is very good, very true to life—haven't I seen the niggers shout all the way up the aisle and back again! How is the work coming on?" (ARM to PLD, December 18, 1897). Regarding working under "Negro women," Alice once wrote Paul: "I hate to work under Negro women, never did it and my heart sank at the prospect" (ARM to PLD, January 7, 1898). Alice told Paul that she "teased" her boss: "My face was better so I was at school to-day and already teased our new 'nigger' head of dept. crazy. She is short and sensitive about it so I've taken to wearing my high collars just for the pleasure

of looking over them at her in a lofty, disdainful manner" (ARM to PLD, January 12, 1898). Regarding a constituent family of the White Rose Mission, Alice wrote Paul: "Two of her boys are in my kindergarten and the oldest one—a boy of ten in my manual training class. She is white, German, her husband a shiftless, dirty Negro. He scurried out when we came" (ARM to PLD, January 23, 1898). Regarding the Brownsville school where Alice worked, she told Paul: "Oh Lord! Brownsville I learned is a district settled entirely by a class of Polish Jews, fairly thrifty and thoroughly dirty. There are about 700 pupils in the school—and *every one* of them are Polish Jew kids. There isn't a single darky anywhere for miles" (ARM to PLD, February 4, 1898).

45. ARM to PLD, January 15, 1898.

46. Ibid.

47. ARM to PLD, February 8, 1898.

Chapter 15. The Wizard of Tuskegee

1. Paul Laurence Dunbar, "The Ordeal at Mt. Hope," in *Folks from Dixie* (New York: Dodd, Mead, 1898), 31.

2. Booker T. Washington, *Up from Slavery* (1901), reprinted in *The Wiley-Blackwell Anthology of African American Literature, Volume 1: 1746–1920*, ed. Gene Andrew Jarrett (Malden, MA: Wiley-Blackwell, 2014), 902.

3. PLD to BTW, July 31, 1896.

4. PLD to ARM, September 19, 1896.

5. Ibid.

6. Ibid.

7. John Wesley Cromwell to BTW, January 19, 1897. Reprinted in *Booker T. Washington Papers, Volume 4: 1895–1898*, ed. Louis Harlan et al. (Urbana: University of Illinois Press, 1975), 255–256.

8. Quotations in *Booker T. Washington Papers, Volume 2: 1860–1889*, ed. Louis Harlan et al. (Urbana: University of Illinois Press, 1972), 366–369. Original publication split over two issues: Washington, "Industrial Training for the Negro," *The Independent* 50 (January 27, 1898): 105–106, and (February 3, 1898): 145–146.

9. PLD to ARM, February 2, 1898.

10. John Stephens Durham, "The Labor Unions and the Negro," *Atlantic Monthly* 81 (February 1898): 225.

11. See ARM to PLD, February 4, 1898, for reference to "Manual Training Class." Also, ARM to PLD, March 19, 1898, indicates Washington's direct support: "Mr. Washington has promised to send a young man from Tuskegee who is to study in college and teach our boys at night. But he will not come until the Tuskegee school closes, and I must prepare his note-books, drawings tc[.] and grade work so the class can go smoothly all next year."

12. ARM to PLD, February 3, 1898; PLD to ARM, February 8, 1898.

13. ARM to PLD, February 16, 1898; PLD to ARM, February 21, 1898.

14. ARM to PLD, February 23, 1898.

15. PLD to WDH, April 30, 1898.

16. PLD to ARM, August 9, 1898.

17. PLD to ARM, January 28, 1898.

18. ARM to PLD, January 29, 1898; PLD to ARM, January 31, 1898.

19. PLD to ARM, February 15, 1898. Together, the stories would appear in *Folks from Dixie*.

20. ARM to PLD, February 16, 1898; PLD to ARM, February 16, 1898.

21. [PLD Submits MS. of *Folks from Dixie*], June 6, 1898.

22. PLD to ARM, August 9, 1898.

23. Metcalf, *Paul Laurence Dunbar*, 129.

Chapter 16. The Wedding of Plebeians

1. PLD to ARM, March 9, 1898.

2. Certificate of Marriage, Paul Laurence Dunbar to Alice Ruth Moore, March 6, 1898, City of New York, New York; New York City Municipal Archives Reference Room, Department of Records and Information Services. Copy in possession of author.

3. PLD to ARM, February 3, 1898.

4. Maud Shannon may be the then-unmarried M. Maud Wilkinson, to whom, for a brief period, Paul had been writing love letters in October 1896: "I love you and poor as I am, if you will take me I will marry you now and take from you this harrowing [case] of self-support.... I want you to think of me darling as your protection, even more than your lover. Know that I wish to shield you from all the severities of life, and take you into the warm shelter of my heart of hearts. You are so much to me, and have grown deeper into my love even in absence. I cannot think of losing you without a hard fight" (PLD to Miss M. M. Wilkinson, October 24, 1896). It is not clear whether this is the same person as Maud Clark, referred to in Eleanor Alexander, *Lyrics of Sunshine and Shadow*, 102–103.

5. PLD to ARM, March 2, 1898.

6. PLD to ARM, February 4, 1898. In his letters Paul would reflect on the times he and Alice enjoyed each other's presence in person: "Do you remember how cozily your dear head falls right into the bend of my arm? Friday, Saturday, Sunday—oh those were three days of Heaven" (PLD to ARM, February 16, 1898). Also, in the days before their marriage, Paul wrote: "Dear heart, it is best that we be not together much before we are married. It is a wise Providence that sent me rushing these thousand miles away as soon as we became engaged and now keeps me chained in another city from you" (PLD to ARM, February 19, 1898). And he had admitted, before their marriage, the temptations that continued to haunt him: "And dear, I have so many more temptations than you can possibly imagine. Temptations you could help me withstand because you could help me bear for oh, my darling, I love you so supremely that I can be anything for your sake; but oh weakness! I need you near" (PLD to ARM, February 21, 1898).

7. PLD to ARM, March 9, 1898. See PLD to ARM, March 11, 1898, for "scolding."

8. PLD to JNM, 1898.

9. PLD to ARM, March 11, 1898.

10. ARM to PLD, March 13, 1898.

11. PLD to ARM, March 13, 1898; ARM to PLD, March 14, 1898; PLD to ARM, March 14, 1898. See PLD to ARM, March 17, 1898, for resting by the window; and PLD to ARM, March 18, 1898, for sponging eyes open.

12. ARM to PLD, March 19, 1898; PLD to ARM, March 19, 1898.

13. PLD to ARM, March 21, 1898; ARM to PLD, March 22, 1898.

14. In ARM to PLD, March 29, 1898, we see the root of the estrangement: "Don't you know I'm vexed now. Here I had gone to work and built up a great romance. Obdurate, hard-hearted mother, stern but loving and inconsolable sister, brother-in-law flourishing a gun, reaction between, amongst and amidst everybody and everything generally—when here to-night's mail deluges me with paternal and sisternal blessings. Without a word of warning mama climbs down from her heights and writes me thusly.—'I am not angry at all about your marriage. I am heartily glad of it—only I would have liked to have given you away. I have worried all the time about you being away from me working half-sick and no one to take care of you. Now you will have a home of your own as you had in New Orleans.' Further on—"

15. ARM to PLD, March 22, 1898; ARM to PLD, March 23, 1898.

16. ARM to PLD, March 23, 1898.

17. Ibid.

18. PLD to ARM, March 24, 1898; ARM to PLD, March 26, 1898.

19. ARM to PLD, March 26, 1898; ARM to PLD, March 29, 1898.

20. Wedding announcement in PLD to JNM, 1898; ARM to PLD, April 10, 1898.

21. ARM to PLD, April 17, 1901.

22. PLD to ARM, March 18, 1898.

23. Will Marion Cook, "Clorindy," in *Readings in Black American Music*, ed. Eileen Southern (New York: W. W. Norton, 1983), 229.

24. Cook, "Clorindy," 230–233.

25. ARM to PLD, summer 1898.

26. PLD to ARM, August 31, 1898; PLD to ARM, September 3, 1898. *Cannibal King* would have a short run in New York City; it would have some incorporated parts overlapping with *Jes Lak White Fo'ks*, *Uncle Eph's Christmas*, and *In Dahomey*. James Weldon Johnson and Bob Cole came aboard, according to Carter, *Swing Along*, 56–57.

27. See Forbes, *Introducing Bert Williams*, 78–83, and Carter, *Swing Along*, 129–137, for Cook's collaborations with Dunbar.

28. ARM to PLD, August 25, 1898.

29. PLD to ARM, August 10, 1898; PLD to ARM, August 12, 1898; ARM to PLD, September 1, 1898. ARM to PLD, December 7, 1898, on consulting Tobey.

30. ARM to PLD, September 13, 1898.

31. PLD to ARM, September 13, 1898. In spring 1901 Alice told Paul that she met Kelly Miller, a historian at Howard University. Miller believed that Paul was "mean" to tell Charles Chesnutt that Miller had offered Paul fifty dollars to deliver a recital there. "I denied that you had said such a thing. Did you?" Alice asked, sensing, due to his history, that Paul's competitive juices had flowed too much (ARM to PLD, March 23, 1901). In denial, Paul replied days later: "I can only drop you a line this morning as I am very busy. About what I said to Chesnutt. It was this, that I thought it foolish to read for less than $50. As to saying that Miller had promised me that, I know nothing about" (PLD to ARM, March 27, 1901).

32. Stephen Crane, "Fears Realists Must Wait," in *Stephen Crane: Uncollected Writings*, ed. Olov W. Frychstedt (Uppsala, Sweden: Uppsala Universitet, 1963), 82.

33. Frank Norris, "A Plea for Romantic Fiction," in *Documents of American Realism and Naturalism*, ed. Donald Pizer (Carbondale: Southern Illinois University Press, 1998), 172.

34. Norris, "Zola as a Romantic Writer," in ibid., 169. For my extended reading of Dunbar in this context of literary naturalism, please see Jarrett, *Deans and Truants*, chapter 2.

35. ARM to PLD, January 15, 1898. Paul Laurence Dunbar, *The Uncalled* (New York: Dodd, Mead, 1898), viii.

36. PLD to Dr. Fisher, August 7, 1897, quoted in *Selected Literary Letters*, ed. Murillo and Nader, 98.

37. Metcalf, *Paul Laurence Dunbar*, 130–131.

38. PLD to Dr. F____, October 2, 1898.

39. ARM to PLD, July 9, 1898; ARM to PLD, August 8, 1898.

40. PLD to ARM, August 12, 1898.

41. ARM to PLD, September 1, 1898; ARM to PLD, September 3, 1898.

42. PLD to ARM, September 9, 1898.

43. Ibid.

44. PLD to ARM, September 10, 1898.

45. ARM to PLD, September 13, 1898.

46. Ibid.

47. Ibid.

48. Alice enclosed a letter that was more pointed than her cover letter: "I have honestly tried to be, but you won't let me—you hold up a barrier every time I approach you—a barrier of 'silly, hysterical.' And then when I go into myself and become uncommunicative you are hurt. Sometimes I have told you things, silly things, incidents, meaningless in themselves. Then when a time comes, when you are half-irritated, wholly nervous, you cast them in my face in derision, and hurt me so that I can not even speak of the simplest occurrence for days after, fearing—" (ARM to PLD, September 13, 1898).

49. ARM to PLD, September 18, 1898.

50. ARM to PLD, September 20, 1898.

Chapter 17. Our New Madness

1. BTW to Emmett Jay Scott, August 23, 1898. Reprinted in *Booker T. Washington Papers*, ed. Harlan et al., 4: 456.

2. Paul Laurence Dunbar, "Our New Madness," in *The Sport of the Gods and Other Essential Writings*, ed. Fishkin and Bradley, 257–258.

3. Dunbar, "Our New Madness," 258. Du Bois would incorporate Paul's line of argument in the chapter "Of Booker T. Washington and Others" in his 1903 book *The Souls of Black Folk*.

4. BTW to Emmett Jay Scott, August 23, 1898.

5. "[American; Mr. T. Thomas Fortune; Mr. Paul Laurence Dunbar; Dayton]," *Leavenworth (Kansas) Herald* (October 27, 1894): 2.

6. BTW to Emmett Jay Scott, August 23, 1898.

7. George Washington Carver to BTW, August 27, 1898. Reprinted in *Booker T. Washington Papers*, ed. Harlan et al., 4: 458.

8. PLD to ARM, September 3, 1898.

9. Ibid.

10. Ibid.

11. PLD to BTW, October 26, 1898.

12. Alice Moore Dunbar, "The Poet and His Song," *A.M.E. Review* 31.2 (October 1914); reprinted in *The Dunbar Speaker and Entertainer*, ed. Dunbar-Nelson, 332.

13. PLD to John Russell Young, October 28, 1898; https://blogs.loc.gov/catbird/files/2013/06/Mears-on-Dunbar-Items.pdf?loclr=blogpoe.

14. John Russell Young to PLD, October 29, 1898; https://blogs.loc.gov/catbird/files/2013/06/Mears-on-Dunbar-Items.pdf?loclr=blogpoe.

15. PLD to BTW, November 7, 1898.

16. For more information about the Wilmington massacre, see H. Leon Prather Sr., *We Have Taken a City: The Wilmington Racial Massacre and Coup of 1898* (Rutherford, NJ: Fairleigh Dickinson University Press, 1984).

17. Paul Laurence Dunbar, "The Race Question Discussed," in *The Sport of the Gods and Other Essential Writings*, ed. Fishkin and Bradley, 260–261.

18. Ibid., 263.

19. Ibid.

20. Ibid., 264–265.

21. Ibid., 267.

22. ARM to PLD, February 26, 1899. For the letter about bronchitis, see ARM to PLD, February 25, 1899.

23. ARM to PLD, February 26, 1899.

24. ARM to PLD, March 7, 1899, for "sassy."

25. PLD to ARM, September 2, 1898.

26. Metcalf, *Paul Laurence Dunbar*, 131–133.

27. PLD to BTW, December 22, 1898.

28. PLD to BTW, January 22, 1899.

29. PLD to BTW, January 29, 1899; PLD to BTW, January 31, 1899.

30. Quoted in Metcalf, *Paul Laurence Dunbar*, 85.

31. PLD to Emmett J. Scott, February 6, 1899.

32. The traditional date of the interview, February 12, 1899, comes from Brawley, *Paul Laurence Dunbar*, 69, 76. The interview was reprinted in the *New York Commercial*, February 14, 1899, found in the Paul Laurence Dunbar Papers, Reel 4, Box 16.

33. PLD to ARM, February 21, 1899.

34. PLD to ARM, February 24, 1899; PLD to ARM, March 3, 1899.

35. PLD to BTW, March 5, 1899.

36. PLD to ARM, March 6, 1899. PLD to BTW, March 21, 1899, for information about the expenses. Background on correspondence between Washington and Bumstead in *Booker T. Washington Papers, Volume 3: 1889–1895*, ed. Louis Harlan et al. (Urbana: University of Illinois Press, 1974), 58.

37. Booker T. Washington, "Extracts from an Address at the Hollis Street Theater: The Influence of Object-Lessons in the Solution of the Race Problem," in *Booker T. Washington Papers*, ed. Harlan et al., 3: 54–56.

38. PLD to BTW, March 29, 1899, regarding keeping his calendar open in April. For a description of the event, see David Levering Lewis, *W. E. B. DuBois: Biography of a Race, 1868–1919* (New York: Owl Books, 1993), 228–229.

39. Ray Julius Sapirstein, "Out from Behind the Mask: The Illustrated Poetry of Paul Laurence Dunbar and Photography at Hampton Institute" (PhD diss., University of Texas, Austin, 2005), 131.

40. Quoted in ibid., "Out from Behind the Mask," 133; on the relationship of the Hampton Camera Club and the Folklore Society, see 136; on the African American membership and racial progressiveness of the camera club, see 128–129, 131.

41. For the Dodd and Mead connections at Hampton, see ibid., 140–141.

42. PLD to MD, June 22, 1899.

43. Dunbar's letter to Frissell, reprinted in Sapirstein, "Out from Behind the Mask," 121.

44. Frissell's letter to Paul, reprinted in ibid., 119; PLD to ARM, January 26, 1898.

45. Sapirstein, "Out from Behind the Mask," 118, on *Southern Workman's* review of Dunbar's *Lyrics of Lowly Life*; and 122, on Dunbar's publications in *Southern Workman* from 1899 to 1906.

46. Ronda, "'Work and Wait Unwearying,'" 863–878.

47. Dunbar, *Majors and Minors*, 118–119.

48. Camera Club minutes reprinted in Sapirstein, "Out from Behind the Mask," 142.

49. These poems are "The Deserted Plantation," "Hunting Song," "Little Brown Baby," "Chris'mus Is A-Comin'," "Signs of the Times," "Time to Tinker 'Roun'!" "Lullaby," and "A Banjo Song."

50. Marginalia reprinted in Sapirstein, "Out from Behind the Mask," 152.

51. Metcalf, *Paul Laurence Dunbar*, 134–136.

52. PLD to Paul Reynolds, August 17, 1901.

Chapter 18. Still a Sick Man

1. "Dunbar in Denver," *Plaindealer* (September 22, 1899): 2.

2. Timothy Thomas Fortune to BTW, September 23, 1899; *Booker T. Washington Papers, Volume 5: 1899–1900*, ed. Louis Harlan et al. (Urbana: University of Illinois Press, 1976), 213.

3. PLD to MD, July 20, 1897, quoted in *Selected Literary Letters*, ed. Murillo and Nader, 96.

4. ARM to PLD, December 5, 1898; PLD to ARM, December 5, 1898; PLD to ARM, December 7, 1898; PLD to ARM, December 9, 1898.

5. "Paul Laurence Dunbar Ill," *New York Tribune* (May 6, 1899): 8. Other publications referring to Paul's illness include "Men, Women and Affairs," *Springfield Republican* (May 7, 1899): 8; and *Morning Oregonian* (May 11, 1899): 3.

6. Roger Clark to PLD, May 6, 1899.

7. PLD to MD, May 7, 1899.

8. John E. Bruce to PLD, October 30, 1899.

9. F. Z. S. Peregrino to PLD, October 25, 1899.

10. By his early forties, Roosevelt had had a distinguished upbringing and career. Born to a prominent family, educated at Harvard, married twice, and the father of five children, he was the youngest man ever elected to the New York State Assembly, which he served from 1882 to 1884. He published three books on his hunting trips and life as a ranchman in North Dakota. A handful of years later, in 1889, he was appointed the U.S. civil service commissioner, a position he held for six years. He resigned to become the police commissioner of New York City. During his tenure, he enacted several major reforms, especially a "war on vice," a moralistic motto capturing his prerogative to clean up the city. He fleshed out his vision of cultural morality in his 1897 book, *American Ideals, and Other Essays*, about what Americans both could and should be. A year later he was promoted to assistant secretary of the navy during the Spanish-American

War, but then he resigned to join the First U.S. Volunteer Cavalry Regiment as lieutenant-colonel and formed the illustrious "Rough Riders," which fought at Las Guásimas on the island of Cuba. With his return as a war hero, he was elected in 1898 as the thirty-third governor of New York.

11. Theodore Roosevelt to PLD, November 17, 1899.

12. Ibid.

13. F. Z. S. Peregrino to PLD, November 7, 1899.

14. Sallie Brown to MD, May 9, 1899; PLD to MD, June 8, 1899.

15. PLD to MD, June 12, 1899; PLD to MD, June 17, 1899.

16. PLD to MD, June 22, 1899.

17. PLD to MD, June 25, 1899.

18. Johnson, *Along This Way*, 152.

19. Ibid.

20. Ibid.

21. "Dunbar in Denver," *Plaindealer*, 2.

22. Ibid.

23. Sheila M. Rothman, *Living in the Shadow of Death: Tuberculosis and the Social Experience of Illness in American History* (Baltimore: Johns Hopkins University Press, 1995), 181; Knopf quoted on 183.

24. Barbara Bates, *Bargaining for Life: A Social History of Tuberculosis, 1876–1938* (Philadelphia: University of Pennsylvania Press, 1992), 28; Rothman, *Living in the Shadow of Death*, 4.

25. Mark Twain, *Roughing It* (New York: Penguin Books, 1981), 188–189.

26. Rothman, *Living in the Shadow of Death*, 132; Tenney quoted on 145.

27. Paul Laurence Dunbar, *Candle-Lightin' Time* (New York: Dodd, Mead, 1901), 25–35.

28. Cunningham, *Paul Laurence Dunbar*, 199.

29. "Paul Dunbar, Negro Poet," *Denver Post* (September 12, 1899): 7.

30. H. A. Tobey to Jeremiah T. Eskridge, July 25, 1899, quoted in *Selected Literary Letters*, ed. Murillo and Nader, 114.

31. Edward Arnold, "Personal Reminiscences of Paul Laurence Dunbar," *Journal of Negro History* 17.4 (October 1932): 400–408; Paul's own descriptions of Colorado on 405. "Prudent" referenced in "Paul Dunbar, Negro Poet," *Denver Post*, 7.

32. PLD to H. A. Tobey, September 12, 1899, quoted in *Selected Literary Letters*, ed. Murillo and Nader, 115.

33. "Dunbar in Denver," *Plaindealer*, 2.

34. "Morning in Denver," *Denver Post* (September 15, 1899): 6. Dunbar wrote other poems as well, including "Yearning" and "Menace," both in *Denver Post* (September 24, 1899): 5. See Gary Scharnhorst and Kadeshia Matthews, "'Denver Took Me into Her Arms': Paul Laurence Dunbar in Colorado, 1899–1900," *Colorado Heritage* (July–August 2011): 16, on the positive reception to Paul's role in the *Denver Post*: "Good and Bad Things Said About the Post," *Denver Post* (September 18, 1899): 5; subsequent references in the *Post* (September 19, 1899): 6; (September 25, 1899): 10; and (September 26, 1899): 6.

35. Paul Laurence Dunbar, "The Carnival Is on in Denver," *Denver Post* (September 27, 1899): 12.

36. Paul Laurence Dunbar, "Home, the Solution of the Negro Problem," *Denver Republican* (September 13, 1899); Dunbar, "Solution of Negro Problem Seen from Two Sides," *Sunday Magazine of the Rocky Mountain News* (September 24, 1899): 7; Dunbar, "The Hapless Southern

Negro," *Denver Post* (September 17, 1899); Dunbar, "A Council of State," *Denver Post* (October 1, 1899): 15. See Scharnhorst and Matthews, "'Denver Took Me into Her Arms,'" 16, for the preliminary title of *Fanatics* as "Copperheads of the Civil War" see 20, for Dunbar's winter project, a Western novel called *The Love of Landry*.

37. BTW to Timothy Thomas Fortune, September 18, 1899; *Booker T. Washington Papers*, ed. Harlan et al., 5:209.

38. Timothy Thomas Fortune to BTW, September 23, 1899; *Booker T. Washington Papers*, ed. Harlan et al., 5: 213.

39. Ibid.

40. PLD to BTW, January 24, 1900.

41. Reprinted in Scharnhorst and Matthews, "'Denver Took Me into Her Arms,'" 21, which published the text of the typescript for the first time.

42. "[Dunbar and Washington in Colorado]," *Denver Post* (January 28, 1900).

43. "Dunbar in Denver," *Plaindealer*, 2.

44. "Colored Poet: Paul Laurence Dunbar to Appear at the Temple Theater Next Thursday Night," *Colorado Springs Gazette* (March 18, 1900): 5.

45. Quoted in Scharnhorst and Matthews, "'Denver Took Me into Her Arms,'" 23.

46. Gilberta S. Whittle, "Paul Dunbar," *A.M.E. Church Review* (April 1902): 320–327.

47. ARM to Lida Keck Wiggins, August 7, 1906; quoted in Eugene Wesley Metcalf Jr., "The Letters of Paul and Alice Dunbar: A Private History" (PhD diss., University of California, Irvine, 1973), 12.

48. In a 1933 interview, Matilda noted: "Paul's doctors told him not to leave, he sacrificed himself for me and brought me back, he sacrificed himself for me" (quoted in Best, *Crossing the Color Line*, 95).

49. E. C. Martin to PLD, January 13, 1900, quoted in *Selected Literary Letters*, ed. Murillo and Nader, 119.

50. Metcalf, *Paul Laurence Dunbar*, 138–140.

51. Metcalf, *Paul Laurence Dunbar*, 136–137.

Chapter 19. A Sac of Bitter Sarcasm

1. Johnson, *Along This Way*, 160.

2. "Education of the Negro," *New York Times* (May 8, 1900): 5.

3. Ibid.

4. Ibid. Paul Laurence Dunbar, "Is Higher Education for the Negro Hopeless?" in *The Sport of the Gods and Other Essential Writings*, ed. Fishkin and Bradley, 279–280.

5. Ibid., 280–281.

6. R. U. [Robert Underwood] Johnson to PLD, December 8, 1894; R. U. Johnson to PLD, August 9, 1895; PLD to R. U. Johnson, April 10, 1896.

7. PLD to R. U. Johnson, August 7, 1900.

8. *Booker T. Washington Papers*, ed. Harlan et al., 5: 661–662.

9. BTW to PLD, November 3, 1900.

10. Whittle, "Paul Dunbar," 320.

11. Quote in Osofsky, "Race Riot, 1900," 17.

12. Ibid., 19.

13. For details on the altercation, see Martha Hodes, "Knowledge and Indifference in the New York City Race Riot of 1900: An Argument in Search of a Story," *Rethinking History* 15.1 (March 2011): 63; and Osofsky, "Race Riot, 1900," 20.

14. *New York Times* quoted in Hodes, "Knowledge and Indifference," 67, 69.

15. Dialogue quoted in ibid., 68.

16. *New York Daily Tribune* quoted in Osofsky, "Race Riot, 1900," 20.

17. Quotations in "Drugged Paul L. Dunbar: The Negro Writer Robbed after Trying to Pacify Men of His Race," *American Citizen* [Kansas City, Kansas] (August 24, 1900): 1. Additional details in Reynolds J. Scott-Childress, "Paul Laurence Dunbar, New Yorker," *New York History* 92.3 (Summer 2011): 195.

18. For details about what Dunbar lost, see "Poet Dunbar Drugged," *The (Indianapolis) Freeman* (September 8, 1900): 7.

19. Hodes, "Knowledge and Indifference," 70–73, on police brutality.

20. Headlines come from "Paul L. Laurence Drugged: The Negro Poet Also Reports the Loss of Jewelry and Money," *New York Times* (August 20, 1900): 2; "A Poet's Hard Luck: Paul Laurence Dunbar Was Drugged and Robbed," *Fort Worth (Texas) Morning Register* (August 21, 1900): 3; "Paul Lawrence Dunbar Robbed: Negro Poet Falls into Evil Hands During the New York Race Riots," *Omaha (Nebraska) World-Herald* (August 21, 1900): 8; "Negro Poet Robbed: Paul Lawrence Dunbar Doped and Loses His Valuables," *Duluth (Minnesota) News-Tribune* (August 21, 1900): 2; "Furnished a Theme: Paul Lawrence Dunbar, Negro Poet, Drugged and Robbed," *Age-Herald* [Birmingham, Alabama] (August 21, 1900): 4; "A Negro Poet: Paul Lawrence Dunbar Drugged and Robbed by a New Yorker," *Butte (Montana) Weekly Miner* (August 23, 1900): 2; "Drugged Paul L. Dunbar: The Negro Writer Robbed after Trying to Pacify Men of His Race," *American Citizen* [Kansas City, Kansas] (August 24, 1900): 1; "Poet Dunbar Drugged," *The Freeman* [Indianapolis, Indiana] (September 8, 1900): 7. For skeptical headline, see the *Kalamazoo (Michigan) Gazette* (August 22, 1900): 4. For more information about the ambiguity of Dunbar's allegation, see Scott-Childress, "Paul Laurence Dunbar, New Yorker," 196n85.

21. PLD to ARM, March 21, 1901. See PLD to ARM, March 31, 1901, for reference to Wetmore. See PLD to ARM, April 13, 1901, for bedtime tuberculosis recipe, corroborated by James Weldon Johnson, *Along This Way*, 160.

22. PLD to ARM, March 24, 1901.

23. Although Dunbar leaves the grandmother nameless in his correspondence, Johnson describes her in detail in his autobiography *Along This Way*.

24. PLD to ARM, March 26, 1901.

25. PLD to ARM, March 24, 1901; PLD to ARM, March 26, 1901.

26. Johnson, *Along This Way*, 159.

27. Ibid., 160–161.

28. PLD to ARM, March 26, 1901.

29. Johnson, *Along This Way*, 161.

30. PLD to ARM, March 26, 1901; Johnson, *Along This Way*, 161.

31. PLD to ARM, March 25, 1901.

32. PLD to ARM, March 28, 1901.

33. Peter P. Hinks and Stephen Kantrowitz, introduction to *All Men Free and Brethren: Essays on the History of African American Freemasonry*, ed. Hinks and Kantrowitz (Ithaca: Cornell University Press, 2013), 2.

34. Ibid., 14, 17.

35. ARM to PLD, March 28, 1901.

36. ARM to PLD, March 29, 1901.

37. Johnson, *Along This Way*, 162.

38. PLD to ARM, March 30, 1901.

39. ARM to PLD, March 30, 1901.

40. ARM to PLD, April 1, 1901.

41. PLD to ARM, April 1, 1901; ARM to PLD, April 3, 1901.

42. ARM to PLD, April 12 and 13, 1901.

43. PLD to ARM, April 3, 1901.

44. PLD to ARM, April 11, 1901. A couple of weeks later, Paul would change his tune about the pin: "Darling, your hubbins has become a crack in masonry and he has the handsomest pin in Florida" (PLD to ARM, April 13, 1901). Moreover, word began to spread around Washington, D.C., about Paul's Masonic honors, according to Hattee Curtis, a common friend of Paul and Alice, who had been in touch with Douglass Wetmore, a Jacksonville lawyer whom they had encountered for the first time in their neighborhood: "Hattee Curtis has been in spending the evening but there isn't any news from her save that Mr. Wetmore wrote her that you had been initiated and had had your lodge named after you, which was quite Masonic in Mr. Wetmore" (ARM to PLD, April 21, 1901).

45. PLD to ARM, March 25, 1901.

46. Paul Laurence Dunbar, *The Fanatics* (New York: Dodd, Mead, 1901), 21.

47. Ibid., 27.

48. Jennifer A. Hughes, "The Politics of Incongruity in Paul Laurence Dunbar's *The Fanatics*," *African American Review* 41.2 (Summer 2007): 299.

49. PLD to ARM, March 25, 1901; ARM to PLD, April 1901; PLD to ARM, April 8, 1901.

50. Metcalf, *Paul Laurence Dunbar*, 140–142.

51. PLD to Dr. F____, September 20, 1901.

Chapter 20. Old Habits Die Hard

1. Emmett Jay Scott to BTW, March 13, 1901; *Booker T. Washington Papers, Volume 6: 1901–1902*, ed. Louis Harlan et al. (Urbana: University of Illinois Press, 1977), 50.

2. PLD to ARM, March 22, 1901.

3. PLD to ARM, March 27, 1901, about pain beneath the shoulder blades; PLD to ARM, March 28, 1901, about loss of weight.

4. PLD to ARM, March 24, 1901; ARM to PLD, March 25, 1901.

5. ARM to PLD, April 17, 1901.

6. John Livingston Wright, "Three Negro Poets," *Colored American Magazine* (April 1901): 404–405.

7. ARM to PLD, April 12 and 13, 1901.

8. PLD to ARM, April 19, 1901.

9. PLD to ARM, April 21, 1901. Paul remarked to Alice, in reference to her attendance of a meeting of the National Social Science Association in 1901: "Your account of the Assn. Meeting was interesting and I am glad I was not there. Niggers will be niggers, the same old rampant fools" (PLD to ARM, April 21, 1901).

10. PLD to ARM, April 19, 1901.

11. ARM to PLD, April 22, 1901.

12. Emmett Jay Scott to BTW, March 13, 1901; *Booker T. Washington Papers*, ed. Harlan et al., 6: 50.

13. BTW to Emmett Jay Scott, March 22, 1901. Paul relays to Alice the invitation in PLD to ARM, March 25, 1901. Paul mentions the ten days at Tuskegee in PLD to ARM, April 7, 1901; PLD to ARM, April 11, 1901; PLD to BTW, April 12, 1901.

14. PLD to ARM, April 17, 1901.

15. PLD to ARM, April 20, 1901.

16. PLD to ARM, April 22, 1901.

17. This poem would be included in Paul Laurence Dunbar, *Lyrics of Love and Laughter* (New York: Dodd, Mead, 1903), 142.

18. PLD to ARM, April 22, 1901.

19. See PLD to ARM, April 24, 1901, for full classes and book sales.

20. Brawley, *Paul Laurence Dunbar*, 90. Alice refers to attending an inaugural festivity in a March 21, 1929, entry to her diary: "So I dressed the doll—Octavie—in glittering lace—a fragment left from the dress I wore to McKinley's second inauguration ball . . ." (Alice quoted in Gloria T. Hull, *Give Us Each Day: The Diary of Alice-Dunbar Nelson* [New York: W. W. Norton, 1984], 313).

21. "Medical History: Austin Maurice Curtis, 1868–1939," *Journal of the National Medical Association* 46.4 (July 1954): 294–298.

22. Charles Mitchell to PLD, March 17, 1894. Regarding Williams's role as a personal physician, Paul wrote Alice in late 1897, "What is most serious in my matter is that my physician and friend has just gone to Chicago (Dan Williams). I have only a little medicine and have grown worse. It is misery to work, but I have to plod on" (PLD to ARM, December 2, 1897). Regarding telling Williams of his marriage, "I have not told the many people you think, here—only my friend and physician Dr. Williams, yes" (PLD to ARM, March 13, 1898). For an example of the socializing between the Dunbars and Mrs. Curtis in late 1897, see PLD to MD, November 25, 1897, and PLD to ARM, December 16, 1897.

23. Theodore Roosevelt to Ethan A. Hitchcock, October 1, 1901; [Secretary to the President] to PLD, October 7, 1901.

24. William Loeb to PLD, October 14, 1901. The letter from the assistant secretary to the president does not state which book Paul left behind—presumably one of his own. Dunbar had published twelve books by this time; the three most recent, published in 1901, were *Candle-Lightin' Time*, *Lyrics of Sunshine and Shadow*, and *The Fanatics*.

25. Newspaper headlines in Edmund Morris, *Theodore Rex* (New York: Random House, 2010), 55.

26. Roosevelt quoted in Morris, *Theodore Rex*, 58.

27. Theodore Roosevelt to Lida Keck Wiggins, August 2, 1906, quoted in Wiggins, *The Life and Works of Paul Laurence Dunbar*, 20.

28. Edward Elder Cooper to BTW, December 12, 1901; *Booker T. Washington Papers*, ed. Harlan et al., 6: 345.

29. Whitefield McKinlay to BTW, December 14, 1901; Edward Elder Cooper to BTW, December 17, 1901; *Booker T. Washington Papers*, ed. Harlan et al., 6: 347–348, 354.

30. Whitefield McKinlay to BTW, December 14, 1901; *Booker T. Washington Papers*, ed. Harlan et al., 6: 347–348.

31. PLD to BTW, December 19, 1901.

32. John R. Thelin, *A History of Higher Education*, 2nd ed. (Baltimore: Johns Hopkins University Press, 2011), 110–111, 127–131.

33. Richard Norton Smith, *The Harvard Century: The Making of a University to a Nation* (Cambridge, MA: Harvard University Press, 1998), 29, 51–52.

34. "Dunbar in Denver," *Plaindealer*, 2.

35. W. H. Grattan Flood, "'Fair Harvard': Irish Origin of the Tune," *Musical Quarterly* 5.4 (October 1919): 463–464.

36. PLD to BTW, January 9, 1902.

37. PLD to BTW, January 23, 1902.

38. Ibid.

39. Louis R. Harlan, *The Making of a Black Leader, 1856–1901*, vol. 1 of *Booker T. Washington* (New York: Oxford University Press, 1975), 34, 67, 93–99.

40. PLD to BTW, January 23, 1902.

41. Ibid.

42. Paul Laurence Dunbar, "Lyrics to the Tuskegee Song," in *Booker T. Washington Papers*, ed. Harlan et al., 6: 403–404.

43. PLD to BTW, February 22, 1902.

Chapter 21. The Downward Way

1. PLD to Paul Reynolds, January 25, 1902.

2. Sapirstein, "Out from Behind the Mask," 161, on the camera club's negotiation with Dodd, Mead and Company.

3. *Southern Workman* review quoted in Sapirstein, "Out from Behind the Mask," 13; Metcalf, *Paul Laurence Dunbar*, 143–144.

4. Paul Laurence Dunbar, "Negro Life in Washington," in *The Sport of the Gods and Other Essential Writings*, ed. Fishkin and Bradley, 275, 277–278.

5. Dunbar, "Negro Society in Washington," 286.

6. PLD to Paul Reynolds, November 7, 1900.

7. Whittle, "Paul Dunbar," 320.

8. PLD to Paul Reynolds, July 18, 1901.

9. PLD to Paul Reynolds, August 5, 1901.

10. PLD to Paul Reynolds, September 26, 1901.

11. PLD to Paul Reynolds, January 25, 1902.

12. Metcalf, *Paul Laurence Dunbar*, 141–145.

13. Paul Laurence Dunbar, "The Negro as an Individual," in *The Sport of the Gods and Other Essential Writings*, ed. Fishkin and Bradley, 291.

14. Ibid.

15. PLD to ARM, January 15, 1902.

16. PLD to ARM, January 16, 1902; PLD to ARM, January 17, 1902.

17. Timothy Thomas Fortune to BTW, February 1, 1902; *Booker T. Washington Papers*, ed. Harlan et al., 6: 388.

18. PLD to ARM, January 30, 1902.

19. Timothy Thomas Fortune to BTW, February 1, 1902; *Booker T. Washington Papers*, ed. Harlan et al., 6: 388–389.

20. PLD to an acquaintance, quoted in Cunningham, *Paul Laurence Dunbar and His Song*, 232.

21. ARM to MD, June 17, 1902.

22. Stories of Paul's abuse of Alice recounted in Alexander, *Lyrics of Sunshine and Shadow*, 165–169; ARM to MD, June 17, 1902.

23. ARM to MD, June 17, 1902; ARM to Lida Keck Wiggins, August 7, 1906; quoted in Metcalf, "The Letters of Paul and Alice Dunbar," 12.

24. Ibid.

25. PLD to ARM, January 30, 1902.

26. Timothy Thomas Fortune to BTW, February 1, 1902; *Booker T. Washington Papers*, ed. Harlan et al., 6: 389. Timothy Thomas Fortune to BTW, February 6, 1902; *Booker T. Washington Papers*, ed. Harlan et al., 6: 391. PLD to ARM, January 30, 1902.

27. PLD to BTW, May 29, 1903.

28. PLD to BTW, February 20, 1903.

29. PLD to W. E. B. Du Bois, January 15, 1903; Du Bois to PLD, January 15, 1903, quoted in *Selected Literary Letters*, ed. Murillo and Nader, 158.

30. Du Bois to PLD, January 15, 1903, quoted in ibid. For Du Bois's correspondence with Charles Chesnutt, see Lewis, *W. E. B. DuBois*, 324.

31. PLD to W. E. B. Du Bois, February 3, 1903, quoted in *Selected Literary Letters*, ed. Murillo and Nader, 159.

32. PLD to MD, March 11, 1902.

33. PLD to ARM, November 19, 1902, which also indicates that, regarding Alice's mother, Dunbar was apologetic: "I am so sorry for what I said to your mother. My heart has bled for it time and time again."

Chapter 22. Waiting in Loafing-Holt

1. PLD to ARM, June 14, 1903.

2. For instance, in 1900 he resided for periods at Brodhead's Bridge in New York and 418 Elm Street, NW, and 321 Spruce Street, NW, in Washington D.C.; in 1901, at 321 Spruce Street in Washington, D.C., and 150 West 37th Street in New York City; and in 1902, at 227 West 33rd Street and 127 West 53rd Street in New York City. During this time, particularly for personal reasons or poetry readings, he also sojourned in Harman, Colorado; Dayton, Ohio; Jacksonville, Florida; Tuskegee, Alabama; Richmond, Virginia; and Charleston, South Carolina.

3. Carter, *Swing Along*, 129–137, for the compositions Cook and Dunbar worked on together. Regarding *Herrick*, Dunbar remarked to Alice on August 4, 1898: "Husband is very down in the mouth and lonesome & sick at heart. Every thing that he has touched lately has failed. McArthur writes that my play is literature but inactable," likely referring to James MacArthur, an adviser to his customary publisher, Dodd, Mead (PLD to ARM, August 4, 1898). For more information about *Herrick*, see *In His Own Voice: The Dramatic and Other Uncollected Works of Paul Laurence Dunbar*, ed. Herbert Woodward Martin and Ronald Primeau (Athens: Ohio University Press, 2002), 3–9.

4. Forbes, *Introducing Bert Williams*, 101.

5. Lester Walton, critic in the *New York Age*, quoted in Forbes, *Introducing Bert Williams*, 115.

6. Walker quoted in Forbes, *Introducing Bert Williams*, 104. Paul's collaborations with Cook also appeared later in life and posthumously, including such songs as "Dreamin' Town (Mandy Lou)" (1904), "A Summah Night" (1906), "Dainty" (1909), and "My Lady" (1912).

7. Reviews of *Uncle Eph's Christmas*, after its debut in Boston in 1900, conjured up such contrasting accolades for Dunbar. Critics quoted in Jonathan Daigle, "Paul Laurence Dunbar and the Marshall Circle," 639.

8. These poems are "A Spring Wooing," "Dat Ol' Mare O' Mine," "Dinah Kneading Dough," "Fishin'," "The Old Front Gate," and "When Dey Listed Colored Soldiers."

9. Metcalf, *Paul Laurence Dunbar*, 147.

10. Paul Laurence Dunbar, "The Debt," in *Lyrics of Love and Laughter*, 141–142.

11. PLD to Alice Dunbar, May 7, 1903, which indicates they were separated, not divorced: "After the first two weeks of our separation, a separation that I have not yet realized, there has not been a day when with heartache I have not longed for you my wife. Nothing can take you away from me. Nothing can unmarry us. Don't you remember when we used to say that we had married for eternity?" Dunbar wrote Alice again when he was passing through Delaware by the end of May 1903 (PLD to ARM, May 21, 1903).

12. PLD to ARM, June 14, 1903.

13. "Paul Laurence Dunbar Ill: The Condition of the Negro Poet Is Regarded as Critical," *Kansas City Star* (June 22, 1903): 1. The newspaper reported that Dunbar had fallen sick a week earlier, with pneumonia.

14. "Reduced Copies of Measured Drawings Written Historical and Descriptive Data," Historic American Buildings Survey, National Park Service, Paul Laurence Dunbar House (Washington, D.C.: Department of the Interior, n.d.), 2.

15. Recent background information may be found in *Paul Laurence Dunbar House: Cultural Landscape and Historic Structures Report* (Dayton, OH: Dayton Aviation Heritage National Historical Park, 2019), 1: 1–4.

16. Ibid. Paul would live in the house with his mother until his death in 1906; and his mother would reside there another twenty-eight years, until her own death, in 1934. In 1937 the State of Ohio would buy the property and turn it over to the Ohio Historical Society.

17. Information about the books in Paul Laurence Dunbar's library was gleaned from a 2008 inventory. I thank Gregg Smith, ranger of the National Park Service at the Paul Laurence Dunbar House Historic Site, for providing me this information when I visited the house in 2015.

18. Verse excerpts of "At Loafing-Holt," published in Paul Laurence Dunbar, "At Loafing-Holt," in *Lyrics of Sunshine and Shadow*, 84–85.

19. "Paul Laurence Dunbar Cannot Come," *Kansas City Star* (November 14, 1902): 5.

20. PLD to Dr. F_____, October 21, 1904.

21. PLD to MD, September 9, 1903; Alexander, *Lyrics of Sunshine and Shadow*, 170–171.

22. Frederick Douglass, "What to the Slave Is the Fourth of July," in *The Essential Douglass: Selected Writings and Speeches*, ed. Nicholas Buccola (New York: Hackett, 2016), 58.

23. Dunbar, "The Fourth of July and Race Outrages," in *The Sport of the Gods and Other Essential Writings*, ed. Fishkin and Bradley, 293–296.

24. Metcalf, *Paul Laurence Dunbar*, 147.

25. Sapirstein, "Out from Behind the Mask," 162 for compensation of two hundred dollars.

26. Metcalf, *Paul Laurence Dunbar*, 147–148.

27. PLD to ARM, February 27, 1904.

28. PLD to ARM, November 16, 1904.

29. PLD to ARM, November 19, 1904.

30. "Poet Paul Dunbar Dying," *Cleveland Plain Dealer* (September 21, 1904): 10; the text of this article was syndicated thereafter in local Ohio newspapers and in other newspapers of the Midwest, such as in Kansas.

31. For letter on California, see PLD to Dr. F_____, October 21, 1904.

32. PLD to Edwin Hackley, November 23, 1904, quoted in *Selected Literary Letters*, ed. Murillo and Nader, 164.

33. Theodore Roosevelt to PLD, November 2, 1904.

34. The first two volumes (or inside the book called "Part One" and "Part Two") of *Presidential Addresses and State Papers of Theodore Roosevelt* were published by P. F. Collier & Son by the time Roosevelt sent Paul the gift.

35. Paul Laurence Dunbar, "[For Theodore Roosevelt]," in *The Collected Poems*, ed. Braxton, 333–334.

36. Parker quoted in Morris, *Theodore Rex*, 362; Roosevelt's responsive letter, on 363.

37. Dunbar, "[For Theodore Roosevelt]," 334.

38. PLD to Edward F. Arnold, February 17, 1905.

39. Morris, *Theodore Rex*, 376, 377.

40. [Postcard of Roosevelt taking Presidential Oath] to PLD, March 14, 1905.

41. Metcalf, *Paul Laurence Dunbar*, 148–149.

42. These poems are "Blue," "Charity," "Curiosity," "Dely," "Parted," and "The Plantation Child's Lullaby."

43. Review reprinted in Sapirstein, "Out from Behind the Mask," 163. The last two books illustrated by Hampton Camera Club, *Howdy, Honey, Howdy* and *Joggin' Erlong*, would be illustrated by Miner, but the decorators would change to Will Jenkins and John Rae, respectively.

44. Metcalf, *Paul Laurence Dunbar*, 148.

45. Ibid., 16, refers to Dunbar's publication, by Dodd, Mead, of a series of dialect verses as *Chrismus Is A-Comin'*, a holiday book. According to Metcalf, not one poem was new; all were reprinted from previous books, and together they recalled the racial realism of *Poems of Cabin and Field*, *Candle-Lightin' Time*, *When Malindy Sings*, and *Li'l' Gal*, although this time without the page decorations and the photographic illustrations of African American life.

46. Metcalf, *Paul Laurence Dunbar*, 148, for "spirit" of his race; and 150 for *Joggin' Erlong*.

47. Paul Laurence Dunbar, *Joggin' Erlong* (New York: Dodd, Mead, 1906), 5.

48. PLD to Reginald W. Kauffman, October 4, 1905, quoted in *Selected Literary Letters*, ed. Murillo and Nader, 166.

49. Dunbar quoted in Scharnhorst and Matthews, "'Denver Took Me into Her Arms,'" 23.

50. "Paul Dunbar. The Dead Poet Laureate's Solemn Funeral Services. Many Unite in Paying Tribute," *Cleveland Gazette* (February 17, 1906): 1.

51. Rothman, *Living in the Shadow of Death*, 7.

52. "The Major of Toledo, Brand Whitlock, Magazine Writer, and Close Friend of Paul Dunbar," *Cleveland Gazette* (March 24, 1906): 1. Full quotation from *Selected Literary Letters*, ed. Murillo and Nader, 171–172.

53. "Paul Dunbar. The Dead Poet Laureate's Solemn Funeral Services. Many Unite in Paying Tribute," *Cleveland Gazette* (February 17, 1906): 1.

54. See William A. Burns to PLD, October 14, 1894; PLD to MD, November 25, 1897; PLD to ARM, January 4, 1898; ARM to PLD, March 31, 1898; PLD to ARM, September 5, 1898; PLD to MD, October 2, 1898; PLD to ARM, March 3, 1900; ARM to PLD, March 25, 1901; PLD to ARM, March 28, 1901.

55. ARM to William Burns, February 14, 1906.

56. Paul's burial date was April 16, 1906. According to his interment card at Woodland Cemetery, his initial location was Lot 3075 W 1/20, section 111; it was later moved to Lot 3465, Section 101, its current location. Paul's final resting place would be moved from its original site to the vicinity of his childhood friends Wilbur and Orville Wright, who died six and forty-two years after he did, respectively. In effect if not in intent, the relocation meant that the poet too embodied the legacy of innovation for which the successful aviators were renowned in Dayton and the broader Midwest. Within a year of his death, some eight hundred literary societies would bear his name in commemoration; see Daigle, "Paul Laurence Dunbar and the Marshall Circle," 634. The first school named after Paul Laurence Dunbar appeared in Washington, D.C., in 1916 (*Paul Laurence Dunbar: Beyond the Mask*, produced by Frederick Lewis and Joseph Slade, 0:00:35).

Epilogue

1. Dodd, Mead and Company to W. E. B Du Bois, February 24, 1906, quoted in *Selected Literary Letters*, ed. Murillo and Nader, 173.

2. In this epilogue, per academic convention, I refer to "Paul Laurence Dunbar" or "Dunbar," rather than "Paul," which I employ elsewhere in the book, as per the narratorial convention of biography to establish interpersonal and intimate proximity between the reader and the subject; in the case of Paul Laurence Dunbar and Alice Dunbar-Nelson, referring to their first names also helps mitigate potential confusion.

3. Recent examples of informative archival discoveries and reprintings include the collection of select letters to, from, and about Dunbar, *The Selected Literary Letters of Paul Laurence Dunbar*, edited by Cynthia C. Murillo and Jennifer M. Nader, published in 2021. Another example is Zachary Turpin, "'Twilight Is Their Child': Uncollected Poems, Letters, and a Short Story by Paul Laurence Dunbar," *Resources for American Literary Study* 40 (2018): 155–182.

4. Jeanne McCulloch interview with Leon Edel, "Leon Edel, the Art of Biography No. 1," *Paris Review* 98 (Winter 1985): 173. The five volumes of Edel's biography of Henry James were published between 1953 and 1972.

5. John Ernest, introduction to *The Oxford Handbook of the African American Slave Narrative*, ed. Ernest (New York: Oxford University Press, 2014), 11.

6. Douglass, *The Life and Times of Frederick Douglass* (Mineola, NY: Dover, 2003), 265.

7. See James Henretta, "Social History as Lived and Written," *American Historical Review* 84 (1979): 1293–1294, 1315. For the academic journals and edited collections instituting the discourse of social history, see Geoff Eley, *A Crooked Line: From Cultural History to the History of Society* (Ann Arbor: University of Michigan Press, 2005), 124.

8. Gene Andrew Jarrett, *Representing the Race: A New Political History of African American Literature* (New York: New York University Press, 2011), 21–25.

9. Although most of the letters by and to Dunbar were legible enough to be read and transcribed, he also wrote in a miscellaneous journal a curious but impenetrably cryptic shorthand that awaits future scholars to decipher.

10. The institutions include Columbia University Library, Dayton (Ohio) Public Library, Duke University Library, Haverford College Library, Historical Society of Pennsylvania, Library of Congress, Newark (New Jersey) Public Library, Pennsylvania State University Library, Princeton University Library, Wellesley College Library, Yale University Library, and the University of Virginia Library.

11. Lida Keck Wiggins, *The Life and Works of Paul Laurence Dunbar* (Dodd, Mead, 1907); Rubie Boyd, "An Appreciation of Paul Laurence Dunbar" (typescript manuscript, 1934); Benjamin Brawley, *Paul Laurence Dunbar: Poet of His People* (Chapel Hill: University of North Carolina Press, 1936); Virginia Cunningham, *Paul Laurence Dunbar and His Song* (New York: Dodd, Mead, 1953); Addison Gayle Jr., *Oak and Ivy: A Biography of Paul Laurence Dunbar* (Garden City, NY: Doubleday, 1971); Eugene Wesley Metcalf Jr., "The Letters of Paul and Alice Dunbar: A Private History" (PhD diss., University of California, Irvine, 1973); Felton O. Best, *Crossing the Color Line: A Biography of Paul Laurence Dunbar, 1872–1906* (Dubuque, IA: Kendall/Hunt, 1996); and Eleanor Alexander, *Lyrics of Sunshine and Shadow: The Courtship and Marriage of Paul Laurence Dunbar and Alice Ruth Moore* (New York: Plume, 2004).

12. For example, I lean on the research in such biographies as Tom Crouch, *The Bishop's Boys: A Life of Wilbur and Orville Wright* (New York: W. W. Norton, 1989); David W. Blight, *Frederick Douglass: Prophet of Freedom* (New York: Simon & Schuster, 2018); Louis R. Harlan, *The Making of a Black Leader, 1856–1901*, vol. 1 of *Booker T. Washington* (New York: Oxford University Press, 1975); Paula J. Giddings, *Ida: A Sword among Lions: Ida B. Wells and the Campaign against Lynching* (New York: Amistad, 2008); and David Levering Lewis, *W. E. B. Du Bois: Biography of a Race, 1868–1919* (New York: Owl Books, 1993). Evident in my biography is the cordial and supportive relationship between Dunbar and Roosevelt, a fascinating storyline that is absent from Edmund Morris's otherwise superb biography of Roosevelt, *Theodore Rex* (New York: Random House, 2010), which is nonetheless important to my framing of Dunbar's perspective on Roosevelt's political reputation.

13. For example, a crucial document of research that I discovered is Rubie Boyd, "An Appreciation of Paul Laurence Dunbar," the core of whose study is an interview he conducted directly with Matilda Dunbar in August 1933 about her own life and her upbringing of Paul Laurence Dunbar. (Boyd also accounts for Matilda's death on February 24, 1934, and the manuscript more or less stops there.)

14. For example, a common myth is that Dunbar attended on March 4, 1901, the inaugural parade of William McKinley, who was elected to his second term as president. Although Benjamin Brawley refers to this attendance in his well-known biography published nearly a century ago, *Paul Laurence Dunbar: Poet of His People* (Chapel Hill: University of North Carolina Press, 1936), 90, he did not use footnotes or citations. (Neither did Lida Keck Wiggins [in her own biography of 1907], Virginia Cunningham [1953], or Addison Gayle Jr. [1971].) Not until Felton O. Best (1996) do we encounter a biography that employs contemporary standards of bibliographical citation. As for the McKinley inauguration, the concrete evidence we have of Dunbar's involvement is Dunbar-Nelson's reference to it in the March 21, 1929, entry to her diary: "So I dressed the doll—Octavie—in glittering lace—a fragment left from the dress I wore to [U.S.] McKinley's second inauguration ball . . ." (Dunbar-Nelson quoted in Hull, *Give Us Each Day*, 313).

15. Although the placement of the comma in the title "Howdy, Honey, Howdy" varies as it appears on the book's title page (only the first comma is there) or disappears on the copyright page, they all settle into place by the table of contents and printing of the book's first poem, "Howdy, Honey, Howdy," whose title and quotations include all commas. This confusion has persisted in later references to the book.

16. For information about Dunbar's recitals from 1898 to 1902, see Paul Laurence Dunbar Papers, Roll 3.

17. The sonnet "To Dr. James Newton Matthews" appears in *Oak and Ivy*, while another sonnet, "Harriet Beecher Stowe," appears in *Lyrics of the Hearthside*. The rondeaus "We Wear the Mask" and "Not They Who Soar" appear in *Majors and Minors*. And the ballad "The Haunted Oak" can be found in *Lyrics of Love and Laughter*, while "A Border Ballad" appears in *Majors and Minors* and *Lyrics of Lowly Life*.

18. PLD to JNM, December 23, 1893; PLD to ARM, January 31, 1898. "Not They Who Soar" appears in Dunbar's second book, *Majors and Minors,* and in his third, *Lyrics of Lowly Life.* "'Twixt Smile and Tear" remains yet unpublished. The sonnet "Sunset" appears in his first three books, *Oak and Ivy, Majors and Minors,* and *Lyrics of Lowly Life.*

19. Ronda, "'Work and Wait Unwearying,'" 864.

20. Virginia Jackson, "Specters of the Ballad," *Nineteenth-Century Literature* 71.2 (September 2016): 181.

21. Major biographies of long-ago literary figures tend not to bear the scholarly burden of historicizing the critical reception of these figures from the point of death until the present. Following this convention, I advise students and experts seeking to understand or reference, in a systematic way, the century-long history of the reception and the scholarship on Paul Laurence Dunbar to turn to two major edited collections of academic essays: the first is *A Singer in the Dawn: Reinterpretations of Paul Laurence Dunbar,* ed. Jay Martin (New York: Dodd, Mead, 1975); the second is *We Wear the Mask: Paul Laurence Dunbar and the Politics of Representative Reality,* ed. Willie J. Harrell Jr. (Kent, OH: Kent State University Press, 2010). In particular, the editorial introductions to these books by Martin and Harrell, respectively, paint this scholarly history in a comprehensive way, buttressed by the essays included in their volumes. Given that my book is primarily a biography, I defer to these two seminal texts for people who wish to understand the history of scholarship on Dunbar's literature after his death in 1906. The recency of Harrell's introduction makes it especially notable for the purposes of taking the longest view of this scholarship.

22. Dunbar also delighted audiences by reciting poems deviating from the sensationalized genres of racial realism, including "A Coquette Conquered" from *Lyrics of Lowly Life* (1896); "Angelina," "The Warrior's Prayer," and "Little Brown Baby" from *Lyrics of the Hearthside* (1899); and "The Haunted Oak" from *Lyrics of Love and Laughter* (1903).

23. As in the case of my reference to "Paul Laurence Dunbar" or "Dunbar" instead of "Paul" in this epilogue, I refer to "Alice Dunbar-Nelson" and "Dunbar-Nelson," the name she publicly preferred and used in the years after Dunbar's death, particularly after she married Robert J. Nelson in 1916. I refer to "Alice" elsewhere in the book as per the narratorial convention of biography, or "Alice Ruth Moore," her maiden name, which on occasion I use to indicate the temporality prior to her first marriage.

24. Dunbar-Nelson quoted in Gloria T. Hull, *Give Us Each Day*, 24.

25. Although Akasha Gloria Hull (or, previously, Gloria T. Hull) has published a number of articles on Dunbar-Nelson, the culmination of her work appears especially in two places: her

original edition of Dunbar-Nelson's diary, *Give Us Each Day: The Diary of Alice Dunbar-Nelson*, which includes, most notably, her introduction and her editorial preface on the research and formal nature of the diary; and the extensive second chapter, "Alice Dunbar-Nelson (1875–1935)," in her book *Color, Sex and Poetry: Three Women Writers of the Harlem Renaissance* (Bloomington: Indiana University Press, 1987). Taken together, these books provide perhaps the most panoramic view of Dunbar-Nelson's life before and during her time with Dunbar; her activities during their estrangement while he was alive; and her life after his death, including her marriages, journalism, political activities, literary efforts, intellectualism, emotional and psychological issues, and lesbian sexuality. (I am not counting Ruby Ora Williams's "An In-Depth Portrait of Alice Dunbar-Nelson" [PhD diss., University of California at Irvine, 1974], which remains unpublished.) Since the publication of Hull's volumes, Dunbar-Nelson's bisexual identity has received increasing attention, and her work has been summarized or collected in volumes celebrating the genre of African American women's or gay, lesbian, and bisexual writing (although they inevitably do not probe Dunbar-Nelson's life with the scholarly intensity and insight of Hull's work). The notable books include Maureen Honey, ed., *Shadowed Dreams: Women's Poetry of the Harlem Renaissance* (New Brunswick, NJ: Rutgers University Press, 1989); Bonnie Zimmerman, ed., *Lesbian Histories and Cultures: An Encyclopedia* (New York: Garland, 2000); and Devon Carbado et al., eds., *Black Like Us: A Century of Lesbian, Gay and Bisexual African American Fiction* (Berkeley: Cleis Press, 2003). The familiar territory covered by Hull is later discussed, if not cited, by Elizabeth Ammons in *Conflicting Stories: American Women Writers at the Turn into the Twentieth Century* (New York: Oxford University Press, 1991) and, more recently, Hugh Ryan in *When Brooklyn Was Queer* (New York: St. Martin's Press, 2019). The most recent substantial biography of Alice Dunbar-Nelson is Tara T. Green's *Love, Activism, and the Respectable Life of Alice Dunbar-Nelson* (New York: Bloomsbury Academic, 2022).

26. For more information about how Dunbar-Nelson redressed mistreatments of Dunbar's legacy, see excerpts of her diary in *Give Us Each Day*, on 50 and 462; she also regularly celebrated his work or missed him, as suggested on ibid., 152, 199, and 415.

27. Dunbar-Nelson quote on "literary consciousness" in her diary in *Give Us Each Day*, 100; her quote on "dialect Dunbar" in ibid., 303.

28. From a scholarly standpoint, the most comprehensive study of Dunbar-Nelson appears in the special issue "Recovering Alice Dunbar-Nelson for the Twenty-First Century," *Legacy: A Journal of American Women Writers* 33.2 (2016), edited by Katherine Adams, Caroline Gebhard, and Sandra A. Zagarell. Not only does it include a thoroughgoing introductory essay by Adams, Gebhard, and Zagarell on what it means to recover Dunbar-Nelson for the twenty-first century (213–253), there is also a comprehensive bibliography of Dunbar-Nelson's published works (254–258); a gallery of Dunbar-Nelson's images (259–266); an essay by Shawn Anthony Christian on Dunbar-Nelson's "Negro Literature for Negro Pupils" (267–285); one by Jacqueline Emery on Dunbar-Nelson's newspaper columns in the African American press (286–309); another by Ellen Gruber Garvey on Dunbar-Nelson's suffrage work, according to a scrapbook (310–335); an article by Gebhard on Dunbar-Nelson's Creole "boy stories" (336–360); another by Anna Storm on Dunbar-Nelson's relation to African American women's literary tradition (361–383); and a reflection by Adams, Gebhard, and Zagarell on the Dunbar-Nelson archive (384–391).

29. ARM to Lida Keck Wiggins, August 7, 1906; quoted in Metcalf, "The Letters of Paul and Alice Dunbar," 12.

INDEX

Note: Paul Laurence Dunbar's works are in **bold** type. Page numbers in *italic* type indicate illustrations. "PLD" and "ARM" refer to Paul Laurence Dunbar and Alice Ruth Moore (or Alice Dunbar), respectively.

abolitionists, 28, 57, 136
Acanthus Club, 178
Accooe, Will, 202
"Accountability" (poem), 229
activism, PLD and textual, 100, 136
Adams, Lewis, 295
Aesop, "The Ass in the Lion's Skin," 233
African Americans: alleged inferiority of, 10, 84, 111, 154, 164–65, 236, 373–74, 401, 451 (*see also* whites: alleged superiority of); in American literature, 230; Broadway firsts achieved by, 7, 315, 422; and classical education, 87–88; Dayton community of, 11, 27, 92, 99–101, 169–70; dialect of, 4, 5 (*see also* dialect poetry and prose); differences among, 376; education of, 57, 62–64, 72, 78, 81, 87, 136, 144–45, 295–96, 327–29, 372–73; elite and middle-class, 177–78, 188–89, 235, 277, 293, 386–87, 399, 410–11, 414, 503n43; family structures of, 49, 60–61, 71; franchise of, 7–9, 480n42, 482n62; and Freemasonry, 383–87; friendships of whites with, 124; gender roles among, 44, 49; intelligentsia's role among, 5; jobs available to, 44–45; and marriage, 56; music of, 200–201; newspapers by and for, 179; in New York City, 375–76; political participation of, 9–10, 49, 332; reversal of Reconstruction gains

by, 9–10; skin color as status marker among, 188–89; in Union Army, 8, 19, 30–34, 36–42, 45–46, 333, 477n98; in Washington, D.C., 177–78, 235, 274, 277, 287, 410–11; white violence against, 332–34, 375–79, 435–36; in Wilmington, North Carolina, 332–33; World's Columbian Exposition's portrayal of, 163–68. *See also* folklore; race; slaves and slavery
African Methodist Episcopal (AME) Church, 28, 65, 67, 167, 186–87, 307, 431, 445
"Afro-American" (term), 219, 329
"Air Ship Soon to Fly" (essay), 102
alcohol and alcoholism: Joshua Dunbar's, 38, 46, 47, 51, 70–71, 103, 272, 291; medical uses of, 272, 290, 352; PLD's, 5, 6, 103, 170, 203, 272, 278, 280, 283, 285, 290–91, 301, 352, 369, 378–79, 394–95, 397, 401–2, 414–15, 433, 503n43; societal attitudes toward, 272; of soldiers and veterans, 38, 46, 51, 479n16; tuberculosis's link to, 352; in veterans' homes, 70–71. *See also* temperance movement
Alcoholics Mutual Aid Groups, 272
Alexander, Charles, 193
Alexander, Eleanor, 453, 460
"Alice" (poem), 194–95, 493n14
Allen, J. Mord, 230

Allen, Richard, 384

AME Church. *See* African Methodist Episcopal (AME) Church

A.M.E. Review (journal), 1

American Anti-Slavery Society, 180

American Historical Association, 451

American Missionary Association, 294, 365

American Missionary Association of the Congregational Church, 205

American Negro Academy, 298–99

American Social Science Association, 372–74

American Sons of Protection, 431

Anderson, Joseph, 372

Andrew, John Albion, 33, 41

Andrews, Marie Louise, 119

"Angelina" (poem), 521n22

Angelou, Maya, 469n8; *I Know Why the Caged Bird Sings*, 2

Anglo-African Magazine, 101

Anglo Saxons. *See* whites

A. N. Kellogg Newspaper Company, 116, 117, 302

"Anner Lizer's Stumblin' Block" (short story), 503n44

Anthony, Susan B., 186

Anti-Caste (journal), 253

Armstrong, Margaret, 409, 437

Armstrong, Mary Alice, 345

Armstrong, Samuel Chapman, 145, 294–95, 300, 344–45, 409, 442

Armstrong Association, 300, 346

Arnold, Edward F., 363

Arrears of Pension Act (1879), 75

Art Club, 178

Association of American Universities, 403

"At Candle-Lightin' Time" (poem), 409

Atlanta University, 343, 357

Atlantic Monthly (magazine), 115, 222, 300, 317

"At Loafing-Holt" (poem), 428–29, 431, 432

Aunt Jemima, 166–67

Baker, Henry F., 265, 500n9

Baldwin, Rebekah, 11, 173–87, 209, 235, 256, 264, 277, 284–85, 287–88, 310, 324

"Ballade" (poem), 468n5

ballads, 455

Ballantine, William Gay, 148

"A Banjo Song" (poem), 140–41, 200, 213, 509n49

Barnett, Ferdinand Lee, 165

Barrett, Elizabeth, 310

Barton, Mary, 380–81

Baucom, Ian, 17

Beecher, Henry Ward, 232; *A Summer in England*, 430

Behman, Louis, 313

Berean Baptist Church, Washington, D.C., 271

Berkeley, George, 120–22

Best, Felton O., 453, 520n14

Bethel Literary and Historical Association, 178, 299, 402

Bibb, Henry, 18, 472n14, 472n22, 474n49

Bible, 406, 444

Black Laws/Codes, 29, 42

Blocher, William L., 130, 443

"Blue" (poem), 518n42

Blumenschein, Ernest, 231

Bohemian (newspaper), 204

bohemianism, 268, 376

Bond, John M., 56

"Booker T. Washington" (poem), 374–75

Booklover's Magazine, 419

Bookman (magazine), 303, 319, 336

Booth, Edwin, 340

"A Border Ballad" (poem), 455

Boston Conservatory, 200

Boston Daily Standard (newspaper), 196

Boston Transcript (newspaper), 371

Boswell, James, 95

Bowditch, Charles P., 40

Bowditch, Henry I., 360

Bowles, W. O., 78, 84

Boyd, Rubie, 453; "An Appreciation of Paul Laurence Dunbar," 520n13

Brake, Laurel, 105

Brawley, Benjamin, 453, 520n14

British Romanticism, 3, 65, 67, 133–34, 337

Brooks, Van Wyck, 222

Brown, Hallie Quinn, 157

Brown, Hattie, 167

Brown, Sallie, 355

Brown, William Wells, 17–19, 230, 452, 471n13, 472n22, 474n49

Browning, Robert, 174–75, 310

Bruce, Blanche K., 182

Bruce, John Edward, 353, 355

Bryant, William Cullen, 134, 137, 455; "To a Waterfowl," 139

Buck, Dudley, 167

Bulwer-Lytton, Edward, *The Lady of Lyons; or, Love and Pride*, 116

Bumstead, Horace, 343

Bunyan, John, *Pilgrim's Progress*, 430

Burleigh, Harry, 200, 202, 339

Burns, Robert, 227, 430

Burns, William "Bud," 87, 356, 446–47

Burt, Stephen, 138

Burton, Elizabeth (Matilda Dunbar's mother), 20, 36, 43, 50, 61

Burton, Elizabeth (PLD's "aunt"), 270

Burton, Rebecca, 48, 61

Burton, Robert, 270

Burton, Willis, 43

"Bus Jinkins Up Nawth" (short story), 268

Butler, Benjamin, 482n62

Byron, Lord, 65

Cable, George Washington, 113, 214, 220

Cahan, Abraham, 113, 225

cakewalk, 202

Callahan, William P., 111

Callis, Arthur, 458

Cambridge University, 180

cameras, 344

Cameron, Julia Margaret, 350

Cameron, Simon, 31

Campbell, James Edwin, 230

Camp Meigs, 33, 40

Canada, 27–30

Candle-Lightin' Time (poetry), 409–10, 424, 437, 441, 468n5, 514n24

canes and walking sticks, 161, 272, 438

The Cannibal King (musical), 315, 421, 506n26

"A Career" (poem), 131

Carlyle, Thomas, 430

"The Carnival Is on in Denver" (essay), 364–65

Carreno Club, 178

Carver, George Washington, 329

Catherwood, Mary Hartwell, 151

census, 17, 67–68, 135

Centennial Exhibition (Philadelphia, 1876), 164

Central High School, Dayton, 79–82, *80*, 85–87, *85*, 90–95, *95*, 102, 106–10, *108*, 117, 142, 432

Central Lyceum Bureau, 148

The Century (magazine), 115, 122, 148–49, 190, 213, 215, 224, 249, 288, 293, 336, 374

cerebrospinal meningitis, 290

Chadwick, Samuel, 426

Chamberlain, Joseph, 247

Chambers, Ephraim, 96

chapbooks, 53

Chapman, Mary Berri, 429

Chapman, W. C., 146

Chapman & Hall, 249

"Charity" (poem), 518n42

Chautauqua Literary Scientific Circle, 178

Chesnutt, Charles W., 10, 124, 224, 225, 230, 317, *318*, 319, 419, 495n14, 506n31; *The Conjure Woman*, 431; "The Goophered Grapevine," 317; "Uncle Peter's House," 317; *The Wife of His Youth*, 431

Chicago, Illinois: Interstate Industrial Exposition in, 153; PLD's experience of, 153, 155–70; socioeconomic conditions of, 155–56; World's Columbian Exposition in, 152–70, *154*

Chicago Daily News (newspaper), 133, 190, 213

Chicago Herald (newspaper), 169

Chicago Inter-Ocean (newspaper), 169

Chicago Interstate Industrial Exposition (1873), 153

Chicago Mail (newspaper), 169

Chicago News (newspaper), 169

Chicago News Record (newspaper), 133, 190, 204, 217

Chicago Record (newspaper), 169, 178, 245, 261

Chicago Tribune (newspaper), 169, 414

"Chris'mus Is A-Comin'" (poem), 509n49

Chrismus Is A-Comin' (poetry), 518n45

Christianity: African Americans' conversion of Africans to, 180; Stowe's *Uncle Tom's Cabin* and, 57–58; Washington and, 406

"Christmas Carol" (poem), 103, 132, 133

"The Chronic Kicker" (poem), 141

Cicero, 87, 430

Cincinnati Commercial (newspaper), 69

Civil Rights Acts (1866, 1871, 1875), 8, 482n62

Civil War, 30–31, 387–89. *See also* Union Army

Claflin, William, 270

Claflin University, 269–70

Clapp, Henry, Jr., 268

Clark, Roger, 353

Clarke, Lewis Garrard, 18, 472n15, 472n22, 474n49

classical education, 81–82, 87–88, 483n15

Clasz, Walter, 133

Cleveland, Grover, 300, 438

Cleveland Gazette (newspaper), 143, 445

Clorindy, the Origin of the Cakewalk (musical), 7, 203, 313–15, 314, 422

Cobb, Rufus Wills, 397

Colborne, John, 29

Cole, Bob, 201, 315, 506n26

Coleridge, Samuel Taylor, 65, 245

Coleridge-Taylor, Samuel, 6, 245, 246

Colorado, 359–71, 416, 432, 438, 444

Colorado Springs Gazette (newspaper), 368

Colorado Statesman (newspaper), 367

Colored American Magazine, 101, 329, 391–92

Colored Americans/Colored People's Day. *See* Jubilee Day

Colored Knights of Pythias, 190, 192

"The Colored Soldiers" (poem), 15

"A Columbian Ode" (poem), 133, 140, 213

Columbia Social Club, 178

Columbus, Christopher, 153

Columbus Dispatch (newspaper), 334

Comité des Citoyens, 235

Compromise of 1877, 9, 10

Conover, Charlotte Reeve, 214, 443, 486n9

"Conscience and Remorse" (poem), 227

Constitutional Convention, 24

consumption. *See* tuberculosis

Conway, Moncure D., 247

Cook, Will Marion, 6, 161–62, 162, 166–68, 201–3, 313–16, 421–22

Cook family, 178

"coon" entertainment, 201, 202, 424

Cooper, Anna Julia, 88

Cooper, Edward Elder, 402

Cooper, W. H., 377–78

Coppin, Frances Jackson, 88

copyright, 412–13

"A Coquette Conquered" (poem), 302, 521n22

Corrothers, James David, 340–41, 392

Cortelyou, George B., 400, 440

Cosmopolitan (magazine), 222, 302

Cotter, Joseph Seamon, Sr., 230–31, 431

Cotton States and International Exposition (Atlanta, 1895), 124, 296, 367

Cottrill, Charles A., 418

"Couldn't Speak from Experience" (story), 104

"A Council of State" (short story), 365

couplets, 139–40

Cramer, M. A. Merritt, 429

Crane, Stephen, 113, 223–24, 225, 276, 320, 430; *Maggie: A Girl of the Streets*, 320

Creoles, 190, 195, 204–5, 245

Critic (magazine), 336

Cromwell, John Wesley, 299

Crouch, Tom, 89, 96

Crummell, Alexander, 6, 180–81, 247, 258, 298–99, 497n16; *Africa and America*, 181, 431

Culler, Jonathan, 497n29

Cunningham, H. S., 429

Cunningham, Virginia, 64, 453

"Curiosity" (poem), 518n42

Current Literature (magazine), 302, 336

"Curtain" (poem), 213

Curtis, Austin Maurice, 399–400

Curtis, Namoyoka Gertrude, 400

Cyclopædia: or, an Universal Dictionary of Arts and Sciences (published by Chambers), 96

Czar of Dixie Land (musical), 421

Dabney, Wendell Philips, 160

Dahomeans, 163–65, 168, 422

Daily American (newspaper), 357

Dandridge, Caroline "Danske," 429

Daniels, William Cooke, 443

D. Appleton & Company, 250, 253, 276

"Dat Chrismus on de Ol' Plantation" (poem), 256

Dave the Potter, 19

Davidson, Olivia A., 298

Davie, Oliver, 429

Davis, Daniel Webster, 230, 392

Dayton, Ohio: African American community in, 11, 27, 92, 99–101, 169–70; Central High School, 79–82, *80*, 85–87, *85*, 90–95, *95*, 102, 106–10, *108*, 117, 142, 432; education in, 57, 61–64, 72, 77, 79–85, 89–90; German community in, 103; Matilda's life in, 36, 40, 43–44, 48, 50–51, 56, 59–61, 67–68, 111, 113; National Home for Disabled Volunteer Soldiers, 68–71, *70*, 75, 76, 152; PLD's residences in, 4, 6, 56, 62–63, 67, 71, 75, 111, 113, 273–74, 426–33, *427*, 445, 517n16; Western Association of Writers meeting in, 110–11, 119–22; the Wright family in, 88–90

Dayton Board of Education, 62, 72, 77, 79, 84, 85, 109

Dayton Democrat (newspaper), 72

Dayton Herald (newspaper), 115, 132, 152

Dayton Normal School, 80–81

Dayton Tattler (newspaper), 11, 91, 97–107, *98*, 115, 132, 179, 218, 219, 302

Deaton, Edward, 445

"The Debt" (poem), 425

Defoe, Daniel, *Robinson Crusoe*, 52–54, 57, 59, 138

Delany, Martin, 384

"The Delinquent" (poem), 239, 468n5

"Dely" (poem), 292, 503n43, 518n42

Democratic (newspaper), 93–94

Democrats, 8–10, 332–33, 387

Denier, Marie E., 437–38

Dennis, Charles, 204

Denver Colored Civic Association, 367

Denver Evening Post (newspaper), 364

Denver Post (newspaper), 362–63, 365, 367

Denver Republican (newspaper), 363, 365

Denver Statesman (newspaper), 363, 438

Derrick, Joseph, 307

Derrick, William B., 307

"The Deserted Plantation" (poem), 229, 239, 347–48, *349*, *350*, 509n49

Detroit Free Press (newspaper), 190

Dewey, Melville, 352

dialect poetry and prose, 10–11, 103, 113, 115, 126–28, 139–41, 145, 213, 218, 225–30, 250–51, 268, 292, 302, 303, 337, 348, 350, 380–83, 391–92, 409, 413, 424, 436–37, 442–43

Diamondback Club, 178

Dickens, Charles, 105

Dillet, Helen Louise, 380–81

"Dinah Kneading Dough" (poem), 409

"Discovered" (poem), 215, 468n5

Dodd, Amzi, 346

Dodd, Frank H., 6, 250, 253, 302–3, 430

Dodd, Mead, and Company, 6, 250, 276, 303, 319, 321, 345–46, 348, 369–71, 387, 409, 412–13, 430, 436, 442, 449 domestic labor, 20–23, 34–35, 44, 60–61

Doubleday, Frank Nelson, 397

Doubleday & McClure, 369

Douglas, David, 234, 251

Douglas, Davison M., 85

Douglass, Anna, 186

Douglass, Annie, 186

Douglass, Charles, 177, 179–80

Douglass, Frederick: accomplishments of, 157–58, 230; autobiographies of, 157; death of, 185–87, 190–91; and Haiti, 158, 186; *The Life and Times of Frederick Douglass*, 431; at Lincoln's inauguration, 451; name of, 17; as news correspondent, 243; personal narratives by, 452; photograph of, *159*; PLD's relationship with, 5, 6, 152, 157–58, 160–70, 177–82, 187, 431, 453; "The Race Problem in America," 167–68; *The Reason Why the Colored American Is Not in the World's Columbian Exposition*, 165–66; and segregated schools, 84; and the Union Army, 33; in Washington, D. C., 177–78; Washington compared to, 367; "What to the Slave Is the Fourth of July?," 433–35; and World's Columbian Exposition, 157–70, 186

Douglass, Joseph, 160, 163, 166, 167, 283, 434, 454

Douglass, Lewis, 235, 265, 500n9

Douglass' Monthly (magazine), 101

Dowling, David, 123

Dowling, Robert M., 202

Down de Lover's Lane (musical), 421

Downing, Andrew, 429

Downing, Henry Francis, 243–45, 247, 258

Doyle, Arthur Conan, 276, 430

dropsy, 36, 51, 479n11

"A Drowsy Day" (poem), 110, 128, 132, 143, 162, 213

Drury, A. W., 41

Du Bois, W. E. B., 88, 296, 329–30, 343–44, 418–19, 449, 452, 453; "Possibilities of the Negro," 419; *The Souls of Black Folk*, 419

Dumas, Alexandre, 230, 430

Dunbar, Elizabeth Florence (sister), 48, 50–51, 448, 478n110

Dunbar, Joshua (father): abandonment of family by, 51, 55, 68; alcoholism of, 38, 46, 47, 51, 70–71, 103, 272, 291; birth of, 17, 453, 471n6; character traits of, 76; death of, 75, 76; education imparted by, 16; marriage and subsequent relationship of, 15–16, 48–50, 55–57, 59–60, 67–68, 89, 91, 97; pension of, 72–75, 83; as plasterer, 17–20; PLD's relationship with, 16, 48, 60, 75–76, 92, 163; return of, from Union Army, 42–43, 45–47, 51, 68–75; as runaway, 23, 27–30; as subject of biography, 4–5, 251, 451–52; Union Army service of, 33–34, 36–42; violence of, 47, 48, 50, 68, 416

Dunbar, Matilda (mother) (née Burton): birth and childhood of, 20–23; in Chicago, 156–57; in Colorado, 362, 368–69; domestic labor performed by, 20–23, 34–35, 44, 60–61; education imparted by, 15–16, 52; emancipation of, 35–36; first marriage of, 31, 35–36, 39–40, 388; Hampton Institute connection of, 346; health of, 148, 369; motherhood and family life, 36, 45, 47–48, 50–52, 60–63, 67–68, 71, 75–76, 111, 143, 155; move to Dayton, Ohio, 43–44; name of, 56; personality characteristics of, 55, 198; photographs of, *21*, *359*, *393*; PLD's works dedicated to, 321; relationship with ARM, 273, 322–23, 353, 416–17, 420, 446; relationship with PLD, 133, 148, 198–200, 234–35, 240, 244, 258–59, 263, 271, 273–74, 277, 287, 322–23, 346, 355–56, 369, 419–20, 426, 428, 433, 444, 517n16; second marriage and subsequent relationship of, 48–50, 55–57, 59–60, 67–68, 89, 91, 97; as subject of biography, 4–5, 251, 451–52

Dunbar, Paul Laurence: alcoholism of, 5, 6, 103, 170, 203, 272, 278, 280, 283, 285, 290–91, 301, 352, 369, 378–79, 394–95, 397, 401–2, 414–15, 433, 503n43; attitudes

about education, 5, 300, 327–29, 338,
342–44, 373–75, 396; attitudes on race,
11, 99–101, 163, 165–66, 217–20, 242–43,
258, 261–62, 277, 292–93, 316–17, 333–35,
339–41, 365, 371, 373–74, 379–80, 392,
410, 414, 433–36, 455, 497n16, 503n43;
autodidacticism of, 144, 180–81, 227, 432;
awards and honors of, 1, 7, 398, 438, 456,
468n4; birth and childhood of, 4–5,
15–16, 47–76, 478n110; canes and walking
sticks of, 161, 272, 438; celebrity/reputation
of, 1, 6–7, 11, 83, 132, 143, 192, 214, 233, 235,
243, 257, 270–71, 283, 285, 289–90, 293,
298–99, 301–2, 307, 324, 329, 356–57, 363,
365, 368–69, 379, 385, 398–99, 410–11,
413–14, 416, 438, 446, 448, 454, 456,
468n4, 503n43, 519n56; childhood and
student literary efforts, 64–67, 91–92, 102;
critical responses to work of, 122–23, 125,
142, 143, 145, 169, 220, 224–33, 239, 247,
249, 250, 252–53, 257, 296, 302–4, 322, 337,
347, 348, 350, 370–71, 388–89, 392, 409,
413, 422, 424, 436–37, 441–43, 496n18,
521n21; clothing of, 357, 386; courtship of
ARM, 1, 5, 11, 188–98, 203–20, 234, 236–38,
296–98, 499n7, 499n61 (see also discussion
of literature with ARM; engagement to
ARM; marriage to ARM); death and
burial of, 6, 438, 444–48, 519n56; dedications
in works by, 321, 374–75, 443; discussions
of literature and ideas with ARM, 190–98,
203–5, 213–15, 217–20, 234, 248–49, 255–56,
268–69, 275–77, 293, 299–303, 313, 342–43,
387–88; doubts and disappointments
concerning career, 12, 124–27, 149–50, 185,
231, 253, 255–56, 293, 319, 382, 389, 498n49;
early career of, 115–30; education of, 15–16,
52, 57, 62–64, 67, 77–90, 93, 97, 106–9,
143–48, 179–81, 198, 403–4; effects of race
on work and career of, 115, 126–27, 217–20,
225–27, 232, 234, 250, 252, 268–69, 286,
292–93, 303, 319–20, 322, 337, 339–41,
370–71, 382, 389, 409, 424, 441–43, 456;
emotional life of (see mental and emotional

life of); employment opportunities of,
111–12, 120, 122–25, 148, 149, 152–53, 156–57,
161, 199, 265–67, 269–70, 285–86, 288, 290,
299, 310, 319, 330–32, 338, 396–97, 486n9,
501n3; engagement to ARM, 238, 240–43,
255–61, 264–65, 270, 272–75, 277–93, 308,
501n30, 502n26, 505n6 (see also marriage
to ARM); in England, 6–7, 234, 238–62;
flirtations with women, 4–5, 150, 212,
241–42, 256, 259–60, 264–65, 283, 285,
307–8, 392–94, 415, 499n7, 505n4 (see also
relationship with Rebekah Baldwin); and
Freemasonry, 383–87, 513n44; gambling of,
414–15; health of (see mental and emotional life of; physical health of); hobbies
of, 356; influences on, 3, 16, 52–54, 57–59,
64–65, 77–80, 133–34; libretti and lyrics by,
7, 203, 313–16, 314, 402–7, 421–22; literary
business and finances of, 5, 6, 7, 124, 126–27,
130, 142, 149, 157, 213, 230, 234–35, 249–53,
258–59, 261, 267–69, 275–76, 289–90, 303,
315, 321–22, 336, 342, 343, 353, 355, 382, 407,
442; marriage to ARM, 1, 6, 12, 307–17,
321–26, 335–36, 369, 390–94, 399, 415–21,
424–26, 437–38, 459–60 (see also engagement to ARM); mental and emotional
life of, 5, 11, 170, 176–77, 183–85, 197–98,
209–10, 280, 283, 286, 289, 316, 324–25,
444 (see also alcoholism of; violence of);
musicianship of, 64; naming of, 47–48;
negotiations with editors and publishers,
6, 113, 129–30, 148–50, 411–12; newspapers
as venue for writing and editorial work, 11,
91–94, 97–109, 152, 156, 179, 190, 192–93,
195, 208, 219, 261–62, 264, 302, 333–34,
336, 338, 363–65, 373–74, 410, 414, 433–36,
453–54; patrons of, 3, 5, 6, 123–29, 143–50,
196, 198, 233, 265–67, 330; personal finances
of, 6, 198–99, 234–35, 244, 258–59, 265,
268–70, 273, 275, 282, 285–86, 288–89, 433;
personality of (see mental and emotional
life of); photographs of, vi, 85, 95, 117, 226,
232, 251, 252, 254, 271, 359, 360, 362, 393, 394;
physical characteristics of, 111, 161, 190,

Dunbar, Paul Laurence (*continued*)
198, 199, 206–7, 211, 225, 241, 357; physical
health of, 2, 97, 233, 282, 289–91, 310, 316,
330–32, 352–53, 355–56, 359–66, 380–81, 387,
390–91, 395–96, 426, 428, 433, 438–39,
443–44, 454 (*see also* alcoholism of); as
"poet laureate of his race," 1, 438, 456,
468n4; recitals and speeches given by, 3,
107–9, 115–16, 120–22, 127, 139, 145–48, 151,
168–69, 196, 199, 200, 208, 213, 232, 235, 239,
242, 244–45, 247–48, 252–55, 257–58, 278,
285–86, 289, 339, 342, 346–47, 352–53, 367–68,
380, 390, 392, 395, 397–98, 412, 433, 434,
435, 454, 456, 521n22; relationships with
women (*see* flirtations with women); relationship with brothers, 52; relationship with
Douglass, 5, 6, 152, 157–58, 160–70, 177–82,
187, 431, 453; relationship with father,
16, 48, 60, 75–76, 92, 163; relationship with
Howells, 231–34; relationship with Johnson, 6, 356–57, 359, 372, 380–83, 385; relationship with mother, 133, 148, 198–200, 234–35,
240, 244, 258–59, 263, 271, 273–74, 277, 287,
322–23, 346, 355–56, 369, 419–20, 426, 428,
433, 444, 517n16; relationship with Rebekah
Baldwin, 11, 173–87, 209, 235, 256, 264, 277,
284–85, 287–88, 310, 324; relationship with
Roosevelt, 6, 353, 355, 399–401, 429, 438–41,
520n12; relationship with Washington, 6,
11, 294, 296–301, 327–30, 337–39, 342–43,
365–67, 374–75, 394–98, 401–2, 405–7, 415,
418, 453; and religion, 67, 436; reputation
of (*see* celebrity/reputation of); robbery
of, 375–76, 378–79; scholarship on, 7, 11,
449–60, 469n12, 521n21; smoking habits of,
396–97, 433; styles employed by, 3–5,
132–33, 139–40, 422, 424, 454–55 (*see also*
dialect poetry and prose; formal English);
suicidal thoughts of, 12, 278, 280; and
Tuskegee Institute, 338–39, 341–44, 367,
392–98, 402–7; violence of, 210, 278–80,
324, 369, 415–18, 425, 460; and World's
Columbian Exposition, 152–70. *See also*
library of PLD

Dunton, Lewis M., 270
Durham, John Stephens, "The Labor
Unions and the Negro," 300
Dustin, Charles W., 111–12
Dvořák, Antonín, 200–201; *From the New
World*, 200
Dwyer, Dennis, 49
Dyer, William B., 350

"An Easter Ode" (poem), 65–66, 119, 133
"Easter Poem" (poem), 125
Eckl, Harry, 445
Edel, Leon, 450
education: of African Americans, 57, 62–64,
72, 78, 81, 87, 136, 144–45, 295–96, 327–29,
372–73; ARM's, 205; classical, 81–82, 87–88,
483n15; in Dayton, 57, 61–64, 72, 77, 79–85,
89–90; Du Bois's philosophy of, 419;
Fireside Poetry and, 138; imparted by
PLD's parents, 15–16, 52; industrial, 144–45,
294–96, 299–300, 327–28, 342, 365, 373–75,
406, 419; PLD's, 15–16, 52, 57, 62–64, 67,
77–90, 93, 97, 106–10, 143–48, 179–81, 198,
403–4; PLD's attitudes about, 5, 300,
327–29, 338, 342–44, 373–75, 396; poetry
as subject of, 139; during Reconstruction,
61, 78, 294; secondary vs. higher, 81–82;
segregation in, 62–63, 72, 78, 84–85, 92;
Washington's philosophy of, 5, 295–96,
299–300, 327–29, 342, 365, 373–75, 406, 419
Eichberg, Julius, 200
Electoral College, 135
Emancipation Proclamation (1863), 5, 32–33,
35, 347
Emerson, Ralph Waldo, 222; *Poems*, 430
England: PLD's recitals in, 3, 6, 239, 242,
244–45, 247–48, 252–55, 257–58; PLD's
tour of, 6–7, 234, 238–62, 254, 290, 454;
queen's diamond jubilee in, 247–49, 257,
259
"England as Seen by a Black Man" (essay),
261–62, 334, 414
Enoch, May, 377
Equiano, Olaudah, 452

Ernest, John, 450

Eskridge, Jeremiah Thomas, 363

Eureka Literary Society, 178

"Evah Dahkey Is a King" (song), 422

"Evening" (poem), 133

Evening Herald (newspaper), 101

Evening Item (newspaper), 97

extradition clause, 23

Faber (newspaper publisher), 93–94

"Fair Harvard" (Gilman), 404–7

Family Fiction (magazine), 317

The Fanatics (novel), 387–89, 412, 413, 443, 514n24

"Farewell Song" (poem), 108–9

fatigue duty, 37–38, 41

Fauset, Jessie, 88

Field, Eugene, 137, 139

Fifteenth Amendment, 8

Fifth Regiment of Massachusetts Cavalry Volunteers, 39, 40–41, 74, 83

Fifty-fifth Regiment of Massachusetts Colored Infantry, 34, 36–42, 46, 70, 74, 83

Fifty-fourth Regiment of Massachusetts Volunteer Infantry, 33–34, 38–39

Fireside Poetry, 3, 134, 136–39, 455

First Confiscation Act (1861), 32

fishing, 356

Fisk Jubilee Singers, 127

Fisk University, 298

Flaubert, Gustave, 195

Flood, W. H. Grattan, 404

folklore, 128, 200–201, 217–18, 220, 225, 227, 345, 347–48, 392

Folks from Dixie (stories), 294, 302–4, 321, 371, 412, 456, 503n44

Foner, Eric, 8, 10

Forbes, Camille, 422

Forbes, George Washington, 503n43

"Forest Greeting" (poem), 468n5

formal English, 4, 5, 11, 106, 128, 132, 134, 137, 140, 151, 226, 251, 302, 337, 408–9, 424, 442, 456

"For the Main Who Fails" (poem), 12

Forthnightly Club, Albany, New York, 352

Forthnightly Spectator (newspaper), 353

Fortune, Timothy Thomas, 328–29, 351, 365–66, 402, 415, 418, 419; *The Kind of Education the Afro-American Most Needs*, 329

Foster, Wilbur F., 295

Fourteenth Amendment, 8, 63, 78, 84, 236, 482n62

Fox, Charles Barnard, 37

franchise of African Americans, 7–9, 480n42, 482n62

Frederic, Harold, *The Damnation of Theron Ware*, 322

Freedman, Estelle B., 279

Freedman's Savings and Trust Bank, 45

Freedmen's Bureau, 44, 49, 55, 400

Freedmen's Hospital, Washington, D.C., 399–400

Freedom's Journal (newspaper), 101, 179

Freeman, J. Arthur, 167

Freemasonry, 383–87, 513n44

Frissell, Hollis Burke, 346

Frissell, Julia, 346

"From Impulse" (story), 104

Fugitive Slave Act (1850), 28, 30

Fuller, Melville W., 441

"The Gambler's Wife" (serialized drama), 104–6

gambling, 414–15

Garfield, James A., 144

Garland, Hamlin, 320

Garrard, James, 17

Gatewood, Willard B., 189

Gayle, Addison, Jr., 453

General Theological Seminary, New York, 180

Gentry, Thomas, 126

Gibbon, Edward, 95

Gibbs, Mifflin Wistar, 429

Gilder, Richard Watson, 249, 288, 293

Gilman, Samuel, "Fair Harvard," 404–7

Glass, David, 20–22

Glass, Sarah, 20–22

Glass, Thompson, 20–22

Goethe, Johann Wolfgang von, 248

"Goin' Back" (poem), 141

"A Golden Chance" (story), 104

gonorrhea, 282, 290

"Good Evenin'" (song), 422

Gooding, James Henry, 37

Grant, Ulysses S., 144, 267

Great Migration, 376

Greeley, Horace, 267

Green, Anna Katherine, 276

Green, John Richard, 95

Grey, John S., "The Bogus Baron De Guyn," 102

Griggs, Sutton, *Imperium in Imperio*, 431

Grimké, Archibald, 178

Grimké, Francis James, 299

Grimké family, 178

Guizot, François Pierre Guillaume, 95

Gutman, Hebert H., 17

Hackley, Edwin H., 367, 438, 444

Hairston, Eric Ashley, 87

Haiti, 157, 158, 186

Haitian Pavilion, World's Columbian Exposition, 157–58, 161, 163, 170, 173

Hall, Prince, 384

Hamilton (Ohio) Intelligencer (newspaper), 222

Hampton Institute, 145, 294–95, 339, 342, 344–48

Hampton Institute Camera Club, 344–50, 409, 437, 442, 518n43

"The Hapless Southern Negro" (essay), 365

Harlem, New York, 376

Harlem Renaissance, 458

Harper, Frances Ellen Watkins, 10, 230, 431

Harper's Cyclopedia of British and American Poetry (edited by Sargent), 144

Harper's Weekly Magazine, 115, 220, 221, 224, 232–33, 301, 314, 340, 372, 410, 456

Harrell, Willie J., Jr., *We Wear the Masks*, 521n21

"Harriet Beecher Stowe" (poem), 455

Harris, Arthur, 376–77

Harris, Joel Chandler, 59, 218, 220, 341

Harrison, Richard B., 205

Harte, Bret, 113

Hartford Press (magazine), 372

Harvard University, 144, 198, 368, 403–7

Hast, Gregory, 245

"The Haunted Oak" (poem), 455, 521n22

Hawthorne, Nathaniel, 95, 222, 430; *The Scarlet Letter*, 195, 320

Hay, John, 245, 398

Hayes, Rutherford B., 9, 144

Haymarket Square, Chicago, 222

Hayson, W. B., 299

Health (magazine), 368

Healy, Thomas, 378

The Heart of Happy Hollow (stories), 441, 443

Henderson, J. H., 307

Henson, Josiah, 57

Herbert, George, 430

Herne, James A., 231; *Shore Acres*, 224

Herrick, an Imaginative Comedy in Three Acts (play), 421

Hickman, Adam, 445

Higgins, Charles, 445

High School Times (newspaper), 94, 106, 142

Hill, Adams Sherman, 144, 368, 403–4

Hinks, Peter P., 384

"His Bride of the Tomb" (story), 104

"His Failure in Arithmetic" (story), 104

"His Little Lark" (story), 104

History Workshop Journal, 451

Hitchcock, Ethan A., 400

Hitchcock, Ripley, 232

Hobart, Garret A., 220

Hobson, Samuel H., 367

Hogan, Ernest, 201, 313, 315

Holmes, Oliver Wendell, 134, 137, 430, 455

"Home, the Solution of the Negro Problem" (essay), 365

Homer, 87

"The Hoodooing of Mr. Bill Simms" (short story), 268

Hooker, Isabella Beecher, 167

Hopkins, Pauline, 10

Horizon (magazine), 101

Horton, George Moses, 230

Hot Foot (musical), 421

Hottest Coon in Dixie (musical), 315–16

Houghton, Mifflin & Co., 319

Houston Post (newspaper), 370

Howard University, 288, 328, 399–400

Howdy, Honey, Howdy (poetry), 442, 453, 518n43, 521n15

Howells, William Cooper, 222

Howells, William Dean, 3, 6, 222–34, 223, 239, 247, 249–53, 294, 296, 301–2, 320–21, 340, 368, 374, 392, 449, 456; *Criticism and Fiction*, 223; *A Hazard of Good Fortunes*, 222–23; *An Imperative Duty*, 223; *Italian Journeys*, 431; *A Modern Instance*, 223; *The Rise of Silas Lapham*, 223

"How George Johnson Won Out" (short story), 268

Hoyles, Euretta A., 429

Hughes, Jennifer, 388

Hull, Akasha Gloria, 458, 460, 521n25

Hulme, Edward Maslin, 429

"Hunting Song" (poem), 509n49

"Hurrah for Captain Kidd" (song), 422

Hutner, Gordon, 470n19

Hyde, Richard, 313

"A Hymn" (poem), 213, 468n7

Impey, Catherine, 253–55, 443

Impey, Ellen, 254–55

Impey family, 253, 424

In Dahomey (musical), 7, 422, 423, 506n26

"The Independence of Silas Bollender" (short story), 408

Independent (newspaper), 150, 190, 261, 276, 299, 300, 302, 327, 330

Indianapolis Freeman (newspaper), 402

Indianapolis Journal (newspaper), 122, 125, 126, 128, 133, 142, 213, 217, 224, 322

Indianapolis World (newspaper), 192–93, 193, 195, 207–8, 219

industrial education, 144–45, 294–96, 299–300, 327–28, 342, 365, 373–75, 406, 419

Ingersoll, Robert Green, 265–67

"The Ingrate" (short story), 19

In Old Plantation Days (stories), 436, 443

"In Summer Time" (poem), 133

"In the Tents of Akbar" (poem), 468n5

"Ione" (poem), 203–4, 249

Irving, Washington, 430

"Is Higher Education for the Negro Hopeless?" (essay), 373–74

Jackson, Virginia, 455, 497n29

Jacobs, Harriet, 452

James, Henry, 223, 225, 320

James, William, 329

James Pott and Company, 418–19

"James Whitcomb Riley" (poem), 137–38, 141

Jarrold and Sons, 412

Jaxon, Helen, 245

J. B. Lippincott Company, 276

Jefferson, Thomas, 426, 451

Jenkins, Will, 518n43

Jes Lak White Fo'ks (musical), 421, 506n26

Jewett, John P., 57

Jewish American writers, 225

Jim Crow laws, 5, 61, 87, 92, 165, 235, 236, 395

Joggin' Erlong (poetry), 442–43, 453, 518n43

"John Boyle O'Reilly" (poem), 140

John Lane (publisher), 250, 253

Johnson, Billy, 201

Johnson, Charles, 142

Johnson, D. W., 38

Johnson, James (father of James Weldon Johnson), 380

Johnson, James "Jim" Weldon, 6, 202, 315, 356–57, *358*, 359, 372, 380–83, 385, 506n26; "Lift Every Voice and Sing" (with Rosamond Johnson), 381

Johnson, James William, 248

Johnson, Lola, 454

Johnson, Robert Underwood, 374–75

Johnson, Rosamond "Rosy," 202, 380–82; "Lift Every Voice and Sing" (with James Weldon Johnson), 381

Johnson, R. U., 149

Johnston, Elizabeth Bryant, 429

Jones, Gavin, 113

Jones, Jacqueline, 22, 60–61

Jones, Samuel M., 429

Jones, Sissieretta, 166–67

Journal (newspaper), 101

Journal of the Lodge (newspaper), 190, 192

Jubilee Day, World's Columbian Exposition, 166–68, 180, 186

Jubilee for Queen Victoria. *See* England: queen's diamond jubilee in

Judge (newspaper), 102

Jump Back (Negro Love Song) (musical), 316

Kalamazoo Gazette (newspaper), 379

Kansas City Star (newspaper), 388, 433

Kantrowitz, Stephen, 384

Kate Field's Washington (magazine), 190

Kauffman, Reginald W., 443–44

Kealing, Hightower Theodore, 419

Keats, John, 65, 430

Keen, Edwin H., 239, 443

"Keep A-Pluggin' Away" (poem), 77, 141

"Keep a Song Up on De Way In" (poem), 468n5

Keith, Prowse, and Company, 244

Kellogg, Ansel Nash, 117

Kellogg, Warren F., 329

Kelly, Patrick J., 74

Kemble, Edward Windsor, 303

Kentucky, 24, 135, 136

Kentucky Negro Education Association, 136

King, William, 426

Kipling, Rudyard, 430

"Kissing as Medicine" (story), 104

Kitching, William, 242

Kline, Walter L., 445

Knopf, Sigard Adolphus, 360

Koch, Robert, 351

Kuhns, Ezra M., 112, 443, 445

Ku Klux Klan, 9, 328

Ku Klux Klan Act (1871), 482n62

labor, 300

Ladies' Home Journal (magazine), 256, 276, 336

"Lager Beer" (poem), 103–4, 140

Lakeside Summer Assembly and Camp Meeting, 208

Langston, John Mercer, 384

"The Language We Speak" (story), 104

Laurie, H. W., 369

Lears, Jackson, 155, 480n42

Leavenworth Herald (newspaper), 329

Legacy: A Journal of American Woman Writers, 459

Leggett, Benjamin Franklin, 429

The Letter (magazine), 214

Lewis, Julia, 501n30

Lewis, Will, 278

Liberia, 58, 180

Library Journal, 267

Library of Congress, 2, 266–67, 285–86, 288, 290, 299, 310, 319, 330–32, 331, 338, 501n3

library of PLD, 6; contents of, 428–32; decorative items in, 432–33; formation of, 144, 148; gifts in, 429–31, 439

"Life" (poem), 213

"Lift Every Voice and Sing" (Johnson and Johnson), 381

Light (magazine), 102

Li'l' Gal (poetry), 441–42

Lincoln, Abraham, 31, 32, 35, 36, 222, 445, 451

Lippincott's Monthly Magazine, 276, 302, 319, 321, 408, 411–12

literary criticism, 231, 250. *See also* Dunbar, Paul Laurence: critical responses to work of

Little Africa, Dayton, 62–63

"Little Billy" (short story), 116

"Little Brown Baby" (poem), 509n49, 521n22

Lloyd, William J., 429

Loafing-Holt (PLD's study), 6, 428–33, 439

Lockwood, Belva Ann, 72–74, 73, 83

Loeb, William, Jr., 400

Longfellow, Henry Wadsworth, 64, 121, 134, 136–37, 139, 455; "A Psalm of Life," 139

Lorimer, George Horace, 443

"Lost Dream" (poem), 468n5

Lotus Club, 178

L'Ouverture, Toussaint, 158

Love, John Lee, 299

The Love of Landry (novel), 369–70, 443

"Lover's Lane" (poem), 468n5

"Love's Apotheosis" (poem), 468n5

"The Love's Castle" (poem), 468n5

Lowell, James Russell, 134, 136–37, 430, 455

"The Luck of Lazy Lang" (short story), 219

A Lucky Coon (vaudeville comedy), 315–16

"Lullaby" (poem), 140, 509n49

"A Lyric" (poem), 194, 493n14

lyric poetry, 248–49, 339–40, 454–55, 497n29

Lyrics of Love and Laughter (poetry), 4, 424–25, 437, 443, 454–55, 468n5, 498n30

Lyrics of Lowly Life (poetry), 217, 250–52, 252, 288, 301–3, 321, 336, 347, 348, 357, 359, 409, 436, 437, 449, 454, 455, 468n5, 498n30

Lyrics of Sunshine and Shadow (poetry), 428, 442, 443, 455, 468n5, 498n30, 514n24

Lyrics of the Hearthside (poetry), 1, 12, 336–37, 348, 409, 424, 443, 454, 468n5, 469n7, 498n30, 503n43

Mabie, Hamilton Wright, *In a Forest of Arden*, 430

MacArthur, James, 319

Macaulay, Thomas, 53

Maclaren, Ian (pseudonym of John Watson), 239

Majors and Minors (poetry), 15, 213–14, 220, 224–31, 226, 233, 235, 247, 249–51, 266, 294, 296–98, 301, 321, 337, 348, 437, 441, 456, 468n5

Manhattan Club, 178

Manning, Alexander, 192

Marcus Whitmark and Sons, 313

Marrant, John, 384

Marshall, James "Jimmie" L., 202

Marten, James, 45–46, 75

Martin, Jay, *A Singer in the Dawn*, 521n21

Mary E. Garst Estate, 113

Masons. *See* Freemasonry

Matthews, Courtland, 452

Matthews, James Newton, 6, 119, 122–28, 132, 137, 142, 143–44, 147–50, 155, 169, 181, 185, 231, 452, 455; *Temple Vale and Other Poems*, 429

Matthews, Victoria Earle, 6, 237–38, 265, 291, 329, 380, 430; *Aunt Lindy*, 237, 431

McCaughey, W. F., 145

McClellan, George Marion, 340–41, 431; *Poems*, 341

McGirt, James Ephraim, 429

McKee, William, 49

McKinlay, Whitefield, 402

McKinley, William, 6, 154, 220, 221, 230, 267, 398–99, 520n14

McLean, William E., 83

McVickar, William Neilson, 397

Mead, Charles L., 345–46

Mead, Edward, 346

Mead, Elinor, 222

Mead, Frank, 346

"The Meadow Lark" (poem), 140, 213

"Melancholia" (poem), 106–7, 109, 183

"Memorial Day" (poem), 133

"The Memory of Martha" (poem), 468n5

meningococcal disease, 290

Merrill, Winifred Edgerton, 352

"Merry Autumn" (poem), 133, 468n5

Metcalf, Eugene W., Jr., 453, 460; *Paul Laurence Dunbar: A Bibliography*, 449

meter, 106, 132, 138–41, 150, 488n18

Methodists, 28, 46

Metropolitan AME Church, Washington, D.C., 186–87

Meyerbeer, Giacomo, 167

Miami Canal, 28

Miami County Temperance Society, 46

Miami Loan and Building Association, 426

Midwest: Chicago's role in, 156; newspapers
thriving in, 93; PLD's ties to, 115, 117, 133,
208, 263; poetry and literature of, 111,
120–23, 134, 137

Militia Act (1862), 32

Miller, A. P., 299

Miner, Leigh Richmond, 442, 518n43

"The Minority Committee" (short story),
408

minstrelsy, 201, 225, 381, 383

Mirror of Liberty (magazine), 101

Mitchell, Abbie, 315

Mitchell, Charles, 399

modernity, 156

Monday Night Literary Society, 178

"The Monks Walk" (poem), 468n5

Monthly Review (magazine), 188, 190, 193,
207

Monthly Review Publishing House, 195

Moon (magazine), 419

Moore, Alice Ruth, (later Alice Dunbar,
Alice Dunbar-Nelson): "Anarchy Alley,"
195; ancestry of, 189–90, 204–5, 316–17;
archives of, 452; attitudes on race, 277,
292–93, 316–17, 392, 416, 503n44; birth of,
204–5; books of, in PLD's library, 428,
432; career of (see teaching career of;
writing career of); "A Carnival Jangle,"
195; in Colorado, 360, 362, 368–69;
courtship of, 1, 5, 11, 188–98, 203–20, 234,
236–38, 296–98, 499n7, 499n61 (see also
discussion of literature with PLD;
engagement to PLD; marriage to PLD);
death of, 458; discussions of literature
and ideas with PLD, 190–98, 203–5,
213–15, 217–20, 234, 248–49, 255–56,
275–77, 299–303, 313, 342–43, 387–88;
education of, 205; emotional life of,
311–12, 324–26, 335, 458; engagement to
PLD, 238, 240–43, 255–61, 264–65, 270,
272–75, 277–93, 308, 501n30, 502n26,
505n6 (see also marriage of); favorite

PLD poems of, 468n5; finances of, 291,
311; Hampton Institute connection of,
346; health of, 192, 280–82, 287, 288–89,
335, 417, 502n33; life after separation from
PLD, 457–58; "Little Miss Sophie," 195;
"Love for a Day," 193; marriage to PLD, 1,
6, 12, 307–17, 321–26, 335–36, 369, 380, 383,
385–86, 390–94, 399, 415–21, 424–26,
437–38, 459–60; name of, 468n1, 468n3,
521n23; photographs of, 189, 360; physical
characteristics of, 188–89; and PLD's
alcoholism, 272, 277, 278, 285, 369; and
PLD's health, 353, 355; and PLD's work
and career, 1–2, 4, 7, 218, 247, 268–69, 293,
315, 319, 321, 391–92, 458–59; PLD's works
dedicated to, 321, 443; "The Poet and His
Song," 1–2; relationship with Matilda
Dunbar, 273, 322–23, 353, 416–17, 420,
446; relationship with Washington and
Murray, 298, 300–301; response of, to
PLD's death, 446–47; scholarship on, 11,
457–60, 521n25; sexuality of, 458, 522n25;
teaching career of, 263–64, 281–82, 286,
292, 300, 310–12, 346, 416, 432, 457;
"Titee," 195; Violets and Other Tales, 193,
195–96, 204; writing career of, 190, 192,
195–96, 205, 215, 256, 341, 457–59

Moore, Joseph, 205

Moore, Leila, 212

Moore, Patricia, 264, 273, 283, 285, 308–9,
311, 312, 420, 516n33

Moore, Tom, "Believe me, if all these
endearing young charms," 404

Moore, W. H. A., 229–30

Moran, Edward P., "Evah Dahkey Is a King"
(with PLD), 422

Morgan, Carrie Blake, 429

Morris, Edmund, 440

Morse, Alice, 348, 409

"The Mortification of the Flesh" (short
story), 408

Moton, Robert Russa, 345

Mott, Frank Luther, 93, 101

Motto, Marie, 245

"Mt. Pisgah's Christmas 'Possum" (short story), 456

The Murdered Lover" (poem), 468n5

Murger, Henri, *Scènes de la Vie de Bohème*, 268

Murphy, Electra, 155

Murphy, Ethel, 155

Murphy, Matilda (mother). *See* Dunbar, Matilda

Murphy, Paul, 155

Murphy, Robert (half-brother), 16, 45, 48, 52, 54, 57, 61, 63–64, 71, 75, 111, 138, 155–57, 199, 212, 263, 478n110

Murphy, William (half-brother), 16, 36, 39–40, 48, 52, 54, 57, 61, 63–64, 71, 75, 138, 155–56, 212, 263

Murphy, Wilson, 31–32, 35–36, 39–40, 43, 48–49, 475n56

Murray, Margaret James, 298, 300–301

music, 200–202, 245, 248, 454

M. Whitmark and Sons, 203

"My Lady of Castle Grand" (poem), 468n5

"My Sort o' Man" (poem), 141, 151, 336

"My Thought–And Hers?" (poem), 256

The Nation (magazine), 303, 336

National Afro-American Council, 353

National Afro-American League, 329

National Association of Colored Women, 237, 298

National Cash Register Company, 111, 435

National Conservatory, New York, 200

National Council of Women, 186

National Era (newspaper), 57

National Home for Disabled Volunteer Soldiers, Dayton, 68–71, 70, 75, 76, 152, 481n57, 482n62

National Institute of Arts and Letters, 372

National Reformer (newspaper), 101

naturalism, 321, 411

"The Negro as an Individual" (essay), 414

"The Negroes of the Tenderloin" (essay), 334–35

Negro Farmer's Conference, 338, 342

"The Negro in Literature" (essay), 392, 395

"Negro Life in Washington" (essay), 410, 414

Negro Problem, 126

The Negro Problem (edited by Washington), 419

"Negro Society in Washington" (essay), 410–11, 414

Nelson, Robert J., 458

New England Magazine, 329, 375

New National Era (newspaper), 84

New Negroes, 3, 219, 293, 413, 458

New Orleans, 188–92, 195, 204–5, 207–8, 212, 220, 311, 317, 373–74

newspapers, 93, 99, 101, 179. *See also* syndication

New York Age (newspaper), 215, 229, 300, 329, 422

New York City: African Americans in, 375–76; PLD's ties to, 263–64; race riots in, 375–79; Tenderloin district, 202, 268, 334–35, 356–57, 376, 411, 500n19

New York Commercial (newspaper), 339–41

New York Daily Tribune (newspaper), 378

New York Herald (newspaper), 102, 267

New York Journal (newspaper), 268–69, 302, 371

New York Times (newspaper), 217, 303, 322, 336, 376, 377, 388, 433

New York Tribune (newspaper), 267, 352, 370

Nicholson, Peter, 18

Nineteenth-Century American Women Writers Study Group, 459

Norris, Frank, 224, 320–21, 430

North Star (newspaper), 179

Northwest Ordinance (1787), 24

"Not They Who Soar" (poem), 455

Noyes Academy, New Hampshire, 180

Nurhussein, Nadia, 115

Oak and Ivy (poetry), 5, 77, 131–47, 149, 157, 160, 181, 196, 200, 213, 251, 321, 336, 348, 443, 455, 457, 468n5

Obama, Barack, 7

Oberlin College, 148

"October" (poem), 133
"Ode for Memorial Day" (poem), 125
"Ode to Ethiopia" (poem), 133, 135–36, 139–40, 146, 160, 213
"Ode to the Colored American" (poem), 168–69, 201
"Of Negro Journals" (essay), 178–79
Ogden, Robert, 346, 397
"Oh, No" (poem), 102–3
Ohio, 23–25, 27–29, 42
Ohio Historical Society, 452, 458, 517n16
"Ohio Pastorals" (stories), 408–9
Ohio River, 26–27
Ohio State Journal (newspaper), 222
"The Old Apple Tree" (poem), 141
"The Old Country Paper" (poem), 151
"The Old Fashioned Way" (poem), 217
"The Old High School and the New" (poem), 117
"The Old Homestead" (poem), 133
Old Negro, 5
Old Sukey (horse), 361
"The Ol' Tunes" (poem), 128, 132, 141, 143, 147, 151, 160, 213, 217
Oneida Institute, 180
"One Life" (poem), 173, 184
"On Emancipation Day" (song), 422
"On the Death of W. C." (poem), 133
"On the Dedication of Dorothy Hall (Tuskegee, Ala., April 22, 1901)" (poem), 397–98
"On the River" (poem), 102, 132
"The Ordeal of Mt. Hope" (short story), 294, 299–300, 303
Oriental America Co., 313
Osofsky, Gilbert, 332–34
"Our Martyred Soldiers" (poem), 102
"Our New Madness" (essay), 327–29, 338, 342, 344, 373–75
Outlook (magazine), 302, 303, 375

Page, Thomas Nelson, 113, 218, 341, 436
Page, Walter Hines, 124, 319
Painter, Nell Irving, 9

Pan Africanism, 180
Panic of 1873, 45
Parker, Alton Brooks, 440
Parker, Benjamin S., 429
Parker, Ben S., 151
Parrish, John W., 287, 502n33
"Parted" (poem), 518n42
"The Party" (poem), 227–28, 247, 456
The Past Before Us (American Historical Association), 451
patrons, 123–24. See also Dunbar, Paul Laurence: patrons of
Patton, Robert, 82
Paul Laurence Dunbar Papers, Ohio Historical Society, 452, 458
Penn, Irvine Garland, 165
Pennington, E. J., 102
pensions, 51, 69, 71–75, 83
People's Advocate (newspaper), 328
Peregrino, Francis Zaccheus Santiago, 353, 355
Perry, Susan, 317
Pfrimmer, William W., 122, 137, 151; Driftwood, 429
Philadelphia Press (newspaper), 338, 342
Philadelphia Times (newspaper), 373
Phillips, Wharton D., 367
Philomathean Society of Central High School, 94, 95
photography, 344–45, 350
"Phyllis" (poem), 191
Pitts, Helen, 186, 235
P. J. Plant (publisher), 441
"The Plantation Child's Lullaby" (poem), 518n42
plastering, 18
Plato, Desiree, 167
Plessy, Homer, 235–36
Plessy v. Ferguson (1896), 235–36
Plutarchus, Lucius Mestrius, 95
pneumonia, 352–53, 355, 426. See also tuberculosis
Poe, Edgar Allan, "Annabel Lee," 116
Poems of Cabin and Field (poetry), 321, 348, 349, 350, 350, 409, 424, 437, 441

Poems of Places (edited by Longfellow), 121
"The Poet" (poem), 4
"The Poet and His Song" (poem), 456
politics: African American participation in,
    9–10, 49, 332; white control of, 9–10.
    See also franchise of African Americans
Pond, Edith, 6, 243–44, 247, 249, 253,
    257–59
Pond, "Major" James Burton, 6, 232–35,
    244, 263, 430
Populists, 332–33
Porter, Rebecca, 20, 36, 43
Possum Am de Best Meat After All
    (musical), 421
Potter, Henry C., 321
"A Practical Suggestion" (story), 104
pregnancy and childbirth, 22, 36
"Preparation" (poem), 468n5
Preston, Charles A., 158
printing, 96
Providence Telegram (newspaper), 338
Puccini, Giacomo, *La Bohème*, 268
Puck (magazine), 317
Pushkin, Aleksander, 230

Quackenbos, John D., *Illustrated History of
    Ancient Literature, Oriental and Classical*,
    144
Quakers, 27, 255, 298
Quincy, Josiah, 404
quinine, 316

race: ARM's attitudes on, 277, 292–93,
    316–17, 392, 416, 503n44; authenticity/
    purity associated with, 4, 6, 115, 190, 220,
    225–27, 250, 251, 348, 370, 392, 422, 442;
    effects on PLD's work and career of,
    115, 126–27, 217–20, 225–27, 232, 234,
    250, 252, 268–69, 286, 292–93, 303,
    319–20, 322, 337, 339–41, 370–71, 382,
    389, 409, 424, 441–43, 456; interracial
    violence, 332–34, 375–79, 435–36;
    PLD's attitudes on, 11, 99–101, 163,
    165–66, 217–20, 242–43, 258, 261–62,

277, 292–93, 316–17, 333–35, 339–41,
    365, 371, 373–74, 379–80, 392, 410, 414,
    433–36, 455, 497n16, 503n43. *See also*
    African Americans; racial stereotypes;
    slaves and slavery; whites
"The Race Question Discussed" (essay),
    333–34
racial stereotypes: art catering to, 3–4, 5;
    in common usage, 339–40, 379; in
    Howell's review of PLD's book, 225;
    PLD's and ARM's use of, 292–93; PLD's
    work and, 115, 218, 286, 303, 339–40, 371,
    382, 389
racial uplift, 3, 11, 166, 178, 219, 296, 298, 334,
    343, 346, 347, 374, 413, 429
Radical Republicans, 7–8
Rae, John, 518n43
rape, 278–79
Ray, Joseph, and Eli T. Tappan, *Treatise on
    Geometry and Trigonometry*, 432
Read, James, 33
Readville, Massachusetts, 33–34, 39
realism, 59, 223, 225, 250, 317, 320–21, 348,
    370, 409, 456. *See also* naturalism
Reconstruction: African American political
    participation during, 49; African Ameri-
    cans in Washington, D.C., during, 177;
    backlash against and decline of, 9–10, 59,
    62, 70, 101, 332–33, 347, 480n42; duration
    of, 7, 469n13; education during, 61, 78,
    294; federal forces deployed during, 9,
    469n13; franchise of African Americans
    during, 7–9, 89; goals of, 7; PLD's life
    during and after, 3, 6; scholarship on,
    470n19; Washington's views on, 499n65
Redemption, 10, 61, 70, 333, 480n42
Reform Leaflets (newspaper), 95
religion, 67, 436. *See also* Christianity
Religious Telescope (newspaper), 89, 94
Renker, Elizabeth, 134
Republican National Committee, 440
Republicans, 185–86, 220, 221, 224, 332.
    See also Radical Republicans
"Retrospect" (poem), 150

"Returned" (song), 422

Revels, Hiram, 384

Reynolds, Paul Revere, 303, 350, 408, 411–13

Richmond, Indiana, 145

Richmond Independent (newspaper), 145

Richmond Star (newspaper), 95

Ricks, William, 378

Ridpath, John Clark, 120, 122

Riley, James Whitcomb, 6, 97, 113, *114*, 115, 120, 122, 127–29, 133, 137–39, 143, 147, 392, 430, 438, 445; *Love Lyrics*, 350

rings, 280–82, 284, 287–88

Ripley, Ezra, 404

"The Rivals" (poem), 146–47, 151

Rivers, Joseph D. D., 367

Robinson, Fay Jackson, 458

Rocky Mountain News (newspaper), 363, 365

Rollin, Horace Judson, 429

Romanticism. *See* British Romanticism

Ronda, Margaret, 455

Roosevelt, Edith, 401

Roosevelt, Theodore, 6, 353, *354*, 355, 399–401, 429, 438–41, 453, 509n10, 520n12; *Presidential Addresses and State Papers of Theodore Roosevelt*, 439

Rothman, Sheila M., 361, 444

The Rubaiyat of Omar Khayyam, 430

Ruffin, Josephine St. Pierre, 289

Rydell, Robert W., 154

"Salutatory" (essay), 91

Sancho, Ignatius, 451

Santayana, George, 329

Sargent, Epes, 144

Saturday Evening Post (magazine), 364, 410, 444

Savage Club, London, 243

Scarborough, William Sanders, 88, 157, 243

Schönlein, J. L., 351

Schoolroom Poetry. *See* Fireside Poetry

Scott, Emmett Jay, 327–29, 390, 394–97, 402

Scott, Walter, 95, 431

Scribner (magazine), 93

Second Confiscation Act (1862), 32

Second Massachusetts Cavalry, 34

"The Seeding" (poem), 213

"The Seedling" (poem), 468n5

segregation: in Canada, 29; in education, 57, 62–63, 72, 78, 84–85, 92; PLD's early experiences of, 5, 6; on public transportation, 235–36; in Union Army, 32, 42; in veterans' homes, 70; in world's expositions, 165

Selkirk, Alexander, 52

Seneca Falls Convention, 158

Senegambian Carnival (variety show), 315

serialized literature, 104–5, 117, 275–76

Shakespeare, William, 430; *Julius Caesar*, 116; *King Richard III*, 319; *The Tragedy of Hamlet, Prince of Denmark*, 197

Shannon, Maud, 307–8, 505n4

Shaw, Anna Howard, 186

Shearer, J. L., 148, 149

Shelley, Percy Bysshe, 65

Shivell, Paul, 231

"Signs of the Times" (poem), 302, 509n49

Sines, Ed, 129

Slaughter-House cases (1873), 9

slave-catchers, 26

slaves and slavery: as artisans, 17–20, 472n15; census counts of, 17, 135; emancipation of, 35, 43–44; female, 22–23, 32, 36; Kentucky statutes on, 135; music of, 200, 245; naming of, 17; PLD's experience of, 135–36; as property or "types," 17, 135; runaway, 19–20, 23–30, 24, 25; scholarship on, 450–51, 453; as subject in PLD's poetry, 135, 140–41

"Sling Along" (poem), 442

Smith, Ella, 310

Smith, Fannie N., 298

Smith, Wilford Horace, 419

Smithsonian Institution Bureau of American Ethnology, 164

smoking, 396–97, 433

Social History (journal), 451

"Solution of Negro Problem Seen from Two Sides" (essay), 365

"Some London Impressions" (essay), 261
"A Song" (poem), 194, 493n14
"Song" (To Miss Alice Ruth Moore)
    [poem], 194–95, 493n14
"Song of Summer" (poem), 409, 468n5
Southern Workman (journal), 300, 345, 347,
    409, 442
"Sparrow" (poem), 213
Sparta Club, 178
Spencer, Herbert, 431
Spofford, Ainsworth Rand, 267
The Sport of the Gods (novel), 321, 408,
    411–14
Spratlin, Paul Edward, 367
Stanley, Henry Morton, 258
Stanton, Edwin, 41–42
Stanton, Frank L., 220
states, racial legislation of, 8–9
State v. Farr (Kentucky, 1841), 24
Steele, Robert W., 62, 84
Stephans, Jacob, 49
stereotypes. See racial stereotypes
Stewart, Frank, 503n43
Stivers, Charles B., 86, 443
Stoddard, Charles Warren, 268
Stowe, Harriet Beecher, 167, 232, 413; Uncle
    Tom's Cabin, 57–59, 138
Straight University, 205
The Strength of Gideon and Other Stories
    (stories), 371, 436, 443
Strothotte, Maurice Arnold, 167
Stuart, Joseph H., 367
Stuart, Ruth McEnery, 218, 341, 430
"A Summer Pastoral" (poem), 133, 141, 217
"Sunset" (poem), 133, 213, 455
"Sympathy" (poem), vii, 1–2, 12, 456,
    468n5, 468n6, 469n8
syndication, 116–17
Syphax family, 178

Talented Tenth, 419
Taylor, William, 52
temperance movement, 46, 272
"The Tenderfoot" (short story), 116

Tenderloin district, New York, 202, 268,
    334–35, 356–57, 376, 411, 500n19
Tenderloin stories, 268–69
Tenney, Edward, 361
Tennyson, Alfred, Lord, 430; Idylls of the
    King, 350; "Lady Clara Vere de Vere," 116
Terrell, Mary Church, 88, 157, 386
Terrell, Robert Heberton, 386
Terrell family, 178
"A Thanksgiving Poem" (poem), 133
Thatcher, Charles A., 145–50
theater, 200–202
"Theology" (poem), 214
Third Civic Division, 398
Thirteenth Amendment, 8, 236
Thomas, Charles S., 366
Thompson, Aaron Belford, 431
Thompson, James Maurice, 120
Thoreau, Henry, 222
Thorpe, Robert, 377–78
Tid-Bits (magazine), 317
Tilden, Samuel, 9
"Time to Tinker 'Roun'!" (poem), 509n49
Timewell, William and Elizabeth, 23, 36
"To a Violet Found on All Saint's Day"
    (poem), 468n5
Tobey, Henry Archibald, 6, 196, 197, 198, 199,
    261, 266, 273, 316, 321, 363, 396, 418, 445
"To Dr. James Newton Matthews"
    (poem), 137, 455
Toledo Bee (newspaper), 149
Toledo Blade (newspaper), 145
Toledo Journal (newspaper), 333
Tomfoolery (periodical), 94
"To Miss Mary Britton" (poem), 136–37
Topeka Plaindealer (newspaper), 351,
    359–60, 363, 368
"To Pfrimmer" (poem), 137
"To the Miami" (poem), 133
Tourgée, Albion W., 236
Troy, Ohio, 27–28, 34, 42–43
Troy Sons of Temperance, 46
Troy Total Abstemious Temperance
    Society, 46

Truesdale, Mrs. (teacher), 110
tuberculosis, 351–53, 355, 359–61, 380, 444
Turner, Henry McNeal, 167
Tuskegee Institute, 182, 295–96, 298, 327–30,
   337–39, 341–44, 367, 392–98, 402–7
"The Tuskegee Meeting" (essay), 338
"Tuskegee Song" (song), 402–7
Tuskegee Student (newspaper), 407
Tuskegee Women's Club, 298
Twain, Mark, 113, 223, 232, 268; Adventures of
   Huckleberry Finn, 303; The Gilded Age
   (with Charles Dudley Warner), 372;
   Roughing It, 361
"Twixt Smile and Tear" (poem), 455
"Two Little Boots" (poem), 468n5

SS Umbria, 239–40, 242
The Uncalled (novel), 250, 253, 255, 263,
   274–76, 302, 319–22, 331–32, 370, 408,
   411–13, 443
Uncle Eph's Christmas (musical), 421,
   506n26
Underground Railroad, 25, 27–28, 33
Union Army: African Americans' return
   to civilian life, 45–46, 68–71; African
   Americans' service in, 8, 19, 30–34, 36–42,
   333, 477n98; alcoholism in, 38, 46, 51,
   479n11; officers in, 42; organization of,
   34; payments by, 38, 42, 74, 477n98; race
   relations in, 42
Union Whigs, 10
United Brethren Church, 48, 49, 88–89, 91,
   94–96
United Brethren Printing Establishment, 94
United Brethren Publishing House, 129–30,
   141–42, 443
United States African News Company, 243
United States v. Cruikshank (1876), 9
United States v. Reese (1876), 9
University of Delaware, 458, 459
U.S. Congress, 68, 135
U.S. Constitution, 8, 23
U.S. Department of the Interior, 400
U.S. National Commission, 164

U.S. Sanitary Commission, Bureau of
   Information and Employment, 45
U.S. Supreme Court, 72–74

vaudeville, 201
Venable, Jack and Margaret, 22, 31
Verdi, Giuseppe, 167
Victoria, Queen, 247–48
Virgil, 86, 87
Virgil, Aeneid, 430
"The Visiting of Mother Danbury" (short
   story), 408
vocational education. See industrial education
Voice of the Negro (magazine), 101

Wadsworth Bennett, 64
Walcott, Joe, 378
Walker, George, 201–2, 313, 315, 421–22, 423
Walker, John Brisben, 222
walking sticks. See canes and walking sticks
Wallace, Walter W., 101
Walters, Alexander, 167
Walters, Spencer, 378
War Department, 41
Ware, Eugene G. (pseudonym: Ironquill), 151
Warfield, William A., 400
Warner, Charles Dudley, 372; "The
   Education of the Negro," 372–74; The
   Gilded Age (with Mark Twain), 372
"The Warrior's Prayer" (poem), 521n22
Warwick, Beatrice, 454
Washington, Allen, 345
Washington, Booker T.: background of,
   294–95, 406; compared to Douglass,
   367; controversial views of, 5, 11, 262,
   296, 298–300, 429, 499n65; educational
   philosophy of, 5, 295–96, 299–300,
   327–29, 342, 365, 373–75, 406, 419; and
   Freemasonry, 384; The Future of the
   American Negro, 431; "The Influence of
   Object-Lessons in the Solution of the
   Race Problem," 343–44; The Negro Problem,
   419; A New Negro for a New Century, 431;
   as news correspondent, 243; personal

narrative by, 452; photograph of, 297; PLD's collection of writings of, 429, 431; PLD's relationship with, 6, 11, 294, 296–301, 327–30, 337–39, 342–43, 365–67, 374–75, 394–98, 401–2, 405–7, 415, 418, 453; and racial uplift doctrine, 11, 296, 298, 374, 429; Roosevelt's dinner with, 401; "Solving the Negro Problem," 366; *Sowing and Reaping*, 431; and Tuskegee Institute, 295–96, 298, 327–30, 337–39, 342–44, 367, 395–98, 402, 405–7; and white–African American relationships, 124; wives of, 298

Washington, D.C.: African Americans in, 177–78, 235, 274, 277, 287, 410–11; PLD's residences in, 273–74, 288–89, 417–18

Washington, D.C. Times (newspaper), 336

Washington Post (newspaper), 365, 371

watermelon, 166–67

Wayland Seminary, 295, 406

Weichselbaum, Anton, 290

"**Welcome Address**" (poem), 110–11, 120–21, 132

Wells, Ida B., 157, 165, 166, 169, 237, 243, 253, 329, 453

"**Weltschmertz**" (poem), 468n5

West End Club, Toledo, 146–47

Western Association of Writers, 110–11, 119–22, 132, 150–51, 208, 219

West Side News (newspaper), 96–97, 102, 115

"**The West Side News**" (poem), 102

Wetmore, J. Douglass, 380

"**We Wear the Mask**" (poem), 268–69, 455, 456

Wharton, Edith, 225, 320, 430

Wheatley, Phillis, 191, 230, 451

"**When de Co'n Pone's Hot**" (poem), 228, 456

"**When Malindy Sings**" (poem), 228–29, 249, 302, 437, 456

When Malindy Sings (poetry), 436–37, 441

"**When the Old Man Smokes**" (poem), 256

White, Robert K., 22–23, 35, 473n34

"**The White Counterpane**" (short story), 408

White Rose Mission, 238, 292

whites: alleged superiority of, 31, 62, 84, 146, 163–64, 333–34, 414, 480n42 (*see also* African Americans: alleged inferiority of); friendships of African Americans with, 124; post-Reconstruction attitudes and actions of, 9–10, 332–34; slavery's harmful effects on, 343–44; violence against African Americans, 332–34, 375–79, 435–36

Whitfield, James M., 230

Whitlock, Brand, 232, 445–46

Whitman, Albery Allson, 230, 431; *Twasinta's Seminoles; or, Rape of Florida*, 340–41

Whitman, Walt, 265, 268, 382–83

"**Whittier**" (poem), 133–34

Whittier, John Greenleaf, 122, 133–34, 136–37, 455

Who Dat Say Chicken in Dis Crowd? (musical), 316

Wiggins, Lida Keck, 453, 459; *The Life and Works of Paul Laurence Dunbar*, 449

Wilberforce University, 182

Wilde, Oscar, 276

Wilkinson, M. Maud, 505n4

Williams, Daniel, 282, 310, 399–400

Williams, Egbert "Bert," 201–2, 313, 315, 421–22, 423

Williams, Fannie Barrier, 160

Williams, Samuel Laing, 160, 165

Wilmington, North Carolina, riots, 332–34, 435–36

Wilmington Advocate (newspaper), 457–58

Wilson, Samuel C., 77–79

Winks, Robin W., 28

Winterer, Caroline, 87

Witmark, Isidore, 313

Woman's Era (newspaper), 289

Woman's Era Club, 289

women: domestic treatment of, 55; PLD's flirtations with, 4–5, 150, 212, 241–42, 256, 259–60, 264–65, 283, 285, 307–8, 392–94, 415, 499n7, 505n4; roles of African American, 44, 49; sexual mores concerning, 279; in slavery, 22–23, 32, 36

Women's Loyal Union, 237

Wood, Charles, 342

Woods, Charles Winter, 339, 340

Woodward, Sidney, 167

Wordsworth, Henry, 64

Wordsworth, William, 64–65

World's Columbian Exposition (Chicago, 1893), 5, 152–70, 154, 173, 180, 186, 200, 201, 403

World's Columbian Exposition Illustrated, 164

World's Industrial and Cotton Exposition (New Orleans, 1884–1885), 164–65

Wormley family, 178

Wright, John Livingston, "Three Negro Poets," 391–92

Wright, Milton, 49, 88–91, 94–95, 97

Wright, Orville, 5, 85–86, 85, 88–90, 90, 91–92, 94–97, 102, 107–8, 113, 115, 129, 453, 519n56

Wright, Patricia, 205

Wright, Susan, 88–89

Wright, Wilbur, 5, 88–90, 90, 91–92, 95–96, 102, 113, 129, 453, 519n56

Wright & Wright, 91–92, 97, 113

Xenophon, 87

"Yellow Jack's Game of Craps" (short story), 268

Young, James (ARM's brother-in-law), 212, 285

Young, James Carleton (also known as Arcadius Yonge), 429–30; *Fantasma*, 429

Young, John Russell, 266–67, 330–32

Young, Leila, 272, 285, 308–9, 311, 312, 338, 425

Young, Pauline A., 452, 458

Zola, Émile, 321, 430